# ISRAEL'S BEST DEFENSE

# ISRAEL'S BEST DEFENSE

## THE FIRST FULL STORY OF THE ISRAELI AIR FORCE

### Col. Eliezer "Cheetah" Cohen

Translated by Jonathan Cordis

Orion Books / New York

*To Ela, who made it all possible*

Translation copyright © 1993 by Crown Publishers, Inc.
Copyright © 1993 by Eliezer Cohen

Published by Orion Books, a division of Crown Publishers, Inc., 201 East 50th Street, New York, New York, 10022. Member of the Crown Publishing Group.
Random House, Inc. New York, Toronto, London, Sydney, Auckland.
Published in different form in Israel in Hebrew by Ma'ariv Book Guild. Hebrew copyright © 1990 by Ma'ariv Book Guild.
Orion and colophon are trademarks of Crown Publishers, Inc.

Manufactured in the United States of America.

Library of Congress Cataloging in Publication Data

Cohen, Eliezer
    [Shamayim enam ha-gevul. English]
    Israel's best defense: the first full story of the Israeli Air
Force / Eliezer Cohen; translated by Jonathan Gordis.
    Includes index.
    1. Israel. Hel ha-avir—History.    I. Title.
UG635.I75C6413   1993
358.4'0095694—dc20                                                93-17855
                                                                  CIP

ISBN 0-517-587904

10 9 8 7 6 5 4 3 2 1

First American Edition

# Contents

# Preface

*I*srael is geographically a very small state. Despite its forty-five years of independence, it is still surrounded by potentially hostile countries, except on one section of its border, which faces the Mediterranean coast. To defend such a strategic depthless area, a very big military force is needed, on a high-alert status year-round. For Israel this would have meant keeping the whole nation in uniform all the time. From the very beginning it was clear to the decision-makers in Israel that such a concept could not prevail in a modern country. Therefore, it was decided that an Israeli Defense Force (IDF) should be established, and that the defense of Israel against a surprise attack would rely upon a thin layer of regular forces supported by a strong and reliable air force.

Colonel Eliezer Cohen, a retired veteran combat pilot, better known in the Israeli Air Force as "Cheetah," has put forward an interesting collection of material, most of which comes from stories of air warriors who served in the Israeli Air Force from the beginning until today.

*Israel's Best Defense* is not an official history book of the Israeli Air Force, but it offers an interesting view of the people, war machines, and decisions that made this force so special and unique in Israel's defense.

Major General Herzle Bodinger
IAF Commander

# Prologue

*In* early 1985, the Syrian Air Force is on special alert. The Israeli withdrawal from its forward intelligence outposts in Lebanon during the previous year has given rise to an intensive regimen of Israeli Air Force reconnaissance flights over Lebanon along the Syrian border. Three years after the downfall of their air force in the Lebanon War, the Syrians feel a need to examine technological developments and to evaluate the 1982 Lebanon War to determine whether any significant change in the balance of power has been brought about in the skies of the Middle East.

An order from President Assad commands his air force "to achieve contact with enemy aircraft in order to create a threat for the Israeli Air Force and its flights over Lebanon."

A pair of Israeli fighter aircraft, accompanied by another pair, head north at high speed over Israeli territory. The bright morning skies are crisscrossed with condensation trails from the early-warning and electronic-warfare planes. The entire Syrian flight-control network awakens in an instant.

Pairs of Syrian intercept aircraft begin to appear on Israeli radar, and their high speed confirms incontrovertibly that the best of these planes are prepared for combat. As the Israeli planes cross the Lebanon border, flying northward, the Syrian MiGs complete their climbing turn and pull west toward the confrontation.

At an altitude of tens of thousands of feet, flying at supersonic speed, are several men who will determine the fate of this battle. To them the entire world is a bluish bubble, several blips on a radar screen, and the lightning speed of the messages being transmitted on the communications channels. They can see neither man nor aircraft before them, but only a dot on the radar, which they have been trained to obliterate.

A missile is fired for an Israeli plane, and an explosion is seen at a great distance. Another missile, and another distant explosion. Panic strikes the Syrians. Shouts fill the communication airwaves and the Syrian planes veer away wildly as the pilots, witnessing their friends exploding in midair beside them, attempt to save themselves. In the Israeli bunkers and the flight-control aircraft, restrained smiles begin to appear, and sighs of relief can be heard.

IDF Military Spokesman Announcement Number 186/85:

"Syrian aircraft attempted to intercept our aircraft along the northern border today, at 10:00 AM. After several provocations, a dogfight took place and two enemy aircraft were shot down in a battle with our planes. All our aircraft returned safely to their bases after completion of their mission. 9 November 1985 13:05."

The spokesman's laconic announcement does not reveal the drama that took place in the skies and on the ground. An entire network of highly skilled professionals had trained for years for these few minutes, and again the network had withstood the test.

The battle was over, and although the term "modest combat" might sound fictional, it is the daily reality of today's Israeli Air Force. It is a force that for years has been able to respond within seconds, and to execute its missions with excellence and power. Through many years and trials, beginning with the War of Independence, the special place of the IAF has been well earned in the eyes of the world's air forces as well as in those of the Israeli people and military.

# 1 The War of Independence, 1947–1949

**May 15, 1948**  Mahmoud Baraka, a pilot in the Egyptian Air Force, took off from the airfield at El Arish, headed toward Tel Aviv. The quartet of Spitfires, a gift from Great Britain to Egypt, its dependent, flew at a moderate altitude, with no fear of enemy planes or antiaircraft fire. The commander of the squadron had guaranteed a quick morning trip to Tel Aviv, where they would drop bombs on the power station that provided much of the electrical power to the Tel Aviv area and then return home. His compatriots who had attacked Sde Dov, the only Israeli air base, shortly after 0500 hours, had reported that they had managed to surprise the Israeli force on the ground and had destroyed it almost completely. They could not recall anything at all having been fired at them from the ground.

Sde Dov was primarily a base for the service flights of the electric company. It had been neglected during the Second World War, and its runway was now covered with sand. The aircraft belonging to the Israeli Flight Club and the Airplane Company used the central and more sophisticated international airport at Lod. The Flight Club, with approximately fifteen relatively inexperienced pilots as members, had a maximum of three light aircraft. The Airplane Company of the Jewish community in the land of Israel, which would become the foundation of El Al, the national Israeli airline, trained pilots for defense missions and flew commercial flights. It had approximately five aircraft and 15 fliers with a basic flight license. After November 29, 1947, the date of the UN partition of the land of Israel, the Lod airfield was left in the center of a hostile Arab area, removed from the center of the Jewish settlements. Arab guerrillas planned to destroy the few Jewish aircraft that were in the field's hangars. A meager but varied collection of aircraft, it was a treasure that the Jews could not afford to lose. With British authorization, the Jewish pilots took the grave risk of flying the planes to Sde Dov, which lacked control and navigation installations to supervise any air traffic denser than that of the Electric Company. There was not even a wind sock. Temporary systems were quickly set up, with the lighting provided by tin cans filled with sand and oil. At this point, most of the flights were already serving the Haganah (the pre-independence Jewish military), but were carried out under the pretense that they were innocent flights of the Flight Club.

The first morning that found the Air Service's base under complete Israeli jurisdiction started off on the wrong foot. The four air attacks it absorbed later in the day would only make things worse. Most of the damage had been done during the first assault. Though they had been told a day earlier to prepare for an Egyptian attack, the response to the notice had been minimal, and the aircraft were not dispersed or camouflaged. The garage was bombed and the munitions warehouse was set afire. Two planes, a twin-engined De Havilland Dragon Rapide and a light Beechcraft Bonanza B-35, were destroyed. The Bonanza was one of two brought to Israel by the base's commander, Boris Senior, a volunteer who had arrived from South Africa. Three additional aircraft, one Dakota and two Austers, were severely damaged, and four others were lightly damaged. Five people had been killed and nine injured. The seaside wall of the power station had also been hit, but its production facilities had not been harmed.

At approximately 0730 hours, Mahmoud Baraka dove toward the power station and had no trouble keeping the building in his simple gunsights as he pressed the bomb-release button. He immediately pulled on the stick and climbed up and to the left to execute one more run, this time on the houses of Tel Aviv. He was to drop a load of pamphlets in halting Hebrew that called for the citizens to raise white flags of surrender before the victorious Arab army. Before he could release the pamphlets from the containers beneath the Spitfire's wings, he thought he heard fire from the ground. Suddenly he saw a stream of smoke spewing from his engine. The propeller began to convulse. Beneath him he could see only the sea and the houses of the nearby city. Mahmoud surged forward, searching for a flat stretch of open ground on which he could land. To his left, far away, he could see the beach near Herzliya, which seemed adequate and safe. He pulled north with the remainder of his dying engine's strength and landed the Spitfire on the water's edge.

An hour later, Baraka surrendered to the Israeli force that had surrounded him. Years later the argument would continue over who would receive the credit for the first plane shot down—the antiaircraft battery at the field, with their 20-millimeter Hispano-Suizas (which had been smuggled into the country in potato containers), or the field's technicians, who had fired with their rifles. They readily admitted that they had missed the enemy aircraft in the surprise morning attack which had caused most of the damage to the field and the squadron simply because they had believed that the Egyptians could not get planes into the air.

**December 1947**                    *T*he transition from two thousand years of foreign rule to independence had occurred quickly. Memories of the throngs who filled the streets in celebration on the night of November 29 had dissipated. For six months afterward, the Jewish population was entangled in a struggle for its survival against Palestinian irregular forces sworn to prevent the UN partition plan from being realized. This resistance existed even though the decision had included the formation of an Arab-Palestinian state in a large part of the Land of Israel. The Arabs desired Arab control over the entire country. Aided by forces from across the Jordan River as well as from Syria and Iraq, the guerrillas threatened the Jewish neighborhoods of Jerusalem and Haifa and even Tel Aviv. They blockaded isolated Jewish settlements and disrupted the Jewish transportation system. In its final weeks, the British Mandate's control over Israel existed strictly on paper.

## The Air Service

The Air Service was a product of the efforts of several men who were crazy about the idea, just as the others had been who transformed Zionism from a dream into a state. The decision to establish the Air Service was reached in the Haganah headquarters on November 10, 1947, three weeks prior to the UN's decision to divide the country into two states, one Jewish and one Arab.

These were days of uncertainty. Even in the last hours preceding the UN vote in New York, suspicions, not supported by solid evidence, began to arise that the Arabs would attempt to disrupt the partition plan, if implemented, through war. It was not only the professional pessimists who understood that this would be a war of survival more bitter than any of the Jewish population of Israel had known since resettlement of the country began in the late nineteenth century. Not numerous, organized, or trained, the military forces under the control of the Haganah lacked even basic arms and equipment, both in quantity and quality. The military thinking of the upper command was limited to lessons learned in the earlier struggle against the British rule, and it saw this new struggle as primarily a ground war. The lessons of the Second World War had yet to be assimilated, and had not brought about the growth of air power needed to plan the War of Independence with the full involvement of an air force.

Aharon Remez and Heyman Shamir, however, already had their wings, having acquired them in the service of the air forces of Great Britain and the United States during World War II. In their eyes, this time had been, far more than a source of pride in itself, a training period in which they were gaining knowledge and experience that would be of use at a later date. While other pilots left the military and moved on to civilian airlines, the uniforms remained part of Remez's and Shamir's souls. Before his discharge from the RAF, Remez had gathered valuable information from his friends in the air intelligence division; this included everything one would want to know about the Arab air forces in terms of organization, technical support, combat methods, operations, and logistics. With this treasure they presented themselves to the commanders of the Haganah and attempted to persuade them that the establishment of a real air force, beyond the amateur proportions of the flight course of the Palmach (the strike force of the Haganah) and the sporty spirit of the Flight Club, was vital. Even the Air Service, which the Haganah command would later approve, seemed to Remez and Shamir to be a ragtag collection of the supply branch's seconds, and a minimal symbol of what it needed to be.

They sought an air force of a size and strength that would be able to affect the battles of the future, and ultimately play the decisive role in them. Most of the Haganah's leaders immediately rejected such visions, thinking it ridiculous to speak of fighter planes and bombers while the Haganah still lacked guns and artillery. Luck was on Remez and Shamir's side, however, since David Ben-Gurion, chairman of the directorship of the Jewish Agency and soon to be prime minister, was attentive to their ideas and agreed with them.

Remez and Shamir (the latter had been a major in the U.S. Army) were held in high regard by Ben-Gurion, who respected veterans of the western armies. Their opinions, backed by a professional education and real experience, were more acceptable to him than any pioneering idea, regardless of its daring, that the commanders of the Haganah and Palmach could suggest. Shamir and Remez were asked to place their ideas on paper, and on October 23, 1947, they presented Israel Galilie, head of the Central Command of the Haganah, with a detailed plan for the formation of a Jewish air force. They requested a budget of 300,000 liroth (approximately $1 million), a sum greater than the entire defense budget. Knowing that these funds were not available, Shamir added a proposal based on information gathered from personal sources on how to raise the money in contributions from Jews in the United States.

The plan had two parts. The first dealt with the procurement of aircraft, the training of pilots in overt programs, and communications with the British. (No one was really certain, a month prior to the partition, whether the British Mandate would actually come to an end on May 15, 1948, as had been promised, or whether the British would leave the country.) The second part of the plan was covert and involved the underground acquisition of aircraft. The chapters of the plan and its secret appendices dealt with all the requisites for forming an organized and equipped air force:

- Organization of the air department in Haganah headquarters, which would function alongside the previously existing departments.

- A census and gathering of all air crew and ground crew in the country.

- Transfer of British airfields and air bases to Jewish control, and preparation of them for use by the planned air force.

- Sending of envoys abroad to purchase aircraft and munitions according to a list of needed types, and the movement of these supplies to Israel.

- Stockpiling of fuel supplies and other necessary materials.

- Delineation of operational plans, targets, and methods.

- Establishment of an air intelligence network.

- Establishment of a system for the early detection of enemy aircraft.

Galilee passed the plan on to Ben-Gurion, who discussed it with two members of the Jewish Agency directorship and then returned it to the Haganah for debate. Two and a half weeks later, the Haganah Command decided to establish the Air Service. Ben-Gurion gave instructions to allocate it a budget of ten thousand liroth for procurement of planes and equipment. Thus began his direct involvement in realization of the plan. When the issue became one of choosing a commander for the Air Service, however, his political weakness overcame him, and despite his respect for the veterans of the Allied forces, Ben-Gurion appointed Aharon Remez operations officer and Heyman Shamir training officer.

Ben-Gurion preferred those politically close to him in the command positions. He eventually chose Israel Amir, a member of the old guard of the Haganah, as the first commander of the air force, despite the fact that Amir had no flight experience or knowledge. Remez was promoted to deputy commander and, after an arduous period, replaced Amir, becoming the second commander of the air force. Remez's backup came from the group of skilled professionals that began to form in the headquarters. Among them was another graduate of the RAF, who was also an engineer.

Dan Tolkowsky had graduated from the elite Gymnasia Herzliya High School in Tel Aviv and had gone on to study engineering in England. At the outbreak of the Second World War, he joined the RAF, where he served as a fighter pilot and was discharged with the rank of captain. He continued his work as an engineer for two years and then returned home to Israel for a visit. Hearing of the plans for the establishment of an air force, he abandoned his career as a British engineer. Though the Remez-Shamir plan seemed too grand for the as-yet-unformed state, its vision excited him. Tolkowsky joined the lead team. Only in 1956, three years after Tolkowsky became commander-in-chief of the IAF, did the air force reach the full number of aircraft and bases that had been stipulated in the original plan.

## The A Squadron—Light and Operational

The operational arm of the Air Service, the A squadron, was established at Sde Dov on December 9, 1947, with the landing of the last of the Flight Club and Airplane Company aircraft that had been smuggled from the Lod airfield. This was a scant but eclectic collection of light and medium-sized passenger aircraft of various types, single- and twin-engined Austers, Rapids, RWD-13s, and Tiger Moths. Like the pilots who operated these aircraft, they were a cross section of civilian air travel in the 1940s. The Palmach pilots joined in, as did another thirty-five people who were found through the two thousand questionnaires distributed by Remez and Shamir. The rest heard about the infant air force through word of mouth. Though more veterans of the RAF and other foreign air forces began to reach the airfield, the number of volunteers from abroad remained small. After sorting through the pilots, it was found that only thirteen of them had at least 120 flying hours. They would constitute the lead team. Two other groups were categorized by those with at least forty flight hours and those with less than forty. While tremendous differences existed not only in experience but in country of origin, education, and worldview, this airborne ingathering of the exiles was first and foremost an ingathering. It was a proud, determined, organized, efficient, and dedicated team with a sense of the groundbreaking nature of its activities. Their commander and the commander of the base were chosen in an open democratic vote.

While this daytime camaraderie was a product of the native Palmachniks and the ramshackle conditions at Sde Dov, the nighttime kingdom was ruled by the pilots who had arrived from abroad. They lived in a spacious hostel in northern Tel Aviv and later in a luxurious hotel on Ben-Yehuda Street in the city's downtown area, one minute's walk from Ben-Gurion's home. Their free hours after work were spent in the bars, trading beers and stories.

The operations of the A Squadron included intelligence flights, as requested by the commanders of the Haganah, over the Arab settlements to gather information regarding preparations of the guerrillas. They also executed liaison and supply flights to the distant Jewish settlements, including the besieged Jerusalem and Gush Etzion as well as those in the Galilee and the Negev. The pilots dropped—or rather threw—packages of ammunition and supplies, transported commanders or important politicians, and evacuated wounded. Even when they did not drop supplies on a flight, they elevated the morale at remote spots simply by maintaining air contact with the center of the country when telephones were either disconnected or nonexistent and wireless communication was faulty. All the flights were executed under the rubric of the Flight Club or the Airplane Company, disguised against the British flight inspectors, who reacted on a few occasions when the cover wore too thin.

In mid-January 1948, three light aircraft took off from Sde Dov carrying crates of weapons and ammunition that were meant to prolong the stand of Gush Etzion, which was fighting for its life. The prohibited weapons had been smuggled to the base from the sea under cover of darkness. The settlements of Gush Etzion in the Hebron hills lacked even the most basic of runways, and the stormy winter weather eliminated any possibility of an accurate parachute drop. It was decided to throw the crates from low altitude onto tires that would be spread out on the ground. Toward the end of the drop, a British patrol plane neared the area. The Jewish planes escaped under the heavy cloud cover that their pilots had been cursing several minutes earlier. The British pilot managed to see only one plane dropping its load. Its pilot was ordered to appear for investigation at Tel Aviv police headquarters. The whipping boy who was ordered to turn himself in was Ezer Weizman, who, in this flight, had been a dropper and not the pilot. Everyone expected him to receive a light punishment that would do no damage to the Air Service. The five others could lose their civilian flying licenses and receive heavy sentences or expulsions from the country, because they were either foreigners or Palmachniks with previous records. Ezer was released without trial following one night in detention.

The first combat flight of the A Squadron had taken place one month earlier, on December 17, 1947, several days after the escape of the planes from Lod to Sde Dov. It was an improvization based on wise use of data and conditions in the territory, and it is a perfect story with which to begin this history of the Israeli Air Force.

In the morning, Pini Ben-Porat, a Palmach pilot and a member of Kibbutz Na'an, was ordered to take off to the Negev with a doctor in an RWD-13. They were to help the wounded from a convoy that had been attacked. Their landing in Beit Eshel proved to be pointless; the wounded had either died or been evacuated. Pini was about to take off back to Tel Aviv when a British official from the then-Arab city of Be'er Sheva nearby delayed him to find out why he was there. His documents satisfied the officer, who informed them in passing that hundreds of members of a Bedouin band were attacking Kibbutz Nevatim, not far from Beit Eshel. Pini decided to act. After the officer left, he easily removed the plane's two side doors and requested the residents of Beit Eshel to look after the doctor who had come with him from Tel Aviv. In the doctor's place, he requested that they give him one of their men with a machine gun and as many magazines, bullets, and grenades as possible. He strapped the machine gunner to the seat and placed the machine gun so that when it was fired, no part of the plane would be hit. He also positioned the magazines next to him so that he could load the gun with one hand and continue flying with the other.

Several minutes after taking off from Beit Eshel, they could see Nevatim, a tiny and solitary square of green in the desert, surrounded by ravines and canyons that could shield the attackers. He could clearly see the Arab forces assaulting the small settlement, and began to plan his attack on them. Light civilian planes are not designed like military ones, for direct forward firing in a dive. Pini calculated that if he banked the aircraft at a downward angle, his gunner would have a wide enough field of fire so that the plane would not be damaged. At the moment when he steadied the plane at the desired angle, he gave the command to the gunner, who opened fire on the Arab forces. The gunner fired one burst, then another and, in between them, dropped grenades. Within minutes the enemy, who had never encountered an air attack, were in a panic and running for their lives.

Pini landed in a field near Nevatim, whose excited defenders reported that they had wounded. Ordering the gunner to remain behind, he evacuated one of the wounded whose life was in danger. He flew back to the doctor in Beit Eshel, who provided first aid, and then immediately took off to Tel Aviv to transport the patient to a hospital. He picked up the doctor toward evening. The sounds of this historic attack reverberated far beyond the expanses of the Negev. In his journals, Ben-Gurion quoted an intelligence report that stated that the attack had astounded even the Arabs of Jerusalem. The British were also quite angry, and announced that any Jewish plane using weapons would be shot down without warning.

Six years later, in 1955, Pini Ben-Porat, by then an El Al pilot, was shot down over Bulgaria. This innocent civilian flight was mysteriously intercepted without warning by fighter aircraft of the Bulgarian Air Force. His Lockheed Constellation was perforated like a sieve and crashed while attempting an emergency landing. All fifty-eight passengers and crew were killed.

In early 1948, the Air Service was about to receive unexpectedly twenty-one light Auster aircraft. They were bought at a clearance sale at a public auction of surplus from the RAF, which had begun to collapse on the eve of the end of Mandate. After renovations, the aircraft slowly began to arrive in the country (though only nineteen of them actually arrived). The purchase had been executed at the command of Ben-Gurion, who had instructed that priority be given to the building of the air force.

Simultaneously, in the United States and Europe, envoys of the state that was yet to be were in the midst of semiofficial or covert negotiations to purchase various types of weapons—fighter aircraft, bombers, and transport aircraft of any sort. An additional supply source developed in Czechoslovakia with the approval and encouragement of the Soviet Union, which supported the formation of the Jewish state, not from love of Zionism but rather because of its desire to evict the British from the Middle East.

Ben-Gurion, tortured by nightmares of the Second World War and the destruction of Europe's cities from the air, was among the few who anticipated an invasion of Israel by the Arab armies if and when a Jewish state was established. He feared aerial bombardments, which could lay waste to the cities of Israel, and expressed that fear in many documents and meetings. At this point he was convinced of the need to acquire a defensive air force as soon as possible, and he used all his powers to remove any obstacles to its formation. The budget was small, and there was no lack of objectors among those responsible for the country's defense. The military thinking of most of them was limited to knowledge and experience gained in minimal ground fighting. The General Command of the IDF would later develop out of this group, and it would take nearly twenty years and two additional wars to convince them that nothing could compete with the decisive power of an air force in modern warfare. Nevertheless, the founders' objections to the preferential treatment given the air force came from honest concern and were not completely arbitrary. Ben-Gurion must receive the credit for his vision and correct timing in ordering aircraft and assembling the first group of pilots to train on them when there was a shortage of weapons. If he had done so any later than early 1948, there would not have been five Messerschmitts in the country to stop the attempted Egyptian invasion of Tel Aviv, which included an aerial attack on the city.

In March 1948, A Squadron had eighteen light aircraft and thirty-seven pilots, more than half of them natives and the remainder volunteers from abroad. The movement of Jewish volunteer pilots increased over the course of the 1948 war, and toward its conclusion they were the backbone of the air force that was growing out of the Air Service. The Service lacked experienced professional pilots, not just pilots with combat experience. Evidence of this shortage appeared in the number of accidents that unnecessarily reduced the already small number of pilots.

The purchase of the Austers allowed for the formation of two sub-squadrons that would belong to the Negev and Galilee fronts. Thus the commanders of the regional brigades would no longer be dependent on the Tel Aviv center. They could now have fast and effective air support upon demand. The southern squadron was based near the headquarters of the Negev brigade at Kibbutz Nir-Am, on an improvised dirt runway. The northern squadron operated out of Yavniel Field, near the headquarters of the Golani Brigade.

Ezer Weizman was sent with two planes, three pilots, and five mechanics to take command of the Negev squadron. It was the first command position for this twenty-four-year-old pilot, who would steadily climb to the top. Ezer, a volatile mixture of fulminate of mercury and boyish mischievousness, was an unusual native of the country, quite the opposite of the Palmach generation. He had not been raised in any of the youth movements, but rather was the product of a wealthy Haifa family. He had learned to fly in the Flight Club when the Second World War was at its peak. Wanting to become an RAF pilot, he volunteered for the British Army. However, he was sent to a flight course in Rhodesia (present-day Zimbabwe) only in 1943.

The training was fundamental, and not superficial as it had been at the beginning of the war. "The lad suffers from exaggerated self-confidence," his instructors warned in his personal file. They were not surprised when he chose operational training on the Thunderbolt rather than on the popular Spitfire. Tremendous daring and bravery were needed to fly this American fighter plane. It was heavier than the Spitfire, but required very careful handling, and a number of pilots had lost their lives through unwise flying of it. In 1946, Ezer left the RAF and returned home.

On the eve of the establishment of the state, the Negev had twenty-three Jewish kibbutzim, most of them fairly new, small, and isolated, some even under blockade. The Negev Squadron was almost the only live connection between the communities themselves and the regional headquarters. The Austers kept watch from an altitude of one hundred to two hundred meters on the movement of convoys, after the Arab forces began to prey upon lone vehicles. Ezer could give early warning of roadblocks or ambushes, and a convoy's defenders would send ahead a rescue force to open the road and secure it. The aircraft took off from a dirt runway that Ezer and the Palmachniks prepared. Flight control took place from a primitive wooden tower. The flights were directed by headquarters, which was located in a shack housing the office and a workshop. If no convoy was scheduled, they executed daily patrol flights along the water pipeline that passed between the kibbutzim, in order to prevent guerrilla actions that could cut off their precious water supply. They also flew routine supply sorties in which they carried medical equipment or vital munitions, not forgetting the mail and newspapers. More than once they were sent to evacuate someone severely wounded, flying the plane with one hand and working as a medic with the other. The kibbutzim attempted to pave landing strips nearby to ease their accessibility to the aircraft, but the shortage of decent strips forced the planes to make risky emergency landings on sand dunes or dried riverbeds in the desert canyons.

In February 1948, they began to act on the precedent set by Pini Ben-Porat in Nevatim. Machine gunners were placed in the Austers and armed with homemade explosives that could be thrown by hand. Thus the flight board was decorated with bombing and strafing runs not only on the assaulting Arab forces that were discovered, but also with planned preventive bombings on villages in the Gaza area. The fleet of aircraft was enriched one morning when one of the brigade's ground patrols captured a Fairchild F-24 Argus flown by a wealthy Egyptian youth who had landed in order to purchase smuggled hashish from the Bedouins. Abstaining even from alcohol, the Palmachniks had no idea what to do with hashish. They threw it into the trash and repainted the plane, adding it immediately to the Air Service.

The Egyptian prize made its way north and was allocated to the Galilee Squadron, which had been formed in early 1948, a month after its southern sister squadron. The northern settlements were not spread out or isolated like those in the Negev, and therefore needed little air service for communications or supplies. Thus the new squadron dedicated itself to combat activities based on the limited experience that the

Negev Squadron had acquired in its operational sorties. Under the command of Pesach "Pussy" Tolchinsky, a member of Kibbutz Kfar Giladi and one of the founding members of the A Squadron, five pilots and one bomb dropper set out in three light aircraft to strafe and bomb enemy positions and installations. After three weeks, Pussy was sent to train on heavy transport aircraft that had been purchased abroad, and he was replaced by Daniel Bookstein.

On May 2, Bookstein appeared in the skies over Ramat Naftali, near the Lebanon border, and saved the kibbutz from being captured and destroyed. Born in Moscow and raised in Tel Aviv, the twenty-seven-year-old commander was among the handful of professionals who joined the A Squadron with five hundred flight hours in the Airplane Company and the RAF.

On that day, three hundred members of the Rescue Army, a volunteer force organized in Syria and Lebanon to aid Israeli Arabs, swarmed down on Ramat Naftali. Prior to this, they had gained control over abandoned police buildings and British military installations along the northern border, threatening a series of Jewish settlements in the area. The assault on Ramot Naftali was aided by armored vehicles and light artillery. The kibbutz had forty-five fatigued defenders with few weapons. They cried out for help from the regional Palmach brigade, but it had been occupied for four days in Operation Yiftah, organized to liberate Safed and to drive out the forces of the Rescue Army that had destroyed communications between the city and the Hula Valley. Ramot Naftali was isolated, on the edge of the front, and its defenders would have to fend for themselves.

They managed to hold on until they saw the armored vehicles nearing the kibbutz's outskirts. Only then did they begin to think of abandoning the kibbutz before falling victim to the mass slaughter that awaited all Jewish residents and fighters who fell into the hands of the Arab forces at that time. The brigade headquarters summoned the squadron from Yavniel, and three aircraft took off to the Machanaim Field, near Rosh Pina. Two of the planes carried explosives, two primitive bombs weighing ten and twenty-five kilograms, which were built in the workshops of the Military Industries, the secret weapons plant of the Haganah. The third plane also carried a machine gunner. The first pair took off to Ramat Naftali, several minutes' flying time away, while the third waited in Machanaim, ready to take off as support or replacement.

Bookstein was the leader. His Auster descended first on the armored vehicles and, flying low, dropped three bombs from the plane's open doors. The explosives landed between the vehicles with thundering explosions that drove panic and hysteria into the enemy forces. Before they had managed to recover, the second Auster, flown by Moshe Feldman (Peled) appeared, and dropped one bomb on the armored vehicles and another two on the nearby Arab village of Kaddesh. He then sprayed a line of trucks on the road from Kaddesh to Malchia with his machine gun until not a single round remained in the twenty magazines he had brought with him. The aircraft returned to Machanaim to reload and returned immediately. The two planes flew nine bombing and strafing sorties that day, with half-hour intermissions between them. Two armored vehicles were damaged and the remainder retreated. Several of the enemy foot soldiers fired strongly at the aircraft and then retreated as well. In their footsteps, the Arab residents of the villages of Malchia and Kaddesh began a massive escape toward Syria. Ramot Naftali had been saved.

Eight days later, on May 10, Daniel Bookstein was killed in the Judean Hills in an operation reminiscent of the breaking of the blockade on Jerusalem. The first great penetration of Operation Nachshon removed the enemy's stranglehold for a few days. The road was again blocked, and the elation was replaced by a depression and frustration the likes of which had not been seen in the previous five months.

The blockade of Jerusalem grew stronger and steadily more airtight starting in December 1947, immediately following the UN partition decision, which recommended that Jerusalem be granted the status of an international city. The riots that erupted in the city the following day were the start of a bloody battle over national sovereignty. The goal of the Jews, like that of the Arabs, both Muslim and Christian, to gain control over this city holy to three religions, was rooted in deep faith and ancient traditions. Each nation based its claim on the city on the fact that at some point over the course of three thousand years its people had ruled it. Beyond the messianic feelings surrounding the conflict, however, both nations in partitioned Palestine understood the city's strategic importance.

The Arabs had no problem cutting off Jewish Jerusalem in late 1947. The new Jewish settling of the country had not created many settlements between Jerusalem and the greater Jewish population centers on the

Mediterranean coast. Jewish Jerusalem's fate depended on a short sector of road, twenty-five kilometers long, that was completely lined by Arab villages. The local Arab forces grew out of them, aided by deserters from the Mandate police forces and mercenaries from other Arab countries and Europe. They disrupted the water supply along the main line to the city and blocked stretches of the road in Latrun, Sha'ar HaGuy, and the Castel, an old Crusader castle on a mountaintop near Jerusalem. Until the end of February 1948, the Arabs had been satisfied with random raids against the Jewish convoys.

The Air Service's planes came to the rescue of the convoys immediately after the first attacks. At first they flew random intelligence sorties and brought back early and vital information regarding ambushes and roadblocks. Starting in early March, the convoys began to receive steady air support. The British military abandoned the main road and transported its troops, who were being withdrawn from the country, along another route. The pressure of the attacks increased daily and required Haganah headquarters to protect the convoys with increased forces. The number of convoys dropped; those that did make their way to the city arrived battered, having left behind the smoking hulks of supply trucks and armored vehicles. The umbilical cord to Jerusalem was in danger of being severed; the distress of starvation and thirst overshadowing the city was now compounded by ceaseless shelling day and night. It would not be able to survive this for long.

The pilots of the A Squadron would take off from Sde Dov approximately an hour before a convoy set out, and would survey the stretches of road that tended to be problematic. The convoys' route was not direct, as they strove to avoid as many Arab population centers as possible along the road. Starting at the bottleneck of Sha'ar HaGuy lay an ancient stretch of road seven kilometers long. Flanked by steep and rocky slopes, the road afforded countless natural spots for cover from which the Arab forces controlled all movement below them. A small roadblock of stones was enough to stop a convoy; no alternate trails existed. The attackers could then pour gunfire down on the convoy. If one heavy vehicle was damaged and could not be moved, the entire convoy would be trapped behind it.

This tortuous path had not reached its end. Eight kilometers farther down the road lay Mount Castel, whose peak, housing the remnants of a Roman and Crusader fort, was now an Arab village that was the center of activities of the bands under the command of Abed Al-Kadr Al-Husseini.

That winter the squadron's pilots were the eyes and ears of the country, serving as flying communication stations that relayed information between the convoys and other forces. The only danger to them was presented by the occasional patrol flights of the RAF. Ground fire was rare and ineffective. A number of times they witnessed from above the assault on Jewish armored vehicles, the fires and the bodies. They could do nothing but report the incident and helplessly grit their teeth.

The hardest and longest battle until then had taken place in late March 1948. A convoy of thirty-three trucks set out carrying supplies from Jerusalem to the four blockaded Jewish settlements in Gush Etzion, which lay in the Hebron Hills. This area, which protected the southern part of Jerusalem, desperately needed 120 tons of food so that it could maintain its stand for another three months. An armed force of 130 defenders in eighteen armored vehicles was distributed among the trucks. Four additional armored vehicles spearheaded the convoy's movement to break up any roadblocks that might be erected.

Daniel Bookstein took off in an Auster from Sde Dov. Next to him lay the first bombs built for the Air Service, less than a day after they had come off the Military Industries production line. The ridiculous-looking metal objects were called "Model 1." An elongated cast-iron box filled with a mixture of explosives, screws, and pieces of metal, this type of device had a tail strengthened by two poles to assure a vertical fall. Though dangerous to anyone struck by it, it was a threat as well to the pilot who had to carry it and execute bizarre maneuvers to protect himself from the bomb as he dropped it.

Bookstein found himself caught in a struggle for survival from the moment his Auster, loaded with Model 1s, left the runway at Sde Dov. The bombs had fuses with a twenty-two-second delay. The countdown began when the safety latch was released, before the drop. He reviewed the operation and safety instructions, which placed the object far out of any accepted standards of safety in air travel. He was simply not to touch the bombs until the moment of attack, and there were to be no sharp movements as long as the airplane was loaded, and no flying at less than three thousand feet. If the safety catch came undone, he was to throw the bomb quickly out of the plane into an open area away from any populated area.

Forty-four days before his tragic death, he beheld the explosives that would pioneer an age of Jewish air bombing in Israel, the insurance policy that would guarantee the convoy's safe passage to Gush Etzion and its return. In a journey of thirty minutes, the convoy reached Gush Etzion and unloaded. Within two hours it was ready to return. The commanders of the Arab forces had not managed to organize themselves for an attack on the convoy on its way south. If the convoy had not been delayed in Gush Etzion for technical reasons, it might have returned safely to Jerusalem. But the extra hour had given the Arabs time to organize themselves. The forward armored vehicle was damaged by a land mine and blocked the narrow road. The convoy, a kilometer long, was halted. Only eleven of the vehicles, including the convoy's commander, managed to turn back and return to Gush Etzion. The 180 others who remained found themselves trapped, easy prey to their attackers, who outnumbered them. The fighters, who were approximately two-thirds of this group, evaluated the situation in that they had no commanders and chose, under the fire which was closing in, to gather their people in the armored vehicles and take cover in a stone house in Nebi Daniel, a Muslim holy site.

After the convoy had left Gush Etzion, Bookstein had been called back to Sde Dov, landing according to the security regulations for landing with live explosives. The cries of those trapped at Nebi Daniel, surrounded by hundreds of attackers, reached the field. The enemy had already set fire to vehicles abandoned in the road. Mordechai "Modi" Alon took the Auster from Bookstein and dropped two bombs on the attackers. Modi, twenty-eight years old, had received his wings along with Ezer Weizman in the RAF course in Rhodesia, and had joined the Air Service. A second Auster took off after him and continued to bomb the Arab forces, which took cover among the olive trees and hills around the house. Dozens of Arabs began to retreat. In the second run, he attempted to strafe them with a machine gun. The two crew members and the passengers were all pilots who rotated functions. They took turns flying the aircraft, dropping bombs, and firing the Bren machine guns, a ground forces gun with magazines holding ten rounds each. This run almost pulled off the plane's wing as the first burst perforated its supports. The designers of this sporty plane had never dreamed that it would serve as a fighter-bomber. The gunner and the pilot had to work at levels of intense cooperation, flying at perfect angles and aiming the gun meticulously so as not to shear off their own wing. Their excitement overcame their prudence, but luckily the second burst jammed the gun. They quickly landed in Gush Etzion, saw that the damage to the plane was not serious, and returned to Tel Aviv.

Modi took off again and bombed. The next aircraft received a welcome of blazing machine-gun fire from the ground, and its bombs missed three truckloads of Arabs. The trapped convoy members had been fighting for thirty hours. That night, in the moonlight, the aircraft attempted unsuccessfully to drop food supplies and water.

Bookstein returned to the area near dawn, this time as the bombardier or "dropper" in a twin-engined, multi-seat Rapid passenger aircraft. In the first run he dropped his bombs, which did not silence the fire from below, but served to confuse the pilot, who missed the house on the next run, as he dropped supplies to the besieged group. The package fell one hundred meters away, and those fighters who attempted to retrieve them fell victim to sniper fire.

The cries of distress increased in the morning. "The Arabs are attacking with mortars! Send planes!" The headquarters of the Etzioni brigade in Jerusalem was helpless. The Air Service was the only lifeline to those in the house. The Austers continued to drop bombs and packages of food and water. In the meantime, the British were called upon to rescue the besieged group, and their armored vehicles set out from Jerusalem. Al-Husseini threatened to attack the British as well if they would not leave the area. The British column was stopped outside of Bethlehem.

Modi returned with Zvi "Chibi" Zibel to bomb the attackers. In the afternoon, Chibi returned again and dropped food packages and ammunition in two low runs under heavy fire. As he pulled out of the second run, he was hit. A machine-gun burst shattered the windscreen and its pieces struck him in his eyes and chest. The bomb dropper bandaged him in midflight. The engine had been hit as well, and Chibi returned to Sde Dov on his last drops of oil.

The besieged group did not give in, and that afternoon the Arab attack slackened. The British were allowed in to evacuate the Jews. The fifteen dead who remained in the building were mutilated by the Arabs, who chose to express their rage and frustrations on those who could not respond and had not managed to escape with their lives.

The Air Service had now executed unprecedented operational activities. It had unquestionably proved its superiority over any ground force, even if its aircraft and weapons were not suited for the mission. During the long battle, the aircraft flew ten bombing and strafing sorties, drop-ping thirty-three bombs, and nine supply sorties in which they dropped a total of one thousand kilograms. They also flew twenty missions on other fronts, all with only fourteen pilots and six aircraft.

Yigal Yadin (whose brother, Mati Sukenik, was a member of the squadron) was commander of the Operations Branch at Haganah headquarters. He congratulated Aharon Remez and requested that he give the pilots a pat on the back in his name. He noted the number of problems in communications with headquarters and the need to improve operational procedures. Remez could conclude, with great personal satis-faction, that the events of those two days in late March 1948 had pulled the Air Service out of its diapers.

Four days after the tragedy that struck the convoy at Nebi Daniel, another convoy making its way to Jerusalem was caught in enemy fire. Pini Ben-Porat and Chibi Zibel, who had quickly recovered from his injuries, were among the pilots of the five Austers that accompanied it. However, they were helpless against the slaughter that took place on the road below them, where twenty-two members of the convoy were killed and sixteen were injured. In Tel Aviv, Ben-Gurion assembled the Upper Command of the Haganah and stated that "the war over the transporta-tion to Jerusalem is now the critical war. The fall of Jewish Jerusalem could very well be the deathblow to the entire Jewish settlement in the Land of Israel."

From this dark moment, Operation Nachshon was born. It was a daring and unusual mission, the product of innovative military thought and a function of time and place. This would not be a series of random defensive battles and meager attack sorties in the cut-and-run style, but rather a dense effort to break through the road to the city in a first-strike attack. Well planned and eclectic, it sought to capture and secure a large area. Israeli representatives had already completed the first deals in Czechoslovakia for the purchase of the light arms needed for this and other operations. The first loaded ship stood ready to depart and smuggle the weapons from the Yugoslavian coast into the country in the third week of March. Because of time constraints, however, Nachshon could not continue beyond the first days of April. Therefore they had to find a quicker means of transporting the shipment to Israel. Israeli purchasing agents in Europe, the United States, and even Africa had thought of this, and were already negotiating with civilian airlines for the purchase or lease of transport aircraft. The limitations imposed by the United States in mid-February on military aid to both of the combatant forces delayed the takeoff of aircraft that had already been purchased, and forced Israeli supply experts to find new underground routes. American diplomats in Europe were instructed to observe the airports and to report unusual flights of transport aircraft with U.S. registration. The envoys managed to deceive them when urgent orders arrived from Tel Aviv in Ben-Gurion's name telling them to accelerate "Operation Balak."

"Balak 1," the code name of the first Douglas C-54 Skymaster transport aircraft, was leased from an American company behind the back of the State Department and the FBI in Washington. It landed in Prague on March 13. Ten days earlier, the Air Service had been instructed to find or improvise a landing strip suitable for a heavy four-engine transport plane, as isolated as possible to allow for covert landings and takeoffs. The airline companies objected to dirt runways, and a search revealed an abandoned British runway in the Arab village of Beit-Daras, near Be'er Tuvia. An emergency landing strip that had been paved during the Second World War, it lacked lighting or any safety or control features. Pini Ben-Porat executed a trial landing and found it usable.

Balak 1 was to land under cover of darkness and take off back to Prague immediately after unloading its shipment of weapons, without the British or the Arabs knowing of its existence. The Air Service was prepared for this landing operation, known as Operation Stork, whose objective was kept secret even from the fighters of the Giv'ati Brigade, who were to protect the area. They had been told that the early patrols around the area were preparation for the capture of Beit-Daras. The true reason would be revealed to them when they were called upon to unload the weapons. The Air Service was to arrange fuel supplies for the plane before its return to Europe, ready a technical crew to check its mechanical state, and provide lighting for the runway. This mission was undertaken by a young man named Avraham "Buma" Shavit, who that night embedded himself in the fate of the IAF for years to come by becoming one of the experts at activating airfields captured in wartime. Buma scoured the country until he found a mobile lighting system in Netanya that could be extended to four kilometers. The system could be unfolded and reassembled quickly and was controlled with one switch. It was connected to a generator that also provided electricity for the communications system with the plane and headquarters. The lighting system was meant to function only for the few minutes required for landings and takeoffs.

The heavily laden Skymaster approached from the sea and landed without a problem on the landing strip, which glowed in the darkness. The lights were turned off and the weapons were unloaded. The hand-pumped fueling of the aircraft and its mechanical check were done with small flashlights. Within an hour the trucks were loaded with a treasure that included two hundred Czechoslovakian Mauser rifles, forty machine guns, and 150,000 rounds of ammunition. In less than eighty minutes the runway was illuminated again. The Skymaster took off, and was swallowed by the black night skies over the sea. A British unit camped twenty kilometers away never woke up. The Arabs of Beit-Daras, accustomed to the flights of the Flight Club, did not suspect a thing. By first light, the landing strip had been cleared of any evidence of the evening's activities.

Though the Haganah command had planned additional air shipments, Balak 1 was immediately grounded upon its return to Prague. Suspicious American diplomats awaited it at sunup. Having heard a mixture of partial information and rumors, they accused the crew of smuggling arms to the Italian communists. The crew was willing to admit only to transporting medical equipment to "a small village in Palestine." Who had hired them? The navigator, the only Jew in the crew, mentioned the name of a British resident of Paris. They were released after being warned not to attempt to return to the Middle East; otherwise they would be charged with breaking U.S. law, and sanctions would be taken against the company. The threat succeeded, and it was six weeks before Balak 2 could take off. To the luck of the Nachshon command center, the boat with arms from Czechoslovakia arrived the next night, on April 1, carrying in its holds 4,500 Czechoslovakian rifles, two hundred machine guns, and five million rounds of ammunition. Ben-Gurion would later claim that this treasure saved the State of Israel.

The Nachshon fighters received the weapons in their bases and embraced the grease-covered guns. The operation began on April 6, and in the twelve days that followed, large areas on the road to Jerusalem were captured. The Castel, the center of Arab activities and a primary obstacle, was taken by one side, then by another, until Al-Husseini was shot and killed there. The blue-and-white Jewish flag then flew from the remnants of the ruin atop the mountain.

For the first time in the history of the Air Service, a force of aircraft had been allocated to a mission and had received its commands from headquarters via a special communications network of a kind that had never been seen before. Pini Ben-Porat prepared a forward base with a dirt runway near his home at Kubbutz Na'an. It had only two Tiger Moth light aircraft that flew reconnaissance flights during the operation. Later they were called in for bombing missions, and recently purchased Bonanza and Norseman aircraft were added to the force.

Operation Nachshon had not surprised the A Squadron, and had not required it to deal with new challenges. The new element was that cooperation between air and ground forces had been improved. The pilots were already experienced and were well acquainted with the variety of aircraft in their possession, and their advantages and quirks relative to the unusual missions they were asked to perform. The accidents that had recently plagued the squadron dropped significantly, and routine damage to the aircraft was now generally caused by antiaircraft fire. The technical crews had also improved; they were no longer auto mechanics, but flight technicians who could find any way, however unlikely, to return a broken or damaged aircraft to flight. They had twenty light aircraft in April 1948, of six varieties. The grounding of any one of them reduced the force by five percent.

Though Nachshon had saved Jerusalem and had broken the Israeli Arabs' makeshift armies, its achievements were limited to the days of the operation. The positions were soon abandoned and the Arabs soon blocked the road again. In early May the number of reports grew of a planned assault on Israel by the regular Arab armies on May 15. There was no doubt that Jerusalem would fall to them sooner or later. It was therefore decided to execute a second joint operation to break through the road to Jerusalem, this time in an attempt to leave it in Jewish hands.

Operation Maccabee, named for Maccabee Mutzeri, a convoy commander who had been killed in Sha'ar HaGuy, began one week prior to the conclusion of the British Mandate and the declaration of the State. On May 1, the A Squadron was called upon to drop a new and experimental bomb on the Arab village of Beit-Mahsir, which overlooked Sha'ar HaGuy. The bomb was a barrel of explosives weighing two hundred kilograms. The mission was to be executed by one of the newly acquired multi-seat Norsemen. Yariv Sheinbaum was the pilot and Daniel Bookstein, by now commander of the Galilee Squadron, pressed to join the flight, even as copilot. By chance he happened to be at Sde Dov on the morning of the flight, and he did not want to miss the historic bombing. He took his place beside Sheinbaum, and behind them, in the belly of the Norseman, sat three munitions experts with the enormous bomb. A graduate of the first aerial photography course joined them as well.

In its last message to ground headquarters, the crew reported identifying the target and entering its bombing run. Immediately afterward, the Norseman could be seen spinning and exploding on the ridge near Beit-Mahsir. The reason would never be known. In the Air Service, it was thought that the heavy bomb might have slipped from its place, causing the pilot to lose control over the aircraft, or that the detonator had been activated too early. There was an outside chance that British fighter planes had shot it down. The six crew members were killed, and their bodies were not found. Half a year later, after the capture of the ridge, fragments of the aircraft were found twenty kilometers west of Jerusalem. The Norseman's engine was left where it fell, and the place became the memorial monument for fallen IAF fighters in Israel's wars. The ridge was renamed Pilots' Mountain.

With Operation Maccabee in full force, urgent telegrams were sent to the Negev and Galilee squadrons, summoning Ezer Weizman and Modi Alon to Air Service headquarters. On his way to Tel Aviv, Ezer attempted to recall what order he had disobeyed in order to be pulled from the front at this sensitive time. The last time he had been summoned was when he had stolen a plane in order to increase the size of his tiny squadron, which was suffering under the pressure of working with only two aircraft. Receiving nearly miraculous preferential treatment, he was not discharged or even grounded for very long.

At headquarters he met Modi, his course-mate from Rhodesia. Aharon Remez greeted them with a dry announcement that caused Ezer's heart to skip a beat. "You are leaving for Czechoslovakia to train on Messerschmitt 109 fighter aircraft and to bring them to the country." This was Ezer's dream of flying fighter aircraft in Israel come true.

He returned to his squadron headquarters at Nir-Am and strapped his pistol to the waist of Eli Finegersh, symbolically transferring to him command of the Negev Squadron. Along with ten other Israeli fliers, including Pini Ben-Porat and some of the foreign volunteers, he took off for Czechoslovakia. These volunteers, American and South African Jews, became a cornerstone in the history of the Israeli Air Force. Ehud Avriel, one of those mysterious acquisitions envoys who could be found in Europe and the United States searching for new weapons to purchase, awaited them in Prague. In essence, Avriel held the rank of unofficial ambassador to Prague, representing the country that was still in formation. While the purchase negotiations were covert, they were not with private vendors but rather with representatives of the new communist government. Avriel revealed to the pilots that ten Messerschmitts had been acquired in the Czechoslovakian arms deal. They still had no idea how they would transfer them to Israel, but in the meantime the group would learn how to operate the aircraft. Everything was taking place under orders from Moscow.

The Russians' intention was to speed up the British departure from the Middle East. The Jewish battle for independence was merely a means of achieving this. Twenty million dollars was paid for the arms, of which $500,000 covered the price of the first ten Messerschmitts—$44,000 per aircraft. No one imagined that things would change so drastically later on, and that within seven years the Czechs would be arming Egypt, with the goal of wiping Israel off the map.

Training began several days later on the grass runways of the Czechoslovakian air base of Ceske Budejovice. The Messerschmitts were of a German model manufactured in Czech factories that had been captured by the Nazis on the eve of the Second World War. Following the war, the Czechs continued their production. The Czechs dressed the Israeli pilots in air force uniforms from other countries to disguise their identities. Modi and Ezer acclimated themselves quickly to the cockpit of the single-engine Messerschmitt, a fighter-bomber armed with machine guns and cannons. On the third day of training, the pilots heard on the radio that in Tel Aviv, David Ben-Gurion had declared the founding of the State of Israel. Almost in the same breath, the announcer stated that Egyptian aircraft had bombed Tel Aviv.

Though they had accrued only seven or eight hours in the planes, less than a tenth of the minimum required for learning a new aircraft, Modi and Ezer knew in their hearts that the course was over. They had not fired a single round, had not dropped one bomb, and had not attempted night navigation, but as the radio told of armored Egyptian columns moving toward Tel Aviv, sitting in the Messerschmitt's cockpit over Czechoslovakia was like sitting on needles. On May 18 the pilots telephoned Avriel and informed him that the course had ended and that they were returning home. Arrangements for transferring the aircraft to Israel were not yet complete. The Messerschmitt had a short flying range, a maximum of ninety minutes. They had to be disassembled and loaded onto transport aircraft that the Israeli envoys had not yet managed to acquire.

Ezer and Modi informed the astounded course commander that they had finished and reassured him that they would be able to make up the exercises missed on the firing range in real life. Returning to Prague, they discovered a C-54 Skymaster, the same type used in Operation Balak, sitting at the nearby Zatetz air base, its belly loaded with the parts of the first Messerschmitt, including bombs, cannon rounds, and replacement parts. It was eleven and a half hours' flying time, without refueling, to the abandoned British air base of Akron near Rehovot, known as Tel Nof. Since its evacuation by the British two months earlier, it was the most sophisticated airfield under Jewish control, serving as a training base and housing a regiment of the Giv'ati Brigade. With early organization and little effort, IAF commander-in-chief Remez's plan to prepare the field and its installations for the landing of the upcoming Balak transport flights was quickly executed. On May 12, Balak 2 arrived and there was no longer any need for makeshift lighting. The Skymaster, loaded with the Messerschmitt parts, was the fifth in the series. Nearing the Israeli coast, it plodded its way through the complete darkness that protected the country from attacks by the Egyptian Air Force. The first fighter plane of the Israeli Air Force arrived on May 20, a perfect and heartwarming present for the week-old state.

The aircraft of the Egyptian Air Force, for the most part Spitfires, returned several times during the week to attack Tel Aviv. Flying sporadically and not in waves, with large intervals between runs, they nonetheless managed to inflict pain. After the relatively heavy bombing of Sde Dov on the morning of May 15, in which the A Squadron's aircraft were damaged and five of its members were killed, they attacked the Tel Aviv Central Bus Station, killing and wounding dozens of civilians. The frequent air-raid sirens sent the city's residents running to bomb shelters. Not many of the city's buildings were actually damaged, and other than in the attack on the bus station, few people were hurt.

The Egyptians also attacked the Negev Squadron's landing strip at Nir-Am, lightly damaging one of its two Austers. Two Dakotas and one Commando were damaged during an attack on Tel Nof. Syrian and Iraqi aircraft attacked kibbutzim in the north and the Galilee Squadron's landing strip in Yavniel. The squadron had to camouflage its aircraft and postpone its liaison and supply flights until nighttime, when they would not be chased by the enemy pilots.

At the outbreak of the 1948 war, the Arab air forces had a total of 131 aircraft. Of that number, the Egyptians had a combined total of fifty fighter and bomber aircraft, Iraq had nine, and Syria had fifteen bombers. This force, however, exhibited limited abilities when sent to military targets whose bombing demanded accuracy. Even when they had no Israeli Air Force or effective antiaircraft defenses with which to contend, they performed poorly. On May 16, 1948, the Air Service officially became the Israeli Air Force, before the formation of the Israel Defense Forces. Its new commander, Israel Amir (Zabeldovesky), a Haganah man and a political crony of Ben-Gurion, was not a professional aviator, which upset people in the Central Command. The IAF had an impressive headquarters, with 675 workers and clerks, and squadrons named "Panther" (the A Squadron), "Camel" (the Negev Squadron), and "Lion" (the Galilee Squadron). These grandiose names did not inflate the forces of the squadrons, which, on the week of the declaration of the State, had a total of twenty-one passenger and transport aircraft, light and medium-sized, of seven different types. Three of these planes were unflyable, ten had various other problems, and only eight were operational. After the May 15 attack on Sde Dov, the number of operational aircraft dropped to five.

The enemy's sorties suffered from a lack of reliable intelligence information and faulty communications at the command level. Thus their aircraft attacked empty airfields such as the one near Kfar Sirkin, or incorrect targets such as the field at Ramat David. On May 22, the Egyptians set out to attack Ramat David, not knowing that the RAF still controlled it and was using it to defend its evacuating forces, which were departing from the Haifa port. The Egyptian pilots, in an assaulting quartet of Spitfires, did not ask themselves where the Jews had suddenly acquired such a large number of fighter planes and why they were exposed on the runway. They descended on the British Spitfires, destroyed several of them, and shot down a British Dakota on its way to land. They then left to clear the area for the second run. The next quartet was caught in a calculated British ambush and was shot down. Egyptian intelligence had been off by forty-eight hours. The last of the British left Ramat David two days later, and the base's sophisticated installations were passed on complete to the IAF. The only thing they took with them was their planes.

Along with its disassembled Messerschmitt, Balak 5 carried five of the eleven pilots who had gone to train in Czechoslovakia. They included Ezer and Modi as well as three volunteers from abroad, Lou Lenart, Eddie Cohen, and Rubie Rubenfield, a strange mix of Jewish intensity and the traits of Anglo-Saxons. Upon arrival, they encountered a situation on the verge of desperation. The Egyptians were nearing Tel Aviv and were closing in on Jerusalem along with the Jordanian Arab Legion. The Syrians were situated just above Degania, near the Sea of Galilee. A mixed Iraqi-Jordanian column was moving toward Netanya and threatened to cut off the center of the country. Ezer explained that the airlift of Messerschmitts would not occur in one day. Though several additional planes were supposed to arrive any day, the tenth aircraft would not arrive until the end of the month. In actuality, only nine arrived, for on May 23 a Skymaster that encountered heavy fog crashed not far from Tel Nof with the Messerschmitt parts in its belly.

At the end of the week, the Czech technicians who had been brought to reassemble the aircraft wheeled four shiny Messerschmitts out of the pandemonium of the repair hangar. They could hardly believe that these untrained pilots were ready to fly. Trained volunteers loaded the 20-millimeter cannons and hung the 70-kilogram bombs from the aircraft. The most symbolic act of all occurred when the Israelis painted, on the body and wings, the blue six-pointed star of David.

Aharon Remez, deputy commander of the IAF, would not allow them to take off until the squadron's first attack plan was complete. They were to attack the Egyptian air base in El Arish and destroy the Spitfires threatening Tel Aviv only several minutes' flight time away. He planned to shoot down the Egyptian aircraft coming from the area of the Suez Canal. Remez hoped for a complete surprise, and therefore strove to keep the existence of the Israeli fighter aircraft a secret as the ground war continued with its Second World War equipment.

On May 29 the reassembly of the fourth plane was completed, and the next day, Saturday, all of Remez's wonderful plans were forgotten. Shimon Avidan, commander of the Giv'ati Brigade, arrived at Tel Nof with an order signed by Yigal Yadin to attack an Egyptian armored column stationed near Ashdod, thirty-two kilometers from Tel Aviv. All that lay between the column and Tel Aviv were a demolished bridge and two and a half rifle companies belonging to the Giv'ati Brigade.

It was decided that Lenart would lead the attacking quartet. Modi would follow him; Ezer would be the deputy leader; and Eddie Cohen would be behind Ezer. Avidan had brought along maps and briefed the foursome. "At dusk, we moved and rolled out to the concrete runway," Ezer recalled in his book. "The distance from takeoff to the battle area was minimal. From the moment we left the ground, we could see ack-ack being fired on us from Ashdod. We pulled toward the sea, climbed to seven thousand feet, and descended toward the Egyptian column. I admit feeling that I was charged with a vital mission as I released my two bombs on that armored column. I accompanied them with a prayer that their strike would delay the column, which was heading almost unstoppably toward Tel Aviv. I returned and strafed the column, expending all of my 20-millimeter cannon rounds. From a distance I could see the first pair executing like me, and as much as we could tell of what was going on down below, we could see the Egyptians scattering in every direction. Then, in the midst of the tumult, I saw Eddie, my number two, diving and diving and diving and then wham!—into the ground, enveloped in flames and smoke. We still don't know if he caught ack-ack or if some problem in the plane caused his first sortie to be his last."

The IAF had lost in this sortie a quarter of the fighter force that it had managed to build up to that moment. Modi Alon's plane scraped its wing on landing and was also pulled out of service for a short time. The next day, Modi received command of the first fighter squadron. The action, though it had all the irregular-forces aura of the Air Service operations, had achieved its goal. The commander of the Egyptian column had not taken into account that the Jews had an air force, and he had crowded his armored vehicles together on the narrow road. Thus they were an easy target for the four Messerschmitts. Although the damage caused by the bombing and strafing was not particularly heavy, the IAF had succeeded in giving the Egyptians a great psychological shock. The column stopped to rest by a canyon near Tel Ashdod, where it had to dig in until the bridge could be repaired. Old light artillery pieces, from among the few that had arrived in the country and were being passed from front to front, were brought by the IDF to the nearby hills and continued to harass the armored vehicles. The Egyptian progress was halted, and Tel Aviv was saved. The column would retreat within days.

The next day, at dawn, the IAF's functioning half, all of two Messerschmitts, set out to attack the Jordanian-Iraqi armored column that was threatening Netanya. The armored vehicles pulled out of Tulkarm and began to shell Kfar Yona with their light 30-millimeter cannons. Ezer took off with Rubie Rubenfield, and they dropped their bombs on the Tulkarm train station, which was the column's base of operations. They then strafed the column with their cannons. On the second run, Rubenfield's plane was hit. Ezer could see a trail of smoke pouring out behind him and the pilot parachuting from his cockpit. He said to himself, There goes another quarter of the squadron's planes.

Rubenfield slowly parachuted over the Jewish village of Kfar Vitkin. The farmers awaited him with murder in their eyes, for no one had informed them of the existence of Israeli fighter planes. Rubenfield was dark-skinned and, from the ground, appeared to be every inch an Arab. Not knowing Hebrew, he knew it would be difficult to convince the farmers that he was an American Jew. Before hitting the ground, he searched his memory for the few words of Yiddish he had heard from his grandmother. It is told that he began to shout to the farmers, "*Shabbes, Shabbes*" (Saturday, Saturday), even though it was Sunday. He then added "Gefilte fish" twice, until he managed to pull a smile of understanding out of them.

On the central front as well, the mere appearance of the pair of aircraft did more damage than the actual bombs. The Messerschmitts, whose existence had not been revealed, were a complete surprise and represented to the Arabs the forward edge of an enormous and terrible air force hidden somewhere underground. Knowledge of the existence of the squadron that had saved Tel Aviv was kept from the city's residents until the evening of June 3, less than a week after its action against the Egyptian column. At six o'clock the air-raid sirens began to wail, just minutes before a pair of Egyptian Dakotas charged in from the sea and randomly dropped bombs from high altitude. Most of the residents had not yet managed to take cover in the shelters. The brave ones who chose to remain outside and follow the course of the bombers suddenly saw a lone fighter aircraft attacking the Dakotas with cannon bursts.

Modi Alon had taken off toward the pair not from Tel Nof but rather from a field in Herzliya, quickly paved in a two-week operation. The British base of Akron was not a safe home for the squadron. Again and again it had been the target of air attacks, and was also exposed to ground operations from the Arab towns of Ramle and Lod. The Messerschmitts could be hidden in the orchards of Herzliya, and packing houses were turned into workshops and hangars. The water tower served as a control tower, and the town's villas as homes for the pilots. The new and well-camouflaged field began to operate on June 2.

The next day the Dakotas materialized in the skies of Tel Aviv. As soon as they appeared over the sea, the warning siren was sounded in Herzliya. By the time Modi could pull the Messerschmitt out of the orchards and take off, the Dakotas had dropped their first payload. He approached them head-on, blocking their path. They were easy prey, slow, crude, and unprotected. Modi, on the other hand, was fast, maneuverable, and aggressive. The first Dakota that turned north was caught in his fire as if on a target range. It dived until it crashed in the sands of Herzliya. The second turned back and attempted to avoid him in heavy rolls. With a few more bursts, it too broke apart on the sand dunes of Bat Yam, just south of Tel Aviv.

From this point on, everything changed. At the end of the month, an Egyptian Spitfire was shot down over Be'er Tuvia. In July, Modi shot down a Spitfire in a short dogfight over Be'er Sheva. By the end of the battles, the foreign volunteers had shot down almost another half-dozen fighter and bomber aircraft. Thus the first fighter squadron slowly pushed the planes of the Arab air forces from Israel's skies, gaining complete control by the war's end.

One by one, and without the knowledge of outsiders, the Messerschmitts were reassembled. Seven of them were in the squadron, along with the Egyptian Spitfire that had been hit above Sde Dov on May 15 and had landed on the Herzliya coast. It had been towed to Tel Nof for rehabilitation, and its damaged parts were replaced with anything remaining in the abandoned RAF warehouses. It served the squadron for a long time until it burned one day on the ground because of a technical problem.

Alongside the fighter squadron, the pilots of the A Squadron also attempted to execute attack sorties. The Egyptian Fairchild that had landed in the Negev on the hashish-smuggling run was passed on to the

Galilee Squadron and then later to the Tel Aviv Squadron. On June 4, the day following the shooting down of the Dakotas, Egyptian frigates neared the coast and began shelling Tel Aviv from the sea. The Fairchild was scrambled from Sde Dov, along with two other aircraft, to drive away the ships. Exposed to antiaircraft fire from the ships' cannons, the defenseless Fairchild descended to achieve accuracy in the hand-dropping of its bombs, which were aimed by eye with no directional mechanism. The bombs missed, and the light plane, hit by cannon fire, went into a spin until it crashed into the sea. The Egyptian fleet fled.

On June 1, the Council of the Arab Legion convened in Amman to decide whether to agree to the UN proposal for a cease-fire. Both sides were in need of it. The two-week-old Israel was on the verge of strangulation after the bloodletting it had suffered on all fronts, with Jerusalem besieged and hungry and the Egyptian army still threatening Tel Aviv. Despite several achievements, Jordan, Iraq, and Syria were in need of a break after their hopes for a quick and easy victory had been shattered.

On the evening of June 2, the IAF, by bombing Amman, tried to encourage the members of the Arab Legion's Council to accept the UN proposal. The mission was allocated to a pair of twin-engine Rapids, which could each carry one ton of ordnance. Their leader was Uri Brayer, who had just returned from a transport sortie to Sodom, whose potash factory, the sole Israeli enclave in the southern part of the Dead Sea, subsisted on resupplies by air. As the Rapids took off from Sde Dov, loaded heavily with bombs and fuel, they were almost certain that the Jordanians would not be expecting this night visit. Israel's extended bombing arm had not been included in their calculations, particularly the use of aircraft generally used for passenger and package transport at short and medium distances. Jordan, however, was still a dependent of Great Britain; RAF aircraft were still stationed there. Brayer knew that even with the Bren machine gun placed in its doorway, the Rapid's chances against the British Spitfires and their cannons were nil.

The Rapids crossed the dark skies of Samaria and navigated by the muzzle flashes and artillery shells of the besieged Jerusalem. A quarter of an hour later they had reached Amman. The capital was lit. There was no welcome from either antiaircraft fire or fighter aircraft prepared for interception, and the Israelis rambled through the city's skies with no interference. The Rapids had no problem identifying their targets near the hall in which the Legion's leaders were convened, close to the palace of King Abdullah, the country's leader and grandfather of King Hussein. They made sure not to damage the palace itself. Before the 1948 war, King Abdullah had held secret meetings with Israeli leaders Golda Meir and Eliyahu Sasson, representatives of the Jewish Agency and what would later be the government of Israel. Both sides intended to harvest the results of the contacts later in the war, or perhaps after its conclusion.

The bombings were a success. The incendiary bombs illuminated the darkened pockets around the targets and aided the pilots in dropping their explosives precisely. Several machine guns and a lone antiaircraft cannon fired diffusely and inaccurately toward the planes. Uri watched the green trail of a cannon shell pass in front of him and miss. He banked the Rapid west and headed home. The planes landed with no problem, and the threat had succeeded. Amman was not bombed again until the end of the war, but, like the attack on the Egyptian column approaching Tel Aviv, this lone sortie had been enough to indicate to the Legion's Council that there was no limit to the IAF's daring. The bombs created the impression that the Jews had a much greater force than they actually possessed. As if these hints were not enough, an Israeli Dakota flew unmolested to Damascus on the night of June 10 and dropped a ton of bombs on Syria's capital. The next morning the first cease-fire went into effect.

It lasted for twenty-eight uncertainty-filled days. Even if the cease-fire had been determined in advance to last one month, no one would have wagered that the battles would not erupt again at any moment. More than any other branch of the military, the IAF had to take advantage of every quiet day to add order and methodology to its operational, technical, and administrative networks, which, through no choice of its own, had grown by leaps and bounds. The command, control, and organizational struc-tures that had been designed a half-year earlier according to the size of the Air Service were proportional to those necessary for a flight club. Within a few short weeks, the image of a flying supply service had been replaced with that of a combat force.

The rapid growth of the IAF occurred primarily during the first twenty-six days of the State of Israel's existence, which were also the days of the war against the combined invasion forces of the Arab states. The missions were allocated to them at a dizzying pace, and it seemed that the fate of the country depended on each one. The IAF's willpower and self-sacrifice being greater than its few weapons, nearly empty magazines, and makeshift means of dealing with inexperience and lack of options, it was a miracle that mechanical malfunctions and poor operating conditions did not claim a greater number of pilots and planes.

The cease-fire could be extended by the request of either of the combatant sides. The IAF needed this extension. At the "Etzion" air base in Czechoslovakia, three heavy bombers, B-17 Flying Fortresses, purchased from the U.S. Army's surplus after the war, were waiting for Israeli crews. The aircraft had been passed under the noses of the agents of the U.S. government, which had forbidden arms shipments to the Middle East. The planes were intended to bomb the Egyptian forward air base at El Arish, Egyptian army concentrations in the Gaza Strip, and Cairo. However, they had been smuggled from the United States to Europe stripped and nonfunctional after a long period of disuse. The process of returning them to operational condition would be prolonged, if it could be done at all.

The commanders of the ground forces were pressuring the General Command to renew the battles at the first possible moment after the cease-fire, in order to initiate a joint offensive attack on all fronts to push out the invaders. The IAF prepared itself for Operation Seedling, which entailed attacking and eliminating the Syrian bridgehead near Rosh Pinna, cleaning up the Lower Galilee, driving out the Iraqi-Jordanian force threatening Netanya and Hadera, and destroying the pocket of Lod and Ramle, thus breaking the siege on Jerusalem. Most of all, they were to force the Egyptians from the roads of the south that overlooked the passage between Jerusalem and Tel Aviv, and liberate the besieged kibbutzim of the Negev. Operation Seedling was the product of calculated and synchronized work in the headquarters, as requested by the General Command and the ground forces' commanders. Every mission was allocated the appropriate aircraft, according to a priority list developed in the headquarters at each front.

The fighting was renewed on July 9 for only ten days. Success on the ground was more limited than that in the air. Operation Seedling had started off on the wrong foot. The operation order had been changed three times during the last week of the cease-fire. Despite the thought that had been invested in it, the plan was still replete with flaws. The four Messerschmitts allocated to attack El Arish in place of the grounded B-17s were not prepared for action on the night of July 8, the conclusion

of the cease-fire. They took off the next morning at dawn, manned by
foreign volunteers and led by Lou Lenart. One aircraft crashed immediately after takeoff. Its pilot was not injured. A second aircraft disappeared. Lenart and his partner failed to locate El Arish. Instead they
attacked Egyptian units near Gaza. In one operation the IAF had lost two
aircraft and one pilot without even attacking the target.

In the north, the bombing of the Syrian bridgehead at Mishmar
HaYarden was canceled for fear of hitting Israeli ground forces preparing
for the attack. Coordination was lacking, and there was no cooperative
planning with the ground forces' commanders. In the south, Egyptian
forces concentrated at Beit Guvrin were bombed by a single aircraft
twenty minutes later than planned. A second aircraft, which was to bomb
other concentrations nearby, failed to find its target and instead aimed its
bombs at a cluster of lights. Luckily it missed, for this was Kibbutz
Ruchama. A third aircraft, sent to bomb Faluja (Kiryat-Gat), also did not
find its target and dropped its ordnance into the sea. The airdrop of
supplies to the besieged Kfar Darom was canceled since the mission's
plane was not fit for takeoff. The bombing of the village of Ananba,
which was to be executed by one Rapid and two light aircraft, was
executed without the Rapid, because its crew arrived at the field an hour
and a half late.

Shlomo Oren, the General Command Operations Branch liaison
officer with the IAF was furious over the first day's faulty execution. The
operations had been planned for three weeks, and the operation order had
been passed to the squadrons nine hours prior to zero hour. He wrote in a
memo, "Most of the operations failed because of late takeoff. When
activities are delayed in such a chronic way, it is carelessness for which
there can be no atonement. Without precision and discipline, things
cannot continue to function."

The Dakotas that were meant to bomb Kuneitra and the Syrian
airfields nearby also encountered problems that night. At the appointed
time, the Dakotas at Ramat David were not ready for takeoff because
there was no truck to fuel them. One aircraft was finally fueled in a
makeshift fashion and took off three hours late. The pilot felt his way
through the darkness like a blind man. His crew had neither a navigator
nor a wireless operator. Two minutes prior to his estimated time over
target, he saw city lights. At the last moment it became clear that this was
Damascus. He turned the plane around and, seeing a smaller city, began

to drop his bombs. Most of them exploded outside of the city, and the estimated location of the airfield was missed as well.

The Flying Fortresses eventually had their own series of problems. They landed in Israel on June 17, at the end of the first week of the cease-fire. For three weeks no one knew what to do with them. Ray Kurtz, a Jewish American volunteer who had recently been a B-17 squadron commander in the U.S. Air Force, felt that no one really cared. He had flown the route between "Etzion" and Tel Nof with Operation Balak's Constellation, and had become exasperated at the sight of the precious Fortresses lying abandoned. Without asking or receiving permission, he took upon himself full responsibility for making the planes operational. Inititally he assigned a crew of Czech technicians to oversee ongoing maintenance, and then began searching for aircrews who could fly them. Upon his first landing in Israel, he began to pressure anyone he could at IAF headquarters to bring these aircraft to operational activity as soon as possible. By his second landing, he had officially received command of the squadron, but was ordered to have them ready to fly to Israel within five days and to bomb Cairo and Egyptian bases at El Arish and Gaza on the way.

Despite the short warning that he received on July 7, just before the end of the cease-fire, Kurtz decided to execute the impossible. He had already compiled a list of Israeli aircrews in the transport division and foreign volunteers who had come to the country seeking employment. The readying of the aircraft was progressing slowly, and the Czechs would not cooperate. The American bombers were foreign to them, and they lacked the equipment and knowledge to handle them. In addition to the horrible weather, there was also a national Czech holiday that week. Of the five mechanics serving him, only one showed up for three of the days that Kurtz had been granted. The Israeli envoys also did not help, and even made things more difficult. The aircrews worked twenty-four hours a day, and on the morning of the sixth day, the aircraft were ready to take off.

Then the cancellation of the operation arrived from Israel. The crews' morale collapsed. Kurtz tried to encourage them to complete the renovations of the aircraft. After three days, on the morning of July 15, they were commanded to take off, and only then did they understand the meaning of the Arabic expression, "Haste is from the devil." Problems began to appear in Kurtz's lead plane during takeoff. Two boosters burned out. The artificial horizon, an instrument flying device, became totally nonfunctional. The first propeller regulator became stuck and limited the number of revolutions to 2,400 rpm. The number-two engine also lost power. Stormy weather over the Alps obligated the aircraft to spread out and regroup over Yugoslavia. In Albania they took antiaircraft fire, but were not hit. Over Crete they split up, and each aircraft headed for its target. Kurtz turned toward Egypt. Over the western desert, he climbed to 25,000 feet, out of the range of antiaircraft fire and Egyptian or British fighter planes. He navigated to Cairo via radio frequencies of the International Airport and the British Faid Field by the Suez Canal. At this altitude, oxygen masks were needed, and the Czechs had provided poor ones. Seven of the nine crew fainted at various times from lack of oxygen. Kurtz opened the oxygen regulator to full and pushed on to Cairo. The crew, which included the IAF's deputy commander, Heyman Shamir, recovered. At 2133 hours, Johnny Adir, the bomber, identified the targets. Within ten minutes he had released four half-ton bombs around King Farouk's palace. Eighty-five people were killed and injured. For the first time, the Egyptians had tasted the bitterness of the war in their own homes. The surprise and shock were complete. No warning signal was sounded, the antiaircraft guns were silent, and no planes were scrambled. Kurtz descended and turned toward Israel. In addition to the problems they had encountered, he understood now that he was also the victim of planning based on faulty intelligence. The Egyptians were not able to intercept aircraft at night, and could barely do so during the day. Cairo had no air defenses. It could have been bombed from a lower altitude, and the oxygen problems that had threatened the crew's lives could have been avoided. The other two Fortresses could have participated in the bombing, which had been allocated to Kurtz's plane because it had the only functioning oxygen system. Kurtz landed at Tel Nof and was told that the bomber sent to destroy the El Arish airfield had not identified its target. Along with the third bomber, it had emptied its bomb loads on Egyptian troop concentrations at Gaza and Rafah. The next night the bombers were scrambled again to El Arish. This time they found the airfield and damaged a number of its aircraft. From there they returned to Ramat David, their base until the end of the war.

In the four days that remained before the second cease-fire, the quality of air operations improved. The Flying Fortresses bombed Arab cities in Samaria, Egyptian forces in Ashdod, and Syrian forces in the

Israeli settlement of Mishmar HaYarden. The Dakotas paid a return visit to Damascus. The fighter squadron also recovered. At the last moment before the cease-fire, the Egyptians attempted to strengthen their positions in Faluja. Modi Alon led three Messerschmitts and bombed them. He did not return to Herzliya, however. He pulled the trio to the Negev, and together they strafed Egyptian armored vehicles near Rekvivim. Over Be'er Sheva, two Egyptian Spitfires appeared. Modi fired on them and they fled. Modi chased them and shot one down with his cannons. Thus the commander of the first fighter squadron created the prototype of a new level of quality execution. He had not only precisely executed the mission to which he had been sent, but had also seized the opportunity of a chance target, initiated a successful attack, and had not been deterred by incidental air-to-air combat, from which he emerged superior.

The war picture and the forecasts of the Arab armies' invasion necessitated rapid procurement of aircraft and recruitment of pilots and technicians. The equipment and personnel were absorbed in the tumult and emotion of the moment, under the pressures of the ongoing operational activities. It would later become evident that a significant part of the air and ground crews, particularly among the hundreds of volunteers from abroad, were not of the caliber needed, and often could not even meet the most basic of standards.

In less than half a year, the IAF increased its aircraft and personnel fourfold. Personnel now numbered 3,600. The aircraft were a random and illogical collection of models, which exacerbated the problems of operation and maintenance. Most were used for combat purposes that their producers had not intended. The balance between operational squadrons, headquarters, and service units was also ruined. The body was large and the head was small. Headquarters was unable to handle the process of decision-making, particularly when the missions became more complex and it now had fighter aircraft. Its ability to supply accurate intelligence information was limited. Its directing, control, and command had not expanded proportionally with the increase in activities and needs. Lacking supervision and control systems for debriefing and for learning from experience, many operations, if they managed to get off the ground at all, were ultimately failures.

These deficiencies concerned commanders at all levels, who flooded headquarters with demands that a meticulous evaluation be done. Headquarters was not unresponsive, but lacked the tools and personnel to execute the necessary improvements. The sense of frustration and helplessness grew. Ultimately, headquarters responded under external pressure from the liaison officer between the IAF and the Operations Branch of the General Command. He would pass a daily operations order to the IAF, and his emissaries would record and pass on to him the criticism expressed by the ground forces regarding the failures they witnessed in air operations. The liaison officer in turn conveyed this information to the General Command, which began to play a crucial role in the struggle between the developing air force, which sought independence, and the Operational Branch, which saw it as a service unit subordinate to the needs of the ground forces. Cooperation with the liaison officer took place with mixed feelings. It was quickly understood in headquarters that the return to its own commanders of full command and control over the activities of the air force was as vital for the strengthening of its professional independence as was the acquisition of additional aircraft and personnel. This stage also demanded extensive planning, organized and methodical administration, coordination, and excellent maintenance of equipment.

## The Wars Between the Jews

The ten days of battle expanded the IAF's foundations. The capture of the cities of Lod and Ramle and their environs removed the threat that hung over Tel Nof and gave the state and the IAF control over the international airport in Lod. The Ramat David air base was added to these two large fields, along with the small and crowded Sde Dov and the provisional fields in Herzliya, the Negev, and Galilee. All that was needed was to fill the frame with proper command and control of Israel's air force.

The second cease-fire, on July 19, was essential for purposes of self-evaluation and reorganization in the IAF. Its extension by the UN to three months was a blessing to both the IAF and the IDF, for everyone agreed that this was enough time for calculating, planning, resupplying, and learning from the mistakes that had resulted from the emergency responses to the Arab invasions. The UN became an overt force, its observers riding around the country in their white cars, watching every border crossing and port. The Israeli government and military were forced to use underground methods to maintain the flow of equipment that had begun to arrive, and to absorb the new wave of immigrants flooding the country. The men were immediately recruited into the IDF along with the foreign volunteers, who arrived separately.

The need for essential renovations was clear in the IAF, even without the criticism expressed by the Operations Branch of the General Command. As always, Ben-Gurion relied on the professionalism and experience of those who had achieved high rank in foreign militaries or who were products of the Haganah. He decided to settle the issues of the IAF's independence through the recommendations of an external expert. He chose Cecil Margo, a Jewish attorney from South Africa, who had been a wing commander with the rank of colonel and one of the outstanding members of the South African Air Force in the Second World War. He asked Margo to critique the organizational problems and the reasons for the faulty performance of the IAF. In particular, he was asked to focus on ways to improve its efficiency. Margo's name had first been mentioned in October 1947, when a trustworthy consultant was needed on the eve of the formation of the Air Service. Margo arrived, studied the functioning of the force, and presented his conclusions in less than a month. His approach had been professional, practical, and aggressive. His starting point lay in a solid definition of the primary goal of the modern air force: the destruction of the enemy's air power. This goal demanded the building of an independent force, equipped for the purpose, well organized, and manned by the most capable personnel available.

Ben-Gurion was one of the few who fully comprehended Margo's approach, which ultimately had its effect and led to the creation of the IAF as an independent body operationally subordinate to the chief of staff and to the Deputy Minister of Air Issues in the Ministry of Defense. During the first stage, this would be partial independence in that in several of the maintenance areas, such as fuel, food, and transportation, the IAF would be tied umbilically to the IDF. This would not be the case with acquisition of operational equipment. The IAF was granted evaluative responsibilities and authority relative to its needs and priorities.

In headquarters, it was thought that the process of reorganization would take one to two years. Margo pressed for it to be completed within weeks or months. His opponents saw that he was receiving the backing and encouragement of the Prime Minister and Minister of Defense, Ben-Gurion, and attempted to hinder several of his recommendations for improvement of equipment. His opponents chose to contest his urgent demand to equip the IAF with sophisticated radar systems, because the maintenance personnel had limited knowledge of this relatively new battlefield tool. They were not bothered, for instance, by the current situation, in which the warning system prior to an enemy air attack consisted solely of visual observations by people who had to notice the approaching aircraft. Margo's opponents therefore rejected the idea of purchasing expensive new radar, saying that he didn't understand the problems of the country, its limited budgets, and its true needs.

Colonel Margo's horizons were wider than the immediate needs of the war effort. He requested the radar in an effort to improve the operational control system, which had been responsible for a number of breakdowns and accidents in the IAF. Ezer Weizman wrote that radar belonged at that point to the area of unattainable technology, and that fighter squadrons did not function with a concept of flight control. One minute after the fighter pilots had been scrambled to their missions, they were alone in the air, untraced and with no guidance from the ground. At best, they had eye contact and communication only with their formation partners. The Israelis generally flew in pairs for reasons of conservation and lack of aircraft.

Ezer remembers an unwritten command passed through word of mouth: "If you meet a quartet in the air, they are not ours. Hit them hard if you can, or disconnect if you are low on fuel." Because of Margo's determination, the acquisition of electronic systems was rescued. Their installation later, and the realization of his other recommendations, including the promotion of pilots and navigators to headquarters positions and the training of flight controllers, proved how professional he actually was, possessing the necessary vision and working for the good of the IAF.

There was no lack of proficient candidates for the top headquarters positions among the experienced Jews who had served in foreign air forces and had come to volunteer for Israel. Though he did not reject the nomination of foreigners if they committed themselves to settle in Israel, Colonel Margo hinted that the best of the Israeli natives, or Sabras, should be used first. He found more support on this issue than on any other. The fighter squadron in Herzliya, for example, had three hundred men, but of its sixteen pilots, only three were native Israelis: Modi Alon, Ezer Weizman, and Sandy Jacobs. The others were American, Canadian, British, and South African Jews who were experienced fighter pilots, having held significant ranks in their respective armies during the

Second World War. Along with the gaps in language and culture, there was a great degree of goodwill and willingness to take risks. However, the group also included thrill-seekers and those looking for a release of some sort. Alongside them was a melting pot of technicians and service workers, few of them Israeli natives and most of them volunteers or new immigrants, primarily refugees from the camps in Europe. It was impossible to command this group or to use any means of discipline familiar to a normal army. Only a natural leader like Modi Alon could, with time, take such a collection and turn it into a fighting unit. Blessed with wisdom and authority that eliminated the need for orders and punishments, he could achieve obedience even in the period when there were no uniforms or ranks.

The first crisis with the foreign volunteers, which began in late June, did not bypass the fighter squadrons, however. They refused to take the oath of allegiance to the IDF, and demoralization and division suddenly threatened the IAF's units. The Americans and members of the British Commonwealth justly claimed that the oath to the IDF contradicted their previous oath of allegiance to the U.S. Constitution or to the King of England. They feared that the oath would annul their original citizenship and prevent them from returning to their countries. On the other hand, without an oath, they would not be obligated to wear uniforms or to obey their commanding officers. In the fighter squadrons, where the lines of discipline were laid down by Modi Alon, the differences in status between the Israelis and the foreigners were somehow overcome. Official uniforms were not required, and everyone continued to wear flight coveralls and work clothes. The previous hierarchy remained.

It was clear to all that the short-term compromises would not last and would not survive Cecil Margo's process of organization, which was rooted in consistent work procedures and discipline. Sooner or later the foreigners would have to choose between Israel and a return to their countries. Under the assumption that only a minority would remain, the Training Division quickly opened a technical school near Haifa's Technion Institute. A series of flight courses, in Israel and abroad, were initiated in order to train a core of skilled Israelis, a foundation for the IAF. Four months after the oath crisis, the moment of truth arrived, and the random group of volunteers found themselves unable to meet the demands while not sharing in the common ideology. As the war pressure decreased, the volunteers began to demand more financial compensation as a condition for their continued service. The government offered poor conditions that did not meet their expectations of high salaries, residence in luxury hotels, and compensation in the event of injury. The members of the Air Transport Command, who felt hurt and discriminated against, presented an ultimatum and began an operational strike. Headquarters decided to terminate the service of those who refused to sign a revocation of the ultimatum, and returned them to their countries.

The revolt faded, but its scars remained. At times, criticism of the state and even anti-Semitic remarks could be heard. Those speaking this way were immediately evicted. Expressions of animosity were rare, however, and most of the foreign volunteers were loyal and performed their work well before coming with demands. All in all, without them, it would be difficult to picture the accomplishments of the IAF in the first stages of the war and the success of the operations during the second cease-fire and upon renewal of the battles. At the conclusion of the war, their bargaining power dropped to nothing. The Israeli replacements, who had been trained in the meantime, made most of the volunteers superfluous. Only 275 of them, approximately one-tenth of the force, were found essential and were given the opportunity to extend their service one or two more years. Faithful to "Margo's Doctrine" and Ben-Gurion's demand, the IAF was willing to invest in those who had achieved pivotal positions by teaching them Hebrew and attempting to persuade them to settle in Israel.

In July 1948, the IAF finally received its first professional as commander-in-chief, Maj. Gen. Aharon Remez. Within one month, he presided over a renovated headquarters with functional divisions established and commanders who had been chosen according to their skills as well as by his personal preferences. Like Remez, the majority were veterans of the RAF. The squadrons took advantage of the cease-fire for exercises and raising standards of performance in all areas.

The Air Transport Command was established largely during the first cease-fire, but its roots were in those first rescue flights, flown in leased aircraft, that brought the munitions from Europe for Operation Nachshon, and in the aircraft that stopped the Egyptians as they neared Tel Aviv. After this, the acquisition of heavy aircraft began with the idea that they would be decisive in transport and bombing. The core of the squadron was formed by two C-47 Dakotas bought from Air France and

Pan American. Later, even in daring procurement deals in the United States under threats of imprisonment, criminal trials, and annulment of citizenship, three Constellations, ten C-46 Commandos, and one C-54 Skymaster were added.

The Air Transport Command flew overseas and back, day and night, importing loads of weapons, ammunition, and disassembled aircraft that were reassembled as soon as they were unloaded. It was the lifeline of the IDF, which had to purchase all its equipment abroad. The multi-runway base of Tel Nof, which could support multi-engined aircraft, was ideal for this function particularly because of its location in the center of the country and its proximity to the critical fronts.

In Ben-Gurion's vision, Israel had no future without a settled and flourishing Negev. A year earlier he had fought to include in the UN's plans for partition this desolate desert within the borders of the Jewish state, forgoing other, more fertile areas of western Israel whose populace was Arab. From Ben-Gurion's perspective, the war over the Negev was not for the small number of settlements holding on to it, but rather for more than half of the country's territory. In this spirit, he was willing to risk a diplomatic conflict with the superpowers and the UN, who were the patrons of the cease-fire, by ordering the IDF to forcibly create a corridor to the cut-off region and assure a free flow of reinforcements and supplies. All attempts at penetration during the first days of the war and in the ten days of battle had failed. The limited transport capabilities of the light aircraft of the A Squadron and the Negev Squadron could guarantee the isolated kibbutzim and the forces of the Negev Brigade a basic stock of supplies sufficient for only one week of fighting.

In a meeting of the Upper Command of the IDF following a first and impressive display of the IAF's abilities to airlift massive amounts of troops, Ben-Gurion asked Remez and Munia Mardor, commander of the Air Transport Command, if the IAF was ready and able continue to fly in troops and supplies. The ground forces were not enthusiastic about the degree of risk involved in breaking through against the Egyptians, who outnumbered them tremendously. Ben-Gurion estimated a lift require-ment of two thousand tons. Remez and Mardor responded that the Air Transport Command would be more than happy to take the operation upon its wings in an acceptable time frame under the condition that it would be allocated the amount of fuel demanded. They mentioned a tremendous quantity, of which part would serve as inventory. The majority of the fuel, however, would be put to operational uses in the bombings and air support of the ground forces, which were planned for after the cease-fire expired. Levi Eshkol, then director of the Ministry of Defense, estimated that there would be no problem with the fuel, and Ben-Gurion concluded the meeting by giving the operation high priority in allocation of aircraft, as well as support by other branches of the military. The priority order was unnecessary, however, for most of the Air Transport Command's aircraft were grounded in Israel and had stopped flying abroad. The United States and England, as leaders of the weapons embargo in the Middle East, had pressured the Czech government to halt the flights of Operation Balak. The flights were reduced until they were completely terminated at the beginning of the second cease-fire.

As soon as the execution of the plan reached the lower ranks, the Jewish internecine wars of those of little faith and the complainers in the operations and supply branches of the IDF began again. It became apparent that airstrips serving the Negev Squadron were too short and narrow for the twin-engined Commando aircraft, let alone the four-engined Constellations that the Air Transport Command had allocated to the operation. Longer and wider runways would quickly have to be prepared alongside them. IAF headquarters and the Air Transport Command organized themselves for intensive work, but instead of bulldozers and operators of heavy equipment, vehicles, and communciations gear, they received smiles that expressed doubts that they would even be able to get the operation off the ground. Munia and his people planned to fly eighty tons daily, calculations based on the experience they had gained during the Balak flights. Eventually the Air Transport Command managed to find a tractor and a bulldozer, all that existed in the Negev, and working day and night, they created a runway near Kibbutz Ruhama, 1,100 meters long and 35 meters wide, the lower limit of the mid-sized Commandos. Its advantage lay in the thin layer of chalklike dust that covered it and would aid the heavy aircraft in braking. The disadvantage was that the first rain would turn the runway into a field of mud. Therefore, every remaining day before the coming autumn would have to be used.

The first Commando to attempt a landing discovered another pitfall. In landing, and even more so in takeoff, the propellers spun the powder into blinding and choking clouds. Thus was born Operation Dust, so named by the foreign aircrew volunteers, who were unused to such a natural desert phenomenon in their countries of origin. The first flight of Operation Dust took place on August 23, and the last landed two months later, on October 21, when Operation Yoav, for the liberation of the Negev, was in full force. On the first day the operation flew twenty-nine tons, and by the end of the second day it had flown in a total of seventy-five tons. In the first flights, ground troops of the Negev Brigade were also rotated. The air bridge was spread out in the night hours, almost above the heads of the Egyptians but out of range of their antiaircraft guns and the intercept capabilities of their aircraft, which could only function in daylight. The Egyptians were not impervious to the air activity fermenting about them, which threatened to destroy all their plans. Under cover of darkness, they sent reconnaissance teams to hills overlooking Dust Field, the nickname of the new runway. From a distance, they could barely make out details. But the sheer numbers of landings and takeoffs left little to the imagination. It was clear that the Jews were preparing an enormous operation.

The Egyptian teams were discovered after a few days, and the rate of the flights was slowed to reduce the impression of a hidden threat. Simultaneously, the brigade command began to send out small patrol parties that initiated quiet confrontations with undirected gunfire. The Egyptians did not respond, but their silent presence became a nuisance. Not wanting to take chances, the Air Transport Command decided to create another runway, Dust 2, at a point far from the cease-fire lines. Given this opportunity, they built the strip longer so it could handle the heavier aircraft as well. Upon its completion, the rate of flights was increased to compensate for the backlog that had been created.

The flights themselves took only minutes, but each round was a trying and fatiguing endeavor, lacking ground flight control at the target. The pilots had to land on a limited runway, and thus every touch of the wheels at the runway's end was a wager against the aircraft's ability to brake before reaching the other end. The crews, none of them Israeli, had to be replaced every two to three runs, and nonetheless were close to collapse from fatigue. The maintenance of the aircraft was even more worrisome. The rushed underground purchase of used planes, often at the junkyard level, did not include an inventory of replacements for those parts that wore out with time. The purchasers simply did not know where to get them. The ground mechanics exhibited resourcefulness and innovation in renovating or creating substitutes for faulty parts. The pilots did not hesitate to take off with patched or barely repaired aircraft that would not have met the standards of any airline. Over the course of two months they completed the airlift of 2,225 tons of food and supplies and 500 tons of fuel, plus hundreds of refreshed fighters who replaced their tired comrades.

Even after the last Balak flight had departed for Israel, the ties with Czechoslovakia were not broken. Another aircraft agreement, involving the purchase of twenty renovated Spitfire Mk 9 aircraft, had been signed but not completed. Unlike the Messerschmitts, which had left Czechoslovakia disassembled in the transport planes, there was no other way to get the six newly repaired Spitfires to Israel than to fly them there. However, the maximum flight range of the plane was 600 miles, and Israel was 1,400 miles away. This was an impossible mission that started on the wrong foot and ended with only one foot; its code name was Velvetta.

The commander of the operation was Sam Pomerantz, a foreign engineer and pilot who had a colorful history of tricks and cunning ideas. He yanked out of the plane every part or instrument that seemed unnecessary for this unique journey, including the radios. In their places he installed additional fuel tanks. The Spitfires were to skip from Czechoslovakia to a Yugoslavian airfield that the procurement people had been granted permission to use, where they would refuel and continue nonstop to Israel. The route was designed along the shortest and safest path, using the last drop of fuel. A Skymaster transport aircraft was assigned to accompany the formation and to provide rescue services (in addition to Israeli Navy boats, which would patrol along the last leg), but primarily to navigate and to provide communications between the aircraft and with the ground. The pilots would have to make do with portable radios, short-range walkie-talkies.

The planes took off on September 24. Their crews included Modi Alon, Jack Cohen, Sid Cohen, Boris Senior, and Sam Pomerantz, who had set out early and awaited them in Czechoslovakia. They were all inexperienced in such long-distance flight, and its beginnings were not encouraging. The first Spitfire was forced to return after taking off from Yugoslavia, and crashed while attempting an emergency landing. While flying over Rhodes, Modi Alon and Boris Senior discovered that their emergency fuel tanks were not transferring fuel, and they were forced to land on the island. They were permitted to continue on to Israel—

without their planes, which had been confiscated. At first they were suspected of espionage, but a Greek pilot, who had been in a course with Senior in England and recognized him, brought about their release. Only half of the formation landed in Ramat David. The loss of three of the Spitfires caused the delay of the operation for an unspecified time, in hopes that safer means of transport would be found. With none found, Sam Pomerantz set out for Czechoslovakia in early December to bring the remaining fourteen Spitfires. They were to be used in Operation Chorev, which was intended to evict the last of the Egyptians from the country and was already under way in full force.

On December 16, Pomerantz led a second formation of six aircraft over the slippery ice-covered Czech runway. A difficult winter had settled on Europe in the end of 1948, and the pilots found themselves feeling their way through the unknown in stormy conditions. Barely an hour after takeoff, before they had crossed the Czech border, the transport plane lost contact with two of the pilots. One was Pomerantz, whose aircraft crashed into the side of a mountain and exploded, killing him. The remains of the plane were found several days later in a nearby valley. Not far from there, the second plane crashed in a horrendous emergency landing.

Four Spitfires remained in the air, a crippled and confused formation that had lost its authoritative and beloved leader. The crew of the transport plane decided to return with them to the exit base, to reorganize the operation and improve deteriorating morale. Among the four pilots of the returning aircraft was Moti Fine (later to be Moti Hod), the sole Israeli in the formation.

Seven months earlier, Fine, a native of Kibbutz Degania, had never sat in a cockpit or held a stick, and felt himself tiny when compared to giants like Pomerantz and his buddies. He had not imagined returning to Israel this way after being away for four years. He had not served in any air force. Flight had been a childhood dream of his, and by chance he had joined a basic flight course started in Italy in May of 1948. Following his discharge from the British Army, he had spent three years in the service of the Mossad, smuggling Holocaust refugees from internment camps and onto boats headed for the Israeli coast. The course in Italy was not unique. At approximately the same time, another course began in California, initiated by Eleanor Rudnik, an American Jew and an avid pilot. Thirteen Israelis were sent to the course, among them Zohara

Levitov and Sarah Makleff, the first two female pilots of the IAF. Levitov was also the first and only woman pilot to fall in the line of duty. Her plane crashed near the Jerusalem airport, which had been paved in a narrow valley during the siege. The course, which was given in Bakersfield, California, was in violation of the U.S. embargo. Eleanor Rudnik was brought to trial and fined, a light punishment compared to those received by other Americans who aided the IAF in smuggling bomber and transport aircraft and risked losing their citizenship.

Moti Fine had not managed to acclimate himself to the training aircraft in the Italian course before he was sent to a quick course in fighter aircraft in Czechoslovakia. He enjoyed flying the Spitfire, with its flexible aerodynamic profile, which allowed for daring maneuvers. After seven flight hours, he did not feel ready for a solo flight, much less for the problems that could arise during this long route in unfriendly weather and over unknown and perhaps inhospitable countries. Shortly after their return to the base in Czechoslovakia, Moti and the others were told to prepare themselves to fly again the next day, with the deal's last eight Spitfires.

Thus a dozen Spitfires set out for Israel, with the risks higher than ever. Flying in the expanded formation was another Israeli, Danny Shapira. Both of the Israelis would accompany each other in long careers together. Moti Hod would become commander-in-chief of the IAF and later chairman of the Israel Aircraft Industries, and Danny Shapira, a pilot and top commander in the IAF, would for forty years be the top test pilot of Israel Aircraft Industries. On that cold morning, though, neither wished for much more than to make it home alive. For four tense hours, the twelve Spitfires and the accompanying Commando aircraft skipped to Yugoslavia. From there they were to fly seven hours nonstop to Israel after refueling.

The first leg passed without problems. But upon landing, the pilots discovered problems in the aircraft. The work executed in the Czech factories was not thorough, but they had managed to overcome the problems until now. They did not want to take any further risks at this point. The checks of the aircraft lasted another week, replacing weak cables and patching leaky fuel tanks. When the order to take off was finally given on December 23, one of the planes was not able to start up its engine and was completely disabled. Another was forced to turn back after takeoff, and also remained behind. Ten Spitfires set out, a respectable number considering the size of the previous shipment and the obstacles facing them.

Toward evening they could see the coastline, and mere minutes separated them from Hatzor Air Base, the new home of the fighter squadron. Suddenly the Commando's pilot was ordered to change direction northward and lead the formation to Ramat David. He passed the command onto the pilots through the walkie-talkies. Moti did not ask why. He did not know one base from another and had no reason to sense a threat in the command to land at the bombers' base in the heart of Jezreel Valley. Only the transport plane had contact with the ground, and received word of the last-ditch Egyptian attack taking place on Tel Nof. Moti was therefore saved the worry of having to wage a dogfight with no ammunition and on his last drops of fuel.

The rejoicing of the ground and service crews who ran toward him, feasting their eyes on the new and unexpected Spitfires, jarred him as if out of a dream. In 1944 he had left the country under British control, with this airfield, one of the strongholds of the foreign rule, far from his reach and beyond his dreams. Suddenly he was surrounded by Jews speaking Hebrew and even English. If he had not recognized the valley fields and Mount Tabor above them, he would have sworn he had landed in another world.

He had missed the war. The contribution of the ten Spitfires to the military victory was marginal. They landed in the last week of December, with the third round of battles coming to a close. However, their moral contribution, as well as their operational capability in the face of anything that might appear, was significant. In a report to the Minister of Defense, Major General Remez reported that by mid-September 147 aircraft of twenty-five different varieties had been purchased. The IAF had received 121 of them, 33 of which had been lost in accidents and combat and another 43 of which were grounded. Only 45 aircraft were operational, and the rest were either out of service for an extended period or on the verge of entering the junkyard. Haste had been necessary.

A month after this report was written, the situation had improved. On the eve of the recommencement of the battles, the IAF and twenty-six aircraft in operational condition (twice the number it had had six months earlier, when the State of Israel was formed), in all the types of squadrons found today in a modern air force. The twenty-nine light aircraft that executed missions of patrol, liaison, and bombing were located in Sde

Dov, Tel Nof, and the Negev. The twenty-two transport and bomber aircraft were in Tel Nof and Ramat David, and only eleven fighter aircraft—six Messerschmitts and five Spitfires—were still hidden in the orchard near Herzliya. The squadron of functional Messerschmitts included only six of the twenty-five brought from Czechoslovakia. Twelve had been lost in action and accidents, and seven (out of the thirteen, six were serviceable) others were in repair.

During the third round of battles, the squadron would receive four Mustangs and seventeen Harvards, all of them American. The Harvard was a training aircraft that could be modified for fighter and bombing missions. The Mustangs, part of the fighter backbone of the U.S. Air Force during the Second World War, arrived disassembled in crates at the end of the cease-fire. They were the last, in Israel and the world, to fight alongside jets eight years later.

The second cease-fire came to a close on the evening of October 15. A group of IAF bombers and fighter aircraft began an assault at dusk on the Egyptian airfield at El Arish. They bombed parked aircraft and strafed the surprised people who darted in between the planes and the hangars. In the original plan, this was to be the inaugural operation of the Messerschmitts five months earlier, but it was executed as a renovated and wider-scale mission. This was the first time the IDF opened a war with an air attack whose goal was to ground and neutralize the enemy's aircraft. This full-force IAF operation, part of Operation Yoav, an overall effort to liberate the Negev, was a turning point in IAF history. From an improvisational band, it turned into a thinking, planning, and ready force. Like the ground units, the squadrons had prepared for the recommencement of the battles through intelligence gathering regarding predetermined targets and through networked planning of attack and support with the other branches of the military. The order to begin firing exactly at the legal end of the cease-fire merely released a tightened spring. Israel was not interested in extending the cease-fire. The General Command had planned to break through to the Negev and evict the Egyptians from the country. The operation became top priority after September 20, when the UN negotiator, the Swedish Count Folke Bernadette, recommended solving the problems in the region by repairing the partition plan. He proposed a new map that would turn the current situation permanent, tearing the besieged Negev from Israeli territory.

Throughout the cease-fire, the Egyptians had not respected the clause that obligated them to allow civilian supply convoys to pass over the Faluja-to-Majdal (Ashkelon) road to the Jewish settlements in the Negev. The airlifts of Operation Dust circumvented the Egyptian blockade, but were actually intended to build up supplies for the renewal of the battles to break the siege. Needing a convincing excuse to begin the battles again, contrary to the written UN decision, Israel reported to the UN Observer Force on October 15 that it intended to send a convoy through. The convoy was attacked and was forced to retreat. The IAF attacks from El Arish to the Egyptian troop concentrations in Gaza, Beit Hanoun, and Majdal began in the evening and continued through the night. In addition, the ground forces began to act to dislodge the Egyptian forces from Mount Hebron and the coast.

Execution of the night assault lagged behind plan. One of the Spitfire quartets assigned to attack El Arish was not ready on time. The trio attacked with two mid-size Beaufighter bombers, new in the IAF line. The Egyptians were taken by surprise, and their Spitfires went up in flames or were perforated on the ground. Antiaircraft fire began to chase the attackers only upon completion of their run, but managed to hit only one of the Beaufighters, which made an emergency landing in Tel Nof.

The twin-engined Beaufighter was similar to the Mosquito and was active in the British bomber squadrons in World War II. Four of them had been smuggled to Israel from England. The procurement people leased them overtly, claiming that the aircraft were needed for a motion picture. The directing of the "production" was flawless. Cameras were set up alongside the runway at the airfield in England, and as ordered, the Beaufighters took off. They did not return, however, despite the "protests" of the director and his team against this "breaking from the script." By the time the British aviation authorities realized what had happened, the bombers were somewhere over the Mediterranean.

Embarrassing problems occurred in the bombing of the large Egyptian forces in the Gaza Strip. Three Dakotas, two Commandos, and a Flying Fortress were allocated to the mission, with cover provided by four Spitfires. One Dakota was not ready and was removed from the force. The Flying Fortress took off late. Most of the bombs, approximately four tons in all, missed their targets, with the Flying Fortress dropping its load into the ocean because of a navigation error. Three additional Flying Fortresses, which were sent in a different sortie to bomb Majdal, departed off schedule and also erred, bombing a village far from the military positions. It was the quartet of light aircraft, each of which dropped three 20-kilogram bombs, that achieved accurate hits. They caused heavier losses for Egyptians than all the sophisticated professional bombers.

Despite all the lateness and misses, the Egyptians were in shock. The second bombing run, in full daylight, was more accurate and effective. In the afternoon the Egyptians began to retreat from Ashdod. In Herzliya, Modi Alon, commander of the fighter squadron, said to Ezer Weizman, "We've got an order to hit them at their retreat, as hard as possible. Let's get flying." On the way to the planes, they argued over who would fly which aircraft. Modi held his ground and flew the sole Messerschmitt. They bombed the center of Ashdod and strafed armored vehicles. Above the city they lost contact with each other, and returned separately. Over Herzliya, Ezer saw a column of black smoke rising from Kfar Shmaryahu. Modi had crashed on his approach to land in Herzliya. He had died at the age of twenty-nine, and the cause of the accident was never discovered. Command of the squadron was passed to his deputy, Sid Cohen.

Late in the day on October 19, Sid was called upon to aid in breaking one of the most problematic spots in the belt keeping the Negev under seige. The foritifed police station in Iraq-Suweidan controlled the eastern side of the Faluja-Majdal road. Repeated attacks starting on the day of the formation of the State of Israel had failed to destroy the stronghold. In the preparations for the sixth assault, a new and unbelievable element appeared. Spitfires began diving in two waves on the fortress, dropping their bombs into its exposed courtyard. The third wave comprised a lone Beaufighter, flown by Len Fitchet. The fortress's defenders at their antiaircraft positions had recovered from the shock of the Spitfires' assault and were ready for him. Heavy and slow relative to the Spitfires, he was hit by their fire. Fitchet barely managed to drag his Beaufighter back to Tel Nof, where he landed safely.

Two days later he again attacked the stronghold, and the next day, October 22, he was called upon to aid in a sea battle taking place off the Gaza coast against an Egyptian fleet led by the flagship *Emir Farouk*. Fitchet was met by a Fury fighter plane, an Iraqi gift to Egypt. Knowing that his chances of surviving a dogfight above the sea against the fast enemy fighter were minimal, he managed to pull the Beaufighter upward. The Fury could not keep up and crashed into the sea. The following day, along with another Beaufighter, Fitchet returned to attack the police station. Having learned from Fitchet's experience, his partner bombed in a quick run at low altitude and immediately escaped. His bombs did not release, however, and he returned to Ramat David. Fitchet decided to replace him, and did not make do with just one hit-and-run strike. He ignored the lesson he had taught his partner, and dived again to strafe the Egyptians with his guns. He was killed, along with his copilot and bombardier.

The fortress fell in the eighth assault, on November 9, after Operation Yoav. The commanders of the Israeli ground forces who entered the stronghold and observed the damage that the repeated bombings had caused were amazed to hear that the daring Beaufighter pilot who had paid with his life was a twenty-five-year-old non-Jewish Canadian volunteer who had shot down the last German plane of the Second World War. In the examination of the lessons learned from the battle, the commanders did not hide the damage to morale that Fitchet's crash had caused in the IDF. In later wars, the IAF would again encounter the strange phenomenon of IDF ground force commanders who would forgo air support if it entailed the possibility of having one of the aircraft crash before their eyes. Even the toughest of fighters found it difficult to function after such an event.

The fall of the Faluja positions was merely a matter of time, and the IAF took it upon itself to frustrate the Egyptian defenders. The targets were stationary, lacking antiaircraft protection, and the region was quickly turned into a target-practice area where the pilots could train in leading formations and attempting new bombing methods, photographing as they pulled out to evaluate results. Every squadron that completed a bombing mission or air-support flight in another region was then sent to bomb the Egyptian forces.

The besieged Egyptian forces dug themselves in and were saved from starvation only by small amounts of food brought in on camelback. One of the high-ranking Egyptian officers was Gamal Abdel Nasser, who placed the blame on the corruption of the monarchic regime. In 1952 he led the Officers' Revolution, which ousted King Farouk. Thus, in Faluja, under the IAF bombings, a new Egypt was created, and Nasser would be its sole and unquestioned leader until his death eighteen years later. His war of revenge could be planned only in 1955, when he entered into a large arms agreement with Czechoslovakia. The Czech weapons, which had placed Israel on its feet with Soviet approval, would then be used in an attempt to bring about Israel's downfall; the Soviet Union had changed its policies.

The IAF flew 240 operational sorties in Operation Yoav, a tremendous number for those days. Aside from fifty sorties initiated by the Egyptians, it had almost complete air superiority. The accomplishments were measured relative to the recent failures that had plagued the force. They surprised the upper command and even silenced their critics in the Operational branch of the General Command. Ben-Gurion concluded after the operation, "We would not have evicted the Egyptian invader and liberated the south and the Negev without the Israeli Air Force."

Between Operation Yoav and the series of operations in the south, the IAF was called upon to provide support for Operation Hirem, the largest and last operation in the country's north, following the capture of Nazareth and its environs during the ten days of battle. The object was to push the last of the Arab Rescue Army's forces under the command of Fouzi Al-Qawugji from the central Galilee. The IAF participated in the planning, and presented detailed plans of support and secondary missions to the Northern Command and to the Operations Branch of the General Command. The IAF sought to present itself as a flexible and mobile arm of the military, willing to respond quickly with firepower according to need at any location or event. Their responsiveness to changing conditions was vital on the northern front; its winter weather and mountainous terrain made movement difficult both day and night. Most of the targets were villages that had been turned into strongholds, or simply provided cover for enemy forces. This was not a regular army, and other than a Syrian battalion that had been brought in, it was a melting pot of bands and groups of foreign mercenaries who blended in with the local population.

The operation began on October 28 and lasted only sixty hours. Its pretext was the Arab attack on Kibbutz Manara. Al-Qawugji claimed that the cease-fire agreement did not obligate his army to anything, since he led a terrorist group. Israeli forces were to block Syrian support arriving from the bridgehead at Mishmar HaYarden, as well as the approaching Iraqi forces. Again the IAF had to improvise because of errors and sudden unexpected problems. In this lightning operation, the IAF did not deviate from the original plan. The number of sorties was small because of limited visibility. The ground operation concluded with the capture of fourteen villages in southern Lebanon, and the expansion of the northern Galilee. The dominant achievement of the IAF lay in the operational experience it gained, which improved the networks for planning and control.

The IAF began to prepare for the final battle. The fighter squadron was moved from the improvised field in Herzliya to the concrete runways in the open and operational field that the British had built in Hatzor. As long as it had remained within range of the Egyptian artillery, Hatzor had been unusable. With the Egyptians pushed far back to areas between Gaza and Rafah in the western Negev, the Messerschmitts and the few Spitfires could now be moved to Hatzor, inaugurating their permanent base, at the point closest to the front. From Hatzor the aircraft frequently took off on intelligence flights, equipped with new aerial cameras but lacking topographical maps. They gathered vital information on conditions in the territory, and on Egyptian troop concentrations. The photographs revealed a secondary airfield near El Arish, which explained where the Egyptian planes could take off from after the Israeli bombing of the central field at El Arish.

On December 22, a force made up of five brigades set out on Operation Chorev; its goal was to push into Egypt and attack the invading army until it dropped its weapons. In a diversionary raid, Egyptian troop concentrations in Gaza and Rafah were bombed from the air and sea, distracting them from the Israeli force making its way toward the Sinai. After five days of heavy fighting, the ground forces penetrated the Sinai, breaking up into five columns. When the road to the Suez Canal and the city of Ismailia lay open before them, Great Britain intervened, citing a twelve-year-old protectorate agreement it had signed with Egypt. It threatened, in the UN Security Council, to move its troops stationed on the Suez Canal to oppose the Israeli forces. The President of the United States added his own warning, and Ben-Gurion yielded, ordering his troops to withdraw to the international border by January 1, 1949.

General Yigal Yadin, commander of the front and the operation, beseeched Ben-Gurion to allow him to outflank the Egyptians at Rafah and to cut them off from the sea route and their forces stationed in Gaza.

Ben-Gurion succumbed to his pleas, and Yadin drove in the wedge. On January 6, the Egyptians agreed to a cease-fire starting the following day, upon which the IDF withdrew from the Sinai.

The IAF flew 243 sorties during Operation Chorev, primarily for target bombing. Approximately 267 tons of bombs were dropped, a record for the war. The B-17 Flying Fortresses paralyzed the El Arish airfield. In a final effort to postpone the end, the Egyptian Air Force sent, from a heretofore unknown airfield in Bir Hama, in the heart of the Sinai, heavy Starling bombers and fighter aircraft to attack the Israeli airfields at Kfar Sirkin, Lod, Ramat David, and Tel Nof, as well as the IDF bases at Tel HaShomer and Castina. Their bombings caused minimal damage. The Egyptian pilots did not find the Ramat David airfield and instead bombed the fields of Kibbutz Mishmar HaEmek. They also accidentally bombed Iraqi forces near Jericho and the Allenby Bridge on the Jordan River. Another group was sent to bomb Tel Aviv, but did not dare approach. Instead, on the morning of January 1, two Egyptian frigates approached the city's coast and fired thirty shells, which struck the water, then retreated. Israeli Navy boats gave chase, joined by an Israeli Flying Fortress, which dropped one and a half tons of bombs, but missed as well.

Fear of the Israeli fighter planes discouraged the Egyptian pilots, who were underdogs in the few air battles in which they had been engaged prior to Operation Chorev. In two dogfights in the skies of Abu-Aweigila on December 28, a pair of Israeli Spitfires shot down two Egyptian fighter aircraft, one Fiat and one Spitfire. The Israeli pilots were both American volunteers, Rudy Augarten-Carmi and Jack Doyle. On January 5, the eve of the cease-fire, a pair of Israeli Spitfires chanced upon a trio of Fiats. One Fiat was shot down, another was damaged, and the third escaped. Egypt begged for air support from the Arab armies that were part of the joint invasion force. Only Iraq responded, stating that since the two Furies it had given Egypt had been shot down, it no longer had any surplus aircraft. Actually, it had donated three aircraft, only one of which had been shot down, but on this side of the barricade, facts had no influence on the moods of the leaders of the war.

On the morning of January 7, 1949, the last day of the war, rumors reached Hatzor that the cease-fire would go into effect during the afternoon. The pilots competed for every sortie, since there might be no more. The Spitfires took off in pairs. Since the arrival of the last ten in

Operation Velvetta 2, the squadron was well equipped. Ezer Weizman, the operations officer, and Rudy Augarten-Carmi took off toward Abu-Aweigila. They attacked the rear flank of the remainder of the retreating Egyptian forces, strafing vehicles and people and then returning. At 0930 hours, another pair, Goldin and McElroy, an American and a Canadian volunteer, returned. They reported shooting down two Spitfires. "British," they added, by the way.

The British air presence was not a surprise. It had been expected from the day the IDF entered the Sinai and received the ultimatum from London. It had also been felt previously, after the bombing of Amman. The British were more reasonable in the air than they had been on the ground during the final days of their rule of the country. They generally observed from the sidelines and maintained a low profile. At most, they sent photographic reconnaissance planes toward Israel. When the frequency of these sorties increased, suspicions began to arise in IAF headquarters that the photographs would be passed on to Egypt, Jordan, or Iraq. In early December it was decided to respond. From the ground they saw the high-altitude contrails of a twin-engined British Mosquito bomber, which they knew could also fly reconnaissance missions. It was flying south along the coast at its peak altitude. Only the Mustangs could climb to such an altitude to intercept it. The Mustangs were already in operational service, and one of them, flown by the experienced Wayne Peake, an American volunteer, rose to intercept the Mosquito. Peake had grown up in the Mustang during the Second World War. He caught the Brit over Hatzor, squeezed a burst out of his cannons, and saw chunks of the Mosquito falling into the sea. The incident was not publicized, and even the British remained silent.

The report that the British had lost an aircraft in a violent confrontation that could give validity to the diplomatic ultimatum was received with mixed sentiments in the squadron. Along with a degree of joy, there was also a certain trepidation about how the British would respond. After two hours, another pair returned from the Sinai. Before landing, Jack Doyle's Spitfire executed a roll, a clear sign that he had shot down an enemy plane. He told how they had encountered six British aircraft. In a short dogfight, Doyle shot down one and his partner might have hit another. The emotion also swept through IAF headquarters, though they felt no trembling of the knees.

Ezer was ordered by telephone to continue the patrols, but to be

careful of further confrontations with the British. The cease-fire had been
set for 1400 hours, and it was now 1230 hours. Ezer was depressed. He
had destroyed Egyptian tanks and vehicles, but had not chalked up one
downed aircraft. At the last moment he called headquarters and proposed
sending two pairs to El Arish to demonstrate their presence and to remind
the Egyptians that they should observe the cease-fire. The planes took off
from Hatzor at 1445 hours, with Ezer leading. Sandy Jacobs was his
number two, and numbers three and four were both Americans, Bill
Schroeder and John Dungot. Flying at seven thousand feet in cloudy
skies, each Spitfire carried two 20-millimeter cannons and two .50-
caliber Browning machine guns. In bone-chilling cold, they flew in an
open formation. Above Haluza, not far from the international border,
Ezer observed several black dots in the distance. Counting them, he
reached eight, decided that they were not Israeli, and waved his wings to
indicate to close the formation. The three others copied and pulled. Ezer
climbed to altitude. He knew that in a dogfight, particularly in the
Spitfire, altitude meant speed. His altimeter read 8,500 feet, and a
quartet was coming straight toward them. The second quartet flew a bit to
their left and above. There was no doubt that they were British. "We're
going in!" he yelled into the radio. The British pilots opposite him
continued to fly as if they had not noticed the Israeli aircraft or did not
expect them to attack now, of all times, when the cease-fire was about to
come into effect.

Ezer saw Bill Schroeder entering the battle, and after a few seconds,
the first British Spitfire began to spin, dragging a trail of black smoke until
it crashed into the ground. It was now four against seven. Ezer grabbed
another and fired all his cannon and machine-gun rounds. The plane
was hit, but did not fall. Within two minutes the battle was over. From
the ground the Egyptians were sending up antiaircraft fire. Ezer looked
around and found himself alone. The skies were empty, and none of his
people could be seen. This was a common experience after a dogfight. In
the distance he could see a British Spitfire climbing to altitude, also
alone. Ezer set out on its trail, but felt the distance between them
growing. He scoured the desert, hoping to find the plane he had hit with
his cannons. Nothing. With slight disappointment he returned to Hatzor. Sandy Jacobs embraced him. He had seen a plane crash and did not
know whose it was. Ezer's Spitfire had survived with only two holes in the
propeller. At 1530 hours, after the debriefing and the reports from the

Sinai, the picture became clear, and he could smile. Five British aircraft had been downed, and one was his. It had executed a belly landing near El Arish, and its pilot had been taken prisoner by Israeli forces, along with another pilot. Two pilots had been killed, and one had been picked up by the Egyptians. Only three had returned to their base.

In Hatzor and Tel Aviv, there was both joy and concern. The pessimists feared retaliatory action, with dozens of RAF bombers and fighter planes wiping Hatzor off the map. After recovering from the ecstasy of victory, a sadness remained. They felt sorrow over the two British pilots who had been killed. The next day, a telegram was sent to RAF headquarters in Cyprus: "Our apologies, friends, but you were on the wrong side of the fence."

For the IAF, the War of Independence actually ended two months after the cease-fire, in a miniature recapitulation of Operation Dust. The Air Transport Command prepared a landing strip, Avraham Field, on a plateau in the Arava Desert, to fly in supplies to the ground units that were competing to be the first to reach Eilat. Operation Ovda was a final and quiet conclusion to the war. Operation Chorev and the rapid advance in the Sinai raised the operational level of the IAF to a new standard. If this hadn't happened, the fatal pandemonium of December 28 in the skies above Ujia and Abu-Aweigila would never have occurred. In this incident, IAF Spitfires mistakenly attacked a convoy belonging to the Negev Brigade, under the assumption that only the Egyptians would be found west of the international border. No one had bothered to notify the pilots in advance of the Israeli entry into the Sinai, and there was no way to update them in the air. If one of the ground troops had not pulled out of his pack the blue-and-white flag of the Jewish brigades, which he had kept since the Second World War, the attack would have ended in an enormous tragedy. The Egyptians also sent aircraft to attack the ground forces, but the Israelis were too confused to intercept them.

Over the course of the following days, Egyptian fighter planes managed to inflict several painful blows to Israeli ground forces in the Sinai. The IAF, which had been proud of its air superiority in Israel, did not always provide the protection that the ground forces deserved. Though the fighter squadron initiated retaliatory attacks on the Egyptian forces after they had departed, the Egyptians managed to envelop the exposed Israeli convoy. Between the time when the warning alarm had reached

IAF headquarters in the center of the country and the planes made the long trip to the Sinai, the Egyptians managed to conclude their attack and retreat to their bases.

Integrated air warfare at large distances demanded centralized control over every plane in the air and on the ground. Thus, through the most difficult and painful of lessons, IAF headquarters came to agree with Col. Cecil Margo's opinion, which stated that the IAF would be considered a modern force only if it would activate a regional radar system. In the winter of 1949, there were only three small and primitive radar sets in Israel, and they all belonged in the Second World War junkyards. One had been taken out of a bomber and reconditioned for ground surveillance at a range of thirty kilometers. It was installed in Haifa, and its operators would turn it using bicycle pedals. The second, taken out of a torpedo boat, with similar range, was installed in Bat Yam, south of Tel Aviv, and a third was placed in Givat Olga, where it was used to seek out illegal immigrant boats approaching the Israeli shores.

With these lessons, the IAF began to equip itself and modify its approaches in order to secure its air superiority beyond the narrow borders of the country. All this had begun little more than a year earlier in the Flight Club, with several tiny sporting aircraft and a large dream.

# 2

## Between the War of Independence and the Sinai Campaign

*O*n April 1, 1949, the first fighter squadron accompanied its commander, Sid Cohen, on his way back to his home in South Africa, where he would continue his medical studies, which had been postponed because of the war in Israel. The foursome of Spitfires stayed close to the passenger plane that was carrying him home to civilian life. They circled him in breathtaking aerobatic feats and parted with a wave of their wings, not only from a beloved commander but also from a period of history.

The war had ended, and the IAF's ranks began to empty of the foreign volunteers. The friendly, adventure-seeking non-Jews returned to their countries, as did Zionist Jews like Sid Cohen. Few of them decided to settle in Israel. The enormous machine that had been constructed under fire, through improvisation and risk, would have to undergo a serious self-evaluation, to the point of disassembly and reconstruction using consistent and appropriate parts. It would have to absorb new equipment, train new pilots, and develop new theories of military action, control, and administrative procedures. All this would be executed while maintaining ongoing security day and night. Though the fire had subsided, the alert to its possible recommencement continued in the IAF. This sense of ultimate responsibility was a product of the war, and was partially a result of the spirit that had pressed them to accomplish the impossible and the illogical in the past year. Dan Tolkowsky translated this into a document delineating the goals of a modern air force, the type that Israel deserved and would need to survive. It would have to be a force that could neutralize the air forces of the enemy at the instant of any hostile action.

This mission seemed tremendous to the few Israeli pilots who remained after the departure of the foreign volunteers. Suddenly they discovered that they would have to conduct the daily business of the IAF in Hebrew and develop a new professional language for daily communication on the runways, in the hangars, and in the air. They would have to translate existing training manuals and write those that were unavailable. Since English had been the official language of the IAF for those long months, the change would entail not only operating in Hebrew under these new conditions, but also thinking and behaving in Hebrew. There was no more appropriate symbol of this shift than the transfer of command of the first fighter squadron to Ezer Weizman.

Many people in the country placed great hope in the truce that had been signed on the island of Rhodes with Israel's Arab neighbors. It was not only the foreign volunteers who saw this as a stepping-stone to peace and an invitation to remove their uniforms. The IDF had lost many of its best fighters and commanders. Ezer even found himself standing before the members of Moti Fine's kibbutz, Degania, pleading for them to allow him to remain in the IAF. "The foreign volunteers are leaving one by one," he told them. "The only people remaining are ones like your Moti. And if he leaves, who'll be left? Do you really want only characters like me to remain in the Air Force?" The kibbutz members approved Moti's remaining in the IAF. He had been one of the first four pilots to receive Israeli wings, along with Danny Shapira (his partner in the transfer of the Spitfires in Velvetta 2), Yeshayahu Gazit, and Tibi Ben-Shachar.

Shortly thereafter, twelve graduates of the first course of the Flight School that had opened at the former British base at Kfar Sirkin joined this group, filling the thin ranks. In May 1949, one month after Ezer took charge of the squadron, it was ordered to leave Hatzor and relocate to Ramat David. Because of a lack of squadrons, Hatzor was shut down for the next two years, and the squadron's remaining Messerschmitts were left there. The twenty Spitfires now constituted the backbone of the squadron. Three Mustangs, packhorses of the U.S. Air Force in World War II, were added to this force. Israeli procurement envoys cleverly evaded the U.S. embargo on arms shipments to the Middle East and soon added more Mustangs to the original three. With only training aircraft being purchased in the United States, fighter aircraft were bought from the military surplus of Europe. The purchasers were not even deterred by the De Havilland Mosquito bombers with their light balsam frames and cloth coverings, many of which were on the verge of decay.

Ezer learned that the role of squadron commander demanded that he abandon his idea of himself as the lone knight of the flying cavalry in order to command and solidify a team that would see their profession as a mission as well. This was even more true of the pilots who were to be not merely airplane drivers, but fighters and commanders. Thus he describes this period in his book, *On Eagle's Wings*.

The old custom of nightly parties would have to end. Pleasures would have to be secondary to an increasingly crowded work schedule. His position demanded constant contact with every skilled worker in the squadron, and development of each unit's sense of its own importance, so that there would be no gaps based on superiority and inferiority. The squadron's combat readiness was dependent no less on the mechanic who tightened the last screw than on the pilot who scrambled to intercept an oncoming enemy plane. This sense could only be conveyed through personal attention and consideration.

The IAF, as opposed to the ground forces, contained professionals and commanders who had reached its ranks without deeply rooted theories of combat brought from other militaries. Ezer therefore found himself spending long nights in his room translating and writing training manuals and course outlines. Through this he reached another personal revelation of the hidden blessing in the lack of experience in a command position. He found himself free to develop new approaches based on professionalism and affected by experience accrued in older air forces, while not imposing foreign traditions and styles on the new generation of Israeli pilots.

There was nothing locally unique in the process of training pilots like Moti Fine and Danny Shapira to be airborne hunters. The combat pilot, regardless of origin or nationality, must learn to sense the aircraft and its weapons as parts of his body; otherwise he will not be able to navigate with intense precision to the best firing position to down enemy aircraft or to strike at an enemy target. Every missed shot or opportunity could lead to tragedy. The one element unique to Israel in the late 1940s and early 1950s was the fact that air superiority could not be achieved on a limited training budget and restrictive "peacetime" conditions, which could lead to quantitative and technological inferiority. The two-to-three-year-old country now had twice the number of destitute immigrant refugees that it had on the day of its establishment. Under these conditions, its advantage lay in the spirit of personal fighting and sacrifice. No appropriate training manuals could be found for the young Israeli temperament; everything began and ended with the personality of the commander, and with his ability to carry his subordinates with him. Even the tremendous motivation of the new squadron members demanded essential processing to withstand operational trials involving the mixture of dangers and natural fears.

While the pilot is the loneliest fighter in war, this loneliness is not a world unto itself for him. It is a cell in a tissue, subsisting in a framework of mutual responsibility. The thought and discretion of the individual, which dictate his actions, affect the group just as they are affected by it. The dilemma of the commander is to clench the range of personal abilities into a fist without the teamwork blurring or dulling their uniqueness. In the IAF, where even official uniforms had yet to be made, there was no place for thinking in average terms. This group had to continue to grow through partnership and a familial closeness whose unique, secret strength lay in friendship and internal discipline and was not limited by the pressures of a rigid hierarchy. However, it was difficult to infuse the spirit of combat into these youngsters, with the skies of the Middle East clear and quiet for the most part. Neither of the two sides sought to break the cease-fire. Even the neighboring Arab air forces were in the process of rebuilding. Their level of preparedness was low, and their chances of being dragged into a conflict were nil. The squadron's attempts to search out signs of an enemy pulse through reconnaissance sorties did not involve dangerous risks or even local dogfights.

Ezer occasionally sent his pilots on intelligence-gathering sorties to "loosen their limbs" from the country's narrow borders, which limited flight and training ranges. They were not allowed to taste live fire even in the accepted training areas, for the expanses of the Negev, quiet and ideal for target practice, were farther away now that the squadron had been transferred north to Ramat David. Even the dogfight tales of the War of Independence told by the few veterans who remained were not enough to kindle their imaginations. Approximately twenty enemy aircraft had been shot down during the war, and most of those who had downed them had either been killed or had left the country.

Thus, even an innocent penetration of Israeli airspace by a British Sunderland flying boat on May 17, 1950, was reason enough for a display of flexed muscles. The Sunderland was on its way from the Persian Gulf to Egypt when Israeli observation points saw it flying over the Sea of Galilee in the direction of Haifa. Ezer heard the news in IAF headquarters in Jaffa and scrambled a quartet of Spitfires to intercept it. After identification and a number of warning cannon bursts, he ordered his aircraft to force the Sunderland to land in the sea near the Tel Aviv coast, where he sailed out in a motorboat to meet its crew. The pilots presented their maps as evidence that there was no mention of a new country named Israel. After several glasses of beer, they departed, promising to update their maps. Some time later, on his honeymoon in England, Ezer was invited to visit an RAF transport squadron. In the operations room, he asked to see a map of the Middle East. Israel was drawn on the map in bright purple, with a tiny flag stuck in it reading, "Any aircraft flying over this region will be fired upon without warning."

## El Hama and Tel Mutila

Barely eleven months after the Sunderland incident, the squadron was given its first opportunity to prove itself in an actual battle, the first since the war. Its aircraft were Mustangs, the Spitfires having been transferred to the second fighter squadron, which had split off primarily for operational training of graduates of the Flight School. This event would serve as a test of the economic training methods being used.

The cease-fire agreement with the Syrians defined the narrow area formed by the Yarmukh River and Hamat Gader as a demilitarized zone. It was the southernmost of five such zones set in the agreement along the Syrian border. After twenty months, Syria found itself undergoing a revolution, which led to military rule in the country, and peace was still remote. Israel began to execute an old plan to dry out Hula Lake and its swamps, parts of which were in the demilitarized zones. Syria viewed these activities as a provocation, and demanded that the status quo be maintained, since control of the area was still in its hands. Israel claimed to be sovereign, and the UN was requested to intervene. This was to be the first in a long series of small, frustrating wars that would last sixteen years. The last of these border incidents for control of the demilitarized zones would ignite the fuse of the Six-Day War in 1967.

A patrol of Israeli soldiers, dressed in police uniforms, was sent to verify a report that a Syrian military force had entered the demilitarized zone in civilian dress. The Syrians had actually blocked the road. The Israeli commander demanded his right to cross, and the Syrian commander denied him permission. When the Israeli instructed his men to break through, the Syrians opened fire, killing seven Israeli soldiers.

Israel decided to respond. A ground action was decided against, because of limitations in topography and time. The next morning, April 5, 1951, the IAF was ordered to be ready to attack. Dep. Gen. Rudy Augarten-Carmi, commander of the Ramat David Base, was Sid Cohen's strict and meticulous deputy in the first fighter squadron, and one of the few foreign volunteers who remained in the country and the IAF. He was summoned to Northern Command headquarters for a consultation. The IDF chief of staff, Lt. Gen. Yigal Yadin, pressured him to attack in the afternoon. If the aircraft approached from west to east at low altitude in the canyon peaks, the sun would be at their backs, blinding the Syrians, and surprise would be guaranteed. Augarten-Carmi was wary of cross fire in the canyon, and preferred dive-bombing from a higher altitude. The representatives of the ground forces did not intervene in the professional aspects of the argument. The chief of staff merely asked about the pilots' morale and their readiness to execute. Augarten-Carmi informed him that his pilots were indeed thirsty for battle. At the end of the meeting he decided to divide the mission between the two squadrons. He would lead the quartet of Spitfires, which would charge in from above, out of the sun, and bomb the police fortress of El Hama at the far end of the canyon in a flat angle, in three runs. Meir Roff, the squadron commander, would lead a formation of four Mustangs in behind him, flying low. He would complete the job with rocket and cannon fire on a nearby tent encampment and bunker.

The assault lasted fifteen minutes. Benny Peled, the Tel Nof mechanic who had been among those who assembled the first Messerschmitts and later became a pilot and commander-in-chief of the IAF, observed from five thousand feet in a Harvard training aircraft that had been altered to serve as a liaison between the attacking aircraft and the Command Center. He did not miss a thing, particularly regarding the Spitfires' bombing. "The bombs fell everywhere, except on the target," he reported. The Mustangs, however, were more accurate. Their rockets hit the bunker and burned the tents. Syrian light-machine-gun fire directed at the planes was to no avail, and no aircraft were scrambled toward the Israelis. In all, the damage inflicted by the operation was minimal, and the diplomatic benefits were none.

Less than a month later, on May 2, the Syrians continued their pressure in the neighboring demilitarized zone. A Syrian unit crossed the Jordan River and took control of Tel Mutila and two additional hills overlooking the mouth of the river and the only road leading to Rosh Pinna and other Israeli settlements in the northern Galilee. This posed an immediate threat.

Confronted by the Syrians, a patrol of the Golani Brigade called for backup from the regiment commanded by Rehavam "Gandhi" Ze'evi. By the time the relief force arrived, the Syrians' positions had been reinforced. When the first Israeli bullets were fired on them, they responded with artillery. The incident worsened and continued for five days. Though it ended with the Syrians being pushed back over the Jordan, four Israeli soldiers were killed.

The Tel Mutila incident revealed not only the decline that had developed in the quality of combat and the motivation in the IDF in the two years since the war, but also the inferior position of the IAF in the minds of the Upper Command. A short and limited air bombing, even compared to El Hama, would have immediately crushed the small Syrian force as soon as it had captured the hills. This would have avoided the superfluous ground battle and prevented the Syrians from attempting further border crossings. However, the General Command failed to regard the IAF as an independent strike force. Perhaps it secretly feared that the use of the IAF against a point target, which traditionally belonged to the realm of the ground forces, would damage the professional pride of the commanders of the ground forces. Lacking confidence in the young pilots, most of whom lacked combat experience, they viewed the IAF as a mere support force.

The aircraft were called upon to help on the fifth day of the battle, when the ground force was on the verge of collapsing because of fatigue and diarrhea. That morning, Augarten-Carmi was testing three Spitfire pilots, flight instructors, in an air exercise over Tiberias. Yoash "Chatto" Tzidon, the air support officer, burst into the communications and called for them to turn north. He sounded hysterical, and was crying that a slaughter was taking place on the ground. Augarten-Carmi responded that he would not enter without approval from IAF headquarters. Chatto reported that he had been trying to request approval since morning, but had not been able to make contact. Augarten-Carmi attempted to make contact and succeeded, but found that no one in headquarters would take responsibility for approving the attack. They would only approve dry runs, without fire. The commander of the Northern Command definitely did not mean more than that. Thus, as the quartet of Spitfires identified the battlefield from 7,500 feet, Augarten-Carmi ordered his trainees to dive in a vertical column and warned them not to open fire. The Spitfires dived eighteen times, freezing the people on the ground with fear. The Syrians began to flee, and retreated in shock to the other side of the Jordan River. The empty runs prevented the battle from resulting in more victims, but could have cost the pilots their lives and their aircraft. A Syrian antiaircraft cannon opened fire on the Spitfires. At first it fired random rounds at the first plane, and then bursts when the dives increased. Augarten-Carmi commanded his aircraft to return home. All of the aircraft had sustained light damage, but landed safely in Ramat David.

That day, Augarten-Carmi flew to IAF headquarters in Ramle to file his report of the incident. Upon his return to base, he was surprised by the warm reception he received from emissaries of the Northern Command, who had come to thank him for saving the soldiers of the Golani Brigade from certain death. Augarten-Carmi did not soften. The goal is not always worth the means, and order must continue to prevail.

Chief of Staff Yadin continued to minimize the importance of the IAF, just as he had not taken it into consideration before ordering the Golani Brigade to evict the Syrians from Tel Mutila. The IAF had no advocate in the General Command who could bang on the table and inform them that there was a more effective and less expensive alternative to the blood about to be spilled in the ground battle. The IAF was functioning at this point with clipped wings. The lessons of the wars of the previous decade and the beginnings of the jet revolution occurring in military aviation throughout the world had not raised the status of the IAF beyond its secondary role, subordinate to the will and needs of the ground forces. After his appointment as chief of staff, Yadin completed what he had begun to create during his period as commander of the Operations Branch. Taking advantage of his superior authority, he halted the process of the building of the IAF as a separate skilled and unique branch of the military, a process that he called "isolationism." The power struggles of the War of Independence that had appeared as operational differences of opinion now became issues of organization and logistics and focused primarily on the distribution of the defense budget.

Yadin adhered to the instructions of the Minister of Defense of October 1949, which stated that there should be no separate command center for the ground forces in the IDF, but rather that the General Command would serve as headquarters for the ground, air, and sea forces. Ben-Gurion's intention had been politically and state-oriented. Justly, he did not want local militias, but rather one unified and disciplined military, subordinate to the government. The chief of staff interpreted this in his own way and subordinated the IAF to the branch commanders of the General Command. The conflicts between IAF commander-in-chief Remez's and Yadin's ideas about the role of the IAF brought about Remez's resignation in December 1950, and the thirty-one-year-old major general found himself out of the military.

Maj. Gen. Shlomo Shamir, who replaced him, was thirty-five years old and seemed to have been cast in the mold of a commander for all seasons. He had served as an officer in the British ground forces and as a regimental commander who had been called upon (relatively unsuccessfully) to aid in the failing battles near Latrun. After the war he had been chosen as commander-in-chief of the Israeli Navy in order to reorganize it from its foundations. Because he had participated ten years earlier in a light flight course in the Airplane Company, it seemed fitting for him to rehabilitate the IAF as well, which was also in need of an organizational house-cleaning. Shamir's entry into the job was accompanied by the Upper Command's instruction to turn IAF headquarters into part of the General Command. Thus it was no longer an autonomous command but first and foremost a supporting service for the ground forces. Several high-ranking IAF officers resigned and left the military. Dan Tolkowsky postponed his resignation for six months until he could find an adequate civilian position. Shamir began to execute the missions that had been approved during the period preceding his command. His only significant accomplishment was the transfer of IAF headquarters from scattered offices in Jaffa to Ramle, near Tel Aviv, where it became a military command post with all the trimmings, including a landing strip for light aircraft.

The new rigid framework emphasized order and discipline. Organizational and administrative issues received attention while other vital and operational subjects were pushed to the side because of the chief of staff's recommendations and misunderstandings of them. Those loyal to Remez who remained in the IAF did not know what to expect, and clung gratefully to Shamir's permission to execute the last goals that Remez had set—the strengthening of the Mosquito bomber squadron and the fostering of the rising leadership (like Ezer Weizman) through courses in military colleges in Great Britain and entrance into the jet age. A first invitation from London to purchase a sea jet aircraft was turned down, but Moti Hod (who had changed his name from Fine) had already been sent to train on the modern aircraft. He became the IAF's pioneer jet pilot.

The new commander and the imposed structure did not withstand the test. Within eight months, Shamir was forced to resign for health reasons, far from actualizing Yadin's plans. It was difficult to view him as directly responsible for the operational faults in the IAF and its involvement in El Hama and Tel Mutila. But they did result from the restrictions from which Remez had sought to liberate himself, and the quest for control that had brought Shamir to the IAF.

## Chaim Laskov, Builder of the IAF Framework

In late August 1951, the next commander-in-chief, Maj. Gen. Chaim Laskov, encountered a listless IAF with a pitiful level of readiness and low combat capabilities. In a report to the General Command, he stated that the operational goal of the IAF and the work of its headquarters opposite the General Command was plagued by a lack of clarity. He found a dearth of commanders, and among the few that did exist, the majority were not trained for their operational or administrative functions. Everything—morale, professionalism, and discipline within the units—seemed to be in a poor state.

Laskov, thirty-two years old, had been more surprised than anyone else when he was informed during a study visit to Great Britain that he had been chosen as commander-in-chief of the IAF. After two years as commander of the IDF Training Division, Laskov's reputation preceded him. Born in Russia, he had lost his father to Arab murderers in Haifa and had reached the rank of major in the British Army. Ben-Gurion appreciated such commanders, and Chief of Staff Yadin was certain that Laskov would successfully bring about integration of the IAF headquarters into the General Command. Who would have believed that an introverted ground forces commander with the personality of a tank operator would bring the IAF to the runway from which it so desired to take off? Laskov was the type of skilled leader whose mastery lay in his ability to be methodically abstract. Such a leader does not have to be skilled or experienced in the field he is commanding in order to raise it to a more sophisticated level. Laskov did not see any blow to his pride in learning from the ground up, through reading and consultations with experts about the elements and characteristics of air power. When he felt that he gained a level of expertise in the field, he began to actualize the ideas with planning and control in methodical and organized work in the headquarters. Procedures and regulations were transcribed, periodic intelligence evaluations of the enemy's capabilities were drawn up, and conclusions were reached regarding arms procurement, training, and troop placement. A positive sign of his healthy thinking appeared when he called upon Dan Tolkowsky, the fiery advocate of IAF independence, to return as deputy commander of the IAF.

In November 1951, in a detailed document, Tolkowsky completed Laskov's initial report on the problems of the IAF. It had two hundred aircraft of seventeen different varieties. Of the 137 fighter and bomber aircraft, only eighty-five were capable of flying. Of the 130 aircrew, only 27 belonged to the fighter squadrons. The diminished level of readiness in the operational squadrons was due to a chronic lack of replacement parts for the aircraft. The devastating shortage of aircrew in these squadrons was a result of the assignment of most of the experienced pilots to train air cadets.

It did not seem that the IAF would be able to pull out of this depression. The General Command, as was proven in the first major IDF exercise in September 1951, was not even aware of the IAF's basic statistics. The chief of staff demanded the participation of twelve Spitfires when only four were in flying condition. The burst forward that the IAF needed would have to come first from within, so that it would merit the trust for which it was striving. Laskov's first year in command was one of increased procurement of new aircraft, planned during Remez's days and accelerated during the Shamir period.

Under Tolkowsky's professional inspiration and Laskov's administrative influence, IAF headquarters created a three-year work plan according to missions it had been allocated by the General Command. The first was defense of the nation's skies. The second involved disabling of the Arab air forces. Transport and attack support of the ground and sea forces was assigned third place. Despite his steadfastness and stubbornness in realizing his goals, Laskov appeared as an individual facing the masses. He had already carved out for himself a place as a permanent member of the General Command and air adviser to the chief of staff. As conditions in the country obligated the IDF to tighten its belt, the IAF was among the first victims of cutbacks. Laskov was repeatedly witness to random and inconsistent division of funds, which undercut the IAF's missions and purpose. He demanded that the IAF's needs be seen as exclusive, and not measured in the context of, or in comparison to, the needs of the ground forces. The defense of the state, he stressed adamantly in a memo to the Upper Command, demanded that the IAF and its headquarters be granted the authority and means given to the General Command in order to achieve superiority over the enemy. The only basis for achieving this goal, he added, was cooperation between the branches, but under no circumstances subordination of the IAF to the IDF.

This controversy ran deeper than personal attitudes, and would continue years after Laskov left the IAF and Yadin the IDF. Laskov understood that rapid response at the outbreak of aggressive actions must be rooted in a strong base of regular forces and not depend on reserves. Later he saw the need for the immediate formation of a flight control network in order to track enemy aircraft and to direct the IAF's planes toward them. Only thus would the best conditions for intercepting enemy aircraft be achieved. The establishment of these two pillars of the modern air force as he planned was halted because of the shortsightedness of the Upper Command, or because it stood in "basic conflict with the capabilities of the military and the State," as Yadin said. While the freeze was not all-encompassing, it was expressed in a miserly budgeting that slowed the pace of growth.

The tension reached its peak in February 1953. After debating the budget for the new fiscal year, the General Command refused to approve the IAF's addition of two hundred men to staff three new operational squadrons whose aircraft had already been purchased. These included British Meteors, Israel's first jet aircraft, which were already on their way. The IDF's chief of staff at this time was Lt. Gen. Mordechai Makleff. At the head of the Operations Branch was Maj. Gen. Moshe Dayan, a devotee of the commando fighting of the ground forces, and one whose vision in regard to security needs was limited to the immediate. The IDF was then focusing on terrorists who were entering Israel from Gaza and Jordan, murdering travelers on the roads and farmers in agricultural communities. The government had ordered the IDF to cut forty percent of its budget, and the IAF was portrayed at the General Command meeting as demanding and pretentious, gorging itself on budgets. Laskov was infuriated by Dayan's statement that there was no justification for the formation of an additional squadron at the expense of canceling another unit from his grand plan for development of the ground army.

The controversy over control of the IAF suddenly seemed secondary, an issue of framework and ceremony. In May 1953, Laskov requested discharge for an extended period of studies. The next commander-in-chief, he wrote in his parting letter from the IAF, must be aircrew, and he was clearly referring to his deputy and spiritual teacher, Col. Dan Tolkowsky. No one in the Upper Comand could contest this last will and testament. In the IAF, Tolkowsky had no competitor, and the General Command was wary of introducing another outsider to take command. On the other hand, they feared that choosing him would deepen the conflicts or be seen as giving in to the "bad boy" from the IAF. Makleff extricated himself from the problem by granting Tolkowsky the position of acting commander-in-chief.

Four months later, they stood on the dais and and surveyed the final formation of Flight Course Number Twelve. I was among those who received pilot's wings at that time, and their internal struggles were light-years away from me.

## Eliezer Cohen, Flight Cadet

"Flight Cadet Eliezer Cohen reporting as ordered to the Preparatory Stage of the Flight Course."

With a quivering hand, I saluted. I was supposed to scream the words almost in a roar. It was not only the ferocity of Sergeant Major Yosefson that caused us to stand before him tense and trembling with every shred of discipline in our bodies. We also had to override the sounds of the training aircraft, buzzing around us like mosquitoes. The IAF Flight School had been established on a former British air base near Kfar Sirkin, not far from Petah Tikva. It was a small airfield of Harvards and Stearman biplanes left over from the combat arsenal of the Second World War. Apparently in our honor, a gorgeous Spitfire ripped the air on that June 1952 morning, flown by one of the instructors, who passed over our heads with the thunderous din of 1,500 horsepower. Respected by all of us, the Spitfire was the object of every cadet's fantasies. For me, a Jerusalem youth, it was the catalyst that had brought me to this ridiculous pose, standing before Sergeant Major Yosefson's mustache, which spat out Rumanian curses with the distinct purpose of shaping us into soldiers.

I was ten years old, toward the end of the Second World War, when I first saw a Spitfire in its true size and within arm's reach. This was not merely a Spitfire decorated with the round symbol of the RAF, but the plane of Douglas Bader, the one-legged hero of the Battle of Britain who had returned from the hospital to fly in combat despite his handicap. As a child I had devoured the stories of the bravery of the British pilots, and there was not a single war film that I had missed. Approximately four years later, immediately following my bar mitzvah, I witnessed other Spitfires through the porthole of the bomb shelter in the basement of our home. They were Egyptian planes, the only ones to bomb Jerusalem in the summer of 1948. Despite my fear that they would hit our home or the bus company's garage, which had been turned into the central food warehouse for the blockaded Jerusalem, I found myself astounded by their ordinary dives and was amazed that they were not aiming at any specific target. The antiaircraft gunner on our roof was even less productive than the planes. To my grave disappointment he never hit a thing.

My high school studies were broken up and irregular. I made every effort to make up what I had missed, at least the minimum that would allow me to pass the IAF's entrance exams. Although the techniques have since been modified and the criteria have become more demanding, the examination stage has essentially not changed over the years. All volunteers for the Flight School were summoned on the day of induction and subjected to days of meticulous medical examinations, psychotechnical tests of compatibility, and, of course, exams to determine their competency if they had no matriculation certificate in the needed fields. Since then the *Gibush* (consolidation) has been added, a sort of prebasic training in which volunteers are tested on a personal level and in teamwork in field conditions and under group pressure for a specific period of time. Those who drop out during this period are saved superfluous frustrations before beginning the obstacle course of the program itself. We had to fool ourselves in order not to succumb to the fears of every flight cadet, a trial of immunization that is a blessing to all and a test of strength in itself. Everyone feared the dismissals that would be necessary to select the elite group that would receive wings. We knew that we must think, act, and look our best in order to satisfy our instructors and the course's commanders. The instructors were remnants of the group of foreign volunteers. The style was British, for the Israeli instructors, only two or three courses older than we, and with no combat experience or heroism about them, had not yet set the tone.

We were terrified of Sergeant Major Yosefson's every displeased glance, which could make its way into our personal files and add demerits, particularly in the Preparatory Stage, with its studies of ground subjects, order exercises, and cleaning jobs throughout the base. Anyone who broke rules of discipline or failed in the interim or final examinations was mercilessly sent on his way. That I managed to pass this obstacle, with my incomplete formal education, was thanks to Gideon Cohen, not a relative but a loyal and supportive friend. Before deciding to become a pilot, he had been an airplane mechanic, and was a sort of walking encyclopedia of aircraft and the history of aviation, and it was his knowledge and expertise that got me through the Primary Stage of my training.

At this point we were allowed to touch the aircraft, Stearman biplanes, and to satisfy the jealous looks we had been giving them from a distance. The structure and content of the studies were a wonderful mix, a product of the foreign veterans, based on the flight courses they had undergone during the Second World War and their war experiences in Europe, the Pacific, and Israel. Of jet aircraft we had only read in the newspapers. Our world still revolved like propellers, and those forty hours of training in the air on the Stearman, exposed to the winds, was a multipurpose combination perfectly fit for this small family air force. The judgment of the instructor who sat in the rear seat was guided more by intuition and straight thinking than by methodical and tested theories. Years later, with wisdom and in retrospective examination, their accomplishments can be seen as astounding.

I was surprised by the Stearman. It was built of an aluminum frame covered by a canvas, and with a strong poke of the finger, one could put a hole in it. I was racked by the fear that with me flying it, of all people, it would be torn to shreds by some strange wind up there. Was it too late to turn back?

I thought about my family and friends who, two months earlier, had barely believed that I would be accepted into the course. We belonged to the "Native Jerusalemites" whose heads had never been in the clouds and rarely produced a pilot. Gideon "Giche" Shapira, a neighbor of mine and a local hero, was enough of a model for me. When I first saw him in an IAF uniform with his wings, I prayed that I would be able to be like him. So far I had not failed. Despite the suspicions and the warnings, I was wearing the blue uniform a week after my induction, with the flight cadet's white stripe on my shoulders. I decided that it was too late to turn back. I climbed into the Stearman and fastened my seat belt, leather helmet, and wind goggles. My instructor was short-tempered. Though he was perhaps a fabulous pilot, he was a horrible instructor, the type of professional who blames his pupils for limited comprehension if they fail to perform perfectly in their first lesson. Because I did not meet his expectations, he passed me on to another instructor. To my good fortune, the new instructor was both patient and tolerant. He did not make do with theoretical murmurings, but demonstrated his instructions—how to start the engine, to rev, to play with the stick and take off, to maneuver and to land. It was complicated, but he demonstrated over and over, allowed me to try, and corrected my mistakes. I imitated his actions as well as I could, even if I did not always understand why. The main thing was that I was up there, though not exactly as free as a bird, for I could see my instructor in the front seat and felt more a passenger than a pilot, still wary of looking down, overwhelmed by the view.

At first the altitude daunted me. However, five minutes in the air, with the sense that you are holding and directing your fate by grasping the stick or pressing the pedals, is enough to dispel any of the ancient questions, like What is keeping this artificial bird up in the sky? What did it matter if they called this "aerodynamic flow," as we had learned in our courses on the ground, or "God," as the elders of Jerusalem thought? I had yet to find out that inattentive steering in too sharp a turn could cancel all those natural forces, causing this bird to spin earthward like a heap of junk. But, showing no signs of instability, it flew, and even the canvas, thank God, held together in the strong winds. We prepared for landing. I recited the procedures to myself, and in my hand and foot I felt the response of the instructor handling the steering mechanism parallel to mine in case I made a mistake. The ground approached, and I hit the runway like a sack of potatoes. The instructor did not get angry. It was good for me to feel the blow, as a reminder for the next landing. Years later, as I lift and land El Al Boeings throughout the world, I am still accompanied by that reminder, so that I may merit the applause of the passengers. After ten flights, when we stopped, the instructor said, "Well, Cohen, what do you think? Can you do a solo flight?"

My heart missed a beat. Fly alone? Was he crazy? True, they did send cadets to fly solo after ten or twelve flights, but what did that have to do with me? I had no idea what was going on. God, what would I do if the engine suddenly shut down? I've already mentioned the fragile canvas. The thoughts flooded me as I repeated the internal command I had given myself at the beginning of the course: Shut up and do what they tell you. They must know better than you! And another rule that I adopted from the outset: Never exhibit even a bit of the storm raging inside you. Pretend. It was this attitude that guided me to the wing ceremony.

"If you think I should try a solo, the decision is yours," I told the instructor with a confidence that spoke of internal tranquillity. The next morning, a hot summer's day, I waited for the examiner near the fueled Stearman.

Bill Levin, blond and handsome, blue-eyed, with a porcupine haircut, was the cadets' terror. A former U.S. Marine pilot with many flight hours, he had decided to emigrate to Israel, and because of his experience he had quickly reached the rank of senior examiner. Throughout the entire examination, the man did not utter a word. You could empty your guts and he would not say a thing. Even on the ground, his words were sharp and to the point.

"Did you check the aircraft?"

"Yes, sir!"

"You know that you are being examined for a solo flight?"

"Yes, sir!"

I did not have the faintest idea what to do. I was counting on him to tell me. We settled into the tandem cockpits and connected to the internal communications, which operated through hollow speaking tubes like those in old ships. I could see him watching me in the rearview mirror, waiting for me to act.

"Should I start the engine, sir?" I asked hesitantly.

He answered, "Do you think we'll be able to fly without starting the engine?"

A stupid question, I gathered. I had probably already failed, so there was nothing to lose. Pretend. I started the engine and completed my checks, again not accustomed to doing so alone. Unsure of my ability to taxi, I promised myself that he would not hear any more stupid questions from me.

I taxied to the takeoff position, and the control hut flashed me the green light. I straightened out in the middle of the runway, waiting for the examiner to say something. He was silent. Endless silence on the lines. Had our communications disconnected? No, everything was connected. I decided to do everything alone. If he didn't agree, he would know how to stop me. I opened my engine to full and took off. Unbelievable.

It worked. Maybe I really was ready to fly alone. Maybe this was the magic secret of this examiner. He would not rattle my brains like the instructor who had something to say about every movement. I climbed and climbed. Two thousand feet . . . four thousand feet. . . . We were in the course's aerobatic area, north of Sirkin, when a miracle suddenly occurred. There was a voice in my headphones.

"Execute a stall!"

Acting according to procedure, I checked that the area below me was clear, and executed one stall and then another, careful not to lose control. Again, silence in the headphones. I started to climb again. At six thousand feet the voice returned.

"Execute a spin!"

I did one downward corkscrew, and then a second and a third. If I did not pull out in time, there was a danger that I would drop below the minimum altitude. But I pulled out of the spin, not sure whether I had performed well or not, and he ordered me to return to circle. Again I did not hear a sound, but I circled again and again in some sort of pleasure, even beginning to come out of the terror of the exam, with that same carefree feeling that leads to self-confidence.

"This is the last time around. Turn to the runway after completion."

I landed, turned off the runway, and the unbelievable happened. Bill Levin climbed out of his cockpit, stood on the wing, and shouted into my helmet, "Circle one more time and pick me up here."

Is that all he had to say to a cadet who had just been sent to a solo? Apparently so. I was alone at the takeoff position. The cockpit in front of me was empty. Green light. I opened the engine up full and found myself in the air, hardly able to believe that this was really me. I reminded myself not to get emotional, and was amazed that I managed not to do so. The altimeter read fifteen hundred feet. Lord! The circle had to be executed at one thousand. I quickly descended and prepared for landing. I was sure I would not make it, not me, never, definitely not today. I advanced to the downwind leg. I was to approach the edge of the base leg and begin to descend. In one minute I would have to straighten out with the line of the runway. The aircraft was a little stubborn, and I responded gruffly. I would not let it get this way. I had to do this well.

I straightened out, shut down the engine, and glided. A second before touching the runway, I pulled lightly on the stick, lifting the nose just like in the books. The landing was smooth and pleasant, like floating.

I braked, stopped, and turned from the runway, completely flooded with joy. Though I still had to circle the field slowly to collect Levin from the takeoff position, my head was in the clouds. I looked in the instructor's mirror on the upper wing and bellowed in a tremendous roar, filled with wild laughter that shot the tension of the last hour out of my chest, "Cadet Cohen, you have completed a solo!"

Bill Levin seemed satisfied when I picked him up. I saluted and we parted. Back at the squadron, I met my instructor, who greeted me by saying, "Levin says we'll apparently make a pilot out of you after all. And he knows what he's talking about."

And he stood there, keeping me in conversation so that my comrades could sneak up behind me with a bucket of water, the immersion ceremony of solo pilots, replete with shouts and kicks in the butt from those who had already undergone the experience.

Several days later I flew a completely aerobatic solo flight in order to experience the exalted feeling that veteran pilots never grow tired of describing. I executed another spin, another loop, another roll. I went wild up there, alone. I laughed and cried until I had nothing left, with that feeling that you and the machine have become one entity. The steering mechanisms felt as if they were part of my limbs, and the engine roared as if from my head, understanding that I had allowed the aircraft to pull me, turn me on my back and upright again, and rotate the world around me as if I were the planet's hinge. Only after this flight did I understand that I really wanted to be a pilot.

There had been many dismissals by the time we moved on to the Primary Stage, where we would use the knowledge we had gathered in operating the larger and stronger Harvard aircraft. This was no aluminum frame with a canvas covering. Day after day we executed more aerobatic exercises, navigation assignments, and night flights. Those who were not dismissed during this period had a good chance of graduating. Afterward, at Tel Nof, we first encountered a large air base. There we underwent the supplementary part of our officers' training course, getting to know the IAF as well as participating in escape and survival exercises. The parachuting course in those days was not a part of basic training, so as not to get the pilot used to bailing out at the first moment of danger. Though this approach did lead to shows of bravery, it was abandoned after lives were lost. From Tel Nof, we returned to Sirkin for the Advanced Stage, the final phase of our training, in which we would learn to fly in formation and execute strafing and bombing runs in preparation for the operational course that would follow our pilot's certification. I told little of this at home for fear that they would not believe me. Even after the fantasy-like graduation ceremony, one of my uncles, unable to hold himself back, said, "Tell the truth. Do they let you fly alone, or is there is always someone watching?"

Lieutenant General Makleff decorated us with the wings. Dan Tolkowsky, already a major general, shook our hands. It was a reception by the new commander-in-chief for the pilots who would later accompany him in their first war.

## Dan Tolkowsky: Pilot, Engineer, and Gentleman

No one could have been a more appropriate successor to Commander-in-Chief Laskov than Maj. Gen. Dan Tolkowsky. In his thirty-two years he had managed to gather knowledge and experience in a wide range of professions and positions. The "British gentleman with Anglo-Saxon manners," as Chief-of-Staff Moshe Dayan would call him, was a native-born city boy, the son of a bourgeois family that had long been part of the Jewish settlement. Having attended the Gymnasia Herzliya in Tel Aviv, with continued studies in London, he was the first commander-in-chief of the IAF who had experience as a fighter pilot and also held a degree in engineering. He had held positions in headquarters, served in operational roles, and been active in acquisitions and training. Years later, this multifaceted expertise, primarily in the synthesis of flight and engineering, would be the litmus test for command of the force. The Laskov period would be considered the time of the solidification of the IAF's foundations in organization, administration, command, and discipline. The salutary overflight during the transfer of command to Tolkowsky was a combination of formations of aircraft from the various squadrons—a symbol of the Laskov revolution.

The Central Command's Intelligence Branch began to warn of a buildup of the Arab air forces in preparation for a second round of war. The lessons of the 1948 conflict had been assimilated faster in the Egyptian, Syrian, and Iraqi command centers than in Israel. Two or three years earlier than Israel, they began to equip themselves with jet aircraft. In the planned Arab attack, the Egyptian Air Force would destroy the IAF in the first strike, while Syria and Iraq would complete the work through the bombing of military targets and population centers. The Jordanian Air Force was still in its infancy. The only doubt raised was in regard to the British. While they were filling the Arab bases with Meteor and Vampire jets, and were training the pilots, Israel was still gathering ancient, piston-engined aircraft. The intelligence network estimated that by early 1954, Arab air power would include 360 fighter aircraft, one-third of them jets. In addition to their rapid procurement, they had significantly progressed in training techniques and were tending toward operational coordination. The inequality in the balance of powers grew even greater in the area of air combat, and the threat to Israel increased as it suffered from a lack of strategic safety within the borders of the embargo.

The operational response developed in Tolkowsky's headquarters was based on four principles:

1. Constant high alert and rapid-response capability must be maintained, twenty-four hours a day, in times of peace and war. With no strategic defense of the country and with a low level of acceptable damage, there could be no substitute for the IAF's aircraft as the first response force.
2. Multipurpose fighter aircraft for attack and defense must be purchased as economically as possible, in order to achieve the greatest benefit from limited procurement capabilities. The plan included increasing the number of fighter squadrons from eight to fourteen during a two-year period. This was the first occurrence of thinking directly correlated to a qualitative and quantitative assessment in consideration of the threat, and it was partially based on the transition to the jet age.
3. Air control, which would allow for operational flexibility and rapid changing of missions, must be established. Only a central command,

with a full regional picture of the situation in the air, would be able to exert timely control over the small force in its possession, transferring it from front to front according to need. This was Tolkowsky's dream, and would demand immediate upgrading of the command and control mechanisms. It would essentially entail the establishment of a modern electronic system and the development of theories for its operation.

4. In the long term, taking into consideration Israel's poor position both quantitatively and qualitatively, the IAF must strive for air superiority at the outset of the war through destruction of the Egyptian Air Force while it was still on the ground. For this mission as well, theories would have to be developed and aircrew specifically trained.

This was an ambitious program, and its goals and methods of operation, products of the commander's personality, brought excitement to headquarters.

## The Jet Revolution

The venture to secure the four objectives began almost immediately. The first step, the establishment of a round-the-clock alert, merely an issue of organization of standing orders and discipline, was the cheapest and quickest to be achieved. The rate of increasing the control system's sophistication was slower and depended on the acquisition of innovative radar systems. Entry into the jet age took place one month after Tolkowsky took command, as he reaped the fruits planted in the Laskov period. The first two Meteor aircraft landed at Ramat David on June 17, 1953, approximately four months after the signing of an agreement for the purchase of fifteen aircraft, products of the Gloucester Company in Great Britain. In Israel, it was a day of celebration. Ben-Gurion gave each of these planes a private name, "Storm" and "Tempest," according to the verse in Psalms 83: "Thus you shall chase them in your tempest and in your storm frighten them." By this time the Egyptians already had forty-nine British Meteors and Vampires. Though the IAF spoke of the need to reduce the quantitative gaps through acquisition of quality aircraft, the only dealer in the market was Great Britain. The British also trained the jet pioneers among the Israeli pilots, including Moti Hod and Benny Peled, as well as the maintenance technicians, led by a young officer named Chaim Yaron. The British even flew the first planes to Israel. The first Meteor squadron had been established ten days prior to the arrival of the aircraft. Its commander, Menachem Bar, and his deputy, Benny Peled, had already completed a transfer course and had added training hours. Because of the experience registered in command of the operational training course in the Spitfire squadron, they immediately began to train the most veteran of fighter pilots for the new age.

Lasting four months, the course had only four training aircraft, which limited each round to four pilots. The first course included Danny Shapira, Aharon Yoeli, Joseph "Joe" Alon, and Yaakov "Yak" Nevo (Millner). After the second course, all eleven of the operational aircraft could be manned. By the end of the next round, there was already a waiting list to fly the planes.

Moti Hod was exempt, since he had made the transition on his own more than a year earlier, during a previous procurement deal that was never completed. Benny Peled was another rising star who had undergone the transition before the others, in England, in a course in which he had gained proficiency in systems and gunning as well. He had spent a year in an operational training course there that was more organized than anything his friends could imagine. This extra training prepared him to take command of the first jet fighter squadron in the IAF.

The jet revolution in the IAF began after its pilots had spent years riding the thunderous piston engines, facing the spinning propeller and the rattling exhaust pipes. Suddenly there was silence, joy to the ear. The exhaust of the jets could only be heard from behind, primarily on the ground. In the air, however, in the clear cockpit shaped like the nose of a missile, now at the front of the aircraft and no longer behind the engine, was born the delightful feeling of smooth floating on wings that had been left behind and could not be seen. At a speed of one thousand kilometers per hour, they were still at the edge of the speed of sound, but had twice the climbing speed of the Spitfires and Mustangs. The transition to the jets was revolutionary in both style and conditions of flight. The silver Meteor, with a pair of Rolls-Royce engines beneath its wings, was indeed a plane from another world. Strong and stable, its structure was solid and its maneuverability excellent, soft, and pleasant to control in the pressurized, air-conditioned cockpit, another revolutionary innovation. The view from the aircraft would change in the blink of an eye, and the pilots enjoyed moments of elation. The change did not occur in one day, however. Pilots called upon to join the course hesitated at first, because of their love for the aircraft they had been flying. The dragging of heels disappeared, though, after two or three flights in the Meteor, and from then on the pilots strove to take off faster and fly higher. The borders of the sky distanced themselves from them, and the heavens themselves were suddenly larger.

Until 1955 the Meteor squadron was the sole jet squadron in the IAF. All of the fighter pilots underwent the transition into the new age, integrating in their day's schedule operational alert and training. The Meteor's weapons were minimal, only four 20-millimeter cannons. They were enough, however, for the limited missions that appeared on the horizon, including intercepting enemy aircraft or attacking ground targets. The purpose the latter was more to threaten or warn than to destroy. The pilots in the piston-engined squadrons, according to a similar training program, learned to gain the most from the aging aircraft in their possession. They practiced air-to-air combat and perfected methods that would became an art form. They learned to assault airfields by practicing on Israeli bases, and to attack vehicles and bomb ground targets for ground support by practicing on the roads of the Jezreel Valley and the Negev. New methods of operation were formed, from technical maintenance and weapons servicing by the Israeli-trained ground crews to quick preflight briefings, reporting and control procedures using control centers, and debriefings after missions. A long and true friendship was woven between ground crews and aircrews. Commanders in both branches invested time and thought in developing this relationship. "Cycle" was the new magic word arising from the joint effort to compensate for the IAF's quantitative deficiency in relation to the Arab air forces. The goal was to fly the greatest number of sorties with the smallest number of aircraft, in an eclectic and flexible series of missions flown at top execution. It could be achieved only when the aircraft returning from a sortie received the best and fastest treatment from mechanics, the fuelers, electricians, and munitions people; this last group was the most efficient and fastest of all. This was the "cycle," the speed with which a plane was prepared for its next sortie. Over the years, it turned into a prestigious competition, with the pilots participating in the teamwork.

## A Friend's Training Accident

When we reached Ramat David for the operational course on the Spit-fire, we gazed respectfully at every one of the select group of jet fliers who would pass by the porch of the squadron's club. Moti Hod, Menachem Bar, Benny Peled, Danny Shapira, Yak Nevo, and their friends were idols to us. The jealousy was not searing, for, to most of us, the Spitfire was the realization of a dream, and we were still deeply in awe of its aerodynamic strength and combat capabilities. "We're also riding in a Rolls-Royce," we would say proudly of the engine. The activities and training exercises included formation flying, cannon strafing, and bomb-ing. After several weeks I got used to the smack in the rear that one received with the opening of the engine on takeoff. I also grew accus-tomed to the confusion involved in moving one's hands from the brakes to the stick and the handle for lifting the wheels, which for some reason had been placed on the far right side of the cockpit. It seemed as if some wacky professor, ignorant of human engineering, had interloped into the team of the producers of this beautiful aircraft in order to mar its perfection.

The day came when I was forced to deal with the death of a friend.
Yitzhak Yalon and I had gone together from Jerusalem to the flight course, and on a morning in October 1953, we took off together from Ramat David in a combat formation headed toward Haifa. As we were about to turn north and leave the hills of the Carmel behind us, I saw from my place in the formation, left of the leader, Yalon's plane charging in from the right and dropping below the leader. I did not understand why it happened and probably never will. Yalon had not received a command to change position. When he saw where he had ended up, he panicked and pulled up. He had not realized how close he was to the leader. Estimating distances in midair while looking backward over one's shoulder is not always easy, even for veteran fliers. Yalon and the leader did not manage to disengage. Yalon's tail struck the nose of the leader's plane, and its propeller, made of wood, sawed the body of Yalon's aircraft in two, reducing it to splinters. I recall emitting a roar louder than those of the leader's engine, which, suddenly having no load to support, increased its revolutions as the propeller disintegrated.

The leader, Ladia Shiovitz, one of the veteran instructors in the operational course squadron, did not lose his cool. He shut down his engine. My formation mates and I immediately pulled to the sides and upward to avoid collision. We then dropped wings and circled above the spot of the accident, in shock and silence. What could greenhorns say at a moment like this?

Ladia broke the silence. "Who hears me?"

I responded immediately. "This is Two. I copy."

"I am executing an emergency landing because of engine shutdown," he said. "Inform the flight controller of the events. Maintain eye and radio contact with me."

I made contact with the controller and informed him of the location of the two aircraft, while observing Ladia's Spitfire gliding below me and Yalon's torn Spitfire, without its tail, sailing toward the ground in an inverted spin.

"Orange Three, Orange Three, jump! Jump! You've got to parachute!" I yelled to him on the communications, without considering whether he could hear me or not, or whether he had any chance of extricating himself from this death trap. I repeated this cry several times, along with the other members of the formation. I dived every now and then toward Ladia, who glided toward a plowed field in the Zevulun Valley and executed a smooth belly landing, straight out of the books. I saw him climb out of the cockpit and wave his arms to signal that he was okay, and then turned to watch the remnants of Yalon's plane fall and crash into the ground. Dazed, I looked around. I had been left alone. My partner had returned to base without my noticing. I reported the facts to the controller in a dry manner, as if hearing someone else's voice. The words were not coming from my throat. I waved my wings at low altitude over Ladia's head, passed over the location of Yalon's crash, and turned toward Ramat David, soaked in sweat.

The next day, at the military cemetery at Mount Herzl in Jerusalem, I attended the first funeral of a friend. A drenching rain poured down, and the cold pierced my bones. The base commander, Ezer Weizman, stood there soaked, a bit bent over, like everyone. He saluted the fresh grave and accompanied the bereaved parents home. I could barely look them in the eye.

In the following weeks, my mood changed. I became serious and melancholy, for I had grown up prematurely. I myself was miraculously saved in an accident when I flipped over on the edge of the tarmac on the eve of the completion of the course. Ten of us had entered the operational training course, and of the nine who remained, one was sent to a transport squadron, four to the Mosquito squadron and four, including me, to the "Skull" Squadron, to fly Mustangs, the choice aircraft in the IAF at the end of the piston-engine era. Though the end of this age was approaching, it was still too soon to eulogize it. The largest operations of that time belonged to the piston-engined aircraft, to the two-engined Mosquitoes with their light balsam frames and cloth coverings and, as always, to the Piper Super Cubs.

## The Mosquito: Photographing the Middle Eastern Skies

While the Mosquito squadron was based for the most part in Hatzor and trained for bombing missions, it was dedicated to a new branch developing in IAF headquarters—air intelligence. In 1952, equipped with standardized photographic equipment, the Mosquitoes replaced the primitive methods of the War of Independence. As was typical of those days, it was not the product of early thinking, but rather the result of a local initiative that had no connection with orders or discipline. On September 3, 1953, Shlomo Lahat, accompanied by navigator Natan "Newtek" Eldar, without asking permission from any of their superiors, took off in a Mosquito to Alexandria and back.

The next day they took off again, this time to the airspace over Cairo. In the Mosquito were sophisticated air cameras. Its flight range could reach 1,600 miles, with a maximum altitude of 35,000 feet. These were ideal conditions for vertical and diagonal reconnaissance flights in the heart of the Arab countries, involving almost no possibility of being shot down by fighter aircraft or by the antiaircraft systems in their possession then. For approximately three hours, Shlomo Lahat's Mosquito cruised seven kilometers above Cairo. Half of that time was spent in the city's skies, photographing the Egyptian airfields, length and width, without being bothered by a soul. The pictures were presented to the General Command and to the Minister of Defense. Their excellent quality, and particularly the fact that they had been acquired without sustaining damage or triggering a military or diplomatic incident, caused them to forget Lahat's violation of discipline. The pregnancy in IAF headquarters lasted exactly nine months from that day until the establishment of the photographic wing in the squadron. Lahat's initiative ended the era of limited and hesitant photographic reconnaissance flights.

Over the course of 1953, as IAF headquarters began to plan attacks on air bases in Egypt and Syria, the existing intelligence information was found to be dated. Lahat's breakthrough gained momentum in July of 1954. The photographic wing's aircraft began to map the Sinai Peninsula fully, and increasingly deepened their penetrations along the Suez Canal, the Nile Delta, the Damascus Basin, and even the forward Iraqi base near Jordan. The aircraft of the photographic wing executed dozens of sorties that provided the essential intelligence information of the Sinai Campaign.

Unlike the Mosquitoes, the Piper squadron executed more-modest patrol sorties, primarily for the gathering of intelligence for the ground forces, from its bases in Ramle (near IAF headquarters), Be'er Sheva, and Eilat. The squadron flew sorties sometimes to the edge of the Gulf of Eilat, along the Saudi or Sinai coast, as it did in Operation Promontory, on March 1, 1954. Five Pipers, which took off from Eilat, rescued the crew of the Israeli Navy boat *Almogit*, which had sailed a day earlier from Eilat to gather naval intelligence along the Strait of Tiran. It had run aground on coral on the Saudi Arabian coast, approximately ninety miles south of Eilat. A Mosquito and a Dakota located it and provided cover throughout the afternoon and evening hours. The operation was postponed until the morning of March 2. At daybreak the Pipers set out and executed one of the squadron's most daring long-range operations as five Mosquitoes and four Mustangs flew above, providing cover. A Dakota circled above all of them, serving as a wireless communications station. The Pipers landed on the beach, rescued the ship's crew, and returned them safely home. The Mustangs, led by Moti Hod, emptied the load of rockets they carried and turned the *Almogit* into a floating bonfire.

## The Ouragans: The Flight from France

In April 1954, Col. Gamal Abdel Nasser, the strongman of the Officers' Revolution, took control of Egypt. A villager whose education and demeanor lacked the polish of the aristocracy, the masses found him to be one of their own, exciting in personality and style and flattering in his diplomacy. He liberated millions of peasants from the bonds of their landlords and easily incited in them waves of nationalistic excitement, not only regarding Israel, but primarily against the British military presence in Egypt. The popular slogan "Egypt for the Egyptians" was indicative of a developing threat to Israel's security. The evacuation of the British air bases that protected the Suez Canal and their transfer to Egyptian control were merely a matter of time. In an evaluation of the situation in the Planning Division of the General Command, it was noted that in this process the Egyptian Air Force would gain substantial advantages in the range of its activities and in the sophistication of its aircraft maintenance. "Through the use of these bases, it will be able to hit us with a surprise attack without our having discovered its preparations," stated the report.

The procurement policy of the IAF, which was intended to provide a preventive medicine before the illness could strike, was limited from the outset to compromise with the limited production of aircraft in the world market. In April 1954, Benny Peled set out for Europe and the United States at the head of a procurement delegation that included experienced commanders who had the foresight to understand the needs of the IAF, the abilities of the pilots, and the maintenance levels of the technicians. From the best of the world's front-line aircraft, the choice was among the Swedish Saab, the American Saber, and the French Mystère.

The Israelis had arrived with the eyes of the poor customer. After investigation, it became clear that the Swedes were concealing credit problems, an excuse for the hesitations of the government. The Saber, which had excelled in Korea in combat against the Soviet MiG-15, was the delegation's preferred model, but American permission, which was needed for its sale, was not granted. The United States feared that such a deal would upset its efforts to add the Arab countries to a Middle Eastern defense alliance that had been planned in order to halt Soviet expansion in the southern part of the Soviet Union. France remained the only option, and the choice was between the available Mystère II, which was already in operational testing, and the more sophisticated Mystère IV, delivery of which would be delayed. The newer plane was on the production line and was designed to serve the NATO forces first.

France was eager to sell the Mystère II, and its decision in August 1955 to sell thirty of the aircraft found IAF headquarters and the upper ranks of the IDF deliberating between the models. The factor of time was weighed against the factor of quality, and they also took into account the fact that the air force of a poor country must strive for multipurpose aircraft in order to compensate for its quantitative disadvantage. The Mystère II was a good fighter plane, but the Mystère IV, in addition to its intercept capabilities, could serve as a bomber as well. The factor of time prevailed. Tolkowsky recommended that the IAF make do with the first model, and quickly sent six pilots to the air force base in Mont-de-Marsan to test the plane and train on it. Among them were Danny Shapira, Yak Nevo, and Dror Avneri, who had graduated from flight course with me and had not managed to warm the seat of the Mustang before he was sent to be among the first of the young pilots to fly the jets. Benny Peled, a doubter who rebelled against convention, was at the head of this delegation. Before long he had changed the balance in favor of the Mystère IV. The first doubt arose when it became clear that the French Air Force had not chosen the Mystère II, deciding in favor of its younger and more advanced sibling. The reason was discovered during a test flight, when all of the Mystère II's deficiencies became immediately evident. Its stability was lost at high speed, and its flight range and munitions capacity were less than needed. Peled pressured IAF headquarters to wait for the Mystère IV. Tolkowsky was convinced, and began to pressure Moshe Dayan, the IDF chief of staff, to forgo the Mystère II and not waste precious funds on "a plane which had undergone and continues to undergo exhausting reincarnations on its way to being operational . . . [an aircraft] whose true operational value will be smaller than the efforts invested in its procurement and absorption." Thus he wrote to Dayan, under the influence of Peled's negative reports. The pressure was to no avail.

Shimon Peres, Director General of the Ministry of Defense, went to France to sign the Mystère II deal. Peled met with him and attempted to persuade him to forget about the idea. Peres consulted with Tolkowsky on the telephone, and the commander-in-chief backed Peled. Peres submitted, and Dayan was furious with Tolkowsky for changing his decision. The French, though, were not angry and did not bargain. They even rushed to satisfy Israel and to fill in the gaps until the arrival of the Mystère IV with twelve Ouragans, which had been withdrawn from the French Air Force. The Ouragan, a single-engined single-seater, was slower than the MiG-15 but faster than the Meteor, and superior to the latter at interception and attack. Its weapons included four 20-millimeter cannons as well as bombs and rockets. Six pilots were sent to train on the aircraft in the Lafayette squadron at the Orange Air Base in southeastern France. In early October, Operation Or-Yesh (Ouragan-Israel) began to transfer the aircraft to Israel. The planes took off in two sextets, flying via Rome and Athens to Hatzor. One sextet was flown by the French, commanded by the deputy commander of the squadron. Benny Peled led the Israeli formation. The French leader erred in his navigation in the first leg of the trip, and Peled took command, leading both formations to Israel. Compared with the hardships Moti Hod had suffered in Operation Velvetta, flying the Spitfires to Israel seven years earlier, this was simply a joyride.

Nasser, whose popularity in Egypt had gained momentum, published his book *The Philosophy of the Revolution.* The Egyptian leader saw himself as leader of the Arab nations and Asiatic Islam. At this time, in response to terrorist infiltrations of Israel, a small Israeli force, numbering less than one hundred troops, laid waste to an Egyptian contingent several times its size. The assaults on Gaza occurred at the height of covert negotiations taking place in Paris between the Israeli and Egyptian embassies. "Black Arrow," the Gaza operation, offended Nasser's pride. He called a halt to the Paris contacts and instructed Egyptian intelligence to increase the terrorist penetrations from the Gaza Strip to the Israeli settlements in the south and the Negev, and to reinforce the terrorists' ranks. They were even given the name *Fedayeen*—those who, according to Islam, go to heaven if they sacrifice their lives in a holy war.

Israeli paratroopers struck again in early September, blowing up the police fortress in Chan Younis, killing and injuring 130 Egyptians. Nasser responded with a sea and air blockade of the Gulf of Eilat through the Straits of Tiran, and secretly flew to the Soviet Union to request military aid. No longer relying on the United States and Great Britain, who had created the central alliance without him, Nasser, in a daring maneuver, linked his interests with those of the Soviet Union. Thus they would both be able to benefit. By the end of September, an enormous arms deal that had been signed between Egypt and Czechoslovakia was exposed. It came under an economic guise: Egyptian rice and cotton for modern Soviet tanks and aircraft. The weapons supplier, which had guaranteed Israel's survival during the War of Independence, changed its policy, altering the entire situation. Though France had agreed a month earlier to sell Israel the Mystère IIs, thirty of those planes would mean little against the 150 MiG-15 and MiG-17 aircraft that had been promised to Egypt along with seventy Ilyushin IL-28 bombers, transport aircraft, and antiaircraft cannons, as well as 430 tanks and armored personnel carriers, and 600 cannons. This threat was unanswerable both in quality and quantity, and its seriousness became evident within a few weeks. The British transferred the large and sophisticated air base at Faid, on the banks of the Suez Canal, to the Egyptians. This combination, estimated Dan Tolkowsky, was liable to grant the Egyptians the upper hand in the air over their own country, over the Sinai Peninsula, and even over Israel.

Another element was playing a significant role in shaping the commander-in-chief's fears. The Israeli flight control network's range of early warning was limited and did not even cover the forward Egyptian base at El Arish. Intercept aircraft could not be scrambled until the Egyptian aircraft had already penetrated Israeli airspace. Thus, in addition to Fedayeen attacks from the Gaza Strip on settlements and vehicles in Israel's south during the summer of 1955, pairs of Egyptian Vampire aircraft succeeded in unchallenged penetration of the airspace over Hatzor and Tel Nof in a show of silent strength. On August 18, a quartet of Meteors was transferred from Ramat David to intercept alert at Hatzor, and two days later they participated in the first dogfight since the War of Independence. Yehuda Peri and Mordechai Lavon turned back a quartet of Vampires in the Negev skies. It was not a momentous conflict. Several bursts were fired, and the Egyptians fled. Lavon reported hitting one of the aircraft, but apparently it did not fall.

Following the assault on Chan Younis at approximately 0700 hours on September 2, central flight control in Ramle reported another penetration by a quartet of Vampires flying at low altitude over Nitzana. This time, flying intercept were Aharon Yoeli and Chatto Tzidon. They turned toward the sea and broke southward. Climbing to 1,500 feet, they were informed by the flight controller that the Vampires were already above Nitzanim, north of Ashkelon. The Egyptians had not noticed that the Meteors had climbed above them and gained the advantage before even a single round had been fired.

"Two bogeys below at three o'clock," Yoeli heard Chatto report on the radio. (*Bogey* was the word used for an enemy plane in the Second World War.) To his right, Yoeli saw only two Vampires. His range to target was 1,200 meters, and he thought flight control had exaggerated with its first warning of four Egyptian aircraft. As Yoeli approached the planes from the rear, Chatto covered him from behind. At four hundred meters he opened fire with his four 20-millimeter cannons. His gunsights were dim, and he was forced to plot his way with tracer bullets. One Vampire slipped, went into a spin, and crashed into the sands of Carmia. The second Egyptian attempted to flee. Yoeli broke east, and Chatto continued to cover him. It did not take a complicated maneuver for Yoeli to position himself on the Vampire's tail and to approach to four hundred meters before opening fire. This time he hit the aircraft behind the cockpit and watched it explode in the air. Its fragments scattered on the ground of Kibbutz Yad Mordechai, named after Mordechai Anilevitz, the leader of the Warsaw Ghetto rebellion.

The battle ended in less than five minutes before the awestruck eyes of the residents of Ashkelon. The chief of staff decorated Yoeli for execution of the combat with supreme efficiency and speed. However, the joy in the IAF did not last even a month. It disintegrated with the revelation of the Egyptian-Czechoslovakian arms deal. Though Israeli pilots had the upper hand in competition with British aircraft of a similar quality, the question now remained whether this superiority would remain against the Soviet MiGs, with Israel flying the unfamiliar and untested French aircraft.

After several days the first twelve Ouragans landed at Hatzor. Benny Peled was given command of the squadron. Within less than a month, a training course began for ten pilots, so that all the planes could be manned. Veteran fliers like Moti Hod, Joe Alon, and Yeshayahu Bareket entered the routine operational training alongside youngsters like Amos Lapidot, Ran "Pecker" Ronen, Rafi Har-Lev, and Shlomo Beit-On. Three of them, Hod, Peled, and Lapidot, would eventually become commanders-in-chief of the IAF. A month later, notification was given of the purchase of another dozen Ouragans. In retrospect, it became clear that the fear of the Soviet Ilyushin and MiG jet aircraft, particularly the MiG-15, was unjustified. American pilots in the Korean War, the first westerners to encounter them at the beginning of the decade, had exaggerated in their evaluations. As always, the fears at the entry of any new weapon into the region were worse than the reality, which would be revealed only in combat.

. . . .

The plan for a possible IDF assault on the Strait of Tiran began well before September 21, the day of Nasser's decree that he would not permit Israeli shipping in the Gulf of Eilat. For more than a year, the Mosquito aircraft of the photographic reconnaissance squadron had been busy mapping the Sinai Peninsula. Those deciphering the photos attempted to locate the few ground transport routes along the length and width of the desert. The missing element was the route along the gulf, through the granite mountains that hugged the waterline for long stretches. The aerial photographs did not reveal how passable it was to ground forces and armored units. On June 9 the Giv'ati Brigade sent reconnaissance teams to investigate the area from up close. They set out from Eilat in the dark of night on the Israeli Navy ship *Eilat,* and landed on the quiet beach of Dahab before dawn. Operation Yarkon, as it was called, was allotted three days for execution. The commandos were to examine the area and return by the sea. A Dakota, flown by Yosef Ofer and Uri Yaffe, linked their communication with the forward command center in Eilat at prearranged times. When the plane dropped packages of food and water at night, only one package arrived intact. The squad was commanded to gather and bury the remnants of the others. On the third day, the General Command received a report that Egyptian soldiers were searching for the squad; a Bedouin had observed them landing on the beach. Chaim Bar-Lev, the brigade commander, demanded that they be evacuated using Pipers, as in Operation Promontory. Dayan objected, fearing that one of the planes would get stuck in the sands, resulting in an international incident. Bar-Lev insisted, and Hanoch Keret (Carter), from the light squadron, was called upon to lead six Pipers to rescue the commandos.

The Pipers' wheels bounced along the ground and the landing gear almost broke. The pilots repeated the acrobatics of Operation Promontory, this time with the additional weight of a commando in each aircraft, which almost pulled them into the ground. That night they landed in Eilat with their precious human cargo.

In a broader plan, which called for the opening of the Strait of Tiran, the IAF stood ready to attack the Egyptian airfields to assure superiority and an umbrella for itself and the ground forces, as well as to prevent the bombing of cities in Israel. The IAF operation order, "Slope," called for the destruction of aircraft, runways, and installations. Twenty-eight Harvard and Spitfire aircraft were allotted for the attack on the airfield at El Arish. The remainder were assigned targets west of the Suez Canal: twelve Mustangs to the Kabrit airfield; eighteen Mosquitoes and Ouragans to the El Maza airfield; fourteen Mosquitoes and Mustangs to the Dewar-Souar airfield; and six Meteors to destroy the Ilyushin bombers at the Cairo West airfield. The dropping of forces and equipment was assigned to twelve Dakotas.

Dayan got carried away and added the capture of the Gaza Strip to the operation. Despite the possibilities of negative reactions internationally, Ben-Gurion supported the plan, saying that it was "not important what the Gentiles will say, but rather what the Jews will do." The government, however, voted to put the plan on indefinite hold.

The equipping of Egypt with new Soviet weaponry added a crippling blow to Israel's shaky confidence and again raised the fears of not so long ago regarding the destruction of the Zionist existence in Israel. At the encouragement of the government, a public movement established a "Defense Fund" to raise money for the purchase of arms, as if the government's funds had dried up. However, this wave of patriotism attracted more children with piggy banks than people of actual wealth. The primary problem was not finances, for retribution payments from Germany had begun to flow, but rather sources for the purchase of modern equipment. While only 44 of the 241 fighter and bomber aircraft were jets, they were already obsolescent, even at the moment when the IAF was striving to pull the piston-engined aircraft out of service. It had begun to sell the Spitfires to Burma. Mustangs and Mosquito bombers were sent to storage. The first fighter squadron was put on hold and was temporarily erased from the operations charts. Canada was still hesitating to sell the Saber aircraft. France, which was about to supply fifteen Mystère IV aircraft, withdrew from the deal at the last moment under U.S. pressure.

Then at the end of January 1956, a socialist government came to power in France, and its Israeli sister, controlled by the Labor Party, found a common language with it. The romance took place behind the back of the Israeli Foreign Ministry and focused on contacts between the two countries' ministries of defense. The French were interested in strengthening Israel under the old maxim that "my enemy's enemy is my ally." Egypt had struck France at two sensitive spots. It had intensified its cooperation with the National Liberation Front in Algeria (FLN) and was striving for exclusive ownership of the Suez Canal. In March, the French agreed to sell Israel the Mystère IV. The deal would include only twelve aircraft, which the French Air Force would not miss in the least.

With more hours flying the Mystère than anyone else in the country and experience in flying formations across the Mediterranean, Benny Peled was called upon to bring the planes to Israel. He had been waiting nearly a year for this moment, and command of the Ouragan squadron in the meantime had been the best option available to him. He easily transferred command of the squadron to Moti Hod, five months after having received it, and departed with the all-star group that had flown over the Ouragans. At Cambrai Field in northern France, they were introduced to the new planes—silvery arrows whose wings slanted backward, their first supersonic jet. On the first takeoff, it carried them to new worlds, at speeds of which they had only dreamed, at steady accelerations generating up to six G's, twice the force they had experienced until now. At first there were moments when they felt as if such forces might tear the skin off their faces, but the blood did not leave their heads and they did not black out. A new coverall surrounded them, a pressure suit with valves that compressed the air on their stomachs and feet to prevent the pooling of blood. Within less than a month they had succeeded at becoming one with the aircraft, and in the beginning of April they readied themselves to skip to Mont-de-Marsan and from there to the familiar route to Israel. This time there would be a slight change. They would not fly via Athens, which had exhibited a cold attitude to the last mission, but would refuel in Brindisi, Italy. With a light tailwind at thirty thousand feet, they could reach Hatzor within three hours, on their last drops of fuel. Hatzor, the base closest to Egypt, had become the primary airfield for the jet squadrons. Along with the operational center of gravity, which they had transported from Ramat David, they had also brought along Ezer Weizman to build the base and command it according to the formula he had demanded on the northern base. It was a mixture of order, discipline, teamwork, and human relations. In honor of the Mystères, they returned the first fighter squadron to active duty; it was by now the traditional home of the most sophisticated fighter aircraft in their generation. Benny Peled was given command of the squadron in France on April 1.

Ezer flew to Italy to take command of the transit station in Brindisi and to set the date of the flight. The success of the operation depended on the weather, for they would not take off without a good wind that could carry the Mystères as far eastward as possible on their fuel limitations. The Italians, along with their liaison, the chief of security services of southern Italy, cooperated. On the morning of April 11, the skies cleared, and on the next day, early in the morning, they took off from Mont-de Marsan. They were to land in Brindisi within an hour and a half without attracting attention. A few Italian planes were parked at the small field. The city's true pride lay in its seaport, from which several refugee ships had sailed to Israel in pre-independence days.

Ezer went up into the control tower, which was full of tension because of the annoying air silence that was being maintained. At the last moment, he heard Benny Peled's voice on the speaker.

"Hello, Brindisi tower. Hello, Brindisi tower."

Ezer grabbed the microphone from the Italian flight controllers and roared in Hebrew, "Hello, Benny, this is Brindisi tower." In their mother tongue, he could shorten the identification procedure accepted in international aviation. Only then did he permit himself to smile.

After a quick refueling, the Mystères took off for the second and more difficult leg of the journey. The upper echelons of the country awaited them in Hatzor from the moment they left Italy. Six sonic booms, thunder unknown to the country's skies, proclaimed the arrival of the planes. They reduced speed and landed one after the other. Everyone was emotional, and several people even shed tears. The Treasury Minister, half in jest and half seriously, exclaimed. "Three hundred sixty thousand dollars per plane, and only one passenger?" The good tidings were not broadcast at the end of that historic day. Instead, the people of Israel heard news of the Fedayeen infiltrators killing four children in a Lubavitch home in Moshav Shafrir. The Mystères remained a well-kept secret even after the second procurement deal, which increased the number of aircraft to twenty-four. In July, with American funding and according to a defense agreement with NATO, the Marcel Dassault factories completed the production of 225 Mystères for the French Air Force. They were looking for new markets. At the end of the month, Nasser nationalized the Suez Canal in order to use its income to finance the building of a large dam on the Nile at Aswan. Great Britain and France began preparations for taking control of the canal. France showed interest in the possibility that Israel might join in the military operation. The positive Israeli response was accompanied by a request to increase the Mystère force. France agreed to sell thirty-six additional aircraft on condition that the deal remain a secret.

The Mystères were ready for flight in mid-August. IAF headquarters dedicated itself to the buildup, though only eleven officers were party to the secret of what was named Operation Shacharit, which means "morning." The remainder of the IAF was told of a special operational course of the French Air Force that would take place in North Africa for Israeli pilots and ground crew. It was a plausible story, considering the close Israeli-French relationship in those days.

This story had one essential advantage in that it would allow the recruitment of Meteor and Ouragan pilots without raising suspicions. In the two preceding months, they had not managed to train enough professional crew to man even the twenty-four existing Mystères in Hatzor. Bringing pilots through the transition to flying jets was a slow process. Only twenty-one pilots were found suitable for the operation, and even the experienced among them had not accrued more than six to ten hours on the Mystère. Thus, in a tremendous effort, it would be possible to organize the transport of the aircraft to Israel in two rounds of eighteen planes each. Each wave would comprise six trios. The leader of each formation would be one of the six fliers who had opened the squadron and knew the way.

The "North Africa Delegation," pilots and technicians, took off on the evening of August 17 in an El Al Constellation and a Nord belonging to the transport squadron. The secret had been kept even from Benny Peled and Moti Hod, who headed the group. The truth was revealed when Benny Peled and the five veterans identified the familiar coast of Mont-de-Marsan at first light. The others had difficulty accepting the announcement that they were landing in France in order to add thirty-six Mystère aircraft to the IAF. Until they saw them standing on the runway in a long line, some of the them with the IAF symbol, they suspected a practical joke. After a quick breakfast, no time remained for celebration. The pilots were immediately divided into trios and began test flights. The veterans did so with pleasure, the greenhorns with a touch of fear. The next day they took off for Brindisi.

This time it was Shlomo Lahat, commander of the Air Division, who welcomed them from the control tower. Lahat had told the Italians a story of breakdowns that had been discovered in the operation of the aircraft in Israel, and of repairs and changes that needed to be executed in

France. The first eighteen Mystères were the glitch-ridden planes being flown from Israel. The next group, of course, would be the repaired aircraft returning to Israel. In order to alleviate any doubts, the Mystères in both waves were given identical numbers. The local representative of the Italian security services even got emotional at the story and told Lahat that he had been keeping a secret to himself. Already at the first shipment, it seemed to him that something was wrong with the Mystères' tails. Politeness had prevented him from sharing his suspicions with Ezer.

At fifteen-minute intervals, the trios landed at Brindisi without problems and then arrived safely in Israel. In the second round, after some time, two of the Mystères used up their fuel over Cyprus and were forced to land at an RAF air base. The British refueled them and sent them on their way without any questions.

The story used to mislead the Italians was also leaked to the press in Israel. At this time, permission was granted to print the description of the landing of the first sextet. Thus the world was led to believe that the IDF had eighteen Mystères that had been returned from France after "adjustment and repairs." In Hatzor, they were not smiling. The internal truth was not far from the cover story. The strengthening of the IAF was only for show; it was not prepared to leap forward. In September 1956, Benny Peled's operational squadron had only twelve planes, and they were able to engage in combat with only a pair of 30-millimeter cannons. The budget did not allow for the purchase of replacement parts and weapons for attacking ground targets. The racks for the bombs and rocket launchers under the wings remained empty. Given the limitations in personnel, it was difficult to put more than sixteen pilots through the transfer course to the Mystère at one time with any reasonable level of expertise while not disrupting the function of other squadrons. The plan to establish a second Mystère squadron at Ramat David was frozen until the first squadron could get settled.

First and foremost, there was a need to accelerate the rate of training pilots for the jet squadrons without going against the principle that the best and most experienced will always receive the newest aircraft. In the flight school, the period of training on the piston-engined aircraft was shortened. The operational training period on the Mustang was canceled, and from the Harvard, the pilots moved straight to the Meteor. An entire squadron of Ouragans was dedicated completely to training. The Mustangs and the Mosquito bombers that had been taken out of service and transferred to storage in the emergency warehouses were the backups of the jet squadrons. The goal was to use every pilot and plane to its limit in order to assure a high level of alert and execution with little warning. In this program, an emergency fighter squadron of Mustangs was formed out of the instructors of the Flight School, soon after its transfer from Kfar Sirkin to Tel Nof. Its commander was Yitzhak Yavne, commander of the Flight School and the originator of the idea. Everyone emerged victorious. The IAF gained another squadron, which would also maintain the skills of the instructors and improve their authority as fighter pilots in the eyes of the cadets. Exercises were held after the wearisome training flights, and each man, according to the free time in his schedule, set out to refresh himself in target flights or night navigation. Before long, a spirit of battle had taken hold of the group. The decline in the country's security situation late in the summer, and the sense of the approaching war, drove even this squadron to a severe series of alerts and increased training flights.

From early 1956, the IAF was involved in a methodical series of exercises whose core goal was the destruction of the Arab air forces—that of Egypt being first and foremost. The attack would involve a surprise integrated assault by most of the squadrons on the Egyptian airfields, with destruction of enemy aircraft during the first run and damaging of the runways and installations in the following runs. The piston-engined aircraft were given circumventing routes over the sea at low altitude. The jets would fly in at high altitude over land. The pilots practiced bombing, strafing, and rocketing, evasion of antiaircraft fire, and of course air-to-air combat. The framework of Operation Slope, planned in 1955 for attacking Egyptian airfields, had not changed, though the content and methods had been modified according to the technological revolution that had simultaneously affected the IAF and the Egyptians as a result of the Czechoslovakian deal.

As opposed to the dynamism of this operation, exercises in ground support plodded forward in the style of former wars. With the use of liaison officers and a hierarchical chain of decision-making and intelligence supply, the efficiency of the IAF was limited. IAF headquarters concluded that greater independence in the choosing of targets was necessary, so that the perspective would be wider and would keep the aircraft out of range of artillery and tank fire. The goal must be to destroy the enemy on his way to the battlefield, and not to wait for contact to be made.

On October 5, 1956, IAF headquarters in Ramle began to update Operation Slope. Dan Tolkowsky sensed the war behind his doors. That morning a special messenger had arrived from the Operations Branch, carrying a brown envelope that held the order for "Kaddesh 1"— classification top secret. The IDF planned to capture northern Sinai and situate itself on the eastern banks of the Suez Canal. The IAF would be requested to achieve air superiority in the opening stages, dropping a regiment of paratroopers to capture El Arish and continuing to protect the nation's skies. The attack on the Egyptian airfields received top priority. Preparations began in closed circles, with an approximate time limitation of at least three weeks. The day and time of attack were still unknown. Even the reason was shrouded in mystery.

Attention was turned in those days to the eastern front. In September, Israeli paratroopers had blown up four Jordanian police fortresses as retaliation for a series of murders and attacks in Israel's center, the Arava Desert and Jerusalem. Iraq had begun moving its military into Jordan, and Israel indicated that the appearance of Iraqi units in the West Bank would be considered an act of war. No one thought that these activities were partially designed to cover for the capture of the Sinai, which would in essence be an excuse for the armies of Great Britain and France to take control of the Suez Canal. Only a few people in the upper echelons of the government were privy to this secret.

The plan was developed in covert contacts between the powers approximately one month after the last British soldier had left the Suez Canal. Nasser surprised the world with the nationalization of the canal on July 26, and was unconvincing in his official economic excuse that its revenues would be used to develop the water project on the Nile. France and particularly Great Britain suspected that Egypt, under increasing Soviet influence, would close the canal to their shipping, as it had done to Israel's.

Operation Musketeer was first developed between Paris and London. Israel agreed to provide support in a separate operation. This cooperation developed through France, for Great Britain was still not regarded as a friend to Israel; the wounds inflicted during its rule of the country had still not healed.

On September 29, a Noratlas Nord 2501 from the transport squadron took off to Paris carrying an Israeli delegation. Golda Meir, the new Foreign Minister, Chief of Staff Moshe Dayan, and Shimon Peres, the Director General of the Ministry of Defense, crowded in among the reserve fuel tanks that would allow them a direct flight. In four days of covert talks with their French counterparts, the fundamental elements of the diplomatic and military cooperation were set. On October 2 they returned to Israel with a French military delegation for talks with IAF headquarters. The French examined the possibility of using the fields in Hatzor, Lod, and Tel Nof if Musketeer's original plan to take off from British bases in Cyprus failed. Britain eventually did hesitate throughout the entire process, eventually ruining the operation when it was at its peak. France was willing to set out on a separate operation with Israel, and the IAF agreed to provide all the logistical support in its possession. On the day following the departure of the French, the chief of staff issued the order for Kaddesh 1.

The General Command thought that the IAF's plan to gain air superiority through a surprise attack on the Egyptian airfields was far too optimistic. However, simple mathematics proved that the MiGs, Vampires, and Ilyushin IL-28 bombers that could take off from the Suez and Cairo bases easily threatened Israel's cities and air bases along the coast. The updated Operation Slope allocated seventy-six aircraft to the mission. Twelve Mystères and ten Meteors would attack the Ilyushin bombers at Cairo West. Six Mystères, eighteen Ouragans, ten Mosquitoes, and twenty Mustangs were allocated to the four bases at Abu-Suweir, Faid, Kabrit, and Kaspirit, where the Egyptian MiGs, Vampires, and Meteors were stationed. The aircraft were the primary target. In aerial photographs, most of them could be seen exposed on the ramp; few of them were even camouflaged. The grand plan was shelved, however, for the General Command did not believe that the IAF would be able to execute it. Still haunted by nightmares of the bombings of the Second World War, Ben-Gurion did not believe that the IAF alone could protect Israel's cities from destruction. His agreement to an integrated operation was conditional on the French commitment to defend Israel's skies.

At a summit conference near Paris on October 22, Israel's role in the operation was presented to Ben-Gurion. It would entail Israel's invading the Sinai and threatening the Suez Canal in order to provide a justification for the powers' involvement and ultimate capture of the canal, saving it from the hands of both enemies. Forty-eight hours later they would present an ultimatum to the Egyptians and Israelis to retreat fifteen kilometers from the canal. They would then invade, claiming that the Egyptians had not retreated. There would be no military cooperation between the IDF and the Musketeer force. Israel would have a free hand in its operations in the Sinai.

Operation Musketeer destroyed the IAF's great dream. The bombing of the Egyptian airfields was allotted to the British and French pilots. Ben-Gurion, at the encouragement of his chief of staff, did not consider this a tremendous loss. Dan Tolkowsky could not convince him that the IAF alone could destroy the Egyptian Air Force within six days. He remained bound in his fears of a large Egyptian air attack in the first two days, when the IDF would be fighting alone. He therefore refused to sign the agreement from the summit conference until the French guaranteed an air umbrella consisting of a fighter-bomber squadron and another squadron of Mystère IVs, in addition to air and ground crew who would man and arm the dozens of Israeli Mystères sitting unused because of financial and personnel limitations. The French backups, approximately seventy ground technicians, landed at Sirkin with equipment while the summit conference was still taking place. They were presented to the surprised Israelis as experts who would aid the IAF in absorbing the French aircraft.

Late on Thursday, October 25, a silent reserve call-up began in Israel, of a size hitherto unseen in any exercise. Guesses as to the reason for this were inspired by the call-up command, which mentioned a possibility of "the entry of Iraqi forces into Jordan." Nothing had been leaked from the summit conference, which had concluded a day earlier. The order for Operation Kaddesh 2, which arrived at Tolkowsky's offices in the morning, still placed responsibility on the IAF for destruction of Egypt's air power. The preparations had apparently taken place before the conclusion of the summit conference agreement. The next day, Tolkowsky was summoned by Dayan to update the plan. The chief of staff informed him of the division of labor with the "partners," and lowered the attack on the Egyptian airfields to third priority; it would be carried out only in the first forty-eight hours, and only if the Egyptians attempted to attack targets in the heart of Israel. Thus the plan for initiating an attack was canceled. The mission for providing support to the ground forces also forbade attacking Egyptian forces outside of the field of battle prior to the Egyptians' attacking Israeli forces from the air. The IAF was granted freedom of action only in defending the skies of the country, in dropping troops and equipment, in evacuation of wounded, and in liaison with the "partners' " air forces. After the entry of Israeli forces into the area of the canal, the attacks on Egyptian airfields would be struck completely from the operations, and the IAF would enter attack alert against the other Arab air forces if the war escalated and they joined in.

Tolkowsky returned to Ramle and convened his command group. IAF headquarters' gates were locked to prevent any chance of information leaking. Operation order Absalom, which was distributed in the afternoon in the wings and bases, set a framework of exercises and preparations for war within ten days. The goals of the war were concealed. Even Tolkowsky's closed circle was not informed of the processes planned for the other branches of the military. The secret was kept airtight, with the command order being issued in twelve copies. The flow of orders from the top ranks was vertical, direct to the various subordinates, with no group orders. That evening an updated version of Kaddesh 2 was issued. In retrospect, even the sharp-witted were surprised that they had not understood the direction of the operation from its code name; Kaddesh is the first chapter of the text read at Passover, telling the story of the exodus from Egypt.

In August 1990, when such a series of activities was repeated with the Iraqi invasion of Kuwait, no one remained in the IAF who could recall the similar process that had occurred thirty-four years earlier.

The rapid movement to war alert and the new distribution of forces put severe pressure on the commanders of the wings and squadrons. The deactivated piston-engined squadrons would have to be awakened from their slumber, and air cadets would have to be distributed among the squadrons according to the number of flight hours they had accrued. A regimen of combat exercises would have to be introduced for the fighter squadrons that had, until that week, been living an easy life partially because of the poor condition of their aircraft, which had become victims of the budget difficulties. Few dogfights or ground-target attacks were rehearsed. Many of the pilots completely lacked experience in providing ground support.

Not much was accomplished in three days, but fortunately the pilots did not know the extent of the ground operation and the support missions that would be allocated to them, so they avoided considerable anxiety and frustration.

There was actually reason to worry about the balance of power. The Egyptian Air Force was situated at three rear bases in the Nile valley, four forward bases by the Suez Canal, and three emergency bases in the Sinai. It had 210 aircraft, 150 of them in eleven fighter and bomber squadrons, all jets. These included four squadrons of MiG-15s and the new MiG-17, three Vampire squadrons, one Meteor squadron, and two Ilyushin IL-28 bomber squadrons. There were also two transport squadrons and a total of 150 pilots who were combat-ready. The IAF had 176 functional aircraft in thirteen operational squadrons. Of the 117 fighter and bomber aircraft, 64 were piston-engined aircraft; they included two Mustang squadrons, two Mosquito squadrons, one Harvard squadron, and one B-17 bomber squadron. There were only fifty-three jets, including one squadron of Mystères, with only sixteen of its sixty-one aircraft in operational condition, one Ouragan squadron and two Meteor squadrons. There were also a transport squadron of Dakotas and Nords and a light squadron for patrol and liaison. The aircrew included 133 pilots, 80 of them piston-engine pilots and 53 jet pilots. The ratio of jet fighters was three to one in favor of the Egyptians. The sole comfort lay in the Egyptians' low level of maintenance, which kept an unknown number of their aircraft out of service, and the limited execution level of their pilots.

Tolkowsky was ordered to reveal the details of the war to the base, squadron, and wing commanders less than a day before its start. On October 28, at 2000 hours, he spread out the plan before their astounded eyes in the conference room of IAF headquarters in Ramle. He immediately began the briefing regarding the first stage, the airdrop of a regiment of paratroopers at the Mitla Pass in the Sinai. Ezer Weizman was the first to leave the room. He rushed back to Hatzor to welcome the sixteen French Nords, which were to land before midnight with four hundred French pilots, technicians, and commanders of the air reinforcements that had been promised to Ben-Gurion at the summit conference. The story of the Sinai Campaign solved only part of the riddle that began to irk him when he was asked to prepare for the arrival of this enormous foreign squadron. The secret of Operation Musketeer had not yet been revealed to him, and he was angry that a foreign army, in foreign uniforms, would use the Land of Israel to serve interests not necessarily those of Israel.

Dan Tolkowsky did his best to shorten the briefing. With his famous self-control he again succeeded at quelling the stormy reactions and imparting quiet and confidence to those around him. However, it was not the rolling war machine that would strike the first blow later the next day, but one lone squadron commander who should have appeared in the orders group, and of whose absence only he and Tolkowsky were aware. The other commanders were too carried away to notice that he did not appear. Immediately after the end of the briefing, Tolkowsky slipped away to the flight control center. The chief of staff was already there waiting for him, before the radar screens and the crackling communications speakers.

Chatto Tzidon, commander of the Meteor NF/3 (night fighter) squadron was cruising at a moderate altitude over the Mediterranean Sea, somewhere between Haifa and Cyprus, searching for an Egyptian transport plane that was supposed to make its way from Damascus to Cairo. Tolkowsky had revealed the secret of the Sinai Campaign to him before the others, when he had summoned him from Ramat David to Ramle at 1400 hours. "By the way," he asked after telling him, "how quickly could you prepare a plane for a night interception?"

Chatto's entire squadron was dedicated to the special model, a two-seater that carried a pilot and a navigator, which the British had designed for night combat with additions of necessary instruments. The commander-in-chief had appointed him to develop the field of nighttime air combat. The squadron had only two aircraft and only Chatto and the chief navigator, El Yashiv, known as "Shivi." The tests had been temporarily called off, and only on the eve of the war were they told to enter an alert status. Even the aircraft's radar, relatively new in the world of aviation, suffered from the instability of youth, and a test flight had to be flown before each night-intercept sortie to calibrate it. However, these were minimal doubts that he could not express, so as not to damage his good reputation. He was there to provide a solution and not to be part of the problem.

"The plane's ready," Chatto responded. "What's the target?"

"The Egyptian General Command," Tolkowsky informed him.

Tolkowsky explained the obvious, that the call-up in Israel and the British military preparations in Cyprus were kindling a natural disquiet among the Arabs. Egypt had no idea where Israel was headed. He then started to read aloud an intelligence telegram that had arrived during the morning. "All the senior officials of the Egyptian General Command are now in Damascus. At their head is Marshal Abdal Hakhim Amar, the commander of the Egyptian Army and Nasser's deputy, who is signing a defense treaty with the commanders of the Syrian and Jordanian armies. In the evening they will return to Cairo in a military transport aircraft."

In the same breath, he continued, "Our mission is to shoot it down. The Kaddesh network needs to catch the Egyptians by surprise. Without a General Command, it will take them time to recover—if at all. We cannot afford to miss the opportunity."

Chatto returned to base and added Shivi, the squadron's navigator, to the mission. After studying the details, they began to calibrate the radar on one of the two planes. Before they realized how much time had passed, as in any such preparation, they received the "green light" notice that the Egyptian plane was in the air and that they were to execute the mission.

They took off toward the sea, climbed to altitude, and began the search. The air was quiet, and the sky was cloud-free. It was a crisp and moonless autumn night. The coastline quickly melted away in the darkness; the Israeli Civil Defense Corps had declared a blackout several nights before.

Shivi was riveted to his instruments, and the flight controller, whose voice could be heard on the communications, aided him in the search for the aircraft. They had taken off with maximum fuel, knowing they might have to wait up to an hour for the target's arrival. In the meantime, the controller dictated directions of flight, and they scoured the skies for an interminable hour.

"Contact, contact, contact," Shivi told Chatto over the internal communications. "Bogey at two o'clock. Range three miles." He told Chatto to reduce speed, and Chatto closed the throttle.

"You're closing range too fast," Shivi said. Chatto saw nothing, but trusted him and began to reduce his speed.

"Bogey at eleven. Range seven hundred meters. Drop down five hundred feet." Shivi guided him. In these stages, the responsibility for leading is in the hands of the navigator. The pilot must fly according to his instructions.

"Eye contact," he reported to the controller.

"I want positive identification," said Meir Roff, the commander of the flight control center, who until recently had been commander of the Mustang squadron.

"Beyond any doubt, positive identification of the aircraft described to me." They approached close to the shadowy shape. Though the plane resembled a Dakota, it had the large windows that could only be found in an Ilyushin IL-14. The tail also matched the Russian aircraft.

"Positive identification," Chatto reported to the control center.

"You have permission to open fire if there are no doubts," Roff responded.

Chatto steadied himself behind the plane, which was flying very slowly relative to the jet. He was forced to lower the landing flaps in order to increase the efficiency of his controls at such a low speed.

Shivi continued to direct him with flight instructions until the target filled Chatto's gunsights. The range was close. No one knew of their presence or interfered with them.

"Opening fire," he said to the control center, and pressed the trigger button of the cannons.

The Ilyushin lost speed as if it had been stopped by the hit, and it could be seen from the distance by the flames that erupted from its left engine. Undoubtedly it was a good hit, but not perfect, and reported the hit to the control center.

Shivi continued to provide instructions, and Chatto again entered firing position from behind. Another burst from the cannon's muzzle exploded against the plane's body. A ball of fire could be seen in the right wing, and the plane began to dive slowly until it struck the sea and broke up.

They returned and climbed to altitude over the burning fragments of the Ilyushin, then turned east and headed home. The lights of the runway, which had been lit, blinked from afar in the darkened country. The fuel gauge did not register any reserve when the wheels touched the ground, approximately an hour after takeoff.

The chief of staff and the upper echelons of the IAF were waiting for Chatto in Ramle to toast the successful mission. Tolkowsky revealed that Marshal Amar was not among the top officers who had been killed. At the last moment he had decided to remain in Damascus.

"Anyhow, you still knocked off the Egyptian General Command," said Dayan, as he shook their hands. "You finished off half the war, so let's drink to the success of the second half."

# 3 The Sinai Campaign

*October 29, 1956, 1000 hours:*
*Tel Nof Air Base*
$\pmb{F}$or three days it had seemed as if all
the IAF veterans from all of the base's squadrons were holding an endless
reunion, exchanging stories, savoring their most vivid memories. They
had never been gathered together in such a way, and only after the third
day did they begin to sense the cause. Of all of the squadrons, only the
transport squadron had expanded to twice its normal size, having been
ordered to call up every one of its reservists. The briefing room in which
they gathered that morning was not designed to hold the eighty pilots,
navigators, and radio operators, but they crowded in, sitting on mattresses
and sacks.

They would be briefed on the mysterious mission for which they had
been recalled from their civilian lives "tomorrow at five," according to the
rumor that had begun to spread the previous evening from the airborne
brigade's headquarters. That meant in seven hours. The sudden addition
of ten Dakota transport aircraft to the squadron's total number served as
another hint; it strongly suggested involvement of paratroopers. The
location of the drop remained hidden behind a black curtain in the
briefing room.

The El Al pilots among them who had participated in the operation
of bringing the Dakotas to Israel were not asked anything, and volunteered no information. The new aircraft, fitted out in green-brown
camouflage colors and the IAF's markings, could not be externally
distinguished from the older planes. A glance inside at the French
operating instructions affixed to parts of the cabin and cockpit suggested
how the squadron had acquired its three "flying eggs," as the crews
nicknamed the new Nord aircraft with their bulbous bodies.

The Dakotas had actually been leased from the French government
and had not been purchased. Using the same cover under which the

thirty-six Mystères had been brought to Israel in August, and French tanks and cannons flown in by night earlier that month, the Dakotas had been smuggled into the country. The French had agreed to let Israel have the planes, since the transport squadron did not have enough aircraft to drop an entire battalion of paratroopers in the Mitla Pass. However, they requested that the lease remain secret since it could expose their role and goal in the war.

In the few days preceding the briefing, Yael Finkelstein had flown one or two of the Dakotas, and their origins were unimportant to her. The transport pilots' feelings about the Dakotas ran deeper than this. They had developed a loyalty to the aircraft, and would zealously preserve each plane's identity and number even when all its parts had been replaced several times over. Five years earlier, during her mandatory military service, Yael had volunteered for the Flight Course. She was accepted into the fifth course, as an understandable exception. The IDF was still living in the fresh memories of the War of Independence, in which many women had fought, and one woman pilot had even been killed. None of the three women who graduated from the Flight Course during that period reached the fighter squadrons. Yael was sent to the transport squadron. Rena Levinson was sent to the Flight School, and Ruth Bookbinder was sent to the light liaison squadron. Though she often felt as though she were merely driving a delivery truck, Yael had maintained her proficiency in the Dakotas since her discharge. As she waited for the briefing to begin on that October day, she had no idea of the battle being waged to exempt her from the General Command's last command order, which forbade women pilots from flying beyond Israel's borders.

The screech of seats and benches being pushed back interrupted her thoughts. Generations of pilots, veterans of the War of Independence alongside youngsters, jumped to their feet and watched squadron commander Yaakov Avisar enter and silently pull the black curtain from the wall. When the map of the Sinai Peninsula was revealed, most faces displayed incredulity; the pilots had heard rumors only about the Jordanian and Iraqi threat crawling toward them from the east. Squadron commander Avisar pointed with his stick to the center of a black circle around the Suez Canal. A dark line connected it to the Israeli border at the Negev. He spoke of an "air armada" that would drop an assault force drawn from the parachute brigade in the circle at 1700 hours to threaten the canal and prepare the ground as the site for landing supplies and evacuating wounded. The remainder of the paratrooper brigade's battalions would arrive over land, following the dark line on the map in tanks, armored personnel carriers, and trucks.

Fighter aircraft would provide cover for the transport aircraft, the convoy, and the airdropped battalion in the territory. The battalion would remain exposed and alone for nearly a day until the arrival of the brigade traveling overland. When the Egyptians deployed their troops against the Israeli paratroopers, the fighter aircraft would maul them. The Egyptians could also use aircraft, new Soviet MiGs, taking off from their nearby bases. The Israeli pilots, however, faced the formidable task of fighting far from home. This could also be the beginning of a war, Avisar added.

The pilots tried to absorb every detail as Avisar delineated the routes and the missions. The airdrop would take place at dusk, and the aircraft would return in the dark. Later that night they would return to drop in equipment, even though the advantage of surprise would be lost. He repeated and emphasized the importance of carrying out this mission fully, no matter what opposition they encountered. Even if the Egyptian aircraft attacked and the armada was scattered, each plan had to reach the target and drop its load at any price.

Before Avisar had completed his talk, an officer entered the room and handed him a note. Avisar smiled and passed it on to the operations officer at the moment when he began to read the crew assignments for the eighteen aircraft. The General Command had approved Yael's flight. She would be the squadron commander's copilot in the lead aircraft.

*October 29, 1956, Afternoon*      *F*or several days, Amitai "Shafan" Hasson, an instructor in the Flight School, had been attempting to devise a new way to use the cables and weights generally employed in towing targets in air-combat exercises. Tzahik Yavne, the commander of the Flight School, had asked Shafan to sever aboveground telephone lines. Israeli reconnaissance photos revealed that such telephone lines were the Egyptians' only means of communication between the forward command centers in the Sinai and headquarters in Cairo. They ran along the roads and primary arteries on low poles, which enabled technicians to repair them while standing on top of their trucks. Shafan had figured out how to strike quickly and efficiently. He was less concerned with safety than with the possibility that he would remain cableless and not be able to execute his mission. Tzahik reminded him of a flight cadet who had once descended too low in a Stearman and sliced through phone lines with the blades of his propeller. The Israeli pilots realized that method could be a last resort.

Tzahik requested his deputy, Harry Crasenstein, to join Shafan, his second deputy, and continue the training exercises. Should the operation take place, it would not be a one-man operation; the planes would form up in pairs. A day earlier, on October 28, IAF commander-in-chief Dan Tolkowsky had summoned them and revealed the secret. Three pairs of Mustangs would pioneer the Sinai Campaign. An hour before the Dakotas neared the drop location, the Mustangs would cut the central telephone lines of the Egyptian Army in the Sinai.

Thus, as Yaakov Avisar briefed the transport pilots, Tzahik gathered Harry, Shafan, and three others in his office. He outlined the details of the mission. Harry and Aryeh Zeitlin would cut the telephone lines from Kusseima and Abu-Aweigila to the city of Suez. Tzahik and Aryeh Fredlis would sever the lines along the central route that Arik Sharon's brigade would use. Shafan and Chaim Naveh would cut the lines from El Arish to Abu-Aweigila. Tzahik, Harry, and Shafan knew the technique: to drag cables so that metal balls, attached to the ends, snagged and tore the telephone wires. But the newcomers to the mission were dazed. That the leader in each pair would do the cutting reassured them, but if help was needed, each leader would rely on his partner to observe the technique and employ it.

At 1330 hours, all of the squadrons on the base were summoned to a final briefing with the IAF commander-in-chief in the officers' club. Tolkowsky described the opening act, which had been placed in the hands of the transport squadron. It would be the first combat airdrop in the history of Israel. Other operations would be carried out, he said, but he provided no details, not mentioning a word about the British or the French. Tolkowsky disguised his anxiety well. And the pilots were too preoccupied with their own nervousness to notice his. As always, he won their trust by exuding confidence and encouragement. "Onward and upward," Tolkowsky said as he saluted them farewell.

The Mustang sextet headed straight from the briefing to their aircraft. At exactly 1400 hours, Harry and Zeitlin took off and headed toward the western edge of the Sinai. Each Mustang carried six fully loaded .50-

caliber machine guns. A few minutes later, the other two pairs departed as well. As they passed over Tel Nof, they could see the paratroopers sitting under the wings of the Dakotas. Only then did Shafan understand that gaining the advantage of surprise in the airdrop was completely dependent on the skill of each pilot.

They flew at low altitude, no more than one hundred feet, and relatively slowly for approximately 250 miles as they maintained radio silence. At Tzin Canyon, they turned west and split up. Each pair was to cut a line at two points. Harry and Zeitlin found the telephone poles near Suez. As they approached the first point, Zeitlin's cable disconnected from his tail. He decided to use the propeller alternative on a second try. As he began to descend, the sun struck both pilots in the eyes. One moment they saw the cables approaching, and in the next, they disappeared. Aiming his Mustang between the poles, he flew through but failed to feel the familiar tug of the wrenching out of the cables. On the third run, almost running into the ground, he saw the cables in front of his eyes and heard the tremendous blow as the propeller hit the cables and ripped them to shreds. At their second point, they cut the cables in the first run.

*October 29, 1956, 1630 hours*          **A**s the Dakotas crossed the border into the Sinai, they hung close to the arid desert floor and canyons, flying at an altitude of tens of meters as they attempted to avoid exposure by Jordan's radar stations. They flew in four quartets, half a kilometer apart, as their pilots maintained eye contact. Two Dakotas remained at Tel Nof on alert, first as replacements if needed, and then later to drop diversionary dummy paratroopers near the Egyptian Kabrit Field and near Ismailiya.

They had been flying for nearly an hour and a half, and had spent an hour before departure preparing the aircraft. Yaakov Avisar had checked the members of the lead team to make sure they had not left any personal equipment behind, and that they all had their parachutes, life jackets, and personal weapons. Pilots also carried an emergency belt with food and water for a day or two, as well as survival equipment including a signaling mirror, a compass, and a whistle. POW cards were essential, in case they fell into enemy hands. The squadron commander glanced over at Yael's feet. No, she had not forgotten to change from her ever-present sandals into regular shoes.

Achikar "Los" Eyal, the squadron's chief navigator, calculated the rate of progress and ensured that the pilots did not stray from the route or alert the enemy radar. Twenty-five helmeted paratroopers sat in each plane, wearing chest and leg packs containing their equipment. Within thirty minutes the paratroopers would experience their first combat jump. For the transport squadron, it was just another work sortie, though farther away and more dangerous than usual. The slow and unarmed Dakotas were, as always, helpless targets for the Egyptian MiGs.

The radio operators, with nothing to do in the radio silence, spent their time in the observation bubbles of the Dakotas to give warning of enemy aircraft. The skies were clean; the Meteor and Ouragan squadrons had spread out in a defensive umbrella far from sight. This was not a close accompaniment, since the fighters' speed was three times that of the Dakotas and since they did not want to reveal the operation to the Egyptian radar.

Though less experienced than many, Aharon Yoeli, commander of the Meteor squadron, was the only pilot who had participated in dogfights with Egyptians, having shot down two of their aircraft. An hour after the Dakotas, the Meteors took off from Tel Nof, and the aircraft were not in visual contact. The Meteors flew at ten thousand feet over Israeli territory, and the transport aircraft, painted in the colors of the desert, hugged the ground deep in the Sinai. Flying separate routes, Yoeli and his pilots watched the skies in order to cover the gaps in speed and to stay near the transport planes or in position to intercept the Egyptians well away from the Dakotas.

Thirty minutes earlier, Eli Finegersh and Meir Livne had set out in a pair of Meteors from the reconnaissance squadron to execute a diversionary mission along the coast from El Arish to the Arava Desert in Israel. Finegersh returned immediately because of a problem in his fuel system. Livne flew sharp zigzags, hoping to provide the Egyptians out of their holes. On his return, he reported no response.

Forced to return to base because of low fuel after an hour of flight, Yoeli's Meteors missed the drop. Moti Hod replaced him, leading a sextet of Ouragans that took off from Hatzor. In contrast to Yoeli, Moti was one of the revered elders of the group. He was a model to youngsters like David Ivri and Amos Lapidot, who now flew alongside him and would later follow in his footsteps as commanders-in-chief of the IAF. Ivri, twenty-two years old and born in Tel Aviv, did not belong to the squadron. He had just returned from England after a course in jet aircraft, and was assigned to the Flight School to be an instructor pilot on the Stearmans and Harvards. Ivri accompanied Yaakov Agassi, a fellow instructor and Moti's deputy, over the Mitla Pass. Their mission was to protect the airdrop, which was to begin within minutes. They saw no enemy aircraft on the horizon, despite their tedious scouring of the skies.

Moti was prepared for the worst. A horrible scenario came to mind in which the Egyptians were counting down the minutes until the Ouragans were low on fuel, and would then attack from their nearby airfields with fresh MiGs. Even if they overcame the Egyptians, it was unlikely that they would be able to return to their now far distant home bases. With the engine filling most of its fuselage, the Ouragan was not designed for prolonged flight. Droppable wingtip tanks had been improvised by the planners to augment the limited capacity of the wing tanks. Without them, the aircraft's range was limited; if a dogfight did develop, the tanks would have to be dropped. But the minutes passed without activity, and Moti realized that he was overestimating the cunning of the enemy.

In the Ramle Flight Control Center, it was decided not to waste the paratrooper dummies on the diversionary drop near Ismailiya, Kabrit, and on the western shores of the Great Bitter Lake. It had been canceled a half hour earlier, at the moment when Benny Peled began to patrol the lake's skies with his Mystère squadron—three quartets led by Yak Nevo, Danny Shapira, and himself. Yalo Shavit was also there, along with Joe Alon and Dror Avneri. Arolozor "Zorik" Lev had been there in a morning flight with Yak. Tolkowsky was taking no chances with the border of the canal; the Bitter Lakes and the Egyptian air bases near them were within reach. However, the pleasure of this first contact with the new view was replaced by a growing frustration. From the perimeter of Kabrit Field, confused antiaircraft fire, sporadic and inaccurate, could be seen. The runway also came to life. A minute earlier the MiG-15 aircraft had been neatly lined up as if awaiting inspection. At this stage the Egyptians began to move them about. Danny Shapira grew hopeful that they were being prepared for takeoff, and he began to stroke his firing switch. But the MiGs offered no clear provocation, and the Mystères were bound by the order not to attack first.

Twenty minutes before zero hour, Yael Finkelstein climbed out of the copilot's seat so that the chief navigator, Los Eyal, could climb in. His job was to identify the drop location and to assist Avisar in congregating the sixteen Dakotas toward it. Precision and timing were of top priority. Los's eyes were glued to the canyon and the road alongside it until from afar he saw the fork of the Nahel intersection and the plateau nearby. Even if they entered the range of the Egyptian radar, this was the moment to ascend to an altitude that would allow the paratroopers' chutes to open and their landing to be as gentle as possible. Relying on the umbrella of Mystères and Ouragans, Avisar focused on the navigator's instructions. Los signaled with his hand; it was almost 1700 hours.

"One." the pilots heard Yael signal as they ascended and turned north in a half-circle, opening the distance between the formations to a kilometer. At five-minute intervals, Yael called out "Two," and then "Three," and then commanded, "Bell!" The copilots in all the aircraft simultaneously hit the switch, and the ringing signaled four hundred paratroopers to jump to their feet.

The signal lights changed from red to green as the crews shouted, "Juuuump!" and the paratroopers spilled out the doors into the darkness. Avisar grasped the stick of the emptying Dakota so as to keep it steady as its load lightened. Within seconds the air was filled with khaki mushrooms. Several human figures below, who had been busy repairing the road, abandoned the red plateau and escaped, running into the hills. Among the paratroopers was a pilot, Yekutiel Altman, who had joined them as air liaison officer. The last Dakota hovered above for several minutes to convey the first messages from Col. Rafael "Raful" Eitan, the commander of the ground forces, to Israel. The drop had succeeded, and the force was preparing to dig in for the night. Moti Hod's sextet was also on its way home. Another sextet of Ouragans had taken its place to provide air cover for the paratroopers until nightfall.

The transport squadron made its way back to Israel in utter darkness so that any approaching enemy plane would not see them. With the aircraft now empty, the threat of attack had also lost its meaning. At 1830 hours, three hours after takeoff, Yael landed the lead Dakota at Tel Nof.

At 2030 hours, the Israeli Radio announcer surprised the country and the world by declaring, "IDF forces have taken control of positions near the Suez Canal." Near the Parker Monument, the paratroopers laid down lights in the shape of a T for the train of Dakotas and Nords that was on its way from Tel Nof to the Mitla Pass to drop them mortars, ammunition, water, and supplies. Near midnight, four French Nords from Cyprus brought new weapons—recoilless cannons carried by eight jeeps. With its rear-opening doors and its tracks down which well-padded vehicles could slide out, the Nord was specially constructed for dropping enormous items like these.

On the night between October 29 and 30, the paratroopers did not shut their eyes. Busy digging in, they failed to see that beyond the hills and under cover of darkness, the Egyptians had taken control of the pass, exploiting the confusion that had led to the battalion's being dropped in the eastern entrance of the Mitla Pass and not in its western end. Raful's sole effort to discover what was taking place beyond the pass had entailed sending a Piper Cub to scout the region late the previous day. Fifteen minutes after the paratroopers had landed, the area seemed empty and silent.

## October 30, 1956, Morning

The Piper pilot, Moshe Even, set out with a second Piper, flown by Moshe Bokai, to inaugurate the landing strip set up by the paratroopers. The Pipers were allocated to the ground forces for evacuation of wounded. Raful's radio had been damaged during the drop, and Even, functioning as a flying messenger, acted as liaison between Raful and Arik Sharon. The good news was that Sharon's battalion was progressing well overland. The bad news was that the fuel and supply trucks, lacking front-wheel drive, had gotten stuck in the sand and were disconnected from the convoy, lagging far behind. Near 0800, Bokai planned to fly out the first of the dozen paratroopers injured in the drop. The paratrooper was being treated for a severely broken leg by Dr. Morris Anklawitz, who had been decorated by the IDF chief of staff for his work under fire during a retaliatory operation against the Fedayeen prior to the Sinai Campaign.

At 0900 hours, the white vapor trails of jet aircraft could be seen in the sky. Bokai wanted to move quickly, fearing that they were Egyptian MiG-15s. Anklawitz claimed that the planes were Israeli. Having loaded his patient into the back of the Piper, he was already outside and Bokai was ready to take off when the MiGs dived, firing cannons and rockets. The Piper's wing and fuel tank were hit. The tank erupted and the fire crept toward Bokai's feet. He jumped out in a roll, to keep from being turned into a living torch, and saw Anklawitz with blood pouring from his chest. Rocket fragments had struck him in the lungs, but he felt no pain. The doctor stood up, and he and Bokai jumped into the fire now devouring the cloth covering of the Piper, to free the wounded man from his straps. The flames had also eaten the belts holding him in, and with his last drop of strength, Bokai, assisted by the doctor, pulled the soldier far from the aircraft. The paratroopers extinguished the fire, which had spread to their clothing. Not a shred remained of the Piper. Anklawitz had fainted, and Bokai was suffering from severe burns. They were rescued and flown to Israel, where Bokai was later decorated for his bravery by the chief of staff.

The twelve Mystères that had provided cover for the battalion airdrop now returned to the Mitla front, this time in pairs, flying at fifteen-minute intervals. The first pair took off from Hatzor immediately after sunrise, and the last left the Mitla Pass at 0830 hours. Only then did the Egyptian Air Force go into action. The picture that developed at the Israeli Flight Control Center was as if described through a broken telephone. Although the French had provided them with new radar systems, even this equipment could not cover the depths of the Sinai. Lacking long-distance radio communications, Flight Control relied on reports from flight inspectors who were with the paratroopers radioing messages to the Mystères, who returned to Hatzor and eventually passed the information on to IAF headquarters. This was one-way communication, replete with electronic and atmospheric problems as well as human error.

The first signs of Egyptian activity came when a quartet of Vampires flew over the Parker Monument at low altitude. A memorial erected by the British for a high-ranking officer who had died there in World War I, the monument lay at the entrance to one of the three main passages through the Sinai. They approached from the direction of Sharon's convoy, and caused the paratroopers to leap out of their entrenchments. The Vampires' patrol showed the Egyptians how large this force, of which all the world was now speaking, actually was. The MiGs followed them. They strafed Sharon's column, failing to inflict any damage.

The first pair of Israeli Mystères passed the paratroopers at 0630 hours and continued toward the Suez Canal. The pilots advised Raful that Egyptian Army convoys were on their way to the Mitla Pass. Raful requested that they be "removed" from the road, and the pilots had problems conveying to him on the open radio frequencies that their orders strictly forbade them to initiate an attack. Raful had no idea what had occurred between the Mitla Pass and the Suez Canal before the appearance of the Mystères that morning. At 0300 hours, two Egyptian battalions had crossed the canal using a floating bridge, and had begun to fortify themselves, according to plan, among the rocks and slopes in the Mitla Canyon. By morning they controlled the bottleneck of the pass, and had camouflaged their positions among the rocks. The forward scouts of this force were five kilometers from the Parker Monument. Reporting from the air, the picture that the Israeli pilots drew for Raful was only partially accurate.

At approximately 1200 hours the first shells began to fall around Raful. The Egyptians aimed 120-millimeter mortars on the paratroopers from their positions at the fork in the roads. An Israeli observation post warned from one of the hills that an Egyptian force could be seen headed toward the canyon. Raful looked up and saw two Israeli Ouragans, silent and passive.

Turning on his radio for the noon news, the duty officer in the Flight Control Center was astounded to hear a strange announcement. "The Air Force has requested permission to attack targets in the Sinai." The telephone rang before the announcer had even moved on to the next story. It was Chief of Staff Moshe Dayan calling from the war room of the Southern Command. He requested that they inform Tolkowsky that permission had been granted.

### October 30, 1956, 1200 hours:
### The Mitla Pass

**R**aful did not wait for salvation to come from the heavens. He ordered his 81-millimeter mortars to silence the Egyptian fire. The hilltop observation point aided in range and reporting. Before he could send a regiment into the canyon, he heard cheers from the two orbiting Ouragans, for they had received permission to attack and were open for invitations! They immediately dropped down toward the forward Egyptian force, which was only two kilometers from the Israeli position. After emptying their ammunition on the Egyptians, they were requested to remain in the air to their fuel limits, to aid in directing the aircraft that were on their way.

The planes, a total of thirty-seven, arrived in wave after wave, using all their ammunition and then returning to Israel. They included fifteen Ouragans, each carrying two quarter-ton bombs, eight armor-piercing rockets, and four 20-millimeter cannons; eighteen Mystères with six rocket clusters and a pair of 30-millimeter cannons each; and four

Meteors with the modest weaponry of four 20-millimeter cannons. The paratroopers lay on their backs in their entrenched positions and watched the rockets shoot out from under the aircrafts' wings, dragging their white exhaust trails. From behind the mountains they could hear explosions and see columns of black smoke rising into the air. The observation post reported that the enemy artillery battery had been destroyed.

*October 30, 1956, Afternoon:*
*Kabrit Field*                     *F*or nearly two hours, Moti Hod's Ouragans pounded the Egyptian forces in the Mitla Pass. While IAF headquarters planned to rescue Raful from the heavy air attack approaching from Kabrit Field, the question remained as to what they would use to do so. Most of the IAF, including ten Mystères, was on its way to bomb in the Mitla Pass or was already there. Only eight Mystères remained in Hatzor. Though the Mystère IV was nearly identical to the MiG-15, it was a new aircraft, and even the French had yet to test it in battle. With this first opportunity in the Mitla Pass, a positive proportion of Israeli to Egyptian aircraft was preferable. The flight controller had no choice, and he scrambled all the aircraft. If they needed assistance, their comrades were already at the Mitla Pass.

They took off in three formations, two trios and a pair for backup. Within twenty minutes the first formation had established eye contact with the canal. Yak Nevo, Shai Egozi, and Yosef Tzuk searched for skies crowded with MiGs, but found only four MiG-15s. This was a good ratio, for each could take on one MiG. With the advantage of the home territory and nearby fuel and munitions sources, the Egyptians were not easy prey. The Mystères were limited to ten to fifteen minutes of combat if they did not want to risk returning to Hatzor on their last drops of fuel. Though this was not an insignificant period of time, the Egyptians knew how to avoid anyone flying on their tails. Yak and his friends were at the start of their careers, lacking experience.

In the meantime, the second trio, flown by Dror Avneri, Dan Gonen, and Shabtai Gilboa, as well as the backup formation flown by Zorik Lev and Amos Lapidot, who had transferred from the Ouragan squadron, approached. The Egyptians saw that the ratio of forces was turning against them. Yak provided the provocation, diving three hundred meters above the field. The Egyptians immediately scrambled twelve MiGs toward him, the goal being as much to protect them from being destroyed on the ground as to intercept the Israeli planes. It was now eight Mystères against sixteen MiGs. At this point it became clear to Yak that quantity would not be the decisive factor. The Egyptians' weak point was the solid and outdated World War II formation in which they entered the battle. The chase provided by the twelve MiGs was not improvised but methodical. At the instant when the smaller and quicker formations of Mystères broke apart the larger formation of MiGs, its responses were clumsy and less calculated.

Thus Tzuk succeeded at catching a MiG's tail and hitting it with a long burst. It spat out black smoke, spun, and crashed. Before he could rejoice about shooting down the first MiG in the war and in the history of the squadron and the IAF, he was struck by a burst to his wing. The Mystère began to shake, and he was forced to turn home. He maintained its steadiness and landed successfully. Avneri hit another MiG, and the Mystères, running short on fuel, disengaged. The Egyptians were not seduced into prolonging the chase.

### October 30, 1956, Afternoon:
### The Mitla Pass

*F*lying his Ouragan, Ran "Ladia" Sharon entered the Mitla Pass according to the topographical features that had been described in the briefing: from the fork in the road, along the route into the pass, and across the mountains. A small hell was breaking out below him. The Egyptians on the edge of the canyon were firing on the paratroopers with all their weapons, thus providing him with a plethora of targets. He had to decide within seconds what to drop on whom first. Two trucks pulling field cannons seemed fitting for the bombs. His precise drop of five hundred kilograms of explosives transformed them into junk. For the second run, he decided to use his rockets. Choosing two trucks loaded with crates, he fired. Breaking upward, he saw in their place balls of fire and billowing clouds of smoke. A chain of explosions followed, glowing like a display of fireworks. The crates had been full of ammunition.

The Egyptian Fifth Battalion, the forward force that had entered the Mitla Pass and had fortified itself near the Parker Monument, remained without vehicles or ammunition. From there the Israeli planes continued on to attack the Sixth Battalion, which was still spread out on its way from the canal. The pilots' reports of severe hits on the convoys of the Egyptian force improved the mood in Raful's command. His people assumed that the bombing had caused tremendous losses to the Egyptians, even though the pilots reported only what they saw before their eyes—that the pass was empty. From the air they did not see that most of the armored and regular vehicles parked by the side of the road were empty and that the soldiers were concealed on the mountainous slopes. Even from the ground it was difficult to identify the makeshift but well-camouflaged positions. The joy that evening in the Israeli paratroopers' camp was premature.

*October 30, 1956, Night:*
*IAF Headquarters, Ramle*                  *F*rom the summary of the debriefing that had been laid on his desk, Dan Tolkowsky had the impression that the first day of war had not justified the prior concerns. While defense of the nation's skies was in the hands of the French, they had not been called upon to stand the test. Over the course of the day, U.S.-made F-84 Thunderstreak fighter aircraft had also landed in Lod, strengthening this force. The Egyptian Air Force did not know that its enemy was bound by an order forbidding it to attack first. Nonetheless, it was caught unprepared. The EAF's responses were slow and characterized by hesitation and a lack of daring. Its combat execution was confused. Not flying beyond the Sinai, even there its pilots limited themselves to participation in the ground battle, using shows of strength and symbolic damage, which they executed only between the flights of the Israeli aircraft. The Egyptians did not dare attempt to intercept the Israeli fighters as they provided cover for the airdrop in the Parker Monument, or to attack the exposed paratroopers at night. Even their participation in the sole dogfight in the skies over Kabrit was forced, and not of their own initiation. The MiGs did not even attempt to disrupt the pounding of Egyptian troops in the Mitla Pass, even though they were only two minutes' flight away.

There were officers in IAF headquarters who had begun to be thankful that the plan to destroy the EAF on the ground at the outset of the war had been taken from them. The situation had allowed them in the first day to expose the points of weakness in the organization and combat effectiveness of the Egyptian pilots and their new Soviet weapons. If things continued this way, one could assume that the rest of the war would be relatively easy.

*October 31, 1956*              **A**t 0410 hours, the Flight Control
Center received an urgent telegram from Israeli Navy headquarters
reporting an anonymous ship that had shelled the Haifa port forty-five
minutes earlier. Since the ship had been detected at 0245 hours, forty
kilometers from the port, and until the chase had begun, events had
occurred in slow motion. For forty-five minutes the ship had been merely
a dot on the Navy radar. At 0330 hours, it suddenly approached to within
ten kilometers of the coast, rained down 220 shells from its four cannons
onto the military port and shipyards, and then escaped. The damage
inflicted was minimal. Two new Israeli Navy destroyers, *Yaffo* and *Eilat*,
were patrolling in the deep seas off the Haifa coast and were prepared for
attacks from the air. Notice of the ship's location was transmitted to them
only an hour after the shelling. The sea liaison officer identified it
through the regional flight control center.

The Egyptian destroyer *Ibrahim Al-Awal* had set out the previous
night from Port Said. So that he could escape to Beirut under cover of
darkness, its captain shelled the port earlier than the morning time set for
him. Twenty minutes after identification of the ship and its location, an
IAF Dakota was sent from Tel Nof to illuminate the region with flares.
The ship was already fifty kilometers from Akko. The yellowish lights that
slowly dropped from the sky blended in with the dawn and illuminated
the enemy destroyer for the *Yaffo* and the *Eilat*. At 0530 hours they
began to shell it for ten minutes, striking its stern.

Hatzor had been on its feet for more than an hour. It had been a short
night for Ouragan pilots Yaakov Agassi and David Kishon after the day of
battle in the Mitla Pass. The sudden briefing about the Egyptian destroyer
did not fit in with their plans to review the images of the day's bombing in
the Sinai. The Flight Control Center had originally ordered the squadron
to prepare four Ouragans for attack, but since the Israeli shelling had
slowed the destroyer's speed, it was thought that two would suffice. Agassi
and Kishon took off at daybreak, 0600 hours, armed with the same
wondrous rockets that had penetrated the Egyptian armor near Suez.
Within fifteen minutes they were over the Haifa bay, and were astounded
by the number of vessels sailing in the area of the target. From ten
thousand feet it was difficult for a pilot's eye to distinguish among the
ships, which all looked alike. The Egyptian destroyer fit itself in with
the U.S. Sixth Fleet, which had come to rescue American citizens from
the war in Israel. Israeli destroyers were also in the area.

The Ouragans wasted a tremendous amount of fuel in useless flight over the sea until they jointly identified the enemy destroyer. The American fleet attempted to ease the situation by departing the battle area. However, the Egyptian destroyer stuck with the Americans until the hits by the Israeli destroyers slowed it down and left it alone, crippled and exposed. Agassi dropped down first. He opened up with cannon fire and then, from short range, used all his rockets. Kishon dived in after him, forgoing his cannons so as not to hit Agassi, and simultaneously released his sixteen rockets. Thick white smoke covered the destroyer's deck. Agassi could see pieces of metal flying in all directions. After thirty minutes the Egyptian destroyer surrendered.

*October 31, 1956, morning:*
*The Parker Monument*                 *D*awn rose on armored track vehicles and trucks, which had not been seen in this area of the desert late the previous day. Before midnight, the forward units of Arik Sharon's ground column connected with Raful's battalion. The area being too small for the brigade, dangerous for a concentration of forces, and overly exposed to attacks from the air and the ground, Sharon was particularly wary of the armored Egyptian force that had entered the Sinai the night before on the central route from Ismailiya to Bir Gafgafa. Yehezkiel Somech, commander of the Mosquito squadron, was the first to see the lights of the enemy convoy, and two of his bombers attacked it during the night. It was not stopped. Sharon felt that the paratrooper brigade must continue forward into the Mitla Pass, for its own security and also to block the entry of the Egyptian support forces from the southern route.

Before dawn he had already begun to move westward, when the General Command stopped him and ordered him to take a defensive position. He was specifically forbidden to enter the Mitla Pass, and would not receive the air support that he had requested during the night. The armored brigade scheduled to attack Abu-Aweigila later in the morning had received priority. While Sharon was dependent on Operation Musketeer, Great Britain and France had informed Israel that they were postponing the operation for the time being. This included the bombing of Egyptian airfields that had been planned for the following day.

Though furious, Sharon ordered the brigade convoy to disperse, particularly so that it would not be an easy target for the Egyptian aircraft. While the vehicles were moving out, the patrol of four Vampires

appeared over their heads again, almost exactly as they had the day
before. The difference was that today two Israeli Mystères were patrolling
at high altitude, invisible to the paratroopers on the ground, who thought
the Vampires were Israeli aircraft and began to wave to them with their
hats. Yekutiel Altman, the air liaison officer, thought they had lost their
minds. He watched the Vampires complete their observational circling of
the area and break upward. This was a clear sign that they were about to
dive and attack. Altman called out to the paratroopers to take cover, and
on the air support frequency asked who was in the area.

Shai Egozi responded. Yalo Shavit was in the second Mystère.
Altman directed them to the Vampires.

"Eye contact," Egozi announced on the radio.

The Mystères descended to ten thousand feet. Egozi saw the tight
formation, with twenty meters between each Vampire. They entered his
cannon range as they climbed to begin their attack. Egozi fired first. The
Vampire closest to him fell and crashed. Its partner, damaged, split off
from the other two as they turned left. Yalo set out on their tails and
downed them in one burst. Egozi did not bother chasing the damaged
Vampire, and it crashed several minutes later, after its pilot had ejected.
Although Vampires were not of the quality of Mystères and had even
been shot down by Meteors in the past, this was the first time in the
history of a jet air force that a pair had downed four aircraft in air-to-air
combat.

*October 31, 1956, Morning:*
*Cheetah's First Sortie*
*in the Central Sinai*  $A$ ccording to the operations chart on
the wall, the "Grasshopper" formation should already have completed its
second sortie. But by 0900 it had yet to take off for the first. After a quick
breakfast in the instructor squadron's club, I sat down frustrated, with
nothing to do. Though the formation included six Mustangs, it was
nothing but an unactivated call sign on the squadron's board.

"Grasshopper to briefing," I heard Harry Crasenstein, the squadron's
deputy commander, announce. I was certain that Harry would be our
leader, and I was extremely pleased. It is good for a novice twenty-two-
year-old pilot to fly his first combat sortie with an experienced veteran
flier leading him. However, Harry informed us that this morning we

would have a leader no worse than he. It was Avram Yaffe, the operations officer in IAF headquarters, who had grown tired of Ramle after two days of combat. Before escaping to Tel Nof, he had chosen for himself and the squadron a distant and interesting target in the heart of the Sinai, behind enemy lines. He arrived at the briefing still wearing his dress uniform. Grasshopper, he explained, would attack the armored column that had reached Bir Gafgafa on its way to the forces at Abu-Aweigila and Umm-Katef. Our tanks had been involved in heavy battles with the enemy since the morning, and we could not allow the Egyptian tank reinforcements to reach there.

The Mustangs were already fueled and armed to their wings' capacity with napalm bombs, rockets, and ammunition for the machine guns. Takeoff would be to tree level, at top speed and with radio silence. Avram led us west, and we crossed the coastline and descended to the sea. Radar was more effective over the sea, and Avram did not want us to be detected. After ten minutes the only thing around us was the sea. Suddenly, at wavetop level, Avram tilted his wings and turned left. Flying over the sea allows room for maneuverability between aircraft even in a closed combat formation at low altitude. I moved from side to side smoothly and lightly and found my place again, making sure to be careful of the air turbulence created by the plane ahead of me. It was not good for a loaded aircraft flying above the water. Avram did not maneuver beyond his pilots' capabilities.

My compass indicated 180 degrees, and for a moment I thought I had become disoriented. Since when had the coast been to the south? Until that day I had been used to encountering the shore flying east. Only the Sinai coast could be to the south of us. We crossed it and began to fly over an endless ocean of yellow sand, extending to the horizon. Suddenly a road appeared. For the pilot navigating in the monochrome landscape of the desert, a road is like an oasis; it provides a point of reference. According to the map, the Ismailiya road, the central route, was the area of our target. Avram led east. If the tank convoy had already passed, we would approach from behind. The road was empty, however, and Avram broke sharply backward and west. From this point on, we knew that every vehicle before us was enemy.

"Grasshopper formation, transfer fuel selector over to a full tank. Arm bombs. Activate weapons systems. I want good hits, and watch your partner's tail." Avram's voice was quiet and confident.

I checked my fuel gauge. My right tank was almost empty. I switched the fuel lever to my left tank, armed my bombs' fuses, and unlocked the safeties on my rockets and machine guns. In the distance rose a cloud of dust.

"The convoy is ahead of us. Get some distance so that we can surprise them from the side. From this moment on, it's every man for himself."

Avram opened his engine, increased speed, and headed off into the distance. I hung close to him. You don't leave your leader and you don't lag behind, especially going into battle.

We charged in from the south, perpendicular to the convoy. The convoy comprised new Soviet T-34 tanks, along with munitions and supply trucks. Each of us had a tank in our gunsights, a hypnotizing spectacle that was approaching with lightning speed.

In training we had learned to release the burning napalm ahead of the target and immediately pull on the stick. At incredible speed the tank grew larger and larger in my gunsights. I released and pulled. With the slightest of delays, the Mustang would have hit the tank. The wing lifted up. Hearing the explosion, I could see the flames of the tank below, in the center of the fire.

Grasshopper attacked in an open formation. Avram led us to the center of the convoy, and six blazes burned below us. We circled and descended again, this time lower. This second bombing run took out another six tanks. The convoy was stopped. Soldiers began to run in every direction, some of them writhing in flames. I swallowed my saliva, and readied myself for the strafing runs using rockets and my six .50-caliber machine guns. Who ever said that a pilot's war is clean and free from human contact? This nightmare would pursue me for years.

The Egyptians did not give up. Whoever had not been injured and had a weapon in his hand began firing on the planes. This included the antiaircraft guns they towed with them, machine guns, and even personal weapons. This was a surprise. They took advantage of our low flight. From the ground, one can kill the pilot of a low-flying aircraft even with an ordinary bullet. The next run to rocket the trucks was carefully calculated. We descended vertically and at an angle and broke higher, the best way to escape the explosions caused by our rockets. Explosions of crates of ammunition on several of the trucks sent scraps of metal flying, nearly hitting us. While the convoy did not return fire, the ack-ack continued even after the final run, in which we riddled it with machine gun fire.

Grasshopper turned home overland, the quickest and shortest route. I felt emptiness, not joy and not sadness. Perhaps even a bit of frustration. The expectations had kept me close to the clouds, but the war had lassoed me to the ground, too close to the fire, blood, and death.

On the return flight, over the desert at medium altitude, we had a long hour to ponder. We kept our distance from Abu-Aweigila and the battle taking place there. Our eyes, searching for enemy aircraft, did not notice the danger lurking below. A dark and quiet patch of desert suddenly began to shower us with antiaircraft fire. Avram was surprised. We spread out, and regrouped after a minute, when the flashes had disappeared.

"Grasshopper One from Three. I'm hit." It was my partner, Uri Schlessinger. He lost altitude and speed and disengaged from the formation. I stayed close to him, trying to see where he had been hit and the extent of the damage. I saw nothing.

"Stay with him," Avram told me on the radio in open language as he distanced himself, leading the rest of the formation with him.

I asked Uri where he had been hit and what had happened to him. He mumbled unintelligibly. There was no question that he had been injured and might be losing consciousness. I called out for him to bail out, but he did not respond. We approached Nitzana. I said to him on the radio, "We are crossing the border. We're in our own territory."

Uri descended to one thousand feet, an altitude at which one does not parachute. He turned the plane and said, "I'm executing an emergency landing."

I felt relieved, believing that Uri would be okay, but when I looked forward, my hopes dimmed. Before us were the swampy sands of Chalutza. I shouted to him to change direction, but he apparently did not hear, and crash-landed in the dunes. I did not see him get out. At least the aircraft had not burned, I thought to myself, and I rushed to the closest base, near Be'er Sheva. On the way, I informed the flight controller of the emergency landing.

At Yemen Field, the emergency base of the Harvard squadron, there was only one paved runway. The Mustang landed easily. I notified the flight inspector of Uri's location, and did not move until I saw the Piper with the doctor take off.

"Our squadron commander was also shot down. He was killed," the inspector told me.

Dan Tolkowsky was on the runway. He had come to encourage the squadron. When he saw me, he jumped onto the Mustang's wing and requested a live description of the bombing of the Egyptian column. "Your story is important to me," the commander-in-chief said, sounding apologetic. "Until now I have been living on the teleprinters and radio frequencies of the formation leaders. Believe me that I would give it all up to fly with you."

I respected him then, and he remains one of a small group of those for whom I still have respect.

After telling him the story, I closed my canopy and took off to Tel Nof. On the way, I heard the Piper report that Uri Schlessinger had been found dead in his cockpit.

The Egyptian column was trapped between Bir Gafgafa (Refidim) and Bir Hama, and never reached the Sixth Brigade to provide support. The defenders of Abu-Aweigila and Umm-Katef, who commanded the central route to Suez, were abandoned to their fates. The Third Armored Brigade, which set out from El Arish to help them, also did not reach its goal. Ezer Weizman and Moti Hod joined the Ouragan force that halted it. From the morning, the Egyptian reinforcements were battered with 110 bombing sorties by formations of Ouragans and Mustangs as well as Meteors and Mosquitoes. There was no precedent in the IDF for this destruction of the enemy's forces so far behind the front. The IAF sought to turn this interdiction into a method of battle, and to be the primary contractor for such actions. According to the results streaming into the Flight Control Center, there were no competitors. A significant number of the sorties were based on the intelligence information received from the pilots. Ground intelligence was not flowing freely and was hazed over by battle vagueness. In several incidents, Israeli pilots erred in this haze and attacked Israeli vehicles whose drivers had failed to paint the proper identification symbol on them.

In the Flight Control Center, a dense picture of the war had been developing since morning. The support flowing to Abu-Aweigila persuaded the head of the Southern Command, Asaf Simhoni, to execute the armored attack on the enemy positions earlier than planned. The schedule of support sorties would have to be altered accordingly, and they would have to be squeezed between the interdiction sorties. All the operational Mystères would have to be brought into the battle to provide protection for the attacking aircraft. Bands of MiGs could already be seen in the area, daring and self-confident. Compared to their appearance a day earlier, they were difficult to recognize. Eight MiG-15s had even succeeded in breaking an assault by six Ouragans on the Egyptian column, hitting one pair and causing another Ouragan to land in the sands of Chalutza. This was the IAF's most difficult day. All the squadrons were sent to battle in a tremendous effort for such a small front. There were also significant losses. Twenty-nine Israeli aircraft were hit, all of them while executing interdiction sorties. Eight of the aircraft had been lost, and some of the damaged aircraft were unable to reach their bases. More than half of the hits and all the losses were in the piston-engined squadrons, particularly among the Mustangs. Two squadron commanders had been killed.

All the damage had been from antiaircraft fire, for the Israeli planes attacking from low altitude were easy prey. The Egyptian ground troops did not give in as had the sailors on the destroyer *Ibrahim Al-Awal*, who had raised the white flag after a rocket attack. They were also not thrown into shock by the planes diving above their heads. Many of them recovered after the first run and returned strong and surprising fire from all their weapons in every situation. The Israeli pilots did not immediately grasp the severity of the danger, and did not rush to warn their comrades. The number of losses increased from hour to hour.

The Flight Control Center cut short the celebration over the shooting down of the quartet of Vampires by the Mystère squadron. Pair after pair was scrambled to cover the aircraft attacking ground targets. They remained at a high observation point to swoop down on the first formations of MiGs, which had begun to charge in from low altitude on the Israeli aircraft attacking the armored column. Though there were many chases, contact was made only twenty-four times, and only two aircraft were shot down, both by Yak Nevo.

At 0900, above Bir Hama, Yak was patrolling with Yosef Tzuk, and encountered three MiG-15s coming out of the clouds. After a fruitless five-minute battle, they began to return home. Above the sea, they met up with another Egyptian pair. Though he was low on fuel, Yak did not give up. He began to chase and rolled himself behind one of the MiGs. His first two bursts missed, and he squeezed out his third until he had closed to within two hundred meters, ripping off a piece of the MiG's wing. The Egyptian pilot attempted to land at El Arish, but crashed into the Mediterranean. At 1230 hours, the story was repeated with the same heroes, at the same place, with only the pair of MiG-15s having changed. This time the final burst was not long, and the pieces did not go flying. The shells penetrated the MiG's body, and it went into a spin. Yak saw the pilot eject, but the parachute did not open.

Such was the air activity that had forced the General Command to forbid Sharon to enter the Mitla Pass, since it could not provide him with the necessary air support. IAF headquarters objected to the division of its efforts. The number of available aircraft barely managed to execute the missions on the central route, which were already beyond what had been planned. Only traces of these activities reached the Israeli forces at the Parker Monument, and the paratroopers had yet to understand how the threat of the armored Egyptian column had suddenly dissipated.

At 1530, a quartet of Egyptian Meteors appeared over Arik Sharon's forces, with six MiG-15s covering them. They attacked the trapped Israeli force in four runs with rockets and machine guns. Seven Israelis were killed and twenty were wounded. This was the EAF's strongest attack in the war, and their daring had substantially increased during this second day of combat. The Egyptian Meteors were not dissuaded by the Israeli Ouragans that were attacking Egyptian vehicles in the western part of the pass. Because of a communications problem, the Ouragans did not hear the cry for help from the air liaison officer. In a moment of weakness, Sharon informed the Flight Control Center that the Egyptians had the upper hand in the situation. He requested air support, but was informed that it was too late. Sharon was not in a position to mark enemy locations for the Ouragans, and the IAF would not risk losing more aircraft. Toward evening, two companies of paratroopers scaled the slopes of the pass and wiped out the Egyptian forces in a hand-to-hand battle. At the conclusion of the day, 38 Israelis were dead and 120 were wounded.

That night, as Israeli transport aircraft evacuated the wounded, un-identified transport aircraft began to fly over the paratroopers. While they feared that it was a retaliatory strike by airborne Egyptian troops, it was actually a surprise party thrown by the French Nord pilots from Cyprus. They dropped packages of food, including pâté de foie gras and cigarettes.

The UN General Assembly, which had convened that night in a call for a cease-fire and a bilateral retreat, caught the IDF with only half of its work completed. Abu-Aweigila was not in their hands. The brigade meant to capture the Strait of Tiran had yet to set out from Eilat. There was almost no activity between Gaza and El Arish. The diplomatic wheels had started to turn swiftly while the action in the field was occurring in slow motion.

That night, even the air was gloomy. For the pilots of the B-17 squadron, the last remnant of the War of Independence, it seemed as if they had returned to those early days. The three heavy bombers had not moved from Ramat David since then, and had almost become museum exhibits. A dual relationship had developed between the squadron's aircrews and the youngsters on the base. While they received the respect they deserved, like venerable grandfathers, they were seen as somewhat useless. The only explanation for their presence was sentimentality of the same sort that had caused Ezer Weizman to preserve one of the Spitfires and to paint it black, flying it during ceremonies and other occasions. The announcement that the Flying Fortresses would be taking off to bomb an undisclosed target sounded inane to the youngsters.

The B-17s were the only aircraft that could fly a heavy night bombing mission. The previous evening they had been commanded to prepare to destroy the Ilyushin bombers at Cairo West and (by accident or not) to drop several bombs on the Egyptian capital. Late that evening, the flight to Cairo was canceled, and headquarters advised that a new target was on its way. They were to bomb Rafah, a closer and less memorable target. Just before 0300 hours, Yaakov "Blackie" Ben-Chaim led two Fortresses over the estimated target area. The pilots could see nothing. The Egyptian camp was shrouded in darkness. Blackie waited for the Harvards from Yemen Field, which were to illuminate the area. Two pairs were on their way, with one plane carrying bombs and the other flares. However, the pilot of the Harvard carrying the flares was struck with vertigo and could not find his way to Rafah. With half the necessary number of flares having been dropped, the area was not sufficiently illuminated. The three Harvards that had finished their work could not find their way back to Yemen Field, forty-five kilometers away. From the ground, they were advised to drop emergency flares to locate the field. The flares were dropped in the western Negev, over the headquarters of the unit that was to invade Gaza the next morning. Fearing that these were the flares to guide the Fortresses' attack, the ground unit canceled the bombing.

Not far from there, at Hatzor, jets were taking off that could exceed the speed of sound, while over Rafah, the language of the War of Independence was being spoken. Time was slipping away. Toward morning the following day, the B-17s returned to the area to bomb Gaza prior to the city's capture by ground forces. This time, with cloud cover from the previous night continuing, they lost sight of the target as well as each other. Since they were being rushed, Blackie changed direction and speed. The original plan was ruined because of the clouds, and suddenly he discovered that they were too close to each other to bomb. Any closer and they would collide. He immediately ordered a dispersal of forces. He told his partner to distance himself and to bomb the northern part of the city while Blackie himself bombed the city's south. It was useless, for only a strike on the city's center, not its suburbs, would have any effect. As they landed back at Ramat David, it was clear that they would encounter obstacles in this war that they had not in the last.

It was a hellish night for the Israeli armored and infantry brigades. Entrenched in the endless dunes, the Egyptian Sixth Brigade had not been broken during the day, even after losing its armored support. They were fully prepared for a night assault against their positions. The Egyptians fought back, and the attacking Israelis became entangled in continuous frontal attacks riddled with embarrassing mistakes. One force got lost; another became stuck in the sands; a third, with all its lights lit, drove into a minefield and became fodder for the Egyptian tanks' cannons. One Israeli brigade commander was killed, and another was removed from his position. Every force acted on its own, and the integrated attack force for which this mission had been designed existed only on paper. By morning the enemy positions were partially surrounded and stable. The IAF was called upon to add sorties to soften the Egyptian positions and to add from the air the pressure that the ground attack lacked.

At 1030 hours, I sat in my favorite Mustang, part of two quartets from the instructors' squadron, on the way to bomb Umm-Katef. In the briefing, they no longer spoke of enemy aircraft but of the dense and deadly antiaircraft fire. This time the flight was brief. Cutting across the Negev via Nitzana, we found ourselves above the target, taking care not to repeat the previous day's mistakes of confusing Israeli and enemy forces. Because of these errors, we had had several unnecessary casualties. This time the Egyptians made it easy for us. Intense fire greeted the

Mustangs, accurately revealing their positions. I started an observation run. A partially buried cannon seemed to be a fitting target for the first napalm run. I straightened out until I saw the cannon in my gunsights. At the moment I dropped the napalm bomb, a chill passed through me as I saw the machine gunner sitting on the cannon firing—at *my* 04. The question of whether to bomb or escape did not exist. My chances of survival were equal in both scenarios. In all my memory, I could not recall any exercise in which the aircraft approaches at such low altitude. The enemy, in these conditions, does not have to be a sniper but merely brave. I released my bomb on him and did not feel the cringing in my heart that I had felt a day earlier at the sight of the burning people in the tank convoy. I even felt respect for the gunner's courage. Like the heroes in a western movie, we drew simultaneously, with the plane having no advantage. The cannon erupted in flames, perhaps incinerating its gunner as well, and my 04 began to spit blood. The machine gun's bullets had pierced the oil-filled radiator in the aircraft's body. The black liquid gushed out, spraying the cockpit canopy, turning day to night. I pulled out of the dive in instrument flight at the moment when the instruments went wild. The oil-pressure gauge spun crazily. The temperature gauge climbed to the boiling point, and the engine emitted its dying sputters. I pulled up and climbed to four thousand feet. Abandoning the aircraft was merely a matter of time, and I wanted to distance myself as much as possible from the enemy's positions. When I shut down the engine and the 04 began to glide, I opened the oil-covered canopy to see the landscape. I was beyond the dunes and approaching a plateau that seemed to be a natural runway. Though still in enemy territory, it was far from their positions. I locked the safeties on all my bombs and rockets and dropped them like stones in an emergency release.

The landing on the Mustang's ski-like belly was smooth. I jumped out and ran from the aircraft. Tremendous thunder above me muted the sounds of the battle rising from over the northern hills. It was a Mustang flown by my formation mate Aryeh Fredlis, who had come out of the battle unscathed and followed the trail of smoke and oil from my 04 to see if I had been injured and where I had landed. He made sure not to approach too closely, so as not to reveal my position. Fredlis waved his wings. Since the IAF had yet to purchase rescue helicopters, I did not expect to be rescued.

I began to organize myself according to the survival training we had received in Flight Course and the topography and state of the forces in the territory that had been described to me an hour earlier by Divon, the intelligence officer. I spent some time studying the territory around me and understood that my problem would not be prolonged wandering in the desert, but my dangerous proximity to Egyptian and IDF tanks. Both sides were likely to consider a lone pilot the enemy, and fire without questions. I trusted that the bright khaki of my flight coveralls would camouflage me in the desert landscape like a chameleon. Just to be certain, I walked with my pistol in hand. My inclination was to head east toward the international border, but my calculation of the position of the forces in the territory led me south. This logic saved me much earlier than I had estimated. Under the relentless afternoon sun, I walked for two hours, resting occasionally.

Suddenly I saw clouds of dust in the distance, moving northward. If my calculations had been correct, these were tanks belonging to the Barak Brigade, Israel's First Armored Battalion, the IDF's elite. It was the only force that the intelligence officer had praised. They had outflanked the Egyptians at Abu-Aweigila and were now threatening from the rear. I placed my money on the dust and headed toward it. By the time I reached the Kusseima-to-Abu-Aweigila road, it was past noon. With not a soul in sight, I hid in a water pipe at the intersection with the canyon. After a few minutes I could hear a command car approaching. I carefully peeked out of my hiding place. The vehicle was Egyptian. It can't be, I thought to myself, for Divon had said with assurance that our forces would take the route before noon. Several hours had passed since then. Was my fate to be buried here? Another command car passed, and familiar voices penetrated to the depths of my nook.

"Moshe! Give me a couple more Pepsis." In Hebrew!

I peeked out. The vehicle was Egyptian, but the voice was Hebrew. It and the Pepsi-Cola were booty. The soda, as yet unknown in Israel, was the hit of the war. America in the Sinai. I climbed up to the road, but the command car was driving away. To attract their attention, I fired two rounds in the air. Certain that the shooter was Egyptian, Moshe and his friends sped up. I sat down by the side of the road. After fifteen minutes, I saw two command cars returning with a Sherman tank, the ancient version from the Second World War, rolling up behind them. I laid my pistol down on the road and raised my hands. I had never raised them so high. The short cannon was pointed straight at my chest.

*"Min inti?"* I was asked in Arabic. "Who are you?" The tank commander, looking out of the turret, almost caused me to burst out laughing.

"I'm Israeli," I said. "An Israeli pilot who just made an emergency landing. Why are you talking to me in Arabic?" I kept my arms raised.

The turret was lifted and the tank commander climbed out with pistol in hand.

"So why are you wearing Egyptian coveralls?"

So that's it, I thought to myself, smiling. That's what tricked them. My dark skin, the coveralls like those worn by Egyptian officers, and the pistol shots.

They took me into the command car. At battalion headquarters, I was fed and given a jeep with a driver to return to my plane to damage the communications equipment and return to the squadron. Since I was unable to remove the frequency crystals, I pulled out the entire machine, and with the heavy box on my back, I appeared six hours later at Tel Nof.

In the squadron they thought I was a ghost, for they were certain that only now, under cover of darkness, would I start to make my way home. My girlfriend received me like a gift. Ela was a soldier on the base, and that day, not long before we got married, she underwent the first test of a pilot's wife. When she had phoned the squadron to ask about me, she was answered with confused stutterings and evasive responses. She had prepared herself for the worst.

On my way to pull out the 04's vital parts, I had seen Ouragans passing overhead. I had not paid attention to the fact that they were not making their way to a defined target, but were waiting for the flight controller to direct them. Upon my return to base, I as informed that they had discovered sand and more sand, as well as large numbers of active and burned tanks; from their altitude they could not distinguish friend or foe. At that time, several Egyptian tanks were attempting to break through from Umm-Katef to the brigade's route. The tank crews of Barak were convinced that the Egyptians' goal was to disconnect the outflanking maneuver. As the Israelis prepared to stop the enemy, their air inspector pleaded for the Ouragans' help. He attempted to break in on the pilots, who were advising each other of topographical points and external guiding signs, but they did not respond. Weakness overcame the flight controller when he saw that the Ouragans had decided to return home and drop the bombs under their wings into the sea. At last light, he was relieved to find three Ouragans returning from the north. Before their eyes was a clear and inviting picture, even without help from the ground. Thirty Egyptian tanks were moving from the south with infantry units behind them. The Ouragans dropped napalm on the lead tanks, and three of them burned. The enemy force dispersed. It did not seem that the Ouragans paid much heed to the antiaircraft fire. The first jet generation in France, they actually had a survivability level greater than any other plan in the area. Their builders still preferred a solid resistant structure over speed and execution. Even the aluminum of the wings was thicker. One of the Ouragans that returned to Hatzor that day had no less than sixty bullet and fragment holes.

The Barak Brigade and the Ouragan squadron did not know of the retreat order that had been sent out that afternoon from Cairo to all Egyptian forces in the Sinai. The bombing of the airfields along the Suez Canal, which had continued relentlessly since nighttime, and the reports of the British and French war fleets sailing to the eastern Mediterranean, made clear to Egyptian President Nasser that he faced an invasion of his country. He needed every tank, cannon, and soldier in order to protect the territory west of the Suez Canal.

The area of Rafah was captured without any prior bombing. Troops from the Golani Brigade and Chaim Bar-Lev's armored brigade assaulted the enemy positions in a short coordinated attack. Twelve Mustangs from the instructors' squadron dropped napalm bombs and used their cannons to strafe the Egyptian tanks retreating from El Arish. The Egyptian forces managed to escape toward the canal. At noon the Israeli forces found El Arish to have no Egyptian military presence. Even the nearby airfield along the sandy yellow coast was silent. The airfield had been the EAF's nearest stepping-stone to Israeli territory even during the War of Independence, mere minutes' flight away. The first Spitfires to bomb Tel Aviv had originated from this base. With only the scorched remnants of aircraft along its outskirts bearing silent witness to its terroristic reputation, it no longer looked dangerous. The IAF runway crews rushed to prepare the field for the use of the liaison and transport squadrons.

The next morning, the Ouragans continued to accompany Bar-Lev's brigade in the chase of the Egyptian columns retreating toward the Suez Canal. Their losses thinned out the convoys, and the antiaircraft fire of the survivors was random and ineffective. The Israeli vehicles had to maneuver through an obstacle course of the remnants of incinerated Egyptian armor up to the line, sixteen kilometers from the canal, which Great Britain and France had established in order not to disturb their planned invasion.

Two six-inch cannons stood at Ras Natzrani, the entrance to the Strait of Tiran, behind a concrete wall. Though they were pointed toward an unseen spot in the mountains of Tiran Island, which protruded from the Red Sea, their actual target was a small strip of water between the island and Sharm-al-Sheikh, the Gulf of the Sheikh, at the southern tip of the Sinai Peninsula. Coral reefs beneath the surface of the water left only a narrow passage for ships, with no possibility of maneuvering. No sailing vessel would be able to elude the accurate fire of the guns. For more than a year they had been commanded to sink any ship, Israeli or otherwise, headed toward Eilat. This sealed the sea blockade of Israel from the Red Sea. The guns therefore became the target of a special mission, Operation Omer, and later, after its cancellation, the primary goal of the Sinai Campaign. On the afternoon of November 1, 1956, the Israeli Ninth Brigade set out, traveling three hundred kilometers overland to Sharm-al-Sheikh to capture the Strait of Tiran. Anticipating Israeli aggression, the Egyptians had retreated after four days according to the order received from Cairo. When the Ninth Brigade arrived after an arduous journey, they found Sharm-al-Sheikh to be unoccupied.

As the brigade was making its way there, the General Command was confused, just as it had been prior to the events at the Mitla Pass. A Meteor from the reconnaissance squadron was sent before noon, and discovered a manned Egyptian position. Did this mean that the retreat had been delayed, or that Nasser would not willingly surrender the Strait of Tiran? The photographs could not explain that the delay was caused by a lack of transportation; the Egyptian forces were waiting to be evacuated via the sea. The General Command felt that Nasser was holding his ground, and ordered IAF headquarters to bomb the area. When the Ninth Brigade reached the target, it would not have enough time or strength to wage a prolonged battle.

Over the course of an hour, thirty aircraft took off from Israeli air bases toward the cannons at Ras Natzrani. They included Mustangs, Mosquitoes, and B-17s from Ramat David; Mustangs from Tel Nof; and Ouragans and Mystères from Hatzor. Though the target had been at the top of the priority list for quite some time, the entire mission was rushed. Having chosen to attack a target beyond their normal range, the IAF's planning was superficial, its intelligence faulty, and its preflight briefings lacking. What they told the pilots about the antiaircraft facilities around Sharm-a-Sheikh was minimal. When the truth was learned, it was too late for several of them.

*November 2, 1956, Afternoon: The Southern Tip of the Sinai Peninsula* **B**enny Peled did not recall anyone warning of such heavy and dense antiaircraft fire. And if the commander of the Mystère squadron was not ready, what would those following him in their less sophisticated and more vulnerable piston-engined aircraft do?

Benny was leading the first of two quartets that had set out from Hatzor. He had always liked to fly with someone from the sextet that had received the first Mystères in France. Danny Shapira was leading the second quartet. This time he had only Dror Avneri and Yaakov Morgan. Number Four in his formation was young and new to the squadron. A daring and wily prankster, Ronen (Pecker) Ran was the type who settled into the cockpit and became one with the aircraft's soul. It was no coincidence that he had been pushed ahead to the elite Mystères.

Benny dived to release his rockets on the military camp, and entered the dense antiaircraft fire. Everything happened within seconds. The cockpit filled with smoke. He tried to climb, and suddenly felt very real burning fire. Although Benny would one day be commander-in-chief of the IAF, he was considered a completely disorganized pilot at this stage of his career. He flew without gloves and with his sleeves rolled up. You could not fly frightened, he felt. But the fire *was* frightening, and it burned his exposed arms, eyebrows, and eyelashes. He had to eject. One of the early models with no automation, the ejector seat did not make things easy. He had to disconnect himself manually and open the parachute by hand. All this took too much time. By the time he ejected, he was at an altitude of less than one and a half kilometers. As soon as the parachute had opened, he slammed into the ground. In addition to the burns on his hands and face, he had a sprained ankle.

He tried to extricate himself from the parachute, but this was not an easy task with the strong northern afternoon wind. He managed to remove it, but was unable to disconnect the rescue kit. The wind filled the canopy and dragged the parachute away. At first he was furious with himself. The rescue kit was the ejecting pilot's survival pack. Without it, his chances of survival, particularly in the desert, were minimal. The next moment he realized that the problem had saved him from being captured and perhaps from being killed. Two Egyptian soldiers from the attacked camp had seen him fall, and had been sent to bring him in. Believing that he was being dragged along by the parachute, they chased it far away from him. Benny hopped on his healthy foot and hid in the nearby hills. A quartet of Mosquitoes was sent to protect him. For half an hour, they hit anything that moved or dared approach him. Benny had only a loaded pistol and a half-empty package of cigarettes—no food and no water. At least it was not hot. Having only a limited knowledge of the area, he tried to orient himself. The flight map had been an aerial photograph, and the faulty preflight briefing was the reason he was here and not home. Looking around, he decided to climb down to the nearby canyon toward nightfall. He certainly had time to think, particularly about the strange combination of events. Of all people, it was he, the squadron commander and the most veteran jet pilot in the IAF, sitting in the first Mystère, the first jet in the IAF, who had been shot down by antiaircraft fire.

In the meantime, he had company. He could see a pair of soldiers approaching, and he curled himself up behind a sand dune. Involved in their conversation, they did not notice him. The sun began to set. Benny attempted to stand up and hop to the canyon, but could not. The ankle had swollen during the long rest, and every light step was agonizing. He began to crawl along the ground, which was covered with thin, sharp gravel. The scraping against his scorched arms increased the pain. Near the canyon's slopes, he began to feel more confident, though he did not know why. He believed that someone would come to rescue him. Not because he was Benny Peled or because of what he represented. His case was different from my incident in the desert, in that he had already heard all the details and had learned from my experience. Such stories travel fast. The IAF had yet to develop theories of rescue, and had no helicopters, or radio beacons that could be given to pilots. However, an awareness of the need to rescue downed pilots had begun to develop in the light squadron. If the Pipers could rescue sailors from ships that ran aground, how could they abandon a pilot? The Pipers were vulnerable, though, and limited to daylight hours and areas where they could land.

Conditions were better for Benny. The Pipers that had been

accompanying the Ninth Brigade flew back and forth along the entire route and encountered no resistance. The location of his ejection, as his formation-mates had marked, was on the southern edge of the route, north of the antiaircraft line at Ras-Natzrani. He believed that they would come to search. Whether they would find him or could manage to land and take off were dependent on the territory and luck.

At 1700 hours he saw a Piper diving behind him. Avraham Greenbaum had spent two hours with the brigade, and had then been called upon to continue on to Ras-Natzrani to search for two pilots who had parachuted. On the rocky plateau, near the coast, he saw two figures. Descending, he identified two Egyptian soldiers. He dropped down even lower, a meter over their heads. They fell to the ground and then ran away. After circling the canyon, he saw a waving white strip. All that remained with Benny from his parachute was the sleeve with which he was signaling. Greenbaum thought it was a trap, and turned to circle again, closer to the slope. Benny heard him shout "Weidenfeld?" and waved joyously with the sleeve. The IAF was still faithful to the original family names. Greenbaum landed in the ravine and sent his scout to rescue Benny.

It would not be easy. The scout was a big man, and Benny could not be described as a weight-watcher. Loading Benny on his back, the scout had trouble carrying their combined weight of two hundred kilograms. Greenbaum tried to help them, and wondered how to get both of them into the aircraft. Somehow they managed to push Benny onto the stretcher in the rear of the Piper, feet in the tail, head on the backseat, under the scout. Greenbaum prepared for takeoff and prayed that the Piper would get off the ground with three passengers instead of two, including the additional heavy communications equipment they had used with the brigade. He squeezed the engine and the stick, and the Piper responded. They took off after an almost endless taxi. An hour later they landed in Eilat.

A Dakota returned Benny to Hatzor. Danny Shapira informed him that his Mystère had also been hit, but had managed to return. Greenbaum was decorated by the chief-of-staff. Benny did not even consider complaining about the failure to mention the antiaircraft fire in the preflight briefing. That was the spirit of the IAF. Once on a mission, you were on your own.

· · · ·

The hasty but heavy bombing of Ras-Natzrani occurred earlier than planned, for the Ninth Brigade was not supposed to enter Sharm-al-Sheikh for another day or two. The General Command was in a panic. Suddenly it seemed that the cease-fire would begin, and that Israel's important strategic goal of the war, control of the Strait of Tiran, would not be achieved. That day the General Command decided on a series of rapid actions that could be taken before the arrival of the Ninth Brigade. The paratrooper brigade sitting idle in the Mitla Pass would be commanded to aid in the capture of Sharm-al-Sheikh from the direction of the Gulf of Suez. Another force, commanded by Raful, would be sent overland via the mountains to the oil city of Ras-Sudar, and from there southward. Two units, under the command of Mota Gur, would take the bridgeheads in an airborne mission.

Thus the transport squadron's Dakotas returned to the landing strip at the Parker Monument to gather the 175 paratroopers who would be used for the mission. The troops regrouped at Tel Nof, strapped on new parachutes and the necessary equipment, and departed in the afternoon in seven Dakotas on the return trip to the Sinai. Six of the Dakotas were to drop their load of seventy-five commandos six kilometers north of Ras-Natzrani until the arrival of the forces from the two gulfs. The other four Dakotas would drop one hundred troops over the airfield at A-Tur, which served the small port town on the coast of the Suez Gulf not far from Sharm-al-Sheikh. From this point on, it would function as a logistical base for supplies and the landing of additional troops. The operation was well under way when the Dakota leader suddenly saw a Meteor flying next to him, trying to attract his attention. It was a friend. The pilot, Mordechai Lavon, a flying emissary of the General Command, had come to inform them from short range of a change in the plan. The Upper Command and the Flight Control Center did not want to convey the information over the long-range communication frequencies for fear of being overheard. There would be no drop at Sharm-al-Sheikh, Lavon announced. All the paratroopers would be dropped at A-Tur. The three Dakotas did not split off, but instead followed the leader of the quartet. At last light, the paratroopers jumped over the empty airfield.

By evening, thanks to the IAF runway unit, it was already a functioning airport with a control tower and ground services. There was nothing to remind them of the landings at the Mitla Pass. Even an El Al

Constellation that was recruited to land personnel and supplies felt at home there.

That night the UN General Assembly was to decide on the cease-fire. The General Command wanted its ground units to be in Sharm-al-Sheikh that day, but one of them had only come two-thirds of the way. That evening a Dakota dropped leaflets over Sharm-al-Sheikh, proposing surrender. Retreat using the overland routes was blocked, and the routes of escape via the sea had been sealed that afternoon. An Egyptian transport ship that had appeared a day earlier opposite Ras-Natzrani had been sunk by two formations of Mystères from Hatzor. Menachem Bar led the first quartet, which scored direct hits on the vessel with rockets. While it was sinking, an unexpected destroyer appeared and began to fire.

Menachem's formation was running low on fuel, so they passed the target on to Danny Shapira's formation, which had come to replace them. When they saw the warship attempting to escape at full speed, the Mystères attacked immediately, without bothering to identify the target. Not dissuaded by the strong antiaircraft fire, they fired rocket clusters in a wide arc, hitting the command bridge, the antenna, the stern, and much water. Other than a small fire, the damage to the ship was not significant.

Its owners did not demand compensation after the war, for the destroyer, the HMS *Crane*, belonged to the British fleet. The haughtiness that the British exhibited toward the Israeli liaison officers in the Joint Command headquarters of Operation Musketeer grew from this episode.

*November 4, 1956, Morning*          *T*he Israeli liaison officers had to leave the Cyprus headquarters in the middle of the war, and were therefore spared the unpleasantness involved in explanations and apologies. Their mere presence bothered several of the British Army officers, even without the IAF's attack on a destroyer in Her Majesty's Navy. The British, who, eight years earlier, had still referred to the Israelis as "natives," now had trouble accepting the surprising accomplishments of the IDF in the Sinai.

While the French did not abandon either of their allies, they capitalized on the Israeli rift with the British. The French squadrons, which were being hosted on the Israeli air bases, acted as they pleased. Col. Morris Fredrigee, commander of the French forces in Israel, could not bear the sadness of his young subordinates who had not participated in the war. How long could fighter pilots who had never fought in their lives sit with their legs crossed or "press" Israel's skies, flying useless patrols looking for Egyptian aircraft that would not dare approach? The Israeli pilots were even getting the first combat experience in flying the French Air Force's gem, the Mystère IV.

The French flew the protective flights over Israel using the Israeli Mystères for which the IAF had not yet managed to train crews. At this stage, though, with the French and British squadrons taking off from Cyprus to attack the Egyptian airfields along the Suez Canal, there was no need for them. No one would notice if the French aircraft stationed in Israel made their own little war on the way to the canal. Thus Colonel Fredrigee proposed that his pilots participate in the bombing of the Egyptian convoys retreating from the Sinai. IAF headquarters informed him that he was more than welcome. They could also bomb the Egyptians beyond the sixteen-kilometer line. In exchange, Colonel Fredrigee would be responsible for destroying the Ilyushin bombers stationed at the Luxor airfield in Upper Egypt. This had been the bombers' base before the war, but they had been moved north to Cairo West at the war's outset. On the eve of the bombing of the Suez Canal airfields, the Ilyushins had attacked Israel twice with ineffective solo runs. Afterward they had returned to seek shelter in Luxor, from whence they could launch retaliatory show bombings. The colonel did not surrender easily, but the intense pressure forced him to consult with his headquarters in Cyprus. The destruction of the Ilyushins could also save French forces if and when they invaded.

The next morning the attack began. The IAF presented the French with a prepared plan, including intelligence information, operational plans, and everything else necessary. The mission was to have been executed at the beginning of the Sinai Campaign, but had been canceled after the Israeli-French accord. The intelligence information had been acquired three days prior to the outbreak of the war, and no bombers had been found at the nearby airfields. A Mosquito from the reconnaissance squadron was sent to look for the Ilyushins in Luxor. The navigator, Elisha Gal-On (Julian), who was experienced at such flights, had yet to visit Luxor, the city of Pharaonic palaces and temples. The flight lasted four hours, and using a telescope, Julian easily identified the thirty Ilyushin IL-28 bombers from an altitude of ten kilometers. On the night before the attack, the photographs were passed on to the French pilots.

Slightly before 0600 hours, the first wave of twelve F-84 Thunderstreak fighter-bombers took off from Lod. At 1120 hours, another sextet took off. They found the Ilyushins exposed and dispersed on the runways, and attacked them with rockets and machine guns. The photographs revealed eighteen burned Ilyushins. The remaining twelve had fled to Saudi Arabia.

On November 5, the B-17 Flying Fortresses proved that they had one advantage over the youngsters. Whereas the piston- and jet-engined fighter aircraft were forced to attack quickly and turn home because of the limited fuel in their tanks, the old bombers breathed easily. The planes remained in the air six hours and spent much of their time over Sharm-al-Sheikh, this time without problems. Their photographs of the area's width and breadth explained the resistance the approaching Israeli forces had encountered. The Egyptians had not retreated, and were prepared for battle. Although they had retreated from Ras-Natzrani, they had taken fortified positions in a belt around Sharm-al-Sheikh, in the rocks that overlooked the routes entering the area.

The Israeli bombings were renewed according to the photographs, and the instructors' squadron followed the directions of the air inspectors of the Ninth Brigade and the patrols of the light squadron, striking at every position that blocked the progress of the Israeli armored vehicles. The next morning, the final bombings were requested. The Mustangs began the attack, with backup support provided by the Mystères. The Egyptian forces began to recede as the uncontested Mustangs struck repeatedly. Early in the war, their troops had lost any hope of receiving support from the Egyptian Air Force, which had been either bombed or grounded.

Following the morning bombing, they finally gave up, 160 hours after the start of the war. The victory flyover was held at Sharm-al-Sheikh on November 6, the day after its capture. The Sharm-al-Sheikh airfield, the third in the Sinai, was added to the network of airfields under the control of the IAF. The chief of staff was one of the first passengers to land there. He carried with him a message from David Ben-Gurion to the hundreds of fighters who stood before him unshaven and covered in dust. For the first time, they heard from the Prime Minister and Minister of Defense that "Yotvat, known as Tiran, which until 1,400 years ago was an independent Jewish state, will return to be part of the third Israeli kingdom." The commander of the southern front, Asaf Simhoni, stood that afternoon on the dais next to Lt. Gen. Moshe Dayan. Afterward he took off in a Piper to Be'er Sheva. In the skies over the Arava Desert, the light aircraft was swept into Jordan and crashed, killing its passengers. The Jordanians claimed it had been an accident. It was the final loss of the war and one of its most painful.

That morning the giant flotilla comprising the British and French fleets neared the shores of Port Said, and the Musketeer forces began to invade the northern entry to the Suez Canal. A day earlier, as the Egyptian commander at Sharm-al-Sheikh announced his surrender to IDF forces, two battalions from the British and French armies had parachuted onto the edge of the Canal and captured the bridgehead. Nasser ordered ships sunk in the canal in order to block it from passage. The two European powers did not progress beyond the bridgeheads. The eighty thousand soldiers, two thousand vehicles, five hundred aircraft, and 130 warships, including seven aircraft carriers, were useless. Even their professional command and centuries of military tradition could not help matters. The generals were controlled from afar, and acted as they had during the Second World War. Their plans rested on faulty intelligence, which overestimated the Egyptian forces and did not consider the element of time in a modern war. They began with prolonged and exaggerated air bombings. Though their airdrop was successful, it was in a poor location and was discontinued. The large and complicated operation was a total failure within less than two days.

The joy of victory in Israel lasted only one day. On November 8, the UN decided on a cease-fire, withdrawal of combatant forces, and the placing of an international force in the Sinai. U.S. President Dwight Eisenhower, who was not a friend of Israel's, was elected to a second term. The Soviet Union suppressed the people's uprising in Hungary, and its Prime Minister, Nicholai Bulganin, threatened Ben-Gurion with Israel's destruction. Similar threats of missile attacks on London and Paris were conveyed to Israel's European partners. According to France and Great Britain, Israel was playing the role of antagonist despite having been guaranteed diplomatic support less than three weeks earlier. But France and Great Britain were now in greater trouble. While Israel had a victorious military and had acquired a broad and strategically defensive territory, the French and British armies were humiliated, and all they had acquired was a small and worthless strip of water. Under pressure, Ben-Gurion announced an Israeli withdrawal.

Dan Tolkowsky estimated that the Soviets would not be able to act on their threats. The IAF meanwhile had its own reasons to be disappointed. It had not been given the opportunity to prove itself and to test the central goals of Tolkowsky's modern air force. Defense of the nation's skies had been placed in the hands of the French pilots, and destruction of the enemy's aircraft on the ground as an opening phase of war had not been permitted. In retrospect, however, this was for the best. For two days, until the bombing of the Suez airfields, the Israeli pilots had the opportunity to prove their superiority in air combat against the new Soviet aircraft. In fifteen dogfights, the ratio of downed aircraft was seven to zero in favor of Israel. These included three MiG-15s and four Vampires. The twelve aircraft that the IAF lost were brought down by the deadly fire from the ground. For nearly all the pilots, this was a first encounter with antiaircraft fire. As in a duel, they found themselves dive-bombing into cannons and machine guns. Their persistence in achieving their objective succeeded in accomplishing the third goal of the IAF, fire support for the ground forces. This was little recompense for the goals they were not permitted to realize. Of 1,900 Israeli sorties flown during the war, 490 were attacks on ground targets.

The division of labor among the squadrons was clearly defined. The Mosquito and Mustang squadrons bombed and strafed. This work was shared by the jet Ouragans and Meteors. The Mystère squadron was reserved for interception and backing up of the vulnerable piston-engined aircraft. The only Mystère to be shot down was executing a rare attack mission. The majority of support was in interdiction as well as in attack and destruction of enemy forces on their way to the front. The IAF shortened and eased the fighting in Abu-Aweigila and Rafah. The ongoing support to the ground troops was particularly decisive in the battle for Sharm-al-Sheikh. Approximately four hundred vehicles and tanks, one-fifth of what Egypt had in the Sinai, were hit from the air primarily in interdictions and attacks on the retreating convoys. With all the benefit gained from the piston-engined squadrons, they were used only because a more modern replacement was not available. This was their final war. The fourth goal of the IAF, providing transport services, nearly became the symbol of the war with the opening phase of the airdrop and the continued flights of the transport squadrons that supplied the units isolated in enemy territory.

The war also revealed many problems. The IAF's flight control network, which was meant to guarantee flexibility and maximum use of forces, was still in its infancy. Owing to a lack of long-range radar systems and an abundance of communications problems, there were repeated breakdowns in the passage of information between the air and ground forces. In several instances, Israeli aircraft attacked their own ground forces. The intelligence network stumbled along in the confusion of battle, and the flow of information among the branches of the military was not fluid or reliable. Most of the aircraft were hit or lost because of a lack of advance warning regarding the strength or location of antiaircraft fire.

Despite this, and with the balance of forces so weighted against Israel, the accomplishments were tremendous. While the Egyptian Air Force was completely composed of jets, Israel had primarily piston-engined aircraft. With enough pilots to man only a third of the Mystère IVs that it had acquired on the eve of the war, Israel was forced to use the French pilots to fill these positions. This was the first war in which the IAF, including the foreign volunteers who remained from the War of Independence, communicated in Hebrew. No longer fighting a war of lone pilots, the IAF functioned as an operative force, organized and methodical, in wings and squadrons, with calculated procurements and professional training. Having fought between the two wars for its position and birthright, it was strengthened by the Sinai Campaign, which proved that a strong air force was vital for security.

Tolkowsky insisted on basing the force on a large standing army that could counter an aggressive enemy and cover for the call-up of reserves. The Israeli-initiated Sinai Campaign made such measures unnecessary. However, the conflict emphasized the importance of a rapid, flexible, and powerful air force in a battle against a new enemy. It also reinforced the element of time. The course of the war was measured in days in a strip of land to which the world was highly sensitive. Even a poor nation, relying on a reserve army, cannot allow itself a prolonged war. The IAF successfully showed it could quickly win battles and a war. Its critics, who resented its pretentiousness and were skeptical of the tremendous budgets that it requested for sophisticated equipment, were forced to admit their error.

It was clear that theories of combat would have to be developed not only from others' experience but according to the personnel, battle conditions, and equipment in the possession of Israel and its air force. Operation Musketeer served as an example of failure; it taught any pilot who idolized such experienced and well-equipped air forces as those of France and Great Britain that a lack of planning, professionalism, and dedication meant certain doom. Ezer Weizman was there and understood this. As the next commander-in-chief of the IAF, he knew that he would have to translate this lesson into action.

On March 7, 1957, the IDF withdrew from the Sinai in exchange for written guarantees of free sailing to Eilat and the placement of a UN police force along the borders. These arrangements would not be enough to prevent another war, ten years later. Although the IAF had emerged victorious, it realized that the Sinai Campaign was merely the end of the beginning.

# 4 The Quiet Decade, 1957–1967

$T$he small and final armored Israeli column evacuating El Arish in early March 1957 was a depressing sight. IDF Chief of Staff Moshe Dayan had announced that he would be the last one to abandon the Sinai Peninsula and would mount the final half-track to depart. About to leave the airfield, Ezer Weizman pleaded with Dayan to fly with him and shorten the agony. Dayan squeezed into the Piper, and Ezer departed sadly. The El Arish airfield, Egypt's stepping-stone to Tel Aviv, mere minutes' flight away, was being returned to the Egyptian Air Force. The suspicions on the eve of the Sinai Campaign, and the order that had forbidden the IAF from bombing El Arish now mixed with the sense of confinement that prevailed in the region following the cease-fire. Would it again be necessary to sneak in long-distance flights to the Strait of Tiran, or to teach the flight cadets navigation between Haifa and Cyprus?

Less than a month after the war, Ezer transferred command of Hatzor to Moti Hod, a process that made Ezer, for the first time, a candidate to head the IAF. He was chosen to command the Air Division of IAF headquarters, the second most important role in the force and one that led naturally to the position of commander-in-chief. Ezer was not guaranteed this inheritance, however, and was more surprised than anyone else by Tolkowsky's choice of him. In the upper echelons of the IAF, there was no dissonance as great as that between him and Dan Tolkowsky. The latter, a cool-tempered gentleman, calm and solid and never parting from his slide rule, had placed a charismatic and impulsive youngster, who had a reputation for unruliness, in a position of responsibility. The paperwork, which included development work, operations, budgeting, and training plans in meetings and conferences, overwhelmed Ezer. In the shadow of a meticulous commander, everything around Ezer was infused with a sense of order and method.

Ezer had been chosen for the position prior to the Sinai Campaign, and though the battles delayed his appointment, they made it all the more crucial. He had learned several lessons from the war. He must rid the IAF of the last piston-engined fighter aircraft, and increase the rate of absorption of the existing jets and newer models being purchased. More and better aircrews had to be trained. The systems of command had to be improved. The next war would be different. The Sinai Campaign had been the illustrious peak of the Tolkowsky period, but also its epilogue. Though he had survived conflicts with two IDF chiefs of staff, the General Command and the Ministry of Defense had grown weary of him. In the debates over the 1957–58 budget, Ben-Gurion hinted to Tolkowsky to stop being "Air Force–minded" and to start being "state-minded." Though he had shown that air superiority was the primary condition needed for victory, the IAF could not stand at the head of the national priority list. Tolkowsky and his new deputy believed that a ready air force must protect its aircraft and equipment in appropriate structures and guarantee its personnel, no less valuable, good food and pleasant accommodations. However, the Israeli government faced a choice. They could build runways and grand quarters for the pilots, or they could pave the Eilat road to build the southern port and lay an oil pipeline from Eilat to Ashkelon.

The defense network found Ezer a more difficult partner than Tolkowsky in assessing the needs of the IAF. In every operational discussion or inter-branch exercise held during his command of the Air Division, Ezer would repeatedly emphasize, to the point of absurdity, that it was preferable to invest in aircraft and pilots than in traditional military apparatus. He pretended that he did not understand why the commanders of the armored corps yearned for more sophisticated tanks, if several squadrons could destroy the enemy's armored corps while they were still on their way to the battlefield. Ezer also proved that an airdrop was the quickest and most efficient method for landing an infantry brigade on enemy territory. He strove to contain his radical ideas so that he would not ruin his chances of receiving command of the IAF. His trial period lasted twenty months. In the meantime, Chaim Laskov replaced Moshe Dayan as chief of staff. Ezer began to feel his chances were diminishing. Laskov had been commander-in-chief of the IAF and was a friend of the family. All his weaknesses were now exposed.

Ezer would remember the seven minutes spent in the company of Tolkowsky and Laskov as sadistic torture. As he describes the meeting in his book, *On Eagle's Wings,* the commander-in-chief "first milked me dry, drop by drop, with perfect Tolkowskian meticulousness." Ezer was shocked when Tolkowsky ultimately recommended him. The transfer of command took place on July 25, 1958, and the thirty-four-year-old Ezer Weizman replaced Dan Tolkowsky. As commander-in-chief of the IAF, Ezer now commanded people as well as machines. The person is the core, he would often say, and the weapons are only a means of expression. He would add that aircraft, though powerful in the air, were helpless on the ground. The tank can at least continue firing even after losing its tread. To fully utilize its air power, the IAF needed skilled pilots. And, ultimately, the teamwork and determination of those pilots would lead to success. Ezer remembered Modi Alon leading the first fighter squadron. Alon's authority rested on personal example and interpersonal communication that had no need for commands. Ezer would have no problem with the pilots, who saw him as a walking legend. The difficulty would be in the relationships with the deputy commanders, a community of noncommissioned officers in the technical branches and in the maintenance and service units. He wanted to inspire them to execute their duties out of understanding of the common goal and identification with it, without feeling that they were being pressured. Ezer won their hearts through humble, friendly treatment. He knew them all personally, and always expressed interest in what was happening in their families as well. Ezer was constantly open to straight talk. Warm and humorous, he knew how to handle overt and relevant criticism. He believed in the simple wisdom that workers are people and that human treatment can turn a large tribe into an intimate family that will loyally follow its leader.

After nearly two years of quiet on Israel's southern borders, the action moved to the north. Egypt and Syria established a diplomatic alliance—the United Arab Republic. Syrian outposts in the Golan Heights, overlooking Galilee, the Hula Valley, and the Jordan River Valley, attacked Israeli farmers and shelled civilian targets every time the residents tried to work any of their land. The tension was local and controlled. No one entered the disputed areas without military accompaniment. The rare exchanges of fire were far from Israeli cities and did not upset the apparent air of peace that had settled on the country.

Ezer encountered greater difficulties dealing with these incidents than with any other problem during his command. He appointed a new intelligence officer who based estimations of the enemy's power not only on the number of pilots and aircraft, but also on their skill level. Operation Musketeer had failed because the allies' espionage had been frightened by the MiGs. They had been unfamiliar with the enemy pilots and their abilities. Absorption of new aircraft was also well organized. These included the Super Mystère, an improved version of the Mystère, some of whose sophistications were the results of lessons learned during the Sinai Campaign or were explicitly designed for the IAF. Its speed was one and a quarter times the speed of sound. Its improvements included an afterburner, two 30-millimeter cannons whose range meters worked on radar, and a more sophisticated bomb sight. The IAF also acquired the twin-engined Vautour, the jet replacement of the Mosquito. Though it was also a fighter plane, it was primarily a long-range bomber (2,000 miles) with a bomb-load capacity of four tons, and sophisticated equipment for night attacks. It provided the long attack arm that the IAF had been lacking.

The IAF became stronger but smaller, for Ezer was unable to man all the new aircraft. Ironically, the best pilots left just as the need for additional aircrew at a high level became greater than ever. Among those who departed were the kibbutzniks, the cream of the crop. The kibbutzim objected to extending their members' service, and limited the number of young men volunteering for the Flight Course. Even after Ezer attempted to convince them that service in the IAF was as Zionist as working the land, a number of the kibbutz pilots still departed. But many remained, in greater proportion in the IAF than in Israel's overall population. Ezer began a public-relations campaign to increase the number of flight candidates and adopted the slogan "The Best to Flight."

The mechanics and the maintenance and munitions personnel, who had experienced his fair treatment at Ramat David, understood and did not protest. The conflict erupted in academia. The intellectuals, far removed from the air force experience, saw this as an attempt to impose an arrogant military aristocracy on the nation. Ezer searched everywhere for as many young and talented candidates as possible, men with high motivation from whom he could create a top team that would bring a quick and decisive victory. He would not settle for polishing the current team and promoting commanders according to their skills. The Flight Course was the key to success, and he therefore set new, more demanding standards. Ezer refused to compromise on quality for the sake of quantity, even after one course provided only one graduate.

Between the time I was a flight cadet in the early 1950s and my return as an instructor, I did not sense the revolution that had taken place in the Flight School. Most pilots felt that the school was an "exile unit," and counted the days until they could return to their squadrons. This was not the institution I had encountered as a flight cadet, and in my years as an instructor, it changed its style and content. In the early 1950s, the Flight Course was otherworldly, in the worst sense of the word. The instructors were foreigners who were signed to short-term contracts. English, which we had not bothered to study well, was the language of instruction, and we even ridiculed it as the language of the rulers of our country not so long ago. The instructors were haughty, and often scolded or degraded students. Breakdowns in communication resulted in expulsions. Theories of training, like aircraft themselves, had undergone subtle changes since the Second World War. The instruction was not methodical, and only rarely were a cadet's mistakes explained to him so that he could understand and improve his execution. Eventually, Israeli instructors replaced the foreigners.

The professional vocabulary was finally in Hebrew, and the thinking, instruction, and evaluation were altered to reflect the Israeli worldview. Though a framework and a direction already existed, sophisticated or consistent theories were nonexistent. Israeli individualism was at its heyday. Every instructor had his own truth, with personally developed experience and methods leading to the creation of a personal relationship between him and the cadet. Nevertheless, the instruction staff shared experiences and lessons among themselves. The common desire not to resemble the instructors of the past taught them to focus on the cadet and his problems. I, for example, quickly understood the importance of the focus of a cadet's attention, and did not burden him with unnecessary talk when he was busy executing a maneuver. I knew he would not hear a word anyway. I learned that the importance of the personal model of the instructor lay in a correct presentation of the exercise, and through letting the cadet share the steering so he could understand what was happening.

A pilot's character was as important as his mechanical ability. Stubbornness, chance, and emotion played a significant role. Ezer and the commanders of the Flight School persistently sought strictly professional sorting and training, a rich program of learning, and impartial evaluations.

I had volunteered for the Flight Course. I had shown up, expressed interest, and signed up. The medical and psychotechnical sorting process was strict but not meticulous. My training was based on ground studies, and the primary course of the Stearman included aerobatics, navigation, and night flight. It also included military exercises and the basic and advanced combat courses on the Harvard. I had received operational training on the Spitfire only after I got my wings. In the process that emerged in the early 1960s, only the skeleton of this earlier program remained.

The first and most revolutionary change took place even before the initial sorting. The IAF no longer relied solely on volunteers. It seemed a shame to lose those who did not volunteer only because they didn't know that they had been blessed with possessing the criteria for the Flight Course. Since that time, the IAF has searched out all those with the appropriate statistics based on psychometric exams given in the recruitment centers. Those who fit the criteria are then invited to volunteer—in other words, to join the sorting stage. A high school or technical education does not necessarily give one an advantage. These are merely two elements among the meticulous medical examinations, physical checks, and tests of mechanical ability, motor coordination, general intelligence, and motivation. The results sort out the candidates who are invited to the *Gibush* stage in the Flight School. This involves seven concentrated and intense days in field conditions, removed from familiar surroundings, with exercises, formations, inspections, guard duty, and even cleaning and KP duty, during which the candidates are examined for their responses under pressure, their adaptability, their motivation, their ability to innovate and survive, and their teamwork, initiative, and leadership qualities. Every volunteer is tracked by instructors and psychologists, and every act receives points and evaluation. Those who meet the criteria according to this method are accepted into the Flight Course. Until 1990, the course of the flight cadet comprised six stages with final examinations followed by an additional sorting process at the conclusion of each stage. This latter process included sociometric examinations in which the cadets expressed their opinions on all areas connected with their activities and their comrades in the course. The Flight School attributes great importance to these personal evaluations, and the cadets learn to phrase them carefully. Many sides of one's personality are expressed in these examinations. The sifting continues throughout each stage, and the number of flight cadets becomes smaller and smaller, with most of those who leave the course doing so in its early stages.

From the late 1960s until its restructuring in 1990, the course of the Flight School and the division of the stages was as follows:

1. The Pre-preparatory Stage, which lasted four months, was a concentrated course in the specific sciences involved in laws of flight, from physics to meteorology, and also included physical training in extended treks and first flight exercises. In the three weeks spent examining the cadet's flight capabilities, only ten hours were spent in the Piper.

2. The Preparatory Stage took place completely on the ground. It continued the building and strengthening of the cadet, and entailed expanded infantry basic training including individual and company exercises in weapons, field activities, treks, and navigation.

3. The Primary Stage took place completely in the basic training aircraft and included the first solo flight. Until 1962, this stage occurred on the Harvard, but after that it took place on the Tzukit, the Israeli version of the French Fouga Magister jet training aircraft. A product of Israeli Aircraft Industries, this was a twin-engined aircraft with machine guns and rockets but without an ejector seat. In this stage, pilots were sorted out for future orientation—fighter aircraft, helicopters, or navigation. The division test took place after eight flying hours ("Check Eight"). Although the criteria for the decision were based primarily on the cadet's skills, the immediate needs of the IAF also played a large role.

4. The "Basic Stage" was concentrated on areas of flight. The fighter cadets continued to train on the Tzukit aircraft, flying formation, navigation, and night flights. From the early 1970s onward, the helicopter cadets flew on the Bell 206. In those early years, the IAF did not yet have enough helicopters or instructors to respond to demand, and groups of cadets were sent to study in the United States. Future navigators studied their field on the Beechcraft, a patrol and transport aircraft, until the time when it was decided who would become a fighter, helicopter, or transport navigator.

5. The Senior Basic Stage did not involve flight, but rather the paratrooping and rescue course, which was considered superfluous until

the Sinai Campaign. It involved four months of officers' training, with workshops in command and leadership. Studies of intelligence, history, and the organization of the IAF were are also included, as well as training in the weapons and operational activities of the other IDF branches, thereby familiarizing the cadet with their jobs and needs. At the end of this stage, the cadets were presented with the company commander pins given to officers in the ground forces.

6. In the Advanced Stage, the final part of the Flight Course, fighter cadets used to return to the Tzukit aircraft. Since 1974, however, they have undergone seven hours of training and solo flights on the Skyhawk, in addition to a first encounter with its characteristics in war, both day and night. The helicopter cadets today train on the Bell 212, and the navigators complete their training on a variety of aircraft according to their future assignments.

By the late 1950s and early 1960s, the cadets were already participating in an organized and methodical training program using aircraft and tools of which no one had dreamed during the early years. Every cadet now had a personal file. He could also request to change instructors if a common language was not found at the outset. The role of the instructor was to aid in reducing tensions and overcoming obstacles, and not to cause additional stress. In those years, I was responsible for the sorting processes in flight. This is the stage in which the cadet meets his fate as a pilot. His character and handling of the aircraft determine his level of flight and his ability to continue in the course. These factors overshadow classroom performance. More than once we encountered a poor pupil who excelled in solo flight. The instructor had to evaluate whether he had a cadet with two left hands or one with latent talents.

We stressed these skills to the instructors, for we did not want to lose a good candidate because of impatience or lack of sufficient observation. In the Flight School, the legend was told of a Messerschmitt mechanic who persisted in becoming a pilot and was expelled from one of the first courses in 1949. He later stole a Piper and flew it to Turkey to prove how mistaken they had been. I prefer the story of Amnon, a kibbutznik, who struggled along as a flight cadet. He was kept in the course solely on the recommendation of the school's sociologist, who thought he possessed latent qualities. As the course continued, Amnon caught up with and ultimately surpassed his friends. Later he became a top intercept pilot who downed MiGs and was awarded the command of a fighter squadron.

The conclusion of the marathon is the wing ceremony. It is a tremendous moment in one's life, standing before parents, friends, and heads of state. At best, fifteen percent of flight cadets who start the race reach the finish line, and this is still far from the moment when the top team will be extracted from this group.

In 1990, the structure of the Flight Course was changed. The internal timetable was shortened and completely altered. The primary changes in content occurred in the material studied, in the formations, in the style of training, and in the appropriate sorting of the cadets according to their skills and the sophisticated systems that the IAF would be using as it approached the twenty-first century.

After the Flight Course, the Operational Training Course still separates the fresh pilots from the certified pilots. In Ramat David, pilots trained on Spitfires, Mustangs, and Meteors, in the spirit of the genesis of the Flight School. After the war, when the course had moved to Hatzor and the Ouragan squadron, it was still held in a catch-as-catch-can fashion, much to the dismay of its new commander, Joe Alon. A man who strove for professional perfection, Joe succeeded Moti Hod, who had replaced Ezer Weizman as base commander. Joe wanted David Ivri next to him as gunning instructor, for Ivri had studied the field in England. Ivri resembled Tolkowsky physically and mentally. Alon needed his orderly approach to instill order and methodology into the operational training.

Ivri, however, had previous obligations. Unhappily, he was forced to return to Tel Nof, to the Flight School, which had been reorganized after the Sinai Campaign. As his comrades in the Ouragan squadron were beginning to delight in the stories of their first war, he was instructing flight cadets in a Harvard that had never looked so primitive to him. Ivri was a role model to many instructors in the course. He even contributed to the Air Gunnery Branch of the IAF by writing a pamphlet summarizing his studies in England and the experience he had gained in Israel. The fighter pilots of the 1980s could not understand what the excitement was all about, for their computers did all the work. In the air combat exercises of the early days, range setting was manual or semimechanical. The young pilot would suddenly realize that though the art of flying was the core, it was actually a small part of air combat.

Joe was not easily satisfied. He made sure the instruction materials were constantly updated. Flight was always taken to the edge—the greatest speed, the greatest altitude, and the sharpest angles. The debriefing, Joe's innovation, was without compromises or excuses. Instead of bullets, they now had gunsight cameras. Every pilot would display his firing film, in the center of which were his gunsights. Success was measured by catching his "enemy," the instructor, in its center. Everyone was victim to everyone's criticism. A new competitiveness developed, creating a professional tension that encouraged excellence. The important films were kept for future generations.

From exercise to exercise, the Ouragan began to prove itself as the best introduction for the training of pilots for all the French fighter aircraft—the Mystère, the Super Mystère B-2, the Vautour, and even the Mirage, which was yet to be purchased. The Ouragan served the operational training network for more than a decade, until the arrival of the Skyhawk, which opened the American era in the IAF.

Joe's neighbors at Hatzor were also undergoing their own little revolution. The first fighter squadron had changed commanders and aircraft. Benny Peled transferred command to Yak Nevo and was sent to study at the Haifa Technion for four years. The Super Mystère pushed the Mystère to a new squadron, according to the tradition that sent the newest aircraft to the oldest squadron. Benny Peled had tested the new planes and recommended them. Yak invited David Ivri to bring the Super Mystère into the IAF. Ivri was not nervous as he climbed into the aircraft's cockpit, for the mystique of the boundary set by the speed of sound had now been broken. Once airborne, it became apparent that other than the light blow one felt when breaking through, the Mach meter was the only evidence of the revolution. Several of the changes, though, were worthy of note. The engine's afterburner added speed to the takeoff and gave the extra push through the sound barrier that the Mystère achieved only in a dive. While intense pressure pulled on the wings in fast turns, there was no need to strain one's muscles pulling on the stick to maintain stability; the "auto command" mechanism, like power steering, conserved the pilot's strength. Ivri was more impressed by the electronic gunsights, which measured ranges and set clear and specific firing data. The improvements were pure comfort after the heavy flight and manual range setting in the Ouragan. They attempted to ignore the price paid for these innovations. The Super Mystère was loaded with sensitive hydraulic systems and lacked the Ouragan's elephant skin. The first bursts of antiaircraft fire that would expose its vulnerability were still unimagined in those days. The Minister of Defense was keeping border incidents under tight control, and issued a severe prohibition against initiating conflicts.

However, the Super Mystère squadron was in need of a real battle. In order to test it, the pilots attempted to replicate all battle conditions that their comrades had experienced in the Sinai Campaign. They incorporated new exercises and unusual techniques in air combat. Yak Nevo was one of the innovators of this process. A quiet and introverted man wrapped in a cloud of pipe smoke, he was then twenty-six years old. The legend that preceded him did not tell of the number of aircraft he had shot down, but rather how he had done so. He was one of the first pilots to think at jet speed. The IAF still had a number of pilots who had been raised on the films of the Second World War, and still looked for the eyes of the enemy pilot. Yak and his comrades in the squadron claimed that there was no time for this anymore. At supersonic speeds, only split-second professional thinking would succeed. The squadron was already familiar with the "Yak roll" and even more so with the "let him pass," trick which turns a disadvantage into an advantage. In air combat, one strives to catch one's enemy by the tail, as in a fight between dogs. Hence the term "dogfight." Yak found a way to shake the enemy aircraft off his tail and to set back in on him. The pilot turns sharply, his opponent is propelled forward, and the pilot executes a wide roll, ending up behind his opponent. All that remains is to place him in the gunsights.

Yak was in need of a barometer, a real battle to test which pilots and aircraft were superior. The lessons learned from actual combat would be incalculably more helpful than the results of any dry exercise or discussion in the officers' club. Ezer understood and agreed. Though he had been ordered to avoid any process that would lead to provocation, the Egyptians played into his hands. In the recent nights, they had sent their Ilyushin bombers to penetrate Israeli airspace on quick reconnaissance missions. Israel's narrow borders and the limited technical capabilities of the early detection systems allowed the bombers to enter and exit within minutes, without risking interception. In the event they might attempt a day penetration, the IAF had to seal the hole in its skies.

The MiG-17 squadron at El Arish was replaced on a monthly basis, and marked the arrival of the new aircraft by flying sorties along the Israeli border. The Super Mystère squadron tracked these new aircraft with suspicion. The change of guard of December 1958 was to occur toward the end of that week, within several days. The route of the Egyptian patrol was parallel to the imaginary line between Rafah and Eilat. In the late-morning hours of Saturday, December 20, Yak led a quartet over Nitzana. A quartet of MiG-17s was executing its patrol over the Sinai. The Flight Control Center tracked the progress of the MiGs minute by minute, and Ezer updated Yak. His quartet dispersed the moment they heard that the MiGs were nearing them. One pair remained behind. Yak and Ohad Shadmi closed in on the border. The Egyptians saw them and turned in a twenty-kilometer arc, one pair on top of the other. They were flying at thirty thousand feet, and Yak set his ambush high above them.

The Mig-17 and the Super Mystère had similar characteristics. They could both break the sound barrier in horizontal flight and had an operation ceiling of forty thousand feet. The MiG's tail assured stability, and tremendous firepower from its three 37- and 23-millimeter cannons.

Yak had the advantage of altitude and surprise, and the MiGs immediately began to escape when they saw the Super Mystères diving toward them. Yak rolled and grabbed the tail of the lower pair. He fired at the leader and missed. The leader opened the distance and left his partner behind. Yak opened fire from three hundred meters and struck the MiG's left wing. He neared and continued to squeeze his cannons, one of which jammed. At one hundred meters he emptied his ammunition and saw fire erupting from the MiG's body. He broke right and saw the pilot eject at twenty thousand feet. The MiG dragged a trail of smoke until it crashed between Nitzana and Bir Lahfan. In Hatzor, they heard of the downed aircraft from Shadmi, since Yak's radio had gone out with his cannon. In those thirty seconds of combat, it was difficult to tell who had discovered whose limits.

The downing of the first Egyptian aircraft since the Sinai Campaign, coincidentally the first MiG-17, took the General Command by surprise. On Saturday night, Ezer was summoned by Chief of Staff Chaim Laskov to report on the dogfight. At the end of the debriefing, Laskov and his aides did not seem satisfied. Laskov was wary of a severe reaction from the Americans or the Soviets, and particularly of the wrath of the Minister of

Defense. David Ben-Gurion had summoned them to his home to hear of the battle. He feared any initiation of action in the air, viewing it as the start of a war. Ezer prepared himself for the possibility that the meeting would conclude with his losing his job. To everyone's surprise, Ben-Gurion was in a wonderful mood, and after hearing the explanations, he blessed the pilots and sent the commanders home with a sense of satisfaction.

Nearly a year passed, and again Yak found himself in need of live battle. He repeated the script. The duty squadron in El Arish was about to be replaced in early November 1959. Assuming that the Egyptians had learned a lesson from the previous encounter, Yak decided to set an ambush. This time, each of the four Super Mystères in the formation had a job. Ivri and Yair Barak would be the bait. They flew in an arc toward the Egyptians and attempted to lure them into Israeli airspace. Yak and his partner, flying in the distance, would intercept them.

The meeting took place at midday on November 4. At the moment when the flight controller warned of the quartet of MiG-17s, Ivri and Barak broke in their arc tangential to the border in the sands over Chalutza. The Egyptian quartet swallowed the bait and crossed into the Negev. Yak's pair dived toward them and intercepted them from behind. One of the MiGs was hit, but did not fall. The others fled. Afterward, the Egyptian military spokesman claimed that an Israeli plane had been shot down in the battle. This obligated Israel's military spokesman to disclose the Egyptian penetration and the dogfight, which took place at 25,000 feet, primarily to deny the Egyptian claim. In this instance, both sides were close to the truth. David Ivri's Super Mystère had fallen, but had not been hit.

It had happened at the conclusion of his luring break, and he had been unable to complete the attack. Although combat procedure obligated the pilot to drop his detachable fuel tanks, Ivri and Barak did not let their half-empty tanks go. Ivri might have turned too sharply, and it is possible that the remaining fuel in the tanks shortened the turn. He stalled and lost control of the aircraft. The spin itself was not a surprise to him. As a flight instructor he had rehearsed it hundreds of times. However, a spin in the Super Mystère was far different from the exercises in the Harvard, and there is no spin exercise in supersonic aircraft. There is only the simulator. Ivri, forced to eject, parachuted into the sands of Chalutza.

Yak returned to Hatzor without a victory roll, and in the sands of Chalutza, Ivri gathered his parachute and folded it. Ivri was awaiting the realization of Uri Yarom's promise of a quick rescue, this time in a helicopter and not after long hours or days of survival, as had been in the past. Of course, this would only be if "Sarah" did not disappoint them. She was always close to his hips and was already transmitting the distress signal. It was strong enough for Uri to home in on its frequency and find Ivri's location. He had spent a great deal of time on the base in the past months and, at every takeoff, urged the pilots to take "Sarah"—their nickname for the Search and Rescue and Homing Device. Uri must have been relieved this day, for if anyone would be carrying Sarah, it would be Ivri. The helicopter approached and landed near him in an enormous cloud of dust. Uri, who sat at its controls, extended his hand to Ivri, and within an hour they landed at Hatzor, straight into the inevitable argument over whether Yak had shot down the MiG or not.

The helicopter squadron had been established twenty-one months earlier. By the time Uri Yarom received its command, in January 1958, and the IAF recognized the importance of the helicopter, it had been the subject of much talk, but had seen little action. Ben-Gurion had wanted helicopters before the establishment of the state in order to maintain contact with the blockaded Jerusalem. The medics of the Palmach had wanted them for the evacuation of wounded. However, in the late 1940s they were new technology, relatively expensive and unreliable. Their virtues had been witnessed during the Korean War in the early 1950s. The newer versions had saved lives and added speed, flexibility, and surprise to the modern ground battle. Since then, chiefs of staff of the IDF had had their eyes on it. Yigal Yadin wanted the helicopters for rapid deployment of infantry battalions. Moshe Dayan saw them landing commando units deep in enemy territory as an alternative to the airdrop. Chaim Laskov felt that they would aid in the destruction of tanks. All this was theory, however, for in the debates over procurement, the conventional fixed-wing fighter and bomber aircraft were always preferred. From the remnants of the budget, five random and miserable helicopters were purchased.

Uri Yarom received two Hiller helicopters with a short flight range and deafening engines, each able to carry two passengers in addition to the pilot. There were also two Sikorsky 55 helicopters, ancient American models with a capacity of five passengers, as well as a light Allouette jet helicopter donated by a generous French Jew. One of the Hillers was almost constantly grounded for repairs, and the other lost oil in flight and often needed battery assistance, sometimes from passing cars. Their operations during their seven years of service included carrying sacks of flour to Kibbutz Palmachim, which was stranded in the floods of 1957, and the rescue of a police officer from an overturned boat near the Nahariya coast.

Uri's body had difficulty with the G pressures of the aircraft in the Flight School, and he was transferred to the light squadron, then to the Mosquitoes, and ultimately to the helicopters. Though the two Sikorskys had been purchased before the Sinai Campaign, they spent the war in storage at the transport squadron. After the battles, they functioned primarily as flying taxis. In the helicopter market, a new generation had developed, including the Sikorsky 58 and the Banana H-21, which were built to carry ten soldiers with their gear or to lift a jeep. The IDF requested to examine them, and the French General Command invited an Israeli delegation to Algeria to follow the helicopter's activities in the battles against the National Liberation Front.

In the IAF, helicopters were still considered transport aircraft. Uri, the air representative in the Algerian delegation, watched the helicopters in combat, landing as well as evacuating troops. The entire Israeli delegation recommended that the "fighting transport" approach be adopted. The Ministry of Defense decided to purchase five Sikorsky 58 helicopters, and the General Command established an inter-branch team to develop theories of combat. There was even a proposal to take the helicopters from the IAF and place them in the hands of the ground forces. Within six months the IAF decided to keep the helicopters. The only thing lacking was new ones. All the money had been spent on the Mystères and the Vautours, and the IAF was left with poor helicopters despite great plans for the transport network. Therefore the helicopter wing was split off, and the Inverted Sword Squadron was born. Till today the insignia is three rotating swords replacing rotor blades. For security reasons this nickname was given, and stuck.

Growth began within several months. Four civilian Sikorsky 58s were purchased at the first opportunity, and in less than a year a new era began in the IAF. Pilots were no longer abandoned after ejecting from their aircraft. The helicopters' primary function as pilot rescue craft kept them in the IAF, but did not improve their status. They remained outsiders to some extent, and fighting transport was seen as fantasy. Being transferred to the helicopters was considered a demotion, beneath the Dakota in terms of prestige. IAF headquarters felt that the drivers of flying ambulances could be trained out of those who had failed in the Flight Course. But Uri thought beyond the terms of troop transport and logistics, and described helicopters armed with rockets and missiles in the future battlefield. When told that it sounded like a fantasy, he responded that life could sometimes be more surprising than any science-fiction film.

Chance brought about my meeting with Uri Yarom and my joining the helicopters. On one of the evenings celebrating the tenth anniversary of Israel's independence, I witnessed an IDF show that included two Sikorsky 55 helicopters charging out of the darkness and landing two squads of soldiers. After the dummy targets had been "attacked," the helicopters returned upon signal, evacuated the troops along with their wounded on stretchers, and disappeared again into the night. Until that show, I had denigrated helicopters. I had already transferred to jet aircraft, and had returned from instructing to the fighter squadrons. My imagination was suddenly struck, and I could see myself flying these aircraft. Along with Yehuda Peri, another helicopter volunteer, I was sent to a helicopter course in France. Returning as licensed captains of the two Sikorskys and at the top of our class, we found the squadron to be flying and on alert around the clock. Exercises tested the aircraft in integrated maneuvers with other units. Uri faced the uphill battle of attempting to persuade the upper command of the value of the helicopters, a feat that was nearly impossible in the glorious shadow of the airdrops of the Sinai Campaign. He was forced to drag commanders to landing exercises so that they could understand the benefits in light of Israel's geographic characteristics. Vital targets in the four neighboring Arab countries lay within the existing helicopters' range, and the more sophisticated models would be able to carry greater loads. He concealed from them the helicopters' primary weakness, which was their vulnerability to the intense desert and dust conditions of the region.

Between the training exercises, the helicopters were on twenty-four-hour operational alert for rescue missions. Though this was only a small part of their activities, it was the outward impression. Their missions included not only rescue of pilots but also rapid evacuation of victims of traffic accidents, both military and civilian. Years later, Uri met the elderly Igor Sikorsky and was amazed that even the father of the modern helicopter was less interested in its combat tales than in the number of human lives it had saved. When Uri had already become the air emissary in the Israeli embassy in the United States, he and I were invited to see the new model of the giant CH-53, which had just come off of the Sikorsky line in Connecticut. The helicopter was the realization of Uri's dreams. The test pilot took us on an aerobatic sortie. Its wondrous maneuvers caused us to recommend it as the heavy helicopter for Israel's future, and within several years it was at the center of the IDF's flight network.

Among all those who began to express interest in the helicopters, Uri found true partnership with Avraham Arnan, the commander of the elite Intelligence Branch commando unit. A cloud of secrecy shrouded them during Arnan's frequent visits to the squadron. Along with Rafi Sivron, the squadron's navigator, they would lock themselves in the intelligence room and then take off for unknown destinations, returning hours later with grins of satisfaction on their faces. No one in the squadron other than they knew of these secret operations. The revolution that the helicopter prompted, in its leaps in time and effort, saved Uri the explanatory conversations and demonstration flights. When the orders were passed through the ranks of the IDF to begin to take Uri's ideas seriously, he suddenly had many friends in the field units and the Central Command. It was at that time that he informed Ezer Weizman that, using the helicopters, he could destroy enemy aircraft on their bases even with axes.

Only upon receiving command of the squadron, four years later, did I learn of the secrets of these operations. I then began to work closely with my brother, Nechemiah Cohen, who was a member of Arnan's unit and the commander of a special operations team. I was their pilot. After one mission together, we were summoned to the office of Chief of Staff Yitzhak Rabin to be decorated. The granting of such commendation to two brothers was unusual, and Rabin forbade us to continue flying operations together.

The squadron was already large enough to receive orders from every Arnan-like unit that needed our help in the execution of missions. The circle of pilots privy to the secrecy also widened. The squadron became operational in 1962, on the day it unexpectedly received twenty-four new Sikorsky 58 military helicopters. The helicopters had been intended for the West German Air Force, and were transferred to Israel in a covert gesture by Minister of Defense Franz Josef Strauss, following his visit to Israel. The gift also included dozens of Fouga Magister aircraft and radar-directed L-70 antiaircraft cannons.

The tradition of rotation in the military, which limits one's serving in a given position to short periods of time in order to assure fresh leadership, did not allow Uri Yarom to reap the benefits of our success for long. He was sent to a new job, and had to train a replacement. Chaim Naveh was the preferred candidate. I was promoted to deputy commander of operations of the Tel Nof base, and commander of the sorting squadron of the Flight School. I also attended the Leadership Training School of the IDF. In 1965, just before the graduation ceremony, Ezer Weizman informed me that the IAF would be receiving a squadron of French Super Frelon helicopters. They were heavy, two-engined aircraft that could carry thirty soldiers to the Nile Valley and back. This was a major step in the direction of Uri Yarom's dream. Since the helicopters would be received by Chaim Naveh, Weizman asked if I was interested in receiving the Inverted Sword Squadron. I returned to the squadron in early 1966, this time as commander.

At first glance it might seem that I had received a well-oiled machine operating with self-assurance; the truth quickly surfaced, however. The squadron was blessed with good helicopters and competent pilots and mechanics, but morale was low. To receive the Super Frelons in France, Naveh had taken the best of the helicopter veterans. The remainder felt that they had been sent to the minor leagues, with a new commander who had less experience than they. Though we had joined the squadron together, they had matured for three years during my absence. A squadron commander in the IAF is judged first and foremost by his professional competence and authority, and that was my main drawback. I had to develop a sense of authority and to strengthen my personnel with the sense of the groundbreaking quality of their participation in a field that had yet to be tested in war. I initiated a series of round-the-clock exercises, more activity and less complaining. "Any mission, anytime, anyplace," I would say, and they laughed until the exercises began to come faster and faster and expanded in scope. At the end of that year, we broke all the records by flying an entire unit for several runs in the dark of night. It was a desert exercise, unlike any other, and was the first in the IDF to test these revised combat theories. It included the flying and landing of hundreds of fighters, equipment, and fuel, and ultimately the evacuation of scores of wounded.

Until that night, in late 1966, we had operated in lone formations, in solitary hit-and-run missions, or in a train of helicopters. We had never attempted a continuous air convoy with a full load of helicopters. All night long, caravans of formations, pairs and trios, flew in a chain on unfamiliar routes, dropping their loads with pinpoint timing and accuracy. The slightest mistake could result in complete failure—the erroneous direction of troops and equipment, or a midair collision. An entire city was formed in the dead of night and had to disappear by dawn. The movement in the forward control center, known as the "Air Head," and in the drop location was reminiscent of airfields on busy nights. Lighting was provided by colored electric lamps that were lit for short periods of time. Every landing site was marked and colored according to the helicopter's mission. All the theories of fighting transport that had been rehearsed in a strictly symbolic framework were now examined and tested in their real proportions. The results gave us reason to be proud, but also to be cautious. In one day and night it is possible to overcome the shortages we encountered in technicians, replacement parts, tools, fuel tanks, and front-wheel-drive vehicles. However, several of the pilots did not receive food and had no place to rest. The brigade's supply unit was naturally unprepared to provide ground services to the aircraft and crews. They would not be able to improvise for another day, because the supply network was not designed for diverse and long-term field operations. We were angry at our own naiveté and at the fact that we had relied on others as we had depended on the supply of intelligence information, vehicles, food, and other supplies. We swore that henceforth we would rely only on ourselves. The squadron began to work in all areas on becoming self-supporting and independent in all its operational needs.

Ezer Weizman's appreciation of the helicopters was limited. Anything with a tinge of ground combat that was not pure air warfare could not compete with his first and tremendous love for the fighter aircraft. He related to the Inverted Sword Squadron and its airborne plans to invade Arab airfields with grenades and explosives as a tangential and unimportant flirt. The idea of destroying the enemy's aircraft while they were still on the ground had preoccupied him since the days of the first Messerschmitt course in Czechoslovakia. The Czech commander who had advised that he overcome the Egyptian Air Force in this way had intended for the work to be executed by real airplanes. Ezer, who had dedicated himself to this goal from the day he received command of the IAF, still lacked the necessary numbers of sophisticated aircraft. He wanted to purchase from France one hundred Mirage aircraft—the most promising and, more important, the most available aircraft. However, the price per plane was $1.5 million, twice that of the Mystére. The total cost, $200 million (including weapons, radar, and replacement parts), was an astronomical sum in 1961, and the General Command thought him to be crazier than all his predecessors. Even at IAF headquarters he found that most people were willing to accept only a small number of intercept Mirages for defending the nation's skies and to return to the less expensive piston-engined bombers. The compromise was twenty-four Mirages. Given the ever-present budgetary problems, it is difficult to know if Ezer would have initiated such a large purchase of new Sikorsky 58 helicopters if they had not been part of a package deal with the Germans. A first model of the Mirage was shown to Ezer immediately after the Sinai Campaign. The first plane came off the Marcel-Dassault production line in 1959, and Danny Shapira, who had been among the sextet that brought the first jets to Israel was there. Flying unknown aircraft had been his personal vocation since the days of the Spitfires and Mosquitoes, and he had accrued thousands of flying hours on dozens of types of helicopters and airplanes. He had been injured twice, and had stopped counting the times when he had to land at the last moment without fuel or with an engine that had exploded. However, he had never abandoned an aircraft. He was the Israeli version of the American Chuck Yeager.

Danny was now sent to a test-pilot course at the factories of Dassault, the manufacturer of the Mirage. One day he was summoned to the production line of the Mirage. The French were attempting to whet his appetite. The plane was classified top secret and had revolutionary delta wings and a powerful engine that could push it to a speed of Mach 2.

Though Ezer was also invited to see the Mirage show, he agreed to come only if Danny Shapira was the test pilot. Though both Dassault and their test pilot were offended, they realized that this was not the time for foolish pride. The plane had yet to undergo operational test flights in the French Air Force. France very much wanted to sell the first series to Israel, which had become an important sales tool for the French aircraft industries. The French attempted to claim that the aircraft was experimental, only a prototype, and that its equipment was secret. Ezer was more stubborn, and demanded to know why they refused to use a test pilot they had just finished training. If Danny did not fly, Ezer would not be there. He added one more condition, that Danny fly at least three test flights before his arrival. The chutzpah worked.

Danny had often said that one needed intuition, gentleness, and a lot of luck for his job. With the Mirage, at first glance, it seemed that he would need all these and more. It was a new creature in its external appearance, and would likely require unique flight techniques. No one, not even the French test pilots, had much more experience than he did on this new aircraft. The Dassault test pilot got even by refusing to provide information. The fuel system? Automatic, there was no reason to touch it. Starting the aircraft? Here, do this and this. Hydraulics? You've got three systems. When the first one goes, the second replaces it. When the third goes, you've got no steering mechanisms, but you have got an excellent ejector seat. "A vous à jouer!" he said—"It's yours to play"—and closed the canopy. For the first time in his life, Danny was sitting in a cockpit designed to cater to the pilot. The seat was fitted to all the body's contours. The field of vision was excellent. All the switches were small and close to the stick and the throttle. Most operations could be executed without stretching one's hands to remote, uncomfortable corners of the cockpit. Even the crossing of the sound barrier was marked on the speedometer with only a few vibrations. By his second flight, Danny was already daring to maneuver at high speeds as much as he could in the narrow air corridor he had been given that was free of civilian air traffic. This plane was amazing, he reported to Ezer. The commander-in-chief could not resist, and flew to Villecoublay, the test field east of Paris, to watch Danny in his third flight.

Ezer followed him from the flight-control car. Danny climbed to forty thousand feet, and the tracking equipment showed him at Mach 1, Mach 1.5, Mach 2, Mach 2.2—approximately 2,600 kilometers per hour. In those days, this still impressed those involved. A year later it would become routine, and for the next generation of pilots it would be standard. Danny slowed down, glided, and landed. On the runway, they presented him with the gold pin of French pilots who had flown at twice the speed of sound. Danny was the twelfth member of this group.

The French had built the Mirage for intercept, with original ammunition limited to air-to-air missiles. Resigned to the idea of a multipurpose, underfunded air force, Ezer demanded that new 30-millimeter cannons with a high firing rate, as well as bomb hangers, be added. One and a half million dollars should not be wasted on an air battle alone, he told the Dassault engineers. Personally, he would prefer to bomb Cairo in a Mirage. The engineers had no objections to the additions, for, after the Sinai Campaign, they had stopped arguing with the Israelis. The concealed faults in the engine would be learned by all much later and in the most painful manner.

Equipped with all the statistics, Ezer returned to Israel with a dream of one hundred Mirages, and fruitlessly attempted to excite the doubting officers of the General Command. Fearing that the new plane would swallow their entire budget, they approved one-quarter of Ezer's request and stated their doubts that he would be able to absorb even this small number. The first team of pilots and technicians was sent to France in September 1960.

One morning they mummified Danny Shapira in a clumsy suit, sealed from head to toe, with a clear face mask, which reminded him of a diving suit. He had been summoned to test the rocket Mirage, an unmatched star in terms of altitude and speed. The rocket engine had been placed in the aircraft's belly, and was fed by a mixture of regular fuel, pure gas, and nitrous acid. It added one and a half tons to the aircraft's force for eighty seconds, three-quarters of a ton for 160 seconds. He was to climb to thirty thousand feet with the primary engine, and from there to increase speed with the rocket to a greater altitude. The suit made movement difficult for him, and the cockpit less accessible. He climbed at Mach 2 and angled the nose upward at twenty-five degrees. Three seconds after turning on the rocket, he stopped hating the suit. He was no longer flying a plane, but riding a missile. As he lifted the nose, the aircraft gained speed. The stick was pulled to his body, and the black dome of space could be seen approaching. He looked behind and heard himself scream "Danny! You're turning ballistic! You're leaving the planet Earth!"

He had been told to stop at 60,000 feet and not to fly above 65,000 feet. The French record was 75,000 feet. But Danny could not resist. Why stop if the aircraft was not losing any of its control? At 65,000 feet he shut down the primary engine so as not to fly beyond 80,000 feet "and leave the gravitational pull of the planet." He even pulled out the air brakes, against all rules of flight. They are to be used in a dive and not in a climb. At 80,000 feet, on the edge of space, he began to feel shaking in the primary engine. He shut down the rocket and turned over. Only forty seconds had passed since he had activated it. If he had not stopped, he might have burst through to a record reached years later by a Phantom, which rose to 90,000 feet. The vibrations of the engine returned him to reality. He opened up his afterburner, and the shaking stopped. At 70,000 feet, he began to descend. In the tests that followed, faults in the engine and problems involving the special fuel were discovered. The rocket Mirage seemed to him to be greater than the needs of the IAF, and its benefits were smaller than its dangers. Even the French eventually abandoned the aircraft.

The first series of multipurpose intercept and bomber Mirages was ready a year and a half later. In the meantime, Lt. Gen. Tzvi "Chera" Tzur replaced Chaim Laskov as IDF chief of staff and oversaw the compromise reached between Ezer and the commanders of the ground forces. He approved the armored forces' purchase of Centurion tanks from Great Britain, and additional Mirages for the IAF. The order was increased to seventy-six aircraft. Danny and a French pilot flew the first pair over in April 1962. They landed at Hatzor on a Saturday, without ceremony. Ben-Gurion respected the sensitivities of his religious partners in the Israeli government, and waited until Sunday to come see them. Fifteen years later the Israeli government collapsed because of a ceremony for the arrival of the American F-15s, which began on Friday but continued a few minutes into the Sabbath. In the fall of 1963, the absorption of the Mirages was at its peak with an operational routine and the gathering of increasing experience. Over three years, Danny Shapira led nineteen formations of Mirages to Israel for the first fighter squadron, which now changed aircraft for the fourth time. Later formations were added to new squadrons formed at Ramat David and Tel Nof. Shapira also flew several two-seat Mirages that would be used for training and navigation. Behind him in one of the flights sat a bright and handsome pilot named Avihu Ben-Nun, who was determined to do all the work himself.

The morning of November 11, 1963, would be recorded in the annals of the IAF as an unusual one. The pilots and mechanics completed their checks and routine maintenance procedures. By afternoon they had to prepare a pair of aircraft for a secret sortie to the Nile Valley, and to guarantee that their speed and their ability to maneuver would enable the aircraft to avoid contact with Egyptian MiGs. The cannons were unarmed so as not to tempt the pilots into combat, and reserve fuel tanks were placed under the wings. The sortie was to take place at low altitude and high speed, necessitating a greater quantity of fuel than usual.

Ran Ronen, the sortie leader, listed it on the chart in the operations room under the simple code name "Navigation Flight." There was no pilot more appropriate for the mission than Ran. His French instructors had said that he was a man for all aircraft, one who attached himself not only to the Mirage's oxygen systems but to its soul. He instructed his partner in the sortie, Amos Amir, and the ground crew to check every part of the aircraft to ensure that there would be no surprises. Amos had not managed to participate in the Sinai Campaign, and had been raised on Ran's meticulousness, which called for one to prepare for every sortie as if it were the first test flight. This time he repeated to Amos that it would be better if a surprise problem ended in death, for it would surely be worse to be in an Egyptian jail. Not only would the pilot be in trouble, but the State of Israel would be dragged in along with him.

Ran checked the camera time and again. It was the core as well as the potential trouble spot of the mission, for the Mirage 3C was not built for reconnaissance photography. Instead of the radar eye, a German Zeiss camera was placed in the plane's nose for automated vertical photography. It was a smart camera, programmed to take a series of pictures at intervals of milliseconds while the aircraft was flown at predetermined speeds and altitudes. The pilot merely had to switch the system on prior to takeoff, then make sure that the green control light flashed throughout the flight. Then he had to bring the aircraft to the appropriate altitude and speed at the predetermined stretches set for photography. For this particular operation, the camera was programmed for a low altitude at which details could be seen even by the naked eye. Such a sophisticated system also had limitations, and was unable to function at high temperatures or in extreme turbulence.

In the briefing room, with the assistance of the intelligence officer, Ran and Amos studied the flight routes and the areas of reconnaissance. It was nearly 1500 hours, and they were ready to depart immediately upon receiving the green light. This would indicate that the skies over the

Nile Delta were clear of both clouds and enemy aircraft. In the Control Center at IAF headquarters, Ezer Weizman and a number of others accompanied them silently. The command to take off was given soon after 1500 hours. They headed south, at "zero" altitude, not climbing above one hundred feet and occasionally almost hitting the treetops. Crossing the border at Rafah, they then cut westward to El Arish. After several minutes the blue strip of water of the Suez Canal glimmered before them. The city of Port Said and the port at the northern entrance to the canal were the first targets of the reconnaissance. Ran climbed while keeping an eye on the altimeter, the speedometer, and the control light of the camera, which continued to flash. The instruments neared the conditions set for the photography: altitude 1,500 feet and speed 540 knots. All that was left to do was pray that the timer that operated the photographic mechanism would stand the test at the crucial moment.

The reconnaissance route began at Port Said and continued along the length of the Damiat, the eastern tributary of the Nile River. The intelligence targets were in the wider parts of the Delta. It was difficult to navigate and locate them among the multitude of details and the fields flooded with water. Ran used all his powers of concentration during those seconds so as not to leave the route and to maintain precise altitude and speed above the targets. While he relied on Amos's backup above him, not a single Egyptian aircraft was in sight. They flew below the radar until they reached the target. By the time they were detected and aircraft were scrambled toward them, they would have completed the photography and would be on their way home with a head start. In the meantime, only the peasants in the fields watched them.

The intelligence stage was completed. The camera had recorded hundreds of photographs from all the requested fronts. However, they had completed only half of the mission. They still had to return the films intact. Climbing to 25,000 feet, they cut northward from the center of the Delta toward the sea, and then east. Egypt quickly disappeared, with the sun setting behind their backs. The skies were clean. Ran looked at his watch; only thirty minutes had passed since they took off. When he saw the Israeli coastline, he broke the radio silence with the code word signaling success. The commanders responded with joy. The flight inspector in the Hatzor tower cleared Ran and Amos on Runway 23. It was nearly 1600 hours. Ran dropped to fifteen thousand feet and slowly shut his engine in order to reduce speed. Coming about with the wind, he prepared to glide. At 2,500 feet, according to landing procedure, he lowered his wheels and pressed the throttle to increase the rpms of the engine, which would steady the aircraft.

The engine did not respond. This was a horrendous but unsurprising conclusion to a respectable mission. The doubtful reliability of the Mirage's engine was already known in those days. Ran was angry at the timing. He was aware of the limitations of the delta wings, which lost twelve thousand feet per minute at a speed of 250 knots. If he lost control, he could hit the ground like a stone. On the other hand, to save himself at the cost of losing the expensive camera and the rare photographs would be a catastrophe and a disgrace. Just as he managed to plan an emergency landing on Runway 29, it passed beneath him. Calm down, keep your head together, and remember how you handled similar predicaments, he told himself. Attempt to execute emergency procedures, such as restarting the engine. He activated the emergency regulator that would replace the paralyzed fuel regulator, relying on the air resistance to bring the engine back to life. Nothing. The engine was dead.

He slowly directed the Mirage toward a plowed field, balanced the steering, and, when he reached four hundred feet, pulled on the ejector-seat lever. He saw ground from all sides, and thought it would be the last image of his life. But he then felt the blow of the wind as the canopy flew free. The seat disengaged and sent Ran rolling in the air. As soon as the parachute had opened, his feet struck the ground. Two and a half seconds between life and death. Before his eyes he saw an incredible sight. The pilotless Mirage had glided on the oncoming southwestern wind and slowly slid along the furrows until it was stopped by a row of thornbushes. Before Ran could extricate himself from his straps, he was surrounded by children from the nearby moshav. He placed his "Sarah" distress device in the hands of an eight-year-old boy and sprinted the two hundred meters between him and the aircraft. First he scrambled into the cockpit and turned off all the switches to prevent fire. The rescue helicopter landed next to him just as he managed to pull the film from the nose of the plane. The rescue squad remained to guard the Mirage, and the helicopter flew Ran to Hatzor.

In the meantime, I flew in an Allouette to the Flight Control Center in order to transport Ezer Weizman to Hatzor. We picked up Ran and continued on to the fields of moshav Bnei-Re'em. At last light we could make out the abandoned Mirage, the first jet aircraft in the world to land without a pilot. At the field, we received notice that the photographs from Egypt were astounding. That night the aircraft was returned to Hatzor on a truck, and experts began to analyze the mysterious problem that had troubled the engineers at Dassault since they began producing this market version of the aircraft. Until that day, seventeen aircraft from that line, all in the service of the French Air Force, had crashed due to engine shutdown. This was the eighteenth overall, and the first in Israel to be struck with complete engine failure. It was also the first that had not been destroyed when it crashed. Therefore the engine remained intact for investigation. The Hatzor mechanics traced the problem to the fuel-system gaskets, which did not hold in the temperature shift between the upper altitudes and ground level.

For this discovery, Dassault Industries awarded the squadron with a new engine and the IAF with a prize of $250,000. One month later, after replacing the engine and fixing the body of the aircraft, Ran flew it again in a breathtaking aerobatic flight.

An unlikely guest had joined the group of officers at the Flight Control Center following Ran's reconnaissance flight to Egypt. Ezer had been required to request the permission of the new Prime Minister and Minister of Defense, Levi Eshkol, for the unusual intelligence sortie because of the diplomatic dangers surrounding it. The last such sortie had been executed two years earlier, over the airfields of Cairo West and the Nile Delta, in a Vautour bomber that had been converted for reconnaissance missions. For greater security, it had taken place at night, and the pilots had nearly lost their way because of a navigational error. But this time they were looking for evidence of the existence of new weaponry— Soviet SA-2 ground-to-air missiles. Photographs of such quality could be taken only during daylight hours.

Eshkol agreed to the mission, and requested to be present in the Flight Control Center. He felt that such an event could quickly turn into a crisis, and it would be best if the senior authority were present in case an immediate diplomatic decision became necessary. The moment was near. Egyptian aircraft began to chase Ran and Amos before they turned to the sea on their return home. They could be seen on the radar, but in the communications silence, the Flight Control Center did not report the danger to the pilots. They would wait until the threat became imminent. Eshkol watched the tense faces of Ezer and his aides as they followed the moving dots on the screen. No one uttered a word until the Mirages increased the distance and the MiGs turned back to their bases. Eshkol was the first to break the silence. *"Kinderlach,* you worried me," he said in his familiar and affectionate mix of Yiddish and Hebrew.

Only five months had passed since Eshkol had replaced Ben-Gurion, and his warmth had begun to affect the military as well as the country as a whole. While many people longed for the early days of Ben-Gurion's authoritative leadership, Eshkol was a kindly man who knew how to extract obedience in one angry or joking word. The suspicion that he would control the defense network with an open account after serving in the Treasury Ministry for twelve years was not actualized. At times he even urged officers to state what they were lacking. Ben-Gurion, on the other hand, maintained until his final day in office that security rested not only on Mirages and tanks, but also on the settlement of the country. Eshkol involved himself in the new resettling of the country and allowed himself to focus on military security without a guilty conscience.

The conclusion of the Ben-Gurion period was only one of the signs of a new age that had begun during the early 1960s. The arms race, combined with Egyptian subversiveness in the region, the aim of which was the creation of an Arab empire under Nasser's control and an increased stranglehold on Israel, indicated the beginning of the changes. The missiles, new weapons of the decade, would have tremendous influence in the future, primarily behind the scenes.

In May 1961, Israel received word that Egypt was planning a first test launch of ground-to-ground missiles on the anniversary of the July 23 revolution. Israel had known since the beginning of the year of missile tests in Swiss laboratories, and of an American deal to sell solid fuel for experimental missiles. Israel had already built its own missile, and therefore moved up its exhibition launch to July 5. Weighing a quarter of a ton, the Shavit 2 rose to an altitude of eighty kilometers. While the official announcement stated that it was meant to be the pioneering stage of Israel space research, its military use was clear. The Egyptian launch was postponed for a year. Egypt unexpectedly displayed four ground-to-ground missiles on July 21, 1962, each bearing inciting names such as "Al-Kahar" (the conqueror) and "Al-Zafir" (the victor). Nasser boasted of their ability to strike any target "south of Beirut."

The Mossad, Israel's intelligence agency, discovered a group of German scientists and European companies behind the Egyptian project. The Mossad then sent mail bombs to the German scientists in Egypt, and deterred the suppliers of equipment and materials. The scientists were injured one after the other, and began to leave Egypt. Only a few remained at the end of the year. Missile production dropped significantly. The arms race moved to the area of antiaircraft missiles. The reports of the first missiles that the Egyptians had received led to the scrambling of Ran Ronen for that historic reconnaissance sortie. Egypt continued to develop chemical weapons and experimented with them in the civil war that began in Yemen, siding with rebels against the monarchic regime. Israel maintained its silence in the missile realm until the public launch of the satellite Ofek 1 in the fall of 1988. Israel would repeatedly deny reports that it had missiles called Jerichos, which could carry nuclear warheads produced in its plant in Dimona.

Tension in the region grew as Nasser outflanked the UN forces, which were to guard the border of the Sinai and the Gaza Strip and prevent infiltrations from the south. Egypt and Syria united in February 1958 at the initiative of the Syrians, who were involved in interparty and ethnic conflicts and hoped a strong leader would emerge. The unification invigorated them to renew the war over the lands in the demilitarized zones. They attacked Israeli farmers and shelled kibbutzim along the northeastern border. On the morning of February 1, 1960, Israel executed its first retaliatory raid since the Sinai Campaign. A force from the Golani Brigade attacked and destroyed Syrian houses and positions in the village of Lower Tufik. Two weeks later, the Soviet ambassador to Cairo informed Nasser that the operation was merely a preparatory stage for a larger Israeli attack on Syria. He also said that several brigades were already gathered in the Galilee. Though they should have been skeptical, the Egyptians did not check the information. On February 18, they secretly sent armored units and three ground brigades into the Sinai. For four days they stood ready on the Israeli border, and Israeli intelligence was unaware of them. The IAF was not in the habit of executing or initiating routine reconnaissance flights; rather, they responded only to the rare requests from the Intelligence Branch. On the fifth day, the Israeli General Command awakened from its slumber. Two Vautour aircraft were sent on reconnaissance sorties in the Sinai, and returned with frightening pictures. Four hundred Egyptian tanks were stationed between Jabel Libni and Abu-Aweigila. Yitzhak Rabin, chief of the Operations Branch of the IDF, commanded Operation Rotem, which was designed to stop the Egyptian force. Ezer Weizman was requested to place the IAF on top alert. The defense of the country during the next twenty-four hours rested completely on his shoulders. By then the Barak armored brigade and the Golani forces would be moved south and another reserve force would have been called up. The thirty tanks of the Southern Command's standing forces and the International Force would be merely a symbolic roadblock if the Egyptian forces entered the Negev. However, Nasser apparently did not intend to invade, but rather to demonstrate his strength.

The Egyptians retreated after two weeks, and Ezer regretted that the IAF had again squandered an opportunity to test its theories of air warfare. Operation Rotem became the code name for one of the greatest failures of the Israeli intelligence community. The Soviet-Egyptian script, which would be repeated in 1967, would lead to the Six-Day War.

Egypt's efforts in the Sinai after Operation Rotem focused on the development of four military airfields. In El Arish, Bir Gafgafa, Jabel Libni, and Bir Thamada, new runways were built. Existing runways were elongated to receive the new jet aircraft. The agreement for the evacuation of the Sinai and the guarantee of a demilitarized desert, which had come about as a result of the Sinai Campaign, disappeared as if they had never existed. In a show flyover in the skies over Cairo in early 1961, eleven MiG-17 squadrons and three Ilyushin IL-28 bomber squadrons were displayed. Hundreds of Egyptian pilots and technicians flew to the Soviet Union to study the operations of the new twin-engined MiG-19.

After Yak's shooting down of the MiG in December 1958, the IAF had no need to set ambushes in order to test its skills. In the two years that followed, the Egyptians tested their strength in six attempts to infiltrate Israeli skies. In four of these conflicts, they were sent running without a shot being fired. In each of two dogfights, one in November 1959 and one in December 1960, a MiG-17 was hit but managed to land at their bases.

The next confrontation took place on April 28, 1961, and led to the destruction of an Egyptian plane. Two Israeli Super Mystères flew toward a pair of MiG-17s over the skies of Nitzana. An Israeli patrol and the soldiers of the Canadian branch of the UN International Force watched from the ground. Prepared for battle, the MiGs dropped their wing tanks and increased speed with the help of their afterburners. The Super Mystères also activated their afterburners. One of the MiGs flipped over in an effort to gain superiority by diving in a direction opposite to that in which he was flying. He was caught by the cannons of Tzur Ben-Barak, one of the squadron's youngsters. Tzur's partner saw the Egyptian pilot eject. The soldiers of the Israeli ground patrol followed the canopy of the yellow parachute and drove to the estimated landing spot to pick up their prisoner, but the Egyptian began to dash toward the nearby border crossing, and managed to escape.

In September 1961, the Syrians dismantled the unification with Egypt, enduring a series of internal military revolutions until the first establishment of rule by the Ba'ath Party in March 1963. Egypt found itself involved in the Yemen War, and Israel's borders were quiet for nearly two years. In 1964, Israel completed its national water-main project and was about to begin pumping water from the Sea of Galilee. Early that year, the Arab nations' summit meeting decided to divert the waters of the Jordan River, which supplied most of the water to the Israeli project.

The mission was allocated to Syria and Lebanon. Israel announced that it would view the diversion project as a provocation for war. In November, Israeli observation posts in the northern Jordan River Valley saw a large concentration of bulldozers and tractors in the area of the Banias, one of the water sources. The Syrians began to prepare features of the canal to divert the spring southward toward the Yarmukh River in order to enrich Jordanian irrigation in the Jordan River Valley. The IDF decided to fortify the sources of the Dan River and penetrated with patrols around the springs and through the dense underbush. Meir Zorea, chief of the Northern Command, walked before the lead bulldozer and made his way through the reeds. He was not deterred by the tank fire that began to come from the Syrian positions. The war over the water had begun.

At noon that day, November 13, the Syrians again attacked, this time striking at an armored personnel carrier on patrol along the Dan River. Israeli tanks shelled the Syrian positions. The Syrians widened their fire, and used cannons to shell Kibbutz Dan and the moshav of Shaar Yashuv. Far from there, David Ivri, the new commander of the Mirage squadron in Ramat David, had planned on a quiet Saturday with his squadrons on regular alert level. Though the northern base was closest to the only "hot" border since the Sinai Campaign, all of the major interceptions of the past years had occurred near the southern base. In earlier years, Ben-Gurion had forbidden the IAF to intervene in the border incidents for fear that it would lead to war. Before now, Israel simply endured the repetitive shelling of its settlements in the Galilee and the Hula Valley. The establishment of Syrian positions in the Golan Heights was altogether different. Yitzhak Rabin, the new chief of staff, proposed to the Prime Minister that they abandon the traditional methods of restraint and silence the Syrians from the air. Eshkol agreed immediately.

The IAF was determined to act on their declaration that the diversion of the waters of the Jordan would be a cause for war. Ezer Weizman received the order in his home and commanded David Ivri to activate Ramat David. Ivri organized a mission force from his Mirages and from the base's Mystère and Vautour squadrons. This would be their first combat activity, as well as the first attack on ground targets since the Sinai Campaign. If Ivri did not want to be suspected of disrupting the balance of the "justice tables," he had to guarantee equal parts in the action to all the base's squadrons. Within forty minutes of his conversation with Ezer and the activation of the sirens, sixteen aircraft were ready for takeoff— Mirages (in their first bombing mission in world history) and Vautours armed with bombs, as well as Mystères with napalm. The members of each team had been given their targets. At the last moment, Ivri ran from plane to plane ensuring that everyone had remembered to cock their cannons and arm the bomb fuses. Ivri's even temper belied the gravity of the situation.

Fifteen minutes later, they dove on the Syrian positions at Tel Azaziat, Tel Hamra, and Nuheila, and ensured a quiet Sabbath for the Israeli communities in the north. Without alert and on short notice, the IAF had been ready. David Ivri viewed the confrontation as the first true test of the top line of those who would lead the next war. The IAF's successful operation tempered relations over the next seventeen months. Eshkol and Rabin, not wanting to heighten the war over the water, removed the IAF and the artillery from the circle. The Israeli tank sharpshooters, who consistently sabotaged the heavy engineering equipment, forced the Syrians to retreat into their own territory. Hoping to avoid a full-fledged war, the Arab countries, led by Egypt, withdrew their support of the project. The Syrians continued alone and covered their diversion efforts with attacks on Israeli tractors and patrols.

As the assaults continued into the summer of 1966, Israel decided to put an end to the Syrian attacks and the water-diversion project. On the morning of July 14, the Ramat David Vautours and Mystères began to bomb and destroy concentrations of engineering equipment at Ein A-Sfira, east of the Sea of Galilee. The Mirages provided intercept backup from high altitude.

Yoram Agmon envied the attackers. The previous evening he had been summoned from the Flight School to his emergency role in the squadron, and he had jumped at the operational opportunity in order to escape the drudgery of training. That day he had been one of four pilots "pressing" the clean skies.

"Turn west at full power," Flight Control commanded Yoram.

Thinking his chances to experience battle were completely gone, he was angry at the flight controller's order. But he obeyed automatically, as he had been trained to do. At first he did not understand that they were preparing him to attack with the advantage of speed.

"Turn east and at the end of the turn, enemy aircraft to your left and below."

Yoram did not have to bother searching. They glimmered below him. He made eye contact with one of them and informed his leader, "I'm on him."

In a sharp maneuver, he released his drop tanks. The chase was difficult, for the enemy aircraft were swallowed up by the colors of the territory. Yoram dove and increased speed, steadying at an altitude where he would be able to see the enemy aircraft better. They disappeared as Yoram neared the ground at five hundred knots. As he cursed and continued on, they suddenly appeared before him again. Two MiG-21s. His heart skipped a beat. They had never encountered these modern aircraft in the air to verify the legends of their abilities. The MiGs were also shocked by the sudden encounter. They broke hard to avoid him. The right MiG disappeared. Yoram maneuvered behind the left one. Aware of the danger, the MiG dropped his tanks. Yoram approached to five hundred meters, cannon range, aimed, and fired. He missed and felt an instant of disappointment.

The Mirage was not a perfect weapon in all respects. Behind the thrills of the speed and maneuverability lay an unreliable engine and control systems. The radar-aimed cannons, which were supposed to be precise, had failed in a number of battles. The pilots, relying on the automatic measurement of ranges, often struck air. At first they suspected that they were improperly calibrating the mechanisms. But later they grumbled about the Dassault factories, which might have provided faulty cannons since they had been forced to add them to the original model. Ephraim Ashkenazi, a pilot and electrical engineer, figured the source of the problem was in the radar system. In a laboratory check, he discovered that it was making mistakes by providing the aiming mechanism with faulty data. Ashkenazi improved the system and received the Israel Defense Award. Yoram had been told that the problem in the Mirages had been repaired, but recalled that they had forgotten to fix the problem in his aircraft.

The MiG pulled in a sharp turn. Yoram stuck to him and closed range to 250 meters. He concentrated on his aim and fired again. Immediately an explosion burst out of the MiG's left wing. It separated from the body of the plane, and the aircraft went into a spin. As he passed over it, Yoram saw the pilot eject. These were two firsts, the first hit scored by a Mirage in combat, and the first MiG-21 shot down. Yoram sang all the way home. Above the runway of Ramat David, he executed his victory roll.

That evening a congratulatory telegram arrived from France, thanking Israel for this wonderful gift on the French Independence Day. The Syrians halted the diversion project.

Ezer Weizman did not preside over the first wing ceremony at the new flight school at Hatzerim, near Be'er Sheva. Around the time of the transfer of the school from Tel Nof, in April 1966, he completed his unprecedented eighth year as commander-in-chief of the IAF. Nearly double the accepted term, his tenure had been extended because of his success and his determination to transfer command to Moti Hod. Ezer essentially felt that his life mission—the creation of an air force that would win the next war—had been completed a year or two earlier. Ever since the War of Independence, he had been developing the idea of destroying the Arab air forces on the ground. He had not even substantially altered the first plans drawn up by his predecessors before the Sinai Campaign. Any skilled commander could transpose them to the jet age and to the new Arab airfields. Ezer had trained his units well. With the exception of one small conflict, he had been spared the battle for the IAF's independence that had embittered the lives of his predecessors. In Ezer's first year as commander-in-chief of the IAF, the Upper Command of the IDF decided that the IAF was important enough that its headquarters should be transferred from Ramle to IDF headquarters in Tel Aviv.

Ezer demanded and received a symbolic fence between the General Command wing and the new IAF headquarters buildings, as well as a separate gate with an IAF flag and IAF guards. At the ceremony inaugurating the new headquarters, Ezer provided a flyover by a formation of Mystères, just so they would know who their new neighbors were.

Several weeks prior to the transfer of command, fourteen months before the Six-Day War, Ezer still elicited chuckles at a lecture he gave at the School for Leadership and Command, in which he stated that the Egyptian Air Force would be destroyed between breakfast and lunch. There could be no other solution to the upcoming war. The acquisition of territory in a short period of time was a necessity.

"Moti Hod will lead you to victory," Ezar promised in the ceremony transferring command. On the Tel Nof runway, following a long and heart-wrenching ceremony marking his departure from the IAF, Ezer closed his twenty-four-year reign. After the ceremony, he climbed into his black Spitfire and took off to wave his wings in farewell.

For the first time in its history, the IAF received a commander-in-chief who was not a major general. Moti Hod, forty years old, had been a colonel only five years. He had undergone a training period for this new role such as none of his predecessors had received. He had been commander of the Air Division and essentially deputy commander-in-chief of the IAF. He and Ezer had shared complete cooperation, even though Moti was more introverted and withdrawn, which sometimes frustrated those around him. In the years preceding his command, he oversaw the functioning of IAF headquarters, supervising budgets and managing IAF priorities. He flew in all the squadrons and became acquainted with every unit to the point where he personally knew everyone.

What Ezer had sown, Moti reaped. In his fourth month of command, he succeeded in terminating the Syrian attempt to divert the waters of the Jordan. He also congratulated Yoram Agmon, who had shot down the first MiG-21 in history. Exactly one month later, on August 15, 1966, he directed a morning of dogfights and bombing over the Sea of Galilee to protect an Israeli Navy landing craft that had run aground near the Syrian-controlled eastern shore. The landing craft was used to protect the Israeli night fishermen, whom the Syrians had begun to steal from and fire at. On one of its patrols, the landing craft got stuck on a sandbar near the eastern shore, and the Syrian positions began to shower them with intensive fire. The exchange of fire increased until Syrian MiGs appeared in the skies. Moti was summoned to the Control Center immediately after the first Syrian aircraft were seen in the air. He placed the Mirage squadron on alert, as well as part of the Vautour squadron in Ramat David. Throughout the years, Syria had avoided using aircraft in the border incidents, and Israel had ceased using them after the El Hama and Tel Muteila incidents fifteen years earlier. While both sides strove not to let the incidents spread beyond the demilitarized zones, the Syrians had now broken the barrier by shelling Israeli towns and diverting the waters of the Jordan River. When Syria began to shell Israel's northern communities in November 1964, the IAF retaliated aggressively. Having destroyed the Syrian equipment a month earlier, Moti expected the intervention of the Syrian Air Force in the next incident. He was ready to respond.

Yehuda Koren's and Avi Lanir's Mirages pressed the Galilee skies, and the Syrian MiG-17 aircraft gave no indication that they intended to cross the Golan Heights border. Suddenly they began strafing runs that began in their own territory, striking at Israeli targets sailing close to the border. Anyone attempting to avoid Syrian airspace so as not to provoke a more serious incident would endanger the Israeli vessels. Moti was given permission to use his aircraft immediately after the strafings. The Syrian MiG-17s, however, were now back deep into their own territory. Koren and Lanir did not regret this. The backup of the MiG-21s was more alluring in its challenge, particularly because they were flying in the gray area between the Golan Heights and the Sea of Galilee. From twenty thousand feet, the border is indistinguishable. The flight controller directed them at the moment when the landing craft was about to recommence its work. The Mirages descended on them from thirty thousand feet, and the battle was short. Koren shot down a MiG-21, the second in one month. The other escaped.

In all, fifteen minutes had elapsed since the strafing of the Israeli boats. The skies were now clean, and the rescue landing craft could approach the sandbar. The Syrian shore positions, not realizing they had lost their air cover, renewed the shelling of the boats. Two shells struck the deck of the beached landing craft, throwing four of its crew into the water. The commander of the fleet demanded that the Syrian positions be silenced before any of his men would be killed. David "Dado" Elazar, chief of the Northern Command, explained that he had no artillery in west of the Sea of Galilee. The chief of staff gave Moti permission to attack the ground targets. Three Vautour bombers were standing ready on the runways of Ramat David. They departed at 0925 hours. Five minutes later they were bombing the banana plantations on the Masoudiya coast. The Syrian positions disappeared, and the Israeli boat and its crew were rescued. The Syrians withdrew from the region for an extended period of time.

The following afternoon, three men dressed in colorful shirts and bathing suits climbed onto the deck of a landing craft. Rabin, Ezer (now commander of the IDF Operations Branch), and Dado had all gathered to plan the rescue operation. A Navy officer asked Ezer if he could not find another time to tan himself at the Sea of Galilee, since such major events were occurring in the IAF. The officer had heard a rumor, but did not know exactly what was going on. Realizing that the tense moments of expectation had now ended, Ezer called Moti, who verified this in two words: "It's here."

It could be seen on the radar screens at an elevation of thirty thousand feet, heading west from Jordan on a route that would cross the Israeli border just south of the Dead Sea. Moti followed the flashing blip on the screen in the Control Center, and ordered that two Mirages from Hatzor be scrambled toward it. He made the pilots swear that they would check meticulously whether it had aggressive intentions and not open fire without his specific command. Until the last moment, he was worried that they had all fallen prey to a clever ruse. The letter he had received a few weeks earlier through a third party in Europe he had perceived as a practical joke. The writer of the letter, Muneir Radfa, had said that he was a pilot in the Iraqi Air Force and wanted to desert. He had personal reasons to seek out a new life beyond the borders of his country, and would arrive with a new fighter aircraft. Would General Hod be willing to promise that the IAF would not injure him and allow him to land in peace? The pilot requested a rapid response and detailed how he could be reached. The letter was passed on to Yeshayahu "Shaike" Bareket, the chief of IAF intelligence. Bareket, a fighter pilot who had flown in Moti's Ouragan squadron during the Sinai Campaign, was Ezer's personal choice for the job. He had been looking for a pilot experienced enough to detect a possible threat.

After an initial check, the pilot was sent an affirmative response, but he was requested to identify himself in a first meeting. He agreed. The meeting was set in a neutral country to which he could travel without raising suspicions. Captain Radfa was a thirty-year-old Assyrian Christian who explained that his progress in the Iraqi Air Force had been halted because of his ethnic-national background. The members of his ethnic group were a minority in Iraq, composing less than two percent of the population. According to him, after five years of bombing the strongholds of the Kurdish rebels, with whom he identified, he had begun to feel frustrated and embittered. During several periods he had been placed under surveillance, and had never been popular among the Muslim fighter pilots. "Almost like the Jews," he said. Radfa expressed his willingness to reach Israel, even with a MiG-21. The Israeli intelligence envoy's impression was that his motives were viable and that his intentions were sincere.

Israel decided to take the risk and receive him. Two years earlier, in January 1964, an Egyptian pilot who had deserted to Israel in a piston-engined Yak-11 training aircraft had been given refuge. The seduction of obtaining the Eastern Bloc's first-line secret aircraft was strong. If Radfa's intentions were aggressive, it would be possible to shoot him down over the Negev or before he reached the center of the country. A date and flight route were agreed upon. However, he would not take off until he had sent his wife and children abroad without raising suspicions, and he still did not know how or when he could do so. He would then have to wait until he could obtain a training sortie in the western desert bordering on Jordan, from whence he could escape with the least risk.

The estimated date was mid-August. The flight controllers were ordered to report any unusual movement in southern Jordan. On that day, Moti followed the suspicious dot and awaited the Mirages' reports.

"It's an unarmed Iraqi MiG-21. Makes a friendly impression," he heard the Mirage leader say, noting the surprise in his voice. From the moment they achieved eye contact, it was clear that the Iraqi had no hostile intentions.

"Roger. Land him at the base."

Besides those at Hatzor and in the Upper Command, Danny Shapira was one of the first people Moti informed of the secret. Announcement of the event was postponed until the safety of the pilot's family, which had already left Iraq, could be guaranteed. I was instructed to keep one helicopter separate from the rest of the squadron so that it could transport Muneir Radfa from Hatzor to Tel Aviv. After embracing Shaike Bareket, he was introduced to Danny, who now received the MiG-21. He would study the aircraft and train others on it. Even the top fliers were not permitted to touch it. First, the blue star of the IAF was painted on the MiG's body and wings, and in place of its original number, 534, they inscribed 007, an expression of the James Bond–like adventure that had brought it to Israel. Muneir Radfa had been thorough, and had brought along the MiG's instruction book. For days he sat with Danny, translating the manual for him piece by piece, and also leading him through the plane, meticulously explaining every lever and switch in the cockpit. In comparison to the elegant Mirage with its "no hands" flight, the MiG had a plethora of levers and buttons in an illogical order. While Muneir agreed that the cockpit was uncomfortable and disorganized, he explained that the plane was easy to fly. The systems were simple and easy to maintain, even for the most amateur of mechanics. Danny encouraged Muneir not to provide too many details. The surprise and the challenge were part of his personal pleasure in a first test flight.

Muneir said to him, "You don't intend to climb into the plane tomorrow just like that and fly it without my instructions?"

Danny answered him, "That's exactly what I intend to do."

"You're crazy," Muneir told him. In Iraq, one earned the privilege of a new aircraft only after an extended period of detailed ground courses and instruction flights in a training aircraft. Danny was not disconcerted by Muneir's exaggerated concern.

Ezer and Moti traveled to Hatzor to witness the first flight.

"You know that all the world's eyes are watching you," Ezer told Danny, for the desertion was big news. The press was convinced that the aircraft had been stolen and smuggled to Israel in an imaginative intelligence operation. The military representative in the U.S. embassy had already begun to attempt to find out when he could view the aircraft.

Ezer wanted to conduct the test flights safely. During his period as commander-in-chief, he had begun to express interest in the U.S.-made Skyhawk and the timetable for its sale to Israel. He saw Israel's future in American aircraft, though up to this point the United States had sold Israel defense weapons only. The IAF's antiaircraft battalions were equipped with Hawk missiles. The secrets of the MiG-21 would be an excellent bargaining chip in canceling the embargo on Skyhawk sales.

Danny harnessed himself into the MiG's cockpit, confident that he could master the aircraft and its flight. But would he also be able to handle himself in the wild trials he was about to put the MiG through? The gauges were the first concern. It seemed that he was flying slower or higher than they registered, for the Soviets measured altitude in meters rather than feet, and speed in kilometers per hour rather than in knots. The conversion process made a difficult flight even more so. Danny had to multiply altitude by three and speed by 1.6. Several flights later, the gauges were changed. Even so, the first flight was fast and easy. To Danny, if felt like the Mirage, but was a bit faster and had a lower peak altitude of forty thousand feet.

In the second flight, he began to maneuver and discovered how the MiG differed from the Mirage. The MiG was difficult to steer at speeds over five hundred knots. Danny had to use tremendous strength on the stick to steady the aircraft in turns, particularly sharp ones. At greater speeds, the danger increased. The nose and the right wing pulled downward. In the first combat test with a Mirage, he proved that the MiG had a true disadvantage that he had always suspected. Since the back of the cockpit was obstructed, the plane's field of vision was severely limited.

Danny set out on a tour of the squadrons with the first lessons learned from the MiG. At each squadron he gained more experience. After a theoretical class with a squadron's fliers, they took off for a practical lesson. This included a series of mock dogfights with the squadron commander, his deputy, and the top leaders. The only weapons used were the gunsight cameras, and when their motion picture films had been developed, they were analyzed by the participants. He flew ten battles with every squadron, each an hour long. In the first half-year, he was in the air more than twice his usual time. The conclusions were as follows: The MiG handled evenly with the Mirage, slightly better than the Super Mystère, and much better than the standard Mystère. If the MiG-21 were given to the veteran top fliers of the IAF, including Yak and Yalo, or Ran Ronen and the up-and-coming star Ehud Hankin, the advantage would clearly be in their hands. Israel's pilots began to learn the aircraft well, and strove to correct its weak points, given its stronger engine and greater speeds.

Relative quiet reigned over the northern border during the first seven months of the learning process. UN observers proposed programs for the cultivation of the lands in the demilitarized zones. The Syrians agreed halfheartedly to a cease-fire. The first condition, which forbade bringing military forces and heavy weapons into the zones, was immediately ignored. In early April 1967, the battleground was in the southern region of the demilitarized zones, the shores of the Sea of Galilee.

On April 7, the Syrians escalated the fire. Two Israeli tractors were attacked with machine-gun and antiaircraft fire from the top of a Syrian cliff. Tanks and heavy mortars joined in the shelling. Two tractors were destroyed, and an IDF officer was killed. At midday the UN negotiated a cease-fire, which lasted an hour and a half before Syrian artillery batteries along the Golan Heights again began to shell Israel. The Prime Minister ordered that they be countered by the IAF. The Mirage squadrons from Tel Nof and Ramat David received the mission. With their operational flexibility, they could attack the batteries and also intercept Syrian MiGs. For two hours they bombed the eighteen fortified batteries in waves. The dogfights continued an hour longer.

At 1400 hours, Yiftah Spector and Benny Romah encountered a quartet of MiG-21s. A dogfight began over Kuneitra and concluded with two MiGs shot down over Damascus, one MiG for each of the Israeli pilots. At 1600 hours, Ezra "Baban" Dotan shot down another MiG-21 over Kibbutz Shamir, following a twenty-minute battle between a pair from each side. It was a longer and more difficult confrontation than his last, in August 1962, against eight MiG-17s over the Sea of Galilee. In that fight he had hit one, but had not downed it.

The third and final dogfight involved the largest number of planes, but ended the most quickly. It took place fifteen minutes after Baban's fight over the Yarmukh Canyon, which crosses from Syria to Jordan. Ran Ronen's quartet faced a Syrian quartet. Within minutes, three MiG-21s crashed in Jordanian territory. Ran, now a squadron commander, shot one down to reinforce his leadership and for personal satisfaction. The other two were shot down by Avner Slapak and Avi Lanir. Avi fired at his MiG from close range, and it exploded at once, forcing Avi to fly through its flames. His plane emerged miraculously undamaged but covered in soot; from that point on, it was known as the "Black Mirage." The three Syrian pilots could be seen parachuting behind the smoking trails of their aircraft. On the Galilee shore, below the cliff of the Golan Heights, five Israeli tractors set out to plow the fields until nightfall.

Danny Shapira was told the results of the day—six to zero—and received them as a personal victory. That evening the chief of staff promoted Moti Hod to major general.

# 5 The Six-Day War

*June 4, 1967, 2100 Hours*  $T$ he third major conflict in the nineteen years since the formation of the State of Israel did not start on the day when the fighting commenced; this was simply one more round in the Arab war against the Zionist presence in Israel, a war that has now lasted, with intermissions, for nearly fifty years, changing its name, its weapons, and its methods of combat.

This third round was sparked by personal motivations and national interests that were no longer in the control of the politicians. The accepted starting date is May 15, three weeks prior to the outbreak of the war. This was the day on which Egypt's president, Gamal Abdel Nasser, moved his tank divisions to the Sinai Peninsula front. However, a more correct date would be April 7, the day on which six Syrian MiGs were shot down by Israeli aircraft. Damascus cried for help from Moscow, and the Russians demanded that Israel cease its attacks on the Syrians. Syria continued shelling Israel's northern settlements, and Prime Minister Levi Eshkol threatened aggressive retaliation. The IDF's chief of staff, Lt. Gen. Yitzhak Rabin, stated that Israel was striving to bring about the collapse of the Damascus government. The Soviets, imagining IDF units stationed in the central Galilee and on the verge of invading Syria, demanded their dispersion. The Soviet ambassador in Tel Aviv invited himself to a night meeting with Eshkol, but refused the Prime Minister's offer to travel to the north to see that the imagined armored and infantry companies did not exist.

As in the case of Operation Rotem, seven years earlier, Nasser availed himself of the false impressions to prove to the Syrians that he was their true savior, and he proceeded to send his military forces to pressure Israel on its southern border. His goal was not war, but rather to "rid Israel of any notion of war." This time he moved his troops in a display of force that began in Cairo. Israel responded by calling up a small reserve unit.

The masses in Egypt and the Arab capitals lauded Nasser for his daring, and swept him away in their enthusiasm. The next day he requested the commander of the UN's International Force to reduce its presence in Gaza, Sharm-al-Sheikh, and Kuntilla. The Secretary General of the UN refused, and stated that forces would remain in their positions along the entire border or would leave entirely. Nasser replied, "Let them go! " and on May 19 the UN flags were lowered from the abandoned positions in the Sinai.

Within one night, the symbolic obstacle that had been one of the primary elements of collateral for Israel's withdrawal from the Sinai after the 1956 conflict had disappeared. The next day a second piece of collateral began to disintegrate as well. A force of Egyptian paratroopers took over Sharm-al-Sheikh, putting a halt to Israel's freedom to sail to its southern port of Eilat.

The IDF called up all its reserve forces. Abba Eban, Israel's Foreign Minister, was sent to Paris, London, and Washington to collect on the collateral it had earned in 1957; he requested that the Egyptians be pressured to evacuate the Sinai and remove the blockade. Eban's requests were brushed aside by the international community, and the message conveyed to him was that Israel had better not start a war. One hundred thousand Egyptian soldiers were already in position in the Sinai. While the regular Egyptian army could flex its muscles with threats of invasion indefinitely, the Israeli economy could not survive a long-term mobilization of its reserve army.

The government could not decide whether to view the Egyptian threat as a pretext for war. None of the familiar signs from the international relations dictionary could be discerned here, and the government avoided drawing any conclusions that would appear rash, even when the voices emanating from Cairo began to leave no room for doubt. Articles in the Egyptian press, patently approved by the president, concluded that war was inevitable, and Nasser declared to a delegation of Arab emissaries that this would be the "total war for the destruction of Israel."

The hesitation of the Israeli government to adopt IDF Upper Command plans to destroy the Egyptian forces with a preemptive strike prior to the completion of its preparations along the border was not due to kindness but rather to a lack of faith. The IAF Commander until 1966, Maj. Gen. Ezer Weizman, boasted that the IAF could lay waste to

Egypt's aircraft in their bases within the first six hours of combat. Chief of Staff Rabin's recommendation to initiate a preemptive strike divided the government. By a margin of one vote, it was decided to give an additional extension to allow for any possible international intervention.

Palestinian terrorists, this time under the guise of Fatah (the Palestine Liberation Organization), which was founded in 1965 under Syrian auspices, again began to cross the border from Jordan, attacking settlements and murdering Israeli citizens. The rare Israeli retaliatory operations had a negligible effect. Public confidence, not only in the Minister of Defense, who had shown a lack of backbone throughout the entire conflict, but also in the IDF as well, was dropping. The public was not emotionally prepared, as it had been prior to Operation Kaddesh, and lacked a sense of confidence in its reserve units. Within several weeks, Israel began to appear to its neighbors and to the world as a weak and frightened nation. Under this impression, Jordan's King Hussein flew to Cairo on May 30 to make peace with Nasser, his lifelong enemy, and to place his military under Egyptian command. In the shadow of this sudden alliance, Israeli Jerusalem was now in danger of being conquered.

Thus, during the first days of June 1967, the Arabs' behavior resulted in something quite opposite to what it had sought to achieve. As the threat to Israel's national survival grew, fewer and fewer Israelis left the country, communal pride grew, and social barriers broke down, reinstilling confidence and creating one large supportive family.

Israel's Operation Moked was devised upon a model similar to that of Operation Barbarossa, the German Luftwaffe operation that, on June 22, 1941, eradicated much of the Soviet air force before it could even take off. For the first time in military history, an air force had been built and trained over many of years with the goal of defeating its enemy in just such an operation. The idea that the best defense of the nation's skies and the achieving of air superiority must lie in a devastating preemptive strike on the enemy's air bases was not easy to assimilate after years of defensive thinking. Dan Tolkowsky had initiated it, and from 1953 he had also issued the operation orders, which included only the front-line bases in Sinai.

In the early 1960s, the Operations Branch commander, Rafi Har-Lev, and the top helicopter navigator, Rafi Sivron, had begun the first discussion in IAF headquarters regarding a new and broad plan for the early neutralization of all Arab air bases. The primary problem of this effort was to involve all the necessary elements of the air force in the planning and development while maintaining the secrecy necessary for the plan's ultimate success. The design was rooted in superior, comprehensive intelligence. The information they needed to assimilate included locations of aircraft, munitions, and fuel supplies, as well as data on pilots and their operational training; on air base design and defenses, including runway thickness and materials; on flight control, radar, and regional control centers; and on aircraft scrambling techniques. The answers to these and countless other questions needed to be organized in an intelligence center and dispersed to every squadron according to its function, so that the information could be used in both planning and training. This change in approach demanded a radical modification of the intelligence network's style of thinking in addition to extensive work by the reconnaissance aircraft and all branches of Israel's intelligence network.

Israel was prepared for war in 1967 with 180 bombers and attack aircraft including Ouragans, Mystères, Super Mystères, Mirages, and Vautours. In addition, the IAF had twenty Fouga Magister training aircraft, which had been modified for limited attack operations, forty helicopters (Sikorsky 58s, Super Frelons, and Bell G-47s), and thirty transport aircraft (Nords and Dakotas). Still, the three enemy Arab air forces outnumbered Israel more than two to one. Egypt alone outnumbered Israel one and a half times with its 420 combat aircraft, which included MiGs and Sukhois, as well as some Vampires and Hawker Hunters, Tupolev TU-16 Badger bombers, Ilyushins, and Antonovs. In addition they had forty-two helicopters (Mi-4s and Mi-6s). Syria had one hundred aircraft of the same types as Egypt's and Jordan had twenty-four (primarily Hunters). Backing up Jordan, Iraq had ninety-eight fighter and bomber aircraft.

The aircraft of the Egyptian Air Force were located at eighteen airfields, four of them in the Sinai, three along the Suez Canal, six in the Nile Delta, and five in Upper Egypt. The Syrians were using six airfields, and the Jordanians two. The first strike would have to include the seven forward airfields in the Sinai and the Suez Canal, and the six in the Nile Delta.

Plans for Operation Moked began in 1963 and were repeatedly updated over the course of the following years as intelligence information dictated. An ever greater number of squadrons were sent on reconnaissance missions whose technical efficiency was constantly improving. These included high-altitude vertical reconnaissance shots as well as low-altitude angle and panorama shots.

The general plan involved grounding enemy aircraft during the first run by bombing the runways, and then destroying the aircraft themselves in the following runs with rockets and cannons. In 1966 came the first trial use of a bomb for runway demolition. The bomb had been developed by the Israeli Military Industries according to the planners' requests. Its power of destruction was reciprocal to its light weight of 154 pounds. It would create a crater five meters wide and one and a half meters deep, much greater than the damage inflicted by the heaviest conventional bombs that could be used. Unlike conventional bombs, the runway demolition bomb would be dropped from an altitude of one hundred meters, slowed down by a parachute that would simultaneously activate a rocket that would propel it with super force through the protective layers of the runway. The explosion would occur after six seconds.

Because of the need for maximum bomb loads to be carried by a maximum number of aircraft in every wave, a greater degree of autonomy would be given to each air base in controlling the activities of its squadrons. To cope with the huge scale of the attack, every plane was scheduled for four to five sorties each day. During the first two runs, emphasis was placed on the technical readiness of the aircraft, with maintenance intervals between sorties reduced to mere minutes. The operational and technical crews would not give up. Shortening the technical break turned into a competitive sport. At first it was between the aircraft crews, but later it turned into an organized series of events between squadrons and bases, with judges measuring times to tenths of seconds presenting awards and prizes at the conclusion. During peacetime, however, they could not rehearse unforeseen technical problems or battle damage to the aircraft. Maintenance control centers were built that held files on each aircraft and the services it had undergone during its history. A communications system was developed to receive warning of problems as damaged or malfunctioning aircraft were returning to base. This ensured that the appropriate experts would be waiting for the aircraft upon its return, with the necessary tools and parts. The system covered all aspects of technical support and guaranteed that the bases' warehouses held the necessary fuel, munitions, and parts while not having more than they could hold.

The aircraft sheds now became a second home for the technical crews. Beyond professional pride, they sought to prove that they were of equal value to themselves and the aircrews, able to prepare an aircraft for operations under any conditions and with top quality. This attitude was the primary achievement of all levels of the commanding ranks of the technical network during the preparations for Operation Moked.

As Ezer Weizman had planned, air superiority would be achieved within six hours of the commencement of the attack through the decimation of the majority of the enemy's aircraft while still on the ground.

In the weeks prior to June 1967, Operation Moked was updated according to current intelligence information. Under the assumption that the Syrians would not be able to respond until the completion of the first wave, almost the entire IAF would be sent to destroy the Egyptian Air Force. The attack on the thirteen Egyptian air bases was designed to cause paralysis and prevent any attempts at defense or the escape of aircraft from base to base, a maneuver that the Egyptians had rehearsed many times.

Targets were allocated according to flight range of the attacking aircraft, level of threat at each target, and the attack capabilities of each type of aircraft. Priority was given to the destruction of the MiG-21s and TU-16s and their air bases. The bases near the Sinai Peninsula were allocated to the Ouragans, the Mystères, and the Fouga Magisters, which were slower and had a shorter range. The faster and more sophisticated Super Mystères and Mirages were assigned the bases along the Suez Canal and the Nile Delta. The Vautours were sent to the distant bases in Upper Egypt. Last-minute changes were necessitated by the discovery of MiG-21 squadrons at the nearby bases, and the original forces were reinforced by several Mirages.

During the first wave, Israeli aircraft would take off in formations of four planes each on three primary flight plans, reaching the Mediterranean together and then diverging according to target. Speed would be under Mach 1, and altitude would not exceed thirty feet, at which height the aircraft would remain undetectable to Egyptian radar. Though still in its infancy, electronic warfare would be used to confuse Egyptian communications and radar systems as well as the missile batteries and anti-aircraft guns. This would occur precisely during the seconds when the aircraft were to pull up and reach altitude prior to diving down to the targets. In actuality, only one Jordanian radar station near Amman noticed the takeoff of the first wave, but its officers attributed this to the presence of the U.S. Sixth Fleet in the region.

After a long period of studying the region of operations in Egypt, gathering meteorological data regarding the desert and the Nile Valley during the summer months, and determining the daily routines of the Egyptian aircrews and technical teams, attack times for primary targets, near and far, were calculated. At 0745 hours, all Egyptian fighter aircraft would have landed after their dawn patrols. Most of the commanders, pilots, and technicians would be on their way from home or to the dining halls, out of reach of communications and flight control. The sun would already have risen, and the morning patches of fog would have dissipated.

Even during this final period of planning, the new IAF commander, Maj. Gen. Moti Hod, was attempting to convince the IDF Upper Command of the operation's reliability. Though Prime Minister Eshkol repeatedly demanded a commitment that "not a single bomb" would fall on Tel Aviv, Hod would only promise that the city would not be damaged by "massive bombings." Never did he state directly that the entire IAF would attack during Operation Moked and that only twelve aircraft would be allocated to defending the nation's skies.

On June 5, at 0700 hours, in the underground control center, the countdown concluded. At Hod's command of "Execute Moked," the formations began to take off from the runways at Ramat David, Tel Nof, and Hatzor, one after another, according to a schedule calculated to the minute and second. A fleet of 160 aircraft, the likes of which had never been seen in this region, turned toward the Mediterranean, flying just above the waves' whitecaps.

**June 5, 1967, 0500 hours:**
**Zvi Umshweif**             Yalo Shavit, commander of the Scorpion Squadron, held in his hand the command order for Operation Moked and read it aloud in a celebratory voice, as if it were the Declaration of Independence. Zvi Umshweif heard him utter the announcement for which most of them had been waiting at least two weeks—that the IDF would be invading the Sinai that morning with three brigades, and that the IAF would open the war at exactly 0745 hours in a strike against all of the Egyptian Air Force's bases. As Yalo began to delineate the

squadron's missions in bombing the Inshas and Kabrit airfields, Zvi suddenly found himself swept into a time tunnel. This had not happened during the days of waiting when the nation feared another holocaust. Perhaps because he was preoccupied with preparations for the operation and knew the facts, he could ignore the rumors. However, the memories returned to him at the instant the squadron commander informed him that Moked was indeed a fact and that in two hours the nightmare would be carried to the enemy's camp. Memories of his own Holocaust, which he had attempted to repress for many years, suddenly flooded him.

"I will never understand why my childhood was suddenly portrayed before me like a hologram on the maps and reconnaissance photographs of the Egyptian airfields, as Yalo drew on them with his finger," he would later say. What he saw was a montage of images of a six-year-old boy sent to Auschwitz with his mother and father. "My father, a well-known chemist, was important and vital to the Nazis. Because of him, a humane German soldier kept watch on me and my mother as Father left to work every morning from our shack next to the longer building filled with living skeletons and shadows of life. They would arrive and disappear, and only we remained. Mother and Father were emotional and concerned, and I did not know why. It continued this way for two years, nearly until the end of the war. We were sent to the Death March, and I suddenly understood what death was. Father disappeared and never returned. Mother fell ill with typhus and never returned. I was placed in a monastery in Czechoslovakia, where one of the nuns acted like a mother to me. I again became like other children. They requested that I change my name, but I refused, fearing that that was all that remained of my family. Because of my name, an uncle succeeded in locating me and decided that I would travel with him to Palestine. Thus a nine-year-old boy took the train from the displaced-persons camp in Germany to Marseilles and from there, with a forged passport, traveled to the Land of Israel. On Kibbutz Ein HaMifratz I learned to eat healthy food and grew addicted to studying, open air, and sports. I returned to life. In 1955, already a pilot and a member of the Israeli national volleyball team, I was sent to the European championship in Czechsolovakia. Between rounds, I set out in search of my dear nun. I found her. I can still see us embracing, and I control myself so that those very tears will not begin flowing again. The entire gang around me would see and not understand. Who ever saw a pilot crying before a war?"

"Hey, Zvika? You with us?" Yalo's thundering voice brought him back to the briefing at the last moment.

"Yeah, I was in the middle of the war," Zvi responded, without specifying which war.

### June 5, 1967, 0500 Hours:
### The Inverted Sword Squadron

*T*he briefing room was crowded with all of our pilots, flight mechanics, and others associated with the squadron. I outlined the basics of Operation Moked step by step and described our missions, dividing up teams for aircrew rescue. I announced the allocation of group leaders and pilots to the evening missions in that we might still be needed for the ground command centers in the Sinai and for the capturing of Egyptian airfields.

Immediately following the briefing, the movement started. The squadron's technical and administrative wings set out in a convoy toward Ashkelon in order to establish the forward field command center. One helicopter was sent north as standby for rescues, and two remained in Tel Nof for rescue missions in the country's central region. Two additional ones flew to Sde Dov to serve the chief of staff and Special Missions. After an emotional parting, I climbed into my helicopter to lead the twenty-four others that would follow me at treetop level. All electrical systems were shut down and absolute radio silence was maintained so as not to attract attention to the dozens of fighter aircraft heading for the Egyptian air bases.

Upon arrival in Ashkelon, we quickly set up a mobile operations center and connected to previously prepared phone lines. Communications with the IAF command was now in order. As our Tel Nof convoy began to roll in, the ground beneath us began to shake. Above our heads at low altitude passed formations of Mystères and Super Mystères. Just north of us we could see formations of Mirages flying low and heavy. It had begun.

### June 5, 1967, 0700 Hours:
### Zvi Umshweif, Hatzor

*Z*vi's Story: All around us, everything was tight and crowded, everything on edge and ready. We were set to take off in two minutes. Precision and order were the name of the game. Everything had been calculated, from takeoff until our turn over the target at the exact time. Though timing is always crucial, in this operation seconds were critical.

We had been trying to pretend that the tension had diminished on our side. On Saturday, two days earlier, the beaches had been packed with thousands of reservists who had received weekend vacations. A few Fouga Magisters simulated the radio transmissions of two squadrons to give the impression that the flight school was having regular exercises. The quiet in my cockpit was so intense that all I could hear was my heart pounding and the sound of my breathing in the oxygen mask. I wondered if the line of MiG-17s in Kabrit would still be waiting for me when I arrived. I knew every corner of that Egyptian base, which was our squadron's target, 280 kilometers from here on a roundabout route over the ocean. Flying time of half an hour, more or less. Every photo and every piece of data was embedded in our memory.

In the air, the G force of five hundred knots pasted me to my seat. Suddenly Kabrit was below us, clearer than any practice range I had ever seen in my life. Black strips of runway on a bright carpet. Even the MiG-17s were just as in the films. Not a single one had been moved. I could not believe that we have surprised them so completely.

We began to execute our mission with no interference. I focused on my dive—angle, speed, altitude. The runway closed in. When the precise moment arrived, I released my bombs. We rolled sharply and began a strafing run. In the midst of our turn we could hear incredible explosions. The delay detonators of the bombs that we had sunk deep into the runways had awakened on time. Every shot a wonderful bull's-eye, and the field was littered with gaping holes. It would take hours to fill them, if there remained any reason to do so. The line of MiGs, our strafing target, came into focus. At full engine power and with clean wings (no bombs, no fuel tanks, no loads), our speed was tremendous.

I was amazed at the quiet. Why had we not heard any antiaircraft fire? It was hard to believe that they had really been caught with their pants so far down. The only panic could be heard on the communication network. Above a nearby airfield, our planes were dogfighting with MiGs. Apparently not everyone was sleeping.

I placed the line of MiG-17s in my gunsights. Slightly before coming into range, I squeezed hard on the trigger. The 30-millimeter cannons roared, and their bullets plowed into the runway beneath the MiGs. The planes convulsed under the cannons and collapsed. An entire line of MiGs was wiped out before my eyes.

We turned in strongly again for a third run. This time we needed to hit only the planes that had not been struck in the previous runs. Only a few remained. A pull of the trigger, and the mosaic of destruction was complete.

"I shot down an IL-41! " I could hear our wing leader calling.

The Ilyushin had been on its way back to Kabrit from a transport mission, and everything had erupted around it. Dazed, the Ilyushin pilot did not know where to go, and flew directly into the wing leader's sights. The enemy plane continued to fly, trailing smoke. On my way to the final strafing, I contributed my own rounds. Below us, almost nothing was left. The control tower had exploded. The fuel tanks were burning. Lone figures darted across the fields. We had ruined their breakfast.

Again I heard the wing commander's voice on the radio. "We didn't down that IL-41? How can that be? I saw him hit the ground two runs ago! Oh . . . sorry. It's another one."

We all converged on it, and it escaped toward Sinai, pouring out smoke. Later that week it was found, crashed in the desert and filled with the bodies of paratroopers who had not jumped.

We had turned to cross the Sinai for the trip home when the wing leader's Number Two screamed, "MiGs in the air!" He sounded almost elated. Opening a war with a bombing and not a dogfight was not his cup of tea. This time it was a pair of MiG-21s, apparently refugees from Faid or Bir Gafgafa. Number Two wanted to add them to his record, but the wing leader denied him permission. We had achieved our goal, and with our cannons all but empty, we had precisely enough fuel to get us home. A dogfight would be nearly suicidal. Still the MiGs pressed us.

"Head east with full engines! Disconnect from them! *Do not* get involved! "

One of the MiGs stuck himself on my tail. I shook him off with two sharp turns, and he passed. Suddenly he appeared in front of me, too close, filling my entire windshield. I fired, and the sputtering of my cannons told me that I had finished my ammunition. To my luck, he turned west and disappeared. Lacking any ammunition and short of fuel, I cut back on the power of my engines and climbed to the minimum altitude needed for the flight home. Each of us was alone. I could see no one from my wing, and could hear no one on the radio. Later I learned that the wing leader had crashed during a sharp low turn. He was the squadron's first casualty of the war, a painful blow.

Above Hatzor, I told the controller that I had only two hundred liters of fuel remaining. He requested that I continue to circle the base. Apparently I was in better shape than most. By the time my turn to land came, I was running on empty as well.

### June 5, 1967, 0745 Hours:
*Oded Sagee*                                           Oded's Story: We had crossed over the Suez Canal at the exact time and place that had been designated. Since we were navigating in an unfamiliar area, we had to choose points of reference about which there could be no error. We pulled the aircraft toward the target on time, and the field lay beneath us.

Unlike Cairo International, which was a mixed military and civilian airfield, Cairo West was purely military and had received preference in the attack plan because of its concentration of heavy and mid-sized bombers. While it also housed squadrons of MiG-21s, SU-7s, MiG-15s, and MiG-17s, the real and immediate danger was presented by its TU-16 and IL-28 bombers. Their mission was to reach the primary cities in Israel and annihilate the civilian population.

Our target was one of the farthest in the first wave, and therefore we were scrambled among the first formations of Mirages. Each of our half-ton bombs, eight of them carrying delay detonators set for seven to fourteen seconds, dug a huge crater in the runway. These were not the new runway bombs, with their rockets and parachutes, but rather the old-fashioned kind whose effect was created through mass and the force of the drop. Without the delay detonators, the bombs would have exploded in the air, causing mere surface damage to the runways.

After bombing, we dropped down for a strafing run. We had an order to follow. First we hit the more dangerous TU-16 bombers. I squeezed the cannon at the first plane. A column of smoke spewed out, and it collapsed. After several strafing runs, the field beneath us was filled with huge mushroom clouds from the dozens of damaged aircraft, particularly the Tupolevs. If we had not been limited by the fuel and our distance from home, some 350 kilometers, we could have continued. Our pre-mission briefing had called for returning with no less than 400 liters of fuel, meaning that we had to break off the instant the red light began to flash.

It lit up, and I was obligated to gather everyone and head home in an organized flight. We were to cross the delta at low altitude, at a point where the area was thick with antiaircraft guns and missiles. We did so before 0800 hours, less than fifteen minutes from the time of entry. Having been among the first to leave Tel Nof, we were among the last to return. The friends we had left worried and tense now received us in celebration. While we walked to the debriefing, the ground crews rapidly began preparing the aircraft for the next sortie. Before we had even managed to remove our G suits, the plans stood loaded like new, awaiting their fresh crews.

*June 5, 1967: Yaakov Terner*          *Y*aakov's Story: Yaakov Terner's squadron of Ouragans, the Lion's Head, carried lighter loads of ordnance than did others. Because the IAF wanted to keep the closest Egyptian airport El Arish's runways and structures intact, two of the squadron's formations set out to attack without bombs. Uncertain whether the armored units would break the defenses around Rafah by the end of the day, the Central Command decided to outflank them and capture El Arish from the air. Mota Gur's paratrooper brigade had been waiting since morning by the Nords and Dakotas of the transport squadron. Part of the brigade would parachute into the base and prepare it for the arrival of the rest of the ground force.

The order not to bomb the runways and to preserve the control tower did not promise an easy mission. It entailed strafing runs on the parked MiG-17s during the first sortie, and running the risk of having several of them escape to the air to intercept our aircraft. The Ouragans were not celebrated for their air-to-air combat ability; this privilege was generally saved for the "quality" aircraft, including the Mystères, the Super Mystères, and the Mirages. The last ones in line in this first wave of attack also stood the additional risk that the Egyptians would have detected the first formations, which had set out twenty minutes earlier. The enemy could now wait for the ones that would follow.

However, the MiGs were parked on the runways, resting after their morning flights. Terner and his men descended upon them immediately, straight from the sea, and left several burning after the first run. Eight Ouragans perforated the exposed rows with their cannons, making them look like cut-out cardboard figures. According to plan, the runways were left intact except for the incinerated heaps of junk that now littered them.

Whatever did not go up in flames during the first run did so during the second and third. Nothing made it into the air between runs, and El Arish ceased to be the Egyptian springboard to Tel Aviv. During the third run, Terner looked toward the control tower. The flight controllers stood petrified on the balcony, dumbfounded or resigned as they watched the spectacle of the burning MiGs that had occurred in mere seconds. Perhaps he was mistaken, but he knew that if they recovered, they would call for help. He had no idea what was happening on the other bases. Despite the order to leave the control tower intact, in the next run he lifted his nose, turned slightly, and strafed the balcony.

### June 5, 1967, 0815 hours:
### The Inverted Sword Squadron

*I*tzik's Story: To Itzik Segev, who sat in Ashkelon listening to the fighter pilots report their achievements on the way home, it seemed that the party would be over before our squadron could even get involved. He turned to Yitzhak Shani and said, "Look how our one chance to be in this war by flying paratroopers to attack airfields is disappearing before our eyes."

Shani, also a helicopter captain, nodded in agreement and added, "Seems unlikely that we'll have a lot of work in rescues either. All reports are talking just about success. We haven't heard a word about injuries or ejections."

"You've got to agree with me," Itzik said. "The picture is too rosy. Even with all our predictions, it doesn't make sense that this would be such a complete surprise." Shani did not respond. Instead he stared out to sea, his eyes fixed on a disappearing dot in the sky. Itzik tried to follow his gaze, and suddenly saw a solitary Ouragan approaching the coast without a formation, losing altitude above the sea.

They both saw the ejector seat flying out of the plane, and then a parachute opening, and looked at each other without speaking a word. Both jumped automatically into the nearest helicopter, turned on the engines, and took off toward the parachuting pilot.

They estimated the approximate point where the parachute would land, and hovered at a safe distance above the waves. Other than the waves and foam raised by the rotors, the sea was relatively quiet. The pilot had hit the water, inflated his life preserver, and now saw them. Segev moved the helicopter above him, and the flight mechanic lowered the rescue cable with its padded belt. Before he could swim five meters or get his clothes more than a little wet, he was already being lifted up. They pulled him in through the door.

"Welcome aboard, Salant." Salant was the commander of an Ouragan squadron.

"What service! " Salant exclaimed. "I had barely managed to report that I was ejecting, and you were here! Is there some telepathic communication in this air force that I haven't been told about?"

On the way to his squadron in Hatzor, he reported that he had finished his attack on the MiGs at Bir Gafgafa and had apparently been hit by ack-ack, which had paralyzed his hydraulic systems. Though the Ouragan had an elephant's skin and few vulnerable hydraulic systems, a bullet had found its way to a weak spot, and the steering mechanisms had jammed. He had been able to maintain direction and had hoped to reach Israel, knowing that he would have to eject at some point. A minute before reaching the coast, he lost all control over the aircraft and it banked toward the sea. Seeing Ashkelon, Salant decided to eject. He was returned to his squadron before they even knew he had lost his plane. Several days later, the sea spat out his helmet on the nearby beach of Ashdod. The city elders, believing that he had been killed, did not check meticulously and memorialized him by naming a street after him. Only after a long time was the mistake discovered and the street name changed.

Eleven airfields had been attacked during the first wave, and during its first minutes, 187 of 420 aircraft of the Egyptian Air Force had been destroyed, eliminating the immediate air threat to Israel's urban centers and to the ground forces moving into Sinai. The eleventh field, Cairo International Airport, had not been included in the original plan. A formation of Mirages, which had had to forgo its target at Inshas because of fog, found itself above the capital's primary airfield. With great caution they dropped their bombs, hitting only the military planes that were parked between the civilian ones.

All of the forward bases and nearly all of the aircraft in the Sinai were taken out of commission. Most of the bombers were destroyed. At several bases, the Israeli planes encountered resistance. Antiaircraft fire from Bir Gafgafa in the Sinai hit an Israeli Ouragan. The plane crashed and the pilot was killed. Antiaircraft fire from Inshas exploded the bombs carried by a Super Mystère, and the pilot was killed. Even Yalo Shavit, the squadron commander, was hit during that attack, but he managed to pull toward Hatzor with his tail ablaze, and execute a belly landing. Yonathan Shahar, commander of a Mystère squadron, was hit by fragments of a MiG he had bombed on the ground. He ejected and was rescued by a helicopter much later, in the dead of night.

The greatest resistance encountered was at Abu-Suweir. Four MiG-21s managed to take off against the twin-engined Vautour formations whose primary goal was to destroy the IL-28 bombers stationed there. While attempting to disrupt the bombing of the runways, the MiGs shot down one Israeli plane and then found themselves entangled in a dogfight with Vautour pilot Ben-Zion Zohar. This was not an easy mission for a heavy plane designed for attack and loaded with bombs, but when the Egyptians began the chase, Zohar played with them for a while. The other Vautours calmly completed the bombing of the airfield. The Control Center sent three Mirages from a nearby field to help out Zohar. Three of the MiGs were shot down and Zohar proceeded to drop his bombs on the field, strafe the grounded planes that had not yet been damaged, and destroy the radar of the SA-2 missiles stationed there. He returned home with nearly empty fuel tanks.

During the first wave, the IAF lost eight aircraft. Five pilots were killed and two captured. This price was not drastic, considering the number of sorties, and did not obscure the success of the missions, which was beyond all expectations. Within an hour, superiority had been achieved in the Sinai. The extent of the destruction was hidden from the Central Command in Cairo and from the presidential palace. Attempting to preserve its prestige, the Egyptian Air Force's command center ordered that all remaining aircraft be smuggled to remote airfields.

At 0900 hours the commanders of the IDF and the IAF in the Central Command were in quite a different state from that of only two hours earlier. Ezer Weizman, commander of the IDF General Command Division, had an I-told-you-so grin plastered on his face. Rabin and the IDF generals still found it difficult to believe, but were less worried and less hunched over than they had been. An hour earlier, in the IAF underground control center, Moti Hod had sent an unusually poetic day order to all of his units:

> The arrogant and provocative Egyptian enemy has raised its hand to consume us. The IAF, the clenched fist of the IDF, has been given the order. We have taken off to battle. The third stage in our war for

independence and sovereignty in our historic homeland has commenced. . . . The immortal bravery of the fighters of Joshua Bin-Nun, King David, the Maccabees, and the fighters of the War of Independence and the Sinai Campaign will serve us as a source of strength and inspiration. . . . Fly on toward the enemy. Batter him into annihilation, destroy his fangs, and scatter him in the desert so that the people of Israel can reside in their land secure for generation unto generation.

Hod's command order for the second wave would be phrased in much simpler language.

*June 5, 1967: Zvi Umshweif*   **Z**vi's Story: Though Umshweif had many reasons for getting emotional as the hour for the second wave neared, he had no time to do so. He ran to the briefing and scribbled down every word. The pounding of the first wave had to be continued immediately before the Egyptians could recover. The element of surprise was not lost. From this stage on, there would be no more combined-operations attacks with that pinpoint timing. Every formation would fly its fastest, and the competition would be tremendous. Even an unofficial scorecard of downed enemy planes was being kept. Within half an hour, Umshweif had returned to the cockpit. His target was Inshas.

The flight in would be at low altitude, but not like the last. Several radar stations had yet to be damaged, and it was still possible that the Egyptians could get several planes into the air. Navigation to the targets that had been attacked was no problem because of the columns of smoke and fire from the previous attack. The remaining antiaircraft guns as well as the SA-2 missiles would present a challenge, however. The Egyptians would be determined to defend the nuclear reactor near the Inshas airfield even more than the field itself. The morning fog that had hidden the base from the earlier formations had yet to dissipate. With not a single Egyptian plane in the air, the antiaircraft guns were alert, knowing that anything flying would be Israeli. They knew that the Israeli goal was their destruction, and they fired wildly with everything they had, including missiles, much of it before any Israeli planes came into range.

For the first time in his life, Umshweif saw the SA-2s, which resembled flying telephone poles, swaying for a second above a cloud of dust, swaggering like drunkards, straightening in their aim, and beginning to chase their targets. As long as they stayed away from him, he could continue on his way. They were fairly crude; with a bit of alertness and cleverness he could avoid them. Again he aimed for the center of the runways, released his bomb load, and broke sharply to avoid the ack-ack. He pulled around low again, and headed into his strafing run. More blazing MiGs. Satisfied with one run, the formation made its getaway. The remaining targets were not worth the risk of the antiaircraft fire.

Their third sortie of the day would be an attack on Mansura, a MiG-17 base, merely a dirt runway in the northern part of the Nile Delta. Warily they took off and navigated to the delta, where their suspicions became a reality. The runway blended in perfectly with the agricultural landscape. Though the leader suggested that they return home with full loads, they would not give up so easily. They proposed returning to the last clear navigation point, the intersection of a railway line and a road, but the search confused them even more. They attempted one more identification of the target, this time from four thousand feet, but all detail disappeared in the green-gray carpet. Dropping the bombs in the sea and arriving besmirched would be too much, so the flight controller had mercy on them and assigned them a mission of assisting the ground forces on the way home.

Slight relief awaited them at home when they heard that the formation following them had initially not been able to locate Mansura either. Fortunately, a MiG on its way home had revealed the location to them. Number Four had locked on its tail, and the rest of the formation had followed them in, destroying the airfield. The lost pride became unimportant, the essential element being that Mansura had gotten what it deserved.

### June 5, 1967, 1000 Hours:
### Oded Sagee

*O*ded's Story: Oded's formation crossed the Sinai and the Suez Canal diagonally at high altitude, flying straight in a southwesterly direction. Their target, El Miniya, was two hundred kilometers from Cairo, almost in a latitudinal line with Sharm-al-Sheikh. It held IL-14 transport aircraft that were similar to Israel's Dakotas and could serve as bombers. They flew at high altitude to preserve fuel, as was demanded by the long flight route. Because most of the fighter aircraft had been destroyed during the first wave, the results of the second wave of attacks on the delta were coming in, they were no longer wary of the Egyptian radar. If anyone tried to intercept them, the IAF planes would have plenty of warning.

Following them was a formation of Mirages from their sister squadron in Hatzor. Oded could hear Lev "Zorik" Arolozor on the communications, leading his group a bit behind them. They spoke freely. Zorik had come to the war from a position in IAF headquarters that involved developing new training theories and methods. At the same time, he was completing his high school matriculation exams.

"Hey, 'Doorframe,' how much fuel have you got?"

Zorik was not asking innocently. He always had something up his sleeve, certain that no one would suspect the sweet expression on his face. Oded fell for it, and told him exactly how much fuel he had.

"We've got less. Would you let us go in before you?"

He was certain that Zorik, who had the same drop tanks as everyone else, was deceiving him. He simply wanted to be the first one in and to collect all the paydirt.

"If you run low, we'll toss you a drop tank," Oded responded.

The high-altitude flight allowed them to identify the Nile Valley from a distance. They could also see the airfield on the western side of the river, which was a green lifeline through the desert. The contrast of colors was phenomenal. As opposed to the atmosphere in the war over the Nile Delta, this region was quiet and pastoral.

The first pair entered and dropped their bombs. The second pair examined the first hits, calculated the wind, and went in, striking with even more success. This was followed by a strafing run in which all four Mirages entered, each destroying one IL-14. By the end of the second run, a large number of fires were burning.

Zorik waited above, pleading anxiously.

"Why don't you do me a favor and give up one attack run?"

"No problem." Oded graciously assented to the request, gathered his formation, and left the target area.

Zorik gave attack orders, and suddenly his voice ripped through the radio. "You bastards, you didn't leave a single plane! "

*June 5, 1967: Herzle Bodinger*          **H**erzle's Story: Herzle Bodinger, who set out for Luxor in a single-seat Vautour, eight hundred kilometers in each direction, thought the flight would never end. They had never before flown this distance, and Luxor, situated in Upper Egypt, with its giant temples from the period of the pharoahs, burial grounds across the Nile, and treasures of Tutankhamen, was like a world out of legends. The Egyptians had flown bombers that survived the morning attacks on Cairo West even to this remote airfield behind the Luxor palace. Only the formation leaders flew the two-seater Vautours, which were designed for night combat. Bodinger had been fascinated by the two-seater since flight school, where he had been trained on its radar systems, which were controlled by the backseat, and aimed the weapons systems. Since then, the one-seater had been developed, and the earlier model had been converted to a daytime bomber and long-distance photographic reconnaissance plane. Because this target was secondary to other fields attacked, they were not given aerial photographs and were navigating with misleading civilian maps.

Though they flew out of range of the Egyptian radar and MiGs, the true enemy of this sortie was the distance. Despite experience with long-range flights, Luxor was on the far edge of the Vautour's range. The planes were loaded with six bombs ranging in weight from 100 kilograms to a half a ton, and ammunition for the four 30-millimeter cannons, which would be used for strafing and self-defense. They therefore flew in an unconventional manner, that of the climbing cruise. As the consumption of fuel decreased the weight of the aircraft, they climbed to a higher altitude until they ultimately reached the Vautour's ceiling. Thus they would also have just a few minutes above the target.

Complete air silence was maintained, as it had been during their morning flight to Beni-Suweif. The Egyptian airfields were constructed in the desert, so as not to waste the precicous fertile land of the Nile River valley, which was needed for agriculture. Dark runways like those of Beni-Suweif were obvious against the bright background.

They executed the bombing in two runs, as in the training exercises, and their precision was even better than the exercises. During each run, the TU-16 bombers, the size of Boeing 707s, were hit too, and within minutes all of the field's runways were out of commission, and all of its bombers were in flames. As he began to ascend, Bodinger began to notice problems with the steering hydraulics, something he had been witnessing in the Vautour for the three years since he began flying them. Having seen worse malfunctions, he overcame this one on his own, so as not to dampen the sounds of joy he could hear on the squadron's radio frequency.

At Luxor, Number Three entered his reconnaissance run alone. Bodinger, flying second position, and Number One waited impatiently by the field's edge. With a bit more fuel, Bodinger would have taken a spin to tour the sights, but Number Three rejoined them for the flight home to Tel Nof, if they were not forced to land at one of the southern bases because of their lack of fuel. Above the Red Sea, Bodinger discovered a fuel leak, and his reserves were quickly depleted. Apparently he had failed to notice the fire he had caught from the ground soldiers attempting to repel their attack. At this point it seemed doubtful that he would be able to make it back to Israel, and he began to plan an alternative route to the Sinai, where he could land and wait for the helicopters to rescue him. Conserving his fuel, he ascended slowly to maximum altitude, where one of his tanks ran dry. One engine failed, and his speed dropped. Numbers One and Two continued on, and Bodinger lagged behind, maintaining radio contact on the squadron's frequency.

Just as he began to see the far edges of the Eilat Gulf in the distance, the second engine ran dry. He hoped to land at the civilian airport there, even though its runway was only 1,500 meters long. No jet fighter had ever landed there, but in Bodinger's mind, a short runway was preferable to a ditched plane. Before he even began his approach to the runway, which began in the sea and ended in the desert, his fuel meters registered empty, though the engine pushed on. Suddenly it shut down.

Before his eyes, Bodinger could see the nightmare he'd lived through in 1964, his first year of flying the Vautour. On a training mission during the first preparations for Operation Moked, he'd been flying a sortie of demanding operational precision, which involved a long and arduous navigation from Ramat David to Ramat HaNegev at low altitude; he'd had to reach specific points at precise times, bomb and strafe, and return home. After an hour the plane had begun to shake, and the two engine-fire warning lights had begun to flash. The sounds of alarms had filled the cockpit. Bodinger had shut down the hottest engine and increased altitude.

As he'd approached his emergency landing in Tel Nof, the nearest base with the necessary repair facilities, he'd attempted to lower his wheels, but the wheel coverings had opened only partially. During the emergency manual operation of the hydraulic systems, the plane had lost altitude. Bodinger had tried to remain calm as they yelled at him from the ground to increase altitude before he crashed. He'd opened the throttle, and his only engine had exploded. At five hundred feet, with no engines, too close for landing or ejecting, he'd had to decide quickly.

Taking his chances with a crash landing before the runway, he'd plowed into the ground and awakened in the hospital, paralyzed and with shattered limbs. Later he'd heard how the firefighters had charged the plane and covered him with foam to prevent fire, and how they had removed him from the aircraft, almost a corpse. Both Bodinger and the aircraft had been sent to rehabilitation, and both had completed their recovery at the same time. Bodinger's first flight after his recovery had been on that very same Vautour.

With this memory haunting him, Bodinger gathered his strength to control the Vautour's glide toward the Eilat runway. Needing to use every inch of the runway, this time at least he had his wheels down. He hit the runway, rode a short distance, and stopped before the end of the runway with one hard push on the brakes. He had forgotten that the plane, relieved of its fuel and bombs, would be so light.

The squadron's top technician was in Eilat within an hour, and connected temporary fuel lines to the damaged system. It was good enough to make it back to Ramat David. By nightfall, both Bodinger and his Vautour were in top condition, ready to return to the front.

*June 5, 1967, 1200 Hours:*
*Ran Ronen*                                    **R**an's Story: Two hours earlier, Ran
Ronen's formation had destroyed two IL-28 bombers at the Abu-Suweir air base, west of Ismailia. In the Bat Squadron's operations room, his next sortie mission was displayed—to attack and destroy the Egyptian airfield at Gardeka with a foursome of Mirages. The briefing was short and to the point. Gardeka, which had not yet been attacked, lay 600 kilometers from their base in the southeastern portion of the Egyptian desert. Its aircraft included MiGs and a variety of helicopters, which commanded both sides of the Red Sea. The Israeli Mirages were loaded with 500-kilogram bombs with short-delay detonators, 30-millimeter cannons, Israeli-made Shafrir air-to-air missiles, and two drop tanks. These were heavily laden aircraft.

The flight over was calm. The isolated Gardeka airfield was not Inshas or even Abu-Suweir, and it seemed to be a relatively easy target. Because of the distance, they flew at 22,000 feet, a high altitude easy for navigation, descending at Sharm-al-Sheikh to sea level. The intensity of concentration in the cockpit grew. At this altitude, the slightest mistake could slam you into the water. They executed a ninety-degree westerly turn to the right at 540 knots. As they crossed the coast at their precisely appointed time, their fuel level dropped and they increased speed to 570 knots. This was not the lush green of the previous sorties. Below them was true desert, a scene of gray and angry beauty, with not a building or a trace of vegetation in sight.

As expected, the twist of the canyon appeared before them. "One pulling," the leader announced. The altimeters jumped forward crazily, and suddenly dense antiaircraft fire was coming at them. At first it was completely ineffective and only helped to guide them to the target, but as they approached, the situation changed. At four thousand feet, Gardeka lay below and to the right. Next to its main runway were an auxiliary runway, a small control tower, hangars for the planes, and quantities of asphalt. The moment had come.

After a quick flip onto their backs and a sharp entry into the bombing run, they found themselves facing an unprecedented spectacle. From all corners of the base and for a radius of several kilometers around it, antiaircraft fire was being spat at them from every possible weapon. It was random fire in a spectral barrage of greens, yellows, oranges, and purples. The Egyptians had been waiting for this attack for four hours; there was no room for retreat. The goal now was to eliminate any temptation to hesitate or think twice. Nose down, with engines at full throttle, at high speed and totally ignoring the ack-ack, they gently focused their gunsights one-third of the way down the runway. At three thousand five hundred feet, the bomb-release button was pressed and they immediately pulled out of their dive to avoid the explosions. Settling into low altitude at five hundred knots, they switched their equipment to strafing settings. A quick glance behind to find the next targets revealed blackness and a barrage of weapons fire from all directions. Even in Inshas they had not received such a welcome.

All the aircraft extricated themselves and rejoined the formation. Eight dark columns of smoke billowed from the runway. The ack-ack stopped, and they lifted their noses to start their eastbound strafing run. Ran warned the others to be on the lookout for the heavy antiaircraft fire. This had been a surprise. When the strategy is to charge in from a different direction every time, one generally manages to disappear from the gunners' sights at the end of every run, leaving a lag time before they catch up. This time it was different and quite unpleasant. The antiaircraft gunners saw them all the time. In the ack-ack hailstorm, Ran steadied his plane as his fuel gauge dropped incrementally. Slightly below him to the left, he could see a hangar with two MiGs, one of which had been haphazardly covered with camouflage netting. The other was naked and in open view. Just as he had been trained, he entered the strafing run with his sights set on the base of the closer MiG. For less than two seconds he squeezed the trigger, from a range of 1,000 to 500 meters. The planes went up in flames simultaneously.

"One moving out. Two, you're clean, a little farther this time. Watch your fuel and keep your eyes open." Number Four notified Ran that both he and Three had gotten out without problem. The ack-ack stopped, but erupted again at the instant they went into their dive. Ran began to think, *Maybe this is enough. Maybe we should return home.* The orders called for three strafing runs, depending on the strength of the antiaircraft fire. With the second run nearly complete, it was still too early to think about departure. The target this time was an Mi-8 helicopter. Ran thought to himself, *You risked your life flying forty minutes to get here and get results in the thirty seconds of the attack run, so calm down, ignore the surroundings, and execute as ordered. If you miss, somebody else is going to have to come here and execute the mission instead of you.*

They continued in a long strafing run. An explosion went off too close beneath the Mirage, and pieces of helicopter flew in every direction. Something dark and large approached and disappeared under the belly of his plane. They turned sharply right and up. Within two minutes the deal would be wrapped up. Gardeka was going up in smoke. Number Three reported he was low on fuel, and Ran ordered him to head home alone. While it might not have been wise to send him without accompaniment, it was clear that between here and Tel Nof there was not an enemy plane available to intercept him. Ran was determined to finish this mission.

The final run began flat, heading in from the west. Its target was three exposed MiGs on the tarmac near the outer garage area. The execution was precise, and Ran pulled out tightly from the run over the roofs of the lone buildings of the base. He felt a tremendous urge to let out a sigh of relief. But at that moment Number Four shouted, "One! Break! They're on you! "

Dropping his nose and looking into the darkness behind him, Ran saw at three hundred meters a MiG-19, which began firing. He recalled immediately that he was not alone, and turned sharply left to pull himself out of the enemy's gunsights. The situation was not good. Three Mirages with little fuel and ammunition remaining, 600 kilometers from home, facing four fresh MiGs defending their homeland, their people, and their lives. Within seconds a wild dogfight had erupted at low altitude over the air base, while the antiaircraft fire did not cease for an instant. The gunners did not worry about hitting their own aircraft. Everyone was firing at everyone.

Over the radio, Ran instructed his formation mates to let their drop tanks go and open full power despite the fuel situation, which at the moment was the least of their problems. He could see the MiG-19 on his tail, its smooth belly colored bright gray and its cannons spewing out inaccurate fire. Ran dropped sharply left over the roofs below and rolled perfectly, letting the enemy pass him. He had known the MiG would respond this way. The Egyptian was struggling to keep up with the Mirage's maneuvers, but managed to keep him in his gunsights. For an instant it seemed that he might crash straight into Ran because of his uncontrolled flying. Ran maneuvered to avoid the collision, and suddenly saw the Egyptian MiG closing at a dizzying speed and then passing him in a split second. The MiG-19 seemed larger than the Mirage, its wings longer, its body dirty, and its dive clumsy. He could see the pilot sitting in his cockpit watching the maneuvering Mirage. His helmet was painted bright brown. The MiG passed forward, straightened his wings, lifted up as if raising his hands, and gave up on the fight.

This was a familiar phenomenon. Young pilots often react the same way in training. One minute they have the advantage, and then, seconds later, find themselves the underdog. This drastic change paralyzes them at their controls. This is what had happened here. Ran completed his roll and came out 250 meters behind the MiG and somewhat beneath him. Aware of his position, the Egyptian began to turn wildly right and left. Quickly organizing himself, Ran got the MiG in his gunsights. It looked enormous at such short range, and its wings extended beyond the outer circle of his sights. After a pause, he squeezed the trigger for a second of fire. The hit was direct, and black smoke poured out of the MiG's center. Parts scattered in the air, forcing Ran to turn sharply to his right so as not to be struck by them. The MiG hit the ground in the center of the base.

The pilot had not ejected since the altitude was low and the speed at which everything happened was too quick for response. After a moment of satisfaction, Ran again had to begin avoiding the base's incessant ack-ack.

"Mine's down. Two and Four, what's your status?"

"Two closing in on one of them, turning left, northwest of the field."

"Four engaged with MiG. Low altitude, low speed, west of the field."

The Egyptians generally flew in foursomes, but Ran had only seen three in this case. Where was the fourth? He completed his low-level turn while intensely surveying the horizon. His eye caught three dots in an asymmetrical row. He had to quickly identify who was who. The second was bright and smaller and therefore had to be his Number Two, who was both chasing and being chased. Ran approached slowly, maintaining eye contact with all three and looking around, particularly at his own tail, for fear of surprises.

"I've got eye contact with a trio. Two, wave your wings."

"Waving," Number Two answered. Ran had been right.

"Excellent contact with you. Pay attention. In addition to the MiG in front on you, you've got another one far behind you. Continue and try to hurry up. I'm going for the one that's threatening you."

Cutting in full afterburners, he took a look at his fuel gauge. This was truly the edge of catastrophe. He checked the ammunition indicator. The right cannon was almost empty, and the left had barely twenty rounds remaining. Clearly they had to leave within a minute, or else they would remain there.

"Pay attention to fuel. One last quick attempt to nail them. And then home!"

Number Two seemed to be in good shape and in range to shoot down his MiG. Ran concentrated on the MiG, which was cutting in Number Two's direction in a left turn. While this let him close in range quickly, he was still too far away. He thought of using one of his missiles, but decided against the idea, since it could endanger Number Two, who was also in front of him. He cut back his afterburners, but his closing speed was too high. Five hundred meters. Three hundred meters. The MiG's silhouette was in his gunsight. Steady aim. Holding his breath. One round left in his barrel. One squeeze of the trigger. He could not allow himself to miss.

"Two has shot him down," Number Two called quickly. "Short on

The War of Independence, 1948. Right to left: Ben-Gurion; Dr. Sidney Cohen; Modi Alon, first commander of the first Fighter Squadron; with unidentified squadron personnel. (Courtesy of *Israeli Air Force Magazine* unless otherwise noted)

Shortly after the Sinai Campaign, 1957. Left to right: Ben-Gurion; Israel Galilee, his deputy; Dan Tolkowsky, Commander of the Air Force; Chaim Laskov, Chief of Staff.

The first team of Israeli jet pilots. All became aces and commanders. Left to right: Yak (Yaakov Nevo); Moti Hod, Air Force Commander of the 1967 Six-Day War; Benny Peled, Air Force Commander of Yom Kippur War, 1973; Joe Alon, Israeli Air Force attaché to Washington; Danny Shapira, "the Israeli Chuck Yeager"; Aharon Yoeli; Menachem Bar; Abraham Yoffe.

P-51 Mustang, 1956. (From author's private collection)

Cheetah (standing third from left) and his P-51 Mustang squadron pals, 1956.
(From author's private collection)

The crew of an Israeli B-17 Flying Fortress, 1957.

Benny Peled welcomed by Ben-Gurion after landing the first Mystère 4, which he had flown from France.

General Ezer Weizman, Commander of the Air Force from 1956 to 1966, was responsible for its modernization.

Iraqi MiG-21 with test pilot Danny Shapira. (Courtesy of Shapira's private collection)

Danny Shapira, center, before test-flying the Mirage III in France, 1962. (Courtesy of Shapira's private collection)

Egyptian airplanes destroyed on the ground during the first three hours of the Six-Day War.

General Moti Hod, Air Force Commander during the Six-Day War.

Hit.

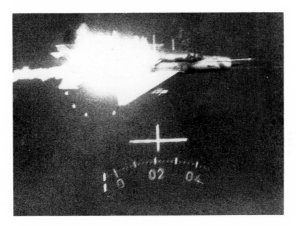

Explosion.

Destruction. A MiG-21 shot down by an Israeli
Mirage during the Six-Day War.

Cheetah in Sikorsky 58, 1967. (From author's private collection)

First class of Phantom F-4 Israeli pilots (standing) with American instructors

Prime Minister Golda Meir visiting the Israeli Air Force.

(kneeling), 1969. (From the private collection of General Ben-Nun)

The first F-4s in Israel, flying over Jerusalem, 1969.

Aviem Sela debriefing after having shot down a Russian pilot flying an Egyptian MiG, 1970.

Bell 205 in pursuit of terrorists in Jordan Valley, 1968.
(From author's private collection)

Three Sikorsky CH-53 giant helicopters on their way to
capture an Egyptian radar installation, 1969.

The radar installation that Israeli forces captured in
1969.

Cheetah climbing the ladder to one of many solos, this time a Skyhawk, 1970. (From author's private collection)

Benny Peled, Commander of the Air Force, Yom Kippur War, 1973.

Cheetah after landing a Mi-8 helicopter that was salvaged from the desert, 1973. (From author's private collection)

Cheetah at Fayid, having escaped from attack the previous morning. (From author's private collection)

General Ivri, Air Force Commander, 1975–1982.

An Israeli-made Kfir, flown by the author's son.

A Hercules C-130, here shown over Jerusalem, the type of aircraft used for the famous Entebbe rescue, 1976.

An F-16 on the monitor of a 707 refueler, 1985.

All Air Force commanders (left to right): General Amos Lapidot; Ezer Weizman; Moti Hod; Dan Tolkowsky; Israel Amir; Shlomo Shamir; David Ivri; Avihu Ben-Nun; Benny Peled. Missing: General Remez, first Commander, abroad at time of photo; General Laskov, died 1982; General Bodinger, nominated after the photo was taken.

The Israeli Air Force today. Front, F-15; second row, F-16D, F-16C; third row, left to right, Kfir, Phantom, Skyhawk.

Major General Herzle Bodinger, present Commander of the Israeli Air Force.

Operation Solomon, rescuing Ethiopian Je[ 1991. (From author's private collection.)

fuel and returning home." An experienced pilot, he had decided for himself.

Ran adjusted his aim and pulled the trigger to the end. A short burst from the left cannon, and it was over. His ammunition and fuel gone, and no time left to waste over Gardeka, which had been sprayed with fire and metal for the past seven minutes. An explosion ripped the wing root of the MiG, and a torch of red fire and black smoke poured out. The engine had been hit. Below, two huge fires burned as evidence of the first two MiGs that had fallen in the dogfight. The third was on his way to join them. In an instant, as the MiG lost altitude and control, a large object flew out of it. The appearance of the canopy and the ejector seat was followed by the opening of the parachute. The pilot who had ejected was a lucky man.

"Four, what's going on with you?"

"I'm still after him, south of the runway."

What Ran saw was really a Mirage. The MiG-19 was slowly approaching the runway to land, its wheels down and its speed low. Behind him the Israeli Mirage was maneuvering so as not to pass him. This was a perfect example of a pilot who was so determined to shoot down a plane that he had become fixated on his objective and had forgotten to pay attention to what was going on around him. Ran and his teammate chased the MiG. Its wheels touched the runway and, seconds later, slammed into one of the craters that the bombs had left behind. The MiG exploded on the runway in a tremendous fiery mushroom.

As they put Gardeka far behind them, the silence was eerie. The field behind them had been devastated by four planes. The only problem remaining now was the lack of fuel. Would they be able to fly the remaining five hundred kilometers back to their base on what remained, the distance between success and failure? They climbed to thirty thousand feet to conserve every drop.

Halfway home, they heard the flight controller looking for a formation with enough ammunition to attack the Amman airport as soon as possible. This was a new chapter in the war—Jordan.

On the approach home, the members of the formation arranged themselves according the amount of fuel remaining. Ran was the last in line. They landed, opened parachutes, braked, turned off the runway, and stopped. Dripping a cold sweat and feeling gloriously victorious and phenomenally weak, they were in a stupor of sorts.

*June 5, 1967, 1200 Hours:*
*Oded Sagee*                              **O**ded's Story: Oded Sagee sat belted
into the cockpit of his Mirage, on intercept alert, waiting to be scrambled.
Anyone listening to the internal frequencies of the IAF would have
blushed in pride at the success of the second wave. Six additional
Egyptian airfields had been attacked, and several others from the first
wave had received a second dose. According to the flight leaders, 110
aircraft had been destroyed in this wave, bringing the morning's total to
nearly three hundred. Three-quarters of the Egyptian Air Force had been
decimated in three hours.

Jordan was now in the war. King Hussein had been swept away by the
victory broadcasts of Radio Cairo. Thirty minutes earlier, Iraqi aircraft
had attacked the Israeli coastal city of Netanya and had fired rockets at a
pharmaceutical plant and a residential neighborhood housing immigrants. There were wounded civilians. Apparently the enemy aircraft had
come in low, beneath the Israeli radar. On their way home, they set fires
in fields, bombed an industrial area, killing and wounding workers, and
destroyed a storage center not far from Tel Aviv. This was the first air
attack on the Sharon area. The runways at the Ramat David air base had
also been lightly hit by cannon fire from the Jordanian "Long Tom"
cannons situated in Jenin, in the West Bank.

IAF Commander Moti Hod had already issued an urgent command
to commence the attack on Jordan. The control center gathered aircraft
from the air formations that were on their way to Egypt and diverted them
to the Jordanian airfields at Amman and Mafraq. This was child's play
after the sorties to Egypt, but Jordan's thirty-odd planes were still reason
enough for Oded to be sitting on intercept alert.

"Scramble! "

The controller's voice brought news to Oded of Jordan's entry into
the war. Jordanian Hunters were attacking Israel's Sirkin airfield. One
Nord transport plane was burning, and there were wounded as well.

What was a Nord doing at this field, which had not been used in
years? It was apparently the victim of a cautious transport squadron that
had scattered its aircraft for fear of enemy counterattacks, but had probably failed to take into account that Jordanian intelligence had neglected
to remove Sirkin from its map of IAF operational airfields. Oded and his
partner took off immediately and saw the smoke of the destroyed Nord as

they began to climb. The flight controller fed them intercept instructions, and within a minute they could see the pair of Hunters.

Oded had an old score to settle with these aircraft, and he had spent many nights planning what he would do when they next met. It had started in November 1964, when the Hunters had crossed the Jordanian border and flown along the Dead Sea. There they had met IAF Mirages. The British Hunter was an older and less capable aircraft than the Mirage in almost every way, other than maneuverability. Because the MiGs were regarded as the real threat and worthy opponents, the squadron had not even thought to train for air-to-air combat against such an inferior aircraft as the Hunter.

The Hunters dragged them into sharp turns and eliminated the Mirage's advantages of speed and strength. Within seconds they had even fired on the Israeli aircraft and photographed them. In the midst of the battle, Number Two had informed Oded that he was out of fuel, and left Oded to handle them alone. Oded had used the speed advantage of the Mirage to break off from them quickly. The great shame, however, awaited them the next day in the world press, where the Jordanians published photographs of the Mirages. It was a clear message—anyone who can photograph them can also shoot them down.

This time, Oded promised himself, he would not let the Hunters get away. Flying east, they approached the enemy aircraft at high speed. The Hunters broke away, apparently having received warning from their radar. Oded's partner attached himself to one of them and they both dived and disappeared for a moment. The controller directed Oded toward the other, and he entered the duel with the advantage. He fired a Shafrir missile, which is guided by infrared rays and is supposed to home in on the heat of the engine, but it dropped downward, below the enemy's engine. This was the first version of the Israeli missile, and it was meant to be something more than a rocket and less than a guided missile. Oded had no choice but to rely on his cannons.

They crossed the Jordan River, and the chase quickly headed toward Amman. Oded shifted around and again came up behind the Hunter. He closed in his range, almost too fast, to two hundred meters. Aiming carefully, he fired one long burst. The Hunter's wing broke off, and the aircraft began spinning.

"He bailed out! He bailed out!" Number Two's cries brought Oded back to reality, and he saw the pilot's parachute. In the style of Hunters, the second one had escaped at low altitude.

Oded returned home after making one roll of pure joy, his first. After the long and trying sorties of the morning, this short flight, topped off by its victory roll, was the true reward.

*June 5, 1967, 1315 Hours:*
*Zvi Umshweif*                    **Z**vi's Story: The Dumeir Airfield, one of the Syrian Air Force's five air bases, lay tucked in between rows of mounts and the desert. Near a small town on the Damascus-Baghdad road, it was forty kilometers east of the capital.

The Syrians had entered the war just before noon. Their first MiGs took off at 1410 hours, a light display of their presence, but definitely not a full-force attack. They sent a duo here and a trio there in a disorganized fashion, somewhat hysterically and with no real preparation. Unfamiliar with the targets, the pilots were ineffective. The impression was that they had not received accurate information about the situation in Egypt. More and more, the air began to fill with Mirages that had become available earlier than anticipated after the attacks on Egypt.

From the scraps of information overheard on the enemy's operational frequencies, it appeared that the Syrians had managed to penetrate beneath the Israeli radar, but had limited themselves to hit-and-run sorties, aware of their limitations. Their results reflected this. A trio attacked Ramat David, but mistakenly identified a nearby crop-dusting runway with a dummy combat plane as their target. One of the Syrians was shot down by antiaircraft fire. The duo that attempted to attack the pumping station to the country's main water lines hit only the Sea of Galilee.

The IAF's formations simultaneously attacked Syria's four forward bases: Damascus, Marj Reiyal, Dumeir, and Sayqal. Situated around the capital, they held the majority of Syria's first-line aircraft, totaling about ninety. They had almost no bombers, and the entire Syrian Air Force, including helicopters and transport planes, numbered no more than 110 aircraft. Though destroying them was a minimal chore compared to the strikes on Egyptian bases during the morning hours, the advantage of surprise had now been lost to the IAF.

The Dumeir MiGs were set up in lines as if awaiting inspection, and it was clear that Damascus was acting according to the news, broadcast by

Cairo, of its purported success in penetrating Israeli airspace during the last hour.

Though the Syrians might have been expecting dogfights, they were certainly unprepared for surprise attacks on their airfields. It was five and a half hours after the Israeli attacks in Egypt, but the Syrians had not even bothered to scatter their aircraft or camouflage them. The bombing and strafing runs were executed in an almost routine fashion, and even the antiaircraft guns put out calmly methodical but dense fire. The IAF's aim, however, was more precise than the ack-ack. The MiGs exploded on the runway and burned, just as had been requested during the preflight briefing.

### June 5, 1967, 1330 Hours:
### Yalo Shavit
Yalo's Story: Yalo Shavit led the second formation of Super Mystères to attack the Sayqal airfield. Situated overlooking the desert, on the edge of the swamps, it was one hundred kilometers from Damascus. He had no navigation problems; pillars of smoke billowed from the runways and offered a beacon from afar. The leader of the first formation, which had just completed its attack, cut his celebration short. He reported that the field was protected by MiG-21s, and warned the following flight to be careful. Since the Israelis had been given a defector's Iraqi MiG and had trained against it, it was now a less frightening contender than it had been. Though the Super Mystère was a less effective aircraft, the IAF pilots had been taught by Danny Shapira, who had flown the MiG, how to take advantage of its weaknesses. Any Mystère pilot who knew these tactics could finish off a MiG.

Yalo instructed the formation to climb to six thousand feet. The Super Mystères would need momentum if they were to encounter the MiG-21s, and strength can be gathered at altitude. Number Three reported a minor fuel leak in his right drop tank. Yalo instructed him to make one bombing pass at the field and then to climb to altitude and wait. He would not have enough fuel to get involved in an air battle.

Upon reaching Sayqal, they surveyed the area but did not see any MiGs. The air base waited passively for their bomb loads. "Clean skies," Yalo reported.

They began the attack, aiming and releasing their bombs. Yalo pulled left and looked behind him. What he saw was an impossibility. The formation leaving the attack was larger than the one that had entered. He counted his inventory: he was Number One, and Two, Three, and Four were following. Where had Five and Six come from? Of course. They were MiGs that were on their tails and closing in. He told Three to break right, opposite everyone, and to stay clear. While it was still three Israelis against two Syrians, Two and Four were greenhorns with no more than four months of experience on the Super Mystère. The two MiGs were at six o'clock and directly behind them—what was known in the trade as "classic conflict conditions," or "having your six waxed."

Yalo instructed Number Four to execute evasive maneuvers and Number Two to place the MiG on Four's tail in a sandwich. He would take care of the other MiG by himself. But the MiG pilot understood and pulled up ninety degrees. It was clear from the start that the battle would be lost if he chased the MiG. The MiG's engine was stronger than Yalo's, and he also did not have enough fuel for a long air battle deep in Syrian territory. The MiG pulled up and Yalo lowered his nose, baring his belly as if he had decided to quit and leave.

The MiG now decided to play hero, and lowered his nose as well. Yalo flipped over and closed in on him from above. The MiG pulled him down—two thousand, one thousand feet. He executed a sharp turn over the base and pulled Yalo through a line of rip-roaring antiaircraft fire. The Syrians fired on both of the aircraft from the roof of every building and hangar. The MiG distanced himself, and Yalo changed direction. The MiG fell for the move, and was now caught in his weak point. In this type of exercise, the MiG's pilot would need tremendous strength to keep his steering controlled. Attempting another diversionary turn, he lost his balance. One long burst, and the MiG crashed in the field among the buildings. Yalo gathered speed and climbed. Doing only 160 knots above an enemy field is a joke.

"Way to go, One," said Three, watching from the side.

"Thank you very much," Yalo answered. "And what's going on with Two and Four?" The response could be heard on the radio.

"I see him now. . . . Now I don't see him. . . ." Without a doubt, it was Number Two. The next question proved it.

"The MiG's in front of me. What do I do now?"

"Pull the trigger, idiot! " Yalo blurted out. He generally tried to speak nicely.

"Wowwwww, he lost his wing! " Number Two whistled after a moment of silence. At the end of the day, during the squadron's final debriefing, Yalo did not forget to mention the phenomenon. Pilots with the experience of students were destroying fields like Sayqal and even shooting down MiGs.

### *June 5, 1967: Oded Sagee*

*O*ded's Story: Oded Sagee did not have time to relish his shooting down of the Hunter, or to absorb the fact that Jordan was now in the war. The time had come to attack Syria. He was already in the air on his way to T-4 Air Base, near Tadmor. The navigation heading north had been much easier. Like everyone, he was less tense, and the sense of his body functioning at its peak overshadowed any fatigue.

Above the Sea of Galilee, he had been contacted by the flight controller. "You've got a change of mission. You'll be heading to T-4 and not to Damir."

Everything, of course, was stated in code. Oded spread out his map and could not find the field. The name had been mentioned in the intelligence briefings, but it was located out of range of the map in his possession.

"You're going to have to direct me," he told the controller, who was not surprised and began to guide him, this time in overt language. This was quite a change from the communications silence of the morning hours. The pillars of smoke from the fields at Damascus and Damir to the left and Sayqal to the right helped guide Oded and his formation. T-4 was a lone base farther north in desert, between Homs and Tadmor (Palmyra), the capital of the ancient Armenian kingdom. The modern name of T-4 came from the nearby pumping station that lay on the oil line from Kirkuk to Tripoli. Smoke also rose from this field because of Eitan Carmi and his formation's attack, which had preceded theirs by several minutes. Oded identified it right after pulling toward the target, and was readying himself to bomb when a MiG-21 suddenly crossed his path. His Mirage, loaded with external munitions, was not in the ideal condition for combat, but why not cap his success with the Hunter by adding a MiG for balance? Appetite comes with eating, so Oded quickly switched to air-to-air and began to chase the MiG's tail, intending to shoot it down. With his finger on the cannon trigger and only three hundred meters behind the MiG, a Mirage appeared in front of his nose and pushed him aside in an air whirlpool. What the hell was going on here?

Menachem Shmul, his Number Two, had seen the MiG near him

and had also charged in. The experienced leader deferred, of course, to the younger pilot. Oded waited for him to finish off the MiG, and suddenly heard him screaming that his engine had failed. This was a familiar phenomenon in the Mirage. The engine's compressor was often deprived of sufficient air flow by a high angle of attack, the precise angle at which Shmul was flying at that instant. He did not shoot down the MiG, but was rather busy saving himself and his aircraft. Like a gentleman in a duel, the Syrian pilot did not shoot him in the back, but instead turned on a healthy Oded, firing a missile at him. Oded did not worry about the missile; he knew its limitations, and saw that it had been fired wildly. He did worry, though, about being in this wrestling match over the Syrian's territory while still burdened with all his ordnance.

Another Mirage suddenly descended from nowhere and saved Oded at the last minute. He had not thought that Carmi's quartet was still in the area, or that his formation had gotten entangled with Oded's in the midst of the battle with the MiG.

Carmi was flying with Giora Rom, Asher Snir, and Eliezer "Leizik" Prigat, according to a familiar recipe. Carmi, the veteran and deputy commander of the Bat Squadron, was accompanied by three young pilots (all of whom would later go far in the IAF). Though two MiGs were awaiting him, Snir initially stuck to the pre-mission briefing, which called for sticking with the ground attack. Only minutes into the attack, however, he could hold himself back no longer. The magnetic pull of the opportunity was overwhelming. As soon as he saw the MiG, he dropped his fuel tanks and charged up from behind, before the MiG even knew that he was there. He fired a burst from close in, and saw two light hits on the MiG's wings. The MiG opened his afterburners to escape, and Snir fired again, but missed. Checking to see what had happened, he saw that one of his drop tanks was stuck under his wing, causing asymmetrical flight and inaccurate firing. Compensating for the problem, he fired again and flew though an explosion. The pilot ejected, and Snir, after satisfying his curiosity to see a burning MiG-21, was now free to rejoin his formation. The second MiG distanced itself for a while and returned toward the end of the attack, attaching himself to Leizik. Giora saw him closing distance to less than a kilometer, warned Leizik, and dropped his tanks in order to shoot the MiG down before the others could. At that moment, Oded Sagee burst in. Two Mirage formations had now equally surprised each other.

Giora saw the MiG firing missiles, but he was not sure whether it was firing at Shmul or Oded. He entered the fight and fired a long burst. The MiG slipped into a spin and burst into flames after crashing in the middle of the field. Giora was gone before Oded could even thank him. Lacking fuel, he headed home alone, following Carmi, Snir, and Leizik, who were already on their way.

In the meantime, Shmul had resuscitated his engine. Oded gathered his formation to hit the target to which they had been sent, and commenced bombing and strafing. A large quantity of MiGs was grouped there. T-4 was Syria's rear base, and the refuge for most of the aircraft that had survived the destruction the IAF had rained down on the fields around Damascus. On his last run, Oded saw two MiG-21s attempting suicidal last-minute takeoffs. He got them in his sights before they even left the ground and shot a long and accurate burst from up close. Though hitting two planes taking off is essentially an attack on a ground target, a moving aircraft that is gaining speed can be considered almost as good a kill as a shot-down plane.

**June 5, 1967: Zvi Umshweif**            **Z**vi's Story: The squadron's operations officer was at his best. "We've arranged Damascus for you as a finale for the day. Hurry up before it becomes night for you over your target. Grab your maps and your intelligence briefings, and move! Your time is precious. The field can be seen clearly even at of the sunset."

It is not every day that one is allotted a target next to an important and sensitive capital with all of its deterrents, including a lot of antiaircraft guns and missiles dedicated to protecting the city. During the past hour, four Israeli aircraft had been hit by antiaircraft fire in and around Damascus. For one base, this was unprecedented and disproportionate to the day's losses. The base was still loaded with transport aircraft, which were easy targets. After bombing and shutting down the runways, Zvi dropped down to strafe. He put a large Antonov in the center of his sights, focusing on the large fuel tanks below its wings. A short burst was enough to ignite the plane. Against the background of the evening sky, the enormous blaze that followed was more astounding than anything they had seen that day. Remnants of MiG-21s could be identified only by the silhouettes of their ashes, and the giant Mi-6 helicopters only by the large rotors that remained resting atop mounds of wreckage.

The flames lit up the area around the capital of Syria, which itself lay in darkness. Had the commanders of the Syrian military and Hafez El-Assad, commander of the Syrian Air Force, gotten the message as they watched from the windows in the buildings of their central command?

Circumventing Damascus in a wide left turn that kept them out of range of the antiaircraft fire, they returned home in the dark, flying by their instruments. Everything became almost painfully silent when they shut down their engines. Exhaustion invaded their bodies; these men had been wound up as tightly as springs for nearly twelve hours. Even the ground crews slowed to a normal pace, calling it a day.

*June 5, 1967, 2030 Hours:*
*Daniel Ilan*                      **D**aniel's Story: After an hour of flight in a lone Vautour laden with six 500-kilogram bombs, Uri Talmor and Daniel Ilan began to plan their approach toward the Jordanian Long Tom artillery battery that had been shelling Tel Aviv. From their range of twenty-five kilometers they had managed to hit the suburbs, and even to land a few shells in the city itself. During the War of Independence, the Egyptians had had to send a Dakota to attack Tel Aviv, only to have it shot down within minutes by Modi Alon's Messerschmitt. Now, from Jordanian Kalkilia, on the border, one cannon could strike at Israel's center. With all of its artillery stationed in the north or the south, the IDF had no way to respond to the Jordanian guns. Thus, in the afternoon, the Vautour was scrambled to silence them.

In the darkness of night, they relied on the sparks of the Jordanian cannon fire to guide them to their target. Time after time, Ilan and Uri dove, in unsuccessful attempts to draw the artillery fire. In their fifth dive, from eight thousand feet, the cannons began to fire. With precision, Ilan released the bomb load, and as the Vautour pulled out, explosions crowned with tremendous mushrooms of fire could be seen. They had apparently struck a direct hit on the munitions or fuel depot. After ten minutes of circling and watching for continued shelling, they turned home, leaving behind the blazing remains of the artillery battery.

*June 5, 1967, 2000 Hours: Yalo*          **Y**alo's Story: That evening, Yalo, commander of the Scorpion Squadron, felt energetic and sharp, as if he had just awoken. He stood on the stage in the briefing room for a long and detailed debriefing. Every formation leader would summarize his missions, short and to the point. Attentiveness was complete, and lessons learned from the day were numerous. Every comment could save lives tomorrow and the day after, and perhaps could have saved those who had not returned. Yalo surveyed those seated before him in the room, seeking out those whom he had nurtured and were now missing. The squadron had paid a heavy price in these losses, because the soft belly of the Super Mystère, so able in terms of range and load, also held the fuel systems and hydraulic steering mechanisms. The antiaircraft fire had damaged them severely. Three pilots had been lost in Egypt, and one in Syria. Eighty-two sorties had been flown to Syria, a large number relative to the number of airfields there. Thus the proportion of downed aircraft was also large. Six of the squadron's twenty-one aircraft had fallen over the course of the day. Of the squadron's nineteen pilots, five were dead or captured. Even the attack on the two Egyptian airfields had exacted a price, one Ouragan and one Vautour. At this hour of personal and group accounting, the empty chairs pierced the heart.

At 2100 hours, Yalo announced a break in the debriefing. The radio was broadcasting the first press conference of the war. IDF Chief of Staff Yitzhak Rabin and IAF Commander Moti Hod summarized. "The Israeli Air Force today destroyed four hundred enemy aircraft of all types at all of Egypt, Jordan, and Syria's air bases, as well as at Iraq's forward base. In essence, the air forces of Egypt, Jordan, and Syria have been annihilated."

### June 5, 1967, 1400 Hours:
### The Inverted Sword Squadron

*M*y Story: By noon it was clear to all that nothing was happening according to plan. Operation Moked was a definitive success, and in half the time predicted.

The armored battalions had also done surprisingly well in the Sinai, and had left the airborne brigade waiting in Tel Nof unneeded. One of the battalions would be heading to Jerusalem, where another completely unexpected surprise had occurred.

No one could believe that King Hussein would be dragged into the war. During the early-morning hours, when the first formations were taking off, Prime Minister Eshkol had sent a message through the UN observers explaining that the war was against only the Egyptians. If Hussein sat quietly, he would not be hurt. Ignoring this, the Jordanians opened fire along the entire meandering border that cut across the country, placing Jerusalem in danger of being captured and the IAF's air bases in range of their artillery. The majority of Israel's military was in the

Southern Command, leaving barely a battalion for preventive purposes in the north. The Central Command was depending solely on the regional defense units, reserve units, and veterans of the War of Independence. They would not be the force to block the Jordanian armored corps and artillery.

The IAF's fighter aircraft included armed Fouga Magisters that had been taken from IAF flight school and turned into artillery hunters around Jerusalem. Veterans of the War of Independence and the Sinai Campaign flew dozens of sorties attacking Jordanian targets around the city.

The Inverted Sword Squadron still sat waiting in Ashkelon. One by one the helicopters were called to rescue pilots who had ejected, or to evacuate severely wounded ground troops from the assault on Rafah.

By 1330 hours, when the majority of the Egyptian air power had been destroyed and the attacks had begun on Jordan and Syria, we began to organize ourselves for the return to Tel Nof. We then received the order to change direction to Nitzana, in the south. Ariel Sharon's battalion had encountered strong resistance, and the Central Command had adopted his plan, allotting him the helicopters of the Inverted Sword.

By 1400 hours I had been summoned to Sharon's headquarters. I quickly arranged the squadron's move with my group leaders, who were well trained. The maintenance and administrative vehicles would be sent out immediately. The road from Ashkelon to Nitzana was 130 kilometers long and already jammed with convoys. At best they would arrive during the early evening hours. I had no worry about the helicopters. On my way to meeting Sharon, I used the squadron's frequency to notify those involved in rescue and evacuation operations to fly to Nitzana after completing their missions. Those who had not heard me would find out from the flight controller.

Sharon's battalion had been fighting to penetrate the fortified defenses along the central road between Nitzana and Ismailia. He had to split two fortified battalion strongholds, including a mixture of bunkers and cement canals around natural barriers, which had been built with the guidance of Soviet experts. The most difficult link lay in Umm-Katef, at the intersection of the Abu-Aweigila roads. The area was comprised of deep sand dunes in the north, fortified trenches along stony mountain slopes surrounded by minefields, and strongholds armed with heavy machine guns and antitank cannons. According to Soviet military theory, the area was impenetrable by tanks.

Not far from here, I had been hit while flying a Mustang during the Sinai Campaign, and had made an emergency landing and returned on foot to meet our troops. Any place where a pilot has a first experience, particularly of this sort, is never forgotten.

Sharon had planned a complicated and varied assault. During the morning hours he made do with eliminating the outer fortifications, leaving the major blow for the night. The primary threat was the Egyptian artillery, which was shelling Israeli forces with 122-millimeter long-range Russian cannons. Several days earlier we had discussed silencing them with a force of paratroopers who would be transported in by helicopters under cover of darkness. I did not believe that this operation, which involved the airlifting of hundreds of paratroopers, would receive high tactical importance or even be approved. The IDF Central Command did not trust the strength of the helicopters, and was wary of heavy losses of aircraft, troops, and pilots. This would be the helicopters' first war, and our combat-worthiness was weakened even more by the air force's promise to destroy the majority of the enemy's aircraft by noon. Sharon considered the darkness of night an insurance policy for the airborne force, if he could outflank the front of the ground war. The noise of the choppers would be swallowed by the explosion of the artillery shells and the chattering of the machine guns. The previous evening we had designed a flight route according to our intelligence information regarding the location of the batteries.

In Sharon's office, I met my old friend Danny Matt, commander of the reserve airborne battalion that would execute the attack on the artillery. Sharon entered the room with something of a smirk on his face, for his forecast of the morning battles had been correct. The dense Egyptian artillery facing us, he said, had become a nuisance that would ruin the complicated process of penetration and cause tremendous loss of life. The general respected the helicopters; there was no other way to surprise the enemy at his rear positions without being detected. We were not meant to land in the heart of the fortified area. Sharon marked the landing spot, four kilometers north of the area's center. Danny was to destroy as many pieces of artillery as he could, and I was to design the airlift, in one direction. At the moment they finished exterminating the batteries, the armored brigades and other ground forces would accelerate the pace of the capture of the Umm-Katef range and connect with the airborne troops in the morning.

The joint command center of the squadron and the brigade was set up on a hill overlooking the clearing where the helicopters would be located in Nitzana. Within minutes, and with lightning communication, we designed a detailed plan that, during peacetime, would have taken us hours to agree upon. The collaborative planning of the commander of the ground forces and the leader of the helicopters is the foundation of joint airborne operations. The ideals of such cooperation had proven themselves in training exercises, and would not stand the test of war in the first airborne operation in the history of the State of Israel.

Navigation in night operations is aided by marking teams who arrange themselves along the flight route in hidden spots, invisible to anyone but aircraft flying directly above. They mark their spots with flashing lights and simple communications equipment that emits a long tone to be detected by an electronic homing device in the cockpit. For tonight's raid we would need only two such marking teams on the ground: one on the border, to mark our entry into enemy territory, and one in the area of our landing, some four kilometers northeast of the Umm-Katef intersection.

At approximately 1800 hours, thirty minutes before twilight, I took off, leading a pair that would mark the border crossing and the landing area for the operation. The captain of the second helicopter was Ehud Hatzroni, winner of the squadron's navigation competition. For this mission, navigation abilities were vital.

The penetration, at zero altitude, scraped the landing gear against the sand dunes beneath us. We stuck to the ravines between the hills, so that the enemy would not sense our presence or that of the teams we were letting off. The landing point that had to be marked was twenty minutes' flight from the border crossing. Despite our anxiousness, we did not rush out of the territory, but rather followed the planned exit route, whose point of border crossing had to be far from the point of entry. This route was checked as well, and found to have no enemy forces.

Our command post lay in complete darkness except for the landing lights. After a moment of rest, we quickly jumped into a wild race. The squadron convoy had arrived with the fuel tanks, and now all we lacked were helicopters. This was cause for worry. Of the twenty-nine helicopters that had been operational that morning, I now had only seven. Most of them now began to land, and their pilots had no idea what was going on. The others had yet to conclude their rescue and evacuation missions.

Hundreds of paratroopers stood waiting for their flights with their gear, divided into groups of ten, and I had only a quarter of the squadron with me. If all the helicopters arrived, we could fly them in two rounds in a maximum of an hour and a half. But zero hour—1900 hours—was approaching, and I decided not to wait and sent off every trio I could find. I gave orders to the first two trios to take off, and they lifted off and disappeared into the darkness one after another, moving toward the entry point in the Sinai Desert. From this point on, we were also part of the game.

Every helicopter that landed became part of a trio, and the captains met in the command tent for a briefing. In the crowded tent, our flight controller traced on the operations map the positions of the formations already en route. On the radio we could hear the pilots conveying code words. No one spoke. The flashes of exploding shells ripped through the darkness, and the thunderous din of the battle drowned out the noise of the helicopters.

For two hours they flew back and forth along the banana-shaped route, with no breakdowns or other problems. Every group of fighters that landed at the target eased the tension just a bit. At the peak of the operation I had no more than eighteen helicopters. Six trios, less than two-thirds of the force, had been slowly put together and lengthened the flight time. At 2100 hours we concluded in the command tent that the operation would come off as planned. Nearly all of the paratroopers were already at the target. Suddenly there were shouts on the radio.

"Watch out! Shells hitting the landing pad!" It was the voice of the brigade's regimental commander.

"Clementina, go around." This was the formation's leader speaking to the captains. He canceled the landing at the last minute, when he saw that the shells were exploding several dozen meters below the formation that was leading them to the landing. Part of the ground force, already on its way to the Egyptian artillery, attempted to mark a new landing area a kilometer away. There too, the artillery fire began to rain down. Through the noise of the shelling, the Egyptian battery operators had heard strange voices. They failed to identify the approaching force and managed to get off only a few mortar rounds, completely out of range.

"Citrus leaders, stop the flights, return to me," I commanded. There was no reason to take such a risk for a marginal addition to the force that was already in the territory. A thick silence overtook the command tent. Around us, the ground shook. The artillery duel glimmered in the sky, and erroneous Egyptian shells landed near us.

Sharon wanted to know what had happened to the airborne force. We reported that the landing was completed and that they should be nearing the Abu-Aweigila road, behind which lay the artillery batteries. It was getting late, though. The force was more than an hour behind schedule reaching its destination, which was a two-hour hike from where it had been dropped. It was nearly midnight, and the elimination of the artillery had yet to begin. The planned distance of the hike had not taken into account the uphills and downhills of the sand dunes, and we could hear their fatigue on the radio. They announced that they could identify the batteries by the incessant light of the shelling. The Egyptians had not seen them.

The order to attack was given at a range of only fifty meters, and the artillery operators were completely surprised. Every Israeli squad decimated one cannon team with bursts from the Uzis and with hand grenades. Those Egyptians who survived jumped out of the trenches and ran for their lives. The work included the bunkers as well, and from there, too, the Egyptians ran away. Several of the enemy had managed to return fire, and there were Israeli wounded. The battles were short. Suddenly a large Egyptian convoy was seen approaching. It included seven trucks running with full lights and loaded with crates of shells. Sure of themselves in the heart of their own territory, the drivers of the trucks went up in flames with their loads.

At the command tent, we traced the success of the attack. Following the destruction of the batteries and the convoy, the paratroopers organized themselves for the retreat on foot. They gathered the wounded and set out on the hike, carrying the stretchers. Suddenly another munitions convoy appeared. Its fate was worse than the first. A larger force than before was available to welcome it, and intense fire poured down on it from all directions. The bodies of the dead and the skeletons of the trucks were all that remained of the full cannons and the incredible stocks of munitions.

The paratroopers made their way through the sands until they connected just before dawn with the force that had completed the attack on Umm-Katef. They were not in a good state. Carrying three severely wounded comrades, they had repeatedly requested an evacuation helicopter and had not received one. After the breakup of the command tent, we remained outside of the joint frequencies of the team and had simply not heard them. I sent my helicopters to various other missions while the cries of the paratroopers rolled from command to command. I heard them only at 0700 hours on the second day of the war. Precious hours had been wasted. After several minutes we took off from Umm-Katef with eight wounded who had already received initial treatment.

We concluded the operation by transporting the brigade's wounded from all the night battles to Soroka Hospital in Be'er Sheva. The last of these evacuations were executed under fire. We flew to the small Yemen Field, west of the city, in order to set up the Inverted Sword's forward base again.

### June 6, 1967: Hanan Eitan and Oded Rappaport

*H*anan and Oded's Story: Rafi Lev ejected from his Ouragan on the return from an attack sortie in the Sinai. On the second day of the war, with Israel holding complete air superiority on the Sinai Peninsula, the fighter squadrons turned to assist the three brigades of ground forces that were progressing into the depths of the desert through day and night combat. The Ouragans were sent to destroy Egyptian convoys deep in the Sinai, as well as stubborn pockets of resistance in the areas that were succumbing to the Israeli forces. Returning from attacking Kasaima, Rafi was unexpectedly hit by antiaircraft fire from a region that was on the verge of collapsing to Sharon's troops. Not far from the area of the ground battle, he ejected and parachuted, injured, into the dunes.

At noontime, Captain Hanan Eitan and Oded Rappaport, his copilot, were scrambled to rescue him. The squadron's helicopters had not managed to set up in Yemen Field after the night's activities in Umm-Katef, and had returned to Nitzana. A Dakota was flying along the border in order to receive Rafi's distress signal. The area had been spotted, but was surrounded by Egyptian forces. Despite his injuries, Rafi had been forced to escape and find cover. Oded and Hanan approached the area and homed in on "Sarah," constantly trying not to lose his signal.

Though under fire and in actual danger of being shot down, they had no choice. The signals were close to the Egyptians' territory. Hanan suspected that the Egyptians had captured Rafi and killed him and were using the "Sarah" signal to lure them into a trap. Suddenly the signal disappeared, and then reappeared after fifteen minutes. Rafi was switching his signal on and off so as not to reveal his hiding place to the Egyptians. By afternoon, still not having found him, they had to return to Israel to refuel for another run.

By the time they reentered the Sinai, darkness had fallen. Returning to search the area where he had ejected, they scanned for "Sarah," but did not detect it. Hanan suggested that they search in the canyon. The darkness shielded them from the Egyptians, but made navigation perilous. Hugging the ground as they were, an incorrect entry into the canyon could lead to a wreck. Oded stuck half of his body out of the chopper to improve his field of vision. As he directed Hanan on their internal communications and it seemed that they were nearing the bottom of the canyon, an enormous mass closed in on them.

"Break! " he shouted to Hanan. "We're going to hit a mountain! "

He threw himself into the cabin and began pulling on the sticks in case Hanan had not heard. The engine screeched in the sharp shift from descent to steep climb. The helicopter lost speed and started sinking. Oded shouted to Hanan to hit the landing lights. Forget security, they were concerned with safety. At the last instant, Hanan managed to break the drop and prevent a crash. The helicopter sat heavily on the slope of the mountain. Like men saved from certain death, they were soaked in sweat and agitated. Now they had to see if they would be able to take off again.

The flight machinist jumped out with a flashlight and returned, smiling. There was no real damage. They took off with pounding hearts. The search in the canyon yielded nothing.

" 'Wrench,' this is 'Topaz.' Discontinue and exit." The Dakota was keeping an eye on the helicopter, and its crew was concerned. They repeated their call, but Oded and Hanan did not even consider calling off their efforts, and ignored the messages.

They had investigated nearly the entire region, and their search was almost over. Still in the proximity of the Egyptians, with the battle to their backs, Oded suggested to Hanan that they activate the landing lights so that the spotlights would blind the remnants of the resistance below. If they began to fire, the lights could be turned off and the helicopter could disappear. Another canyon lay ahead of them, and they entered. For some reason the lights were weak. Hanan dropped down sharply to the floor of the canyon to fly low and slowly along its length.

"Something's moving there! " Oded shouted. Hanan pulled them into a hover.

Rafi came skipping toward them, waving his tiny flashlight. With a slight jerk of the helicopter, they stopped near him. He seemed calm, considering his situation.

"I was certain you would come to get me at night," he said. "I saw how you flew around me during the day, and how they fired at you. I had no doubt you'd return at night."

They cut east rapidly to Israel and Be'er Sheva, where they dropped Rafi at Soroka Hospital for treatment. On their final stop, at Yemen Field, the helicopter became stuck, sitting on the runway at an unusual angle. It could not roll on its wheels. They shut down the engines and, jumping down to check, beheld a frightening sight. One of the tires had exploded, and the rear wheel was completely gone. There were two holes in the belly from the stones on which they had made their heavy landing. All of the belly's antennae and one of the spotlights had been wrenched off. They now understood the reason for the dim lights during their last run.

In later years, Hanan transferred to fighter aircraft. During the Yom Kippur War, six years later, both he and Rafi were killed in fighter planes. This was not the last war, as they had then believed.

**June 6, 1967: Herzle Bodinger** *H*erzle's Story: With the takeoff of Hunters from their forward base along the Jordanian border on June 5, the Iraqis entered the war. H-3 Air Base lay on the oil pipeline from Kirkuk, Iraq, to Lebanon's Tripoli and Israel's Haifa, the branch that had run dry after 1948. Though it had been a civilian landing strip during the British period, the Iraqis had developed it into a military base.

Destruction of the field had been postponed until the following day, when Israeli air superiority would be assured in Jordan as well. The plan was rushed and superficial. With no maps or intelligence information about the field other than its estimated location, Herzle Bodinger took off from Ramat David in a quartet of Vautours backed up by a pair of Mirages. They would have to cross the border at the southern coast of the Sea of Galilee and fly straight and low along the pipeline until they hit the field. It was impossible to go astray with this type of navigation. The

Vautours were to bomb, while the Mirages intercepted any aircraft that were scrambled toward them.

They had been meant to take off early in the morning, but during the last check at the hangar, Herzle saw a large, bright plane with no markings or camouflage approaching from the east at one thousand feet. "It's a Boeing," said one of the mechanics. *What would a Boeing be doing at Ramat David?* Herzle thought. Then he realized. "It's a TU-16 coming to bomb our field! " They ran for cover. Sirens sounded on the base, and antiaircraft fire began to pour from all directions. The Tupolev turned right, and its gunner rained fire on the base. Two seconds later, a pair of Mirages was behind it. One fired its guns and the other a missile, and the Iraqi bomber crashed into a military camp near Megiddo. Twelve Israeli soldiers were killed, and many others were injured.

This was the second time that Ramat David had been attacked. Following the Jordanian shelling the day before, ground and armored forces had been sent toward the hills of Jenin in the West Bank to eliminate the cannons. The Vautours set out along the pipeline road toward Iraq in order to prevent any additional attacks. As planned, they flew very low, with the Mirages at their heels. Along the way, they passed a parking lot with Iraqi military forces on their way to the war. Gritting their teeth, the Israelis flew on and did not touch them. They identified H-3 by the clouds of dust rising from its runways. Two MiG-21s were taking off. The Mirages headed toward them as the Vautours pulled into a bombing run from the east, igniting a Hunter on its way to land. A second Hunter was on its way to land, but, seeing what happened to his compatriot, its pilot turned toward the Vautour flight leader.

"Break! They're on you! " everyone shouted at him. He broke, and Number Three entered to deal with the Hunter. After the first bombing run, Herzle realized that he had enough ordnance remaining for another run. As he pulled into position, he saw a third Hunter about to land. He switched his gunsights to air-to-air and closed in. Suddenly the Hunter broke left at low altitude, having apparently received warning from the control tower. Loaded with bombs, Herzle decided to forgo the endeavor. An antiaircraft battery fired densely on him from the edge of the runway. Out of shock, he acted stupidly by straightening his wings and laying himself out wide for all to see. Within a split second he entered his bombing run, using his guns to fire on the antiaircraft. Following one more strafing run on the line of planes sitting on the runway, his leader called for him to return home. Behind him he could see a MiG-21 ablaze on its way into the ground. On their way home they emptied the rest of the ordnance on the parking lot loaded with Iraqi forces.

*June 6, 1967: Yitzhak Glantz-Golan* **Y**itzhak's Story: They set out for the third attack of the day on the Iraqi airfield, a foursome of Vautours with backup provided by a foursome of Mirages. Their welcoming party included murderously strong antiaircraft fire as well as Hunters and MiGs that were waiting for them at every corner. The problems of navigation and fuel supply were immediately forgotten. Trying to maneuver their way between survival and executing their mission, they had barely hit one plane on the ground when the Hunters were on all of them. Several distracted the Mirages, and the rest went after the Vautours. Everything had occurred within seconds.

Shlomo Keren, the flight leader, shouted, "I'm hit!" and headed south, dragging a trail of smoke. There was no way out, only steadfastness in attacking the target. Glantz dropped down to strafe, and refused to entertain the possibility that there might be a Hunter on his tail. Suddenly he was on fire as well. Should he eject or crash? His survival instinct dominated. He ejected at low altitude and parachuted near the airfield. Iraqi troops took him prisoner, and he gave himself up without fear. Glantz had gone through the Holocaust as a child, and he would survive this as well. He had already seen death much closer than he did on his way to the jail in Baghdad.

In the run on one target—H-3 Air Base—Israel had lost three planes and four men. One had made an emergency landing on the Iraqi-Saudi border, and the Saudis had found the two aircrew dead. Glantz and Gideon Dror were taken prisoner.

What distinguished Operation Moked was its awesome and smashing speed, along with its execution according to plan and the lessons learned from exercises leading up to the operation. The Egyptians were paralyzed. The primary achievement of the operation could be measured by the shattering of the enemy's air power, which was its spinal column, and by the prevention of their ability to organize themselves into a second-strike response. The number of aircraft destroyed was considered secondary. The level of resistance was on a par with the level of readiness and the daring of the antiaircraft gunners and the pilots on each base. Despite the surprise, many of the air bases were not at a loss to respond, and they fought bravely even during the first wave. The IAF's loss rate on the first day—ten percent of the attacking force—was high. Nonetheless, the level of success was astounding, and it pushed aside the pain and criticism regarding the final and unplanned leg of the operation, the attack on H-3. This had been a nonessential target whose attackers were victims of the routine of the plan, sent in repeatedly on unvarying routes and methods, and falling into a well-planned and executed ambush. The heavy toll was relatively greater than the attack on any Egyptian, Jordanian, or Syrian air base attacked, and was not worth the light damage that the Iraqi Air Force sustained. If they had dared penetrate Israeli airspace after the second day, the Iraqi planes could have been dealt with in air-to-air combat.

The air superiority achieved during the first day allowed the entire power of the IAF to be turned toward assisting the ground forces and deterring the last-ditch sorties attempted by remnants of the demolished enemy air forces, which sought to disrupt the processes taking place on the three fronts. At this point, the initiative to decide where and when to attack was removed from the IAF, and it became a supportive and not always decisive force, subordinate to demands from the ground. After two days that had demanded a total effort by every pilot and plane, the IAF's ability to supply was greater than the demand. The average daily number of sorties dropped by a quarter, from four on the first day to three on the following days. Few of the ground force's commanders requested IAF support.

Three Israeli divisions penetrated the defensive Egyptian positions in the Sinai within thirty-six hours. Twelve hours later they were within range of gaining control of the Suez Canal. Hundreds of attack sorties aided in demolishing the convoys of Egyptian artillery and armored vehicles. Most of the destruction was done by the Vautours, Mystères, and Super Mystères. Preventive bombings blocked the flow of support to the forward positions and, jamming the routes of escape, shortened the battles.

Israeli aircraft, primarily Ouragans and Fouga Magisters belonging to the flight school, also participated in the armored units' combat. The training squadron had forty-five Fouga Magisters, and the lack of equipment brought about, after deliberations, the altering of twenty of them to combat missions, just as the Harvards had been altered during the Sinai

Campaign. The decision was a risky one. The combat abilities of the Fouga Magister were makeshift and limited to attacking ground targets. It had no ejector seat and was easy to shoot down, with the pilot standing little chance of survival. The dangers had been taken into account. The emergency Fouga Magister squadron had been formed in 1964, and comprised fresh young pilots and veterans of the previous wars, who fought for the chance to serve in it. The oldest member of the squadron was Eli Finegersh, forty-five years old, one of the first pilots in the IAF and the only reserve pilot for whom this was his third war. Both Aryeh Ben-Orr, the squadron's commander, and his deputy, Arnon Livnat, were killed during the war.

The squadron's first formations were scrambled fifteen minutes after the bombings of Moked's first wave. Each plane was loaded with twelve 80-millimeter rockets capable of penetrating armored vehicles, or two 50-kilogram bombs, as well as two .30-caliber machine guns. The Fouga Magister squadron dealt alone with attacking ground targets during the morning and the afternoon, because all of the IAF's fighter aircraft were occupied in destroying airfields. In dozens of sorties, they demolished artillery batteries and tank positions in the Gaza Strip and the northern part of the Sinai, which had been shelling settlements in the Negev and threatening the armored division attempting to break through the Egyptian defenses at Rafah. Its greatest display of bravery, however, would take place in an area that few ever dreamed they would be fighting over.

Throughout the years, Israel's security had rested on King Hussein's silent agreement to keep the majority of his military on the other side of the Jordan River, in a way similar to the distribution of forces in the Sinai after the Sinai Campaign. The entry of the Iraqi army into Jordan and the reinforcement of the Jordanian forces on the West Bank were understood to be a cause for war. Out of this developed Hussein's double error of June 5, 1967. In the morning he was lured into joining the war without having an accurate picture of the events taking place on the Egyptian front. Several hours later he hastened to attack Jerusalem, Tel Aviv, the settlements in Israel's central region, and the Ramat David air base, prior to bringing his armored brigades across the bridges of the Jordan River. Hussein had more British Centurion tanks than the IDF, and a large quantity of sophisticated American Patton tanks. The Israeli armored reserve units relied on the ancient Shermans and the light French AMX.

Only a few of these poor-quality Israeli tanks were stationed in

Jerusalem, while approximately one hundred Jordanian Pattons were in the Jordan River Valley, ninety minutes' travel time from the eastern part of the city. By noon the Jordanian tanks had crossed the Abdallah Bridge to Jericho, and had begun to climb toward Jerusalem. At the point where the road was carved into the mountainside, the Fouga Magisters set their ambush, firing rockets and blocking the tanks' progress. Thus these training aircraft saved Jerusalem before its defenders even knew the size of the threat crawling toward them.

### June 7, 1967, Afternoon:
### Cochav Hess

Cochav's Story: By the afternoon of June 7, the Jordanians were in the midst of an organized retreat from Jerusalem. The Fouga Magisters and the Ouragans relentlessly attacked their rear on the road to Jericho, and even across the Jordan River. Burned and shattered tanks, cannons, and armored personnel carriers lay strewn by the side of the road. The Jordanian antiaircraft defenses were formidable, and every diving plane was met by fearless fire. An Ouragan pilot named Zike was hit while attacking a Jordanian Legion base near the Abdallah Bridge, and was forced to parachute east of the Jordan River, almost at the foot of Mount Nevo. His flight leader guided the helicopter's crew to the area.

Cochav Hess and his crew flew through the canyons of the Judean desert north of Jerusalem, avoiding the main thoroughfares. The dangerous area began in the Jordan River Valley, an exposed plain with short canyons. The helicopter circumvented Jericho, a large tray of water and vegetation. Across the Jordan, a hellish barrage of fire awaited them, but they continued to fly, evading the enemy. They reached a ravine and the Legion camp, praying and eluding while attempting not to lose the direction of their entry to find Zike. Only thus would they be able to reach his area in order to track his "Sarah" signal.

Cochav could hear the thuds of bullets striking the body of the helicopter. The flight mechanic reported a leak from the fuel tanks. The sharp smell permeated the cabin. This was not the place for an emergency landing, but the threatening possibility that they might, at any moment, turn into a ball of flames intensified the pounding of their hearts. The sound of the "Sarah" coming from the control panel eliminated any thoughts of landing. It was best to take the risk and rescue Zike. What did they have to lose? Even if they landed, they would not be taken prisoner; the Jordanians were too riled. They had to reach Zike before the Legionnaires found him. There was no doubt that the Jordanians had seen him parachute near them and had already sent out patrols to search for him. They had also seen the helicopter, and the fire was now coming to them from the direction of the "Sarah" signal. *If we survive this fire, we're liable to reveal Zike's position*, Cochav thought to himself. They had to concoct a solution quickly.

"First let's check with Zike to see what his condition is," said the copilot.

"Sickle Two, Sickle Two, do you copy?" Cochav called into the homing frequency. If Zike heard, he would respond with a tapping. "Sarah" was not designed for two-way conversation. The receiver in the helicopter blurted out two agitated clicks, the agreed signal for a positive response. One click meant negative. Zike could hear.

*He must be running like mad to get away from those bullets. They can hit us as well. I don't care. I'm going to give my all to get him out. We're in the same boat*, Cochav told himself.

"Sickle Two," he called, after quickly surveying the area, "Run east and cut in toward their area. There is a hill, and behind it a flat valley. If you can get there, we'll pluck you out from under their noses."

Flying as low as possible, Cochav headed toward the hidden valley, encouraged by Zike's affirmative response, which accompanied him as he disappeared from his pursuer's eyes. The Jordanians aimed a mortar at the helicopter, and Cochav realized he had to convince them that he was retreating. He turned and banked around their position, behind the hill. This seemed to be the safest spot in the area. He would wait on the ground for Zike's appearance, grab him, and flee into Jordan. Once he had achieved a safe distance from the Legion, he could turn south and cross into Israel over the Dead Sea.

"Sickle Two, do you see us?" Cochav returned to the radio.

The response was one click. Negative. This was a good sign, for if Zike did not see them, neither did the Jordanians.

"We are holding at the meeting point over the hill," he notified Zike. Two clicks.

The shelling drew nearer. The Jordanians were closing in not only on Zike but on the helicopter as well. Several minutes passed that seemed to last an eternity. Suddenly, Zike appeared from behind the hill, running, soaked in sweat. Cochav hopped the helicopter over to his position. The mechanic extended his arm and pulled in the Ouragan pilot.

"Take off! Take off! " he cried, as the mortar shells closed in. They flew east and then south. The odor of the fuel struck Cochav's nose. They had been too busy to remember the fuel leak. The flight controller directed them via the Jordanian airfield in Kalandia, the location of the Israeli settlement of Atarot, which had been destroyed in 1948 and had now been returned to Israeli hands. Cochav would later receive one of Israel's highest medals of bravery for Zike's rescue.

## Air Battles in the Six-Day War

The Egyptians who survived Operation Moked did not forgo the remaining opportunities that would allow them to regain their lost pride, at least in their own eyes. By the fourth day of the war, Israeli ground forces held the passes in the Sinai and were positioned facing the blue stripe of the Suez Canal's waters. They were in the final stages of eliminating the remnants of the Egyptian divisions that were waging hopeless last-ditch battles. It demanded incredible bravery for the Egyptian pilots to take off from the devastated airfields in the Nile Valley and to provoke the Israeli ground forces, who, from the outset, were in a position of advantage. They did not hesitate to take position opposite the Israeli Mirages that controlled the skies, in attempts to draw them into suicidal air battles.

The IAF umbrella was incontrovertible, largely due to the flight-control network that had been developed since the previous wars. Whereas, a decade earlier, the Israeli radar had barely covered the country's borders, it now extended to great distances and provided early warning of low-altitude penetrations. Though Mirages patrolled and waited in ambush at potential points of penetration, they were called several times to other distant missions and caught the intruders because of this sophisticated air detection and control. This network had proved itself in its adaptable and advanced management of the bombing runs of Operation Moked by transferring formations from planned targets to new targets of greater importance. The shooting down of the intruders was inevitable in that the Israeli pilots had the advantage of knowing the traits of the enemy aircraft, including the MiG-21, the toughest of all.

The air battles of the Six-Day War added sixty enemy aircraft to the number destroyed on the ground, a quarter of which were shot down by four pilots. Giora Rom, the ace of the war who would later become deputy commander of the IAF, shot down five. Oded Sagee, Menachem Shmul, and Asher Snir each shot down three enemy aircraft in this, their first war.

Sagee completed his trio on the day following the downing of the Jordanian Hunter that had attacked the lone Nord at the Sirkin Air Field. In the morning he shot down an SU-7 that was part of a quartet attacking Israeli ground forces. Later that afternoon, he and his partner simultaneously shot down two MiG-19s in central Sinai.

Shmul shot down his trio during the final two days of the war. The first, a MiG-19 that was part of a quartet, was downed over the Suez Canal using only his instincts, since his gunsights were out of commission. That afternoon he was scrambled to the canal again to contend with a quartet of IL-28 twin-engined bombers that, protected by MiG-21s, were attacking Israeli ground forces. When one of the bombers suddenly changed direction toward Israel, Shmul suspected that it was headed to attack civilian targets in the country, and departed his formation on a lone chase of the bomber. The gunner in the bomber's belly opened fire, which Shmul returned, ripping the tail, along with the gunner, from the rest of the plane. Shmul returned to his original mission at the canal, observed a MiG-21 in front of him, closed the distance, and splintered the aircraft in one burst.

Asher Snir's first victim, a MiG-21, was at the T-4 Air Base in Syria. The last two were shot down in one air battle on the fifth day of the war. The MiGs were flying hit-and-run missions, attacking airborne units near the Suez Canal, setting trucks ablaze and escaping back to Egypt. Snir was part of a pair patrolling at high altitude above the Mediterranean coast. Seconds after the paratroopers' cry for help, the aircraft were in a sharp dive toward the attacked force. The MiGs could be seen fleeing westward at eight thousand feet toward their base. Above the outskirts of Ismailia, the enemy leader crossed Snir's sights, and his tail went up in flames in the first burst. Snir immediately found the second MiG directly in front of him. If he had fired, they would have both exploded. Snir's leader attempted to fire, but reported that his guns were jammed. The MiG broke too sharply, and, knowing his limitations, Snir was able to plan a turn approach from behind, and rip off its right wing in a cannon burst from five hundred meters. Burning and broken apart, the MiG flipped on its back and crashed in the center of its airfield in the Nile Delta.

In their last moments, the Syrian and Jordanian air forces did not exhibit even this symbolic and respectable show of bravery.

### June 7, 1967, 1200 Hours:
### The Inverted Sword Squadron

*M*y Story: At 1030 hours I brought thirteen helicopters to Eilat. We had crossed the Negev Desert for nearly an hour, flying at low altitude from Yemen Field. Our orders were to stand ready under cover. The Jordanians in Aqaba were watching Eilat, which appeared abandoned in the afternoon hours. Every iota of movement raised suspicions. If they could guess our intentions, they would report to the Egyptians or simply begin shelling out of fear for their lives. Our goal was to capture Sharm-al-Sheikh in an airborne operation. Under the threat of an imminent cease-fire that the UN Security Council was devising, we were in a rush, as in the Sinai Campaign, to capture the Strait of the Tiran, which had sparked the war. The helicopter and transport squadrons were ordered to give priority to airlifts.

The paratroopers dispersed to the helicopters. For the first time we were working with three Super Frelon helicopters, which had transport capacity almost identical to my thirteen. We took off without ceremony, with no fear of war. Though we were flying at low altitude, it was a day flight with nothing to threaten us other than what might be waiting at Sharm itself. Above us, the umbrella of fighter aircraft provided protection even though there was no attacker in the area. To be safe, we flew along the desolate Saudi Arabian coast, which was of no interest to anyone, even the Saudis. After less than an hour we saw Sharm-a-Sheikh. We approached cautiously, circling and recalling the brave battles in which the Egyptians had held on to the last stone until they had been defeated from the air. We surveyed the entire area with our eyes and binoculars and discovered it to be abandoned.

This was a joke of fate. A bloody war waged for free sailing in the straits, which had been closed to Israeli shipping, and not a soul remained to guard them. We landed on the dirt runway of the airfield. The force we carried spread out and secured the area. Our flight controller set up a control tower with his crew, and called for the transport squadrons to inaugurate the field. The planes were loaded with paratroopers who had hoped to capture the field in an airdrop. The glory of the transport squadron had been dimmed during this war. They had worked hard and well, flying and dropping supplies, but the Egyptians had now taken away their last chance to perpetuate some of the renown of the last war. The transport aircraft began to land and unload soldiers and equipment, and within two hours the place had an Israeli presence that seemed to have been there forever.

Someone peeked over the cliff toward the Suez Canal and could not believe his eyes. What was the Navy doing here? A squadron of torpedo boats was harbored there, and there was no question that they were ours. Although we had not been told that we were in a race against them, it seemed possible that they had arrived first. Still, we had not seen a single sailing vessel along the entire route. The upshot of the situation was that the Navy had set out before us and had been the first to raise the Israeli flag at Sharm-al-Sheikh.

In the dark of night we returned to Eilat. On the way home, as the fatigue of three days without sleep began to take over, we could hear the news of Israel's liberation of Jerusalem on the radio. At our hotel in Eilat, we tumbled into the showers and called our wives for the first time, immediately afterward falling into our first deep sleep of the war.

At 0600, I was brought back to reality. The head of operations, Rafi Har-Lev, telephoned with new orders: "Gather your pilots and helicopters. You've got a big job in the north. Rafi Sivron is being sent to you. He put so much into planning this damned war—make sure he has some fun from it as well."

Formation after formation, we departed from Eilat, each leader having mission orders to execute. One foursome headed to the recently captured bridges of the Jordan River, to aid the ground forces there. Another unloaded to be on alert for pilot rescue anywhere in the country. Thus, by the time I reached Poria, in the north, most of the helicopters had departed, though in was clear to all that once they had finished their missions, they would fly north, from whence we would set out to our next front of operations. The Syrians were the ones who had begun to push this war, and they had made sure to remind us of this for the past four days. They had relentlessly shelled the settlements in the northern Galilee and the Jordan River Valley, and had even attempted a fruitless attack on other, more central settlements. On June 6 they sent a division with ten tanks that came within one hundred meters of the Israeli forward position at Kibbutz Dan. Tank and aircraft fire dispersed them within an hour, but since then the artillery shelling had not ceased.

We flew from Eilat to Tiberias, stopping to refuel at our home base. I picked up Rafi Sivron, who, along with Sagee, became my partner in planning and flight. He had the full picture regarding the missions that the Northern Command had planned for us for the upcoming days.

When we reached Poria, just above Tiberias, I was quickly summoned to the office of the chief of the Northern Command, Maj. Gen. David "Dado" Elazar, at the forward post. This was an uncommon situation. Majors are not usually directly invited to the office of a major general without the presence of a mediating rank and representative of headquarters, who can provide operational instructions. Dado directed me to prepare for a large night landing operation beyond the mouth of the Yarmukh River, in order to capture the Golan Heights.

The only Israeli activity along the front was of fighter aircraft that were attempting to silence the artillery. They bombed not in waves but in lone sorties, paying the toll of lost aircraft in the effort. In the evening, notification of a cease-fire with Egypt and of Nasser's resignation was heard, but within a short time it became clear that these announcements were inaccurate. In the field, the changes were noticeable in the radical instructions that were given.

Opposite Rafah, in the Mediterranean, a strange occurrence took place involving Israeli aircraft and torpedo ships and a ship belonging to the U.S. fleet. It was an unidentified vessel, flying no flags, bristling with antennae, which was sailing in the area of the war front. Only after Israeli Mirages had strafed it with cannons and the torpedo boats had fired two torpedoes, did the ship's crew begin to wave an American flag. It was the *Liberty*, a spy ship of the CIA. The attack had severely damaged it, with dozens of dead and wounded left on the deck. The crew refused Israeli aid. The Israeli government apologized and, years later, paid damages and compensation.

After the war, it became clear that responsibility for the ship's proximity to the battle front lay with erroneous instructions given by the command of the Sixth Fleet. Since there was no coordination between the Sixth Fleet and the Israeli Defense Forces and government, the headquarters of the fleet was the primary cause for the development of this mistake in the field.

Upon arrival at the northern front, the helicopters of the Inverted

Sword Squadron were summoned to various evacuation missions of wounded soldiers, often near fire by the front lines. Others were involved in transporting equipment, primarily using equipment slings, for brigades that were organizing themselves for the attack on the Golan Heights. The helicopters spent all of June 9 and 10 flying dozens of sorties to rescue pilots and wounded soldiers and transport supplies.

On the afternoon of June 9, at the peak of the assault battles in the northern Golan Heights, Dado proposed a night landing in the southern part of the Golan above the Yarmukh ravine. Speaking to me and representatives of IAF headquarters, he explained that his intention was for our forces to capture the vital intersection at Peak-El-Al. Though he feared that Syrian forces, armed with antiaircraft weapons, might be fortified there, the general was convinced that this was a decisive tactical move.

IAF headquarters was uncertain whether the operation should be approved. Throughout the afternoon we worked on the plan with the operations and intelligence personnel. For the first time in my life, I had been assigned a mission about which I was not convinced. The night was too dark, and the area was replete with enormous topographical obstacles. The accrued fatigue of the squadron's crews would only make things more difficult. The ground forces that were to be flown in were also not organized and had not concluded their regrouping from Jerusalem and the Sinai. All of this did not guarantee a successful operation. I explained to the general that the tactical advantage he hoped to gain would be diminished because of our partial execution of the operation. He agreed to postpone the operation until the next night.

On the morning of June 9, Israeli ground forces attacked a number of Syrian positions at Kineitra and Tel Fachar. Fighter aircraft attacked positions in the southern Golan from which Israeli settlements had been shelled. All this was in preparation for the ground forces' attack. Top IDF officers, Defense Minister Moshe Dayan, and Prime Minister Levi Eshkol decided to spend these hours with the chief of the Northern Command.

At the end of the day, following the penetration of two brigades into the Golan Heights, Dado spoke with the chief of staff.

"The Syrians are broken! " he yelled. "They're retreating, terrified. They've been seen blowing up their artillery and munitions. Refugees have abandoned their villages and have escaped." By Saturday morning, the picture had changed completely.

By 1000 hours, Dado said, "Let's get on with the Golan Heights. The paratrooper force and tanks will head to Touefik, above Tel Katzir. A second airborne force will be flown in by helicopter and placed in the forward Syrian positions in control of the cliffs of the Heights."

At Poria, the helicopters of the Inverted Sword Squadron stood ready. This was to be the final undertaking of this war.

Dado proposed moving the landing to the early afternoon, another idea that did not seem too plausible to me. From the Americans' experience in Vietnam, we had learned that such a landing demanded a force of helicopters several times greater than I had at my disposal, even if the other helicopters of the IAF were included.

I informed him that we would execute any operation. It was difficult to say no twice. By 1400 hours we had taken off. Members of the kibbutzim crept out of their bomb shelters and could not believe their eyes—eight helicopters flying to the Syrian Heights. Next to me, Rafi Sivron navigated to the police station, which had been a forward Syrian outpost. The paratroopers stormed out of the helicopter and discovered it to be empty. I proposed to the commander of the force that we secure the building as our first acquisition in the southern Golan Heights. On the way back to Poria, en route to fly in the next round, we had to change our plans and skip quickly to the next points. This was the Peak-El-Al intersection—the target of the night landing that had been so important to Dado, and had been canceled the previous evening.

We flew east along the Yarmukh ravine, south of the intersection, breaking north and landing at the intersection itself, on top of the Syrian antiaircraft forces. We were deep into enemy territory. Astounded by our arrival, the Syrians turned their cannons toward us, but, leaping out of the helicopters, our paratroopers attacked with gunfire and subdued them within minutes. On the communications network, I openly directed the other choppers from Poria to the intersection. They flew back and forth until we had a platoon-sized force, including Danny Matt, the battalion's commander. The brigade advised us that the cease-fire would go into effect at 1600 hours.

Danny and I did not want to end this war without completing our task. We decided that we had to capture the length of the road up to the Botmiya intersection so that we could assure ourselves a large part of the Heights. For this we had to receive approval from high up. Back at headquarters, we proposed that we continue until we reached the organized Syrian army, but the chief of the Northern Command was not there, and his approval was needed. He was flying with Chief of Staff Rabin to Kuneitra. We tried to reach them on the radio in their helicopter, and could hear their pilot yelling that at that moment they were being chased by a MiG-21. Frozen, we listened to every word as the pilot attempted to conceal the helicopter in a deep canyon. We could no longer hear him. The flight controller informed us that they had evaded the MiG, and it became clear that we would not find any high-ranking officer to approve our plan.

Elad Peled, the brigade commander stationed at Poria, would approve a scouting run using only one helicopter. Depending on what we found, he would decide whether to let us transport the ground forces farther. Rafi and I set out on a combat reconnaissance sortie, flying very low. Occasionally we saw an armored vehicle or a small force of foot soldiers who fired on us. We flew to the end of Rafi's 1:100,000 map, not having planned such a penetration. Rafi was well organized, and pulled a 1:500,000 map from his pocket.

"We're going too far," I told him.

"Hogwash," he said. "We're only sixteen kilometers from the Peak-El-Al intersection." Below us were well-entrenched Syrian divisions, who greeted us with dense ack-ack. We avoided the fire and landed quickly two kilometers southwest of Tel Fares. "Last stop," I told the paratroopers who piled out of the helicopter.

On the way back to the Peak-El-Al intersection, Rafi and I deliberated on whether we had made a correct decision. It is a fine line between victory and defeat in such instances. Danny Matt agreed with our decision, and managed to get approval for a limited airlift to Botmiya if we didn't run into trouble. I prayed that we would succeed. From the Peak-El-Al intersection, the settlements of the Galilee were still within mortar range. If we succeeded in capturing Botmiya and gained control of the eastern positions, we would put the settlements out of range of the artillery as well.

We were followed back to Botmiya by three helicopters carrying thirty paratroopers. The first group had marked the spot and had set up a homing mechanism to aid the helicopters' navigation. With the airlift working perfectly, we returned to Poria for another round. This was one of the squadron's greatest moments.

The Super Frelons joined us, transporting jeeps with recoilless cannons. The force also received personnel carriers and anti-tank weapons. By nightfall, Peak intersection had two hundred paratroopers and Botmiya four hundred. Thus we had established the farthest border of the Golan Heights. Armored forces and commando units that had been approaching overland reached the paratroopers several hours later, and around midnight the capture of the southern Golan Heights was sealed.

At 1800 hours the cease-fire took hold, at the very moment when the paratroopers at Botmiya completed a battle in which they devastated a Syrian convoy retreating from Kineitra. Sixty vehicles were destroyed and hundreds of Syrian soldiers were killed and wounded, more than in any other battle in the Golan Heights. The war was over.

The next morning, after a short debriefing, I led a formation of a dozen helicopters, for the first time in the history of Israel, in a daylight flight over Judea and Samaria. We arrived in Jerusalem, executed a wide turn over the city before the amazed eyes of all those on the ground, and turned home to Tel Nof.

Yaakov Agassi, who had taken over as acting commander of the base, greeted us. Schmuel Shefer, the base's commander, had been hit in his Mirage and had ejected in the Golan Heights. One of our helicopters had rescued him. After Agassi had met with all of our pilots and shaken their hands, he took me aside to the squadron's office, where he informed me that my brother, Nechemiah, a platoon commander in the paratroopers, had been killed leading the force that spearheaded the capture of the Gaza Strip on the first day of the war. Throughout the entire war, everyone had known, but had concealed it from me, so as not to affect my leadership capabilities. In the heart of the victory celebration, my world was shattered.

Mount Hermon, the most important strategic point for the defense of the northern region of the country, had been forgotten during the thirty-six-hour battle for the Golan Heights. The error was discovered several days after the cease-fire, when UN observers requested a helicopter to mark the new border. The Northern Command was astounded to discover that Mount Hermon was in the territory captured from the Syrians, even though there was not even a symbolic force of Israeli soldiers securing it. The flight of the UN observers was postponed until an Inverted Sword helicopter could fly a team of fighters to one of the mountain's peaks that seemed to our commanders to be high and decisive enough. The fighters settled in and raised the Israeli flag. The cease-fire line around that peak was signed by the observers, and within days Israel began to erect an intelligence outpost and detection systems. The Syrians quickly set up their own outpost on a nearby peak, the highest in the region. Israel regretted choosing the lower point and, years later, lost this vital outpost to a surprise Syrian attack.

The Mount Hermon observation post was one new point in the newly acquired territories that provided wide and distant horizons for the Israeli air defense and flight-control network. The new territories' significance was measured in IAF headquarters by the critical four minutes they added to the warning Israel would have as enemy planes neared its border. This period would allow for early scrambling and interception of enemy aircraft. The June 5 borders had been anywhere from several meters to a few kilometers away from population centers, and allowed for a warning period of only thirty seconds or less. This had made possible the surprise penetration of Syrian aircraft to the Haifa Bay and Jordanian aircraft to Netanya on the first day of the war. The Jordanians had been able to attack the Sirkin airfield without even crossing the border of the West Bank. The planes could be attacked only after bombing, and only in their own airspace. On June 9, Israeli Mirages engaged Egyptian aircraft that took off from the Nile Valley for Sinai and Israel, *this* time on the border of the Suez Canal.

In these new, wide-open spaces, the pilots felt as if they had been liberated. After years of having to use the narrow skies above the Negev Desert, they had now been granted large expanses of training grounds far from population centers. The airfields in Sinai would now breathe down the necks of the Egypt's rear positions. Nevertheless, the plethora of accomplishments did not quiet the criticism. At one of the war's concluding debriefing sessions, held by IAF headquarters and senior pilots, the level of mutual reproach was intense. Moked had been accepted as self-explanatory. Its unpredicted success turned the critics' anger on those responsible for the weaknesses that appeared during other attacks in the war. The bombing of H-3 in Iraq, the epilogue of the war, which had lacked the inspiration of the incredible opening scenes of the war, was a special target of criticism. Not part of the original plan, this attack had not received the attention that had been given to the airfields in Egypt, Jordan, and Syria. Day after day, aircraft had been sent in with superficial preparation, lacking maps and intelligence information, on the same flight route. This allowed the Jordanians radar and the logical minds of the defenders of the Iraqi fields to prepare the ambush on the third wave. The damage to H-3 was peripheral, and the losses—a killed pilot and navigator, two pilots captured, and three aircraft downed—were heavier than at any other base. In the eyes of the critics, this was a warning indicator of faulty functioning of the system, which operates best with early planning and extensive training, and fails with improvisation.

The pilots criticized the fact that full air support of the ground forces had not been used until the second day of the war. But they were pleased with the concept of the massive crushing of the Egyptian army in the Sinai mountain passes and the decimation of the Jordanian army while on its way to the Judean hills and Samaria. In their striving for perfection, they did not even boast of the sorties flown by the Fouga Magisters on the first day of the war, which had blocked the Egyptian tanks, essentially saving Jerusalem. The critics furiously accused the ground forces' commanders of adhering stubbornly to the pace and methods of previous wars. They had failed to feed the air force early intelligence information about their next targets, and so, instead of receiving close and organized support, they had received only partial assistance. In the battles for the liberation of Jerusalem, the paratroopers had lost precious lives in frontal attacks instead of calling in aerial bombings of the targets. Other fronts had benefited from such support, owing to the initiative of squadron commanders who had taken advantage of personal connections to commanders on the ground. In the wisdom of hindsight, they forgot that those commanders had not had tremendous expectations for the IAF prior to the war.

In his conclusion, IAF commander Moti said that if he had been requested to summarize the results of the war according to the criticisms and analyses stated during these sessions, one would think that Israel had lost the war.

On the eve of the war, the IAF had only 210 fighter and bomber pilots and 180 aircraft, to which were added the twenty Fouga Magisters from the flight school. Along with the 40 helicopters and 50 transport aircraft, the IAF had no more than 270 aircraft all told. Of these, only 160 attacked the eleven Egyptian airfields during the first wave of Operation Moked, approximately four formations of quartets to each field. In the second wave, 164 aircraft attacked fourteen Egyptian fields. In the subsequent strikes, in which the two Jordanian and five Syrian fields were attacked and the assault on the five remaining Egyptian fields was completed, only 120 to 130 aircraft remained. This force destroyed 391 aircraft on the ground and another 60 in air-to-air combat, a total of 451 aircraft. In the attacks on ground targets, Israel lost forty-six aircraft; twenty-four pilots and navigators were killed, seven were taken prisoner, and fifteen were rescued. Three aircraft were shot down in dogfights. The rate of loss was considered low relative to the 3,250 sorties flown during the war, and it balanced the disproportion of the first day, during which nearly half of the planes lost during the war fell, and most of the aircrew were killed. The lightning work of the ground crews and adept performance of the flight control center allowed each plane an average of four sorties per day on the first day, and created the impression that the attacks on the Arab airfields were executed by a much larger number of aircraft.

During the days following the war, all Israelis, including the pilots, felt that they had been born into a new geopolitical era, and were floating in elation. A week earlier the pilots had been alone in their confidence regarding the war, while the average civilian saw himself sentenced to death between the walls of the state. On the morning of the seventh day, a sense of strength prevailed. The pilots tried, perhaps, to immunize themselves against the feelings of invulnerability growing around them. But slowly even they were swept into the joy of this indisputable success.

# 6 The War of Attrition

*I*t was a morning in mid-July of 1967, and my squadron was busy shaking off the final dust of the Six-Day War. We had just concluded two weeks in the Sinai, chasing the remnants of the Egyptian Army. They were battered and desperate for food and water. My pilots wanted to sleep and recuperate from the tension and fatigue that had accumulated over the recent months. The rapid victory created an illusory sense of security, as if a show of strength were enough to bring us closer to peace. The spirit of the times in Israel tended toward passivity and introspection, when initiative was needed to produce diplomatic gains from the military success. Few people understood that this was merely another victory on the battlefield, and not the final war.

The wailing of the alarm siren shattered the sense of calm.

"We've been told to scramble a quartet to aid the Central Command's 'Charoov' commando team near Ramallah," my operations officer told me. "And since it looks like serious business, they want a top leader. A large terrorist squad is on its way to Jerusalem, and we have to catch it before it enters the capital."

The terror squad had been sent by Fatah, a branch of the Palestine Liberation Organization. Fatah's terror squads had penetrated Israeli territory prior to 1967, but their operations had been less impressive and threatening than those that the Fedayeen had executed during the first decade of the State of Israel.

The Central Committee of the PLO had met in Damascus two weeks after the Six-Day War and had decided to transfer its field of operations to the territories captured by Israel during the war, and to Israel itself. Terrorists recruited from the refugee camps and from the cities' lower classes received basic military training in Syrian army camps. With the aid of an Iraqi force, they were transferred to Jordan, which became the stepping-stone to the West Bank, now under Israeli control.

In the helicopter squadron, it did not occur to us that a random chase in the Ramallah area would lead to the development of an entire theory of airborne combat against guerrilla forces.

We assembled crews to fly a quartet of Sikorsky 58s, the old version, with transport capacity limited to ten to twelve fighters. I took my place as the leader.

" 'Blossom,' this is 'Bird.' We'll be near you in five minutes. What are your instructions?"

" 'Bird,' this is 'Blossom.' Our trackers found the squad's tracks two hours ago. You've got to transport our forces forward to block its way before Jerusalem."

"Okay. Mark your location with smoke."

Our landing was quick and deliberate. In telegraphic language, the Charoov team's commander described the situation that had developed several kilometers east of our position, in the southeastern hills of Samaria. The quartet of helicopters split up into pairs and took off loaded with fighters in order to connect with the commando force alongside the trackers.

I was disappointed. I had not expected that they would use my services merely as a flying command car. This would not be making the best of our operational capabilities. I proposed that on our way to the trackers, we search the territory to the point of body-searching every suspicious figure we found. I didn't mind landing and taking off frequently. That was the helicopters' primary function. Though the ground force's commander felt that it was not in his authority to use the helicopters for anything more than a simple transport mission, he accepted my surprising offer, and began to search every hilltop and canyon with his telescope. By the time we reached the trackers, we had landed several times and had questioned everyone who did not look like an innocent passerby from our bird's-eye perspective. When one helicopter landed, its partner hovered nearby, searching the area and providing cover.

The trackers informed us that they estimated the terrorists were approximately two kilometers away, though a meticulous search of a wider area was necessary to ensure that we were not chasing in the wrong direction. The trackers had spent hours in their mission, and were amazed to hear that the airborne force had scoured most of the territory and found it to be clean. In a short meeting, we improvised a plan of operations: one helicopter would remain near the trackers; two would search the rest of the territory; and the fourth would jump forward to the end of the estimated route that the terrorists were following, on the road from Ramallah to Jerusalem and not far from the hilltop on which King Hussein had started building his castle.

After an hour, "Bird Three" informed "Bird One" that it had identified five figures who had seen the helicopter and were running from cover to cover.

"Immediately mark your location with smoke grenades and get out of their line of vision," I told him. "They'll begin shooting at us the minute they discover they're trapped."

"Bird Three" did as told, and the rest of the "Birds" followed his signal and landed the fighters on the hills around the smoke. The pilots indicated their location on the maps to the Charoov team, and the force spread out. The trackers were right. The terrorists had been discovered three kilometers from the first point. We returned to the commando base to acquire an additional company of fighters. Thirty minutes later, a short battle ensued. Two terrorists were killed, one was injured, and two were captured. The quantity of weapons and ammunition they were carrying seemed sufficient "to capture Jerusalem," explained one of the young fighters.

Later the helicopter crews and the Charoov force commanders gathered to debrief at their base. We analyzed every stage of the operation, according to IAF tradition. Working with utmost seriousness, we learned immediate and detailed lessons from everything possible. We dealt with many problems. But our main goal was to strengthen the cooperation with the helicopters in order to better our performance at cutting off the terrorists as quickly as we could, starting at the moment of their discovery. During the recent battle, we had accomplished this. But we wanted to be capable of succeeding every time.

The squadron that had concluded the Six-Day War by landing paratroopers in the Golan Heights had now opened the next war, and played an essential role in the period of airborne chases. In the following years, the helicopters would become vital components of the IAF.

In the months following the Six-Day War, some three thousand to four thousand armed terrorists situated themselves on the eastern side of the Jordan River Valley. During the first weeks they crossed the shallow riverbed and, hiding in the vegetation on its banks, attacked IDF patrols with rocket-propelled grenades. Chasing them proved futile, since they knew the twists and turns of the thick greenery, and the Israelis did not. Eventually, IAF aircraft were scrambled toward them. From the moment an Israeli patrol set out in its vehicles along the river, a plane loaded with napalm bombs stood at the edge of the runway, waiting to take off. If the patrol encountered an ambush, the aircraft would appear overhead within minutes and turn the riverside undergrowth into an inferno. They were not always successful, however. When terrorists managed to escape, helicopters then began to chase them on the ground and in the air. The fighter aircraft waited to enter the attack, even if the terrorists lured them into Jordanian territory. It was ironic, for the air force that had managed to annihilate the Arab air forces in one powerful blow was now chasing three or four terrorists on foot.

When air attacks became more frequent, the terrorists began to operate at night and more frequently. Even in winter, when the waters of the Jordan River rose and flowed strongly, they did not hesitate to cross the river on rafts or using ropes. Thirty to fifty terrorists crossed each time, in teams numbering up to a dozen or more. Some were sent to carry out missions in Israel, and others acted as couriers, carrying arms, explosives, and instructions to the PLO's terrorist squads organized in the villages and cities of the West Bank.

The mission of putting a halt to these penetrations was allocated to the paratrooper brigade in the Jordan River Valley, and to the Charoov commando unit. Until early 1968, the Inverted Sword Squadron's helicopters were scrambled once or twice a week for chases lasting anywhere from several hours to several days. It was an all-out manhunt. The fighters would not rest until they had killed or captured the infiltrators, for it was clear that the terrorists were on their way to attack civilian targets and would not hesitate to murder women and children. The operations were overseen by the chief of the Central Command, Rehavam "Gandhi" Ze'evi, who also participated in many of the chases.

The terrorists generally crossed over between 0200 and 0300 hours. The trackers would discover evidence of their penetration at first light, around 0600 hours, after searching the dirt path along the fence that had been erected by the river. The path was smoothed over every evening, and could not be crossed without leaving signs. Thirty minutes later, the helicopters arrived with the squad of chasers. The time and territorial advantage that the terrorists had gained was reduced by the helicopters, which were directed by the trackers. The trackers were sharp-eyed and experienced Bedouins from the tribes of the Negev and the Galilee. These desert nomads quickly adjusted to the "flying machines," as they called the helicopters. After several flights, they managed to adapt their senses to the tools of modern flight.

The helicopter captain commanded these operations, even adding fire from airborne positions. When the terrorists' route and estimated location had been determined, the helicopters landed the paratrooper squads at the points at which they were to block the progress of the terrorists and counter their fire. The encirclement and attack would be executed under the cover of mortar fire, with artillery often coming into play as well. All the helicopters could do was hover between the cliffs near the caves or other places where the terrorists took cover. Troops would fire from the helicopter's door with machine guns. More than once, we pinned the terrorists down deep in their hideouts, thereby allowing the fighters to progress until they were in range to fire or attack from short range. The terrorists often fought to their last man. Sometimes they would surprise their chasers by hiding in villages sympathetic to their cause. They would then be able to fire at them from behind the cover of a wall of women and children. The paratroopers paid for their caution with their own blood, losing many soldiers and commanders.

As the chases became more sophisticated, the helicopters' limited firing capabilities became a hindrance. We needed more devastating weaponry than the mid-sized machine guns in our doors. Before every landing or low-altitude search, we attempted to clean the area. But we proved to have weak responses to ground fire. While we hoped to get American-made Cobra helicopters, which had served the United States very well in Vietnam and were armed with rockets and cannons, they did not arrive until years later. In the meantime we received the Bell 205, another combat transport helicopter from the same family, which replaced the Sikorsky 58 on these chases.

By early 1969, the line of the Jordan River was essentially sealed, thanks to the chases and ambushes that had occurred for eighteen months. Hundreds of terrorists had been killed and captured. Kibbutzim and moshavim were built along the Jordan River Valley, and a mined fence with electronic defense systems was erected. The terrorists transferred their activities to other fronts, and the helicopters of the Inverted Sword Squadron followed them.

The Sikorsky 58s had completed their service in the IAF, and within a short time, I was one of those recommending that the Sikorsky CH-53, a helicopter that could carry an armed company, be purchased. My squadron quickly absorbed large quantities of Bell 205s, and other helicopter squadrons were created and expanded. There would no longer be only one veteran helicopter squadron. by the end of the War of Attrition, we would have a helicopter training squadron, an operational squadron for Bells, a Super Frelon squadron, and a CH-53 squadron. Uri Yarom's dream had been realized in full, faster and better than either he or I had imagined. The IDF could no longer function without helicopters.

Heavy cloud cover hung over the Israeli coastal region on the morning of March 21, 1968. For the first time since the war, the Inverted Sword Squadron took off carrying fighters from the paratrooper commando unit. The formations were larger than the pairs and quartets that had been used in the chases. Among them were four Super Frelons flying east, loaded with jeeps. The goal was to land a surprise attack in the enemy's core, striking at their primary base, Karameh, on the other side of the Jordan River Valley. This was not a military camp, but rather a large village, visible from Jericho. Its population had tripled because of the influx of refugees from Jericho who had escaped eastward during the Six-Day War. The terrorists recruited the refugees into their ranks, and trained them under the civilian guise of the village. Karameh became one of the central bases from which terrorist squads set out toward Israel, organizing terrorist networks in the West Bank and among Israel's Arabs, as well as executing their own actions in Israeli territory.

The first activities had begun in September 1967. Explosive devices were planted in movie houses, in the streets, and in factories. Jerusalem was the primary target. By early 1968, fifty such attacks had been attempted in Israeli territory. Information had been received regarding a large terrorist operation being planned in Karameh, one that would ruin Israel's Independence Day celebrations, and particularly the victory march planned by the IDF in Jerusalem on the first anniversary of the reunification of the city during the Six-Day War. The General Command's armored assault on Karameh, Operation Inferno, would be the first operation across the new borders since the war. An armored column would cross the Allenby Bridge, near Jericho, and destroy the terrorist base. The tanks were to storm the village, destroy its huts, and kill as many terrorists as possible. Israeli paratroopers would await the escaping terrorists in the surrounding hills.

The IAF had a double mission. From the early-morning hours, fighter aircraft dove on the Jordanian artillery base in the valley and silenced it so that it would not interfere with the invasion. A helicopter squadron was to land the paratrooper commandos in the eastern alleyways of the village. The fighter aircraft attacked on time, and the tanks crossed the Allenby Bridge. Fifteen minutes later they were ready to shell the houses. The only problem was that the commandos were still making their way in the fog, and their ability to block the terrorists' routes of escape was in jeopardy. I had postponed their takeoff, hoping that the fog would lift. However, this was one of those late-winter and early-spring mornings in which the cold and heat collide, creating a thick haze. Experience had taught me that the fog often lifted after sunrise, and even if it remained, it would not rise above two thousand feet. I instructed the squadron to take off, but to remain in a tight formation so as not to lose eye contact.

The first goal was to get out of the cloud cover in as rapid a vertical climb as possible. But as we neared five thousand feet, its end could not be seen. Heavily loaded as they were, the helicopters could not climb over eight thousand feet, and were about to reach their maximum altitude. The throttles were completely open, but I would not give up. I decided to take a chance and fly east toward Karameh, through the cloud. If we did not reach the cloud's end, we would break west according to the flight controller's instructions, descend to sea level, and then return to base. On the operational frequency we could already hear the echoes of the armored invasion and the first reports of armed terrorists escaping to the hills. The cloud was unending, so we continued to climb.

Suddenly the top of the cloud bank vanished, and we found ourselves in blue skies. I had almost given up a moment earlier, when I saw how difficult it was for the other helicopters to keep up with me. We straightened out to gain speed and tighten the formation again. The air was crystal clear, but we could not see the ground. Where were we? Using this navigation equipment, my copilot managed to plot our position near the Jordan River, and from the distance we could see the valley, knowing that when we reached the arid desert region in a few minutes, the fog would disappear completely.

This is exactly what happened. I had to respond quickly. The fog, which had provided us with cover, had now dissipated, and our helicopters were exposed to ground fire. I dived, and the formation followed me. The navigator quickly got his bearings. I headed toward the hills that had been set for the landing, and dropped to near ground level along the Jordan, flying fast along the country's spectacular landscape. Karameh's huts and checkered streets could be seen from the south, shrouded in the smoke and dust of explosions. Shells were exploding all around. I was giving final orders before landing east of the village, when my breath suddenly stopped. Armed figures were running around the landing area. Should I land? According to plan, the paratroopers were to surprise the terrorists, and not vice versa. The decision was in the hands of Matan Vilnai, the paratroopers' commander and the one in charge of the ground operation.

"Cheetah, land!" he commanded in a cold, authoritative voice.

The terrorists saw the landing helicopters and the fighters jumping from their doors. Instead of opening fire, they took off, running for their lives. The commando squads shot out like released springs, spraying fire on anyone in their way, striking dozens of escaping terrorists. The Super Frelons unloaded their jeeps in the nearby valley and took off to bring the armored vehicles. The paratroopers were suddenly turned into a mobile force, unaffected by obstacles on the ground. We left the landing area, which had begun attracting Jordanian artillery fire. With no loads to carry, the Sikorskys took off in a wild westward climb toward the "air head" near the forward command unit. We were ready to take off for any mission that might arise.

By nightfall the helicopters had executed another dozen sorties, landing fighters, executing chases in Karameh and the nearby areas, and evacuating wounded. There were many more casualties than we had expected, with a total of thirty Israelis killed and ninety-three injured. The operation to clean out the village had not been easy, for not all the terrorists had run for their lives. Those who had remained had fought ferociously. In the course of the sorties, we searched for the terrorist commander, Yasser Arafat, then an almost unknown engineer whose face was recognizable to very few. In July 1967, he had established a headquarters in Nablus and had often set out for Syria to receive instructions. Later he moved to Karameh and conducted his affairs from there.

On our return from Jordan to Israel, carrying the paratroopers, the squadron passed over the village's homes, destroyed by a day of integrated attacks from the ground and the air. The terrorist base had been destroyed, and the operation had disrupted Fatah's activities in the Jordan River Valley. However, we had failed to get the organization's leader, and the terrorists regrouped in other places. The attacks in Israeli territory grew worse, and the question of whether the bloody price paid during the assault had been too high remained unanswered. Nevertheless, the experience at Karameh was a preparation for future airborne operations. Operation Inferno was the final operation of the old Sikorsky 58s, which soon afterward were taken out of service.

Six months after Karameh, the Inverted Sword Squadron was flying the Bell 205, with a capacity for ten fighters or a ton of cargo, in a small, compact helicopter. The small jet engine provided it with high speed and maneuverability relative to the Sikorsky, which had a large and crude piston engine.

On the morning of December 1, 1968, the squadron was told to prepare eight helicopters for a night operation. A maintenance convoy had been organized on base to set out toward the Dead Sea. The terrorists had begun attacking Israeli targets near the border in areas where the chase could not be completed, and were shelling population centers with Soviet-made Katyusha missiles. The previous night they had struck the potash factories in Sodom. Operation Iron was designed to send a signal to King Hussein that life in his country could be disrupted as well, if Jordan did not stop supporting the terrorists who were upsetting life in Israel. I was called upon to participate in the planning of the operation which took place in the command center of the paratrooper brigade. Twelve hours passed from the morning warning until the evening execution, and I had never seen any operation develop so quickly.

I learned that the target points were the main roads from Amman to Aqaba and the parallel railway line. The bridges that had been chosen to be destroyed crossed a wide canyon east of the Israeli potash plant. I now understood why the maintenance personnel had loaded "sprinkler" bombs on the trucks headed toward the Dead Sea. The technical wing received instructions from headquarters to load the bombs, which were packaged in giant metal cylinders that looked like innocent fuel tanks when tucked under the helicopters. At 1600 hours the Inverted Sword Squadron took off in four formations in its first operation in this new incarnation. Though only eight helicopters had been called for, we sent twelve, almost the entire squadron, so that the four extras could serve as backups in case of technical problems or a need to evacuate wounded.

The Bell 205 brought along with it the newest helicopter technology. It was also the product of previous large airborne missions and a response to greater demands for such missions from the IDF. The cumulative experience of the U.S. Army in Vietnam, using thousands of these helicopters, also added to their prestige. The Bell 205 was designed from the outset to be comfortable and simple in field conditions for both fliers and fighters.

Every formation was given its own timetable, with the synchronization precise to the second. In the lead formation, my three helicopters, loaded with paratroopers and their equipment, landed by the Dimona-Sodom road for a final briefing and a review of the aerial photographs. In the forward command center in Sodom and in the nearby "air head," a large group of high-ranking officers had gathered. The reworking of the plan and equipment continued to the last minute as the crews worked all day in a race against the clock. At exactly 1900 hours the scramble notice was given, and the three paratrooper helicopters took off toward the bridges to take control of the surrounding area and block the routes of access to all Jordanian vehicles. For fifteen minutes we flew along the ground, swinging through the awesome canyons, which seemed to be the products of a sculptor's chisel. At the landing spot, the paratroopers disembarked in an instant. The Bell 205's two large side doors were an improvement over the Sikorsky's one.

The three helicopters of the second formation, which carried the "sprinkler" bombs, started their engines and waited in Sodom. One carried two 250-kilogram bombs for the railroad bridge, and the other two held one 500-kilogram bomb each for the roadway bridge. The pilots waited for word to take off. But first the engineering officers, who were flying with the paratrooper force, would mark the weak spots on the bridges where the bombs should be placed.

The scramble code was not coming. Instead, the commanders of the force called on the third formation, two helicopters armed with mid-sized and heavy machine guns, standing on alert to assist the teams sent to block the roads. The movement of the vehicles on the road was heavier than expected in both directions, and beyond the ability of the small force to control. The Jordanian drivers did not understand what these uniformed "traffic officers" wanted from them, and why they should stop in the middle of the desert. Frightened, they began to speed up. The paratroopers did not seek to harm them, and the traffic did not stop. Two helicopters were called upon to hover over the road and to fire at the vehicles' wheels. Several of the cars were hit and created a roadblock for those following them. Within an hour, large traffic jams had developed on both sides of the bridge which would block the approach of any Jordanian Army vehicles if they would begin to wonder what the confusion was on the desert roads.

The "sprinkler" formation was then scrambled and arrived at the bridges within minutes, hovering over them as the paratrooper sappers directed each "barrel" to the explosion spot that would guarantee the quick collapse of the slab of concrete. The bombs were placed on the bridges, and their harnesses were released as the helicopters took off, their carrying cables pulling and activating the delay fuses. The paratroopers distanced themselves and took cover. Three minutes later, four tremendous explosions shook the ground. The amount of explosive in every "barrel" was specifically calculated for each structure, and upon detonation the full force of the explosion was propelled downward. The bridges collapsed simultaneously, and the roads were disconnected. The paratroopers returned to the landing spot, where my trio was already awaiting them. Within fifteen minutes we were all in Sodom.

The following day, the entire world saw photographs of the destroyed bridges and read dramatic descriptions of the helicopters firing from the air. IDF Chief of Staff Chaim Bar-Lev, who decorated the squadron, was amazed by the meticulous planning and perfect execution. "Operation Iron again proved that there is no limit to the fruitful imagination, capability, technical skill, and, most of all, dedication and bravery of the Israeli helicopter pilot," he wrote to me three days later.

The following day, there were those in the Upper Command who expressed doubts about the value of such a complex integrated operation. They asked why we could not have bombed the bridges from the air. The response to their queries was more political than tactical. The dropping of bombs from fighter aircraft would not have provided the same threat to the Jordanian king as did the capturing and blocking of two central transportation routes in the middle of night by an airborne force.

Nearly two years passed before King Hussein felt the threat of the terrorists' presence and ordered his military to destroy their bases. In the meantime they had opened a new front in Europe. On July 23, 1968, three terrorists boarded an El Al plane in Rome and hijacked it to Algiers. The passengers and crew were held hostage in an extended and degrading haggle. Minster of Defense Moshe Dayan succumbed to the terrorists' extortion and released twelve of their comrades from Israeli jails. Thus a precedent was set for a series of hostage-taking incidents in the bartering over terrorists being held in Israel and other countries. The PLO found the method to be successful, and five months later, two terrorists set out from Beirut to Athens to destroy an El Al plane loaded with passengers on its way to New York. They reached the airport on December 26, 1968, and attacked the aircraft with gunfire and grenades as it began to take off. It was severely damaged, primarily in one of its engines, which was hit by a grenade. The passengers had to lie on the floor, and bullets perforated the walls of the plane, killing an Israeli engineer. The complete destruction of the plane was luckily prevented, and the two terrorists were captured by Israeli security agents who had begun to accompany El Al aircraft.

This was the beginning of a long series of hijackings and aircraft bombings by the People's Front for the Liberation of Palestine (PFLP), a radical wing of the PLO, which sought to frighten the world and to publicize the Palestinian plight. While the showy operations held the attention of the press, the world's airlines and airports responded slowly. Checking of passengers' baggage and bodies, as well as heavy security on aircraft, would become routine only in later years.

Beirut began to develop into a central base and exit spot for the terrorists. In the General Command, a plan sat waiting the day following the Athens attack which involved striking at the Beirut airport and aircraft belonging to the Arab airlines. It was designed according to the concept of passing diplomatic messages the painful way, as the assault on the Jordanian bridges had done. The Beirut plan, called Operation Gift, was limited and symbolic from the outset. Prime Minister Levi Eshkol approved it on the assumption that only three or four aircraft of the Lebanese Middle East Airlines would be hit. It was forbidden to strike at civilians or aircraft belonging to foreign airlines. Raful Eitan, the chief paratrooper officer, was chosen to command the operation.

The force took off on Saturday night, December 28, two days after the Athens incident. Three large teams from the paratrooper commando unit and another command unit were flown in Super Frelon helicopters under the direction of Chaim Naveh, the squadron commander. The Super Frelons were larger than the Bells and served as the primary vehicles for airborne assaults deep in enemy territory until the arrival of the CH-53s. Two Bell 205s took off first, led by me, carrying the mission's commanders, including Raful. I had one additional mission as well. After landing the command group in the area near the passenger terminal in Beirut, my partner was to return to Israel. I was to hover over the highway leading to the airport and block the routes of approach. The exit routes were to remain open to anyone wanting to escape. One goal was to empty the airport as much as possible, and the other was to block the arrival of backup forces.

While the entire operation was to last thirty to forty minutes, I was given an hour. My helicopter was particularly heavy, carrying not only soldiers but also machine guns and sacks of slippery gel and spikes, which I was to spread along the roads in order to create a roadblock of drivers who would lose control of their cars. The lesson from the firing on the Aqaba road had not been forgotten.

In complete darkness and communications silence, we flew over the sea after refueling in Haifa. We continued on at low altitude and at a distance close enough to the shore to navigate by the lights of the coast, but far enough away for the sound of the helicopters not to be audible. Though our identification lights were not lit, we could see each other because of plates made from a radioactive plastic that were connected to the edges of our rotors, creating a glowing halo around the helicopter as they turned. The "lanterns," which could not be seen from far away, were the creation of Professor Saadia Amiel, a nuclear physicist and a member of the Atomic Energy Commission, who had developed them according to my request. I had been searching for a means of lighting that would not be dependent on the helicopter's electrical systems and whose visibility would be limited to the helicopters in the formation. Professor Amiel worked on his invention in the laboratories of the nuclear reactor at Nahal Soreq, and the IAF's engineers found a way to connect the plates to the aircraft. They were soon attached to all the IAF's helicopters as well as those of foreign militaries who purchased the plates from Israel Aircraft Industries.

We maintained stable altitude in order to avoid colliding with the Super Frelons that were to cross before us near Sidon. The assault was to begin after the hour of peak traffic at the airport, when the passenger terminal would be nearly empty.

"Five minutes to landing," my young copilot said to me, but five minutes later, opposite Beirut, we had trouble finding the field. The runways were dark, and the landing lights were not lit.

"What's going on here?" Raful asked. For a moment we began to suspect that word of our assault had been leaked to the Lebanese intelligence network, but a moment later the lights were turned on. It had probably been a routine check of the lighting system. The first formation of Super Frelons landed the paratrooper commandos at the eastern side of the field. One of the helicopters, loaded more heavily with fuel than the others, quickly departed to hover over the sea as planned, on alert to evacuate wounded if necessary. As soon as it turned toward the sea, the second formation landed its commandos at two locations on the field. Raful, seated next to me at the head of the command group, observed them from nearby. At first he had planned to land at the field's periphery, but at the last moment he saw the open central area and instructed me to land there instead. The following day, tales would be told of how he had walked into the terminal's coffee shop, ordered a cup of coffee, and paid with Israeli currency. There were approximately one thousand people at the field. They saw the helicopters hovering around the terminal and landing nearby, and, guessing the purpose of our visit, they began to flee. The control tower went into panic as its crew saw dozens of fighters jumping out of helicopters and running toward the planes of the Lebanese airline, which were parked near the garages. The next day the aircrafts' technicians told how they were ordered in fluent Arabic to save their skins. Before they escaped, they saw the commandos checking the Boeing 707 aircraft to see if anyone was left on board. Only then did the Israelis begin to prepare the explosives, which they placed near the landing gear, the fuel tanks, and the engines. Workers and passengers with cars hurried toward the highway and were surprised to see a helicopter overhead nonaggressively blocking the entrance to the airport.

I had started toward the road immediately after dropping off Raful and his party, and I hovered at the level of the streetlights that lined it.

Beirut is only five kilometers from the airport, and I flew over this stretch, dropping sacks of gel, which burst on the road and turned it into a slippery mess. Vehicles that attempted to cross the area began to spin and collide, creating the desired traffic jam, blocking routes of access. Gunfire echoed from the field. I could hear on the communications frequencies that the backup helicopters were circling over the sea, ready to enter the field if necessary. Within five minutes the Lebanese aircraft were ready for destruction.

I turned toward Beirut one more time, and saw ambulances and fire trucks rushing to the field. When they saw the blocked highway, they crossed the divider and continued driving against traffic. I changed my route, and my crew quickly emptied a bag of spikes onto the road below. They punctured the first cars' tires, immediately creating a traffic jam involving dozens of vehicles.

On the communications frequency, we could hear the final words of the operation.

"Uzi force ready to explode . . ."

"HaNegbi force ready to explode . . ."

"Digli force ready to explode . . ."

"Explode," ordered Raful.

The teams activated their detonators, and I could see them retreating to their evacuation points. Explosion followed explosion as the fuel tanks turned into balls of flame, and rivers of fire flowed around them. I climbed to five hundred feet to avoid damage, and counted thirteen burning aircraft. One Lebanese plane had only its nose destroyed, to prevent damage to a Greek airliner parked nearby. Four Middle East Air planes that were flying at the time were the only aircraft to survive.

On the flight controller's frequency, I heard the familiar voice of my former commander, Ezer Weizman. I gave him a short report of what was taking place.

"I expected nothing else," the commander of the IDF Operations Branch responded.

At the sensitive time when the Super Frelons were leaving their waiting stations to evacuate the forces, an armored vehicle and half-tracks could be seen approaching the field on a dirt road. I ordered the deputy technical officer to fire at their wheels with the mid-sized machine gun. He fired several bursts, and the bullets ripped into the ground in front of the first armored vehicle. It continued on. Raful commanded the helicopters to begin evacuating the fighters, and the first formation landed, swallowed up its commandos, and took off above the glare of the blazing aircraft. The second formation landed, and the armored vehicle entered the field. I turned the helicopter around to get within range of my heavy machine gun, which was set in the door.

"This time, aim to hit them."

The technical officer aimed and fired, perforating the armor. It was stopped forever.

"Five minutes to evacuation," Raful announced.

Within five minutes the Bell had swallowed up the command group, and the final formation of Super Frelons took off as well. We made one final circle around the field. Hundreds of people stood along the road, watching the huge bonfires. The helicopters broke south and disappeared into the darkness over the sea. All the way home, everyone was ecstatic, for the operation had been successfully completed, with no injuries.

We would later learn that Prime Minister Eshkol was not pleased. He had approved a small operation, and was upset that thirteen aircraft had been destroyed instead of the three or four he had been promised. His fury was nothing compared to that of French President Charles De-Gaulle, who was bothered by the use of French helicopters to attack Lebanon, traditionally a French protectorate. The shock of the strike on Beirut spurred him into enacting an embargo on all French military aid to Israel. It was this embargo that propelled the IAF into the era of American aircraft.

The American chapter in the history of the IAF was to have begun in early 1968. Nearly two years earlier, an agreement had been signed with the United States regarding the initial supply of forty-eight Skyhawk aircraft. Until then, the Americans had provided Israel with defensive weapons, including Hawk antiaircraft missiles, and they preferred to finance Israel's purchases from France in the area of offensive weapons. The date for transfer of the aircraft had been set for November–December 1967. No one had dreamed of the Six-Day War at the signing of the arms agreement, and after the war it became clear that this was definitely the time when the IAF would need these new aircraft. Though the loss of aircraft in the war had been relatively small, there was no other source from which the IAF could replenish its ranks. The American aircraft represented Israel's sole hope of arming itself for the next war and for the small conflict on the Jordanian border. Though the number of bombing missions assigned to the IAF Mystères, Super Mystères, and Mirages increased, these aircraft were not designed for massive attacks on ground targets. While Israel still had the Vautour fighter-bombers, France had already refused to sell Israel more of these aircraft in 1966.

The A-4 Skyhawks were workhorses compared to existing aircraft. They could carry four times the amount of ammunition to the heart of every Arab country in the region as could the aging Mystère, which had been reconditioned for attack missions. They could also remain in the air twice as long as any other IAF plane. However, the United States delayed supply of the Skyhawks because of the war, and even France postponed a shipment of fifty advanced-model Mirages that the IAF had helped design and had also paid for nearly in full. At that time the Soviet Union renewed its policy to subsidize Egypt and Syria with advanced aircraft.

The Skyhawk deal was Ezer Weizman's baby from his final days as commander-in-chief of the IAF. Prime Minister Eshkol had sent him to Washington in 1965 with a delegation to persuade the Americans to sell arms to Israel in order to free the country from its dependence on France. Ezer gave the responsibility to Benny Peled, then a base commander, for preparing a document to explain the reasons. Peled was a fighter pilot and an aeronautical engineer with wide-ranging vision and foresight, who had dealt with all of these issues in the purchase of the French aircraft. The IAF's needs necessitated multipurpose aircraft for interception and bombing. The realization of the dream after the positive experience with the French fighter aircraft would be the F-4 Phantom aircraft. But it would be a long time before Israel added Phantoms to its force.

The IAF decided on the Skyhawk, whose specifications were less optimal than those of the Phantom, but answered the needs of the day. Under the Skyhawk's wings were a large number of hangers for bombs and missiles, weighing up to four tons. Capable of refueling in the air, it could remain aloft without ammunition and with drop tanks for up to eight hours, until it finished its oil. Carrying a dependable engine, it was easy to fly and maintain. All of these advantages were enhanced by its relatively low price, less than $1 million per aircraft. The Mirages had cost $1.5 million per aircraft. Of the 220 aircraft needed, the Americans decided to sell only 48 Skyhawks. Because of a partial embargo set after the Six-Day War, supply was delayed.

Eshkol again sent Ezer to Washington to smooth relations. In this mission, there was no need for him to put on the face of the pitiful hero, as he had had to do during the previous meetings. Though Ezer was the first high-ranking Israeli officer to visit Washington since the war, he was treated to a cold reception in his first meeting with fifty top U.S. generals. How could he win their support? He made use of Uri Yarom, the air envoy to Washington, who had come along to help in the presentation. Uri told a story of what had once happened to him as commander of the helicopter squadron. One day he had been scrambled to rescue a wounded sailor from the deck of a merchant vessel in the Mediterranean. On his way home, realizing that he was short on fuel, he had decided to land on a U.S. aircraft carrier. The Americans had been amazed by the audacity of this stranger who had descended on them without a permission and was now asking for fuel. However, Uri had felt at home. "I apologize," he had said. "I thought this was one of our aircraft carriers."

The generals began to laugh, and things warmed up. Ezer began to talk seriously in a language to which his American peers, who were immersed in the deep mud of Vietnam, could relate. During the Six-Day War, he said, Israel had also fought the Russians. In the next war, signs of which were already beginning to appear on the borders, Soviet involvement would be even greater. Although the Arabs could afford to lose the next war as well, Israel could not. If it did, it would be its last. In 1967, Israel had won the war using French weaponry. It wanted to prevent the upcoming war using American weaponry. With pressures from other sources as well, Ezer's argument succeeded. The delay in the delivery of the Skyhawks was lifted.

The first planes arrived in August 1968, and they were used in 1969–70 in heavy bombing missions. The radar station on the top of Ajaloun Mountain was attacked at night, using flares for illumination. They also attacked the long-range cannons of the Iraqi forces in Irbid, whose shells were reaching Tiberias as well as the Saudi forces near the Dead Sea, which were aiding the terrorists heading west. While other targets throughout Jordan suffered similar fates, these bombings were minimal compared to the war that was about to begin on the Egyptian front. The Skyhawks bridged the tremendous gap that existed between the IDF and the Egyptian Army. On the static combat line along the Suez Canal, the ratio of soldiers and equipment was thirty to one in favor of Egypt. Israel executed dozens of bombing sorties along the Canal and in Egypt, and invented the term "flying artillery."

The War of Attrition was one of the longest and most difficult the IDF had ever encountered, lasting one thousand days, in which all the IAF's aircraft attacked targets in Egypt, Syria, and Jordan. The Skyhawks flew at the center of these ground-target attacks, replacing the Mystère, the Vautour, and the Ouragan, which were taken out of service. Of all the French aircraft, only the Super Mystère remained for the attack of ground targets alongside the interception Mirage. The Super Mystère was equipped with an American engine at IAI, and flew until the 1973 Yom Kippur War. The Mirage continued to serve interception missions, and was the last of the French aircraft to leave the IAF, concluding its operational service after the Yom Kippur War.

The Skyhawk quickly replaced it as the backbone of the IAF in ground-target attacks. It further enhanced IAF capabilities, in that it could be loaded with varied and sophisticated weaponry and could be refueled in the air and enter its long-range attacks on full tanks. Now one could avoid, deceive, and enter at low altitude even at long distances, using such new attack methods as "sneak" and "toss" bombings, from which one could quickly pull out of the attack. Each method added a plethora of potential to combat. As the French aircraft were pulled out of service, more Skyhawk squadrons were added. New sophistications were added to the aircraft with the operational experience accumulated from the dozens of sorties flown. The Skyhawk was praised during the War of Attrition, and later received a new and better engine and sophisticated electronics systems. By the early 1970s, a navigational computer and then a bombing computer were added so that the models flying in the war were nothing like their predecessors and were truly flying electronic stations, loaded with electronic-warfare canisters and batteries of airborne weaponry.

The Egyptian front first erupted three weeks after the Six-Day War. An Egyptian commando force crossed the Suez Canal and was repelled after a day of combat. An Egyptian MiG-21 was shot down in a dogfight. Less than two weeks later, on July 11, 1967, two Egyptian torpedo boats were sunk near Port Said. The Egyptians took revenge three months later, and on October 21 they used sea-to-sea missiles to sink the Israeli destroyer *Eilat*, which was on a routine night patrol in the region. Israeli Nord aircraft illuminated the area and dropped lifeboats into the sea. Sikorsky 58 helicopters from the Inverted Sword Squadron rescued 135 sailors from the sea, and another 50 were pulled out by the Super Frelons.

For nearly a year after this, relative quiet existed in the region. The first Egyptian shellings began in September 1968, and by October 26, ten Israeli soldiers had been killed and eighteen had been wounded. This was followed by the "Black Sabbath" on which the Egyptians aimed their artillery at an Israeli soccer match, killing fifteen soldiers in the shelling. Another thirty-four were wounded and were evacuated by Inverted Sword helicopters under heavy fire. The IDF, which, sixteen months earlier, had swiftly won a major war, decided to dig itself in. A line of fortifications known as the Bar-Lev Line (for Chaim Bar-Lev, then chief of staff) was built under the mistaken assumption that these structures could prevent an Egyptian invasion of the Sinai.

Since several quiet months were needed for the construction of the fortifications, the General Command decided to distract the Egyptians by attacking strategic targets in the Nile Valley. This new series of operations disrupted civilian life in Egypt and to a certain extent called into question the sense of security that existed in the country. The Egyptians were compelled to use their forces to protect sensitive locations that were being attacked deep in their territory. Though these actions would not be decisive in the conflict, they provided the Israeli military and civilian population with a boost to their morale.

The Intelligence Branch proposed an attack on three sensitive and prestigious civilian targets in Upper Egypt, between Cairo and Aswan. They included the hydroelectric dam and switching station at Nag Hammadi, and the bridge spanning the Nile at nearby Qena. The power station provided electricity to the Cairo suburbs, some five hundred kilometers north of the town, and the dam controlled the irrigation system of a large area, 250 square kilometers in size. The Qena bridge, seven hundred meters long, was considered Egypt's second greatest construction project after the Aswan dam. The intelligence files on these targets were replete with information, the results of routine information gathered over many years. They were completed and updated at the last minute by fresh reconnaissance sorties. There was data on the thickness of the bridge and the dam's concrete walls, which would determine the type and quantity of explosive needed to destroy them. There were also descriptions of the area around the targets, including the type of seasonal agricultural work taking place, so that the planners could choose a land-

ing spot for the helicopters to raise the least dust possible and to cause
minimal damage to the rotors. There was also information regarding the
security of the targets, including the height of the concrete walls surrounding the switching station.

The paratrooper commando unit was allocated the mission, and
Matan Vilnai was given five days to plan Operation Shock, which was set
for October 31. The General Command considered an airdrop of the
paratroopers at Nag Hammadi and a pickup by helicopters, but Matan
felt that their chances of coming home alive from such an airdrop were
minimal, and that any navigational error in the heart of the Nile Valley
could doom them. He pressured the IAF to provide him with helicopters
in both directions. The Super Frelon squadron, commanded by Chaim
Naveh, was the only one that could fly such a long-distance mission.
Chaim and his pilots had experience with long flights in the squadron's
seven helicopters, having brought them over in a direct flight from
France, flying via Rome and Athens, with a refueling stop in Rhodes.

The round trip between Israel's Ofir airfield in the Sinai and Nag
Hammadi was approximately seven hundred kilometers, similar to one
leg of the distance from Marseilles to Tel Aviv. The success of the flight
depended on conditions in the territory and the weather information that
the intelligence network would provide. In the initial plan, the helicopters were to skip to their targets, and would defend themselves while
refueling. Chaim did not like the idea, feeling that once an engine was
shut off, there was no guarantee that it could be restarted. He preferred a
direct flight, even though it necessitated precise calculation of every drop
of fuel. The entire squadron would be used for the mission. Two
helicopters, commanded by Zevik Matas and Shaul Shefi, would lead
Matan's force to the switching station. Two others, led by Nehemiah
Dagan and Chaim, would carry the bombs to the Qena bridge and the
dam at Nag Hammadi. A fifth helicopter was placed on rescue alert, and
the two remaining helicopters stayed at Ofir, one as reserve and the other
loaded with fuel tanks for emergency refueling if need be.

Preparations continued until the day of the operation. At midday
they flew to the Ofir airfield. Minister of Defense Moshe Dayan came to
bid them farewell, along with Chief of Staff Chaim Bar-Lev and Ezer
Weizman, who exuded distress and concern. Vilnai recalls that they
made him feel as if his force were departing on a one-way trip. Dinner
was eaten in silence, "like the last meal of those sentenced to death," in

Vilnai's words. Three hours had been allocated for the round-trip flight and another ninety minutes for the operation itself.

Where Operation Iron, the destruction of the Jordanian bridges, had been executed using "sprinkler" bombs flown under the bellies of the Bell 205s and operated by paratroopers, the 500-kilogram bombs would be treated differently in Operation Shock. They would be packed into the helicopters and lowered by a special crane operated by the flight mechanic as the helicopter hovered over the target.

As evening fell, they took off. Matan's force set out first, and the "sprinkler" helicopters shortly thereafter. Matan's landing spot was several kilometers from the switching station, and the commandos would make their way there on foot. The assault on the station was set for 2200 hours. Five minutes earlier, the bombs were to be loaded on the dam and the bridge. Timing was set under the assumption that the region's electricity would be shut down by the Egyptians as soon as the station was attacked. Chaim and Nehemiah's helicopters needed light in order to place their bombs in their specific locations. After seventy minutes of flight, they saw the dark Nile Valley and the silvery stripe of the river glimmering in the light of the half moon.

Zevik's helicopter was the first to land, and Matan and his team jumped out. Not far from there, Bedouin campfires could be seen burning. Matan pulled out his flashlight and signaled for Shaul's helicopter, carrying the second team of commandos and the explosives on a hand cart, to land. Fuel became more of a problem as they continued to fly, for the weather was far different from what the intelligence had stated. The fuel calculations had been specifically based on these provisions. While they had predicted winds of four to six knots and temperatures of nineteen to twenty-two degrees Celsius, the helicopters encountered winds of thirty knots and temperatures of thirty degrees. These differences weighed heavily on the helicopters and necessitated the use of additional fuel. Chaim quickly calculated and realized that even if everything took place as planned, they would return home on their last drops. The paratroopers ran to the switching station, pulling the cart with its explosives. Near the outside wall, they performed as trained. While Matan climbed on the shoulders of one of his men and attached a rope ladder, he saw the station's security guard sitting directly below them. Matan tensed, for time was working against them. They were already fifteen minutes behind schedule, and the bombs would soon be activated on the dam and the bridge, destroying the element of surprise. He jumped down and decided to kill the guard. The Egyptian shouted, *"Min hada?"*—"Who's there?"—and Matan answered him, *"Ta'al hone."* "Come here." His accent sounded strange to the guard, and he cocked his gun. Matan fired and missed, and the Egyptian took off screaming.

The commando force burst into the switching station and found itself facing four guards whom they mowed down with Uzis. They then began to attach their explosive charges. Far from there, Chaim and Nehemiah were hovering over their targets, counting the minutes to 2155 hours when they would place the "sprinkler" bombs and activate the detonators. Five minutes later, if all went according to plan, darkness would encircle the area. Every second had been calculated. Chaim approached the dam at Nag Hammadi, where the engineers had chosen the specific spots where he should place his bombs in order to cause maximum damage. Chaim began to hover over the spot, and suddenly saw an armed guard nearby. The man was rigid with fear as he watched the heavy helicopter descend over him out of the darkness. The flight mechanic prepared to lower the bomb from the crane, and the man did not move. Chaim told himself that his job was to destroy the dam and not to take human life. He told the mechanic to stop and return the bomb to the helicopter. He moved the helicopter over the guard's head, and this time he turned his on heels and fled. They returned to their assigned spot, and the bomb was slowly lowered as the helicopter continued to hover. The mechanic steadied the barrel on the concrete floor and activated the fuse. Three minutes to explosion, and Chaim took off. They continued to hover at high altitude, counting the seconds. At 2200 hours exactly, when two explosions shook the ground below the helicopter, the paratroopers kilometers away had still not finished attaching their explosives.

The syncopation between the two operations had failed. The dam and the bridge had been destroyed, and the noise had woken everyone. The guard who had fled returned with four comrades, and they began to fire on the paratroopers, who immediately returned fire and killed them from a range of five meters. Gunfire began to fall on the commandos from inside the station as well. Matan was amazed. The intelligence report had spoken of three or four guards at most. The final part of the operation was executed in the midst of a battle for their lives. The delay fuse of fifteen seconds was attached. Matan checked the connections, and they dove over the wall. As they ran, the explosion went off behind their backs, throwing them to the ground. A sea of flames soared over their heads.

Several minutes later the evacuation helicopter arrived. Hovering, it lowered its ramp and swallowed up the commando team. The flight mechanic dropped the two reserve fuel tanks, and at exactly 0200 hours they took off toward Israel. When they arrived with no dead or wounded, they were received as if they had returned from the dead.

The following day, the Mirages took off on a reconnaissance sortie to Upper Egypt. The photographs revealed that seven of the nine transformers had been destroyed or severely damaged. Cairo's southern suburbs were disconnected from the electrical system, and the Qena bridge was irreparably damaged. Though the dam had been less damaged, Egypt was forced to transfer large forces to defend the Nile Valley, and recruited a special militia for this purpose. The construction of the Israeli fortifications along the border continued unmolested for four months. When the shelling along the canal commenced again, more airborne missions, of a more sophisticated nature, were executed in the Nile Valley. Israel hit the dam at Nag Hammadi again, and attacked other bridges as well as electric and telephone lines in the region.

The series of Israeli fortresses along the Suez Canal sprang up in the spring of 1969. From March, the official starting date of the War of Attrition, the region was dominated by a seventeen-month conflict between Israeli and Egyptian positions, reminiscent of the battles of the First World War. Vast empty stretches of land lay between the Israeli positions. They were therefore vulnerable to Egyptian artillery and commando infiltrations. The Egyptians took full advantage of these gaps, and Israel lacked the firepower to retaliate. A day did not pass without Israeli deaths. Dozens died and were wounded every month. In March alone, forty-four Israelis were killed and forty more were wounded.

While the airborne assaults in the Nile Valley continued, Egyptian President Nasser was not dissuaded from his decision to liberate the Sinai. He declared that he would achieve his goal even if one million Egyptian soldiers died as a result. His tactical intentions along the front were unclear. No one in the Israeli General Command knew whether he intended to invade the Sinai, with these shellings serving as an introduction, or whether he was merely testing Israel's nerves. Therefore no clear

line of response developed. No one spoke of a massive crossing of the
canal.

Activation of the IAF seemed to be the only useful replacement for
the lacking ground artillery. However, this idea had several detractors.
Although more and more Soviet advisers were being absorbed monthly
into the various branches of the Egyptian military, there had been no
clear Soviet response to Israeli air activities. Israel's diplomatic circles
were wary of the U.S. response. The supply of the Skyhawks was evolving
slowly, and a deal for the acquisition of Phantoms, the IAF's dream, was
brewing in the background. Israel had not received new aircraft. And
considering the losses from the Six-Day War that were not being filled
because of the French embargo, the IAF's commanders hesitated to
endanger the current force. They wanted to save what little air power they
had in the event of an Egyptian invasion. The new Egyptian missile
batteries began to firghten them; although such missiles had been encountered during the Six-Day War, the entire system had been improved. In addition to these problems, many in the IDF claimed that the
air attacks along the canal would not stop the Egyptians, but merely
weaken the IAF. A new reality had taken control of the region, forcing
Israel into a weakened position and affecting its ability to deter the
enemy.

It was midday at the Ofir airfield in the Sinai. The black asphalt
runway burned in the heat of the June sun. Hell itself could not have
been hotter. Asher Snir readied himself for a long run. Four Mirages
stood waiting at maximum takeoff weight; it would be difficult to create
the flow of air needed under the wings for lift. If they did not have a long
run, they would not get off the ground.

The scramble code was issued, and after releasing brakes and opening
the afterburners to full, they set out. Amos, the leader, stayed low and
turned toward one of the canyons. They passed Mount Sinai and regrouped into pairs, dropping even lower and increasing speed toward the
Suez Gulf. Within two minutes, flying at six hundred knots, they were in
Africa, between the rocky shores and the desert sands, striving to remain
in the cover of the dark mountains. Behind them, the entire IAF watched
tensely. If the planes were detected and MiGs were scrambled toward
them, it would be seen on the radar, and the commanders at home would
order them to return to Israel. The Egyptian shore was lined with

observation posts that were familiar to Israel from previous flights, and one had to sneak between them to avoid contact.

Asher wanted to continue on, for this was no ordinary sortie. They were flying to photograph installations around Cairo, and to shake the capital with a sonic boom. A sonic boom is created when an aircraft flies at supersonic speed; air resistance builds up in front of it, creating a shock wave of tremendous force, like that of an explosion. When the boom takes place at high altitude, the sound is startling but harmless. At lower altitude it can be destructive, shattering windows, throwing objects off shelves, and cracking weak buildings.

In the confusion that the Egyptian shellings had caused along the canal, the boom was more important than the reconnaissance photographs, which had been shot in the Nile Valley many times over. There was no more frightening or cleaner method than the boom to deter the Egyptians from stretching the tense rope of the conflict too tight. The IAF's ability to penetrate Egyptian defense systems would make the point without spilling a drop of blood. The pilots strove for precision along the flight route, taking into consideration wind force and temperature, and hoping to reach the Nile at the precise moment they had chosen to be detected. However, the wind was strong and pushed them off course, driving them directly over one of the observation posts. Asher and his friends saw the frightened Egyptians running for cover, and there was no doubt that their planes had been seen. In a little while the communications silence would be broken, and they would be called home.

But the silence continued. If the observation post had reported the penetration, they had apparently not been believed. The quiet had only one meaning: they were to continue to Cairo. The dark stripe of the Nile appeared on the dusty horizon, jutting out in the afternoon sun through a tight weave of roads, railroad tracks, and clay villages. They crossed the valley at their precise spot. Quietly, without a word uttered on the communications frequencies, the quartet split into two pairs. Amos and Reuven turned right, toward central Cairo, and Asher and Eitan turned toward the northern end of the city. They flew very fast and low, under the radar, stealing precious extra seconds from the Egyptian defense system. When they pulled up and were detected, it would be too late to catch them. The smoggy cloud grew thicker, and below it lay the city.

The silence was suddenly shattered by the radio. They had been detected, but the sortie was not being canceled. They were merely to speed up and execute the mission earlier than scheduled. This was the moment to rid themselves of the large drop tanks. A quick shake of the wings, and the tanks spun downward, crashing in the desert. Increasing speed, the aircraft opened their throttles to full engine power. The camera was set to work at the flip of a switch. Their speed increased: 540 knots . . . 560 knots. . . . The desert disappeared below them at nearly three hundred meters per second. The pyramids at Giza sprang up quickly before them, and the city spread out below.

A quick pull left on the throttle, and the red ignition light lit up. The fuel in the afterburners had burst through the turbine, and the engine was working at full strength. This extreme situation could continue for no more than ten seconds. One had to watch the gauges to make sure that the light turned yellow and that the burner "caught." The lights changed, and Asher and Eitan climbed together. Within several seconds they were at the altitude of the first reconnaissance run.

The Mirage's nose plowed through the sound barrier. The furnace in the Mirage's tail did not disappoint, and provided the necessary power, where the increase in air pressure would have torn older aircraft apart. A double shock wave passed under the two pairs and exploded over Cairo's homes. They were flying at moderate altitude, and inflicted great damage beyond the frightening noise. Windows shattered, and many hearts skipped a beat. The city disappeared behind the Mirages, with the Delta to the left and the desert to the right. Within a few seconds the nuclear reactor at Inshas would be beneath them. Their hands were steady, and the camera switches were activated. The cameras clicked in the noses, and the control lights in the cockpit transmitted reassuring messages. They climbed over the military airfield at Inshas, which Asher had attacked in the first quartet of the Six-Day War, two years earlier.

He had no doubt that the entire region, from Mansura to El Hamed, was filled with MiGs taking off and chasing them in crazed scrambles designed to cut them off. However, the initiative was in their hands, and their accurate planning kept them several seconds ahead of the enemy. They would not be caught. They took one more photograph of the Biblis airfield and successfully eluded the MiG-21s attempting to chase them. The thirty remaining miles contained most of the Egyptian military. Gunfire from here had brought down planes in the past. They turned off their afterburners and dropped to zero altitude. In three minutes they would be home in the Sinai. The adrenaline slid out of their blood, and their pulses slowed down, along with their breathing. Suddenly they discovered quantities of perspiration under their G suits, and they had to turn off the air conditioning. Two days later the world's papers carried the news of the boom, displaying ridiculing caricatures of the Egyptian defense network and the Soviet innovations. However, Cairo merely replaced its windows and sealed its ears.

On July 10, an Egyptian commando force assaulted an Israeli tank unit stationed near the southern entrance to the canal, at Port Taufik. Six Israeli soldiers were killed and one was taken prisoner after having been wounded. Several days later his body was returned. The assault had taken place under cover of heavy artillery fire, and it broke the restraint in the area. The number of victims of the recent wave of attacks totaled thirty-one Israelis killed and eighty-one wounded. The go-ahead was given for an Israeli assault on Green Island, the first in the series of "Boxer" operations, which were scheduled to begin on July 20.

That day, as man was about to take his first step on the moon, an integrated force comprising naval commandos and another elite commando unit landed at the stronghold on Green Island, not far from the city of Suez. The force destroyed the Egyptian radar station that scanned the region. At 1400 hours, IAF fighter squadrons attacked the western bank of the canal. Every type of aircraft was employed, including the Mystères, the Super Mystères, the ancient Vautours, and particularly the Skyhawks in their maiden attack. The Mirages provided cover from above. For three hours, 171 sorties were executed nearly unchallenged, aside from a few instances of light antiaircraft fire. One aircraft was hit, but its pilot managed to return to the Sinai, where he was ordered to abandon the plane. By last light, approximately two hundred tons of bombs and napalm had been dropped on the Egyptian positions at the northern end of the canal, including two SA-2 missile batteries, antiaircraft batteries, artillery, and tank concentrations. The canal carrying fresh water from the Nile to the Egyptian Army was also attacked, placing the troops in danger of a severe water shortage.

The Egyptians recovered and began to respond only at 1700 hours. MiGs sent to attack in the Sinai played right into the hands of Mirages awaiting them in an intercept umbrella. In the ensuing dogfights, the Egyptians lost five aircraft and Israel lost one Mirage, whose pilot parachuted in the Sinai.

The Boxer bombings continued until July 28. For six days the attack squadrons executed approximately five hundred sorties, and the intercept squadrons dozens more. Among the installations hit were six missile batteries and five radar stations. The freshwater canal was attacked twice. In all, approximately three hundred Egyptians were killed. Another ten Egyptian aircraft were shot down, seven of them in one day. Among them was a MiG-21, downed by an Israeli-made Shafrir air-to-air missile. One of the Egyptian pilots shot down was Maj. Nabil Said, who had been flying a Sohoi SU-7. He was familiar to Israel because of the famous photograph in which Nasser was seen embracing the pilots of the Egyptian fighter squadron on the eve of the Six-Day War. Among those faces smiling ear to ear was that of Major Said.

The IAF entered a new period on the Egyptian front with the entire weight of the combat placed on its shoulders as the armored and infantry corps dug into the sands and absorbed assaults and heavy shelling. The Boxer operations were concluded successfully. In August, the attack squadrons continued their sorties against the Egyptian ground units, with the Skyhawks dominating the attack aircraft. Day by day, over the course of the month, the squadrons attacked Egyptian positions along the canal, crushing concentrations of armored vehicles, artillery, and munitions. Dozens of sorties were executed daily, disrupting civilian life as well as industry along the canal. The cities emptied out, and refugees flooded the already crowded Cairo. Egyptian losses could be measured through aerial photographs of cemeteries. The numbers were frightening, but much lower than the million soldiers whom Nasser had been ready to sacrifice for the liberation of the Sinai.

After the Boxer operations, IAF headquarters knew it would have to deal with the missile infrastructure along the canal, which had yet to be hit. These were still the old versions of the SA-2, which had been encountered during the Six-Day War and which could be neutralized with electronic warfare. The Mirage pilots had attacked them in 1967, and had returned in one piece. The missiles fired toward them had been described as flying telephone poles with a cloud of dust under them. While the problem was avoiding contact, the aircraft had enough time to maneuver, since ten to fifteen seconds at jet speed is substantial.

It became clear that the missile was a threat only when it took off behind the pilot's back. The pilots managed to overcome the limitations in their field of vision incurred by the restricted cockpit. Pilots now maintained eye and radio contact with all members of their formation and divided the skies among themselves so that everyone covered his formation-mates' blind sides. The first Skyhawks did not have electronic defense systems, and their pilots had no choice but to activate and sharpen their senses and intuition. During the Six-Day War, Israel's pilots had no difficulty attacking and destroying the missile batteries in their path, for the batteries were alone in the territory and exposed, without protection.

However, they encountered a new challenge during the War of Attrition. Now the batteries were built in bunches and protected one another while receiving strong cover from antiaircraft cannons. The IAF's pilots quickly discovered that this new system was not hermetic, either. They analyzed the missiles' habits as well as the detection range of the batteries' radar, the response time between detection and firing, areas of mutual protection, and the dead zones between them. Anyone who treated these variables with precision, processed them, and reached the proper conclusions came out safely and generally managed to put the missile batteries themselves out of commission.

The Egyptians were also aware of the weaknesses of the SA-2. Until the arrival of more sophisticated versions, they pressured the Russians at least to provide protection for the missiles. For the first stage, their ally provided them with radar-guided antiaircraft cannons, designed to strike at the aircraft diving on the missiles from tree level, where the SA-2 batteries were helpless. The Israeli attack pilots discovered a method of overcoming the problem, but it only worked until the seconds when the nose of the plane was headed toward the ground in an attack run. The antiaircraft radar was then a definitive target, and the plane dove into a funnel of dense fire from the battery's cannons. Survival was dependent on the shortest dive possible. The Americans' experience in Vietnam had shown that the period of greatest hits occurred when the aircraft's aiming mechanisms were locked on the target. Crushing the missile batteries therefore became a matter of repeated strikes rather than a single operation.

The massive and methodical pounding of the missile batteries, which had either not been hit during the Boxer operations or had since been rebuilt, continued throughout August. As the Israeli air strikes continued, the Egyptians realized that only missiles could block the aircraft, which were already penetrating deep into their territory. For every battery destroyed, the Egyptians wanted to erect another two, and IAF headquarters began to develop a plan to wipe out the swelling missile system completely.

The missile was an appropriate weapon for the Egyptian fighter, for its operation did not demand any special skill, bravery, or innovation. It was enough to detect the aircraft on the radar, lock one's systems on it, and press the button. The Russians did not hold back in supplying the missiles, and the Suez Canal front, like distant Vietnam, soon became a testing ground for new weaponry. The Russians replaced the missiles and support equipment destroyed by Israel, and provided the Egyptians with more than they needed. Where accepted calculations called for firing three missiles to hit one aircraft, the Egyptians fired six and sometimes ten along the canal. Even then they were not assured of a hit. The Israeli attacks recommenced in early September in an assault on another series of ground targets. Two SA-2 batteries were destroyed near the Suez Gulf, and an Israeli Skyhawk was shot down by antiaircraft fire. Its pilot was killed.

On September 9, IAF attack aircraft provided support for Operation Drizzle, the first integrated naval and armored assault on the western shores of the Suez Gulf. The armored corps camouflaged themselves in Soviet tanks and armored personnel carriers captured from the Egyptians during the Six-Day War. For a full innocent day, they roamed along fifty kilometers of shoreline between Ras-Zaafrana and Abu-Darag, wreaking havoc on the Egyptian military. They destroyed outposts, military camps, guard stations, radar stations, and numerous vehicles. One hundred fifty Egyptian soldiers were killed, among them a major general and a Soviet adviser holding the rank of brigadier general in the Soviet Army. Two days later a large dogfight took place along the northern front. Sixteen Egyptian aircraft attacked Israeli positions. Israel retaliated with attacks on Egyptian positions and intercept aircraft, which chased them halfway to Cairo. Eight MiGs were shot down from the air, and three Sohoi aircraft were hit by Hawk missiles and antiaircraft fire. An Israeli Mirage, flown by Giora Rom, was shot down by an air-to-air missile. Rom, the ace who had downed five MiGs during the Six-Day War, was taken prisoner.

The largest pounding of the Egyptians took place two months later. The day after an Israeli patrol plane was shot down by an SA-2 missile, one hundred Israeli aircraft swept down on eight batteries that had been rebuilt or renovated in Abu-Suweir, between Ismailia and Cairo. Over the course of eight hours, 240 tons of bombs were dropped on the batteries. Though the Egyptians fired at least twenty-four missiles in response, only one Israeli Skyhawk was hit by fragments of a missile that exploded near it. Its pilot returned to base and landed successfully.

The area of the Suez Canal was again free of missiles, although it was not clear for how long, because of the Egyptian ability to recover and rebuild. The length of this period would be somewhat dependent on the initiatives of the General Command and the momentum of the diplomatic echelons. However, they chose not to use this quiet period to attack the Egyptian positions around the canal, and did not initiate a large ground action beyond the armored assault on the Suez Gulf. Henceforth, they relied only on the IAF, and it paid the dear and bloody price for its enforced role of initiator and attacker.

In the final week of September 1969, on the eve of Rosh Hashanah, the Jewish New Year, the Phantom became a reality. The first four American-made McDonnell-Douglas Phantom F-4Es were flown in a nonstop flight from the United States by the USAF. They refueled in midair, and Israeli Mirages were sent to accompany them over the Mediterranean. Moti Hod welcomed them from the control tower at Hatzor. One month later, in the large mid-October bombing, the Phantoms participated in their first attack on Egyptian positions and missile batteries on the banks of the Suez Canal. Before the Phantoms arrived in Israel, large fund-raising drives were held both in Israel and abroad. This ceremony at Hatzor was designed to celebrate the success of these efforts.

Israeli attempts to procure the aircraft had begun in the United States immediately after the Six-Day War. It was difficult for U.S. President Lyndon Johnson to decide, and he found himself in a tug-of-war between the support of the head of the Joint Chiefs of Staff, Gen. Earl Wyler, and the objections of Secretary of Defense Robert McNamara. Wyler claimed that of all the new models of aircraft, the Phantom had the varied and flexible characteristics to satisfy Israel's defense needs. McNamara feared that he would find himself lacking Phantoms for the Vietnam War, which was growing ever more complicated. President Johnson leaned toward approving the deal, and during a visit by Israeli Prime Minister Levi Eshkol and IAF Commander-in-Chief Moti Hod to his Texas ranch on January 7, 1968, he gave his tentative approval for the U.S. to supply the aircraft to Israel. Moti returned to Israel believing that the Phantoms would arrive since the president had commanded the USAF to order more planes from McDonnell-Douglas so that supply would not be delayed. The official negotiations over the procurement of two squadrons of twenty-four Phantoms each began in late 1968 after cancellation of the U.S. delays and the arrival of the first Skyhawks in the IAF.

In early 1969, five IAF aircrews, a pilot and a navigator in each, were sent to George Air Force Base in California to learn to fly and maintain the Phantom. Shmuel Chetz, who would later become squadron commander, led the group, which included Avihu Ben-Nun, Yoram Agmon, Rami Harpaz, and Ehud Hankin, the youngster in the group. The multipurpose Phantom was an ideal aircraft for interception and bombing deep in enemy territory. It astounded veteran pilots from the moment they sat in the double cockpit.

This was nothing like the two-seat Vautour, which had been difficult to fly and was replete with problems, particularly in its hydraulic systems. The navigator would now be responsible not only for the navigation equipment, but also for the weaponry and other sophisticated electronic systems. It took the pilots some time to get used to having a partner, but they soon discovered that two were truly better than one. One flew, and the other looked behind, as if they were actually in two planes and not one. Teamwork allowed them to make full use of the aircraft's flexibility and effectiveness. Aviem Sela would later attest to the fact that without his navigator he would not have shot down his first MiG in a Phantom. The navigator spotted the MiG, aimed, and locked the target into the radar system. All Aviem had to do was fire.

If the Skyhawk had been the revolution of the decade for the IAF, the arrival of the Phantom was clearly the revolution of the century. Each plane cost $3 million, three times the price of the Skyhawk. The F4E Phantom, which Israel desired, surpassed the advanced Soviet-built MiG-21 as well as any aircraft accessible to the Arab air forces. It also stood out in the amount of weaponry it could carry—six tons of bombs and air-to-air missiles, as well as the accurate and dependable Vulcan 20-millimeter cannons. The fact that it had two engines added to its thrust and survivability in the air. Its aerodynamic design allowed it to reach a speed of Mach 2 with its heavy load. Its maximum altitude was seventy thousand feet. Taken together, these traits made the Phantom excellent at maneuvering in dogfights even at altitudes much greater than what was then the accepted norm.

Moreover, the Phantom was equipped with the most up-to-date electronics. It had radar for the detection of enemy aircraft at much greater ranges than had ever been possible before. The weapons-control system for accurate firing of missiles at targets in the air was complemented by a navigation computer and an electronic warfare system. Israeli experts would later improve these electronic systems, integrating the navigational and weapons control systems. The Americans expressed amazement that they had not thought of this earlier. Within less than two decades, more sophisticated systems were developed, executions were improved, and a model of the Phantom was developed for the year 2000.

With the first aircraft still being improved while on the production line, the Israeli teams continued their training in California with emphasis on the operation of the complex weapons systems in bombing sorties and dogfights. By springtime they felt themselves torn. Their hearts were at the Suez Canal, where the action had heated up, while their minds were in the training routine. Their American counterparts were sympathetic and hung daily notices on the announcement board stating the number of MiGs shot down in the Sinai. The American instructors felt throughout the course that they had much to learn from their Israeli students who had so much experience in air warfare.

After one of the first flights on the Phantom at George Air Force Base, Ehud Hankin remained locked in the debriefing room for an extended period with the commander of the course. Though the Americans excelled at methodical and detailed debriefings, this one lasted longer than usual. After an hour, the American and the Israeli exited the room, smiling and lighthearted.

"We finished my first dogfight on the plane," Ehud said in his characteristically calm voice. "In every battle, I managed to either hang on his tail or shake him off quickly and then get on his tail. After I came out on top every time, he pulled me into the debriefing room and said, 'I've been flying on this aircraft for years. I did an entire tour in Vietnam and consider myself an extremely competent pilot. How can a young pilot who has just begun flying this aircraft defeat me? We will not leave this room until we dissect every exercise, one at a time. You will teach me every trick, so that I can pass them on to our flight instructors.'"

In analyzing the elements of the flight, Ehud did not reveal that he had already, at a young age, bested his own more experienced compatriots on the Mirage squadron and the other scramble squadrons.

After the debriefing, they were no longer instructor and student, but friends. They approached one of the Phantoms and flew it together as a team to demonstrate the trick they had analyzed.

In August the first crews arrived back in Israel and immediately started training new crews. In September the first four Phantoms arrived and started a new era in the Israeli Air Force. These first four Phantoms joined the operations of the War of Attrition, and on November 4 they rocked Cairo with the first F-4 supersonic Phantom "boom." Soon after, they provided support for the armored assault, which exposed weak links in the Egyptian antiaircraft network. Distant from each other and undefended, the radar stations along the gulf were easily destroyed in the first attack run. The Israeli intercept aircraft dominated the region and allowed for the attack squadron to execute its missions unhindered. The radar network covering Egypt was comprised of forty-seven stations, all Soviet made. Most of the stations along the canal front had been damaged during the first wave of the Boxer operations. Several months later the Egyptian radar stations, which had been erected in Jordanian territory for early detection of Israeli aircraft taking off toward Egypt, were bombed.

Unfortunately for Israel, the results were only temporary. New weapons and equipment arrived from the Soviet Union, flown in by the dozens of transport aircraft that landed in Egypt weekly. These new installations soon became a vital target for the IDF General Command's Intelligence Branch and the IAF's Intelligence Division. The electronic war was, first and foremost, a war of brains. Exposing the secrets behind the radar would allow Israel to control Egypt's forces from afar, and to neutralize or trick their operations. The Soviet radar installations that had been captured by Israel during the Six-Day War had been studied, and with electronic warfare devices developed in Israel, it was possible to affect similar machines still being used by the Egyptians. Every secret they revealed was overcome through the development of a more sophisticated instrument. Two years after the Six-Day War, Israeli pilots began to report that the new radar installations in Egypt were not affected by Israel's electronic warfare devices. The aircraft were being detected at early stages of their actions, and their operations were being disrupted. It appeared that the Egyptians had an improved and evasive model that could continue to function on a different frequency as the electronic jamming confused the previous frequency. Low-altitude flight became the primary defense against early detection.

Intelligence experts in the IDF and IAF yearned to peek into the heart of the new model. This urge grew after the armored assault, for the radar stations along the assault front were apparently of the old model. Their easy destruction had proved their weakness to the regional air defense commander. They had not done their jobs, and had even made it easier for the Israeli aircraft to locate them. Within several weeks, IAF experts discovered that the new deployment of radar in the region, which had begun to disrupt the activities of Israeli aircraft in the western Sinai, was of a different type that was difficult to decipher. The station's location was a mystery. Intelligence estimated that it was a lone station, remote and well camouflaged, which was detecting the Israeli aircraft entering Egypt. It executed its operations with the knowledge that discovery from the air was unlikely.

After one of the reconnaissance flights, Israeli photo interpretation experts disocvered a strange object on the beach of Ras-A'rab. The quadrant was enlarged several times, and electronics experts were called upon to express their opinions. The lights burned all night in the photo-deciphering unit, and by dawn no doubts remained that this was the secret installation they had been looking for, a Soviet-made P-12 radar station. The spontaneous response was to bomb the station, and attack aircraft stood ready for the mission.

When radar was still an innovation in the Second World War, 115 British commandos stormed a German radar station on the French coast of the LaManche Canal in February 1942, taking the device that had been disrupting RAF sorties. Churchill himself had come up with the idea. This mission in its modern version was pushed forward in Tel Aviv by Lieutenant Yehiel and Sergeant Rami from the Operational Intelligence Division. Operation Rooster 53 was instituted on December 24, 1969. It was primarily a logistical operation, dependent first and foremost on Israel's ability to transport the heavy installation, estimated at seven tons, quickly and safely over the Suez Canal. The only transport tool that could be considered was the newly acquired Sikorsky CH-53 helicopter.

At that time, I was serving in IAF headquarters in the Operations Division as commander of the Integrated Operations Branch. Yehiel and Rami came to my office in the morning after spending a long night deciphering the photographs. On my desk they spread aerial photographs of the radar station and its environs, which revealed the astounding fact that the installation lay exposed without antiaircraft defenses. Rami proposed that attacks on all Egyptian installations in the area be stopped, including those planned for "our target." He had grown attached to it like a child to a toy.

I was filled with respect for these two young men, whose initiative was typical of how large operations developed, even when they had a relatively marginal job to execute. This time they acted with diligence and persistence, tracking the activities of the Egyptian regional air defense commander until they had deciphered his secret and had reached the proper conclusions. Their idea won my heart, and I felt that this was a golden opportunity. We immediately went to David Ivri, chief of the Operations Division. He had already read the intelligence reports and was pleased with the initiative. On the spot, he drew up the essential points of a possible action. A force of paratroopers would be landed at the installation by Super Frelons. They would get control of the target and would check the radar. If it was possible for it to be flown whole, the CH-53s would come to get it. If not, they would take the sensitive parts of interest to intelligence.

The commander-in-chief, Moti Hod, gave the project his seal of approval, and the planned bombing attack on the site was canceled. The IDF chief of staff, Chaim Bar-Lev, did not reject it, but wanted to be convinced that all possible technical solutions had been found. I began to organize the plan along with Raful, the chief paratrooper officer. Moti Hod demanded that we work fast, telling us that we had better not miss the chance because of preparations that took two weeks. We had already saved some of the time, for the informal personal connections allowed us to agree on the operation that very day.

The race against the clock began the following day, December 25, and the timetable was shortened to half a week. Nehemiah Dagan, commander of the CH-53 squadron, said that the new helicopter could lift three tons and perhaps a bit more. This meant that the installation could not be carried whole, but would have to be dismantled. We began to test the helicopters, and the following day the CH-53s began to lift weights. It became clear that under operational conditions their peak load would be nearly four tons, about half the weight of the radar installation. We prepared ourselves for the idea that we would have to split the installation into two primary parts, the station and the antenna. The pilots would be Nehemiah and Zevik Matas, and this operation, which we named "Rooster," would be the maiden mission of the new helicopters. They practiced carrying a P-10 radar station captured during the Six-Day War, and after several experiments they recommended that one helicopter lift just the station while the other carried the antenna. They also suggested that the strongest of the paratroopers be chosen for the mission. Giants would be preferable. They would have to tie the station to the connecting hook on the helicopter's belly. This would occur in the midst of the whirlwind of dust raised by the helicopter as it hovered over the desert trench where the radar installation was situated.

The aerial photographs revealed that the radar installation was strapped onto the back of a truck with cables. Throughout the night, the ground troops trained at welding, cutting, dismantling, and assembling the steel cables and giant bolts. Ezra, the radar maintenance man who accompanied the mission throughout, strolled among them and made certain that their work was gentle enough not to damage the precious machine. He also taught them how to take apart the antenna so that its sensitive parts would not be damaged. The paratroopers completed their preparations on December 26. The chief of staff approved the plans, but did not set a date for execution. He was amazed that only forty-eight hours had passed since he gave the green light.

It was agreed that the attack aircraft would execute a diversionary action by bombing Egyptian forces near the installation. Before noon, the operation order was issued, and the time was set for 2200 hours, Friday night. The forces moved to the Ofir airfield and from there to the exit base along the Suez Gulf, opposite Ras-A'rab. At 2100 hours the attack aircraft took off, and the bombing began.

The noise of the three Super Frelons flying the paratrooper force was swallowed up by the engines of the Skyhawks diving on the western shore and by exploding bombs. Because the helicopters were filled to capacity with personnel and equipment, the landing was difficult. They maneuvered for ten minutes under the noses of the Egyptians. They were six kilometers from the radar station before they managed to land. After the operation, it became clear that the paratroopers had carried much more equipment than had been planned and agreed upon.

Hod's force of fifteen fighters turned to block routes of access. Israel's force of twelve fighters prepared themselves to terminate the security force in the Egyptian tent encampment. Nehemiah's three teams were to dismantle the radar and to load it onto the helicopters. The pilots, Nehemiah and Zevik, waited on the other side of the gulf to be summoned.

The Egyptians were surprised. Their security force was smaller than expected, comprising only ten soldiers. Several of them were killed and the rest were taken prisoner. The paratroopers approached to disassemble the radar installation, and Ezra jumped on the roof of the station and dismantled the antenna while the others took apart the cables. The frustrating work took more than an hour; some of the tools did not fit, and others broke. The welding machinery covered for what was missing. Finally the parts were connected to carrying cables for the helicopters. At 0200 hours, later than planned, the CH-53s were called upon to cross the gulf. Nehemiah took the station, which weighed four tons, and Zevik took the communications station and the antenna, a total of two and a half tons. They took off slowly, grinding and moaning, and disappeared into the darkness over the water. The paratroopers danced with joy, and on the other side of the gulf the forward command post joined them. In their elation, they nearly forgot to send back the Super Frelons to evacuate the paratroopers.

Despite hydraulic problems, Nehemiah managed to execute a safe emergency landing. Zevik struggled to land as well, and placed the radar on the bed of a truck that waited to take it to the center of the country. The electronics and intelligence experts waiting for him on the gulf coast excitedly began to examine the equipment at the landing spot. By Saturday morning, not a trace of the operation remained on the shore.

The operation was first revealed abroad. Germany published a caricature in which an Israeli helicopter was portrayed stealing the presidential palace in Cairo, while the Sunday Times of London showed the Israelis lifting one of the pyramids. There was no longer any reason to withhold the story from Israeli readers. In the week that passed before the IDF removed the censorship on the operation, the installation was dismantled and all its new parts were studied. Particular focus was placed on the elements that allowed for early detection of low-flying aircraft. The data and lessons were passed on to the various branches of the IAF, and the Soviet-Egyptian advantage was nullified. The threat on Israel's continued air superiority in the region was lifted. Some time later, the American press reported that the station had been sent to U.S. intelligence experts for examination, as had been done with the MiGs and the SA-2 missiles captured in previous years.

In August the Phantom aircrews returned to Israel accompanied by technical teams who had also undergone training in the United States. They began to train others, as the first aircraft were to arrive within a month. In September the first four arrived, with one of them flown by Moti Hod in a celebratory flight over the base and Tel Aviv. It was his first flight in a Phantom. The remaining planes were brought over by McDonnell-Douglas test pilots while the first ones were already charging to the battles over the canal.

On November 4, the Phantoms repeated the operation executed by Asher Snir and the quartet of Mirages in June. They penetrated deep within Cairo; flying at only seven hundred feet, in a tight formation, they nearly shaved the roofs off the capital and the presidential palace with a sonic boom that shattered windows and cracked houses. The EAF was helpless, for its planes were unable to catch the Phantoms. Their air defense network was punctured and helpless. Despite the increase in the number of missile batteries and antiaircraft cannons, the Egyptians would have to add another ring of antiaircraft defenses for the heart of the country. The IAF commander-in-chief's sense of confidence drove him to draw up lofty plans for the new planes to strike at Egypt's core.

Until then, the War of Attrition had developed through a series of punitive actions in response to Egyptian provocation. The bombings by the IAF's aircraft along the front, the crushing of the missile batteries, and the airborne assaults incrementally increased the level of punishment, often at a level greater than the intensity of Egypt's original shelling. Every stage in the conflict therefore became more severe than its predecessor. The fact that every retaliation was worse than its provocation did not deter the Egyptians. Rather, it inspired them to attempt to inflict greater damage. The intensification of the conflict was rapid and uncontrollable.

Every Israeli-proposed operation to defeat the spirit of the Egyptian leadership and to convince it that this was a lost war was limited by the understanding that Israel's ground forces would not cross the canal. Crossing the canal would be seen by the world as an overt act of war, and Israel's government was searching for means of winning with the minimum amount of danger, not only militarily but also diplomatically. Israel had no desire to occupy additional territories. In other words, the enemy had to be defeated in half a war. Thus the idea of bombing missions deep into Egypt developed in late 1969.

Indicators were received from the United States that it would no longer object to an intensification of the operations. Extremism was increasing in the Arab world, which was shedding itself of pro-Western leaders. While Muammar Khaddafi, the new leader of Libya, was the most radical of them, Washington felt that Egypt and its president, Gamal Abdel Nasser, were at the forefront of those encouraging this subversiveness, and might even be inciting unrest. But the United States failed to foresee the possibility that the Soviets might respond to the Israeli bombings by increasing their involvement and their presence in Egypt.

The goal was to upset the foundations of the Egyptian military and to halt its preparations for an all-out war and an invasion of the Sinai from the air. Moti Hod believed that these bombings could create an imbalance in the Egyptian military, and would eventually break the spirit of the Egyptian people as well. "We will bring you to a point where you will no longer be able to live in your country if you continue this war," he announced.

His sense of security was based not only on the ability of the Phantoms to execute bombings and to contend with opposition on their way to and from Egypt—something that the Skyhawks lacked—but also on the fact that Egypt's home front was vulnerable because of weaknesses in its antiaircraft network. Moti was not concerned by the small number of Phantoms that had been absorbed in the IAF by early 1970, providing for only two squadrons.

On January 7, 1970, a series of operations dubbed "Blossom" began. The IAF's top pilots led the first four Phantoms to targets far from the Suez Canal. The official announcements were conservative, for the IDF did not want to declare a new policy. It merely began to mention new names that were unfamiliar to all but those who had memories of the Six-Day War and even World War II.

One pair attacked a training base for SA-2 operators and some large warehouses in Dahshour, southwest of Cairo. Aviem Sela's pair descended on the commando command center in Inshas, not far from the nuclear plant and industrial zone in Halwan, also near Cairo. Aviem would never forget the incredible destruction he dropped from the sky, wiping the command center off the face of the earth. Before the Phantom era, it would have taken many aircraft to execute such a mission, but now a group of four Phantoms completed the job, dropping twenty tons of bombs that were guided with computer precision to their targets.

The surprise was complete. The Phantoms charged in and disappeared in an instant, dropping awesome tonnage in one run. The residents of Dahshour and Inshas were certain that it was the Egyptian military in training, until the blazes brought home the new reality. Over the next four months the scene was repeated almost weekly, though sporadically. Each time, Israel attacked on a different day and at a different hour. The EAF felt defeated and ashamed. When the radar warning was given, it took the MiGs two minutes to take off toward the conflict. Those 120 seconds were enough for the Phantoms to bomb and disappear. The MiGs' chances of overtaking the Phantoms were almost nil, even if by chance they were in the air while the bombing was occurring. This actually did happen, exactly one month after the first bombing. On February 8, the Phantom pilots received what they had been waiting for, and Ehud Hankin shot down the first MiG to be destroyed with an American-made Sidewinder air-to-air missile. In this attack they were accompanied by the Mirages, one of which shot down another MiG. The Phantom pilots came to understand that it truly was possible to set out on an attack mission, bomb one's targets, and then down enemy aircraft in air-to-air combat. The Phantoms' capabilities seemed unlimited.

During the four months of the Blossom operations, the Phantoms executed 118 bombing and intercept sorties. This number does not include the almost daily bombings executed by the IAF's squadrons on Egyptian positions along the Suez Canal. In January the Phantoms attacked the camps at Tel El-Kebir, which were familiar to the veterans of the Israeli units in the British Army during World War II. Columns of smoke could be seen rising out of Cairo. On a number of targets they dropped bombs with delay fuses that were detonated after several hours, increasing the damage and particularly the confusion. In February the Phantoms began to attack the missile batteries deep in Egypt. In one swoop, fourteen tons of bombs silenced the batteries in Dahshour and Halwan. SA-2 missiles fired toward the Phantoms missed. In all, during these months, twenty-four large military bases, four radar stations, and dozens of missile batteries, along the Red Sea as well, were attacked. Only twice did the Phantoms err and bomb unintended civilian targets.

The first error, on February 12, occurred because of a mistake in the navigational computer of one of the Phantoms, combined with the pilot's erroneous identification of his target. The bombs were dropped on the metal plant at Abu Zabel instead of on the nearby Dahshour artillery base. From the Phantom's cockpit, the structures looked like buildings in a military camp. Approximately seventy workers were killed and dozens were injured. When the error became known, Israel's Minister of Defense notified Egypt through the International Red Cross that a 400-kilogram bomb with a delay detonator was buried in the building and would explode in twenty-four hours. The second error occurred three months later, but not because of human or technical error. A school building near a military command post in Tzalhiya was hit as well, and forty-seven people were killed. By mid-April, Cairo was encircled by a crown of bombed targets. The city was shrouded in the atmosphere of war. Hundreds had been killed and wounded. The hospitals were filled. Blackouts were enforced at night, and daytime activities were disrupted. The Egyptian General Command was confused and depressed. All of Israel was elated. Most of the missions were executed with success and precision, and without injury to the Phantoms. Egyptian bases were emptied out and their units dispersed in the desert. Their aircraft sought refuge in Sudan and Libya.

On the morning of January 22, fifteen Super Frelon helicopters landed a paratrooper force on Sadouan Island, in the Suez Gulf. The island was controlled by sixty Egyptian commandos who were to protect the sea radar station and its Egyptian Navy operators along its southern coast. The force captured the island after a seven-hour battle. Israeli Skyhawks sank two Egyptian torpedo boats that attempted to bring support from the nearby port of Gardeka. A support boat that ran aground nearby was also hit. Operation Rhodes lasted thirty hours, with nineteen Egyptians and three Israelis killed. The Israeli force was evacuated the following afternoon, and took with it sixty-two prisoners along with equipment belonging to the new radar that had protected the entrance to the gulf.

That night, Egypt's president took off on a secret flight to Moscow. Shortly before this trip, in an interview with the French newspaper *Le*

*Monde,* Nasser admitted that the IAF was three times stronger than the EAF and that he saw no reason to send his pilots to compete with the Phantoms bombing Egypt's heartland when Israel's technological advantages had predetermined that Egypt would lose the battle. He beseeched the Soviet Union to eliminate the gap if they sought to erect their bridgehead in the Nile Valley. Within less than a month, a Soviet air convoy began to land in Egypt, loaded with experts and sophisticated weapons. IAF intelligence reports told of the arrival of squadrons with their crews, and of ground-to-air missiles with their operators. The Soviets established themselves in Egyptian bases throughout the month of March. Although IAF headquarters was not worried about this increased force, it was said that Minister of Defense Moshe Dayan was concerned about a direct conflict with the Red Army. He instructed the chief of staff to examine every operation plan to make certain that it would not provoke the Soviets. Most of these missions were part of the war against the terrorists, who had increased their activities and were hijacking planes and taking hostages.

Moti Hod proposed to the chief of staff that Israel take advantage of this period while the Soviets were getting settled by attacking one of the new missile batteries that had been placed near Cairo. He wanted to show the Soviets that Israel was displeased by their increased involvement and that they should halt the extension of their presence. The plan was postponed but not discarded. Moti believed that they would be left with no other option.

In the meantime, attention was focused on the area between Cairo and Ismailia. Israeli reconnaissance planes flying missions to check the results of the bombing runs returned with interesting photographs of unusual activity. The interpreters quickly enlarged the photographs and saw thousands of Egyptians, with Soviet supervision and assistance, recruited for large engineering operations to dig trenches for the new missile batteries. They would protect the new SA-3 missile batteries, which were even better than the improved SA-2s and could hit aircraft at low and medium altitude.

These sophisticated missiles were not the only surprise up the Soviet sleeve. They had mobile SA-6 missiles as well, also designed to work against low- and medium-altitude aircraft, which the Israelis had yet to see. Slowly one of the most sophisticated and dense air defense systems in the world developed along the western banks of the Suez Canal. Though the new system was designed to block Israeli penetration into Egypt, it also threatened the airspace over the Sinai.

The flying artillery expanded the area of the bombings. Skyhawks, Super Mystères, and Phantoms executed nightly assaults on concrete bunkers being built to protect the radar units and fire-control centers of the batteries as well as the missile supplies. These sorties were flown at low altitude, and there was no problem in identifying the targets. Dozens of tons of bombs were dropped on the bunkers. Reconnaissance photographs taken the next day gave evidence of tremendous destruction and loss of life. Hasnin Heichal, editor of the Egyptian daily *Al-Ahram*, would write several years later that at least four thousand civilian engineers and technicians had been killed. He did not mention the number of soldiers.

On the surface, it seemed that the Egyptians were willing to pay any price as long as the air defense system would be built. Egyptian tenacity in the face of the Israeli bombings only emphasized the severity of the threat to Israel. Though approximately forty targets were attacked in April, eighty were bombed in May. In July, 106 bunkers were attacked. It is difficult to tell how these attacks would have escalated if a cease-fire had not been declared. With tremendous blows to Nasser's military as well as to the morale of the country, it seemed that he had little option but to agree. However, the events of late summer 1970 proved that Egypt's agreement to the cease-fire was not only a means of self-preservation, but also a ruse that would allow them to complete the construction of the missile system.

On June 30, 1970, two Israeli Phantoms were shot down over Egypt. The first Phantom of the war had actually been shot down two weeks after the arrival of the planes. Ehud Hankin was flying it in a bombing sortie against the Jordanian radar station in Ajaloun, which was watching Israel's airspace. The Phantom was hit by antiaircraft fire, and Hankin and his navigator ejected near Nablus in the West Bank. Two months later he evened the score by shooting down the first MiG in a Phantom.

In the squadron, the Phantom that was hit over Jordan was considered a work accident. After the downing of two Phantoms in a missile ambush over the delta, and the capture of two Israeli pilots and one navigator, some felt Israel had been dealt a devastating blow. Aviem Sela's attitude to the new plane was academic and sober. He considered it merely one more step in the gradual improvement of the IAF, not a leap to seventh heaven. He thought of the enemy missiles in a similar fashion. They were not a threat in whose shadow Israel could not live. Dealing with them was easier than any dogfight. He even understood how the two Phantoms had been shot down on June 30. The pilots had simply not seen the missiles fired toward them.

Only after he had experienced the phenomenon for himself did he begin to see things differently. A new and high-quality threat suddenly appeared in the crowded Egyptian missile system. The SA-3 was not the "telephone pole" of the SA-2, which took off slowly in a cloud of dust and was only effective at high altitude. It was small, swift, and dangerous at relatively low altitude. Worst of all, it was difficult to see. On one of Aviem's bombing sorties, the Egyptians (and perhaps the Soviets) fired three SA-3 missiles toward his plane. He saw one of them headed in his direction, fast and tenacious in an unfamiliar way. The chase took place at a moderate altitude, in the dead zone of the SA-2. Aviem responded automatically, as he had been trained to do with their old SA-2 adversary. He attempted to drop down, but the missile followed him. It did not leave its path, and did not plunge nose-first into the ground. Instead, it simply closed range. Aviem turned left, and the missile followed him. He turned right, and the missile followed again. Suddenly he felt as though he were in a dogfight with an enemy whose tactics were unfamiliar to him and against whom no trick seemed to work. He saw the missile approach, and was suddenly uncertain whether he would get out of this alive. An instant before the missile was about to strike him, he broke hard upward, using all his remaining power. The missile exploded at the point from which he broke.

In July, the last month of the war, Phantoms were shot down in unprecedented and unforeseen numbers. The loss of the best of the IAF's pilots and navigators shocked the General Command and the diplomatic circles, and caused morale in Israel to plummet. The decision-makers began to hesitate at initiating new operations. Navigator Uri Talmor took off on June 30 as part of a quartet of Phantoms headed for the daily bombing of the SA-2 missile batteries. They were to strike at a battery near the 101-kilometer mark on the Suez-Cairo road, not far from the canal. Three and a half years later, this would be a historic spot on the way to peace. Israeli and Egyptian representatives would meet there to discuss the separation of forces after the Yom Kippur War.

This late-afternoon sortie was preceded by a long night of discussions on ways of dealing with the SA-3 missiles. Talmor saw the new missile headed toward his formation partner over the canal. At the last moment he shouted, "Break!" and the Phantom did so, avoiding the missile. The formation completed its bombing and turned home happily, for they could handle this new missile as well. Several minutes later they heard of the other formation, flown by Rami Harpaz and Yitzhak Pear, which had been shot down.

Fragments of the exploding missile had torn holes in the Phantom flown by Yitzhak and his navigator, David. A blaze burst out in the right engine, and thick white smoke filled the cockpit. They activated their oxygen masks. Yitzhak turned off the burning engine, hoping that he would be able to survive this with the left engine only. He compensated for the loss of power by activating his afterburner. It was then that the plane was hit again. The meters all went dead, and the steering mechanisms froze. Yitzhak ordered the navigator to eject, and David was propelled helmetless from the aircraft, into a mushroom of exploding antiaircraft fire. The parachute opened quickly, and out of the corner of his eye he could see an SA-2 missile flying by him as their Phantom crashed into the ground. He could not see Yitzhak, but heard him on the distress signal that was to guide the rescue helicopter and allow contact to be maintained. Yitzhak reported a group of Egyptian soldiers approaching him, and knew he would soon be taken prisoner. Hoping to save himself from this fate, David pulled on the parachute's cords and landed in the sand dunes, where he buried himself from head to foot.

Evening fell, and the Egyptians did not bother to examine the remnants of the aircraft. They had taken three prisoners—the pilots Pear and Harpaz, as well as navigator Achikar Eyal. They did not check for the fourth crew member. David continued to transmit his distress signal, which was eventually picked up by Nehemia Dagan, who was flying the rescue helicopter. He crossed the canal but could not find David's hiding place. Tron, the copilot, lit the helicopter's spotlights in the heart of the Egyptian positions, and David saw them.

"Ninety degrees to the right," he transmitted. He then opened his coveralls, took off his undershirt, and began to wave it until it was caught in the spotlight. Within seconds they had snatched him up, and the helicopter turned toward the Sinai, chased by dense Egyptian antiaircraft fire. Hugging the sand dunes in a series of evasive zigzags, the helicopter managed to cross the canal and landed the navigator in the hands of his waiting mother and his wife, who was eight months pregnant.

The pain of the air war taking place around the canal did not dampen the joy at the Flight School graduation on July 16, 1970. This was also a day of personal celebration for Ran Ronen, who was to finish his tour of duty as commander of the Flight School and then depart for a year of studies in England. As the ceremony was breaking up, he felt a hand on his shoulder. It was Shmuel Chetz, the Phantom squadron commander. Shmuel's thin face was clearly troubled. Ran had received Shmuel into the Mirage squadron seven years earlier, and had immediately been drawn to his modest but glowing personality. After Shmuel's recent successes in the Phantom squadron, which had earned him the nickname "Terror of the MiGs," Ran had begun to believe that Shmuel stood a good chance of someday receiving command of the IAF. As a relatively young commander, Shmuel often found Ran to be a good sounding board for his thoughts and feelings. He now told him how troubled he was by the absorption of the Phantoms even as they were flying the bombing sorties in Egypt, which prevented the IAF from properly assimilating the essence of the sophisticated weapons systems. He was bothered also by the increasing number of missile batteries, and by their slow crawl toward the canal. Most of all, he was worried by the Phantoms that had recently been shot down and whose pilots had been killed and captured. Ran listened in silence as Shmuel told him of the new electronic warfare equipment that had just arrived from the United States following the recent events. He also described the missile battery attack planned for July 18 under the protection of these new wonder devices.

The following day, Ran transferred command of the Flight School and went to vacation in a hotel for the weekend. The attack of the missile batteries in the delta was to take place on Saturday at 1240 hours. Shortly afterward, Ran snuck away from the hotel pool and called the IAF Control Center. The operations sergeant recognized his voice and informed him that Shmuel had been killed and that his navigator, Menachem Eini, had ejected and had been captured.

Two formations had set out for the attack. Shmuel led the first and was also the sortie leader. Avihu Ben-Nun, commander of the northern Phantom squadron, led the second formation. The instructions were to rely on the new electronic warfare devices that were designed to disrupt the activities of the missiles if and when they were fired. The missiles did not actually hit the planes, but exploded nearby as the Phantoms crossed the canal and entered a wall of planned antiaircraft fire. Shmuel's plane was hit first, at the moment he entered his bombing run. Menachem Eini saw the missile and felt the concussion. The aircraft was damaged, but all was not lost. They immediately broke east for home, flying low. Within seconds they lost control of their steering. There was no time to lose, for a series of actions has to be taken before ejecting. According to protocol, navigators eject first. Menachem was ejected and parachuted near Ismailia, where Egyptian soldiers found him unconscious, with numerous broken bones. Shmuel remained in his cockpit in the hope that he could manage to cross the canal in thirty seconds. Perhaps he thought it was bad for a squadron commander to be captured. Or perhaps he was relying on his good luck, which had extricated him from death's grip in similar situations at the last second. This time he was trapped. The plane spun and crashed in a ball of flames. Avihu saw the missile fired at Shmuel, and decided to destroy that battery first. He entered to bomb, and fate had its way with him as well. The missile fired did not surprise him or his navigator. They saw it, but thought that they would be safe from its hit, as they had been promised. They executed several evasive moves, but relied primarily on the American device. It was too little and too late, and the missile exploded next to them, puncturing the cockpit like a sieve. One engine was extinguished, and the second began to burn. All the lights and emergency control systems chimed and blinked. The hydraulic pressure gauge dropped to zero. The steering mechanisms functioned only partially.

Avihu's Number Two dropped his bombs in the heart of the missile battery and annihilated it. The damaged and smoking leader barely pulled himself out of the bombing run. With the rest of the burning engine's power and his half-paralyzed steering mechanisms, he turned toward the Sinai and dropped his precious bomb load on the desert floor to lighten his plane. All he wanted was not to fall prisoner.

"We can eject," the navigator told him as they crossed the canal.

"Why eject when the airplane's still flying?" Avihu asked as he attempted to stretch those final minutes remaining before they reached the forward Israeli airfield at Refidim.

The runway could be seen, but it was still very distant. In order to control the damaged plane, he had to land at high speed without the hydraulic pressure to lower his landing gear or flaps, and without brakes. Though it seemed impossible, he decided to continue.

He lowered his wheels with the emergency system, and when he hit the runway and attempted to brake with the secondary emergency system, nothing happened. The Phantom shot along the runway in a crazed sprint. Avihu released the braking parachute, but it tore and was ripped off the plane because of the intense speed. The only thing left was the tail hook. As on aircraft carriers, the IAF's bases had flexible braking cables stretched across the runways, which the hook could catch. However, the plane veered off the runway far from the cable, and without ground steering, it rode through the airfield uncontrolled, passing among buildings and obstacles, miraculously missing every one of them. It continued until the nose struck a sand embankment and the aircraft came to a halt.

In the debriefing held in the squadron, they heard of the missile batteries that had been destroyed. Half in scolding and half with a commiserating wink, they were told that they should have ejected, even on the ground. The risk they had taken had been too great and unnecessary, for the mission had already cost the life of one squadron commander.

Ran Ronen attended the General Command debriefing on the day after the mission. During the meeting, a note was passed to him from one of the forward benches: "Are you willing to take command of the squadron?" It was signed "Moti," no description and no rank. This was a commander who was also a friend. Ran did not think twice. In such a situation there is no place for deliberations. He knew that this sacrifice would be greater than any he had ever asked of his wife, and he hoped that she would understand this time as well, and perhaps even forgive. Without hesitation, he wrote on the note's margins, "Affirmative and immediately." He saw the commander-in-chief confer with the IDF chief of staff. In the recess, they called him over. After a two-minute discussion, they approved his new position.

For his thirty-fourth birthday, on Sunday, July 19, Ran received a Phantom squadron. By 0800 hours, all the squadron's air and ground crews were gathered at Hatzor. Wearing flight coveralls and work clothes, their faces tired and their eyes red from a long night and perhaps from tears, they faced their new commander. Shmuel's death was the greatest blow the squadron had ever faced. Ran understood this, and spoke straight from his heart.

"Shmulik is gone. We have to better ourselves and fight for him as well. If he could express it, this would be his wish. Good luck."

Ran had never flown a Phantom before, and he promised the crews that he would get to know them and the aircraft as quickly as he could. Meeting with his deputies, he attempted to persuade them to run him through a concentrated version of the Phantom course. They agreed, but would not promise him a date of completion. After several days of ground training, he coerced his instructors to take off with him for eight training flights. His ninth flight was his first operational sortie in a Phantom. It would be another attack on the SA-3 missile batteries. Yoram Agmon, one of his deputies, would be the leader. David, Yitzhak Pear's brave navigator, took his place behind Ran, also serving as an unofficial instructor. The aircraft was armed with eleven half-ton bombs, more than Ran had ever carried. He was still not adept enough in the details of the rapid automatic operations, for there was no time to learn. Yoram shoved a piece of paper into his hand with a list of the fourteen weapons switches that he needed to activate before the attack.

Yoram entered first, with Ran flying behind him. Antiaircraft fire rained on them from everywhere. Ran's amazement at the Phantom grew from moment to moment. He was completely focused on the gunsights, ignoring the glowing bullets and missiles being fired at him. His fear of physical damage shrank behind his desire to complete a successful mission. Relying on fate and luck to protect him from the antiaircraft fire, he counted on himself for the rest. A commander cannot miss or be humiliated during his first operational flight. He was glad David was behind him, as he heard his deep voice over the intercom calling out altitudes. With a sharp press on the end of the stick to release the bombs, the aircraft became light and rose easily, pulling out of the threatening plunge to the target. Ran climbed in a sharp pull while squinting at the ground below. The bombs had struck at the center of the battery, and it was wrapped in a cloud of smoke.

Only after departing the missile area and crossing the Suez Canal could one begin to sing. While he had sung a lot in the Mirage, this time he was silent. A pair of curious eyes were piercing his back, and though he might be a risk-taking and somewhat crazy commander, he still had to behave properly.

· · · ·

Throughout this period, the Soviets slowly gnawed away at the Egyptian authority and control over the front. Though their involvement was generally covert, evidence of their presence could be seen even in the shellings and the Egyptian commando assaults along the canal. The Soviets manned the missile batteries and radar-guided antiaircraft guns in the areas of Cairo and Alexandria. They provided support for the positions between the delta, the Nile, and the canal. Soviet pilots manned the MiG-21s in Cairo, Mansura, Kotmiya, Kum-Ushim, and Beni-Suweif. While they began by providing air defenses for Cairo in order to prevent the collapse of Nasser's regime, they slowly gained control of the entire airspace that was prey to the Israeli bombings, which stretched from the canal to the Western Desert and from the Mediterranean coast to the Suez-Cairo line. Their squadrons were based in this area, and everything beyond it remained in the hands of the Egyptians.

It is not coincidental that the deep Israeli bombings ceased on April 18, 1970, the day of the first conflict between the Phantoms and the Soviet MiGs. The Phantoms were sent on a reconnaissance mission to the Cairo area. The Soviets were scrambled to intercept them. While the MiGs carried the markings of the EAF, the pilots spoke Russian with the control center and among themselves. The Phantoms did not respond to the provocation, and were commanded to disengage and return to Israel. The silent confrontation was not publicized internationally. Because of the intensification of the war in Vietnam, it seemed that the Soviet Union was plotting an attack on Western positions throughout the world. Moshe Dayan publicly hinted that he was willing to draw a line from the canal to the Nile Valley. He would guarantee that Israeli aircraft would not cross it to bomb the heart of Egypt, under the condition that the Soviets would not appear along the canal front. For the next three and a half months, the Soviet pilots in Egypt maintained a modest profile along the canal.

After this, the MiGs began to appear on the radar as they slowly neared that imaginary line, twenty to thirty kilometers from the canal. At the last moment they would turn on their heels and disappear. Once they attempted to approach Rami Harpaz's Phantom, and he fled. On July 25 the Skyhawks attacked Egyptian positions along the canal, and Soviet MiGs appeared. This time their voices were again heard on the radio, with distinct intentions of intercepting the Israeli aircraft. The Skyhawks were ordered to disengage, but the Soviets chased them and even crossed into the Sinai as one of their MiGs fired an air-to-air missile. Its fragments struck the tail of one of the Skyhawks, and it was forced to land at Refidim.

This incitement eliminated even the hesitations of Moshe Dayan, the primary advocate of moderation in the defense network, who feared any confrontation with the Soviets. Passive response to the border incident with the Skyhawks was clearly giving in to Moscow's desires to dictate the course of the war. After a delay of more than four months, the Minister of Defense and the chief of staff accepted Moti Hod's plan to initiate a direct air confrontation with the Soviets. The Israeli government approved the plan.

Over the course of weeks, the plan for the battle developed in the IAF operation rooms, down to its every detail. It would be a pure Israeli-Soviet battle whose results would leave no room for excuses. It had to conclude with many downed MiGs and not a single Israeli loss so that the Soviets would understand one important lesson—that this was not their field or their league. In the script, the front was set one-third of the way between Suez City and Cairo, not far from the Soviet base at Kotmiya airfield, and distant from their home base, which was protected by their own radar and flight controllers.

When aircraft of similar capabilities meet, it is their pilots who determine victory. The IAF's top team of twelve pilots, who would man the Mirages and Phantoms, had downed fifty-nine enemy aircraft. The Soviet capabilities were an unknown factor. Since the Second World War, they had not participated in dogfights. It was not known what weapons, tactics, or tricks they would use. The Israeli trap was therefore designed on assumptions that provided the Israelis with an excellent opening advantage. Nonetheless, the Soviets had the advantage of the home field as well as quantitative superiority.

On July 30, 1970, somewhat after 1400 hours, two Phantoms attacked the Egyptian radar station at Sohana, near the Suez Gulf. Amos Amir led a quartet of Mirages that covered the Phantoms from above, even though the Phantoms could easily take care of themselves. The Soviets did not respond. The Mirages extended their range and were on the verge of penetrating deeper into Egypt. The Soviets still hesitated. Twelve minutes passed until they swallowed the bait and scrambled two quartets of MiGs from the Beni-Suweif airfield. First contact was established at

1420 hours, and Amos pulled them toward Cairo. As they were seduced into following his quartet, a second quartet of Mirages suddenly charged in from behind, led by Yiftah Spector. The balance of forces was maintained for several seconds, but the desire to get the Israelis was too strong. From the moment the Soviets awoke, they began scrambling every formation that stood ready on their bases.

Within half a minute, the MiG force was reinforced by another three quartets that arrived from the Kum-Ushim airfield. The Soviet flight controller almost clapped his hands in glee. The Israelis were sitting ducks. What could eight Mirages do against twenty MiGs?

Suddenly, Avihu Ben-Nun's quartet of Phantoms appeared on the Soviet radar screens and drove into the swarm of aircraft. They began to split up. In addition to Avihu, the Phantoms were manned by Aviem Sela, Ehud Hankin, and "Gal," surprising the enemy in a rapid climb from low altitude. The Phantoms rattled the confidence of the Soviet flight controller. Within seconds a sixth MiG quartet was in the air, arriving from the nearby Kotmiya airfield to join the battle taking place above.

This was Aviem Sela's first mass battle. It was crowded in the sky, and he was used to more modest dimensions, a pair against a quartet or, at most, a quartet against an octet. However, in this devilish dance there were thirty-six aircraft, everyone chasing, everyone firing. The sight reminded him of films about the First World War, run at high speed. Every second, another MiG passed in front of his nose, and between them flew missiles and drop tanks. Only an experienced and sophisticated flight-control system like Israel's could guide every Mirage or Phantom toward its goal and prevent confusion between friend and foe.

Aviem quickly latched onto a pair of MiGs at the exact second in which he heard Asher Snir's voice on the radio, stating that he had shot down the first MiG of the battle. Aviem envied Snir, since he had not yet shot down a single aircraft. Aviem was tense and pressured by the responsibility to succeed and the desire to have one Soviet aircraft to his credit. The second hand inched forward, and he could find no Soviet pilot in his gunsights. The first MiG he headed for was already being chased by someone else. The second was too far away. The third charged in on him, flying too fast to provide an opening, and he lost him. He had already participated in battles against MiGs, but had never encountered such pressure. He had to remind himself to remain calm.

He then saw his target, flying toward him with an advantage. After spinning and flipping over, as he had learned in the basic exercises on the Mystère years ago, he had not only shaken off the MiG, but was on his tail as well. In one second, it was in his gunsights. "Ben," his navigator, was glued to the weapons control system, waiting for the beep that would tell him that their missiles were locked on the heat from the MiG's engine. It beeped, and Aviem fired. The missile flew like an arrow, and though Aviem saw it explode and hit, the MiG remained whole. He was furious with the missile. Had the detonator been activated too early? Was it his fault? He decided to fire another, and waited for the word from "Ben." Everything occurred in an instant. The missile flew out from under his wing, and the MiG exploded. Aviem was amazed. In the heat of the battle, he had not given the first missile enough time. However, he did not trouble himself about the extra missile he had used. No one would argue with his success, for he had just shot down a Soviet MiG. He saw the pilot parachuting, and waved his wings at him as he passed by at nearly the speed of sound. Aviem and "Ben" allowed themselves a second of celebration, and then returned to the discipline of battle. They looked for another Soviet, and saw a parachute sailing down. Avihu Ben-Nun had downed another MiG with a missile. The Soviets also saw their comrades falling, and panic struck them. A slew of Russian curses filled their communications frequencies. At the peak of the battle, after "Avik" 's Mirage cannons had brought down a fourth MiG, the Soviets began to give in, and the skies grew less crowded. Some of them retreated to their bases, and others moved to the edge of the battle to maintain a safe distance. The Mirages and Phantoms chased them into Egypt and were on the verge of more confrontations.

"Everyone disengage. Shake them off and get out immediately."

The adamant voice was that of the flight controller, but the hands were those of Moti Hod. After two and a half or three minutes of battle, he had decided that a final score of four to zero was better than a score of six to one. The planes were also low on fuel, and there was still a long journey home.

They exited with their job well done. It was a perfect victory, and Aviem executed the traditional roll over the base. He did not land with exaggerated pride. His respect for the Soviet pilots had not diminished even after he had shot one of them down. A superpower, he concluded to himself, can allow itself several mediocre pilots.

The ground crews did not understand the meaning of the celebrations. Only four Egyptian aircraft? What was the big deal? They had had much better days than this in the past. They had not been included in the secret of the operation, and the IDF military spokesman maintained silence, as did Cairo and particularly Moscow. A long time passed before the ground crews were allowed to replace the emblems of the downed aircraft on the bodies of the Israeli planes that had shot them down—either the three concentric circles of the EAF or the red star of the Soviet Air Force.

Snir, who had shot down the first MiG, was certain that he had managed in the final seconds to shoot down the fifth as well, before he himself was almost downed by a missile that exploded behind him and struck his tail. He had managed to cross the canal and to land at the Refidim airfield. The approval of the downing of the fifth MiG was received in a roundabout way when, two months later, the story was leaked to the London *Daily Express*. The results of the battle in the British headlines were five to nothing. Three Soviets had parachuted, and two had been killed. The source of the leak was apparently Egyptian.

On August 4, 1970, Yehezkiel Somech, deputy commander of the IAF, telephoned the southern Phantom squadron. The cease-fire would go into effect that day, and the squadron was to prepare itself for a final bombing. The sorties across the border would continue until the afternoon. By last light, they had to destroy the Firdan Bridge, at the heart of the canal, near Ismailia. They took off in two pairs. Levi Tzur led the first, and Ran Ronen the second. Every available inch below the wings, including the hangers for the drop tanks which had been removed at the last moment, was loaded with bombs. They flew at high altitude and maximum speed. The flight controller spurred them on. The clock had begun ticking toward the cease-fire. Five more minutes . . . Three more minutes . . .

Two minutes until the cease-fire. The area around the target was quiet, for the Egyptians apparently believed that the bombings were over. The bridge looked like a thin pencil line, a small and narrow target that would be easy to miss. They had to focus on their gunsights. Ran dropped down to improve his chances of a good hit. The navigator called out the altimeter readings. With one press on the bomb-release button, all twenty-two of his explosives dropped onto the bridge at once. The quartet dropped a total of eighty-eight bombs, folding the bridge into the water. Ran then pulled sharply out of the attack dive, turned on his back, and joined the formation to return home. The cease-fire had begun.

On the evening of August 7, 1970, Prime Minister Golda Meir appeared on Israeli television and announced that a cease-fire would take effect at midnight along the Egyptian border. The War of Attrition, or "the War After the War," had come to an end. The cessation of the fighting was part of a package deal negotiated by U.S. Secretary of State William Rogers. The "Rogers Plan" aimed at achieving a peace settlement between Israel, Egypt, and Jordan on the basis of an Israeli withdrawal from most of the territories occupied during the Six-Day War. The plan led to tremendous internal political strife within the Israeli government as well as strained diplomatic relations with the United States. Thus Israel was sending a mixed message to the world that would unintentionally sow the seeds for the next war.

Though the eastern front had quieted down as well, in September 1970 it appeared that the war everyone hoped would never begin was about to erupt. During this month, terrorist activities in Jordan reached their peak, turning King Hussein's welcome policy and military support into a threat to his political power. The terrorists were ravaging Jordan with outbreaks of random violence. While Israel and Jordan, encouraged by the United States, were in the midst of covert talks regarding the future of the West Bank, King Hussein relied on the superpowers to help control the Palestinians, who were doing all they could to shake the foundations of his rule.

Palestinian terrorism reached its peak with the hijacking of three large foreign airliners, which the terrorists blew up in the Jordanian desert near Az-Zarqa. In September 1970, Hussein ordered his army to attack the terrorist bases and destroy their support among the Palestinian citizens of Jordan. A civil war began that led to an invasion by Syrian armored units, which came to aid the terrorists. The United States and England were called upon to help Hussein. Israel was asked to provide local pressure along the Syrian border of the Golan Heights. The Syrians withdrew, and King Hussein was again saved. The terrorists were defeated. Through Egyptian moderation, an agreement was reached between them and King Hussein, clarifying exactly who was landlord. "Black September" was another gloomy chapter in the Palestinian struggle, and it became the name of a new radical faction founded, one month later, by the PLO's number-two man, Abu Iyad. The terrorist actions shattered the tranquillity that Israel experienced after the battles of Suez.

Except for a few outbreaks from late 1969 until June 1970, only the Syrian border along the Golan Heights remained quiet during the War of Attrition. Internal dissension within the Syrian Ba'ath party, which eventually brought to power the commander of the Syrian Air Force, Haffez Assad, ignited the conflict. The IAF was involved throughout these battles, which began with Syrian artillery shellings and climaxed with an attempt to overrun Israeli outposts along the Golan Heights. The IAF engaged in dogfights, landed forces that attacked Syrian military bases, constructed high-voltage lines and bridges deep in Syrian territory and around Damascus, and later participated in concentrated bombings of Syrian military camps. In these battles, thirteen Syrian MiGs, as well as one Israeli Mirage and one Israeli Phantom, were shot down. Two Israeli pilots and one navigator were taken prisoner. They spent three years in the Al-Maza jail in Damascus and were released in exchange for five senior officers of the Syrian General Command who were kidnapped from Lebanese territory in a daring operation by an elite IDF commando unit.

Seven Syrian MiG-21s were shot down in one battle in July 1969 as they attempted to disrupt a reconnaissance flight being executed by a pair of Israeli Mirages. A quartet of MiGs was scrambled toward them as they began to photograph Syrian military positions along the Golan Heights and the Eastern Desert from an altitude of 35,000 feet. The Syrians did not pay attention to the quartet of Mirages waiting in the skies of the Upper Galilee, ready to cover the reconnaissance Mirages, which were carrying only photographic equipment. The backup aircraft flew at low altitude, hidden from the Syrian radar, until the MiGs attacked the photographing Mirages. The Israeli flight controller scrambled the waiting quartet toward the Syrians, while the reconnaissance aircraft were still fleeing the area. Three MiGs were shot down in a short battle. The fourth lowered its wheels. The pursuing Mirage pilot, who already had him in his gunsights, halted his fire, for this was the international sign of surrender. It seemed that the MiG pilot was seeking to land in Israel. The Syrian took advantage of the confused moment, raised his wheels, flipped over, and disappeared.

The skies cleared, and the reconnaissance aircraft returned to Syria to continue their mission. Near Damascus, a second quartet of MiGs approached them. Having foreseen this, the IAF commander-in-chief had kept another quartet of Mirages in the air to cover the second run of the photographing Mirages. The four MiGs were shot down within seconds, two of them by the formation leader, Giora Foreman. The reconnaissance pair again returned to Syria to complete its mission. This time they photographed over Damascus and farther east undisturbed.

In the meantime, the Arab positions had hardened, echoing the declaration of the Khartoum Conference of Arab leaders in September 1967, which had declared, "No recognition of Israel, no peace, and no negotiations." UN Resolution 242 obligated the Arabs to recognize Israel, and did not require Israel to withdraw from all the territories it had captured during the Six-Day War. Together, these resolutions made peace seem remote. Egypt, Jordan, and particularly Syria immediately rejected the American proposal of compromise based on the concept of "territories for peace," which stood behind the Rogers Plan. In Israel, the idea was accepted a bit more readily, though an opposition camp slowly grew in strength, recognizing the strategic and emotional significance of the territories. With the IDF-controlled Sinai serving as a partition zone and the Suez Canal as a water barrier, the threat of an Egyptian invasion of Israel's population centers seemed to be reduced. The IAF had a double advantage. The range of advance warning of Egyptian attacks had been increased, and the distance between Israeli aircraft and the Nile Valley population centers was now reduced. The West Bank remained not only a strategic advantage but also a chance to realize the dream of controlling the whole of the biblical Land of Israel.

In the War of Attrition, 594 Israeli soldiers, including 33 aircrew, were killed. Another 2,659 were wounded. This was a heavy price to pay for a series of battles that had ended inconclusively, with both sides emerging battered and weakened. The IDF had no goals or missions that included capturing territory during this war. It had been commanded only to maintain the existing borders and put a halt to the bothersome enemy actions. Therefore, when the cease-fire took hold, no one criticized the quiet until it became clear that the Egyptians had availed themselves of this time to complete the processes that had been halted by the repeated Israeli bombings of their bunkers. A mere forty-eight hours after the beginning of the cease-fire, Egypt began to move its missile system toward the Suez Canal, and to reinforce it. In the fifty-kilometer-wide belt along the canal, only sixteen missile batteries had remained after the Israeli actions. With no option, Israel had accepted their presence under the condition that the situation would be frozen. The United States guaranteed this stasis, and promised that its patrol aircraft would ensure it. Nevertheless, within a month, approximately fifty missile batteries crossed the fifty-kilometer line, operated by or with the support of some three thousand Soviet military people and advisers. Approximately one-third of the dense and dangerous new network comprised SA-3 missile batteries. By the outbreak of the Yom Kippur War, in October 1973, this system would have been reinforced with mobile SA-6 missile launchers. If the battles began again, IAF aircraft would not be able to approach the canal without the danger of being shot down, even fifty kilometers away in the Sinai.

Israel did not take any military actions to rid the region of the new missiles, and its government restricted itself to diplomatic protests. The United States did not respond to the Egyptian violation of the cease-fire terms. The downing of the Phantoms on the eve of the cease-fire had led to the suspicion that another encounter with the missiles would not end well. It could even lead to an unnecessary confrontation with the Soviet Union. The entire Western world was surprised by the intensity with which the Soviets operated the missile systems for the defense of the Egyptian skies. Until the War of Attrition, the West had been familiar with only the SA-2, primarily through encounters with them in Vietnam. The Americans had also encountered the small, swift SA-3, but had not dealt with it at the intensity that Israel had along the canal. In addition to these, the Soviets possessed the SA-7 Strella shoulder-held missile and, even more important, the secret and mysterious SA-6 mobile missile. Both were designed to hit low-flying aircraft.

Israeli pilots were the first and only ones in the world to encounter all these missiles together in an enormous and tight-knit formation that sealed off the skies, complementing each other. An entire Soviet antiaircraft division, dozens of missile batteries, and radar-guided antiaircraft cannons were pushed into the narrow zone between the canal and the Nile Valley, a strip 150 kilometers long and 50 kilometers wide. These were supplemented by five Soviet fighter squadrons that flew under the colors and symbols of the EAF. Along the other fronts, well-fortified antiaircraft and EAF units were stationed. They were improved by constant operational activities over the course of months. Along with the

Soviet reinforcements, the missile network in Egypt in the summer of 1970 included approximately one hundred batteries of every type, nearly four times the twenty-four SA-2 batteries that the Egyptians had possessed in 1967. It was a lethal and almost impenetrable system.

Moti Hod claimed that the Soviets had brought in the SA-6 to avenge the downing of their five MiGs in July 1970. They knew that the IAF was focusing on the SA-2 and SA-3 batteries. The Soviets did not make particular efforts to camouflage the batteries against Israeli reconnaissance photography or electronic intelligence. Hod was convinced that they had persuaded the Egyptians to continue fighting until they could prove to the Israelis that they possessed viable weapons against the Phantoms.

On August 3, the Phantoms set out to bomb SA-3 missile batteries that had been moved near Ismailia. The Israeli aircraft fell into a well-placed trap of SA-6 missiles brought from the Soviet Union and covertly set up in the area. An Israeli Phantom was downed. Four days later, Egypt agreed to the cease-fire.

Aviem Sela would later explain that "the War of Attrition concluded in Israel with a feeling of discomfort, largely because of the SA-6. We had no response to the overlapping missile systems, which complemented each other. We knew that the SA-6 could do everything but brew a cup of coffee and sing the national anthem. This was no longer a missile fired from a bunker but one fired from a vehicle, something tiny, seeing but unseen, with almost unlimited range of operation. It transmits, but can also operate perfectly well on someone else's frequencies. It can shut down its engine, look with its optic eye, and then run to its target. It gives its opponent no prior warning until it is seen in the air. The pilot's response time is reduced to almost nothing. A lot of time passes before the aircraft's radar detects the location of the firing and until the opposition missile homes in on its target. In this time, the mobile missile carrier can turn and run, and it is not worth wasting ammunition chasing it."

Moshe Dayan promised Israel's Defense Prize to anyone who captured and brought in an SA-6. The General Command spent 1971 planning an assault on the missile batteries in Egypt or Syria. In the summer of 1972, Israeli intelligence accumulated data on the movements and locations of the mobile batteries in Syria. It was decided to photograph them from the air. The mission was allocated to a pair of Phantoms. Amnon Factori would lead, with the assistance of Aviem Sela.

Describing the mission, Aviem said, "The sortie was designed for complete surprise, with no diversion or electronic warfare. We were therefore total partners in the discussions and deliberations regarding the date of execution until the final minute. Intentionally a holiday and a time when there would be the least wakefulness were chosen. It was planned that we would fly over five batteries. Though there were general aerial photographs, we did not know exactly where the batteries were. It was decided that we would execute two serious plowing runs from the forward line in the Golan Heights toward Damascus, and from there south to Druze Mountain. We would fly at low altitude, almost at ground level, in order to guarantee close and detailed photographs. Speed would be on the edge of the speed of sound without breaking the sound barrier, so as not to disturb the cameras. The flight demanded prolonged training and preparation. Navigation had to be precise to the hairline measurement. We were forced to train in the Sinai, for it is difficult to fly low in Israel without frightening the population.

"On that day, one minute before takeoff, my leader indicated to me that I should take command. His navigation system had broken down. I was not exactly pleased, for I had trained for months as Number Two, and this sortie was one of those historic missions for which you are not always happy to receive responsibility. However, we had been ordered to maintain communications silence, and I could not argue or refuse. We entered from the area of Mount Hermon, flying toward Damascus at more than six hundred knots, with full burners so that they would have no time to respond. I missed the first battery near Damascus by three hundred meters. We were flying so low that from three meters you could see nothing from the side. It is difficult to be precise at this altitude, when you are busy avoiding electrical wires and antennae. I missed the second battery by two hundred meters, and Factori passed right over it. I was furious with myself. 'The third time,' I told myself, 'it has to work.' "

Only after we had plowed through Syria for twenty minutes, and had photographed everything possible without being bothered, did we understand how complete the surprise had been. Not a single missile had been fired toward us. That night we saw the pictures. They were successful. The special cameras had covered the missiles from every possible angle. It was the first time that the SA-6 with all its accessories had been seen from up close in the west, exposed to the naked eye. The photographs were a strategic advantage of the highest degree, and provided a tremendous boost to our ability to deal with the missile. They were eventually passed on to the United States. Shortly before the Yom Kippur War, they were shown to me during a work visit there. The USAF personnel were proud of the photographs, and told me how the pictures had helped them develop theories of combat against the missile. I could barely hold myself back from telling them who had taken the risk for those photographs."

At first the cease-fire was set for ninety days, but it was then extended almost automatically. Life returned to normal. The lessons from the War of Attrition were not quite evident, and the effects of the missile threat did not extend beyond the IAF. The IDF remained, in its own eyes and in those of the public, undefeated, and the battered enemy remained a subject of contempt. The makeshift Israeli bunkers that had been dug during the war, in haste and under fire, were replaced by sophisticated structures built at tremendous expense. The construction operation took place in a race against the clock and in fear that the battles might begin again at any moment. The false sense of security and happy living balanced each other. Nothing could have been further from the Israeli mind than a new war.

There was no room in the IAF for complacency. The War of Attrition increased the importance of the Air Force and the range of expectations regarding its operations. It was no longer viewed as a body whose sole purpose was to guarantee Israel clean skies and air superiority. It was now the only force in the country with a fast, strong, far-reaching arm that could postpone or thwart a surprise attack. The IAF had been forced to prove itself as a capable replacement for other forces lacking in the territory.

Imbalance in the distribution of duties came down harder on the IAF than on the other arms of the IDF. It was obligated to execute most of the ongoing security missions and simultaneously to prepare for the next war with new and sophisticated tools. The need to bomb the missile batteries or to wage air battles in a screen of unknown sophisticated missiles brought about the development of theories of combat that the members of NATO followed with curiosity. Thus, explains Moti Hod, he also would have decided on the cease-fire if the decision had been in his hands. The IAF needed room to breathe in order to acclimate itself to the new generation of American aircraft, the Skyhawk and Phantom, which had been absorbed under unnatural pressures straight into the battlefields. The Mirages and the Super Mystères, remnants of the aging French generation remaining in the IAF in 1973, were already equipped with American engines. The missile problem necessitated new technology and budgets far beyond those to which the IAF had grown accustomed.

The main objective was to gain time. The IAF had to have a clear head to absorb the lessons learned under fire, and to cultivate better responses. This would mean massive acquisition of precious electronic equipment and weapons. Not everything could be found on the shelves or even on the production lines. The problematic missiles had yet to be studied to their core. Even the most promising of solutions were still on the laboratory drawing boards. Development and production, even in the top manufacturing facilities in Israel and abroad, would need at least three years. The IAF prayed that this time would pass quietly. In the meantime it would fill in the gaps by purchasing available equipment. This would include light unmanned aircraft for gathering information on the missiles without risking human life; metal dust that would be dispersed in the air to confuse enemy radar; and American-made Shrike air-to-surface missiles, which could home in on the radar of the missile batteries' fire-control centers.

The Shrike missiles had first been tested on September 18, 1971. A day earlier, an Israeli Stratocruiser aircraft had been shot down by an Egyptian missile ambush, even though it was flying over the Sinai, twenty-three kilometers east of the Suez Canal and at an altitude of thirty thousand feet. It was executing an angular photographic surveillance of the Egyptian missiles. Seven of its crew were killed; only one, the mechanic, survived. The following day, the Phantoms were sent to bomb the missile batteries, using twelve Shrike missiles. It was too little and too late, and the damage was inconsequential. The IAF had now paid the price for the negligence of the diplomatic level, which, for more than a year, had not responded to the movement of the missiles toward the canal.

Its planners continued not only to refurbish the IAF with new and old technology for attacking missile batteries and for air combat in the presence of missiles, but also began to develop theories of combat for such situations. Plans based on the experiences of the War of Attrition were developed, along with training exercises. In them, the IAF would operate even if the ground forces were not prepared, and the ground forces readied themselves to act in case the IAF had to be occupied in other operations. These plans were expanded in the summer of 1972, after Israel studied the war exercises of the Egyptian and Syrian armies. Israel began to prepare itself for a joint surprise attack by Egyptian forces, which would cross the canal, and Syrian armored units, which would appear over the Golan Heights. The plans focused on concentrated attacks on the missile systems, which would lead to their destruction or at least to their substantial weakening, so that the IAF could function freely. The series of plans was referred to as the "Scratch File."

It would be a long while, however, before the plans were ready to be implemented. The IAF was not the only body involved in deciding whether and how to activate war plans. A series of rotations in the Upper Command proved how far away the war actually seemed to be as of early summer 1973. On Janaury 1, 1972, the IDF received a new chief of staff, Lt. Gen. David "Dado" Elazar. A year later, most of the commanders who had developed the "Scratch" plans concluded their tours of duty and were replaced. Maj. Gen. Benny Peled was to take over command of the IAF from Moti Hod. Several other command generals in the IDF were to be replaced as well.

While the General Command was now composed of men relatively inexperienced in their new positions, a new president took his place on the other side of the Suez Canal. Anwar Sadat replaced Nasser, who had died of a heart attack in September 1970. Though he was a villager like his predecessor, Sadat differed in his character and style of thinking. Nasser had been swept away by feelings of revenge and his megalomaniac desire to become the leader of the Arab world and the African continent. Sadat, however, was more pragmatic and rational. He tempered his personal goals and faced the reality that Egypt was on the verge of internal collapse and population explosion. Sadat was no great lover of Israel. He had even cooperated with the Nazis as they were about to enter Egypt during World War II. But he was thirty years older when he took over the presidency. He was now concerned about providing food and housing for his country's poor. A man of pride, Sadat waited a year in hopes that American pressures would soften Israel. By July 1972, his wish had still not been fulfilled. He announced that he would continue the plans of his predecessor. He then evicted the Soviet advisers from his country. Thus Egypt began to plan the war that was to restore its pride without the help of foreigners. Israel preferred to believe that the evictions merely diminished the threat of war.

Moti Hod left the IAF in April 1973, after a parade celebrating twenty-five years of Israel's independence. Four hundred aircraft participated in an air show the likes of which had never been seen in the Jerusalem skies. He was the commander who had led the IAF in two wars and had prepared it for three. He had passed through two generations of aircraft and had begun the design and production of the Kfir and Nesher, the first fighter aircraft produced in Israel. Years later, as chairman of the board of Israel Aircraft Industries, he would close this historic circle by working on the development of the Lavi, an aircraft for the 1990s, which was shelved after its maiden flight because of budgetary constraints.

In the summer of 1973, the Egyptian war machine rolled into gear. An Egyptian war game that propelled the IDF into high alert proved to be a false alarm and left its imprint on analyses of the situation issued in the IDF. The only damage to the peace since the cease-fire was in the area of Palestinian terrorism. At Lod International Airport, Japanese terrorists in the service of the PLO killed dozens of passengers and those waiting to welcome them. Palestinian terrorists kidnapped and murdered eleven athletes from the Israeli Olympic team in Munich. In London, an Israeli diplomat was murdered with a letter bomb. That year, top PLO officials were killed in European capitals in a variety of ways. Israel did not take responsibility for these events.

Late that summer, between Rosh Hashanah and Yom Kippur of 1973, chances for war along the Egyptian and Syrian fronts seemed slim. The Israeli defense network began to call for mandatory military service to be shortened and for budgets to be cut. Even the IAF was told to trim its procurement and building plans. At that time I was commander of the Refidim airfield and the airspace in the central and western Sinai. My heart cringed when I was commanded to halt plans to install an underground control center to be used if the aboveground operations center was damaged. Shortly thereafter I was transferred to the IDF School for Command and Leadership, and took command of the Air Subjects School. I nearly paid with my life for the cuts when, six months later, I returned to Refidim in an emergency role on the eve of the Yom Kippur War. The control tower and the operations center were the first targets of the Egyptian attack aircraft. They were bombed as I stood in them.

I wouldn't have been there if the fortified control center had been built.

The new IAF commander-in-chief, Benny Peled, had received a large, modern air force, well equipped with aircraft and sophisticated systems. The new forty-five-year-old commander had begun his service in the IAF as a technician. During the War of Independence, he had assembled the first Messerschmitts, which had arrived dismantled. After the war, the mechanic became a pilot and a brilliant leader. He was one of the pioneers of the jet age, a commander of the first Meteor, Ouragan, and Mystère squadrons, and the first Mystère pilot to be shot down while attacking during the Sinai Campaign. In the Six-Day War he had been a base commander, and later he was among the first to see that flight and air superiority toward the year 2000 would not involve only flying, but also the integration of advanced technology. As deputy commander of the IAF, he fought for aeronautical engineering, both in Israel and abroad, to be included in the training of future pilots who sought positions of upper command in the IAF.

In August 1973, Benny updated the "Scratch" file. In his opinion, the plan was too complex, and was overly dependent on elements not in his control. However, in the two months remaining before October 6, in a public and military environment that denied any possibility of a war, it was difficult to develop a more promising alternative plan. The agendas of the presidents of Egypt and Syria were much more definitive than the procurement schedules of the IAF, which was in need of sophisticated antimissile weaponry. Just as Israel would be surprised when Sadat invaded the Sinai, it would be shocked when he was welcomed in Jerusalem in November 1977, on his way to give his peace speech in the Knesset.

# 7 The Yom Kippur War

$O$n the morning of October 6, 1973, Avi Lanir, commander of the Mirage squadron, summoned Michael Katz to his office at an IAF base in the center of the country. "As of now, you're going to be the only one flying on Yom Kippur. It will apparently be a reconnaissance sortie, but a very important and special one. Its results will prove whether the reports that a war is about to break out tomorrow are true. Your target is Egypt. Take Yair as your partner, chart your maps, and call me for the briefing when you're ready."

The command did not surprise them, for everywhere around them was confusion. This was unusual compared to the two years of quiet that had passed since the cease-fire ended the War of Attrition. People were running in every direction, and some reservists were even being called up. At twenty-six, Mickey was among those who had accrued the largest number of hours in high-altitude reconnaissance flights. He was the first Israeli pilot to fly a Mirage less than a year after finishing the Flight Course. Often a leader in intercept formations, he was also a member of the IAF aerobatic team. Now he had to update himself, plan the flight route, and prepare himself for the obstacles and dangers that might await him. On his way to the plane, the confusion grasped him as well. Avi suddenly told him to change direction, to Syria and not to Egypt. *What's going on here?* Mickey asked himself. If Egypt was so important, why was he suddenly flying to Syria? However, he quickly understood that this was not the time for pondering. By the time he had equipped himself with new maps and was familiar the new route, and sat waiting in the underground hangar, he heard Avi on the telephone.

"Listen," the squadron commander said to him. "I don't understand what's going on here either, but you're going to Egypt after all. And immediately. According to the original time over target. Everything is urgent, and you can't delay even for a minute."

Within moments his maps had been changed again, and Mickey was in the air, climbing to sixty thousand feet. It was 1000 hours. In synagogues around Israel, the worshipers thought it strange to hear the sound of a plane on Yom Kippur, the holiest day of the year. But they did not stop praying. The reconnaissance sortie was executed at high speed with top precision, completely undisturbed by the enemy. Upon landing, the crew encountered a strange sight. Instead of the usual soldier from the photo division who would take the films to be developed, there stood a group of top commanders, waiting impatiently. They grabbed the films and ran. No one knew or dared ask to where. Several days later, Mickey would learn that the photographs had been placed on the desk of Dado, the chief of staff, after they had been studied by Minister of Defense Moshe Dayan, who had conveyed their results to the government. They were the conclusive evidence that the Egyptian Army was on the banks of the Suez Canal, standing ready to cross and invade Israel.

IAF Commander-in-Chief Benny Peled received the word at his home at 0500 hours. Dado called and told him that a "well-informed source" in the intelligence community had stated that Egypt and Syria would begin an integrated attack on Israel that evening, immediately after Yom Kippur. Benny and Dado decided to focus on a preemptive strike against the Syrian Army's missile system, and not to diffuse the effort according to the Scratch Plan, which was limited to the Egyptian front. The destruction of the Syrian missiles would guarantee clean skies for the following stage of thwarting the armored invasion. The threat coming from the Golan Heights was closer to Israel's population centers and was therefore more relevant. The chief of staff asked when the IAF's aircraft would be prepared to attack. Benny explained that he would need five to six hours from the moment they received the green light. Dado gave the command, and the time for the attack was set for 1100 hours, depending on the approval of the government, which had yet to be informed of the events taking place. Benny hurried off to IAF headquarters. Before he had even arrived, operation orders had been pulled out of the war room.

For the commanders of the Phantom and Skyhawk squadrons that had been allocated to the mission, the morning telegrams were the conclusion to a long, frustrating, sleepless night. They had received the order to pull out the attack plans they had received the day before, and update them as IAF headquarters began to receive bits of information regarding the status of the imminent war. Their pilots were summoned to final briefings. The ground crews were told to prepare the aircraft, and to arm them with bombs for the specific targets they would attack. Saturday, let alone Yom Kippur, was a strange day for such activities. The crews had already undergone several false alarms, and even in these days of calm, the level of alert was like that of a tightly coiled spring. They hoped that this day would end with nothing as well.

The tension had been continuous for three weeks, since September 31, when the Syrian Air Force had lost twelve MiG-21s that had attempted to disrupt an IAF reconnaissance sortie. The reconnaissance aircraft had approached from the sea, heading toward the Syrian coast north of Lebanon, as Mirages flying at high altitude provided cover. The Mirages swooped down on the Syrian MiGs and downed eight of them in the first battle, using missiles and cannons. One Mirage was hit by a Syrian missile, and its pilot parachuted into the sea. While Israeli rescue helicopters were on their way to him, the frustrated Syrians decided to attack the pilot in the water, even though one of their own pilots was floating in the water next to him. The Mirages again descended on the MiGs, and downed another four.

IAF intelligence analyses of the day of battle concluded that the Syrians might attempt to avenge their defeat with a limited attack on Israel. No one was thinking in terms of war. If he had paid attention to signs, Benny Peled would have been able to predict these events in light of the precedent that had been set in the not-too-distant past. The Six-Day War had also started soon after a day of battle in which seven Syrian MiGs had been shot down. That battle had been Moti Hod's first as commander-in-chief of the IAF, and this was Benny's first in his new job. In any case, the experts did not estimate that this would develop into an all-out war, which, according to their calculations, would not begin for another two years, when Egypt and Syria had procured long-range aircraft that would allow them to strike at IAF bases in Israel's center. Thus, as Israel readied itself for a localized Syrian response, the IAF sufficed with reinforcing air defenses in the country's north, and with execution of more reconnaissance sorties.

In the week between Rosh Hashanah and Yom Kippur, the flow of reports increased from both fronts regarding a worrisome strengthening of enemy positions. The IDF Intelligence Branch latched onto reports that the Egyptian Army was about to execute a large exercise, and classified the danger of war at a low probability. The attention of the Israeli public was focused on Austria, where terrorists had hijacked a train loaded with Soviet Jews emigrating to Israel. The IDF maintained its silence, and censored all efforts by foreign and local journalists to hint that war was imminent.

The shift came about in the late-morning hours of October 5, Yom Kippur eve, when IAF headquarters received word of the landing of a Soviet air train at the airports of Cairo and Damascus. Eleven Aeroflot airliners had evacuated the Soviet military advisers and their families from both Egypt and Syria. Benny convened his top officers. Though he was convinced at this point that war was about to begin, he limited his forecast to Syria alone. He ordered that the IAF alert be raised to medium level, and that a partial reserve mobilization begin. He also spoke of the first action of the war, which would entail attacking the tight network of twenty-five SA-2, SA-3, and SA-6 missile batteries protecting the Syrian ground forces in the Golan Heights.

At 0700 hours, the meteorology duty officer reported that low, dense morning clouds would cover the Golan Heights until noon, and could disrupt that attack on the missile batteries. However, the skies over the airfields deeper in Syrian territory were clear, and it was decided to change the targets and the time of the attack. The airfields would be hit first, but the time would be moved from 1100 hours to 1200 hours, since the aircrews had to be briefed again and, more important, since the airplanes' munitions had to be changed. By the completion of these preparations, Prime Minister Golda Meir had informed the chief of staff that she objected to any sort of preemptive action. The Minister of Defense agreed. Though they trusted the reliability of the information indicating that a war was about to begin in the evening hours, they still had doubts. Meir did not want the world to have the impression that Israel had fired the first shot. The reconnaissance photos that Mickey had brought back from his morning sortie reinforced the picture, but did not alter any of the governmental decisions.

Just before noon, Benny held a meeting in his office. The mood had been tense since the squadrons had received orders to cancel all their plans and unload the bombs from the aircraft that were to attack the Syrian airfields. In essence, they were to enter a state of alert to absorb any kind of offensive enemy action. As confident as they were of the IAF's superiority, it was difficult to display it when the initiative lay in the hands of the enemy, whose intentions were unclear. Col. Rafi Har-Lev, commander of the IAF Intelligence Division, was attempting to unravel and predict Syria's plans when, at 1350 hours, blips of enemy aircraft began to flash on the radar screens. Their origin was Syria. Benny immediately ordered aircraft scrambled to protect the country's north. Many of them were still unarmed, or had yet to unload the bombs they had planned to drop on the Syrian airfields. Because they were scrambled to emergency blocking missions, they first had to turn over the sea and discard their bombs so that they could hurry to intercept the attackers.

It was noontime, and before Mickey could finish the debriefing of his reconnaissance sortie over the Suez Canal, he was quickly summoned to a briefing for the attack on the Syrian airfields. As they concluded, the cancellation arrived, and they were told to remain on alert. Confusion was everywhere. After a few minutes he was called to intercept position, to sit on alert for immediate takeoff. Before he could even heat up the Mirage's seat and make contact with Uri, his partner, the alarm sirens began to wail.

"Scramble! Scramble!"

They took off like mad, and Mickey turned toward the Sinai as he had originally been instructed. Suddenly he heard the voice of the flight controller.

"Climb over the base and execute territorial defense of the center of the country."

Mickey would never forget the shock and surprise he felt at that moment. Thoughts careened through his head. An attack on the center of the country, after they had been trained all these years to propel the war into the enemy's territory? A quick glance down revealed that this really was war. The streets of the country, generally completely empty of cars on Yom Kippur, were jammed with traffic. There was clutter on the communications frequencies. Mickey and Uri were not alone. Many other formations were in the air. Several turned north to block the Syrians, and others headed south toward the Egyptians. Syria and Egypt were in this war together. Mickey found it hard to believe. The flight controller's voice suddenly spoke again.

"Direction two-seven-zero to intercept an enemy formation coming out of attack and headed west. Range fifteen miles . . . Range ten miles . . . Low altitude over the sea . . . Direction two-four-zero . . ."

He saw a quartet, and thought to himself that to be coming *out* of an attack, they must have entered it without being shot down. Looking at the planes from afar, he saw their wings loaded with bombs and their drop tanks still in place. "I don't buy this bull," he said to himself. "Aircraft coming out of an attack don't look like that."

"Eye contact," he heard his Number Two say. "I'm taking the right pair."

"Number Two, *keep your position!!!*" Mickey commanded. It was a rare command in an air force where initiative was rarely censured.

He was right. As they approached the quartet, they saw that these were Israeli Super Mystères, the first formation that had been scrambled to block the Egyptian armored column that had begun to cross the Suez Canal.

*This war is not starting well,* Mickey told himself as he began to circle over the base. First there had been the confusion about the reconnaissance sortie, and now the flight-control center could not tell Israeli aircraft from the enemy. Below him, Mickey could see cars evacuating women and children from the base's residential quarters.

"One to the operational telephone immediately!" I heard them calling me.

The flight controller from the Regional Control Center did not try to disguise the emotion in his voice.

"Sir! True report! True report!" He continued to speak, as if I would not believe him. " Many formations of enemy aircraft en route to all IDF units in the Sinai. Several on their way to you, and one on its way to us. All aircraft on alert in the center of the country have been scrambled. Your aircraft will be scrambled immediately. You have permission for antiaircraft fire on any attacking aircraft. . . ."

Dorit, the operations sergeant, was well trained. She immediately patched me into the control tower.

"The war has started! The war has started!" I shouted. "We will be attacked within minutes. Activate sirens from all positions without delay. Activate procedures of a base under air attack. Priority to scrambling aircraft from intercept positions." Before I could finish speaking, the warning alarms began to wail all around me in a frightening barrage of sound.

From the jeep, on my way to the control tower, I saw dozens of dazed male and female soldiers running, some to their positions, others to the shelters. *This is good,* I thought to myself, *it works. They're taking me seriously.* I had feared that the two years of calm would make them listless, but it was not so. Since the War of Attrition, the base had looked like a passenger terminal for anyone flying to the Sinai. But on this day it became the IAF's forward base of the war. The alert of the past day had injected a bit of adrenaline into the last of the doubtful, who had grown accustomed to false alarms.

A pair of Mirages were already taking off from the runway. They climbed and pulled west.

"Turn off the sirens," I commanded. Everyone had already gotten the idea.

I requested to speak on the secret telephone with the flight-control unit in charge of air activities in the region. They would be busy identifying enemy targets on the radar and directing our aircraft toward them.

"I'm sorry. There's no answer."

"Try again. I want to speak to the commander-in-chief."

This time I was answered by an impatient but apologetic voice.

"You have no idea what's going on here. Everyone is scrambling everyone toward everyone. I'm sorry, but you have no chance of speaking to anyone."

Persistence paid off, and I got Giora Foreman, the commander of the Flight Control Center and a veteran flier, on the line.

"Cheetah, we know your situation. But we have no time for you. The Syrians and the Egyptians are attacking at every corner. You're on your own. Shalom!"

You're on your own. In the shortened language of the IAF, that meant nobody gives a damn about you right now.

"Good God!" I said to the operations officer standing next to me. "The war hasn't started, and we're already in total panic. I don't recognize this air force."

It was 1400 hours, and there was silence in the control tower as we sat waiting for the enemy. As we exchanged glances, no one was willing to reveal his thoughts. I could see the fear on the face of the sergeant standing next to me, and I thought to myself, *If he could only know how terrified I am.*

Exactly twenty-four hours earlier, the IAF commander-in-chief had found me at a Tel Aviv restaurant and ordered me to go take command of Refidim in place of the commander, who was abroad. I knew the base, for I had been its commander until six months earlier, before I received command of the IDF School for Leadership and Command. I had been promoted to colonel a year earlier as I worked for two years building the IAF's regional command system. This experience allowed Benny to forgo much of the explanation.

"Chances are that a full or partial war is going to begin tomorrow. Get down there and start to work."

I wanted to know if all the requirements of the alert files had been updated and acted upon. But for the first time in my life I received an unclear response from a commander who was known for his sharpness. Benny said we would "have to make do." I had never felt such discomfort at receiving an operational job. This was not how Benny acted or had trained us to act.

Refidim went on alert without knowing why, just as many of the officers were taking off to the north to spend Yom Kippur with their families. That evening, when the transport aircraft returned them to the base, they heard the forecast of war and my warning that I would take action against anyone who did not complete his preparations by my morning inspection. I could see in their eyes that they were resentful of the fact that they had been called from their homes by an acting commander who seemed to be taking things much too seriously.

In the five minutes between 1403 hours and 1408 hours, I underwent the greatest change of my life. From complete confidence in IDF and particularly IAF initiative and intelligence, I encountered this bubble of confusion and doubt that gnawed away at all strata of the country and revealed the dimensions and disgrace of the situation.

I suddenly saw four quartets of aircraft headed straight for us at low altitude.

"Affirmative identification!" the antiaircraft command shouted. "All Egyptian Sohoi SU-7s!"

"Free fire command in effect!" I yelled.

The radar-aimed 40-millimeter L-70 cannons began to roar. Several of them were below the control tower. The Egyptians were flying at three hundred feet in horizontal flight, perfect for the cannons. But no. The first quartet released its bombs on the center of the runway and on its far side, and continued on in an open formation. A tremendous explosion could be heard, and then several less thunderous blasts. The cannons continued barking, and the aircraft continued to attack.

The second quartet created more craters in the runway's center and final third, and also disappeared without injury. It seemed that the Egyptians were looking at me and laughing at the fruitless efforts of the antiaircraft guns. When the third quartet appeared, I was filled with fear and violent anger. They were ripping my base apart as in a movie, and no one was doing a thing about it. Why was the ack-ack not hitting them? And where the hell were the intercept aircraft that were supposed to eliminate the attackers before they began?

*That's it*, I thought to myself. *We're done for.* Nothing was going as it should, and this worried me more than the bombing. The third round of bombs landed right in front of the control tower. I managed to see the last one falling and passing by the window. My instinct for survival made me take cover under the apparatus table in front of the window. It was the only metal shelter in the glass structure. I managed to drag the air inspector and the antiaircraft officer along with me.

A fierce explosion ripped the roof of the tower, and it went flying off into the distance. We could not understand how we had not been injured. Luckily the table had been well bolted to the tower's metal frame. However, metal was also a death trap. Electric wires were torn from their connections. Their contact with the metal caused deadly sparks to fly in every direction.

"The tower is electrified!" I yelled as I pulled them to the operations bunker, which was the nearest building and was surrounded by thick defensive walls.

When we had taken cover behind the concrete, all of us in shock, the last quartet released its bombs. They landed near the bunker and sent its roof flying as well. After we had shaken the sand and dust from our bodies, we went outside. We could see the last of the enemy aircraft disappearing undamaged and with no threat to their tails.

And suddenly there was quiet. No sirens. No explosions.

From now on we expected the worst. We had to work well and fast. IAF aircraft had to land, and the runway was a ruin. We had no damage-control unit, since it was made up of reservists who had not been called up. I had requested a day earlier that a unit be mobilized, but Benny Peled said that Minister of Defense Dayan had refused to activate reservists. We would need to improvise to survive the upcoming days.

Before we knew it, a Phantom whose gas gauge was on zero was on its way back to base. It was one of the aircraft involved in intercepting the Sohois. The pilot had three to four minutes to decide whether to risk his life with a landing on the damaged runway or eject and lose the aircraft.

The damaged and electrified control tower was disconnected from the base's electricity. The communications system was silent. The only survivor was a small portable communications unit used in light field conditions. The flight inspector tuned in to the attack frequency. We made contact with the Phantom pilot, Ran Goren. None of us was considering abandoning the aircraft. I told Ran where the trouble spots were on the runway. I knew that he was risking a crash landing. I left the decision in his hands. Ran chose the correct route when he decided to attempt the nearby runway, which was only partially damaged.

He passed close by us and quickly braked as he hit the runway, maneuvering around a pile of dirt and raising a thick cloud of dust behind him. He then straightened out in the center of the runway and stopped. After several seconds we could hear him speaking in an incredibly quiet and somber voice on our frequency.

"One engine shut down because of a lack of fuel. I am moving toward the hangar using the other."

Inspection of the damage revealed that the taxiing runway had escaped almost undamaged. All we had to do was sweep away the pieces of the main runway that had covered it during the explosion, as well as several bombs that had not exploded. With the operations officer, we used our hands to push away the pieces of concrete, planks, and iron rods before dealing with the bombs. Each was relatively light, weighing approximately 150 kilograms, for the Soviet Sohoi aircraft had limited carrying power for external ammunition. If they could have carried quarter-ton or half-ton bombs like the IAF's aircraft, it is doubtful we would have survived after they exploded near the control tower and operations center. The base would have looked different as well.

We did not know if any of the bombs had delay detonators, so we had to work carefully. We tied the tail of each bomb to the jeep and slowly dragged it away from the runway. Throughout this procedure, we dared not look at how pale each of us was, and we ignored the cold sweat that poured off our foreheads and down our backs. After that bomb clearance and the miracle in the control tower, I began to believe that I had truly been given my life as a gift.

. . . .

Like Mickey's formation, Eitan Carmi's Mirage had received the morning order in the first round after the alarms sounded.

"Direction two-seven-zero. Full speed west."

Eitan, a veteran leader in the squadron, had several downed aircraft to his name from the Six-Day War and the War of Attrition. As he turned, he could see the large, strong shadow of a target approaching on his radar screen. The flight controller was directing him to it when it suddenly began losing altitude at tremendous speed. Eitan identified the mid-sized Tupolev TU-16 bomber, and was amazed at the cleverness this large, ancient aircraft was exhibiting. The Western air forces had just begun to install electronic equipment for the detection of approaching aircraft in their sophisticated bombers, and it would take time for the Soviets to discover and imitate the idea. There was no such innovation here. The TU-16 had descended to drop an air-to-ground missile from its belly, and it then turned back to Egypt. The Kelt missile that it dropped was actually a MiG-15 that had been transformed into a giant, pilotless flying bomb. It was automatically programmed to home in on the radar waves of the flight-control stations and hit them with one and a half tons of explosive.

When the Tupolev disappeared from his radar screen and was replaced by the smaller target of the Kelt, the flight controller directed Eitan toward it. At the first moment he was fairly amazed by the shape of the MiG-15 and wondered why the Egyptians had again begun flying these junk heaps, which had barely proven themselves during the Sinai Campaign. However, when he approached and saw that the MiG was flying without sensing the danger closing in, Eitan began to suspect that this was not just a plane. What did it matter if there was no pilot in the cockpit and if this UFO was a plane in the guise of a missile or a missile in the guise of a plane? Since it was racing east and the closest and most appealing target in that direction was Tel Aviv, there was no time to fool around. Though a large city emits no radar waves, it is a wide target with a dense population. This fact alone was enough to cause tremendous damage at any random location the missile would hit.

Eitan attempted to block the path of the MiG with a Shafrir missile. As the missile shot out from under his wing, something happened that had begun to puzzle him a second or two earlier. The large engine flame on which his missile was meant to home in was suddenly extinguished.

The Shafrir lost its course and dove into the sea. Eitan had been amazed to see the flame when he thought he was chasing a plane, for the MiG does not have an afterburner. He could not know that this was a plane turned into a flying bomb, and that the source of the flame was a small rocket engine that had replaced the jet's heavy compressor and increased its carrying capacity for explosives. The rocket speeded up the bomb to a starting speed of Mach 1. It was then shut down and the missile glided to its target. The Shafrir had missed its target since it had lost the heat source it required to guide it. Eiten knew he had to respond quickly as he had learned, without thinking about the risks he was taking. He approached to within three hundred meters of the aircraft, squeezed his cannon trigger, and saw the shells rip off the aircraft's right wing, sending it into a spin. Eitan distanced himself and watched its enormous explosion. The shock waves rattled his plane. His head was banged into the top of the cockpit. Only then did he understand what he had been fighting, and what a miracle had saved his life. If his cannon shells had missed the wing root by centimeters and struck the body of the missile, it would have exploded next to him and torn him to shreds.

With the first downed aircraft of the war to his credit, Eitan attempted to find the Tupolev in order to shoot it into the sea. But the bomber had broken west and dropped down. Eitan knew that he had no chance to catch it in this race, for the Tupolev's greater fuel capacity would outrun the Mirage by far.


It was midday at the IAF's Ofir air base at Sharm-a-Sheikh. Amir Nahumi and "Shuki" were each strapped into the seats of their Phantoms, waiting to be scrambled from intercept alert in the well-protected underground hangars. The planes were connected to all the ground equipment, and the mechanical crews stood by waiting. Whoever had sent these two to be on duty alert at the southern tip of the Sinai Peninsula clearly had not dreamed of war. They were both young inexperienced pilots and had just begun their training on the Phantom. Neither was accredited as formation leader in operational flight. The navigators, "Binu" and "Moore," who were to operate the radar and weapons control equipment, were also new to the field, having just graduated from Flight School.

Until 0900 hours, the base lay deep in innocent sleep. Nahumi's wife, Naomi, had awakened him at 0600 with a phone call from their home in the center of the country. She had informed him that she was going to her sister's in Ashkelon, their agreed signal to inform him that the base was being evacuated. She then called again to tell him of unusual traffic on the roads. Nahumi was furious at whoever had sent him to this distant place, just as the serious action was about to begin. According to the intelligence reports and the partial alert, he was certain that the war would be centered in the north.

At 0900 hours, the flight controller told him to go on full alert. By noon he could already smell the war, his first. According to all the briefings, he assumed that they would only receive a taste of the combat, if anything at all. Yak Nevo, the hero of the Six-Day War dogfights, had been sent to Ofir as reserve commander of the base. He explained that intelligence estimated that at most they would have to deal with airborne commando forces. Nahumi thought to himself that even shooting down helicopters at low altitude would be acceptable. He walked to the intercept position, carrying his gun. Yak arrived later to tell them that the war would begin that evening.

The sirens began to wail at 1350 hours. Nahumi, Shuki, and the navigators were quickly strapped into their cockpits. Making contact with the flight controller, Nahumi could hear the panic in his voice as he said, "Your instructions are to remain on alert." However, two seconds later, the controller said, "I see a lot of low-flying formations of combat aircraft on the radar. Very close to you. South of Ofir . . ."

To Nahumi it did not seem plausible that the flight controller was going to instruct him to remain on alert as the skies filled with Egyptian MiGs. Without asking a soul, he abandoned procedure and signaled to the mechanics to send him on his way. He taxied onto the runway, activated his afterburners, and climbed. Shuki joined him.

In the air, he turned his head and his eyes darkened. The skies over the base were filled with low-flying MiGs. The runway was dotted with the small mushroom clouds of exploding bombs. *What luck*, he thought to himself, for the fact that they had taken off had saved their lives. If they had waited thirty seconds, the bombs would have fallen on them as they taxied along the runway.

"They're destroying our base," Shuki said. The flight controller affirmed this.

"Number Two, we'll climb with full burners to Snapir Island, direction zero-four-zero. From there we'll return to the fight with the advantage of altitude and speed."

Nahumi had now taken charge. As he had climbed the ladder of command in the IAF, he had lived by the words "You must take authority. You never get it as a gift."

"We've got to throw the drop tanks," his navigator reminded him. Nahumi wanted to kick himself for forgetting this important detail before entering combat.

"Number Two, throw your drop tanks," Nahumi said with the confidence of a commander. "There are a lot of them, so we'll have to split up. I'll stay east of the base, and you take the other side."

Shuki broke hard and disappeared for a moment. The next instant, Nahumi saw him on the tail of a MiG-17. Nahumi looked for more prey. Below him, he could see a MiG-17 diving in a return bombing of the Ofir runways. In a series of quick motions, he set in on the MiG according to the book. With correct direction, he would be in position to fire his heat-guided Sidewinder missile within seconds.

"Don't fire!" Binu cut him off. "We haven't gotten the locking beep."

Again, Nahumi had to bite his lip and control his pride. The navigator had done his work well. The missile's system had a control mechanism that guaranteed efficient and precise firing, not too close and not too far, at the angle appropriate to the flight, and only after the infrared sensor in its nose had "smelled" the hot target. If all conditions were met, the crew heard a sharp beep.

With one more move and one more repositioning, the shrill beep filled the cockpit. Nahumi squeezed the trigger. Less than half a second passed before the missile set out on its way but it felt like an eternity. The Sidewinder exploded, and the MiG, which had been so beautiful and full in the gunsights, turned into a red-black mushroom of fire and smoke. It was his first downed aircraft, and it was a hypnotic sight. Only then did he begin to feel the tremendous power of the experience of which veteran pilots speak with such passion.

Binu again brought him back to reality. "Break!" he screamed on the intercom, according to all the rules he had learned. Whenever you are busy with your prey, his partner, whose job it is to defend him, can climb onto your tail. You must therefore immediately leave the attack route by breaking sharply. Nahumi responded automatically, pleased that despite the intense conditions, he and his navigator were working as a team. He turned toward Ofir and found himself passing between two MiGs that were diving on the field. It seemed they were more frightened than he was, for they quickly cut off their dive and climbed so that they could escape.

There were shouts on the communications network. The flight controller wanted to know exactly what was going on, since he was not used to a battle in which he was not directing the action. Nahumi and Shuki were doing everything without him, Shuki said. Shuki reported to Nahumi and asked his location to find some encouragement and also get his bearings in the craziness around them. Binu was also shouting, for he knew that Nahumi was so absorbed in his job that he would not hear if he did not scream. *In this kind of wild action*, Nahumi thought to himself, *you've got to free yourself from the pressure of the screaming on the radio.*

Everywhere he looked, there were MiGs. In the debriefing he would learn that they had been attacked by seven formations, a total of twenty-eight aircraft. They were a pair. To Nahumi and Shuki's luck, the Egyptian attack on Ofir was slow and highly inefficient. After Shuki reported shooting down his first plane, Nahumi was pleased and thought that the Egyptians must now be feeling the presence of the Israeli force. Israel must capitalize on the moment. When he saw a pair of MiG-17s diving to attack a Hawk missile battery on the periphery of the field, he turned to follow the leader. The Hawks were holding their fire so as not to hit Israeli aircraft. The MiG dropped low, apparently because of a warning he had received from his partner. He hugged the terrain to escape his chaser. Nahumi followed him, and in one of the turns, the MiG appeared in his cannon gunsights. The Phantom cannon is a 20-millimeter Gatling gun, and its barrels revolve at astounding speed. Nahumi pulled the trigger for a split second. At a firing rate of 6,000 shells per minute, and with 640 shells in the Phantom's belly, he had only six draws on the trigger. He missed. But the MiG abandoned the bombing mission, and this satisfied the requirements of Nahumi's job to keep the skies clean.

The MiG began to take evasive action, and seemed to be panicking. The MiG has a distinct advantage over the Phantom in its ability to turn. But it is slower and rolls less easily than the Phantom. Nahumi tried to use his advantage and was amazed that the MiG was escaping. "Something is not right here," he said to Binu, and upon checking, they discovered that their right engine was out. The last maneuvers had been executed with half-power, for the engine had apparently shut down during the cannon fire. It could not have been a breakdown, for they had not received any signal from the warning system.

Nahumi started the engine, and with a quick burst from the burners, he caught the MiG. The weapons control system emitted its beep. Nahumi pulled the trigger and watched the MiG disintegrate before his eyes. This time he was less emotional. The other MiG escaped. Nahumi wanted to return to base and was looking for Shuki when he saw another pair of MiG-17s attacking the Israeli communications unit on the shores of the Suez Gulf. He expected the MiGs to break toward him to attack. But he had frightened them so much that one of the MiG pilots fired his entire load of air-to-ground missiles at him. As the rockets flew in every direction, Nahumi fired a missile at the MiG. It ripped open the jet's front end and then blew it into pieces, six hundred meters away.

"Three MiG-17s until now. Not bad. What about the fourth?" Binu said. The navigators had done spectacular work in this battle. The sight of two burning aircraft in the distance proved that Shuki was doing his share as well.

"What's going on over there?" Nahumi asked.

"I've shot down three and am looking for the fourth," Shuki responded. He had downed two MiG-17s at the beginning of the battle and, after several minutes, had encountered a pair of MiG-21s. He had shot one of them down immediately, and the second had crashed into the ocean as it attempted evasive maneuvers.

Nahumi felt that he too needed a fourth, and he found a pair of MiGs. He pulled hard. They broke, as did he. From above, the Ofir field seemed to be devastated but quiet. Shuki announced that he was low on fuel and would attempt to land despite the damage to the runway. Flipping onto his back and at tremendous speed, Nahumi was blinded by the flash of light reflected off the pair of MiGs. It was apparently the last pair left in the area. Their routes met, and it was tight. Nahumi fired another missile. One of the MiGs crashed into the ground. It was the fourth MiG-17, which he had been so desperate to shoot down. Its partner escaped into the mountains. That was it for the day. They headed home.

However, it was only the end of the beginning. Where would they land? In low flight, they surveyed the damaged runway. Upon conferring between themselves and with the flight inspector in the control tower, they decided to land on the parallel runway, which was shorter but less damaged. If they had not stopped abruptly after a short run, they would have concluded their flight in a deep pit in the middle of the runway. Several of the flight mechanics remained riveted to their places, frightened to come out to refuel the aircraft and rearm them. Nahumi climbed down himself, dragged out the missile wagon, and began to attach the missiles to the hangers. Shuki grabbed the fuel hose and connected it to his fuel tanks. Seeing the pilots at work, the mechanics' professional pride overcame their fears. They quickly completed the work on their own as they occasionally lifted their heads and looked at the skies with a worried expression. All four of the pilots and navigators were decorated because of this battle.

The extent of the Egyptian crossing of the Suez Canal was greater than the Israeli positions at the Bar-Lev Line could halt or contend with. On the eve of the war, five Egyptian battalions were stationed on or near the canal. Each included an armored brigade. There were also two independent armored brigades and a commando brigade. Israel faced them with one IDF battalion in the Sinai and its Bar-Lev positions. The Egyptian force crossed the canal, using hundreds of boats and amphibious vehicles at first, and then floating bridges that were constructed for the armored corps and mobile infantry units. They outflanked the Israeli positions and essentially infiltrated between them as intense Egyptian artillery kept the Israelis at bay. In this situation, only the IAF's aircraft could disrupt the crossing and attempt to halt the movement of the Egyptian columns into the Sinai.

The areas of the crossing were protected by a tight network of SA-2, SA-3, and SA-6 missiles that the Egyptians had moved forward to the canal in direct breach of the cease-fire agreement. Thus, in the early afternoon hours, the IAF bombed the bridge crossings and the armored and infantry concentrations while executing evasive maneuvers to avoid the missiles. They also attacked the batteries. The aircraft struck from low altitude or used "toss" bombing, in which the plane dives toward the target and climbs in a path that resembles a loop as the computer releases the bombs at a precise point just before the aircraft is to flip on its back. The bombs are dropped in an arc on their target as the plane is fleeing, also in an arc, though in the opposite direction. Thus the aircraft is exposed to the missiles for a minimal period of time. Even if a missile is fired, it has a relatively low chance of hitting.

The bridges were struck with high-powered bombs. Cluster bomb units were dropped on several of the infantry concentrations. CBUs are dropped in one piece. Their packaging then opens automatically over the target, and a shower of dozens of small bombs, the size of grenades, then explodes on the ground or several meters above it. They cause much more damage and affect a much greater area than regular bombs. The CBUs only partially disrupted the Egyptian crossing of the canal, since the bombing was inconsistent and sporadic. The bombing of the Egyptian bridges was more impressive, for it involved direct strikes (on only half of the fourteen bridges) that could be seen in the aerial photographs, though it also did not prevent the crossing of the canal, because only seven of the fourteen bridges were struck.

After the last of the Egyptian aircraft had left the skies over the Refidim air base, the taxiing runway was readied in less than an hour to replace the main runway, which had been bombed. Within two hours the main runway was partially repaired as well. I had spent the afternoon transferring the control tower and operations bunker to new locations and operating them with ridiculous replacement equipment. The air activity increased, for Refidim was the primary air base in the western Sinai. Transport aircraft landed and took off in an air train as they unloaded troops and equipment to reinforce the ground units. By dark, the base was buzzing with personnel and activity, as if the afternoon attack had not occurred.

On the evening of the second day of the war, I was standing at the intercept position, talking to Ran Goren, when the ringing of the telephone cut short our conversation. It was the flight controller again. He reported that in the second Egyptian attack wave, a large number of helicopter sorties had been detected. A quick call to battalion headquarters confirmed the report. The helicopters were landing commando forces that had already assaulted the primary transport route in the northern Sinai leading westward from El Arish. They had also attacked the first reinforcement units headed toward the canal.

All the units in the area had received warning that they were vulnerable to airborne commando assaults during the day or the approaching night. The Refidim air base and the nearby battalion headquarters were high on the priority list. Having been denied an early reserve call-up, my guard force was small. Using my experience in the helicopter squadron, I calculated that the Egyptians would land their forces east of the base, since that area was not manned by Israeli units and it contained many quiet and hidden landing spots.

I recruited the antiaircraft cannons for the mission. Moving from battery to battery, I reminded the gunners that they had the ability to shoot down helicopters if they flew near the base. This could be done even at night, since the guns were radar-guided. I wondered if they would disappoint again as they had when the MiGs attacked the day before. In the worst case, I told the gunners, if they did not hit the helicopters, they could fire on the commando units if and when they assaulted the base's fences.

The air-raid sirens sounded again. Ran Goren and his partner were scrambled from the short runway after they chased away the soldiers who were busy improvising lighting for the field from old oil lamps. The flight controller's next phone call arrived just as Ran's Phantom and his partner's Israeli-made Nesher climbed into the sky.

"Sir, there are several large formations of helicopters in our area," the flight controller said. "They are apparently Egyptian commando helicopters, since we have no helicopters in the range of our radar. One formation seems very close to your base, and actually a minute ago we detected a formation between your base and ours."

Since the flight-control center was ten kilometers north of Refidim, I knew the Egyptian helicopters were at our doorstep. I ran to the makeshift control tower. Through my binoculars, I could see Ran's Phantom descending near the flight-control center, diving and surveying the area as he approached Refidim. On the communications frequency that we shared with the flight controller, I heard him report a formation of twelve large Egyptian helicopters. He began to dive on them, using his cannons. The sun had already set, and the flashes of the shells missing their targets and striking the ground glittered in the twilight. Panic struck the Egyptian formation, and its leaders broke to the sides. I made a quick calculation. If every helicopter could carry forty fighters, I was facing an entire regiment of commandos. If Ran missed again, the Egyptians would escape into the darkness and return fifteen minutes later without our being able to track their landing spot. The capability of these helicopters' captains to execute night maneuvers was unknown.

Ran understood that his high speed was a disadvantage, and he slowed down for his second strafing. It was clear that he sensed the weight of the responsibility on his shoulders. The target of his strafing was a formation of four helicopters that had turned right toward Refidim. A long burst took care of the lead helicopter, which exploded at low altitude. Burning soldiers could be seen flying through the air as the helicopter crashed into the ground and was consumed by a ball of fire. The remaining helicopters broke wildly and escaped westward. Ran continued to search for them, but had difficulty finding them because of their closeness to the ground and the darkness, which was growing thicker. As he readied himself to land, he realized that the improvised lighting system was not yet functional. Lacking the fuel needed to wait, he decided to return to the center of the country to land.

For more than two hours, Shlomo Egozi had conducted the war of the Phantom squadron. The squadron commander was participating in the sorties, and he, as deputy commander, was replacing him in the operations room. When the squadron commander returned, Shlomo grabbed his equipment and ran to get in one flight before dark. He was sent to the canal to intercept Egyptian aircraft attempting to attack Israeli forces organizing themselves to block the large crossing of the canal at last light. Over the desert, the flight controller directed him and his partner toward the Suez Canal. Hawk missile batteries there had detected dozens of helicopters flying at low altitude toward Abu-Rhodes. The Phantoms descended toward the canal in a wild dive, for every moment was precious. Shlomo was worried by the twilight. Small units were already dispersed in the territory. A successful commando assault under cover of darkness could cause tremendous losses and lead to the capture of the vital territory of the oil fields.

On the backdrop of the bright horizon, Shlomo saw thirty giant grasshoppers cross the shoreline and begin to descend into the canyons. There was no doubt that they were Soviet-made Mi-8 helicopters. He saw them all clearly, and asked the flight controller to send him any support possible. There were enough targets for everyone. Until the backups arrived, Shlomo and his partner would begin the hunt on their own. Helicopters flying close to the ground have a great evasive advantage over fighter aircraft, which have limited maneuverability at low altitude and low speed. If the helicopter detected the airplane headed toward it, the attacker would have little chance. At the moment the plane went into its attack dive, the helicopter would turn under him, and the aircraft stood a good chance of crashing into the ground before hitting its target.

Shlomo repeated this to himself and, in a split second, readied himself for the confrontation. He decided to deal with the closest formation of helicopters, and he split up the targets between him and his partner as they descended and decreased speed. Countless thoughts streamed through his head. When he attempted to set the gunsights so that he could get firing data, he did not know where to begin. Relative to the Phantom, the helicopter was a ground target. On the other hand, it was airborne. Should he attack it with missiles or cannons?

By the time he made up his mind, the helicopters detected them and began to disperse and descend even further. Several of them scattered into the canyons and were swallowed up by the darkness. Before the chase had even begun, he began to feel that they would catch only a few, and that they would not be able to prevent the large assault. The helicopters beneath him were moving so anxiously that he thought they would crash into the ground and do his work for him. It was a strange dogfight, for though there was no danger to the fighter pilot, the enemy was still difficult to catch. A helicopter flew into his gunsights, and Shlomo fired a missile, which struck the ground and exploded. The helicopter escaped. At this point the navigator came to his assistance and took over the tracking, the search, and the weapons control, so that he could concentrate on flying. Under the evening light and mountainous conditions, with the Phantom almost running into the ground, any small mistake could cost them their lives.

"Turn hard here, and on the other side of the ravine you'll find your helicopter," said Roy, the navigator.

Shlomo turned and caught the helicopter. This time he used his cannons. It was a hit. With the helicopter falling in midair, a second entered his gunsights and a third entered his partner's. With two cannon bursts, the helicopters were smashed into the ground. The giant bonfires lit the region and functioned as spotlights under these difficult flight conditions. At that moment, Shlomo's partner reported that he was low on fuel. If he did not return immediately, it was unlikely that he would even be able to land at the damaged Refidim airfield. Shlomo dismissed his partner and was left alone in the darkness, facing a deep canyon and a helicopter whose pilot was frightened and nervous and flying wildly, up and down, right and left. When he saw the Phantom's cannon shells exploding around him, he pulled his pursuer toward the bottom of the canyon like a trap's lure.

Shlomo was not duped, and suddenly had a brilliant idea. He suddenly opened up all his burners, and the almost-empty Phantom shot forward with full engine power and closed the short distance between them. When he was several meters above the helicopter, he climbed steeply and sprayed the helicopter with the tremendous turbulence of the jet engine's exhaust. The helicopter flipped over and crashed.

As they pulled out of the attack, they saw a helicopter on the ground below them, unloading troops. Shlomo fired at it, and the helicopter exploded before the commandos could get away. His Phantom was low on fuel and ammunition, and the darkness was making things difficult. However, at the moment when he decided to finish the war for that day, he saw the shape of a helicopter in front of his nose, number five. Shlomo straightened out and squeezed the trigger until his cannons were emptied. The helicopter was hit by one of the final shells, and exploded. After his five and his partner's sixth, a pair of Nesher aircraft appeared, having followed the light of the bonfires, and shot down a seventh.

Over the course of that day and the next, the Egyptians landed five commando regiments, approximately 1,700 fighters in seventy-two helicopter sorties, which were to strengthen the effects of their crossing and to disrupt the flow of IDF reserve reinforcements. Their airborne operations were large and daring, but only a few of the ambushes along the El Arish–Al-Qantara road achieved their goal. Twenty helicopters were shot down, almost a third of them in Shlomo Egozi's and Ran Goren's one-man efforts. The Egyptians lost 750 commandos, and another 330 were captured. Less than one-third of the original force survived in the territory, and they were more concerned with escape than with the missions for which they had flown there.

Shlomo Egozi apparently holds the world record for shooting down helicopters in the short period of fifteen minutes, and he might be the first pilot in the world to have downed a helicopter with jet exhaust. When he landed at his base on his final drops of fuel, he had difficulty analyzing each stage of the action in an organized manner. "It was a catch-as-catch-can battle," he said. "I used all my knowledge and experience in air combat in those fifteen minutes. They were the most dense and insane moments of my life."

. . . .

The Mirage, Skyhawk, and Phantom squadrons had expected the war to begin differently. They had planned to attack the Syrian missile system at 1100 hours and later the airfields deep in Syrian territory. However, heavy rain clouds covered the Golan Heights in the morning, and by afternoon the government's clouds of doubt hung over the entire region. Trained to dictate the course of fighting, the IDF and IAF were now turned into preventive and responding forces, riddled with distress. Three Syrian armored and infantry battalions broke through the lines along the Golan Heights; their 1,500 tanks began rolling forward toward the Upper Galilee and the Jordan River Valley under the cover of heavy shelling by five hundred artillery cannons, aircraft, and a tight umbrella of anti-aircraft cannons and dozens of mobile and stationary ground-to-air missiles. Israel faced them with 180 tanks, two infantry regiments split into small teams dispersed among the forward positions, and the IAF.

Syria's aircraft included MiG-17s, MiG-21s, Sohoi SU-7s, and Sohoi SU-20s. They attempted to penetrate to the Galilee and the valleys, to attack the emergency warehouses that had been opened, and thus to disrupt the IDF's reserve call-up. The Skyhawks, which set out on missions to bomb and rocket armored columns, found themselves in the midst of dogfights. One of the pilots who returned on the verge of a crash landing began to realize that this was war when he saw the confusion in the air. They were flying along the border at eight thousand feet when, during a 180-degree turn, he saw a trail of smoke and a tremendous explosion in his gunsights, five hundred meters ahead of him. He fired and thought he had helped down an enemy aircraft when the leader interrupted and said, "It's mine." In the meantime, over the Sea of Galilee, the formation's number-two aircraft was hit and exploded. He saw pieces of it raining down in flames. Out of the fire, a parachute opened. The other planes in the formation broke in all directions and began diving toward the lake.

"Who hears me?" spoke the voice of the pilot who had ejected, over the communications frequency. "I've been hit in my left foot. I'm still in our territory, but I'm being pulled eastward." He parachuted into the inferno near the border, but luckily landed in a dead area and was undetected by the enemy. Under the cover of darkness, he made his way westward and was rescued. His wedding was scheduled for two days later.

Over Kuneitra, the first IAF aircraft of the war had been shot down by a ground-to-air missile. Four Syrian "Frog" ground-to-ground missiles landed in Migdal HaEmek. The Syrian armored assault was halted by last light, but it began again after nightfall.

Around midnight, Eliezer "Leizik" Prigat, commander of a Phantom squadron, set out on his fifth sortie. The commanders of the Israeli Navy, like those of the units in the Golan Heights, were pleading for air fire in order to relieve some of the pressure they were under from the joint Syrian-Egyptian assault. The IAF was unable to respond to all the requests. Leizik was summoned to assist in a sea battle against Egyptian missile boats north of Gaza. With his partner, he planned to attack the boats intermittently, with one aircraft dropping flares for his partner. However, immediately after takeoff, the partner detected a malfunction, and Leizik flew off to attack alone.

He had been scrambled to his first three sorties on that busy day without understanding exactly what was going on. On the communications equipment, he heard that many aircraft were being sent to intercept enemy aircraft; a number of them reported difficult dogfights and losses. After each sortie, as his aircraft was being refueled, he was passed small notes with incomplete bits of information. His third sortie was in support of the Ofir air base. When he landed between the craters on the bombed runway and heard Nahumi and Shuki's stories, he no longer needed to hear officially from Yak, the base commander, that this was really war.

Toward evening he was scrambled from Ofir for his fourth sortie to intercept enemy aircraft. He would never forget the flight controller's voice instructing him as it suddenly rose and began to shriek for help when the Egyptians began to attack the flight-control center. Without the flight controller, the pilot's "eyes," he unsuccessfully felt his way through the darkness in search of the attackers. He later learned that these were attack helicopters that had fired their missiles and then fled. He was instructed to return to his base in the center of the country, where he prepared himself for his fifth sortie of the day.

Along with a pair of Skyhawks that dropped flares, he attacked an Egyptian missile boat. The Egyptians maneuvered and managed to escape the aircraft's bombs and the missiles fired on them from the Israeli missile boats. As the Skyhawks returned to their base, Leizik decided to take the boat on his own. On his second run, with one bomb remaining, he dropped flares and headed toward the boat. He placed it in his gunsights, dropped, and then pulled up sharply to avoid crashing into the water.

"We got 'em!" his navigator shouted. "It sank! It's gone from the radar!" The rest of the Egyptian boats fled.

That night, after midnight, as he sat at his desk at the squadron, his acting squadron commander placed a pile of messages in front of him with operation orders for the following day. He had almost forgotten that he had a squadron to command as well.

Anwar Sadat would later write in his memoirs that only 5 of the 222 EAF aircraft that attacked Israeli in the first wave were shot down. He described severe damages inflicted on all Israeli command centers and functions. Just as Cairo tried to underplay the severity of the damage to the EAF during the first days of the Six-Day War, preferring to believe the erroneous reports that Tel Aviv was in flames, they overestimated the accomplishments of the first day of the Yom Kippur War, when they had the advantage of surprise. Actual damages, as described in the reports placed on my desk and sent to the commander-in-chief of the IAF, were only inflicted on the runways at the Ofir and Refidim airfields. The airfields were taken out of action for only a few hours in Ofir and for one hour in Refidim, and reopened after a series of emergency repairs. The regional flight-control center in the southern Sinai was attacked. But the flight-control center in Refidim, apparently a target of the commando raid, remained untouched. The three antiaircraft systems along the canal, each containing Hawk missile batteries, L-70 cannons, and other operational units, were also not damaged. Rumors began to circulate that the bombing of the Refidim tower had killed all those inside, including me. I phoned home to report that this was untrue. I tried to imagine how the Egyptians were imagining the picture of their attack on the Sinai airfields when this was how it was being described in Tel Aviv.

The mood was not a good one in IAF headquarters that night. Anyone who sought comfort in the fact that overall the IAF had managed in the past ten hours to actualize the theories of Dan Tolkowsky, which called for the stopping of any enemy invasion until the mobilization of reserve forces and the moving of the war into the enemy's territory, knew that these were theories of the past. Any superiority achieved in a dogfight, and any damages inflicted while attacking ground targets, could not balance the public disappointment in the IAF and the frustration of its fighters, who had guaranteed clear skies through pressure attacks if not by a preemptive strike. Though the IAF had grown more sophisticated and innovative, even relative to the War of Attrition, its forces had been caught in a confusing and embarrassing surprise attack.

The IAF's aircraft were scrambled to dozens of sorties, most of them toward Egypt and a few toward the Syrian front. They dealt with 120 Egyptian sorties and 60 Syrian sorties, and stopped the movement of enemy ground forces while under the threat of missile systems for which they still had no response. Egyptian armored and infantry units were attacked and hit at the crossing spots along the canal, from Port Said through Ismailia and the Great Bitter Lake. Though the bridges across the canal were damaged, their modular pieces were quickly repaired. Egyptian ships were attacked at Ras-Zaafrana, and missile batteries south of Al-Qantara were also hit. Other than the Syrian missiles that landed in Israel and the Kelt missile that was intercepted, clean skies were maintained over the country. Antiaircraft fire and dogfights brought down thirty-seven Egyptian aircraft.

Along the Syrian front, armored and infantry columns were attacked and bombed on the Damascus-Kuneitra road. Everything possible was done to block the passages in the southern Golan Heights, to prevent the armored columns from reaching the Jordan River Valley and the Sea of Galilee. Five Syrian aircraft were shot down in dogfights. Four Israeli aircraft were shot down over the Suez Canal and two over the Golan Heights.

The initiative was in the hands of the enemy. Two fronts had been penetrated, and the assault had not been stopped. Israel's plans for the destruction of the missile systems were not executed, and the Arab air forces had yet to be demolished. The skies over both fronts were not completely clean, and the IAF's pilots were often called upon as the last hope in places where the ground forces could not withstand the onslaught.

The following day, I heard the authoritative voice of Benny Peled on the other end of the secret telephone, calling me like a command order.

"Cheetah Cohen! Minister of Defense Dayan and General Rehavam Ze'evi, his aide, are on their way to you in a helicopter. They're to meet with commanders in order to make crucial decisions. The situation on both fronts is difficult, very difficult. I know Dayan, and I suspect that he'll want to fly to places that will be dangerous for him, like the forward battalion and brigade command posts. I want you to fly him yourself, in a well-armed and well-protected helicopter. And I'm personally instructing you to avoid flying him to places where we might lose the Minister of Defense at the beginning of the war. That's all we'd need now. Actually, it's the only thing that didn't happen to us during the first day. . . ."

Discipline is no less important in war than in peace, I thought to myself as I put on fresh flight coveralls and shined my shoes.

When the VIPs arrived, I saluted the Minister of Defense and he looked right through me, as if I were made of glass. He turned to the side of the landing pad and began to urinate in front of everyone. Astounded, I turned to Ze'evi.

"What's going on here? Is he that tired?"

"No," Ze'evi responded. "He's that much in shock. The entire way over here, he did not stop muttering about the destruction of the Third Temple."

I transported them to the Forward Command Post of the Southern Command at Umm-Hashiba, flying through the desert canyons. The outpost was built in a well-protected underground bunker set into a cliff whose midsection was a small town of fortified underground command centers, including intelligence installations that overlooked the canal and could see deep into Egypt. The helipad on which I landed was not far from the command center.

As I turned off my engine, I could hear aircraft approaching. Sticking out my head, I saw four MiG-17s pulling sharply upward and turning to attack us from the southwest. In less than a minute, the MiGs would shower the area with cannon fire after dropping their bombs. With my rotor still spinning, I jumped out. All my concern was focused on the Minister of Defense, who was walking slowly toward the command center. I ran to him and pointed at the MiGs, which were already diving toward us. Dayan continued in his leisurely gait, as if to display complacence, and ignored the thunder of the antiaircraft cannons.

Ze'evi tried to speed him up. I shouted that we were too far away to enter the command bunker. It would be best to take cover in the nearby communications canal. Ze'evi agreed with me, and as we attempted to persuade the Minister of Defense to run for his life, the antiaircraft cannons at Umm-Hashiba proved their efficiency.

The lead MiG absorbed a direct hit before completing its turn to enter attack. A large burning red hole gaped in the center of its belly, and it did a low barrel roll and slammed into the ground before everyone's eyes. Immediately afterward, we heard another explosion above us. A second MiG began to burn from a hit by one of the L-70 cannons. It dove and crashed into the ground at the base of the cliff. The two remaining MiGs dove west of the cliff and fled. Ze'evi was ecstatic; the attack had been quelled almost before it began. To me, this was a good sign of Israel's recovery from the shock of the surprise attacks that had begun the war.

However, Dayan continued to show reticence, as if nothing had happened. I entered the central command room. The events that I witnessed there caused me to forget my responsibility to report the incidents outside to the IAF commander-in-chief. Shmuel "Gorodish" Gonen, the chief of the command, a hero of past wars who had just started in this current post full of self-confidence, described a horrible picture of the Israeli attempts to take new positions along the road parallel to the Suez Canal at a distance of twenty miles. From Dayan's responses, it was clear that he was interested in disengaging from the Egyptians in order to establish a line far from the canal. He sought to take a stand with the existing forces in order to allow for backup forces to be sent to block the Syrian invasion, which presented a greater threat to Israel's security.

The command team turned pale. According to the Minister of Defense's proposal, the Egyptians would receive all of the western Sinai like a gift, less than a day after the invasion. Gorodish continued to reassure himself with hopes of the arrival of two reserve battalions that would allow him to reinforce his positions. If it was decided that Israel should retreat, not only would the invasion be completed without interference, but the Egyptian SAMs would be pushed into the Sinai, further limiting the IAF.

"Mr. Minister, is this a suggestion or an instruction?" Gorodish asked. "Because if it's a suggestion, I'm not accepting it. And if it's an instruction, I have to receive it from the chief of staff."

I heard Dayan murmur a response that indicated it was just a suggestion. A small group of commanders exited to another room to speak with the chief of staff by telephone. After five minutes, Gorodish returned with orders from Dado to continue without changing the plans. Dayan quickly left the bunker, and Ze'evi instructed me to fly straight to Tel Aviv. The Minister of Defense was interested in reaching the General Command as quickly as possible.

When I returned to Refidim, I went to battalion headquarters to get updated. As I entered the command bunker, I felt as if I had walked into a funeral. Everyone had sour faces. On the maps were red labels indicating the movement of five Egyptian battalions, fifty thousand soldiers, toward the eastern banks of the Suez Canal. I looked at the maps, and found it difficult to comprehend the size and severity of the invasion. Such a tremendous force? How had they managed? Why hadn't they been stopped?

Since the early hours of the war, Benny Peled had continued to believe that the IAF must give priority to the Syrian front. A high-ranking and responsible representation of the IAF had already been chosen to advise and aid the Forward Command Post of the Northern Command. Former IAF commander-in-chief Moti Hod would be the personal adviser to the chief of the command. This was the beginning of a new system of forward command posts that were to relieve the IAF's Main Control Center of the tactical management of the war. The forward command posts had authority over aircraft and used them according to their needs. After several days, once the northern front had stabilized, Moti went to Umm-Hashiba to establish a forward command post for the Southern Command as well. In the meantime, he was stationed in the north alone to face the reserve battalion commanders who were pessimistic at the sight of the Syrian tanks flooding into the Golan Heights. "We have nothing to stop them with," they said. Moti requested the Minister of Defense and the chief of staff to provide him with two more squadrons so that he could block the invasion in the southern portion of the Golan Heights until the arrival of a third reservist battalion. He received one Skyhawk squadron, which blocked every penetration through air bombings. Moti was proud of his people, stating that "at our front, not a single tank got through."

On the morning of October 7, Ehud Hankin strapped himself into his seat in the cockpit of the lead Phantom, knowing that the experience of the great morning of Operation Moked in June 1967 would not be repeated. At thirty-one, Hankin was one of the IAF's top fliers and a member of the aerobatic team. During the Six-Day War and the War of Attrition, he had shot down three MiGs and had been shot down twice. The first time, he had been in a Mirage that was struck by pieces of an Egyptian MiG he had shot down in 1967, on his way home from attacking the Egyptian airfields. The second had occurred two years later, when he was hit by antiaircraft fire while attacking a Jordanian radar station. Both times he had parachuted and had been rescued. Though he was the first Phantom pilot in the IAF to be shot down, he was also the first Phantom pilot to down an Egyptian MiG.

The Egyptian airfields marked on his map were in Kotmiya and Mansura, and were different from those bases he had encountered six years earlier. The aerial photographs of the Kotmiya field, halfway between Suez City and Cairo, showed a pair of parallel black runways jutting out against the background of the bright desert. Like the other Arab air forces, the Egyptians had learned the lessons of Operation Moked, and now housed their aircraft in hundreds of concrete underground hangars. Though not enough hangars had been built on all the bases, only a few aircraft remained exposed on the runways. Any surprise attack would encounter strong radar-guided antiaircraft response. The Egyptians had built new airfields and had improved the existing ones, which had been attacked in 1967. Primary and secondary runways had been added in order to reduce the danger of their being shut down if they were attacked again. Seven of the twenty-five Egyptian airfields had been chosen for the IAF's morning attack. Three more would be added in the days that followed. There was no need to expand this to other targets. Israel made do with attacking the forward fields from which air activity in support of the canal crossing was taking off.

The Phantom squadron outflanked the wall of missiles along the canal, and split into formations that made their way to their allotted fields. Ehud broke and descended on Kotmiya, releasing his bombs with precision on the hangars. Other aircraft in his formation struck at the runways. They then turned toward Mansura and home. The antiaircraft cannons had not managed to disrupt their attack. EAF fighter aircraft were more of a bother, however, for it was difficult to surprise them. From that morning, the Egyptians had dozens of aircraft in the air to protect their airfields. They succeeded in blocking some of the IAF planes. The time spent in the dogfights also meant that these Egyptian aircraft would not be available to aid the ground battles or to attack targets in Israel. By the end of this day, twenty-two EAF aircraft had been shot down in this and other battles. The Kotmiya airfield was shut down for forty-eight hours two days later, after a return attack, and the Mansura airfield was closed for six days after seven MiG-21 aircraft were destroyed on the ground. Its runways and concrete underground hangars were also severely damaged.

As soon as the Phantom squadron had landed in the center of the country, it received the high-priority operations order for which its pilots had been waiting. Within two or three hours they were to prepare to destroy the missile systems and radar stations along the Syrian front. These systems had managed to hermetically seal the deep, narrow corridor between Damascus and Kuneitra, which was the main route of the Syrian forces, as well as other routes along the Golan Heights, which were now functional and in better condition than they had been during the Six-Day War. Even if the IAF had air superiority over the enemy air forces, the missile threat would still have limited their freedom of activity in the region and their abilities to aid the ground forces along the front.

The front line along the Golan Heights was protected by sophisticated SA-6 missiles, which were lighter and easier to use and repair than the older missiles. After firing, it was nearly impossible to track their flight. The missile was fired with a rocket engine that left a small trail of smoke for the first six seconds. A jet engine that reached high speed without leaving an exhaust trail then took over, and the pilots had trouble detecting it or avoiding its hit. The primary advantage of this missile was its mobile launcher, which made it difficult to find or destroy from the air. The second and third lines along the Golan Heights held SA-3 missiles, which were efficient at low and medium altitude, and SA-2s for medium and high altitude. Thus all levels of the Syrian skies were protected.

For more than two years the IAF had invested tremendous effort and special budgets in developing plans for the destruction of the Egyptian and Syrian missiles as the opening stage of the next war. The lessons of the War of Attrition were studied and used to crystallize and rehearse clever and sophisticated attack tricks. These were aided by the development of ELINT (electronic intelligence) for detecting the radar emissions of the missile batteries and the communications systems; by new electronic warfare equipment; and by large procurements of advanced weaponry such as Shrike missiles and optically and electronically guided missiles that were in the early stages of production.

When the time came to activate the plans and to test the efficiency of the tremendous investment, execution began and ended on the wrong foot. On October 5, after it was decided to attack the Syrian systems, it became clear that Israel lacked up-to-date information on the location of the missile batteries. The attacks were then canceled because of weather conditions and because of the government's fears of being considered the instigator of the war. The plans were not used during the first days after the Egyptian and Syrian attacks because the IAF was pressured by the air threat and by the distress cries of the ground forces. Its efforts were therefore dispersed, and it could not gather the forces needed for successful execution of the operations.

On the second morning of the war, when the decision was reached to attack only the Egyptian missiles along the canal, where more and more aircraft were being shot down, two more Skyhawks were downed. The plan fell victim to confusion, loss of self-confidence, and lack of conviction. Everything was prepared for the attack when the chief of staff, responding to Moshe Dayan's fears that the country would be destroyed, ordered the IAF to change direction and move on the Syrian missiles first, while it was still morning.

Operation Dugman 5 was scheduled for 1130 hours. The sudden change in target under the pressure of time would, in the best of circumstances, have caused problems only of the type that had affected the aircraft's alert, for when the battles had broken out, they had been forced to contend with intercept missions while they were armed for ground-target attacks. However, a more serious problem hovered over the morning's changes. Though the ELINT system could provide updated pictures of the location of the missile batteries and their equipment, Israel was still lacking details to complete a precise picture of the system, particularly regarding the location of the mobile SA-6 launchers, which could camouflage themselves among the forces in the territory by turning off their radar.

The Phantom squadron took off toward its targets with almost all its aircraft. Three formations, each comprising five aircraft, split into smaller formations of pairs and trios before crossing the border eastward. Each formation had a target. They flew in a horizontal line so that they could maneuver when starting the attack. At the moment they entered the deadly firing range of the antiaircraft missiles and cannons, their paths twisted and coiled as they broke in sharp diversionary moves and flipped over to avoid being hit. The dense fire made it difficult to identify the targets, whose precise location was not even known. Under such fire, from which they had to worry about getting home alive, it was difficult to focus on the attack.

Of the thirty-one batteries in the Syrian system, only three active missile sites were identified. Several SA-6 batteries were discovered to be empty, since their missiles and mobile launchers had escaped to other locations along the front. The two first pairs executed a successful attack. The next two formations executed a flat and imprecise run. One pilot was unsure of his identification of the target, and in the second formation, the exhaust of the leader blurred the vision of his Number Two, flying behind him. They scored only partial hits. Their bombs were released too late, and only one battery was destroyed while another was damaged.

Ehud Hankin and his navigator, Shaul Levi, were no longer sharp after the morning attack on the Egyptian airfields. They identified their battery in a different location from where they had been briefed to find it. Flying low, Ehud realized his mistake and attempted to climb to improve his attack route. This was a big risk, though it was typical of Ehud, who believed that he could overcome even the most difficult of situations. Flying amid the exploding mushrooms of the antiaircraft fire, and facing the missile batteries, his chances of striking the target and getting out safely were in inverse proportion to the amount of time he spent over the target. Ehud decided to gamble and execute a second attack run.

His comrades could not see whether he had been hit by antiaircraft fire or if he simply flew into the ground. Both Ehud and Shaul were killed. Five other Phantoms were shot down that day; nine of their crew members were taken prisoner. Six aircraft, nearly half of the force, was a dear price to pay for an operation that had barely touched the periphery of the missile system and had definitely failed to silence it. Instead of availing themselves of the partial shock by sending in stronger and more frequent blows until the goal was achieved, the failure paralyzed the IAF, a phenomenon more frustrating than the catastrophe that had cost Ehud, Shaul, and the others their lives.

At 1630 hours, Benny Peled corrected the reports he had previously sent to the chief of staff. It was not two bridges that had been hit by the IAF bombings on the canal, but seven—half of the fourteen that the

Egyptians had constructed. Dado used this report to encourage the government ministers, who were desperate for some sign of success from the front. "Then come and get a kiss," said Dado, inviting the IAF commander-in-chief to the Upper Command, which was crowded with his advisers, former chiefs of staff.

"And now the IAF is going to blow up the bridges and everything will look different," one of the advisers said. Another added, "If I heard correctly, this changed the face of the war."

Several days later, Dado sobered up and said, "We destroyed seven of their bridges, and everyone was happy. The next day the bridges were functional again. [IAF aircraft] destroyed every bridge twice, and there are now eleven bridges spanning the canal. [The aircraft] drop a bomb weighing a ton, one of the bridge's sections is destroyed, and after an hour another piece is brought in and the bridge continues to function. . . ."

However, during those afternoon hours of the first day, the true picture of the situation at the fronts had yet to be drawn; the gloomy reports took a long time even getting to the forward battalion command centers. The concentrated and methodical bombing of the forces crossing the canal had failed. The top commanders were still shrouded in the confusion of battle.

After the failure of the operation to destroy the Syrian missiles, there was no one of high rank who was daring enough to shake off the sense of degradation and initiate an assault. A number of young officers in IAF headquarters, including Avihu Ben-Nun, were unwilling to accept the failed sorties of Ehud Hankin and his comrades as the end of the story. They felt that the IAF needed to strike continuously for two days in order to destroy the missiles. It was decided not to attempt to try an all-out operation again. While IAF aircraft continued to gnaw away at the system's edges, only three of the thirty-one missile batteries were destroyed by the end of the war. Five others were listed as damaged. The pilots could comfort themselves with the small victories they had achieved in dogfights that developed while they attempted to block the Syrian armored columns that continued to press toward the center of the Golan Heights. They had downed nineteen Syrian aircraft in total.

On the morning of October 8, I was pulled out of the shower by the operational telephone. The flight controller informed me of several formations of Egyptian aircraft in the area, which might attack Refidim and the control and radar units nearby. "My advance warning will be very short," he said.

"Did you scramble my intercept aircraft?" I asked.

"No," the flight controller said. "We just put them on alert. They're standing with engines on at this moment."

"Not exactly," I said loudly, over the thunder of the Mirages' engines and burners. "Their leader decided to take off, and he was right."

To make sure I was correct, I jumped outside almost naked. I barely managed to put on underwear. The sight before my eyes nearly froze my blood and returned me to the scene at Refidim, seventy-two hours earlier. A quartet of Sohoi SU-7 aircraft was flying in from the north at low altitude, east of the base. They turned hard to the right in order to begin their attack. The defense system that had detected them had also activated the air-raid sirens. The radar-guided L-70 cannons barked out their rhythmic firing.

The Sohois began to dive from east to west, with one formation flying over the officers' residence toward the nearby battalion command center. The other pointed its nose toward the runways. I grabbed a Kalashnikov submachine gun from the jeep and fired a long burst toward the Sohoi dropping its bombs on the battalion command center. "Congratulations to the sons of bitches. They caught us with our pants down again!" I yelled to my friend Uri Yarom, when I did not manage to shoot down the aircraft.

"You're telling me. Look at you!" Uri could not let go of his sense of humor even at such pressured moments.

We then saw the Mirages in the air.

The antiaircraft fire did not cease. Someone had gone crazy, and I had butterflies in my stomach. Our planes were chasing the Sohois, and the ack-ack continued firing! Its shells could not tell the difference between our aircraft and the enemy's. At that instant, I saw a Mirage flip on its back, place the rearmost Sohoi in its gunsights, and fire a Shafrir missile, which blew up the enemy aircraft before the eyes of all those caught on their way to the shelters. In a flash, we saw the second Mirage fire a missile at the lead Sohoi, which had managed to drop its bombs on the field. Suddenly there were two more Mirages, which latched onto the Sohois attacking the battalion camp. They all then flew out of sight.

The control tower heard that all the Egyptian Sohois had been shot down. The quartet of Mirages landed after four victory rolls. In the underground hangars, the ground mechanics embraced the pilots and carried them on their shoulders. The battle had lasted forty-five seconds at most. Just as with Nahumi and Shuki at Ofir two days earlier, everything would have ended differently had the leader at the intercept position obeyed orders and only taken off when he heard the scramble order. Instead they had acted without permission and without coordinating it with the flight controller. They were unwilling to sit there waiting, loaded to their maximum capacity, only to become easy prey. Ultimately they had eliminated all four MiGs.

The bombs that had been directed against the battalion command post had hit its canteen, killing and injuring many soldiers. The field's runway was not hit. Two bombs with delay detonators that had not exploded were dragged to the nearby sand dunes. This time I did not have to pull them off by myself; those who were normally responsible for this job had been called up. I was about to take off to Tel Aviv in a Cessna, headed to a new job. Amitai "Shafan" Hasson, the commander of Refidim, had returned from abroad. The downing of the four Sohois was a proper finale for three days of temporary command over the base, three of the stormiest days of my life. There could have been no better omen for my departure, and it also signaled that we had passed beyond the stage of confusion. The IAF was back.

Avi Lanir, commander of the Mirage squadron that had verified the outbreak of the war with Mickey's reconnaissance sortie, decided to grab a flight and was in the midst of a patrol mission along the Jordan River. The flight controller informed him of a quartet of Syrian MiG-17s that had just attacked in the Golan Heights and was disrupting the movement of armored reinforcements to the front. He directed Avi to fly north, where he would encounter the MiGs at an altitude of several hundred feet. At this altitude, the MiG had better maneuverability than the Mirage. The Mirage also had difficulty firing its missiles accurately, since the nearby ground would disrupt the guidance mechanism of the missile. Low clouds covered the area, limiting visibility and disrupting cannon fire. Though there were already a number of clean areas along the Egyptian front, the dense missile system along the Syrian front was making things difficult for the Israeli pilots.

Maneuvering between the clouds and the missiles, Avi and "Adi," his

Number Two, dropped down to close on the MiGs. Suddenly they found themselves together on the tail of one of the Syrian aircraft. Though the right of fire is generally in the hands of the veteran leader, Adi, who several hours ago had left a position at headquarters, did not want to miss the opportunity. Aside from that, he told his leader, he was in better firing position. Avi gave in, and Adi fired. The missile slammed the MiG into the ground, and the three others fled.

The skies did not clear that night, and when dawn broke, it seemed that winter was about to arrive. Thick and low cloud cover hung over the Golan Heights all the way to Damascus. The previous night, a Frog ground-to-ground missile had landed at the Ramat David air base. In view of the missiles that had landed in the country's center and the failed attempt to destroy the Syrian ground-to-air missile system, the government decided to strike at Syria with a bombing of its nerve center as well as strategic and economic targets. The first ones chosen were the Central Command and the Syrian Air Force headquarters in Damascus. The two buildings lay next to each other, in the heart of the capital, on the central square and near parks and the sports center.

The attack was to carry a double message; it was to inflict a physical blow as well as psychological and morale damage that would disrupt the operation of the Syrian Upper Command, if not completely silence it for a period of time, thereby reducing the pressure on the front. It would also prove that the missiles were not a significant obstacle along the front, for IAF aircraft could skip over them or fly through them.

Throughout the night, sixteen crews worked on the plan in the intelligence and briefing rooms of the two Phantom squadrons, an octet from each. The leader of the attack would be Arnon, a reserve pilot who was considered one of the best and most daring commanders in the fighter squadrons. Arnon created for himself a mission force, choosing every pilot and navigator according to his qualities and limitations. Early in the morning, in the base commander's final briefing, a number of top commanders were present. It was vitally important to succeed in this mission, because the war would take a drastic turn for the worse if it failed. In addition to the weight of the operation, it would be necessary to penetrate through the belt of missiles and antiaircraft batteries along the front and around the targets. Along with the problematic weather, Arnon and his comrades felt the weight of a national responsibility, as if the fate of the country lay in their hands.

They took off and gathered together at low altitude and in communications silence, navigating along their route according to plan. Suddenly one of the planes in the lead formation had a problem. Its pilot advanced and broke toward home. The team was now lacking one member. The weather as they entered the Golan Heights was reasonable, but the deeper they flew into Syrian territory, the worse it became. Heavy clouds and high winds made navigating, holding formation, and primarily low-altitude flying difficult. This was to be the essential element of surprise, for they were certain that the Syrians would provide them with a welcoming committee.

The cloud cover continued to thicken to the point where they were almost feeling their way in the dark. Navigation was nearly impossible, and Arnon was certain that all was lost. He gave himself a one-percent chance when he recalled the pep talk of the base commander before their departure. He decided to take the risk. He broke the communications silence and informed the formation that they would continue, and to hell with the weather. A hole in the clouds, which they discovered as they approached Damascus, allowed them to see the ground. Luckily, Arnon had prepared a series of topographical markings ahead of time, so that he could correct his route. Looking into the hole, he found one of his landmarks and redirected their flight.

Damascus welcomed them with a suspicious silence. Was this an ambush, or had they actually managed to surprise the city under the assumption that no plane could penetrate this cloud cover? The antiaircraft cannons only managed to turn their barrels, but did not fire a bullet. Someone shot up a shoulder-held Strella missile, which passed by Arnon. The Syrian air-raid sirens did not begin sounding until after the first round of bombs had been dropped.

One after another, the seven Phantoms of the first formation started the bombing run, climbing, flipping over, and diving while placing the targets into the gunsights and releasing the bombs. Five tons from each aircraft, a total of thirty-five tons. The hits were good. Thus far, Arnon's formation had evaded the intense antiaircraft fire that had begun to fill the skies. But now one of the Israeli aircraft was hit. Its pilot was killed, and its navigator would be taken prisoner. A second aircraft was hit in its wing and engine. Fire engulfed its tail. The engine slowly began to burn. Arnon pulled up to within several hundred meters to advise and encourage the pilot. The important thing was to hold on until he was over Israeli territory, where he would probably have to eject. Arnon pushed him on, and the pilot managed to pull the Phantom to Ramat David, straight into the hands of the fire and rescue crews, who covered him with foam and extinguished the fire, saving the pilot and the navigator.

Upon landing, they were informed that the second formation had turned back, for the hole in the skies had sealed up, and Damascus was covered by clouds. The octet was transferred to the command of Moti Hod, who was responsible for coordinating air activities with the Northern Command. He sent them to break up the armored Syrian concentrations along the Golan Heights, which were about to begin a counterattack against Israel.

The intelligence network reported that the attack on Damascus was a success. The Central Command had been hit on its top floors. The Syrian Air Force headquarters had been partially damaged. Several of the bombs had fallen around the buildings, striking a television station and the Soviet cultural center. Several Soviet clerks had been killed. The two military command centers transferred their activities to other buildings. After the war, in the exchange of prisoners, it became clear that during the attack, four captured IAF pilots were being interrogated in the basement of the Syrian Air Force building. Upon their return, they told of how their captors had been convinced that the hits were partial compared to the severe damage inflicted on the Central Command building, because the Israelis knew their comrades were being held prisoner there.

At approximately 1000 hours, the firing of missiles along the Syrian front stopped. Moti Hod conveyed the joyful announcement to the chief of staff to compensate for the disappointments of the past day. The Israeli counterattacks along the Suez Canal, on which Israel hung hopes of a reversal at the Egyptian front, had not succeeded. IAF attacks had failed to destroy the bridges along the canal. The missile batteries hit during the attacks were quickly rehabilitated. Along the Syrian front, the destruction of the missile batteries had failed. Syrian tanks had reached the entrance to the battalion headquarters in the central Golan Heights, and Raful, the battalion commander, was involved in combat that was nearly hand-to-hand. Since the remainder of the battalion reserves were still being mobilized, the IAF was the only force blocking the progress of the Syrian tanks along the southern end of the Golan Heights. With ceaseless bombing waves, the Syrians were prevented from descending to the Sea of Galilee and the Jordan River Valley. The IAF lost aircraft and pilots during these attacks. A number of planes were damaged and managed to return to base, where they were grounded for repairs. Outwardly it appeared that the morale of the aircrews had not been shaken. The ratio of downed aircraft was heavily in the IAF's favor.

The bombing of the Syrian airfields, which had begun a day earlier, along with the attacks on the missiles, had still not achieved the desired results. Like the Egyptians, the Syrians had proven their ability to absorb damage astoundingly well. Airfields that were attacked by three quartets of Phantoms who struck at their runways and hangars were again scrambling aircraft within less than an hour. For Israel, nothing was going according to plan. Nor did the Israelis expect that within hours they would be fighting in enemy territory.

When Benny Peled informed the chief of staff, almost simultaneously with the announcement of the successful attack on Damascus, that the Syrians were no longer firing missiles on Israeli aircraft, Dado was elated. "No missiles! Do you hear? No missiles!" he shouted on the telephone to the chief of the Northern Command. "If the missiles are destroyed, I'm giving you the IAF for free range of activities." The chief of staff, having experienced the premature joy that had spread after notice of the bombing of the Suez Canal bridges, was more subdued this time. *If* the missiles were destroyed, he had said. In truth, the missiles were not destroyed. Though a number of batteries had been hit, the system was silenced because it had used up its supply of missiles. Until the Soviets replenished them, the IAF could act freely to stop the Syrian armored corps. The missile silence lasted twenty-four hours.

Benny Peled knew that a Soviet air train had begun landing in Syria on October 9. Central Flight Control continued sending Phantoms on dozens of bombing sorties against strategic targets throughout Syria. After the attack on the Syrian Central Command, the Phantoms bombed primary power stations, refineries, fuel storage locations, bridges, and water supply centers. Half of Syria's fuel and electrical supply was destroyed. Several bridges were damaged. While the civilian population was distressed, there was no sense of siege, and the Syrian war effort was not disrupted.

The bombing of the Syrian airfields that began on October 8 elicited hopes of immediate results along the front. In the first attack on the Natzaria airfield, a formation of MiGs in the process of landing was caught in its tracks. Three of its aircraft were destroyed. Over the next six days, the IAF struck at the intercept network of the military airfields at Halhoul, Blei, Dumiar, Seiqal, and T-4, on the Iraqi border. Five radar stations, from the Jordanian border to Damascus and Tartus on the Mediterranean coast, were attacked. During the first days the fields returned to activity after several hours. But as the Israeli efforts continued, their ability to absorb the attacks decreased while the time between the bombing of the runways and the return to operation increased. The bombings had an additional effect, in that the Syrians were forced to allocate many additional aircraft to defend the fields, and thus had to remove them from the front. This eased the efforts of the IAF to provide support to the ground forces and to complete the expulsion of the Syrian tanks from the Golan Heights. On October 11, the IDF began an assault toward Damascus.

On October 14, eleven Syrian aircraft were destroyed on the ground and another twenty-one were shot down in dogfights over the airfields. Though four Israeli Phantoms were shot down, signs of fatigue in the Syrians' execution and in their antiaircraft network began to appear.

A Phantom pilot who had attacked many installations at the Dumiar airfield that week reported that on his way home he had managed to evade five ground-to-air missiles that were fired after the replenishing of the supply by the Soviets. However, he felt that the intensity of the ground fire was relatively weaker than it had been at the war's outset. Another pilot reported that six MiG-17s had appeared as he was bombing runways and nearby missile batteries. The MiGs had attempted to disrupt his activities, but were stopped. "We didn't have the time or the appetite to shoot them down. We had to concentrate on bombing the runways. The MiGs flew around like mosquitoes until they ran out of fuel. When they discovered that they couldn't land on the bombed runways and couldn't reach another base, the pilots parachuted from their undamaged aircraft." These pilots' squadron had shot down thirty aircraft since the beginning of the war. Their pace was so quick that between sorties on the ground, they often did not have time to paint the symbols of the Syrian Air Force on the aircraft to match the number of aircraft shot down.

In the meantime, the Soviet air train had begun to arrive. Heavy transport aircraft arrived, carrying a fresh supply of ground-to-air missiles to replace those that had been fired or had been destroyed during the Israeli attacks. They also brought significant quantities of weapons and ammunition that had been lacking, and guaranteed that the Syrian military would be well equipped for an extended period. The rapid replenishing of the missile supplies exposed the Syrians' weak point, for any damage to the missile system was dependent on the Soviets for recovery. Though the IAF was attacking Syrian airfields, the Soviet transport aircraft were not among their targets, and the process was not disrupted. The situation along the Syrian front did not justify missions that could lead to active Soviet involvement in the battles.

On the morning of October 12, Benny Peled's face, like those of the other generals at the meeting of the General Command, was gloomy. Though they had had a difficult week, they were more troubled by what tomorrow would bring. Israel's forces were being steadily reduced. There was still no assurance of replacements for the aircraft that had been shot down, the tanks that had been burned, and the munitions supply depots that were emptying out. The Americans were not replicating the Soviet air train. Washington was maneuvering between the pressures from Jerusalem and its own desire to gain advantage from Israel's weakened position. The situation in the Sinai had the potential to be a turning point toward an Israeli withdrawal and enactment of the Rogers Plan. However, the situation was not clear, even around the tables of the General Command. The armored battalions were holding on largely because of the air support they were receiving. How long could it last?

The chief of staff and his generals looked toward the IAF commander-in-chief. Deputy Chief of Staff Israel Tal recalls that Benny Peled looked them in the eye and stated that the current rate of erosion of his force would reduce his ability to protect the nation's skies within several days if there was no change along the front. The chief of staff understood that any local effort to reinforce the ground forces would not reduce the rate of damage to the IAF. None of the generals could paint a rosier picture. Under these conditions, he summarized the Central Command's view to the government, saying that he saw no choice but to request a cease-fire along the existing lines, even at the risk that it would ensure an Egyptian presence in the Sinai.

The government decided to inform the United States, and thus Egypt, that Israel was interested in stopping the war and was willing to accept a status-quo situation along the front. Cairo, encouraged by the signs of weakening in the Israeli camp, did not accept the offer. The battles continued.

At this time, I was in my fourth day as commander of the IAF Search and Rescue Center, my new job after I had left Refidim. They had appointed me because of my experience as a helicopter pilot and my involvement in pilot rescue. I found the center manned by officers and soldiers working around the clock with their maps and communications equipment, all doing incredible work. Several groups were involved in tracking and rescuing pilots who had ejected. From the moment a plane reported an ejection or its partner reported the aircraft's location, the area was marked on the map and its coordinates were used to guide the rescue helicopters, which carried sensitive radio receivers that could home in on the pilot's distress signal and determine the precise location of his landing. The method of rescue and instructions to the helicopter were determined by the available information and a priority list. First priorty was given to those who had landed in enemy territory. This started a race against the clock to prevent their capture. Preference was also given to wounded aircrew. Those who ejected in Israeli territory without injury often had to wait or, in the early days of the war, find a way to rescue themselves. One pilot who parachuted in the Golan Heights got a lift on an Israeli tank in the midst of a battle.

A second group dealt with the difficult task of searching for the missing, including those who had ejected early in the war and had yet to be found. This was a bitter and almost impossible struggle. Pilots in a formation who discovered that one of their aircraft had not come out of an attack run would sometimes have no idea where the pilot had ejected. In the beginning of the war, this happened to a number of pilots whose location remains unknown. The search for them did not stop during the war or after it. One of them was Col. Arlozor "Zorik" Lev, commander of the Ramat David base, who took off on the fourth day of the war to attack missile batteries along the northern part of the Suez Canal in a display of leadership and personal example. He dove to attack and did not return.

I thought they had found me a simple though frustrating job, but after a few hours I realized how exhausting it was in the Search and Rescue Center. It was a difficult and important war I had been given to wage from this sensitive nerve center.

In the late morning of October 13, a Phantom pilot named Mati had been floating in his life vest in the Mediterranean Sea opposite Beirut for nearly an hour. Only his head protruded. The rest of his body was immersed in the cold water. His navigator, Dekel, floated next to him, counting the minutes. An air battle was raging over their heads. Too much had happened to them in the past hour, he said to Dekel, his navigator. Mati, a reserve pilot who was generally a controlled and calculating type, could only think of the dogfight taking place above because of them. Its results would determine their fate. He also watched the rescue helicopter attempting to reach them like a redeeming angel from above.

He had awakened before dawn, while everyone else slept, so he could prepare the attack sortie on the El Mezzeh airport in Damascus. It was still dark as they headed toward the aircraft. They took off in four quartets, with Mati leading the second formation.

The sun shining in their eyes as they flew east made the low-level flight and navigation to the target difficult. The day was not starting well, he thought to himself as they reached the field and released their bombs directly on the target, despite the intense antiaircraft fire. Then he heard something slam into his plane, most likely a fifty-seven-millimeter shell. Mati saw several missiles pass him by. He avoided one missile and then another. The navigator told him their wing was ablaze. He then dis-covered that some of his systems were not working.

"You're on fire!" his Number Two shouted on the communications system.

The quick response was to break west and get out of the battle area and Syria in the shortest route possible, even if it passed through southern Lebanon. The flight controller estimated that the crew would eject soon. Even if the Phantom could continue to fly, its rear end was wrapped in flames, and its engines, though working, were uncontrollable. They passed over Mount Hermon, and the coastline appeared in the distance. Number Two informed him that his aircraft was burning up, but Mati continued to hope that the fire would go out before they reached the sea. Just before crossing the shore, the steering mechanisms froze, and he lost control of the Phantom, which could have exploded at any instant. They ejected and pulled hard on the parachute lines to direct their fall toward the sea—anything to avoid falling into the hands of the enemy. They could see Beirut. Their emergency transmitters began to send signals of their location. From the Search and Rescue Center near the Central Command in IAF headquarters, I had scrambled a rescue helicopter to them from Haifa while they were still in the air. We had known that their ejection was merely a matter of time. The battle to save Mati's and Dekel's lives now began.

Twenty minutes after they landed in the water, the helicopter pilot reported that he was hovering over them. As his crew began to prepare the pulley to fish them out of the water, the pilot informed us that he was the target of mortar and machine-gun fire from the shore. We ordered him to move away and then return. The helicopter climbed and broke west, but every time it tried to approach the pilots in the water, the firing began again and threatened to sink it as well. He was ordered to get out of there. I went to get help.

The IAF Central Command was swamped with more than it could handle, and told me to manage on my own. The unit that provided air support for the gound forces agreed to give me a pair of Skyhawks. I requested the Flight Control Center to scramble them to the shoreline in order to silence the mortar and machine guns. The Skyhawks arrived and dove on the enemy guns. In the process they sank a motorboat that had set out from Beirut to capture the crew in the water. Afterward they flew over the men like a protective umbrella and waited for the helicopter to return. It had run low on fuel and had returned to Israel to refuel. The intercom from the flight controllers began to click in the Search and Rescue Center.

"What's going on with you opposite Beirut? What kind of war are you running?"

Instead of the rescue helicopter, a large number of MiGs coming from Syria could be seen on the radar screens, heading for the Skyhawks. The flight controller did not speculate on what had brought the MiGs there. Every second was vital. He scrambled a quartet of Mirages toward them while returning the Skyhawks to Ramat David. Two MiGs were shot down in the short battle. One pilot parachuted into the sea. The others fled. Only then was the second helicopter, which had been waiting for the signal to rescue, able to enter and pull out the crew. A third helicopter was scrambled after it, and pulled out the Syrian pilot.

That afternoon, Avi Lanir, commander of the Mirage squadron, also ejected from his burning aircraft over the Golan Heights. He had fallen victim to a new Syrian ploy of which his friends, under the pressures of the moment, had not managed to warn him.

Herzle Bodinger had first noticed it two days earlier, in the midst of a dogfight. Suddenly all the Syrian aircraft broke east very hard, as if attempting to escape. As soon as they had seduced their chasers into pursuing them into Syrian territory, they immediately dove and cleared the stage for the missile batteries. The batteries had held their fire so as not to hit their own aircraft until the moment when Herzle and his comrades sensed that they had been pulled into a clever ambush. The missiles were fired, but the experienced Herzle saw them coming. Along with the other aircraft in the formation, he managed to escape uninjured.

The following day, the Syrians attempted the trick again. Since they were the underdog in the air battles, they used their aircraft as lures toward the missiles. Herzle reported the new phenomenon to IAF headquarters. His friends told the other intercept squadrons. Avi Lanir was not in the squadron that morning, when his deputy briefed his crews to beware of the ambush. When there was a need for another formation for an intercept sortie, he grabbed a plane and led a formation of Mirages in a chase of the Syrian MiGs. Seeing them break eastward as if they meant to escape, he followed them in. No one had the time to stop him and say that this was not the right moment to exhibit leadership and perseverance in completing the mission. Avi fell victim to the ambush, and a Syrian missile struck him. He quickly ejected from the burning aircraft.

The Search and Rescue Center went silent when we heard the distress signal. On the map we could see the spot where Avi had ejected. He was still parachuting, and was over Tel A-Shams in Syria, the area where Israeli armored forces were attacking Syrian ones as they pushed eastward. The area was crawling with Syrian tanks.

The IDF Operations Center managed to connect me to the frequency of the armored regiment commander whose forces were closest to Avi's estimated landing spot. I did not want to repeat the story of Gabi Gerzon, a Skyhawk pilot who had been shot down over the Golan Heights. The rescue helicopter that had set out toward him was hit and grounded by strong antiaircraft fire. A second helicopter had to be sent to rescue the crew of the first. In the meantime, Gerzon attempted to survive. Though he took shelter, the Syrians found him and took him prisoner. He returned after the war with one of his feet missing.

"Do you see a parachute in the air?" I asked the regiment commander.

"Affirmative! A parachute landed several kilometers from here just now. My forward tanks reported a downed MiG. Its pilot is parachuting into their hands."

"Negative! Pay attention. That pilot is ours! No MiG has been shot down in that area. He's ours! Ours!"

The communications frequency went silent. Every word was extraneous, for the regiment commander knew what to do. After two or three eternal minutes, we heard his voice again, this time with the vigor that conveyed the atmosphere of the front.

"Roger, roger! I've sent tanks to him. They're speeding toward him." Another minute passed. "I see him in my telescope. He has taken off his parachute and is running toward our forces. He is well aware of the territory and his situation."

Five more minutes passed. Everyone in the Search and Rescue Center had abandoned what they were doing to listen to the voices.

"The Syrians are close to him, and have begun to chase as well. They fired some artillery toward him to get him to stop running. We are starting an armored battle here."

There was no need to scramble a rescue helicopter. It was doubtful that fighter aircraft would be able to help either, because of the proximity of our tanks and Avi's location.

Three more agonizing minutes passed.

"I'm sorry. I'm very sorry. We had to stop the battle here because we were endangering the pilot. The Syrians are beginning to surround him."

Silence. Everyone turned pale and felt defeated.

"This is my final message on this frequency. They have put him in an armored personnel carrier, which is leaving the area and heading toward Damascus."

I returned my teams to normal duty and reported Avi's capture to the commander-in-chief. The commanders around him froze when they heard the news. Benny Peled requested to let the Syrians know through the proper foreign diplomatic channels that we had seen Avi reach the ground safely. Though our past experience had shown that such an announcement regarding the known condition of a pilot could prevent his being injured in captivity, it did not hold for this war. At first the Syrians claimed that they did not have him. Later they claimed he was injured. Even later they reported that he had died of his injuries. Essentially, the Syrians murdered Avi Lanir in prison. His body was returned after a long and difficult struggle, and he was decorated posthumously for his activities as squadron commander and for his behavior in captivity.

On October 17, several hours before Arik Sharon's battalion crossed the Suez Canal, IAF Central Command received word that the missile system along the northern front around Port Said had been completely destroyed and had not been restored. Over the past ten days, IAF aircraft had bombed the batteries three times. Each time, the missiles had been functional again within hours. The missiles and installations that had been destroyed or damaged were replaced with new ones. The Soviet equipment was easy to use and maintain. Even the crews that were injured and killed were replaced. If there were no Egyptians available, Soviet personnel operated the equipment. After days of depression following the failed operation for the destruction of the Syrian missile system, the mood in Central Command improved. A group among the younger generation of pilots continued to pressure the upper echelons to act against the missiles in a comprehensive operation. However, the Upper Command had chosen to gnaw at the periphery of the missile systems along both fronts or at any stretch that was particularly troublesome to IAF planes. Fifteen radar stations deep in Egyptian territory and five in Syria were also bombed.

On the morning following the beginning of the Israeli crossing of the canal, as initial signs of fatigue were beginning to appear at Port Said, a methodical attack began on the seventy canal missile batteries, from Al-Qantara to Suez. Six Israeli aircraft were shot down during the first day. These were the majority of Israel's losses during the operation. For four days it received more sorties than did the support of the ground forces. A total of forty-three missile batteries were destroyed or damaged after repeated attacks, which also included Shrike attacks on radar installations. The armored and artillery battalions crossing the canal destroyed another eleven batteries, most of them SA-6s. The missile system was paralyzed. On October 22, IAF aircraft reported that they no longer sensed any threat from ground-to-air missiles along the Egyptian front and could grant greater support to the ground forces.

· · · ·

On October 16, David Ivri, the IAF's deputy commander-in-chief of operations, summoned me to his office. The number of Israeli aircraft being hit in dogfights or from the ground was decreasing steadily. The number of pilots ejecting was nearly zero. The Search and Rescue Center was almost completely quiet except for the unit dealing with the missing.

"What do you think?" Ivri asked as he pushed across the table an aerial photograph that he had been given during one of the first days of the war. It was an Egyptian Mi-8 helicopter, one of those that had attempted to land commando troops. It could be seen parked in a canyon near Abu-Rhodes, abandoned but giving the impression that it was ready for takeoff. Until that morning, no one had found the time to deal with this discovery.

Ivri requested that I examine the helicopter and see what could be done with it. In the simplest case, he proposed that I dismantle every part that could be of service to the technical intelligence units, in order to become more familiar with the helicopter and its executions. These would include the flight control boxes, night-vision devices, and special armaments. I was given a Bell 205 and a technical crew. Within several hours we were in the air on the way to the Sinai. It suddenly occurred to me that everything in the helicopter would be labeled in Arabic or Russian, and I asked if we had a translator in the crew.

We had not thought of this, since none of us had even considered that the helicopter might be in flight condition. I thought to myself that it might be good nonetheless to recruit an expert for this purpose. Recalling the Egyptian helicopter pilots who had been captured, I decided to stop over in the makeshift prisoner-of-war camp that had been erected in the Sinai. In the camp office, I was permitted to peruse the captive pilots' files. Two seemed fitting for the mission. I summoned them to an interview and chose one of them, a major named Ibrahim. He was a pleasant fellow who had much experience on the Mi-8 and, most important, fluency in English. We blindfolded him and walked him to the Bell 205 with an armed escort.

Flying over the Sinai, I interrogated him about the helicopter. Ibrahim was astounded. An hour ago he had been a prisoner, and suddenly he was being spoken to with the respect reserved for a squadron commander. He was filled with curiosity.

"What are you planning to do?" he kept asking.

Silence.

"You're probably executing a military operation against my people using one of our helicopters." Silence.

"Colonel, don't ask me to act with you against my own people."

I noted that the man was wise and sensitive, and I liked his last request. I calmed him by explaining that we simply wanted to learn about technical aspects of the helicopter.

"You will remain completely neutral," I promised Ibrahim.

We landed next to the helicopter and executed a quick check in and around it. Outside, near its nose, lay a body. Ibrahim looked at it and let out an agonized, heart-wrenching groan. He had identified a good friend from flight school. It was not difficult to reenact the last moments of the helicopter and the pilot. Loaded with troops, the Mi-8 had landed at twilight in the rocky ravine. It had been a hard landing; instead of having the commandos jump out as he hovered, the pilot had descended and slammed into the ground. The forward wheel had broken from the weight of the load and the blow. The nose tilted forward. The pilot had climbed out to check the damage and had not noticed that the rotor, which was still moving, was leaning downward at a sharp angle, threatening anyone who approached the front of the aircraft. The pilot was beheaded. The copilot and the fighters escaped through the safer rear door, where the rotor was tilted upward. They must have been terrified, for otherwise it is difficult to understand why they left all their equipment in the helicopter and left its engine running. The rotor continued to operate until the fuel ran out. For more than an hour, Ibrahim was dumbfounded. The technical crew cleaned the helicopter. After a quick check, I had the impression that it could fly. From that moment I had a challenge. Why should we dismantle parts and boxes, if the entire aircraft could be flown north as a gift to Benny Peled and David Ivri?

In the meantime, Ibrahim had recovered and was almost calmed. I requested his help in testing the engine and rotor. We called for barrels of jet fuel from the airfield in Abu-Rhodes, in order to rinse and fill the helicopter's dry tanks. When we had done this, the engine came to life, and the rotor began to move. Everything sounded okay. Could we really get this thing off the ground? The technicians wanted to be certain. Opening every control panel they could find, they searched and checked and were amazed. This aircraft could fly. From a nearby unit, they requested a squad of soldiers to guard the helicopter until we could fly it the following day. Afterward, they took off in the Bell 205 toward

Refidim, to arrange the flight and get some rest. I asked the ground technicians in Refidim to lay out tires on which I could set down the Egyptian aircraft instead of on the broken front wheel. I planned to land at Refidim before flying to the center of the country, in order to check the aircraft after flight and to refuel.

The following day, at first light, I returned to the canyon. Barrels of fuel were waiting by the helicopter, sufficient to allow us to reach Refidim. The mechanics refueled and replaced the batteries. Before entering the cockpit, I approached Ibrahim and asked him to accompany me and fly by my side. That was the reason we had brought him. Ibrahim attempted to avoid it as he again began to believe that we were taking him on a secret operation in Egypt.

"I don't understand you," he said in a half-pleading, half-rebuking tone. "How do you plan to fly a helicopter that has crashed?"

I tried to calm him. All we were doing was repeating the rotor test of the day before. Ibrahim was satisifed, and sat down next to me. I secretly signaled to the head of the technical crew. One by one, his men snuck off the helicopter. The Egyptian's armed escort sat behind him and blocked his view of what was going on. When the last of the technicians had gotten off, the escort tapped my shoulder. That was our signal to take off.

Ibrahim began to shriek. "Colonel, you're crazy! This helicopter crashed! Oh my God, oh my God, oh my God . . ."

I intentionally took off in a steep climb, for the helicopter had been exposed for many days to the desert sands with its door open and its windows shattered from the hard landing. In a normal takeoff, the strong winds would create a prolonged sandstorm in the helicopter. At the moment our Mi-8 whipped up the sands, I quickly dropped the nose to gather speed, and within half a minute the last grain of sand was gone. It was like flying in an open jeep.

The pilot of the Bell 205 flying next to us described the confusion on the communications network. Anyone who saw us reported the penetration of an Egyptian helicopter. I was not frightened of interception, for we had informed the flight controller, and he had us on his radar screen. I was a bit wary of spontaneous fire from soldiers who were not privy to the secret, and we could not complain about their sensitivity to Egyptian helicopters. I gained altitude.

Ibrahim was comfortable again, and had even begun to enjoy the flight after his fears of the covert operation had been dispelled. He was now certain that he had been brought along for safety reasons. He even asked to steer the aircraft. After an hour, before we landed to refuel in Refidim, the escort started to blindfold him again. Again, Ibrahim began shrieking.

"Colonel, you have never landed an Mi-8 in your life. It's missing a wheel, and we're going to crash if you don't let me land it."

"Okay, Major, you land." I gave him control of the helicopter, and he tried to hover over the tires laid out on the ground as a replacement for our forward wheel. Ibrahim could not believe the simple and un-conventional solution that would prevent the crash landing of which he was so terrified. He pulled the helicopter into a tremendous shaking, which was about to smash us into the ground. I drew on all my experi-ence as a flight instructor handling a cadet who had begun to panic.

I violently grabbed the steering mechanism and screamed at him to let go as I took off and came around again. I told the armed escort to place a bullet in the barrel of his gun and to lay it against Ibrahim's neck. On my command to fire, he should do so without hesitation. He should just be careful not to damage anything in the cockpit. I told Ibrahim in English, in well-chosen words, that he was not to touch anything or utter a word. His life was hanging in the balance.

The landing on the tire was smooth and perfect. Ibrahim released himself from his safety belts, burst out of the helicopter, and took off running. Though the escort chased him with his gun drawn, Ibrahim was not thinking of escape. Even the events in the cockpit were the result of misunderstanding. He feared that we would crash, and had no inten-tion of dying a hero's death with his enemy. After he was some distance from the helicopter, he sat on the edge of the helipad and stared at the sky.

On my way to the center of the country, I tested the helicopter's basic capabilities. I found it to be a strong and clumsy aircraft, but very stable. Typical of the Soviet design, its finish was crude; every knob in the cockpit was the size of a tractor wheel. I began to understand why Ibrahim and his comrades enjoyed flying it, for the helicopter was easy to maintain and comfortable to fly. However, everything in it was the reverse of what I was used to, from the direction of the opening of the throttle to the movement of the rotor. When we landed, I parted from Ibrahim with a handshake and requested that he persuade his country-men, when he returned home after the war, that they not consider another round. Even in another war, they would have no chance against the IAF.

"Yes, Colonel," he said, and smiled. "But you don't expect me to tell them what I did for you, do you?" Then he went back to being a POW.

Mickey Katz's quartet of Neshers was one of many scrambled eastward toward the canal and beyond, during recent days. They headed toward the bridgehead to Africa that Arik Sharon's battalion had set on the west bank of the canal, flying almost at ground level. For four days, since October 16, Egyptian aircraft had attempted to deter the Israeli forces crossing the canal and to strike at them in hit-and-run bombings. The Egyptians no longer had the protective cover of the missile batteries that they had possessed at the war's outset, for most of them had been destroyed from the air and by the ground forces. The IAF's superiority had cost the EAF many aircraft. They began to attack in snatched bombings, arriving in large waves at low altitude as they flew parallel to the canal. They would bomb, break, and attempt to flee.

Mickey crossed the Suez Gulf at wave level, an altitude at which the Egyptians would not be able to intercept him and might not even detect his presence. As his formation broke to the north, the flight controller breached the communications silence and warned the aircraft of MiGs that had begun an attack run on Israeli forces that had propelled the bridgehead deeper into Egyptian territory. In a climb, the Neshers rose to catch the MiGs and encountered the wall of Egyptian antiaircraft fire. The range between them and the MiGs grew smaller. Twenty miles . . . Fifteen miles . . .

Mickey's Nesher suddenly received a strong blow.

He had no doubt that it was an antiaircraft shell. His control gauges began to spin. The engine shook and suddenly went dead. His speed was still high, and this was good, for he could break eastward and quickly pass over the Egyptian Third Army, which was dug in on the east bank of the canal. From there he could climb and glide until he ejected. He dropped his precious external cargo of drop tanks and missiles and pulled on the stick. The Nesher climbed. Two thousand feet . . . Six thousand feet . . . He attempted to start the engine in the air, but it was irretrievably dead. He tried again. His speed fell to five hundred knots . . . Three hundred fifty knots . . . At three hundred knots, the best speed for the glide, Mickey lowered the Nesher's nose and prepared to eject.

Mickey was the project officer for the absorption of the Nesher into the IAF, and it was a precious weapons system that had been placed in his hands. The Nesher had developed out of the Mirage after a mysterious incident that involved a Swiss citizen and the stealing of the Mirage plans in the mid-1960s. Extremely familiar with the Nesher, Mickey operated it capably. He began to regret that he would have to let it go.

Eitan Carmi, his Number Two, who had shot down the Kelt missile on its way to Tel Aviv, covered for him. The flight controller was also watching out for him.

"Whip One, I've sent a quartet of Phantoms to protect you."

Four Phantoms, on their return from an attack, began to patrol above him, even though they were low on fuel and ammunition. Over the Greater Bitter Lake, Mickey decided that it would be better to eject over land. The temperature in the cockpit rose, and he feared that fire would break out at any moment. When it was clear that he had passed the area of the Third Army, he ejected from his Nesher.

The landing was hard. It had been a long time since he had practiced parachuting and rolling. A sharp pain shot through his back, and he lost consciousness. When he awoke, he could not move a limb of his body. The rescue helicopter transported him to Refidim, from whence he was flown to a hospital in the center of the country, tied to a stretcher. Benny Peled found time away from the war, and came to visit him. After four months of treatment and rehabilitation, Mickey returned to a transport squadron. That morning ended the combat career of the pilot who had photographed the war three hours before it began, and had led the formation that shot down the Sohois that had attacked me during my last day as commander of Refidim.

"Guri" 's Nesher was sitting ready in the underground hangar at Refidim even before the pieces of Mickey's shattered aircraft spread about the sands of the Sinai. The flight controller ordered him and his partner to take the alert position, prepared to scramble at any second. Guri waited impatiently for his turn. The minutes that passed were interminable to him, particularly after his unexpected feast of five enemy aircraft in the last forty-eight hours.

From the outbreak of the war, he had held a position in IAF headquarters and had heard the sounds of the war through the Central Command's communications networks. Here and there he saw pieces of battles and bombings that had been filmed. A day earlier, he had grown tired of it, for he wanted to participate in the war before it ended. He had flown to Refidim and managed to take off at dusk to prevent an attack on the sole Israeli bridge across the canal. In the lingering twilight, all he had been able to see were the rivers of fire ignited by the napalm bombs, and the shape of the Mi-8 helicopter that had dropped the barrels (napalm bombs). He placed the Egyptian helicopter in his gunsights and blew it up over the water.

The following day, Guri was granted a precious prey, two Sohoi SU-7 aircraft that were part of an Egyptian octet bombing the area from which IDF forces were setting out to cross the canal. He blew up the last SU-7 in the formation with a missile. Afterward, Guri downed the leader with cannon fire, a split second before it snuck out of Guri's gunsights behind a wall of antiaircraft fire. That afternoon he returned and shot down two Sohoi SU-20s that had returned to repeat the same attack.

Before the second battle, a quartet of Phantoms on its way to a bombing entered the area. Egyptian Sohois found them, but did not see Guri, who was closing fast. The Phantoms were caught in a dire situation, for they could be hit by either the Sohois' fire or by Guri's. Suddenly they heard a shout on the communication frequency.

"Phantoms, break!"

They did not recognize Guri's voice, which had burst into the frequency without knowing the formation's code name. They broke without asking questions and without understanding why, thereby clearing the way for Guri to shoot down the second Sohoi before they even noticed his existence.

He spent the morning hours that day "ironing" the skies of the canal, quietly patroling back and forth. From the early-afternoon hours, the flight controller had kept him on standby. By 1600 hours, he was on alert. In the underground hangar, during those minutes of tense waiting with nothing to do, he was always flooded with memories. He now realized that he was closing a long account that he had with the Egyptians.

It had started during his childhood at Kibbutz Negba. After the War of Independence, when the Egyptians were pushed out from the entrance to the kibbutz and did not leave a single house intact, he began to seek revenge and was elated to see the first Israeli Messerschmitts chasing the

Egyptian Spitfires. Since then, he spoke only of airplanes. Guri planned to continue the chase after Flight Course, but the doctors eliminated him because of a heart murmur. He volunteered for the paratrooper corps and excelled in the skydiving team, proving to the doctors that the only heart attack would be the one he gave others. At the end of his mandatory military service, they let him join the Flight Course under the condition that he become a helicopter pilot. After the wing ceremony, he did not stop bothering the commanders of the helicopter squadrons and the commanders-in-chief of the IAF until they finally transferred him to a fighter squadron. He concluded the operational training unit at the top of his class.

During the Six-Day War he had flown a Mirage and shot down his first Egyptian aircraft, a Sohoi SU-7, on the second day. When the War of Attrition began, he was already known as a hunter. He was a trickster who could think quickly, had excellent strafing skills, and could read the map one step ahead of his opponent. Guri always managed to position himself on his enemy's tail or above him, so that he could rip him to pieces with accurate cannon fire. Over the next twenty months, he added four more symbols of the EAF to the side of his Mirage as he downed another SU-7, two MiG-21s, and a MiG-17. The last one was shot down at tree level over the Nile Delta.

After shooting down five aircraft in less than two days of this war, he expected that the Egyptians would again return at last light as they had the day before. Maybe it would then be his turn to be scrambled. In the meantime, the account was still open.

Yigal, the flight controller, was Guri's good messenger, informing him, at 1630 hours, that a large Egyptian attack on the canal crossing was beginning. He immediately scrambled Guri, with a pair of Neshers and a pair of Mirages, toward the Bitter Lake. Guri reported clean skies, and the flight controller instructed him to continue westward to meet the attackers in Egypt. Suddenly he saw two MiGs pulling north toward them from the direction of Jabal Obeid, southwest of the lake.

"Release drop tanks," Guri ordered. "Open afterburners." The fuel tanks fell off the wings, and the burners were squeezed to maximum strength.

In a sharp right turn, they pulled toward the MiGs. Guri had begun to come up behind them when he saw approximately ten pairs of MiG-21s and SU-20s climbing toward them at ten thousand feet. Guri's formation was not alone, for another Mirage quartet was already in the region. The flight controller scrambled them to the battle to replace the four Phantoms, which were fighting eight MiGs on their last drops of fuel. The Phantoms had encountered the MiGs on their return from a bombing mission. Only after they had shot down two of them did they leave the area.

The two formations split up. It was eight against twenty. Anywhere you looked, you could see a Mirage or a Nesher on the trail of a MiG or a Sohoi, as its partner covered.

In his Nesher, Guri was paying attention to a solitary pair, apparently a lure designed to draw his formation into an ambush. He set on the rear MiG and downed it from about one thousand meters with a Shafrir missile. He always opened his dogfights with a missile. When the victim is caught unaware of the danger behind him, the hunter can maintain steady speed, angle, and range, and can therefore direct the missile without worrying that he might miss because of a sharp turn by the target. He reserved the Mirage's cannons for the later stages, when the enemy pilot was quite aware of his presence and would attempt to avoid him.

Guri attempted to chase the leader. But, seeing what had happened to his formation-mate, the Egyptian tried to escape with wild moves. A chase began toward the ground at tremendous speed, which, in a sharp turn, places tremendous pressure on the wings. The aircraft lost speed. In order to gain speed, it became necessary to dive and then climb again. Guri thought the MiG would crash into the ground with the force of the dive. But it pulled upward at the last minute before crashing. The highly experienced Guri pulled early and maintained his advantage in a vertical climb.

Thus they rose and descended, as all around them the chases criss-crossed. Only a miracle prevented confusion between friend and foe. Adar, Guri's Number Two, took on a pair of MiGs and was thrown out of the battle after the first missile, when his Nesher's engine stalled. As he lost speed and altitude, Guri ordered him to return home.

Guri was still chasing his MiG when he saw Harry, his Number Three, passing next to him on the trail of another. There was only two hundred meters between pursuer and pursued.

"Why don't you shoot him down?" Guri yelled on the radio.

"I can't seem to hit him," Harry responded.

The MiG was evading Harry's cannons. After a second, Harry opened up the distance and fired a missile.

"Downed," he reported in a calmer tone.

Guri had not had time to congratulate him before he heard Kole, his Number Four, report that he too had fired a missile that had hit its target, but he was not sure whether the MiG had fallen.

Guri was certain that there was no need for him to waste a missile. The cannons would suffice, even if he had to close in to less than five hundred meters to be in effective firing range and to avoid being hit by parts of the enemy aircraft. This was not an easy chore. Guri had developed the cannon strafing exercise into an art. He closed range and squeezed out a long burst from three hundred meters. His second MiG exploded.

Suddenly, Harry also reported a problem and had to turn home. Kole, who for some reason found himself short of fuel, followed him. In the meantime, the second quartet had shot down a Sohoi SU-20. The ratio of forces was turning against them. It was now fifteen against five. Guri, however, thought he was left alone. Perhaps as many as ten MiGs were flying around him. The number of attackers made it difficult for him to gain the advantage. He had to use every ounce of resourcefulness to respond quickly and correctly if he wanted to win, let alone return home in one piece.

He broke left. A pair of MiGs closed in on him from ahead and behind, and attempted to hit him with cannon fire from five hundred meters. He rolled between them. The MiGs flew forward like missiles. He maneuvered in the opposite direction, flipped over, and took position behind them. As he was readying himself to shoot them down, two blinding flashes passed in front of him. In a frontal assault, two MiGs had fired a pair of missiles at him from four hundred meters.

It was too late to respond by diverting the aircraft. Guri bent over instinctively. The missiles and the MiGs passed over him. He turned and began to chase them. Before coming into firing range of the rear MiG, he saw another pair closing on him from the right. In another roll, he was on the tail of the second plane in the formation. With a short burst, he blew up his third MiG.

Guri had not managed to break backward before another pair tried to close him off from both sides. He squeezed between them in sharp twists right and left. The MiGs cut through each other's routes and flew off into the distance. Guri rolled and steadied above them. This time he was in good position for a missile. He aimed at the rear MiG. The missile disconnected from his wing, but plunged toward the ground like a drop tank. The MiGs disappeared.

He broke back again. Finding two more MiGs, Guri did not know if he had seen them before or if they had entered the combat freshly. They sped forward and vertically, in a loop. He climbed after them. When he caught one of the MiGs in his gunsights at the peak of its loop, he fired a short burst from below. The shells exploded the cockpit. From ten thousand feet, he followed the path of the MiG as it plummeted like a stone, straight into the ground.

Looking around, he saw clean skies—no MiGs, no mushroom clouds, no parachutes. Nothing. One after another, all the aircraft whose partners had been hit had fled the battlefield. Guri scanned his control panel. He was running low on fuel. Each cannon had only thirty shells remaining. Deciding that four MiGs in one battle would suffice, he broke eastward, descended to altitude, and pulled toward Refidim.

In the underground hangar, he was unable to climb out of the seat. It was as if someone had melted lead onto his feet over the course of the battle. The intense pressure had contracted his muscles. The G force, which works steadily and at top force in such a battle, weighed heavily against him. The mechanics had to pull him out. That evening, after a rest, he returned to his post at IAF headquarters. Benny Peled ran to greet him. Disgraceful, Guri thought to himself, as he attempted to shake off the hugs and kisses of the commander-in-chief. But he admitted to himself that he knew of no other pilot in the IAF who had shot down nine aircraft in two days.

On the morning of October 21, two Israeli CH-53 helicopters took off from the Umm-Hashiba cliff. Immediately after leaving the ground, they dropped their noses and dove sharply, as if in an aerobatic exercise. The enormous helicopters descended and turned west, hugging the ground as much as possible to avoid detection by enemy radar. Within minutes they passed over the Suez Canal. They flew over the seam between the Egyptian First and Third armies through which IDF ground forces had penetrated. The route was littered with hundreds of incinerated and destroyed vehicles, often stacked one on top of another. Along the northern and southern horizons, clouds of smoke and fire billowed, signs of the ongoing battles against the Egyptian armies. Below them floated the IDF's two temporary bridges across the canal, loaded with convoys transporting an entire army to the canal's west bank. A third bridge was in the process of being built. To their left, the morning sun illuminated the Great Bitter Lake. West of the lake lay the helicopters' target, the Egyptian Faid airfield, newly renamed Nachshon. Yigal Yadin had conceived of the name in a flash a day earlier. Meeting him in IAF headquarters, I told him that I had been appointed to take command of the Faid airfield, which I was to make operational. Yadin, the former IDF chief of staff turned archaeologist, immediately said that according to modern estimates the airfield was close to the spot at which the Israelites had crossed the Red Sea in their exodus from Egypt. Legend says that Nachshon Ben-Aminadav was the first one to jump into the sea after the waters parted.

Of the several abandoned airfields in the region, Faid was the largest, and was situated almost at the center of the Israeli penetration into Egypt. It was easily accessible to the battalions crossing the canal, and could be protected by them. Intelligence information stated that the airfield's runways and installations could satisfy the needs of the Israeli forces. Three Israeli brigades were in need of a base that could receive large quantities of airborne equipment and troops, and allow hundreds of soldiers to be flown daily to the center of the country and back. The crowding along the routes through the Sinai and along the bridges turned the journey from Israel into a torturously long one, taking at least a day. The IAF needed a forward base that would allow for partial operation of its fighter aircraft, and airborne evacuation of wounded in helicopters and transport aircraft. The abandoned hangars at the runways' peripheries would be turned into a field hospital.

A day earlier, at midday, I had been sent to open the field. I was given two CH-53s and an elite paratrooper unit with two jeeps. I was guaranteed that at Faid I would receive a tank unit as well. During our flight to the airfield, Captain Amitai Nachmani, the commander of the paratrooper unit, explained that the guarantee could not be backed up. Though the armored corps had been in the area the day before, when the promise was made, it had been decided to capture Suez City. So those troops had left the area. We landed almost in the center of an armored battle in which Israeli Pattons were firing at Egyptian T-62s. In this mess, I was expected to open up the field for air traffic. We executed an initial careful patrol. The control tower was empty. The base itself seemed like a ghost town. The runways were pitted. The warehouses were filled with bombs and large quantities of fuel. Although Faid had ceased to serve as an operational airfield since the Israeli attacks in the Six-Day War, and had functioned since then as an antiaircraft and missile base, the quantity of armaments there indicated that the Egyptians planned to reopen the field if their forward forces in the Sinai needed support. As we made our way back to the control tower, things seemed calm, and we began to grow accustomed to the place.

Suddenly a screeching whistle pierced the air, followed by a tremendous explosion.

I flew through the air. All of my belongings were ripped off me—my glasses, my watch, my dogtags. I did not let go of my Kalashnikov. All those who had been sitting with me in the jeep were thrown as well. I fell from two meters straight onto my bottom, next to the jeep, which began to burn. Amitai, who had been sitting on the fuel tank, was killed instantly. I pulled myself out of the ring of burning fuel around the jeep, and then heard the horrible cries of the young officer who had sat next to Amitai. He had been caught by the flames, which had scorched his face and eyes. I also helped Amiram, Amitai's deputy, who had broken both legs and was pulling himself along on his belly. He had not lost his clarity of thought.

"There are Egyptians here," he said with his last drops of strength. "We were probably hit by an RPG. We've got to get on the other jeep and get out of here fast. Run to the tower and make contact with the ground forces. Tell the armored corps to send us support."

As I began to run, bullets started to whistle around me and the wounded, so I dragged them into a nearby garage. The Israeli paratroopers in the control tower began firing in every direction. The wounded were loaded on the remaining jeep, and we crowded onto the battered vehicle to ride out with it. Though wounded, Amiram navigated westward through the open enemy territory, where we would be less likely to meet up with another ambush. As we were riding along the edge of the damaged runway, a quartet of MiGs dove toward us, following the trail of dust we were raising. We took cover behind an ammunition depot. The MiGs passed over us, looking for another target. Within seconds they had gone or had been shot down by the Mirages that appeared. We did not have time to watch the dogfight.

We called for a rescue helicopter from the nearby armored unit to pick up the wounded.

Back at Refidim, before taking a night's rest, I met my old friend Yehoram Gaon, the well-known Israeli singer, who had come to perform before the troops. "You're dripping blood from your ear," he told me. In the medical unit, they found damage to my inner ear as a result of the explosion. The doctor was Sid Cohen, a South African pilot who had volunteered for the IAF during the War of Independence and was Ezer Weizman's commander in the first fighter squadron. After returning to South Africa to study medicine, he had moved to Israel with his family and had continued to serve as an airborne doctor in the IAF reserves. He told me I needed an operation, but the procedure had to be postponed for two months. Overtaking the Nachshon airfield could not wait. The following morning I took off with the two CH-53s and a paratrooper unit that had arrived after me that evening. This time the tank unit was waiting for us after having cleaned out the field. Nine Egyptian corpses lay in the hangar near where our jeep had exploded, remnants of the Egyptian force that the tank fire had destroyed. Buma Shavit accompanied me to the field, serving in reserve duty as the commander of the unit responsible for activating forward air bases. They began to work on the communications and lighting systems. The construction unit began to fill the craters on the runways. Three and a half hours later, the Nachshon airfield received its first aircraft, an Israeli Nesher that had been hit by antiaircraft fire and had been forced to land at the newest Israeli airfield.

Yuval Efrat, commander of the helicopter squadron, softly landed his CH-53 near the bunker-turned-hospital. The helicopter was loaded to capacity with wounded. The doctor in charge was near tears. He asked Yuval how many more wounded he could possibly fit in.

"Four," Yuval said, exactly the number of severely wounded he had been told to pick up at the "Sweet Tooth" outpost when he took off from Nachshon an hour earlier. For their sake, he had removed four less severely wounded troops from the helicopter at the last minute. The doctor burst into tears. Yuval also felt his heart breaking. He had been evacuating wounded for the past day and night, with barely a minute's rest. The transport of the hundreds of paratroopers who had recaptured

Mount Hermon from the Syrians the day before, in a series of packed CH-53 flights, seemed incredibly simple compared to this.

The Nachshon field hospital was overflowing with wounded from the battles at the Israeli penetration beyond the canal and from the frequent Egyptian shellings. Many Israeli troops were wounded by the artillery before they had even managed to cross the canal. It was a dark and foggy night when Yuval was scrambled to Nachshon. He flew low, never rising above four hundred feet. If he had not been heard on the communications frequencies, they would have sent out a rescue force to find him. But when he landed, much later than planned, everyone understood the reason for his delay. On the medical frequency, Yuval had heard the cries of the wounded units along the route leading to the bridges. Ignoring the weather, he had descended to pick up those who had been hit by the Egyptian artillery. Thus he moved from unit to unit, following the makeshift lighting along the ground, landing and taking off at great risk.

After bringing the wounded to Nachshon, Yuval picked up those who were in the most urgent need of treatment in Israel. The thick blanket of fog that hung over the base limited visibility to several meters. With calm determination, and ignoring both Buma's and my trepidation, Yuval took off vertically, straight into the pitch darkness of the night and the threat of missiles. In this instrument flight, he could easily err in his navigation. After a minute or two, we heard his voice, which eased our nervousness. The fog was hugging the ground and reached up to only two hundred feet. Yuval could safely continue on to "Sweet Tooth" to pick up the other four wounded. The doctor's tears greeted him. Yes, he had requested four places, but the number of severely wounded was much greater. The doctor was having trouble determining a priority order for their evacuation. He had dozens of wounded from the shelling. Yuval ordered the medics to ignore the standing order that limited the number of wounded in the CH-53 to twenty-two. When he landed at Refidim, the hospital personnel could not believe that he had squeezed so many wounded into one helicopter. Yuval slept an hour or two and then set out with the squadron's helicopters for another round, until they no longer heard the calls for evacuation on the communications network.

The IAF's air train to Nachshon was flying day and night. Every transport aircraft in reserves was called up, from the new Hughes C-130

Hercules to the ancient Dakotas. They would unload their contents on the runways, often while taxiing slowly so that they would not have to stop. They transported everything from food and fuel to weapons and clothing. Antitank missiles and artillery shells arrived straight from the United States after a short stopover in Lod. USAF Galaxy aircraft were now being called up for an air train to match that of the Soviets, who were resupplying Egypt and Syria. IAF aircraft accompanied the Americans along the last stretch of their flight before Lod.

Before breakfast, a Dakota landed at Nachshon and unloaded a strange cargo. It was a group of men dressed in casual clothes and safari outfits, somewhat uncomfortable at their landing in a battlefield rather than at a plush airfield in Israel's center. Benny Peled requested that I host this group of international journalists in "IAF style." I was told to make sure that they saw with their own eyes how extensive the Israeli presence in Egypt was, and who was really winning the war. For two weeks, no one had believed the announcements of the Israeli military spokesman.

After a tour along the bridges over the canal and through the units and command centers, the reporters returned convinced that the IDF was truly spread out and well established on the road to Cairo. However, during lunch at the "Faid Hilton," as we called the relatively comfortable residential quarters at Nachshon, it was clear that they were lacking a bit of "action" with which to color their stories.

"Colonel," one of the journalists said to me, "we've heard that there are tremendous daily dogfights here, and that many MiGs are shot down by your aircraft. Where and when does this take place?"

"In recent days, it has occurred just about at this time," I told him. "If you're willing to wait, I'm sure you won't miss our matinee."

The international press thought I was mocking them. I did not reveal that in the past three days, Nachshon had undergone three attacks from the air, all of which had been stopped before they could succeed. An hour earlier, IAF Mirages had chased away a formation of Libyan aircraft. But at that moment the IDF's reliability was affirmed. The air-raid sirens began to wail.

In the operations room, the flight controller informed me that a large number of enemy formations were organizing themselves to attack Nachshon and the forces around it. The base's personnel rushed to the shelters. I invited the press to the roof of the base headquarters. If we were attacked, we would be able to jump into a nearby underground cover.

A quartet of Mirages thundered over the base at low altitude and gathered speed as it climbed to ten thousand feet, where the shining pinpoints of the enemy aircraft, mostly MiG-21s, were approaching. I watched through my telescope and explained to the journalists that a dogfight was developing between an Israeli quartet and twelve MiGs. Another quartet of Mirages was on its way. The reporters, mostly high-ranking reserve officers in foreign militaries, grew as excited as spectators at a basketball game. In order to add sound to the sights that were unraveling before them, I ordered the flight supervisor in the control tower to connect the communications frequency to a loudspeaker. On the speaker, we could hear Guri determined to join the battle. "We are not leaving the frequency. We are going to battle!"

He requested data and received no response. Looking toward the Great Bitter Lake, he found the battleground. We saw Guri let his drop tanks fall and enter the combat, ignoring the flight controller.

The reporters on the roof could understand only part of what was taking place around them. They saw one pilot parachute, and then another, and knew that a rapid battle between four thousand feet and ten thousand feet was taking place above them. A MiG attempted strafing bursts, and a Mirage closed in from behind and shot it down.

What we were witnessing was Guri's fight, described earlier. We saw him down three enemy aircraft. Twenty aircraft participated in this massive battle—eight against twelve. Seven MiGs were shot down, and not a single Mirage. The journalists were excited, for it was not every day that they were able to witness such a dogfight from the ground.

But the special prize still awaited them. I took them to meet the two Egyptian pilots who had parachuted, and who had now been brought to Faid by helicopter for treatment. One was large and dark, and had been wounded in his foot. The second, a short, chubby man, was nervous and tended to shout. They both spoke good English.

"Why were you shot down?"

"There were more Israelis than us. Everywhere we looked, we saw only Israeli Mirages." The pudgy pilot took on the role of spokesman as the other sank into self-pity.

"Are you aware of the fact that the IDF is in Egypt?"

"Lies. We weren't even shot down over Egypt. For two weeks we have been flying deep into the Sinai."

I took him to the roof and showed him the location of the sun. Having convinced him that he was looking east, I gave him the telescope and pointed toward the Great Bitter Lake.

"If we are in the Sinai, could you please explain to me what that large lake is, and what those boats anchored there are?"

The pilot lost his confidence and fell silent.

An American journalist commented to one of his companions, "The Israelis are back to winning, and the Arabs are back to believing their own lies."

An hour later the journalists were on their way back to Tel Aviv in a Hercules, along with a respectable group of Egyptian POWs, including high-ranking officers and pilots. The reporters wanted to meet the Israeli pilot who had shot down three MiGs in front of their eyes. Guri, however, was far from there, for he was on his way back to his home base in the center of the country. His base commander contacted him on the communications frequency.

"How many did you shoot down?" Amos Lapidot asked.

"Seven," Guri answered. "I got three. Cheech got two. Avik and Sari each got one."

"Nice, but no cigar," Lapidot said. "Goni and Barry's quartet, which was with you, also shot down seven."

Fourteen aircraft in one battle, Guri thought to himself. Not bad at all. His personal tally in this war rose to twelve. It did not seem that any other pilot would manage to take this top position from him.

"By the way," his commander said, interrupting Guri's thoughts, "in two hours the cease-fire takes effect. The war is over. Over and out."

Benny Peled would have preferred to forget the first four days of the war. He was convinced that it was a bad set of coincidences that had tied the hands of the IAF, and that circumstances had forced it to function other than it should have from the outset. The IAF returned to form only on the fifth day. Until then, the commander-in-chief believed, they had been victims of the faulty decision of the Prime Minister and the Minister of Defense.

In a conference of high-ranking officers, Peled stated that the government's ministers did not comprehend the importance of the preemptive strike that the IAF had wanted to execute as the opening step of the war. The lack of approval, despite the support of the IDF chief of staff, had led to the tremendous gap between the expectations and the reality. There is a large difference between an initiating air force and one that merely responds to the enemy's moves. As a result of the cancellation of the preemptive strike, the IAF's aircraft found themselves immersed in preventing the assaults of the Egyptians and the Syrians.

No official information is available regarding the number of aircraft in the IAF's possession at the war's outset. Accepted estimates by foreign military research institutes spoke of approximately five hundred aircraft. According to statistics published by the American journal *Aviation Week* in December 1973, the IAF lost 114 aircraft in the Yom Kippur War. Sixty aircrew were killed. Ground-to-air missiles or antiaircraft fire downed 109 aircraft. Only six were shot down in the war's 117 dogfights. The aircraft downed were thirty-five Phantoms, fifty-five Skyhawks, twelve Mirages, six Super Mystères, and six helicopters of various types. According to *Aviation Week*, the IAF lost eighteen percent of its total force, indicating that it had 660 aircraft at the war's outset. The American air train supplemented this force toward the end of war, adding another forty Phantoms and forty-three Skyhawks. Approximately half of the aircraft (fifty-four) and half of the aircrew (thirty-one) were shot down during the first four days of the war, primarily by missiles or antiaircraft fire. This was the most painful blow for the commander-in-chief and the IAF's greatest problem during the war. It had been unable to eliminate the threat from the ground as the opening step of the conflict, as had been done that first morning of the Six-Day War. This type of destruction was impossible during the Yom Kippur War, in which the Arab aircraft were protected in underground hangars. Also, in front of the airfields were walls of missiles and antiaircraft batteries. In retrospect, IAF commanders admitted that the force was unprepared to handle the threat and to destroy it with the speed and efficiency that had characterized Operation Moked in 1967.

On highest alert possible, the Egyptian and Syrian armies were well prepared for the conflict on the eve of the Yom Kippur War. Any attack on the missile systems would have cost the IAF dearly. A surprise action under such conditions would clearly have had only a marginal affect. The missile networks were designed for rapid response, as opposed to grounded aircraft incapable of quick reaction in response to a surprise air attack. At the war's outset, the Egyptians had fifty missile batteries, and toward its conclusion they had seventy. The Syrians had thirty-one batteries near the end of the war. The types of missiles were known, but all their secrets were not. Though some technological and tactical lessons had been learned from the confrontations of the War of Attrition, any Israeli attack using the full potential of the available means would have led to tremendous losses and no gain. The missile networks, as had been proven during the second day of the war, had astounding survivability and recovery capabilities. Batteries that were damaged or even destroyed were quickly rehabilitated. From all Israeli actions until the end of the war, only forty-three Egyptian batteries and eight Syrian ones were taken out of commission, most from air attacks and several through ground attacks. This survivability should not have surprised the IAF, for it had encountered the same phenomenon during the War of Attrition. What, therefore, was the source of the self-confidence that the commanders of the IAF displayed prior to the war, when they claimed the ability to destroy the missiles?

Here as well, in their retrospective wisdom, IAF commanders admitted in debriefings and closed inner-circle meetings that the estimations regarding their response capabilities were unrealistic. The turnabout came too late. In opposition to this stands the claim of Avihu Ben-Nun and the other young officers that the missile networks could have been completely demolished from the air if the IAF had mobilized all its attack and airborne capabilities in waves over the course of two days. Instead of such an action, the upper echelons of the IAF were frightened, and hesitated because of the losses and poor results of the operation on the second day of the war. Ben-Nun's claim was not tested adequately, for the attack aircraft were busy preventing the invasion. From the perspective of the IAF, it was not allowed to act according to its own considerations. The IDF, on the other hand, felt that the prevention of the invasion had top priority. With the recovery capabilities of the missile networks well known, no one would wager on how quickly the results of the IAF's efforts would be nullified.

Prior to the Yom Kippur War, when the glorious feeling of invulnerability reigned in Israel, everything looked different. The IAF's certainty that the missiles were within its reach was somewhat a result of the hope (and the misimpression) that the precedent of the Six-Day War would be repeated in the next war—in other words, that the IAF would begin with the same advantage of landing the first strike and would be able to focus on its primary purpose, the elimination of the threat of enemy air superiority. However, the political elements bound the hands of the IAF and ultimately did not grant it the priority it had sought. At first the IAF was prevented from executing the preemptive strike. After the invasion, it had to provide support in blocking the enemy forces, and absorbed heavy damages from antiaircraft fire.

The IAF's level of alert on the morning the war began was incomparably higher than that of the ground forces, primarily because the IAF was not dependent on mobilization of reserve forces. According to Israel's defense strategies, the IAF's purpose is to provide cover in the event of a surprise attack. In the Yom Kippur War, it executed that mission as well as it could. Deputy IDF Chief of Staff Israel Tal stated that the IAF performed as it was expected to, providing maximum operational flexibility when the circumstances of the outbreak of the war had destroyed its sense of equilibrium, just as had happened to the IDF. Since the secret of strategic power clearly lies in second-strike capabilities, the IAF managed to recover from this first blow and move on to victory.

On the other hand, the course of events does not side completely with Moti Hod's criticisms that the root of the problem during the first days of the war lay in the decision of the political element not to permit a preemptive strike. The chief of staff and the commander-in-chief agreed on the eve of the war to a limited attack against the Syrian missile network. This plan was ultimately canceled, not because of a governmental decision, but rather because of poor weather conditions. The optional plan for the attack of the Syrian airfields would not have led to a significant deterrence of the armored invasion, just as it did not, several days later, manage to upset the taking off of enemy planes from the attacked airfields. In any case, the plan did not include the Egyptian front at all.

Even if the desired priority had been granted, it became clear on the eve of the war that the plans for the preemptive destruction of the missile systems were flawed. There was not enough updated intelligence information regarding the movement and location of the mobile and sophisticated SA-6 batteries. The batteries could be camouflaged by shutting down their radar systems, and could home in on aircraft using optical systems. When the pilots set out to attack them, the missile batteries were not always where they were expected to be. Even when they were found and attacked, it seemed that tactics could not always serve as a viable substitute for missing technology. Only a tight-knit synthesis of the two can provide the full answer to the problem.

After some time, the pilots learned to live with the missiles, and the rate of losses decreased. Part of this was thanks to two American Jewish pilots who volunteered for the IAF, providing a great deal from their experience in the Vietnam War and their dozens of Phantom sorties against the Soviet missiles. They taught their new compatriots how to take full advantage of the responses and limitations of the SA-2s and SA-3s in order to avoid them if they were detected with enough advance warning. The lessons of the American pilots and their tricks developed during the War of Attrition were forgotten for some reason during the first stage of the Yom Kippur War. To this day, no comprehensive solution has been found for dealing with the missile batteries.

In all, the missiles caused less damage to the IAF than they did to the USAF in Vietnam. The number of missiles fired was also lower. In the Yom Kippur War, the Egyptians fired approximately one thousand missiles. Though there is no verified number of missiles fired by the Syrians, it is estimated that the quantity was in the hundreds. Most of them missed. Anyone seeking comfort in statistics could be relieved by the fact that fewer than one in ten found its mark.

In the nineteen days of war, the IAF flew 11,223 sorties. Thousands of these were in support of the ground forces. A total of 117 dogfights were fought (as opposed to 60 during the Six-Day War and 97 during the War of Attrition) involving 456 aircraft, often more than once. Many of these were long, massive, and difficult battles in which the new element of close contact with short-range firing was encountered.

Egypt and Syria began the war with 1,040 aircraft and lost 450. The ratio of forces in dogfights was always against the IAF, one and a half to two times. Nonetheless, the ratio of downed aircraft was 18.4:1 in the IAF's favor. While 277 Egyptian and Syrian aircraft were shot down in dogfights during the war (173 others were downed by Hawk missiles and IAF antiaircraft guns), Israel lost only 15 aircraft in air combat, 6 of which were shot down by enemy aircraft and the rest by support fire from the ground. The IAF fought against familiar aircraft, MiG-17s, MiG-21s, Sohoi SU-7s, and Sohoi SU-20s. The American aircraft flown by the IAF allowed for a technological advantage that was enhanced by improvements made in the aircrafts' electronics.

The IAF's air superiority in the dogfights owed much to the EAF's conservativism. Its success was achieved despite the daring exhibited by the Syrian pilots. The Egyptians maintained tight formations and did not enter every encounter. The Syrians, however, surprised the Israeli pilots more than once by entering dangerous situations with effective fire. The Israelis' qualitative advantage was maintained not only in the level of flexibility, but also in its cunning and bravery. The Israelis won many battles or hit their targets because of their ability to move beyond combat procedure or the set plan. The maps were read more quickly and correctly by the pilots over the actual territory than by the flight controllers or the commanders in Central Command. Often without requesting permission, the pilots maneuvered and reached their targets.

Had it not been for the missile problem, Israeli air superiority would have been unchallenged. But by maintaining its superiority against the Egyptian and Syrian aircraft, the IAF executed its primary mission, to provide cover for the mobilization of the reserve forces and to maintain clean skies. No military or civilian targets deep in Israel were attacked from the air, even during the confusion of the first days. Even though the IAF could not guarantee clean skies along the front as well, it did block the Syrian invasion of the Golan Heights. A correct evaluation of the IAF's contribution to the war effort must compensate for the psychological dimension that developed as a result of the 1967 war. There remained an expectation of a speedy and awe-inspiring victory of the kind that the Six-Day War had produced. The level of disappointment was inversely proportional to the level of expectation. It was not only because of the missiles that the IAF played a relatively marginal role in this war. The one great victory of the Six-Day War was more impressive than the dozens of smaller achievements in the Yom Kippur War, even if the IAF did eventually threaten the entry to Cairo and Damascus at its conclusion.

# 8 The Second Generation

*T*he Yom Kippur War burst into the lives of the Israeli POWs sitting in Egyptian prisons as they were watching "Flipper" on television. Their captors at the Abbasia jail entered the joint cell holding the six pilots and navigators captured during the War of Attrition, confiscated their television set, and dispersed them to separate cells. The isolation did not prevent the leakage of information. The fears that took hold for a day or two turned to controlled joy when they learned of the war. This news was their first glimmer of hope in the two and a half years since Egypt's president had sentenced them to life imprisonment with no chance for pardon, as his revenge for the IAF bombings deep in Egyptian territory.

A day earlier, the pilots had been deep in their seemingly endless depression, feeling defeated and degraded. There were moments when they envied the Israeli ground troops in the nearby cells, for they thought that the shift from liberty to imprisonment must have been much less drastic for them. For the aircrews, the world collapsed in a split second. A direct hit meant a quick and sure disaster. Such an event was not described in training, and they were not prepared for it. Having convinced themselves that it would not happen to *them*, they had sublimated any conscious sense of the danger. If uninjured, a pilot was trained to return his aircraft home if it was even partially functional. At the very least, they should distance it from enemy territory. They would abandon the aircraft only upon complete loss of control. This act would not be condemned, for there is no bravery in suicide. Being captured under such conditions never entails a loss of prestige or respect. Returning POWs generally receive a hero's welcome.

The glory of the return, however, does not soften the shock of abandoning the plane. Imprisoned pilots are often overwrought with feelings of guilt over losing their precious aircraft. The numbered seconds after the ejection seat is activated, in which their lives hang by a parachute between sky and earth, are the few moments a pilot has to make this drastic shift. Once he is imprisoned, the supersonic speed of the open skies is reduced to the stagnation of foul dungeons. After June 1967, the Egyptian and Syrian captors and interrogators loved to abuse and degrade the pilots, much beyond the intelligence needs. Their blows were apparently meant to shatter the monstrous myth that had developed regarding the omnipotent air force. The prisoner felt, in those first days of physical and emotional weakness, that he was not a traitor. The questions asked of him gave the impression that the enemy's knowledge of the IAF and his squadron in particular was much greater than he had imagined. The script was a patchwork of unclassified information and crumbs gathered at other interrogations. The interrogators covered for what they did not know by pretending and by assuming that the prisoner was in too much shock to differentiate between truth and trickery.

If the prisoner swallowed the bait, he became entangled and would rebuke himself for the information he let slip. The following day he would try to atone by telling new stories to confuse or contradict the others he divulged. This would cause him to lose his equilibrium. Weeks of physical and psychological torture followed, including murderous blows using wooden and rubber sticks. Prisoners were often beaten to unconsciousness. Captors would also strike at a prisoner with blows to his ears, cigarette burns on his body, electric shocks, and the pulling out of fingernails. Days of hunger in the freezing or broiling dungeons, with hands tied, would add greater agony to the wounds. The imprisonment exercises they had undergone in survival training helped them to know what to expect, but did little to ease their extreme pain.

Rami Harpaz, a kibbutznik who had been part of the team that received the first Phantoms, did not play the role of the silent hero. He decided to talk so as not to anger his interrogator. He saw no reason to protest and endanger his life, or to wallow in self-pity. His problem was to survive without seeing himself as a traitor. He chose to tell of the older French aircraft. The Egyptians were not stupid and wanted to know about the Phantoms. He refused to answer, and the inquisition began with blows to his back that almost shattered his spine. They beat on his tailbone, sending shocks through his body. The torture continued periodically for several weeks and then months. Between interrogations, he was thrown unconscious into a cell, blindfolded, his hands and feet bound.

He was tied for hours to a high window with his hands bound behind his back. Rami constantly hovered on the edge of suicide. He would often return to consciousness under a steaming tin roof where he would have to lick mop water from the floors or lap up filth from the garbage cans on his way to the interrogation.

In research that took seventeen years to complete, and was finally published under the title *Other Than Birds*, psychologist Amia Lieblich recalls how Harpaz mentioned that he received only "dry blows." Torture, to him, was the one-time effort to frighten him by waving a kitchen knife in his face as if they were going to chop off his leg. In retrospect and from a distanced perspective, Harpaz can also speak highly of his "beaters," as he called them, who preserved his human pride. They did not strip him naked, but always left him in his underwear. They did their work silently, without curses and screams, and they made sure not to injure his genitals. In all, "they acted like soldiers doing their job." This level of forgiveness was a function of his reasonable and rational stance, which, to his interrogators, bespoke bravery. They reciprocated to the extent that the rules of the game would permit. Though he spoke less than other prisoners did, the torture did not go beyond blows to his body.

After the interrogations were over, the prisoners were placed in a joint cell and allowed to recuperate. They developed a communal life, as on a kibbutz, with a committee that deliberated every large and small issue. There was even a vote on the naming of a cat they adopted. Because of the strength of his personality, Harpaz became the leader of the "squadron." Wounds began to heal in the cell. Though each of them tried in his own way to rebuild his self-image, no group dynamic really developed. The horrors of the interrogation and pains that had been pushed aside were not revealed. Yitzhak Pear would later tell Amia Lieblich that they were all ashamed of what had happened to them during the interrogations, and therefore maintained their silence.

With a television and a record player in their cell, and trips to the pyramids, the prisoners in Egypt had a more pleasant life than that of their compatriots in Syria. The relative security in which they were living distanced their release. Yitzhak Rabin, then Israeli ambassador to the United States, hinted to the families that they should prepare for dozens of years of separation. The IDF exchanged five heads of the Syrian General Command who had been kidnapped along the Lebanese border for four Israeli prisoners. The Yom Kippur War added another twenty-four pilots and navigators in both Egypt and Syria to the six who remained in the Egyptian jails. After the war, prisoner exchanges occurred more often, primarily with Egypt, because of the large number of high-ranking Egyptian officers who were captured along the front. The exchange began one month after the war, and was completed half a year later.

Almost all the prisoners resumed service in the IAF shortly after their return to Israel. They wanted to forget the "black hole" from which they had emerged, and downplayed the hero's fame that they received upon their return. Gabi Gerzon, who returned without a foot, was determined to fly again, and did so. His model was Douglas Bader, the British hero of the Second World War.

Yigal Shochat was one of the first Israelis to fly a Phantom. After a missile ripped through his plane, he found himself floating down in his parachute over the Egyptian Delta. Shortly after he hit the ground uninjured, a mob attacked and almost lynched him. The riot concluded with a truck intentionally running over his foot. He sat in the jail for weeks, and his foot would not mend. He returned to Israel after it was amputated. The entire country was filled with sorrow when a photograph appeared in the newspapers of Prime Minister Golda Meir welcoming him on his stretcher. After recovering, he began to hobble around on crutches. Though he improved, his family life fell apart.

It was during this period that I first met him. We worked together for several months in the Operations Division of IAF headquarters. We were able to use every Phantom pilot after the War of Attrition to learn lessons from the combat and to prepare for the next war. Yigal joined the division in order to actualize his potential and to try to return to a normal life. After hearing of his troubles, I decided that nothing would be better for his rehabilitation than to fly again. My personal example was my French instructor, who had lost a leg in the Algeria operations and was an excellent helicopter instructor.

One morning, after working together in the underground headquarters of the General Command, we drove to the nearby airfield at Sde Dov. I did not tell Yigal my plan. I had requested that an Allouette helicopter, a small jet-engined vehicle flown by the light squadron, be prepared. We climbed into the helicopter and I started it up as Yigal found a comfortable position for his prosthetic leg on the steering mechanisms. After an hour, he was flying the helicopter with complete confidence. The next flight was more organized, with theory studies before takeoff. Yigal made progress and began to enjoy himself. All that remained for him to learn before his solo flight was to execute an autorotation and a helicopter's emergency landing. Helicopters can be flown for a distance without engines, for the glide maintains the rotors' motion and allows for safe flight. After completing his solo and proving himself before the IAF's chief doctor and commanders, Yigal was a happy man. To this day, he is one of the IAF's helicopter pilots. He also completed his medical studies and went on to command the IAF's medical unit.

The release of the thirty POWs from the War of Attrition and the Yom Kippur War was of primary concern to Benny Peled. He recalled how he had been miraculously saved from capture during the Sinai Campaign, when he played hide-and-seek with the Egyptian patrol until the Piper came and rescued him. There had never been so many Israelis, let alone pilots, in enemy prisons after a war. During the Sinai Campaign, only one pilot had been taken prisoner. Only five had been captured during the Six-Day War. The commander-in-chief invested tremendous effort in securing their release. He felt as if he were sitting with them in the cells.

The number of prisoners only increased the feeling of disgrace and degradation. The IDF and particularly the IAF, which had not repeated the swift victory of Operation Moked, had disappointed in the war. There were mutual accusations within the military and between the military and the government. The people of Israel blamed both. A small strip of the Sinai remained in Egyptian hands, and the IDF had managed to capture significant areas in both Egypt and Syria. Cairo and Damascus were now only a short ride away, or within artillery range. Three Egyptian battalions were surrounded in the Sinai, and the IDF sat on both banks of the Suez Canal. At the 101-kilometer mark on the Suez-Cairo road, the first talks over the division of forces between Israel and Egypt began. The United States collected its repayment for the military support it had provided during the first weak days of the war by coercing a diplomatic settlement.

Even the IAF was caught in the mistaken idea, which had grown out of the victory of the Six-Day War, that Israel possessed an invincible military. In the squadrons and command centers, they admitted that they had not realized the expectations. The accounting and evaluation continued for weeks and months. This time, unlike 1967, the self-condemnation was merited. Numerous investigations and evaluations did not eliminate the deep pain of the war. Two core aspects of the IAF had been lost. It had not served as the preventive force before the war, and had not emerged feeling itself the victor. The false impression that the IAF had a response to the missiles was shattered, and the supply of aircraft was quickly diminished by antiaircraft fire.

Benny Peled set out to reorganize the IAF. The shock of the war would enable him to shorten the process, which he had begun to plan before the war began. David Ivri was his right-hand man in both thought and execution. He was responsible for evaluating the lessons of the war. They were to investigate why the IAF had lost 105 aircraft, nearly a third of its force. How had the expectation of a powerful victory turned into a bloodletting that had led to numerous casualties and POWs? There had been many achievements, but any sense of victory was impossible. In the Six-Day War the IAF had also paid a high price, but its rate of loss was still low relative to the number of sorties flown. The relative price was of no comfort in light of the hard numbers, which caused tremendous pain. The data was not easy to digest, particularly considering that among the dead and wounded were a number of personnel who had been expected to climb the various ladders of command. The void created by the war demanded the creation of a new and relatively large tier of commanders.

As in 1967, most of the losses had occurred in the opening stages of the war, when missiles and antiaircraft fire dominated, diplomacy was limited, bad weather conditions prevailed, and the unexpected alliance between both fronts stole the opening initiative from the IAF. The IAF was disappointed that it had not been allowed to execute its plans. The ground forces were disappointed no less by the fact that they had not received the air support they anticipated. As the ground forces secretly eulogized the upper hand of the IAF, they began to hope that they would be able to gnaw away at its tremendous budgets.

The first lesson learned was that in order to minimize the damages of a surprise attack, even on several fronts simultaneously, the IAF could not rely on the initiative of opening air force operations. It had to be prepared for any combative event possible, and to expect the worst of all combinations. It was no longer possible to rely on enormous operations that were dependent on countless elements, from weather to governmental decisions, or to count on plans that depicted an IAF able to respond within seconds. Support for these conclusions can be seen in the method of operations of the USAF and its allies during Operation Desert Storm in January 1991.

Though most of the IAF aircraft hit during the first days of the war were victims of antiaircraft fire, it seemed over time that the missiles were the source of the catastrophe. Finding a response to them overshadowed all other lessons learned during the war. The missile failure, as was proven during the debriefings, was not a problem but a syndrome. Problems arose when the IAF attempted to counter them with the sophisticated tactics of conventional air warfare. Even after the War of Attrition, they sought methods of tricking the batteries and the missiles using the aircraft's capabilities and the pilots' skills, altering attack altitude and angles at which they pulled, and reducing the amount of time spent over the battery during bombing. They even attempted to devise ways to avoid a missile once it had begun its chase. It was now clear, however, that bravery and trickery would not suffice.

The era of the innovative and daring pilot had come to a close. There could be no solution to the problem without intelligent weapons, electronic warfare, and equipment that would provide intelligence data in real time. Only a synthesis of these innovative weapons with the correct tactics could guarantee early detection, blocking, and diversion of the missiles, as well as their destruction. Technological thinking had begun during the days of the War of Attrition. Until the Phantoms were shot down in August 1970, the IAF had blindly trusted the electronic pods under the Phantoms' wings. Disappointment struck, and when the best of the IAF's pilots were killed or captured, no effort was made to determine whether they had received equipment for the missiles used in Vietnam, as opposed to the newer versions stationed along the canal. Instead of progressing with the proper machinery, they retreated into the familiar paradigms of tactical methodology. In the early 1970s, air-to-air missiles were still considered the "scaredy-cat's weapon." A hero was one who approached his opponent's tail to within cannon range. The easy part of educating the pilots to use the air-to-air missiles was teaching them new tactics of detection and firing. The difficult part was to find a substitute for the sense of personal bravery. The young pilots of the 1980s, only ten years after the Yom Kippur War, did not mind shooting down an enemy aircraft from a range of kilometers. In the unromantic mentality of the sophisticated systems, the bravado of the past succumbed to security concerns. However, in the summer of 1970, there were few prophets in the IAF. The unfinished war had been cut short, and everyone preferred a cease-fire to finding a solution to the missiles. Over the next three years, tremendous sums were invested by Israel's defense network in strengthening the fortifications along the canal. Technology was secondary. The IAF made do with weaponry existing in the world market. They ordered and received Shrike missiles to use against the SA-2 and SA-3 batteries, but did not find a way to overcome a battery after it had turned off its radar, on which the Shrike homed. No independent or thorough Israeli development of sophisticated armaments was undertaken. Research occurred at a crawl, under the belief that the cease-fire would continue forever. In Benny Peled's first five months as commander-in-chief until the start of the Yom Kippur War, it was difficult to change practices and beliefs that had developed over the past five years.

The IAF, which prided itself on always thinking one step ahead, found itself, at the critical stage, one step behind. At the moment when Israel's lag became evident, a push was given to close the gaps. The results could be seen even before the lessons of the war had been concluded and written down. One year after the war, the Shrike missiles were significantly renovated, and their capabilities improved. Extra pressures provided additional solutions that could have prevented aircraft from being shot down during the War of Attrition, if they had been thought of previously. Emphasis in research shifted to scientific development and advance procurement of the last word in electronic warfare, self-driven long-range missiles, linked tracking of mobile SA-6 and SA-9 missile batteries, and computers for flight control in complex electronic systems. The rules of this new arms race, after the disappointment of the Yom Kippur War and the decline of the IAF's image in the eyes of the ground forces, necessitated budgetary maneuvering. With the available resources, it was necessary to choose weapons that could inflict greater damage with fewer aircraft. Choosing the correct weapons for a target was also given more careful consideration. Before firing, the IAF would need accurate intelligence information to time the target for optimal destruction. They also needed a flight-control system that could pinpoint targets for the ground forces and control of the air force sent to the front.

The IAF functioned as the primary contractor and as a full partner with the ground forces. It received many compliments from the IDF for its activities. While air support of the ground forces had improved by the conclusion of the war, it had still fallen short of expectations. The ground forces' main lesson of the war had been the falseness of the promises of close air-to-ground support. Years of experience taught that the error was part of a deeply ingrained idea that no one had attempted to dispel, even after the appearance of the combat helicopter, which was designed for such support. When the forward control centers were constructed in 1973, Benny Peled treated their creation as an act meant to pacify the ground forces. At this time, the IAF had yet to comprehend fully the importance of the interdiction sorties flown in 1967, which had blocked the Egyptian armored columns in the Mitla Pass and the Jordanians on the road to Jerusalem. Benny used the confusion of the Yom Kippur War to illustrate how the destruction of the enemy's ground forces while on their way to battle must be a primary mission of the IAF. In his approach, the enemy's tanks were to be detected close to their exit base and destroyed before they could reach the battlefield. Detection and identification would be easier there, and would minimize the risk to Israeli forces.

The demands of the ground forces also strengthened his desire to be better equipped with updated intelligence reports regarding the movement of forces, both Israeli and enemy, and speeded up the internal evaluations that he planned to execute in IAF intelligence. The first step after the war was to establish an autonomous IAF branch responsible for ground intelligence. He had been disappointed by the IAF's dependency on the IDF's Intelligence Branch in the General Command. The support to the ground forces during the war had failed more than once because the intelligence that the IAF received had already grown old. By the time the aircraft had reached their targets, the picture on the ground had changed completely. Pilots sent to photograph the Egyptian crossing of the canal during the first two days of the war were furious at IAF headquarters for sending them out to bombing missions hours after the photos had been taken, thus limiting them to attacking only bridges. They claimed that they were missing their chance to affect crossing operation when the enemy troops were crowded at the entrances to the bridges. When they later bombed the bridges themselves, the structures were rebuilt within hours. Soldiers and tanks would not have recovered so quickly.

The pilots were unaware of the strange procedure that defined the IAF as the chief photographer for the IDF. The photographs had to be passed on to the IDF Intelligence Branch prior to any action. The IAF was not authorized to analyze the ground targets or to order attacks on them.

Benny saw the photographs of the crossing only during the third week of the war. This lesson led him to replace the commander of IAF intelligence and to grant budgetary preference to the radical development of the unit, including the establishment of a branch that would deal with ground intelligence. Amos Lapidot, the new commander of IAF intelligence, was considered a thorough officer whose steps were conservative. The mission would involve the long-term training of new professionals and the study of previously unknown subjects. Benny felt that the delay was not technical. Summoning Amos to investigate the matter, he discovered that the new commander was also serving the needs of the general intelligence community, and was not focused on the IAF. Amos claimed that the establishment of the ground intelligence branch in the IAF might cause a duplicity that would not be to their advantage in relations with the IDF Intelligence Branch. Benny was furious. "I don't want to hear another word about duplicity," he shouted. "Bring me the intelligence that I want, or you're out of here." Amos had been scolded, and Benny received the services he requested. Nine years later, Amos would become commander-in-chief of the IAF.

David Ivri was much tougher as he executed Peled's reorganization of IAF headquarters. Commanding the IAF's top unit, the Air Group, he disagreed with his commander's insistence that the operation planning and control units be separate. The reason for this change was pilots' criticism during the war and in the debriefings that analyzed the IAF faulty planning. Yiftah Spector, the commander of a Phantom squadron during the war, explained that the lesson he learned in the war was that "the planner is your greatest enemy. Everything he plans is exactly what you must not do." This was how he acted in his squadron. He concluded the war with fewer injuries than the other squadrons sustained.

Benny and Ivri had differing explanations of this criticism. Benny thought the planner would work better if isolated and freed from pressures. Ivri claimed that the planner was the pilot's best friend, since he was familiar with past operations, lived the lessons of the analyses of these events, and was able to correct their errors by extrapolating into the future. Ivri had learned from the War of Attrition that only the planner could order a change of direction or innovate tricks if problems in the territory called into question aspects of the original plan. He explained that managing air combat since the War of Attrition had been an art and a synthesis of changing variables, emotions, and intuitions. One man must have his controlling finger on the pulse, closely and constantly, in order to respond to unexpected situations. More than once, late in the War of Attrition, original flight routes for the attacks on the missile batteries were altered when less dangerous "holes" for penetration were discovered. Benny recalled how, as commander, during the Yom Kippur War he had had to hold back Avihu Ben-Nun, the planner and commander of the Attack Planning Section of the IAF, who was applying the pressure to execute a massive assault on the missile systems with a large force. He had assumed that after the heavy losses of the first days, the additional price would be worth the result. The issue was complex and replete with problems. The debate ended in a tie. The commander-in-chief's opinion prevailed, as usual.

In analyzing the war's problems, they found it difficult to isolate the responsibility of the planner from the confused, erroneous, and misleading intelligence picture or from the problems in the communications networks. These difficulties led to the creation of a much-improved operational communications system. The IAF's new command post, which Benny began to plan and build, vastly improved air control. Modern and rapid communications systems replaced the slow and noisy teleprinters. The map tables in the war room, with their toy airplanes, and the charts, with their wax pencils, disappeared. In their place appeared monitors for the sensitive long-range radar networks and electronic displays of geography and meteorology, technical statistics and updated intelligence information from the advance warning systems, and sophisticated detection and identification systems. Thus a control center that allowed the commanders personal and ongoing contact on many levels was built. They now had contact with a maximum number of people, aircraft, and munitions as well as status reports on the near and distant fronts, all at the press of a button.

In February 1973, on the eve of Benny Peled's inauguration as commander-in-chief, a tragedy took place that emphasized the tremendous danger that lay in the clear division of responsibilities and authority within the IAF and between the IAF and the IDF. A Libyan passenger airliner on its way from Tripoli to Cairo crossed into closed military areas in the Sinai. A pair of Israeli Phantoms called for it to land at Refidim. The plane lowered its landing gear, but suddenly turned to escape. Moti Hod reported to the chief of staff. Dado gave permission to open fire. At that time, Palestinian terrorists were threatening to crash aircraft in suicide runs on Israeli targets. They suspected that this plane might be one of them. The Phantoms repeated the intercept procedures on the radio, and used hand signals as well. The Libyan aircraft did not respond. The pilots fired in front of its nose and toward the wings. The Libyan pilot attempted an emergency landing and crashed, killing 104 passengers and crew. An international uproar ensued. Benny, then Moti's deputy, was sent to Washington with the black box to prove that the airliner's pilot had ignored fifteen warnings over the course of a half hour, and had taken his reasons for this with him to the grave. Israel was saved from sanctions, but the commander-in-chief was viewed as solely responsible for the incident.

Benny did not forget that Dado's public expressions of regret over the downing of the Libyan airliner avoided taking responsibility for the order. Benny foresaw an increase in the war with the terror organizations, and met with the Minister of Defense to predetermine his range of authority in a more severe crisis. The IDF's weakness in fighting terrorism lay in the tremendous force it had built to overcome large standing armies. The terror strikes had the advantage of surprise if they were not thwarted by intelligence information or by swift military responses whose goals and limitations required prior knowledge. The commander-in-chief requested that the minister instruct him on what to do if terrorists, working under the guise of a civilian aircraft, attempted to execute a suicide dive on a city or a sensitive target in Israel. The problem was not so much when the intentions of the aircraft were clear as when there was a chance that the plane might also be carrying Swedish children to a vacation in Eilat. Minister of Defense Shimon Peres pondered the issue.

Benny requested that the instructions be given to him in writing. However, Ministers of Defense were not used to providing the IDF with set instructions that would provide a backup for its commanders' actions, regardless of the results. Benny postponed the test of responsibility with the governmental element almost a year and a half after he took com-

mand of the IAF. Such a conflict over responsibility and ultimate authority was destined to failure. The Yom Kippur War and the conclusions of
the Agranat Commission, which investigated the war's problems, reinforced his criticisms and suspicions. The commission placed the blame
on the chief of staff, the commander of the Intelligence Branch, and the
chief of the Southern Command. The Prime Minister and the Minister
of Defense were not implicated, because of the vagueness surronding IDF
laws. Dado resigned. In April 1974, after the conclusions were publicized, the entire government was forced to resign under public pressure.
Golda Meir left political life. Yitzhak Rabin became Prime Minister. He
chose Shimon Peres as his Minister of Defense. Mota Gur was appointed
chief of staff. The government never issued instructions on how to deal
with unusual cases of terrorism.

On Sunday, June 27, 1976, seven Palestinian terrorists hijacked an
Air France airliner with ninety-seven Jewish and Israeli passengers on
board. The flight was scheduled from Tel Aviv to Paris. The terrorists
boarded after its stopover in Athens. They landed the plane in Bengazi,
Libya. They then flew it to Entebbe, Uganda, where they demanded the
release of dozens of terrorists imprisoned in Israeli jails. The Israeli
government floundered, having no diplomatic response or plan. It did
not rush to use IDF solutions, and wasted precious days on useless
thought. Israel almost succumbed to the cries of the hostages' families.

On June 29 it was still unclear what Israel would do. Benny Peled
attended a meeting of the board of directors of El Al. Gidon Alrom, a
pilot and former commander in the IAF, asked him if it was possible to
get to Entebbe to rescue the hostages. Benny responded, "It is not
important whether we can or cannot. One thing is quite clear to me. If
we give in to the terrorists again, as we did in Algeria, and release
terrorists for hostages, I will resign. I truly did not intend to be commander-in-chief of the IAF after two such colossal cases of backing
down."

That night he was summoned to an urgent meeting with the chief of
staff. On his way there, Benny passed by the underground headquarters of
the Upper Command. They were already planning, and had summarized
on two pages, what it was possible to transport to Entebbe, and how.
Mota Gur opened the meeting with a wide grin. The Minister of Defense
has asked him about the operational possibilities. It's a ministerial ques-

tion, Benny thought to himself, and not a command to execute. Benny pulled out the papers and said that the IAF could fly up to 1,200 soldiers and their equipment to Entebbe in the twenty-one Hercules aircraft that had been purchased at the end of the Yom Kippur War and in eight Boeing 707s. They could be maintained for several days. The flight time was six hours. Refueling problems could be dealt with on the return trip. He outlined the solutions and recommended that they use four Hercules aircraft that would land the rescue force at the airfield and evacuate them with the hostages. The chief of staff laughed as if it were a good joke, and asked what the Navy had to propose. The commander-in-chief of the Navy said that if the naval commando unit was airdropped into Lake Victoria, it could assault the airfield, gather the hostages in a hotel on the shore, and call for UN intervention. He also proposed that the forces be flown to Nairobi and be transported to the Kenyan shores of Lake Victoria, from which they would go by boat to Uganda. The chief of staff listened and did not laugh. These ideas sounded rational to him.

The commanders then set out to the office of the Minister of Defense. Mota said that he had brought a solution, and proposed that Peres first listen to the IAF commander in chief, noting that in his opinion Benny's plan was deceptive, rash, and irresponsible. He stated that he did not support it, but felt it should be heard. Benny repeated his plan, and the chief of staff again expressed his doubts. The commander-in-chief of the Navy presented his plan. Peres did not decide. Benny chose to use the time to work on the plan. Along with Maj. Gen. Yekutiel "Kuti" Adam, the commander of the Operations Branch of the IDF, a plan was developed quietly. Kuti appointed Ehud Barak, who became IDF chief of staff in 1991, Muki Betzer, and Yoni Netanyahu, from an elite IDF unit, to work with particular officers from the Joint Operations Unit and from the transport network. There was almost no intelligence information.

Four days after the hijacking, the naval plans that the chief of staff had liked so much were examined. It became clear that the Navy lacked the equipment needed for the operation. A quiet check with Kenyan authorities proved, as expected, that they vehemently objected to an operation against Uganda setting out from their territory. At most, they would be willing to receive the hostages and wounded, if there were any, after the rescue. It was a small but vital gesture. In the meantime, Ehud and Ido's team completed the plan. Four Hercules aircraft would land at the airfield in complete surprise. One force squad would attack the old passenger terminal where the hostages were being held, and free them. Other forces would take control of the airfield and its environs. The aircraft would disperse, each to its specific area of action, and evacuate the hostages and the fighters immediately after completion of the operation. Two Boeing 707s would be added to the Herculeses. One would be for command and control, and the other would be an airborne hospital. The problem of refueling on the return trip remained unanswered. The possibilities included using the Ugandan fuel supplies at the airfield, refueling in midair, or landing in Kenya to refuel. Maintaining tight secrecy and abandoning every other mission, Benny and Kuti began to push Operation Thunderball forward.

On Friday morning, six days after the hijacking, the forces began to train on models chosen according to descriptions of the airfield and the passenger terminal that were gathered from the non-Jewish passengers who had been released over the course of the week and were now in Paris. Photographs and other intelligence information were gathered from a variety of other sources. The squadron trained at an airfield in the Sinai, near the sea. The rescue unit trained by executing assaults on a building resembling a hotel at another field. That evening Chief of Staff Mota Gur began to change his mind. Now he wanted to be in the picture and to observe the forces training on the models.

For Shani, the commander of the Hercules squadron, this was a difficult test. The flight itself was actually the easy part, even though it involved dangers that could ruin the operation. The approach route for landing was from the direction of the sea. The runway was difficult and completely dark. During the practice landing, Shani veered to one side of the runway, but at the last moment straightened out and landed well. Benny was not pleased, but trusted his crews. The conditions in Entebbe would be much easier. Mota, in the cockpit, had not noticed Shani's near mishap; he was not familiar with instrument flight.

After hearing the chief of staff's approval, Peres announced that he would recommend the operation to the government. On Saturday afternoon at 1500 hours, the forces set out to Sharm-al-Sheikh. A cancellation order could return them from there or even in midflight on their way to Uganda. The Hercules took off separately and quietly. Before getting on the plane, Amos Lapidot told Benny that the intelligence community had managed to get hold of updated photographs of the Entebbe airfield.

Benny wanted to show them to the pilots. However, Amos had passed them on to the IDF Intelligence Branch, which infuriated Benny. At the last moment the photographs were passed on to Yoni Netanyahu's fighters, who conveyed them to the pilots.

Shani recalls that on that Friday evening the commanders boarded the aircraft with the chief of staff to check them. They flew to the Sinai airfield and, over the course of two and a half hours, executed a number of runs on the target model in which they proved time and again, until everyone was convinced, that they could execute the landing as planned. On one of the runs, they placed the guests, commanders from all branches involved—ground, sea, and air—on the side as spectators so that they could check what could be seen and heard from the ground. The visitors were not able to detect the approaching aircraft, even though they knew all the stages of the arrival by heart. The complete surprise was the core of the plan; the responsibility for it rested on the pilots' skilled execution. There remained no more time for rehearsals. Many of the foreseen problems would have to be encountered and solved in the mission itself. On Saturday evening, a final pre-operation briefing was held. Outside, the Herculeses were being fueled. The Ofir airfield at Sharm-al-Sheikh was Israel's closest point to the distant target. Every drop of fuel was vital. All the participants, including fighters and pilots, were gathered in the dining hall and told the full script of the operation. The speaker was Dan Shomron, the chief infantry and paratrooper officer and the commander of the operation. Until that moment, the operation had been a secret well kept in a small circle.

Planning to arrive in Uganda near midnight, they had six hours of flight before them. The plan was to slip in between civilian aircraft landing at the Entebbe airport. The commander of the lead squadron would land first, with the fighters from Yoni's unit. They would disguise themselves as Idi Amin, the Ugandan leader, and his bodyguards, and would act as if he were paying a routine visit to the hostages. The Hercules would carry exact replicas of Amin's black Mercedes and the Land-Rovers that carried his entourage. Using this disguise, they planned to reach the old passenger terminal and to kill the terrorists and guards responsible for the hostages. Immediately afterward, the second Hercules would land with the paratrooper commandos, and the third with a commando squad from the Golani Brigade and their vehicles. Their job was to take control of the airfield, ground the aircraft of the

Ugandan Air Force, and block all avenues of approach for support forces that might arrive. The fourth Hercules would land last, carrying fuel tanks, pumps, and technical equipment. This equipment would be left behind as a gift to the Ugandans, for the entire belly of the aircraft would be used on the return trip by the hostages and the crew of the French aircraft, approximately one hundred passengers. This fourth Hercules would be the first to take off from Entebbe. The others would follow in reverse order from their landing. Thirty minutes after departure, they would meet at the Nairobi International Airport in Kenya to evacuate wounded, if there were any, and for repairs and refueling before the return to Israel.

The four-engined Hercules aircraft that the IAF had received at the end of the Yom Kippur War were precisely fit for this mission. Their tremendous carrying capacity of nearly one hundred fighters or twenty tons, their cruising speed of six hundred kilometers per hour, and their maximum range of four thousand kilometers with a full load or twice that when empty, were ideal. The aircraft could climb to an altitude of ten kilometers. From the moment the IAF acquired the aircraft, the transfer to its operation was not rapid, primarily for the reserve pilots. This was the first problem in planning Operation Thunderball, for there were few experienced pilots with a large number of flight hours on the Hercules. This operation, for which there was no precedent in the squadron, would demand the Hercules' all and much more than in routine flight. It was not easy to prepare the aircraft, the pilots, and the flight under conditions of such intense secrecy. It was necessary to demand the maximum, in the minimum number of hours, from a large number of personnel in operations, maintenance, meteorology, and intelligence, without informing them of what was taking place.

The flight itself was dangerous. Flying with full loads, the aircraft would reach a variety of altitudes, starting at sea level in the hundred-degree heat of the Israeli summer to the cold, thin air at 22,000 feet, above the mountains of Ethiopia. The air-pressure regulator would face an unprecedented test. The six or seven hours of tense flight without the automatic pilot because of the extreme conditions would make it a difficult night.

They took off on Saturday evening before sundown, to reach Entebbe by midnight. The Herculeses shook on takeoff because of the tremendous load on their wings. Turning wide and flat, they crossed into Saudi

Arabia, for they had no other option. At that point they increased speed to 250 knots, at which they were to continue all the way to Uganda, and dropped down to minimum altitude. The thunder of the propellers and the turboprop engines revealed the aircrafts' efforts.

Thirty minutes before landing, they woke everyone and began preparations. The fighters checked their gear. Over Ethiopia they entered a huge cumulonimbus stormcloud that reached to the northern end of Lake Victoria, exactly at their point of entry. Shani maneuvered his aircraft, and the others stayed closer to him than they would have in any other tight formation. If the formation collapsed, they could crash into each other in midair. Regrouping the formation in the dark of night at low altitude over the water could do severe damage to the timetables, and, more important, the heavy thunderstorm could cause them to lose the British civilian airliner that Shani and the others planned to follow in. They could already hear the British pilot on the radio, talking with the Entebbe control tower. He was descending to land.

They maintained radio silence and overcame the desire to utter a word, even to keep the formation. The cloud caused the aircraft to shake and made contact difficult to hold. Shani exited the cloud and entered an open formation as he followed the landing British plane. He stayed close to the airliner and took advantage of its noise and the support of the lights that were activated for it, and distracted the control tower from the "hitchhikers" who followed it in. He landed without problem and taxied to the edge of the airfield, where he waited for the others to land and take their positions on the ground.

In the meantime, the team disguised as Idi Amin and his guards, with the black Mercedes and the Land-Rovers, prepared for their devious parade. For much of the way they drove with their lights off, and then lit them with the full official pomp expected of a visit by the head of state. The Ugandan guards were fooled, and saluted the convoy as it turned toward the old passenger terminal. Everyone breathed easier. The final stage had begun, exactly on time and according to plan. The second aircraft, with the paratrooper commandos, landed on the lit runway. The runway lights suddenly went out, and the third and fourth aircraft had to struggle in the darkness and land using the emergency lights.

The Mercedes and the entourage approached the old terminal where the hostages were being held. Shani taxied his Hercules to the area of the new terminal. The forces that had arrived in the other aircraft dispersed to guard the field and the aircraft, which had not shut down their engines. A pair of Ugandan soldiers who stopped Yoni's convoy before the terminal requested identification, and Yoni's men killed them using pistols with silencers.

Suddenly a burst of gunfire was heard. One of the Israeli fighters had understood the elimination of the guards to be a sign to open fire. He fired his Kalashnikov at the Ugandan soldiers on the building. The surprise was gone. To the Israelis' good fortune, the terrorists responded slowly. Most of them were sleeping, and were awakened by the noise of the gunfire. The guards who were awake began to check who was firing and why.

The fighters wasted no time and burst into the passenger terminal in a wild run, while there was still no response to the fire from inside. In a short battle from room to room, they killed all the terrorists before they could harm the passengers. The hostages were shocked when they heard the loudspeaker voices in Hebrew, calling for them to lie on the ground. All of them obeyed except one, who began to run crazily. Thinking he was a terrorist, the Israeli force killed him. Two others nearby were injured.

All that remained now were the Ugandan soldiers on the roofs and around the terminal. Gunfire suddenly opened up from the control tower on the command group standing at the entrance to the terminal. Yoni was fatally hit in his neck. Another commander was shot in the back and paralyzed. The others responded with fire and destroyed the control-tower outpost. The paratrooper commandos assaulted the new terminal and wounded the few soldiers stationed there. They continued on to the MiG-21 aircraft stationed nearby. The operation was fast, and all resistance was elminated within minutes. The Golani commandos blocked the entry routes to the airfield from every access road. When they saw that nothing was coming, they turned to help evacuate the wounded to the Hercules carrying the medical crew. Others volunteered to march the dazed hostages to the other Hercules, which had already been emptied of its refueling equipment and had approached the passenger terminal.

As the passengers began to board, Amnon, the Hercules pilot, picked up the microphone and requested that they push forward and check their spouses, friends, and new acquaintances from the incident to make sure that everyone had boarded. The loading continued for twenty minutes and seemed as though it would never end. The hostages climbed on board groggily, with their clothes disheveled, but smiling. When the Hercules was loaded to maximum capacity, Amnon requested a precise count. Using the Air France passenger lists, they knew who should be present. The French captain, Michel Bacchus, who had not abandoned his responsibility for the passengers from the moment of the hijacking, and had refused, along with his crew, to be evacuated with the non-Jewish passengers, helped with the count. When the rear doors of the plane were shut, the Hercules took off over the dark lake. Once in the air, with Entebbe behind them, the code was transmitted indicating that the passengers were in the air, on their way home. Amnon invited Captain Bacchus to join him in the cockpit. "Let's finish together the flight you started," he said, and made room for him until the landing in Lod.

When the crews of the other aircraft saw Amnon's plane with the hostages take off and disappear, they felt relief. From that moment, only the fighters remained at the airfield. As planned, they congregated and departed the airfield in reverse order of their landing. Thirty minutes later they met in Kenya for their refueling stop in Nairobi. The airborne hospital in the Boeing 707, a faster plane than the Hercules, had already landed and waited to gather the wounded and evacuate them to Israeli hospitals.

The worries returned at 0300 hours. IDF radio quoted the story of the operation from a London BBC broadcast, and the aircraft still had to pass by Sudan, Egypt, and Saudi Arabia. However, after several more hours of tense but peaceful flight, they landed in Israel and were greeted by festivities at Lod. Crowds of relatives and fellow citizens broke down the barriers and crowded around the aircraft that had carried the hostages back to freedom.

The celebrations after Entebbe lasted two months. Because the public was not aware of the covert units that had participated in the operation, the transport squadron was the only element of the joint force that attracted waves of respect and love. Such glory had been forgotten since Operation Moked. In those celebrations of the summer of 1976, they did not realize that Operation Thunderball symbolized a turning point in the strategy of the Israeli-Arab conflict. The center of gravity was now shifting toward the war against terrorism. This change demanded new approaches, for the IDF was not designed for urban guerrilla warfare. The chases in the Jordan River Valley after 1967 had been merely an episode. There was no way to prevent the preparation of car bombs. The General Security Service (GSS) was responsible for dealing with terrorist organizations in the occupied territories. Terrorist leaders in Europe were eliminated after the Munich Olympics bloodshed by anonymous teams who devised ingenious traps. The foreign press attributed these activities to the Israeli Mossad. On the eve of the Yom Kippur War, these activities stopped when an innocent Moroccan waiter in Norway was killed by accident. The wave of violence began again after the war. Although the IAF could rescue Israeli hostages, it was not designed to combat the terror itself.

After 1973, the Arab standing armies and air forces received new aircraft from the Soviet Union and then from the west. As the MiG-23 and MiG-25 appeared in Syria, Egypt received its first Phantoms. These forces were being constructed according to the requirements of an all-encompassing war in the future. After 1967, the IAF would never again achieve air superiority by destroying the enemy's aircraft while still on the ground. Operation Moked was the end of World War II tactics. Its lessons were learned by all the world's air forces. Aircraft were now hidden in protected underground hangars, polished like laboratories, with fueling equipment, munitions supplies, maintenance garages, and residences for ground crews who worked in clean white coveralls. A number of them were buried in reinforced scramble positions at the runway's edge. These sophisticated defenses limited the attacks on airfields and returned the lost pride of the massive dogfights. The destruction of aircraft for the achievement of air superiority coincided with electronic warfare, radar stations, and airborne command and control centers. The ideal aircraft for the Middle Eastern air battlefield in the 1980s would have to excel in flight capabilities and air combat, and would have to include intelligence weapons and avionics systems. Aircraft production facilities in the United States and Great Britain competed to meet those needs in the early 1970s. Economic pressures within those countries sacked political embargoes and spurred weapons sales. A poor and ostracized client like Israel was now a target of the producers' forecasts. The IAF became an excellent marketing tool and model for imitation after 1973.

During the previous twenty years, the sources of vital arms had retreated, and the Israeli government had decided in the meantime not to rely solely on imports. It chose to develop local production of sophisticated aircraft, tanks, and naval vessels. Great Britain, which had turned its colors a number of times, promised to sell Israel an advanced version of the sophisticated Chieftain tank after tests in the Sinai. At the last moment, however, it canceled the deal. The French embargo after the Six-Day War was cruel and unfair from every moral or commercial vantage point. Shipments of the Mirage V were stopped, even though the producers had benefited from the lessons of Israel's wars. The transfer of a fleet of missile boats that were already constructed and paid for was also halted. In response to President de Gaulle's treatment, Israel deceived France. The missile boats were smuggled out of the port of Cherbourg.

Plans for the Mirage and the Atar 9C turbojet engine were sold to Israel by Alfred Frouenknecht, a forty-two-year-old Swiss military engineer who worked in the factory that produced Mirages for the Swiss Air Force. "It was an unfair act to abandon the Israelis," he would later tell his friends. He was apprehended and tried, and served three years in jail. Most of the $200,000 he had received for the plans was confiscated. The French had now received a double blow. They had lost their prestige to the Americans in the world of military flight as well as revenues from the Mirage, which now began to appear under an Israeli name. The development of an Israeli fighter-bomber had begun during Moti Hod's days and had made use of the American market, which had been opened with the procurement of the Skyhawks and the Phantoms, which were better than any advanced-model French aircraft. Israel Aircraft Industries chose to design a local mixture with a French-style body and an American-style motor. The secret was kept five years and was revealed on the eve of Israel's Independence Day in 1975, after the IAF received its first Kfir ("Young Lion"). The foreign press, which had hinted of this in years preceding, referred to it as the Nesher ("Eagle") or the Barak ("Lightning"), and did not understand that there were two models.

The Nesher was the Israeli Mirage, almost identical to the newest model that had been withheld by France. It was produced according to the drawings received from Frouenknecht, in addition to parts that continued to arrive from France through a third party. These parts also allowed Israel to maintain the Mirages already in the IAF's possession. The Nesher was superior to the Mirages in attack capabilities against surface targets, and had additional armament and an increased fuel capacity that extended its flight range. None of these additions detracted from its original advantages as an intercept aircraft carrying air-to-air missiles. Its inefficient radar was replaced with a telemeter, which is an accurate range meter for the gunsights. The Nesher attacked and shot down many aircraft during the Yom Kippur War, but primarily proved to IAI that it could produce a locally built aircraft.

The first model of the Kfir was designed according to the silhouette of the Mirage, with changes necessitated by the changing of the engine. Instead of the French Atar, which was a constant headache to the pilots and maintenance technicians, the Phantom's J-79 engine was installed, a strong and reliable engine produced by General Electric. Thus IAI thought to produce a functional and relatively cheap aircraft— approximately $3.5 million apiece, about half the price of the Phantom in the early 1970s. However, the production of the first model was delayed and did not meet expectations.

After his maiden flight, Herzle Bodinger, who had experience in the Vautour, Mirage, Nesher, and Phantom, thought that the mountain had produced a molehill. The first model of the Kfir was presented to the IAF in 1975, and was an achievement for local production. However, its capabilities were no leap forward relative to what already existed in the IAF, or compared to the American F-15 and F-16, which were already being used by the United States and several other countries. Though it carried more munitions, Herzle and his squadron mates who received the Kfir found that it was inferior to the Nesher and the old Mirage 3C in air combat. The Nesher consumed more fuel, and was heavy and difficult to maneuver because of its body, which was long and thick relative to its wings. The American engine was short compared to the French Atar, and the addition of the radar systems, navigation computers, and weapons-control systems in the nose led to the shifting of its center of gravity forward, tilting the nose downward. Herzle felt a definite decrease in maneuverability and ability to maintain speed in battle conditions. He had to use more strength to steady the aircraft not only in sharp turns but also in straight flight. After losing force, it was difficult to rebuild it. A tendency of the cannons to jam and problems in the plane's ability to carry advanced missiles and communications equipment were also discovered. Replacement parts for the engine as well as spare tires were lacking. After two years, the Kfir became the Canard, French for "duck." The new model stood out with its pair of small wide wings on its nose, which made it look like a duck's bill. These wings improved the flow of air over the rear wings and returned the center of gravity to the plane's rear. The nose straightened out and the maneuverability improved.

Herzle immediately felt the difference in the palms of his hands. The Kfir-Canard carried twice the amount of munitions that the Mirage did, and was better than the Skyhawk in its range with a full load of weapons—four tons of bombs as well as air-to-air missiles. The flexible maneuvering provided stability without effort, a fast maximum turn of 20 degrees per second, and comfortable and easy flying at any speed, even at very high attack angles. Its executions at low speed were even better than the Phantom's

The navigation and bombing computer and the system for guiding air-to-air missiles, which were installed in the aircraft in addition to the electronic warfare apparatus, added for self-defense against missiles, were Israeli developments that were constantly improved in the IAI laboratories. The avionics system, one of the most advanced in the world, gave the Kfir an advantage that appeared in the third model, which entered service in the early 1980s. In this model, the engine and body had barely been altered, but the cockpit was made more comfortable, which eased operational executions, and its electronics systems, which were updated according to the times, went far beyond the original Kfir and turned it into a light and inexpensive fighter aircraft, one of the most precise in the world. The price doubled to $7 million, but it was still one-third the price of the Phantom, which was even less expensive than the advanced American aircraft of the 1980s. Unfortunately, the Kfir had a shorter flight range than these aircraft, as well as an older engine and a lack of modern radar equipment. It would be a solution for a limited time, but was not meant to replace the aircraft of the future, which had yet to arrive. Therefore, only a small number were produced.

Benny Peled was the godfather of the Kfir project at IAI in the 1960s. He quickly left the project after realizing that his demands were not being met. Afterward, Benny fought against every local initiative that was destined to entail tremendous waste. With an investment of $4 billion for the Lavi, the minimum needed to develop a new airplane whose qualities and advantages were still unclear, it would have been possible to fund the purchase of the fleet of modern aircraft that the IAF needed. There were not many quality aircraft on the market, and the choice among them was relatively easy when the needs of the IAF to the end of the century were taken into consideration.

Benny had tested and studied a large number of aircraft in the past, and had always chosen the best. It was in this spirit that he directed the Hadish ("Modern") Team, which would undertake the search. He established the team when he was still deputy commander-in-chief in the late 1960s. The Hadish Team began its work with the planning of the Nesher and the Kfir. It also wrote an entire library on what was needed as compared to what was available on the world market. Delegations of top pilots were sent to test the prototypes of the five American "F" aircraft, from the F-14 to the F-18. On the eve of his taking command of the IAF, Benny himself stood at the head of a delegation that included David Ivri and Amos Lapidot. Benny felt that the best purchase would be a combination of F-15 and F-16 aircraft. The F-15 was an excellent intercept aircraft with attack capabilities. The F-16 had similar capabilities. David Ivri attempted to influence the decision in another direction, recommending a combination of the F-14 as a launching station for Phoenix missiles, which could down enemy aircraft from a range of one hundred kilometers, alongside British Harrier aircraft, which take off vertically carrying air-to-air missiles. The British planes eliminated the need for runways and enormous bases. After test flights and checks, the F-15 was chosen without any additional deliberations. Amos, who took control of the Hadish Team after Benny received command of the IAF, continued to investigate the F-16 until it was chosen.

The first prototype of the McDonnell-Douglas F-15 Eagle took off in July 1972. Aircraft were first transferred to the USAF in 1975. The IAF's first quartet landed in Israel on December 10, 1976. The date of their arrival was set for Friday afternoon. The ceremony continued into the Sabbath, causing a crisis with the religious political parties over the violation of the sanctity of the holy day. The government resigned, and the elections, which were moved ahead to May 1977, eliminated the Labor Party government, which had controlled the state since its establishment. The F-15 had achieved an unprecedented feat, for before it could down its first enemy aircraft, it became the first plane in history to topple a government.

With two engines and a double tail, the F-15 can reach a maximum speed of Mach 2.5. Its operational range is approximately five thousand kilometers, farther than any fighter aircraft in existence. For its maiden public appearance at the Paris Air Show, it crossed the Atlantic Ocean from the United States without stopping or refueling. A drop tank slung under its belly, an Israeli development, even added to its stability. The

F-15's inelegant shape held a series of electronic systems that were hidden from the eye, and placed it twenty years ahead of the Phantom. It was equipped with modern radar that could detect aircraft from great distances, both at high altitude and from above. It was protected from ground disturbances and could distinguish between moving and stationary targets. The radar fed a central navigational computer guiding the weapons systems, which controlled the flight systems, electronic disruption and blocking of enemy systems, and attack modes. It could carry a variety of air-to-air missiles (such as Sidewinders or Sparrows) for short-range or long-range combat (up to forty kilometers, which would ride an electronic ray, television, or heat-guided signals. The system would signal to the pilot, "conversing" with him when it sensed the enemy's presence. It presented all the data and suggested methods and weapons for a solution. It would receive his commands from the pressing of switches on the throttle or the stick. The missiles could be fired simultaneously toward several targets while being controlled by the system and the pilots' eyes.

Those who revered the Mirage and the Nesher, which had reigned during the dogfights of the last decade, expressed their doubts at their first encounter with the F-15. But after an initial run in the sky, the F-15 seduced them to chase it, then disappeared before their eyes with a swift maneuver. Within seconds it reappeared on their tails, both literally and symbolically overtaking the older aircraft.

The Hadish Team concluded that the F-15 was the best and most expensive aircraft on the market. Its unit cost was $30 million, including equipment and munitions. "Robbie" was one of the pilots who quickly placed the Mirage in his photo album and entered the world of the F-15 with seriousness and awe. In the cockpit of the downturned nose, he felt as though he were riding *on* the aircraft and not *in* it. The panoramic field of vision and the quiet flight gave him a sense of mastery and power. Though its aerodynamics were excellent, it responded shakily to extreme operations. The flexibility of maneuvering was almost limitless. The warning signals that sounded as it approached maximum G were the only sounds in the cockpit. The combination of the power of the engines and the new aerodynamics gave him the feeling of leaping a full generation forward.

A triangle on the radar screen and the computer depicted the battle front. Enemy aircraft appeared as dot targets, and locking on one was executed with the movement of a finger on the hand that held the "keyboard" of switches on the throttle. The data appeared on a screen, including everything the pilot would want to know about speed, distance, and direction. In a quick, sharp maneuver he could catch the enemy's tail and fire a missile that would lock on the aircraft with the press of a button. The F-15 pilot could accelerate vertically, opening up a wide range of possibilities that would attempt to justify its place as the "invulnerable air platform" the literature described.

The F-16 was one man's gamble, for the Hadish Team rejected it almost unanimously, saying that, as a flying fuel tank, its survivability level was low. Any small injury would blow it up, not leaving a trace of the aircraft. Though the criticism in IAF headquarters was powerful, none of the critics studied or even understood its phenomenal execution capabilities. Its revolutionary flight and weapons controls resembled those used in computer games. It represented a breakthrough in the world of aviation, in which the steering mechanisms were operated by the "fly by wire" technique, which uses electronic cables.

Ze'ev Raz, a Phantom pilot in the Yom Kippur War and later a squadron commander, did not understand why Benny Peled demanded so stubbornly that the IAF purchase this aircraft. It was new and untested, and apparently would not deliver the perks that McDonnell-Douglas had provided for the purchase of the Phantom and later the F-15. General Dynamics, the manufacturer, was new to Israel, as was the aircraft, which did not have the F-15's two engines, fuel tanks that sealed themselves upon injury, or other defense systems such as protective plates for the pilots.

Benny was adamant, because he had read every article written about the aircraft during the period when General Dynamics was in an economic slump after its F-111 had disappointed in Vietnam. Continuing to inquire, Benny discovered that the U.S. Defense Department had a new regulation against purchasing aircraft on paper. The government presented the aircraft industry with open tenders and even composed a slogan: "Buy Before You Fly." The prototypes of the world's future aircraft were presented for the contest. Of the five that reached the final stage, the Americans chose two—the F-16 and the F-18. The Hadish Team mingled with the generals at the Pentagon and deliberated along with them. Most preferred the F-18. The U.S. Navy wanted it, and the

Pentagon thought that what was good for the Navy would also be good for the Jews. Benny was not convinced. Though he agreed that the F-18 would serve the IAF excellently, he believed the F-16 was even better, as if it had been designed for the IAF. Amos Lapidot, who was assigned to execute the study, agreed. They stood almost alone against the critics. Pressure built because the Americans could smell a large deal in the making.

In the final test of the lightweight fighter, the F-16 emerged victorious. It was chosen as the front-line aircraft of the NATO forces, and the commander-in-chief of the IAF decided against the critics even before the commander-in-chief of the USAF had expressed his opinion. The relatively low cost, $14 million, was less than half that of the F-15, yet another good reason to choose it. The decision was reached in the mid-1970s, and Israel took its place in line, receiving a favorable spot behind the U.S. Army, the NATO countries, and also Iran, which ordered 150 aircraft.

The aircraft destined for Iran were ready for shipment when the Khomeini revolution began and the Shah was removed from power. The new Iranian government rejected the planes. Therefore, Israel had its date of supply advanced. David Ivri, the IAF commander-in-chief after Benny Peled, received them and opened new squadrons. In July 1980, test pilots from General Dynamics landed the first quartet at Ramat David after eleven and a half hours of flight direct from the United States. Refueling in the air, they had flown a route that crossed the Atlantic Ocean and the Mediterranean Sea, circumventing territorial skies and international flight routes in order to avoid explanations or political friction.

The "Fighting Falcon," as the F-16 was called in the United States, was designed for air-to-surface attack. Somehow its creators had been lucky and had produced an aircraft that also had excellent air-combat capabilities. Benny Peled was not surprised; the pilot-engineer felt that a good aircraft was a good aircraft, for dogfights as well as attack missions. The veterans of the Mirage world found it difficult to comprehend the new toy, with all its modern amenities.

The youngsters who flew the Skyhawks and the Kfirs felt at home in this aggressive game. The older fliers, after several hours of training, were convinced. They did not understand how they had not thought of it earlier. The flight computer eliminated all the unnecessary calculations and estimations that determine altitude and range. Five years later the C version was born, with its strong General Electric engine that allowed for the transport of heavier and more intelligent munitions in addition to advanced avionics, improved radar, data displays on the front of the canopy, and electronic equipment for night combat.

After Israel's bombing of the Iraqi nuclear reactor in 1981, and the Lebanon War in 1982, the pilots of the IAF named it the plane of the decade. The F-16s flew to Baghdad and back without refueling, each plane carrying a pair of bombs, each one weighing one ton. In Lebanon, they participated in dogfights and attacks on ground targets. All returned without a scratch. The F-15s were hit, but managed to return and land safely. One F-15 even lost a wing in a training flight in the Negev and survived. Ze'ev Raz approached one of the F-16's greatest critics in IAF headquarters and asked him about the "low survivability rate" that had frightened him so. "I was not wrong!" the expert answered. "I just said that if they were hit, nothing would be left. Is it my fault that none of them were hit?"

The F-15 and F-16 became the backbone of the IAF, both in quality and quantity. The IAF purchased fifty F-15s and 150 F-16s to add to its Skyhawks, Kfirs, and the Phantom 2000, which was being developed. All the aircraft were improved and equipped with advanced avionics, most of which were produced in Israel. The radar systems and the navigation and weapons-control computers, when wisely used by the pilots, were products of the electronic age, and created operational capabilities that were greater than the optimal forecasts of the designers of the original models.

In 1987 the F-16 downed the Lavi ("Lion"), a prestigious Israeli-made aircraft and a brother to the Kfir, which was born of the Hadish Team. It was conceived because of political considerations and fell to pieces because of political quarrels. The Hadish Team had recommended a decade earlier that an inexpensive attack aircraft be developed to replace the Skyhawk and the Kfir as a second-line aircraft after the F-15 and F-16. The aircraft would serve as a cover in case the American sources of arms would disappear. IAI proposed the Aryeh ("Lion"), a small, single-engined jet bomber or a two-engined, multi-mission model that would be stronger than the Phantom. The Shah of Iran wanted to be a partner and to achieve Israeli-type air superiority. In 1974, Israel decided on the larger Aryeh. In a secret document to the Committee of

External and Defense Affairs of the Knesset, Benny Peled stated that the decision had been reached against his recommendations. The failure of the first model of the Kfir was enough to prove that the development of another aircraft would be difficult for the local economy, even with the support of the Shah's treasury. The investment of billions of dollars for the development of a quality aircraft did not justify the relatively small quantity needed by Israel and the Iranian Air Force. It would therefore make every aircraft more expensive than the best available on the U.S. market, which appeared to be open and stable and beyond all suspicions at the beginning of the decade. Toward the end of the decade, the IAF began to focus on the American aircraft. Even the Shah began to transfer part of his investments from Israeli equipment to American.

Work on the development of the large Aryeh continued for five years. In 1979 the Shah was overthrown, and the shipments of the F-16 came faster than expected. Benny Peled proposed that IAI request the concession to assemble the F-16 and eventually to produce it. IAI was offended, claiming that it was "not a garage." Beside the Israeli national firm stood a Prime Minister with national pride and a Minister of Defense with a background in aeronautics. Menachem Begin wanted an Israeli bomber at any price. Ezer Weizman proposed that they make do with the smaller Aryeh. The United States also felt that Israel was planning a brother to the Kfir and transferred, in an unprecedented move, part of its military support funding to development of a variety of systems for the Israeli aircraft. Thus the Lavi was born.

In 1980, Ezer decided to recommend to the government to produce a small and inexpensive fighter aircraft—the "little bastard," as he called it. It would be based on the General Electric 404 engine, which was used in the older F-5 aircraft. The IAF found the proposed version to be equal to a "jet Spitfire," far from the attack and air-combat needs of the modern battlefield. David Ivri recommended the Pratt & Whitney 1100 engine, which was stronger, and Prime Minister Menachem Begin, an admirer of the commander-in-chief, immediately gave the recommendation his blessing. The next Minister of Defense, Moshe Arens, pushed to expand the sophisticated avionics. Arens understood how the plane of the future should look, and how one furthers a state-owned aircraft industry. He was first and foremost a professional—an aeronautical engineer, a lecturer at Haifa's Technion, and a former employee of IAI. Only after this did he become a politician. In October 1982, the development of the Lavi began. Arens persuaded the United States to divert a substantial portion of its support to the project. On December 31, 1986, the prototype Lavi took off on its maiden flight. Over the course of four years, the budget had grown beyond any prediction, reaching a cost of $1.5 billion and calling into question the value of the aircraft's production. It seemed superfluous, and the question of its continued development was transferred to the political battlefield.

In 1985–86, the American civilian aircraft industry began to lose its local market, and foreign military industries competed with the American dominance over the fighter aircraft market. The Lavi was a low-cost and high-quality fighter plane based on the operational experience of the IAF, and was considered a threat to the international air force market. The American government began to pressure Israel to abandon the Lavi project, which was partially funded by the United States. It proposed alternatives, and eventually threatened to cut support beyond its part in the Lavi budget. U.S. representative Dov Zackheim managed to win favor for the U.S. position, based on the historic jealousy felt toward the tremendous budgets of the IAF. The decision to stop production of the Lavi was reached by a margin of one vote in the Israeli government.

Benny Peled would later admit that Israel should not have frozen production of the Lavi after such a tremendous investment and such great achievements, even if its development was superfluous from the outset. The continued production would be the best option after Israel had rejected the idea of assembling the F-16. If the concession had been requested as compensation for the Lavi, it is likely Israel would have received it. The United States had already granted assembly and production licenses of modern quality aircraft to a variety of countries in order to reduce competition. IAI missed a golden opportunity to produce a large fighter aircraft and eventually to install in it the weapons, electronic warfare, and avionics systems that were developed for the Lavi.

The pilots of the 1990s are of a new generation whose skills vary much more than those of previous pilots. Once the Mirage had climbed toward the edge of space, speed and altitude were no longer as much of a challenge as the weapons systems, whose importance grew with the arrival of the Phantom. Since then, the various firing systems and weapons control have been linked to navigational computers and systems for early warning, defense, and confusion of enemy networks. A pilot whose only skill is flight is no longer considered a pilot, and the virtuoso soloists of the 1960s and 1970s reign only in the storybooks. Processed information is now presented to the pilot on computerized flight and radar screens, flashing in a spectrum of colors or chiming out in musical notes. Every sign, color, or note indicates an instruction or warning in an electronic code that is understandable to the pilot who is fluent in all these languages. With all his human weaknesses, only the pilot's awareness and sharpened senses can turn the flying machine into an effective war machine. The technology finally liberated the pilot from the burdens of calculation, so that he could concentrate on the complex operations of the battle.

No comparison can be drawn here to the Arab missile battery operators who shot down Israeli aircraft at the press of a button, without excessive bravery or intelligence. Aircraft and systems, which are becoming more sophisticated daily, are creating ever greater possibilities. Dogfights that once took place within eyesight now develop at a range of 120 kilometers, also extending the autonomy of the pilot. Moti Hod was the last commander-in-chief to advise pilots in mid-battle or to measure the fighting time with a stopwatch, ordering them to return home before the pilot forgot his fuel gauge. Today the pilot decides, but his discretion necessitates sorting the relevant data from the plethora of numbers streaming at him, all in seconds. The pressure is tremendous. There is no room for excuses, for every step is photographed and recorded on color video and is judged in the debriefings.

David Ivri was certain that the extent of this responsibility would place the Israeli pilot far above his peers in other countries. He could not be satisfied with personal accomplishment, but rather carried group responsibility for the quality of the squadron and for the achievements of the entire IAF. The Israeli pilot sees the defense of the country placed in his hands. Much is dependent on the speed and precision of the IAF's response. Every one of its personnel is under constant pressure for immediate self- and group improvement, and knows that the entire system is checking him and will respond quickly and steadily. In serious operations, the eye of the upper command is watching. The American squadron commander in Vietnam did not report on his operations directly to the commander-in-chief of the USAF in Washington. Other air forces in the world have no central control like Israel, or tracking by the commander-in-chief of a pilot's progress. Though no larger than the IAF,

the French Air Force, for example, has no such communication network. The commander-in-chief of the force is not everyone's friend. His
familiarity with the aircrews under his command results from debriefings
or from the reports written by their commanders. Only in the IAF can the
commander-in-chief be involved in any small or large battle and choose,
through his personal knowledge of the pilots, which will be the best team
for execution of a mission.

In the early 1990s, the IAF is appearing more as a technocratic
institution than as a human one. Herzle Bodinger recalls the story of
"Pesach," one of his subordinates and the commander of a Kfir squadron,
who was designated to provide support to a paratrooper unit in an Israeli
assault on a Palestinian refugee village in Lebanon. It was a tight criss-
cross of clay and brick huts. The Israeli force, trapped without an escape
route in the alleyways of one of its quarters, requested that their surrounding area be bombed. Leading the formation, Pesach said that from ten
thousand feet it was difficult to distinguish between the terrorists' guns
and the homes of the innocent residents. He requested that his target be
defined. The commander of the paratrooper force demanded that he
bomb indiscriminately. Pesach was torn, for the lives of the paratroopers
were held in the balance by the lives of dozens of civilians. There was no
guarantee that random bombing would save the force, though it was
certain that the bombs would fall on innocents. He explained that he
would be happy to destroy the terrorists if a specific target could be
defined. The paratroopers were unfamiliar with the territory, and could
not provide a specific point of the terrorists' location. The paratroopers'
cries wrenched his heart. The terrorists had learned to play on the world's
sensitivities, and displayed civilian casualties to the international press.
Afterward they would mingle with the civilians, some of whom were
supportive of the terrorists' actions. Deeply disturbed, Pesach decided to
abandon the paratroopers without bombing. Upon his return to base,
Pesach threw the Kfir's tape on Herzle's desk and demanded that he listen
and judge whether he had acted correctly. Herzle listened to the hysterical dialogue and backed Pesach up completely in the debriefings. Herzle
explains that the old story was repeated in the Lebanon War years later,
when the IAF filled the sky with aircraft waiting for ground targets to be
delineated. Instead, all they received were complaints on the faulty
support they provided.

The lesson from Pesach's experience was that in the future aircraft should not take off without specific targets. However, his dilemma would continue to occupy the IAF in the battleground of the future. On the one hand, there is a tremendous IAF network that can decimate an entire country with the bombs hung on its wings. On the other, according to strategic forecasts, the battleground will comprise specific point targets of local terrorism rather than missions aimed at large-scale destruction of enemy armies. The IAF entered this era in 1967 as its helicopters chased the terrorist squads in the mountains of the West Bank. The problems began with the bombing of terrorist headquarters set up in the heart of the refugee camps in Jordan and Lebanon.

The quality of aircraft and pilots continued to grow, but it would not reach full expression without backup from the ground. The shock of the technological explosion did not bypass the mechanics. Though maintenance in the "cycle" system had been improved and revolutionized since 1967, the new aircraft were creatures from another world. The experts who arrived from McDonnell-Douglas estimated that these "flying laboratories" would be too complex for the local tecnnicians, and they planned on a long trial period. However, the Americans did not understand the professional egos of their students, who pressured them to reveal all the technological secrets quickly, so that they could handle the sophisticated systems on their own in a short period of time. Any foreigners who had not witnessed their activities in wartime could not understand the internal competition and the intense need for personal and group achievement. In their desire to improve daily and to be the best in the network, the mechanics' tenacity resembled that of the aircrews. They displayed openness toward the most complex innovations, and the foreigners' doubts regarding the "Israeli arrogance" were quickly replaced by respect for their speed in learning and their ability to assimilate the material. The list of changes that the Israelis recommended to the McDonnell-Douglas representatives a year later for the improvement of the check and treatment systems of the F-15 was long and astounding.
Chaim Yaron was no longer there, but his presence still hovered between the underground hangars and the central garages. After incorporating the lessons of the war, he concluded his twenty-six years of service and departed the IAF. During the Yom Kippur War he was commander of the Equipment Division in IAF headquarters, and the best man for the job in that war, which destroyed more of the IAF's

aircraft and equipment than any other. He had participated in all of them. Chaim had started with Benny Peled as a Messerschmitt mechanic in the War of Independence, but had continued on the technical route. Their paths had crossed twice more, when they studied together for their engineering degrees at the Technion and late in the War of Attrition under Benny's command at IAF headquarters. The maintenance centers he established in the bases incorporated the lessons of the Six-Day War and grew increasingly sophisticated until it became necessary to coordinate their work in a technical control center that was activated during the Yom Kippur War. Their primary mission was to accelerate the return of damaged aircraft to operational activity within a day.

During the Yom Kippur War, the IAF lost 105 aircraft. At least twice that number were damaged. A total of eighty-one aircraft that were damaged and executed emergency landings away from their bases were rescued, repaired, and returned to service. Within a day, and often within hours, the 290 aircraft that were damaged and landed at their home bases returned to fly. This number includes aircraft that were hit more than once. Even the twenty aircraft that were severely damaged returned to fly after a number of days or before the conclusion of the war. The usability of aircraft in most of the squadrons remained at over eighty percent throughout most of the war. Repairs were quick and were designed to return every aircraft to the air. Evaluations done after the war on the Phantoms and Skyhawks revealed that only thirty percent had to undergo another more comprehensive repair. The technical crews' high level of service under the pressures of battle, around the clock and under tremendous loads and fatigue, amazed even the commanders of the maintenance network. Without them, entire squdrons would have been grounded within two weeks.

In addition to this work, the network had to develop technical "counter" devices when it appeared that many of the damages were of similar types. For instance, many Skyhawks were hit by heat-guided SA-7 missiles. Maintenance experts added a long sleeve to the engine's exhaust pipe, and the damages were reduced, limited to marginal hits that missed the engine and tail steering mechanisms.

The complex network used approximately four thousand replacement parts daily, four times the number used on a routine day. Over the years, the IAF had invested enormous sums on replacement parts but relatively little on storage and management. The warehouses were at the bottom of the priority list of construction plans, and were left in ramshackle buildings, most of which were remnants of the Second World War. Only after the Yom Kippur War did the IAF begin to heed the words of a maintenance officer named Avraham Ofer. A dedicated officer with a great deal of vision, Avraham almost had to struggle before he was able to gather a group of high-ranking officers from IAF headquarters on a bus to take them on an organized tour of all the installations. The officers were shocked by the sight of equipment valued at millions of dollars being managed with logbooks and file cards under rusty and leaky roofs. Filled with mice and rotted walls, the installations were not even fit to house junk, and were an entire generation behind the technology they were protecting.

Benny Peled provided financial backup to the organizational and administrative revolution in the technical warehouses. Ofer flew to visit foreign air forces. Though he saw modern storage facilities, he did not find computerized or advanced management methods. He discovered the system he was looking for in a giant American bakery, Sara Lee. The system used by the bakery to classify, sort, and send cakes, and receive raw materials for baking, was precisely what the IAF needed, though slightly modified. Engines would replace cakes, hydraulic systems would replace flour, and tires would replace eggs. The technical specifications of the system were translated to computer programs and a management system that began to function in 1978. By then, Chaim Yaron and Avraham Ofer were civilians.

The technical wonder was the operation of a robot in computerized control, which would gather the ordered parts from the shelves, carrying them in its arms and packaging them in the correct box for each squadron or for a base's maintenance unit. The central computer that controlled it also kept track of the supply in every branch and issued instructions for the procurement of missing parts. Everything was executed under the watchful eye of a supervisor, but without his intervention. The Lebanon War was the first in which the automatic supply network was used. It was said in the computerized control center that if during the Yom Kippur War they had managed to return aircraft to function within days using the old system, the robots would now be able to shorten the process to hours or minutes. However, computers in the operational branches of the IAF prevented the aircraft from being hit. The great test would have to wait.

• • • •

The IAF was also faced with an urgent need for real-time intelligence. Despite the disagreements over responsibility for the introduction of pilotless aircraft into the service of the IDF, the truth is that the idea was not Israeli. The first American pilotless aircraft executed espionage flights over China in 1964. The aircraft, which were guided from a distance or had a preprogrammed computerized flight system, revealed the efforts of U.S. intelligence to find a substitute for manned espionage flights after the catastrophic downing of a U-2 aircraft over the Soviet Union and the imprisonment of its pilot.

Before Israel's purchase of the professional pilotless aircraft, there were small, hobbylike experiments like that of Shabtai, an Israeli intelligence officer in the Sinai. He was apparently the first to fly a small radio-operated model airplane, the kind that can be purchased in toy stores, over Egyptian positions at the Suez Canal. With a small automatic camera attached to its belly, the model airplane passed over the canal at low altitude, and the pictures that Shabtai developed less than an hour later were not inferior to those taken by the reconnaissance aircraft. This method saved money and particularly time. Shabtai received fresh information on the positions of Egyptian forces in the last hour. Aerial photographs from sorties requested from the IAF would have been received a day or two later. The commander of the IDF Intelligence Branch congratulated him on his initiative and instructed him not to repeat it. Almost simultaneously and without connection to Shabtai's model airplane, two IAF headquarters pilots were attempting to bring pilotless aircraft into the IAF's service. In their spare time they were building and flying models of the types they wanted. Ezra "Baban" Dotan and Yehuda Munk often flew miniature radio-controlled planes. Late in the War of Attrition, Baban had shot down the first MiG using an air-to-surface antitank rocket. Along with Benny Peled, Yehuda served in the IAF's armament development unit. Their pilotless aircraft were designed to peek "behind the door," or at the dead area behind the mountain and the missile battery, which did not merit a jet reconnaissance sortie and the endangering of pilots' lives in an area protected by the SAMs. They also proposed that the aircraft be armed with bombs that could be dropped according to preprogrammed routes or by radio signal. While their friends ridiculed them for playing with toys, IAF headquarters took the experiments seriously.

Around the time that the Phantoms were shot down over Egypt and

Syria at the end of War of Attrition, the search in the U.S. market for a pilotless aircraft suited to Israel's needs stressed the need for a replacement for the reconnaissance aircraft. Israel purchased the Fire Bee, an expensive aircraft costing half a million dollars, and the Checker, which was more of a target aircraft for antiaircraft gunners and cost $50,000.

Produced by Teledyne, the Fire Bee was designed for long-range reconnaissance sorties, both day and night, along a predetermined flight path. It could fly up to two thousand kilometers, depending on altitude. Until the Yom Kippur War and throughout it, these aircraft executed a large number of sorties. Oded Erez and his team began to fly them toward Egypt from Refidim, where I was commander. From Israel's center and north, they were sent to Lebanon and Syria. All the aircraft that Syria prided herself on having shot down after the war were pilotless.

The missile damage in the Yom Kippur War necessitated an intelligent and inexpensive tool that could bring in updated and precise intelligence information, particularly regarding the mobile SA-6 launchers. Manned air patrols that attempted to track the batteries in mid-attack did not endanger themselves in low-altitude flight over the missile sites, so their intelligence information was partial and lagged behind the pace of the war. Benny Peled's pressure to receive intelligence in real time, as a condition for the efficient destruction of targets, returned the wheel to Shabtai, Baban, and Yehuda's model airplanes, with the modern addition of a video camera. For the enemy's antiaircraft guns, the light, pilotless aircraft was a target the size of a fly.

According to IDF instructions, IAI and Tadiran, an Israeli company, each developed its own pilotless aircraft (the Scout and the Mestiff), which had strong, stable bodies and engines, sensitive cameras that were not affected by flight turbulence, and reliable guidance and transmission systems. The images were displayed on a television screen in the control station before the eyes of the aircraft's flier and the navigator, who used a small stick similar to that of the F-16. Controlling the cameras as well, they could receive wide-angle pictures of the entire region and enlarged close-up shots when the pictures were received in the station. Both of the pilotless aircraft could remain in the air up to six hours and could cover an area of one hundred square kilometers, reaching the necessary altitude over any Middle Eastern topography. Their operation was simple, their survivability good, and their cost high—approximately $1 million each, including the control station.

In 1978 the IAF, under David Ivri's command, was the first military to use the pilotless aircraft. Until 1982 he was still laughed at for playing with toys. However, after the silencing of the Syrian missiles in the Lebanon War, and the reports of their numerous intelligence sorties in Syrian territory, other militaries, led by the United States, began to purchase the more sophisticated models. The "toys," along with Grumman E-2C Hawkeye surveillance aircraft with radar dishes on their backs, provided the IAF's command with the advantage of being able to live the action of the front from far away, directing their attack aircraft to specific targets with response time reduced to seconds.

The antiaircraft cannons were the adopted children of the IAF. The only ground fighters in the force, they were separated from the Artillery Corps at the end of the War of Attrition. Until their adoption, the antiaircraft units were small and poorly armed, particularly compared to the enemy antiaircraft "armies" along the front lines that included hundreds of thousands of fighters and thousands of guns. The IAF's aircraft guaranteed air superiority with a minute chance of enemy aircraft penetration to population centers and sensitive targets in Israel. Hawk missiles, the first modern antiaircraft weapon, which the United States sold to Israel in the mid-1960s, were first received by the IAF and not the ground forces.

The transfer of the antiaircraft units to the IAF expanded the force. According to the lessons of the War of Attrition and the Yom Kippur War, they were dispersed in wide areas and between the battalions. The operational demands on them were increased. The IAF also received new weapons intended to cover the aircrafts' weak points in the air defense network. Israel purchased the 20-millimeter multi-barrel Vulcan cannon, which is carried on an armored personnel carrier. With a firing rate of thousands of shells per minute and a sophisticated control system, it is highly effective against low-flying aircraft. In ongoing security operations in the north and during the Lebanon War, its strengths were revealed in ground fighting as well. The old radar-guided 40-millimeter L-70 cannon underwent a series of changes in the Yom Kippur War. Because of the extent to which it disappointed during the war, sophistications were added so that only its original name remained. It was capable of radar and optical tracking at a range of dozens of kilometers, using a simple and inexpensive gunsight and rangefinders that utilized lasers to feed the firing system precise data. The radar was durable yet complex. It emitted a web of unseen beams issued by set containers on the body of the aircraft. These joint systems, with the assistance of Mohawk electronic surveillance aircraft, cover each other to disrupt and trick any aircraft or missile system.

The mobile American-made Chaparral missiles, which were Sidewinder air-to-air missiles altered for firing from the ground, were added to this surface-to-air missile force. Heat-guided, they have high homing capabilities under any weather conditions and at all hours of the day. The battery is carried on armored personnel carriers that house an independent control center. Like the Soviet SA-9 missile, it is inefficient above five thousand feet and is therefore good for defending airfields or as a complement to a dense missile system. Standing alone, without backup, the batteries could be attacked as were two Syrian batteries in Lebanon.

In its wars, Israel captured a large number of Soviet-made SA-7 personal missiles. Red Eye missiles, which home in on infrared signals, were purchased from the United States, completing the protective net against low-flying aircraft. In early 1990, IAF gunners were waiting for the arrival of American-made Stinger personal missiles and the new surface-to-air missile, the Patriot, which finally arrived, later than scheduled, in the middle of the Persian Gulf War. The first batteries were American and were operated by American teams, as part of the effort to prevent Israel from entering the war against Iraq. The Patriots' effect was primarily to boost morale, and the American operators were welcomed in Israel with love and warmth. Their operational results were disappointing.

The old mobile Hawk 23 missile batteries were given modern radar and optical systems that enabled them to track and identify enemy aircraft from great distances. They follow the enemy and, from the moment of the firing, lock on the target relentlessly. The improved Hawk 238 was added to this network. It functioned on a par with the Soviet SA-6, even bettering it at certain executions. It had an accurate weapons control system and lacked the childhood ailments of its predecessors.

Through great and small inventions, the fighters and commanders of the antiaircraft batteries developed sophisticated weapons systems and could speak proudly of their accomplishments in the air. Since the new systems began to enter the IAF's service in the mid-1970s, the antiaircraft network has downed sixty-eight enemy aircraft.

# 9 Baghdad, Beirut, and Tunis

$O$n October 29, 1977, Benny Peled transferred command of the IAF to David Ivri, leaving him with the foundations of an air force growing in a new and sophisticated direction. The transition occurred smoothly, since Ivri had previously been considered a contender for the job, despite his dreams of becoming a chemist. Only after he had commanded the Flight School on the eve of the Six-Day War, the Operations Division during the War of Attrition, and the prestigious Tel Nof base afterward, did his steady climb to the top commence. Benny treated Ivri as a successor and sent him to study at the Technion. In two years, Ivri received his degree in aeronautical engineering and took command of the IAF at the age of forty-three. Menachem Begin was Prime Minister.

In Egypt, the pressure to conclude the state of war with Israel had begun during the War of Attrition and had increased after 1973. It came from elite families whose sons had been called into the field units after the failures of 1967. There was hardly a family who had not lost a relative. Israel did not attempt to use the victory of 1973 to achieve a secure and guaranteed diplomatic arrangement, but instead was willing to accept a cease-fire and separation of forces. The right-wing Likud government, which was elected in 1977, prompted Egypt to regard the situation in a new light. Anwar Sadat's willingness to compromise came about only after he had restored his country's pride through the destruction of the Bar-Lev Line. In November 1977 he came to Jerusalem and spoke in the Knesset, offering peace for the Sinai. Though his historic journey had been preceded by covert meetings in Morocco between his personal emissary, Hassan Al-Tohami, and Israeli Foreign Minister Moshe Dayan, this was the second time in four years that an initiative by the Egyptian president had managed to surprise Israel.

David Ivri was as astonished as everyone else, and thought that history had given him a mission to shift the IAF's mission to peaceful endeavors. The withdrawal from the Sinai meant giving up strategic territory, a large air training area, and systems for early warning and electronic warfare. Ivri was to dismantle five airfields that the IAF had constructed in recent years, two of them—Eitam, opposite El Arish, and Etzion, near Eilat—being among the most sophisticated bases in the world. The price was high, but seemed worthwhile. The positive spirits dissolved over the course of the sixteen months of frustrated bargaining before the peace agreement was signed.

Sadat's peace initiative estranged Egypt from the rest of the Arab world. The Palestinians declared him a traitor and felt themselves the primary losers in Egypt's withdrawal from the circle of war. Though Sadat had declared that the peace agreement must include Israel's commitment to create a Palestinian state in Judea, Samaria, and Gaza, the Palestinians doubted that he would demand their rights after he received the Sinai. The terrorist organizations increased their actions. On Saturday, March 11, 1978, a terrorist squad from Lebanon landed on the Israeli beach of Tantura, south of Haifa. They hijacked a busload of Israeli vacationers on the coastal road and murdered some of them near Tel Aviv. Four days later the IDF assaulted southern Lebanon and cleaned out the terrorist bases with the support of the IAF.

Nearly a decade had passed since the terrorists had turned Lebanon into their primary base and the hub of their activities. The IAF bombings and IDF assaults on their bases in the Jordan River Valley and their expulsion from Jordan in the "Black September" of 1970 pushed them to the southwestern slopes of Mount Hermon and to the valley along the Hatzbani River. At first they flocked to the natural shelters of the caves in the area, then slowly moved to nearby villages, the southern portion of the area between the Litani River and the Upper Galilee, and to the 1948 refugee camps along the coast from Tyre and Sidon to the outskirts of Beirut. Lebanon, with its small, helpless army, was enmeshed in an ongoing civil war between private militias.

The first aerial bombings of terrorist installations and artillery spread throughout Fatah-land (the terrorists' first autonomous area, at the foothills of Mount Hermon), and occurred after a year of mortar and Katyusha shellings on Israeli communities in the north, including Kiryat Shmona. Identifying the terrorists' guns in the checkerboard of the

Lebanese villages was almost impossible, for they were spread out and camouflaged under innocent civilian cover. Even the random accurate hit caused minimal and irrelevant damage.

The shellings and assaults on Israel continued, and the IDF forged a route to Mount Hermon to get footholds for its ground operations, which would rid the villages and hills of the terrorist bases. The "Uproar" assaults, as the missions were called, involved Israeli tanks and special forces. The second series of Uproar operations, which began on May 12, 1970, was assisted by Ezra "Baban" Dotan's Skyhawk squadron. Baban had destroyed one MiG-21 of the six that were shot down on the eve of the Six-Day War. He had also executed a miraculous landing of a Mirage that had lost its tail during the failed attack on the Iraqi H-3 airfield during the war.

"After several turns around the area," Baban would later tell, "we found the terrorists' armored vehicles and went into a dive in an effort to destroy them. At that moment my Number Two informed me that he saw a pair of MiGs in the area. We had not expected them, since Lebanon, as we all know, has no air force. They could only be Syrian, the regional patrons. We were a pair of Skyhawks. I asked the flight controller if we had any additional aircraft in the valley, and he informed me that intercept aircraft were being scrambled and were on the way. I ordered my partner to follow me, since I had no intention of missing an opportunity to attack them. I quickly found myself on the tail of a pair of MiG-17s, which are known for their excellent maneuverability. The Skyhawk is also not a bad aircraft for this kind of territory even though it was not designed for dogfights. Its gunsights are meant for surface target attacks.

"The Syrians detected us immediately and began to maneuver. We did so as well. Luckily we were loaded with armor-penetrating rockets and not heavy bombs, which would have made it hard for us to move. After a maneuver or two, I was close to the tail of one of the MiGs and could see, out of the corner of my eye, my Number Two firing at the other. His cannon shells just missed the tail, and the MiG began to go crazy because of the danger so close to him. These two MiGs were quickly turned from hunters into prey running for its life.

"My MiG's pilot knew his stuff. He executed a sharp turn and entered the canyon steeply. I had to make the best of my Skyhawk so that he wouldn't escape from my gunsights. I decided to do something not usually considered acceptable—to fire my rocket honeycomb, which was hung from my wingtips for attacking terrorist armored vehicles, instead of using my cannons. When he steadied in my gunsight, I pressed the button and released the honeycomb toward him. The rockets, which were typical air-to-surface weapons, missed.

"I did not give up. I raised my gunsights, approached, and fired a second round. This time the rockets covered the entire area, and the MiG broke into pieces.

"At that instant my Number Two shouted that I should break, since the second MiG had fled from him and was now on my tail. The rascal was firing his cannon enthusiastically, and the shells passed right by my steering mechanisms. I attempted a few favorite maneuvers that I recalled from my days in the Mirage squadron. I pulled hard right to several good G's, and brought him to a position he could not understand how he had gotten himself into, flying straight into my nose. When I could see the pilot's helmet, I told myself that this was a good time to shoot him down. This time I checked my tail before focusing on him, and found a pair of MiGs behind me, as if they were waiting for me to shoot down their comrade before taking care of me. If I had attacked, they would have gained the advantage.

"My Skyhawk already had thirty-millimeter cannons, the first in the IAF, and I turned toward the leader of the pair chasing me. He opened his burners and tried to escape, taking full advantage of the low speed I had been flying at when attacking his friend. Nonetheless, I fired more rockets, and they exploded below him near Mount Hermon. The two other MiGs took advantage of the break and escaped home. I decided I could not give up on this guy so easily when he had tried to shoot me down, and I told myself that I had to do everything in my power so that he would not return home, at least not easily. A MiG in one's gunsights in the air is worth much more than several armored vehicles on the ground.

"The terrorists were not making things easy for us. Throughout the battle, they did not stop firing from the ground. They didn't know that there were MiGs in the air, and continued firing indiscriminately.

"When I had decided to chase the lone MiG, I heard our Mirages approaching. They requested that I direct them to the enemy, but I told them that he was mine and that they should look for other targets. They must have thought I was insane. A Skyhawk in a dogfight? Who had ever heard of such craziness? But I followed my MiG deep into northern

Fatah-land. The pilot began to get frustrated and to fly wildly from ravine to ravine, increasing his speed to over five hundred knots. At such low altitude, in between the mountains, it was not easy or comfortable flying. We were both starting to go crazy when he suddenly filled my gunsights. I was close to him, and since I had no more rockets, I fired a burst from my cannons and hit his wing. It was torn off, and the MiG spun and exploded as it hit the ground."

Baban was the first pilot in history to shoot down two MiG-17s with antitank rockets and a cannon burst from a Skyhawk. He was decorated for his heroism.

Baban later found out that the daring pilot, his second victim, was a squadron commander like him, and was the one who had penetrated Israeli skies a year earlier and executed a sonic boom over Haifa. It was Syria's response to Deputy Prime Minister Yigal Alon's declaration that the IAF had hermetically sealed Israel's skies. The Syrian action served as a reminder that no skies are ever completely sealed from hit-and-run missions.

The Syrians chose to ignore the presence of the Palestinian terrorist organizations in Lebanon. Their MiG-17s flew over Fatah-land in order to keep away the Skyhawks that were aiding the IDF Uproar forces, primarily to stop them from penetrating into Syria and not with a goal of supporting the terrorists. The Syrian connection to the terrorists was limited to providing several training bases; their strong inclination was to the Arab oil states, which provided most of their weapons and funding and requested in return that the violent conflict with Israel continue. Over the course of the 1970s, Lebanon was the terrorists' largest training base and their primary weapons depot. Beirut was the hub of planning and command of terrorist actions against Israel and Israeli and Jewish targets in western Europe.

Southern Lebanon and the hills of the Upper Galilee are a continuous topographical system, and the Litani Valley can be considered the natural northern border of the land of Israel. It is a mountainous area that makes armored vehicle movement extremely difficult. Ongoing assaults like the Uproar series could not efficiently serve Israel's purpose in southern Lebanon, which is several times larger than Fatah-land. It was much more dangerous to search out the terrorists' guns in the villages or refugee camps. Artillery shellings would not provide the solution, either. Air attacks on small ground targets could miss and create innocent victims. Ultimately this war of attrition was also placed on the IAF's shoulders, though there can be no clearcut military solution in a war against a federation of terrorist organizations. Air actions are the quickest, cheapest, and most efficient of all means. Activation of the aircraft would necessitate close cooperation with the intelligence community. The IAF would have to find weapons and attack methods that would guarantee direct hits, even on a single house in the heart of a village, neighborhood, or refugee camp, under the condition that the specific target was predetermined.

The limited military profit created by these attacks led to diplomatic losses. The destroyed civilian targets, displayed on television around the world, tremendously damaged Israel's image. Lebanon presented them as evidence of Israel's wild, indiscriminate vengeance, the aim of which was to strike at Lebanon's sovereignty. No one requested that Lebanon explain its sponsorship of the terrorist organizations. While Israel relied on the belief that the cumulative damage would deter the terrorists, the aircrafts' sorties were not routine or methodical enough to destroy the command centers, weapons dumps, and training bases in the villages of the "wild south" and the refugee camps. Most of the actions were solitary responses to terrorist incidents, at random intervals and of little use. In a system of underground tunnels, a large supply of weapons, primarily Soviet-made, was gathered that had been bought with Saudi or Kuwaiti funding and was openly unloaded at Lebanon's ports. Volunteers from the Palestinian diaspora throughout the Arab world trained in the logistical foundations and were turned into a semi-standing force that included two battalions by the end of the decade.

The growing force began to threaten the delicate weave of relations among the various clans in Lebanon. The civil war began again in 1974. The Muslims demanded that the 1943 constitution, the basis of the current regime, be altered, and that the hegemony and presidency be taken from the Christians. The Christians gathered their forces and requested Israel's help. In April 1973, in the dead of night, an Israeli force had assaulted the apartments of four terrorist leaders in Beirut and killed them as they slept. Memories of this operation were deeply embedded in the Lebanese consciousness.

The slaughter conducted by the Christians against Palestinians in the A-Zatar refugee camp upset the entire Arab world. Syria transferred its support to the Muslims and encouraged the Palestinians to avenge the blood of their brothers. The Muslims attacked Christian villages in the mountains, and burned the town of Damour, near Beirut. The Christians increased their pleas to Israel.

The terrorist assault from Lebanon on the coastal road in March 1978 was additional evidence of the lack of method being used to disrupt such actions. Four days after the hijacking, the IDF assaulted southern Lebanon and Fatah-land to destroy the military foundations of the terrorist organizations and to disrupt their supply routes from the sea. Operation Litani was essentially a ground operation that lasted six days, between March 15 and March 21. Approximately an hour before the IDF forces entered, IAF F-15s executed their first operational sorties in the skies of Lebanon. Their purpose was to block Syrian aircraft from entering the area. The Syrians did not get involved, and the F-15s flew their patrols undisturbed.

Under conditions of guaranteed air superiority, the IAF focused on attacking surface targets that the ground forces had trouble reaching. These were primarily terrorist hiding places and arms caches in secret nooks along the slopes or mountaintops, which vehicles could not easily reach or which would endanger Israeli forces trying to reach them. The operation allowed IAF headquarters to actualize the models of cooperation with the ground forces that had been designed after the Yom Kippur War. Air coordination officers who were IAF representatives were allocated to the ground forces and acted under the limitations set by the planners, who were striving to limit losses. For this reason and considering the topographical conditions, they were prevented from providing heavy ongoing air support to the ground forces. Phantoms, Skyhawks, and Kfir aircraft dropped fragmentation bombs on terrorist installations in only sixteen villages, but managed to destroy the sea supply bases at the ports of Tyre and Damour, and silenced dozens of artillery positions that had been shelling Israeli forces and communities in the Upper Galilee. The aircraft encountered light local antiaircraft fire from several cannons and shoulder-held missiles. Only two aircraft were lightly hit and managed to land.

The activities of the helicopters were limited to the evacuation of wounded; they were not used to kill or capture terrorists fleeing the attacking Israeli forces. A panicked escape from the bases in Fatah-land and southern Lebanon began with the start of the assault and the bombings. Few of the terrorists defended their positions. Most of those escaping availed themselves of the Israelis' slow and disorganized progress, and fled to the camps around Beirut. The logistical infrastructure along the battlefront was severely damaged, with large weapons depots being bombed or captured whole. The human infrastructure was barely injured. Approximately three hundred terrorists were killed, small losses relative to the size of the force that was stationed in the assault area. Shortly after the IDF's withdrawal, the terrorists returned and began to repair their installations. The new UN police force (UNIFIL) and the Lebanese villagers were unable to stop them.

In the vacuum created in south Lebanon by the terrorists' departure following Operation Litani, an "independent Lebanese state" was formed after the IDF pulled out. It was a Christian enclave around the Upper Galilee and Israel's northern border, relying on the strength of a new local militia under the command of Saad Haddad. Their arms, equipment, training, and liaison officers were Israeli. The Christians' alliance with Israel intensified the Syrian sponsorship of the Palestinians. The civil war grew in strength and increased security problems in the Galilee. For every round of Katyusha missiles or other terrorist actions in Israel or abroad, the terrorists in Lebanon received punitive treatment that became almost routine. Their training bases, weapons warehouses, and command centers were destroyed in attacks that displayed ever-growing sophistication. IAF pilots executed extremely precise high-altitude bombings whose damage was limited to targets that had been specified by intelligence, even if it was in the heart of a crowded area, such as a refugee camp or the center of Beirut. Apartments were hit without the floors above or below them being damaged.

The cumulative effect of the aerial bombings was not ultimately destructive or deterrent. In this routine, the Israeli planes' control of the Lebanese skies was solidified, at least over the terrorist concentrations in the refugee camps and Beirut. This dominance began to threaten the Syrians, whose border with Lebanon was not protected like the skies of the Golan Heights. Beyond their concerns for their own security, they also had their undeclared commitment to those they were sponsoring in Lebanon. In April 1979 the Syrians first sent their aircraft into Lebanon's skies. Though it was a silent display of presence that was limited to closing the gap in the shared border, it was intended to call into question the absolute Israeli dominance of the Lebanese skies.

Several weeks later the Syrians moved on to controlled provocation. They appeared opposite the Skyhawks and Phantoms that were attacking the terrorist bases, but did not manage to incite a dogfight. David Ivri had issued a strict command that Israeli pilots must disengage and return home if attacked, even if they were in the middle of a bombing mission. While the Upper Command did not want to intensify the conflict with Syria, the controlled response elicited increasingly violent provocations.

In June 1979, Ivri persuaded Chief of Staff Raful Eitan that the time had come to set things straight in the Lebanese skies, and to put an end to the Syrian incitement. The Skyhawks executing the bombing missions could not defend themselves; the Phantoms, which could participate in a dogfight, had trouble doing so while carrying their full bomb load for the attack of surface targets. However, a defensive umbrella of F-15s and Kfirs could set an air ambush for the MiGs with a distinct message. Ivri did not tell Raful that the need to shoot down aircraft had been tingling in the fingers of the F-15 pilots for nearly two years, and that they felt frustrated relative to the pilots of the past. The Mystère, Mirage, and even Phantom pilots had managed to shoot down enemy aircraft soon after their planes were received by the IAF.

Raful granted Ivri permission to eliminate the MiG nuisance. The first quartet of F-15s allocated to the mission took off to provide cover for IAF aircraft attacking a terrorist base. On the traditional "justice chart," this privilege was reserved for the veteran fliers, though many of those who had received the first aircraft had moved on to other positions in the IAF in the meantime. This role was reserved for "Manny," who had already been chosen as commander of the fighter wing in the Flight School. During the first days of the IAF's relationship with the F-15 at the McDonnell-Douglas factories, he had promised the Americans that he would be the first to shoot down an aircraft from an F-15. The promise, which could have sounded boastful to foreign ears, was taken seriously in the squadron. "Benny," the squadron commander, scrambled him to the sortie from Hatzerim, but nothing came of it. It was as if the MiGs had guessed what was awaiting them, and they did not approach the area.

On the morning of June 27, Manny was again scrambled from the Flight School, this time to be ready for a sortie within thirty minutes. The air ambush split into two forces. The quartet of F-15s, with Benny as the leader and Manny flying as his Number Two, provided cover for the aircraft attacking terrorist positions in Sidon. A second quartet, comprising a pair of F-15s and a pair of Kfirs, provided cover for the formation attacking near Tyre. Slightly after 1000 hours, Syrian MiGs appeared on their radar screens. In addition to the warning apparatus and the weapons computers, the F-15s relied on sophisticated control systems that received rapid intelligence data that had been so lacking during the Yom Kippur War. The IAF had also purchased the Grumman E-2C Hawkeye, an airborne control unit carrying a radar dish on its back, which could penetrate beyond the mountaintops and direct the battle with excellent simultaneous warning, target identification, and vectoring of several formations. These were almost ideal conditions for Manny and the others.

In the meantime, it seemed that this confrontation might also leave them empty-handed. Manny thought that if he missed this opportunity, his historic promise might never be actualized. Six advanced model MiG-21B aircraft saw the intercept aircraft and began to turn back. Ivri, from his distant position in the new Flight Control Center, decided to get clever. He instructed the attack aircraft to continue with their mission, and told the F-15 intercept aircraft to turn westward over the sea and away from the battle. Though the Skyhawks objected, explaining that they were out of bombs, Ivri demanded that they continue to dive as if they were bombing, so that the MiGs would be seduced to return and attack under the assumption that they had managed to drive away the Israeli intercept aircraft. The attack continued, and the MiGs swallowed the bait. They returned to the Sidon skies with backups. Manny was not able to count them, but assumed that the enemy force included two or three quartets. The events of the following seconds were well described by one of the Syrian pilots who survived the battle and was interviewed the following evening on Syrian television. "We waited in ambush for the Israeli aircraft, and when we didn't see them, they attacked us in their treacherous way."

Benny's quartet moved in first. The MiGs approached in tight formations, in a flat line. For Manny, the enemy was a dot on the radar screen, and the spirit of battle that had tensed his muscles suddenly lacked the emotion that had been described by veteran fliers. The F-15's advantage is also its drawback, for it eliminates the need to fly close to the enemy and suffer the pain of the eye contact with the enemy pilot who explodes at the touch of a missile. The systems are designed to execute most of the work, and enemy aircraft are shot down almost through remote control. It is a matter of a second between target identification and the locking of the radar. Several seconds after the button is pressed, the missile reaches its target.

Manny will never forget the moment when the skies filled with the trails of missiles fired from every direction. He asked Benny to fire first, but Benny did not respond. In the meantime, missiles were on their way. No aircraft were exploding at the end of their paths. Manny then decided to contribute his skills to the brilliant electronics. He raised his eyes from the gauges, and saw two MiGs crossing his path and turning in a circle whose purpose was clear. They were after him. Within five seconds he locked one of them in the radar and fired a missile.

The MiG broke in two. It was the first MiG to be shot down by an F-15, and immediately afterward, a second and a third were downed by missiles from Benny and "Tzuri," the formation's Number Three. It was now the turn of the mixed quartet. They shot down only two MiGs, one by an F-15 flown by a second-generation IAF pilot whose father was a top flier, and one by a Kfir. Returning to base in an arrowhead formation, they executed their traditional victory rolls and landed straight into the embraces and kisses of the ground technicians. That afternoon, Minister of Defense Ezer Weizman sent them five bottles of whiskey with a letter of commendation. Survivors of the battle revealed on Syrian television at the end of the day that two of the pilots shot down were wing commanders.

The battle for the control of the Lebanese skies had begun. In September, four additional MiG-21s were shot down under the same conditions. In two dogfights that took place in 1980, three more were shot down over Sidon and Metulla. In February 1981, the first MiG-25 was shot down near Beirut. MiG-23 aircraft, which had been involved in previous battles, were not hit. Within nineteen months, the score was twenty-one to nothing in Israel's favor, and it had only one message. Syria's skies were essentially vulnerable to penetration by Israeli aircraft from Lebanon, which were now also threatening the Syrian divisions stationed in Lebanon.

In April 1981, Lebanon's president, Elias Sarkiss, flew to Damascus and requested that Syrian president Haffez Assad send additional military units to support him in the civil war. The Syrians penetrated to the Bekaa Valley and took control of the city of Zahla, not far from the Beirut-Damascus road. The Christian forces requested that Israeli aircraft delay or disrupt the Syrian movement. The alliance with Israel was now almost overt. The Syrians moved their forces in helicopters to Mount Sanin, overlooking Zahla. A pair of Israeli F-16s shot down two Mi-8 helicopters and thereby received credit for another world first. This was somewhat less impressive, however, because helicopters have small chances of survival even against aircraft that are inferior to the F-16.

The downing of the helicopters signaled to the Syrians that Israel would not sit with its arms crossed if they attempted to turn Lebanon into part of their dominion. However, it did touch a sensitive nerve. The last dogfights proved that the Syrians could not hold air superiority, and revealed that the Syrian skies were highly vulnerable. They sent SA-6 missile batteries into the Bekaa Valley and placed them in pre-dug bunkers, under the assumption that they would deter or at least limit the activities of the IAF. Israel's government approved the IAF's destruction of the missiles, and it began to prepare to attack them. Severe weather conditions caused the operation to be delayed. In the following days, the Syrians did not provoke the Israelis into destroying the batteries.

In the meantime, the IAF's aircraft were given more urgent targets. In those spring days of 1981, they silenced the terrorists' Katyusha missiles, which were disrupting life in Israel's north and causing residents to flee to the center of the country, but many of the mobile missile launchers managed to escape. Bombing the launchers' home base did not reduce the shelling. Israel demanded that the Christians keep their part of the bargain and strike at the Palestinian population centers deeper in Lebanon. Philip Habib, a Lebanese-American and President Ronald Reagan's emissary, arrived and proposed a cease-fire. Yasser Arafat, the chairman of the PLO, quickly agreed, for he felt the growing strength of the Christian force, which was being assisted by Israel, and feared his vulnerability from the north and the south. His promise to call a halt to the shellings and the terrorist attacks in Israeli territory was given on condition that the Christians not attack his people. The Syrians also agreed to the red line that ensured their presence in Lebanon at a safe distance from the Galilee. Through the United States, Israel silently joined the agreement. Arafat claimed that this was de facto recognition of his organization. Though Israel denied this, the peace of the Galilee was not disrupted for a year.

In 1981, before Philip Habib's cease-fire, David Ivri's office was like a noisy intersection with traffic coming from two main directions, and often a third.

Penetrations by MiG quartets and provocations of IAF aircraft indicated that the Syrians were preparing for war. The Syrian wall of SAMs that had been erected in the Bekaa Valley after the first dogfights provided Israel with an opportunity to use the plan that had been developed for their destruction and to repair the failures of the War of Attrition and the Yom Kippur War. For eight years, critics in the IDF and the media had not stopped pressuring the commander-in-chief to find a solution to the missile problem. The critics examined the system according to public information, and did not incorporate other elements of the air power being built behind the scenes. This unbalanced analysis raised false concerns with the appearance of a new missile in the region. The SA-9 was discovered on armored vehicles near Sidon after the downing of the first five MiGs. The exaggerated suspicion regarding its strengths was shattered on May 28, the following day. Guided bombs destroyed the vehicles carrying both SA-9 batteries, which were manned by Libyan troops that had been sent as part of the inter-Arab deterrence force. The press began to exult that a solution had been found to the missile threat. Ivri stated that the joy was premature and was the result of a misunderstanding of the situation. The SA-9's name, containing a higher number than the other SAMs, caused it to be considered more sophisticated. Actually, it was a small heat-guided missile for use against low-flying aircraft and was no more dangerous than the Strella and no more effective than the Chaparral used by Israeli antiaircraft units.

The pilotless aircraft squadron continued to fly almost daily, photographing the missile batteries in the Bekaa Valley. Their pieces of information were collected to create an overall picture. The Syrians were aware of the intelligence problem and began to fight it. One pilotless aircraft was shot down by antiaircraft fire. Another was chased by a MiG-21. The aircraft's remote operators maneuvered it to avoid the MiG, but the Syrian pilot would not desist. At a certain instant, the MiG attempted to pass below the small aircraft. The pilot lost control and had to eject. The MiG crashed. This incident was a first in the history of flight. The battle was preserved by the pilotless aircraft's television camera. The operators sent David Ivri a photograph of the MiG a minute before it crashed, and gave the squadron a document confirming their having downed an enemy aircraft. In his journal he wrote, "After all, there is someone stupider than the pilotless aircraft."

As war began to stir in Lebanon, IAF headquarters was busy preparing to evacuate the Sinai after the peace agreement with Egypt. Israel was to lose a number of settlements and its airfields, and was to grant Palestinian autonomy in the territories of Judea, Samaria, and Gaza as a step toward independence. The U.S. president, Jimmy Carter, had agreed to build replacement airfields in the Negev, north of the Ramon crater and in the Ovda Valley, not far from the Etzion air base, which would be abandoned.

American companies began to build the new airfields in 1980. The evacuation of the Sinai was to conclude in the spring of 1982. Though the new bases were not poor substitutes, there was no replacement for the skies of the Sinai if the peace agreement did not succeed in turning the Egyptians into friends. Nonetheless, the limited size of the Negev necessitated that the IAF replace the dimension of width with that of height and to organize itself for safe flight at tight altitudes so as not to cross the border of Jordan and Egypt which were now so close.

The evacuation of the Etzion airfield was delayed to the last minute to keep it as the only scramble base for an operation being planned for the destruction of Iraq's nuclear reactor. The plan was woven secretly throughout that year alongside the enormous operation for the destruction of the Syrian SAMs in Lebanon. A small group of commanders participated in the discussions in the spring of 1981 among the Prime Minister, the chief of staff, and the commander-in-chief to determine which operation should be executed first. The attack on the Syrian missiles was an understandable and natural action that had been debated in IAF headquarters and had been rehearsed by the squadrons. The attack provided the perfect distraction from the plans being developed to attack the Iraqi reactor.

Osiris, the name of the reactor, was taken from Egyptian mythology. Saddam Hussein, Iraq's president, was the first Arab leader to decide to develop atomic weapons, and he did not conceal the fact that his intention was to use it to destroy Israel before crowning Jerusalem as the Islamic capital. "The Butcher of Baghdad," as he was called after the enormous slaughter of the Iran-Iraq War, had risen to power in the military and was the strongman under President Al-Baqr from 1971 until he became the sole leader in 1979.

He had used the energy crisis of the mid-1970s and the Western dependence on Arab oil to persuade three Western countries to sign contracts with Iraq that would make their oil supply dependent on developing Iraq's nuclear power. Brazil promised to provide enriched uranium, which would be separated and processed in a French-made reactor using Italian technology and installations. Outwardly, Osiris, known as "Osirac" to the French, functioned under the cover of innocent scientific research. However, its capacity of seventy megawatts and estimates by nuclear physicists indicated that it was capable of producing the plutonium needed for production of the bomb. Even the French and Italian experts who built the installations in the nuclear center in one of Baghdad's suburbs, and trained the scientific and technical staff, knew that these tremendous efforts would not be limited to peaceful needs.

The completion of the first bomb was only a matter of time. Meanwhile, Saddam Hussein developed means of firing it. The flight range to Israel was not great. Iraqi aircraft, which had taken off from forward bases along the Jordan-Iraq border, had bombed Israel during the Six-Day War. Since then the Iraqi Air Force had added long-range bombers such as the Tupolev TU-16 and TU-22, and the MiG-23. This was the type of MiG smuggled to Israel by a defecting Syrian pilot in October 1989. Nuclear warheads could be attached to SS-21 surface-to-surface missiles if Iraq received them from the Soviet Union, and also to the improved Scud missiles that bombed Tehran during the Iran-Iraq War. Thirty-nine Scuds were fired at Israel during the Persian Gulf War ten years later. A nuclear warhead, even limited in strength, would be enough to destroy Israel's population centers, which are not widely dispersed and would not survive massive killings with tens of thousands of victims.

The first discussions of the Iraqi nuclear threat were held in the Israeli government alongside the discussions of the peace with Egypt. In August 1978, the ministers heard a situation evaluation from representatives of the intelligence community. They had already traded information with the Shah of Iran, who was just as likely a victim for the Iraqi leader. Cooperation with the Shah continued until he was overthrown in 1979. That year, 150 Iraqi experts flew to Italy to study the operation of installations for the separation of uranium. Another large group flew to

France, which had produced the reactor. Israel put diplomatic pressure on France, via the United States. Leaders of nations, UN organizations, and international groups working against the proliferation of nuclear weapons received detailed and updated information on the reactor and the Iraqi plans for it. These pressures were to no avail, even when Israel claimed that France was helping Iraq plan a second Holocaust against the Jews.

By the end of 1979, a war had broken out between Iraq and Iran, after Khomeini overthrew the Shah. The Iranians attacked the reactor twice from the air, but did not inflict any significant damage. The French experts left Baghdad, fearing for their lives. Claims by the French government that they could prevent the Iraqis from using enriched uranium to activate the reactor were never validated. The fleeing experts had left behind, unsupervised, the first twelve kilograms of uranium, which had been received from Brazil and were meant for production of the bomb. The attacks increased the pace of the work, and the experts returned after greater protective measures were taken. The reactor was surrounded by batteries of dirt and by an enormous protective wall, thirty meters high. Shoulder-held missiles and SA-6 batteries were added to the antiaircraft network. Helium balloons anchored to the ground with steel cables were sent to float above the center as a physical barrier against low-flying aircraft. These made the nuclear center obvious and easy to detect from above.

Preparations for a military action against the Iraqi nuclear reactor began in November 1979 and increased as the chances for preventing the development of the bomb through diplomatic channels decreased. IAF headquarters and the Operations Branch in the IDF General Command developed separate plans. Ivri informed Aviem Sela, commander of the IAF Operations Division, of the secret. The ideas were tested in routine exercises that were assigned to the squadrons without detailing their target. After a long hiatus, the Skyhawk and Phantom pilots again began to train in their air refuelings in long-range flights to the center of the Mediterranean Sea and to the Red Sea. Ivri demanded perfect refuelings, and concentrated on developing methods of precise meetings with fueling aircraft in areas that lay beyond the reaches of Israel's flight-control network. In an IDF General Command meeting in February 1980, Ivri stated that the IAF could execute the plans. The General Command considered and rejected several ideas. Chief of Staff Raful Eitan recommended to Minister of Defense Ezer Weizman that an air attack be used. He was not asked to explain why this plan had the greatest chances of success.

Ivri presented three possible plans of attack to the Minister of Defense and the chief of staff, each based on a different combination of Skyhawks and Phantoms. He described the dangers of refueling in the air for every combination according to training sessions. When they had already decided what squadrons would participate, and had begun installing the improved fuel systems on the aircraft, word arrived from the United States that the F-16 shipment that Khomeini had rejected would be arriving sooner than expected. Ivri informed Raful that these aircraft could eliminate their need to refuel in the air and could attack and protect themselves in air combat. Their suitability to the mission would be checked immediately after the aircrafts' arrival in early July.

When the F-16s arrived, Ze'ev Raz, the first squadron commander, returned from the training course in the United States to begin a series of exercises in long-range attack. He assumed that they were preparations for the next war. Aviem loaded him with different missions daily, when the only common denominator was the graph they were creating of the aircraft's ability to carry different loads at different distances. When they were certain that the plane was suitable for the mission, Ze'ev was summoned to Ivri's office with the squadron's navigation officer. Aviem sat next to Ivri, smiling. The commander-in-chief looked straight in their eyes and, in a quiet voice, informed them of the secret target. From now on they would function as a theory and planning team, and led by Aviem, they would develop ideas, analyze them, and reject or recommend them. Aviem would turn the results into the operation order with the assistance of Pesach, the veteran Kfir pilot and squadron commander.

Aviem distributed many questions to various channels by a method designed so that they would not be able to guess what he was talking about and what the information they were providing him meant. His team wanted to know meteorological conditions in various areas of the Middle East at all seasons, and the angle of the sun in various countries at different times of day. He expressed interest in the power of specific bombs to penetrate through concrete of varying thicknesses, and the sophistications of different delay detonators. Another expert was asked about the quantity of smoke and dust that each bomb would raise, and the cloud's thickness and time of dispersion. He wanted to know not only the brightness along the flight route to Baghdad in all seasons, but also the easiest hour to fly it in terms of light, and how many seconds should separate the entry of every diving aircraft so that the cloud of an aircraft's bombs would not obscure the area for the one following him in. From another source he gathered all the relevant intelligence details regarding the reactor building, its structure, and the rate of work. Pesach wrote the command order by hand, for Ivri had demanded this for security reasons and trusted that his handwriting would be legible. The number of copies was minimal.

On October 29 the chief of staff summoned Ivri to his office. Raful conveyed the Prime Minister's order to attack the reactor. All the ministers except Deputy Prime Minister Yigal Yadin were in favor of the attack. The operation would take place after the U.S. presidential election on November 4, less than a week away. Raful explained that Begin hoped to persuade Yadin by the day of the attack since he wanted the decision to be unanimous. Raful decided that the attack would take place on a Sunday, and Ivri felt that it was Begin's sensitivities speaking through Raful under the assumption that the Christian French experts would not be working on Sunday. Ivri returned to IAF headquarters, summoned Aviem, and told him to increase the pace of the preparations.

The F-16s would fly to Baghdad and back without refueling, by using drop tanks. The Americans had forbidden the use of drop tanks by aircraft loaded with bombs, since they feared a fatal collision between the two. After debates, Aviem decided to take the risk and ignore the American prohibition, since the chances of such an accident were minimal. Drop tanks would also be necessary for the F-15s that would accompany the bombing force to protect it from Iraqi and Jordanian aircraft and to block missiles with electronic warfare.

November 4 passed. Ronald Reagan defeated Jimmy Carter. He would take office in January 1981. It was difficult to know what his relationship with Israel would be, and how the United States would respond to Israel's bombing of the reactor. The primary concern was that it would terminate the delivery of the F-16s.

On November 10, Raful convened the General Command. He estimated that the government would determine the date of the attack within several days, and decided to include his generals in the events to prepare for the worst possible circumstances. Ivri outlined the plan, and the generals were asked to predict the military responses of Iraq and other Arab countries. Aviem's team related to these dangers in terms of the immediate threat they would pose to the aircraft on their way to and from the target. Jordan would probably not respond, particularly if the aircraft circumvented Jordanian airspace. Syria would watch from the side. Egypt was out of the circle of tension. All that remained was Libya, which was not an immediate threat. There was no doubt that the international community would denounce the operation. But Israeli officials estimated only a verbal reaction by all, except those countries directly affected, i.e., France, Italy, Brazil, and the United States.

Ivri felt that the immediate danger was an Iraqi military response. The possibility of war must be considered. The IDF's Intelligence Branch had received reports that the air defenses around the reactor had been reinforced. However, the most important piece of information could not be verified by the intelligence units. When were the Iraqis planning to insert the uranium rods into the core of the reactor, initiating the nuclear reaction? The bombing of a "hot" nuclear reactor would have a deadly effect on its civilian surroundings. Menachem Begin would not consider such an attack. It was vital to know whether the rods that the Iraqis had purchased in Brazil were of normal or enriched uranium. If the bombing were delayed and the reactor received the enriched rods, Iraq would be on the road to producing a nuclear bomb. It was doubtful the process could be stopped. Israeli intelligence could only provide estimations regarding these subjects.

On New Year's Eve 1981, reports began to accumulate in the ministerial Defense Committee that the Iraqis were beginning to produce plutonium, the preface to nuclear weapons. Saddam Hussein was declaring his intentions to destroy Israel. Raful informed Ivri that Yigal Yadin had added his support to the operation. The government unanimously approved.

In the meantime, additional F-16 aircraft and the first belly drop tanks arrived. However, it was the heart of winter, a season of drastic change in weather. Aviem pressed the meteorologists to put forth special efforts to update the data on winds, types of clouds, and the sandstorms between Israel and Iran. With every passing day, he polished the tools of the attack, improving the execution. His team worked on the plan, and the squadrons trained on the models. In Baghdad, the bombs would have to pierce the concrete dome of the reactor at an angle of forty-five degrees and penetrate its core in order to guarantee complete destruction. Israeli experts provided estimated engineering details on the thickness of the structure and the solidity of the concrete; these calculations stated that a bomb weighing one ton could do the job after gaining velocity in its fall. The bombs would be equipped with delay detonators to ensure that the explosion took place inside the reactor, inflicting the greatest damage possible. For one of the trials, Aviem and the chief of staff joined the pilots in two-seat F-16Bs. Raful saw with his own eyes that the approach and bombing were executed smoothly and precisely. Aviem believed that a force of six F-16s, each carrying two bombs, would suffice. Two tons of explosives on each plane was the maximum load for such a flight with the large quantity of fuel. To this group, Aviem and Ze'ev added a reserve of two aircraft and four pilots. The force that trained for the mission included twelve pilots and ten F-16s, to which they would add the protective aircraft.

In the spring, the Lebanon front began to heat up, and the Syrians erected their wall of missiles. The government approved the IAF attack on the system, and Raful had trouble deciding which to attack first—the reactor or the missile system in Lebanon. Ivri assured the governmental ministers that he had the tools to destroy the missiles quickly. Moti Hod proposed from the side that they signal the Syrians by destroying one battery. After conferring with the Prime Minister and his generals, Raful gave priority to the attack on the Iraqi reactor. Begin agreed, since intelligence forecasts estimated that the reactor would be "hot" between July and September.

The date of the attack was set for May 10, 1981. The decision gave them just over a week to complete preparations. Aviem and Ze'ev briefed the ten pilots on the details of this secret mission. One of them was the commander of the F-16 base, who had received the assignment after a personal plea to the chief of staff and despite Ze'ev and Ivri's objections. He was accepted under the condition that he disregard his superior rank and act as one of the pilots. It was decided that they would fly in two quartets. Ze'ev would be the primary leader, and Nahumi, commander of the other F-16 squadron, would be the secondary leader. The Etzion airfield, from which they would depart, was not the home base of the F-16 squadrons, and logistics and communications preparations had been made during the previous weeks. Alert orders were also passed on to the rescue force that had been chosen from the helicopter squadron. In the event that any of the planes was hit, instructions dictated that they pull the aircraft as close as possible to the Israeli border. Ze'ev estimated that two of the aircraft would not return. He did not tell his comrades of these thoughts, but he prepared himself for the possibility that one pilot would be captured and another would be rescued. He had been given Iraqi dinars with which he was to equip the pilots, so that they could survive if they ejected. He returned the money. This was not the Second World War, he said, and Iraq was not occupied Europe. An Israeli pilot downed in Iraq, a stranger in flight coveralls not speaking the language, would be helpless with or without money.

On Sunday morning, May 10, a group of men landed on Etzion's side runway. Raful, Ivri, and top officers from IAF Central Command secretly made their way to one of the briefing rooms and stood before the "Baghdad crew." The pilots already knew Aviem and Ze'ev's operational texts by heart, just as they had emblazoned the reconnaissance photographs of the route and the reactor in their memories. The presence of the chief of staff and the commander-in-chief was a sign of the joint responsibility they had in this mission, with its supreme national importance. Ivri spoke directly. A quick attack was of vital importance to him. They should not remain over the target for more than three minutes, meaning less than thirty seconds for each aircraft. Anyone who found himself off angle in his first dive and might miss the target should abort and return. He forbade returning for a second run, for any aircraft that did so would delay the others and complicate the situation. The team had an extraordinary number of experienced pilots. Nearly all of them were accredited as formation leaders. Several were of a rank equal to the leader, one even higher. Ivri emphasized that there was only one leader-commander, Ze'ev Raz. Every decision connected to the overall operation, because of a sudden problem or unforeseen territory conditions, would be his alone. He also emphasized the need to avoid contact with the Jordanian Air Force and instructed them how to behave if they had to abandon their aircraft and be rescued. He had no doubt that the mission would succeed, not only because of its importance but because of his familiarity with the capabilities of those executing it.

It was Raful, whose strength was never in his words, who sounded sensitive and emotional. He spoke of the nuclear threat to Israel's existence, but said that nonetheless, despite the national importance of the mission, he did not want it to be executed at the cost of Israeli lives. His speech was short and full of concern for the pilots. He gave Ze'ev authority to stop the operation if they encountered problems. It was not a one-time chance, and could be repeated. If someone was shot down or taken prisoner, he should do everything he could to survive. Those who listened to him felt a pain in their hearts for this man who had been determined enough to come to this base, from which his son, Captain Yoram Eitan, had taken off on a training flight less than a month earlier and crashed and been killed. At the end of the briefing, Raful asked to be shown the house in which his son had lived. He entered the house alone. Afterward he joined Ivri and his officers, and they took off northward. The scramble was set for the afternoon, and there were still several hours for final preparations.

The countdown went according to plan. The patrol aircraft took off, and the rescue helicopters were dispersed to their locations. From Etzion, the commanders were informed that the F-16s were armed and fueled. The pilots were on their way to the aircraft. Suddenly the chief of staff was called to the phone. It was the Prime Minister. Short and to the point, Begin ordered Raful to stop the operation. He did not explain, and Raful did not press. There was no time for arguments, for they had to fold up quickly without raising suspicions or giving a hint that this was merely a delay before a later execution. Security limitations made a normal fold-up difficult as a last-minute procedure. They fabricated stories and ridiculous excuses, and in several of the responses, Ivri heard the chuckles on the other end of the line.

It was clear to Begin that there had been a leak of information and that people who were not meant to be privy to the secret, even at the upper levels of government, knew of the preparations. Word of the operation had reached the head of the opposition, Shimon Peres, who quickly warned Prime Minister Menachem Begin of its potentially horrific results. Begin was more worried by the leakage of the secret than by Peres's fears. He instructed that the operation be dealyed because of his concerns for the pilots' safety.

In retrospect, Ze'ev revealed to Ivri that the delay was a godsend. After they had taken the bombs off the planes' wings, they discovered that several of them had been put on by mistake with delay detonators a fraction of a second too short, errors that might crucially affect the effectiveness of the bombing.

. . . .

Two weeks later, at a meeting of the IDF General Command, Raful slid a note over to Ivri. "David. Last time! The date has been set for May 13, Sunday. Don't say a word to anyone. I told them—either yes or no. If not on this date, then they should stop bugging us. Until further announcement—this is the date. Raful."

The detection of the problem in the delay detonators was not the only benefit to arise out of the postponement of the operation. Every day that brought them closer to summer guaranteed more stability in the weather. In the meantime, additional drop tanks had been completed at IAI. The order had also been reworked and its name changed. The computer that issues random code names for operations printed one word: "Opera."

Three days before the operation, Ivri received another note from the chief of staff.

"David! Delay of one week because of the summit conference next week. The Prime Minister and Sadat will be in Ofir. Raful."

The new date was eventually set for June 7, the eve of the Jewish holiday of Shavuot. It is a time when many people take an extended weekend vacation, and the F-16 squadrons had planned a unit trip. Its cancellation would raise suspicions. Ivri instructed that all vacations and trips should continue as scheduled and that the commanders of the units involved in the operation should receive notice on Thursday, June 4. On that day he was to fly to Naples with the chief of staff and the commander-in-chief of the Navy for the change of command of the U.S. Sixth Fleet. Even their one-day trip to Italy was not canceled. On the return trip from Naples, the Command Center instructed Raful and Ivri to prepare themselves for a meeting with Begin immediately after landing. A helicopter, with Aviem standing next to it, was waiting to take them to Jerusalem. He summarized the forces' preparations and the operation plans.

"Weather?" Ivri asked.

"Can't be forecasted," Aviem responded.

This cloud hovered over their meeting with the Prime Minister even after they received his approval to execute Opera. Meteorology reported desert sandstorms on the way to Iraq that were limiting visibility in some areas to five hundred meters. However, the clouds over Baghdad were high and thin, with light winds. Visibility was ten kilometers.

On Sunday, at 1400 hours, the pilots at Etzion were strapped into their seats in the F-16s as the ground crews checked every part for the thousandth time. The planes were loaded to the maximum with a drop tank and a one-ton bomb under every wing and another drop tank under the belly. Ze'ev double-checked with the technical officer that the timing of the detonators was matched to each bomb's target according to the order of the attack. The first bombs would split open the reactor building, and the following ones would destroy its contents down to the underground floors and the basement, collapsing the roof.

The aircraft rolled to takeoff position. The 2,500-kilometer trip was calculated to the last drop of fuel. Because of this operation, the evacuation of the Etzion airfield had been delayed beyond the timetables of the Sinai withdrawal. Its location was part of the calculation.

The aircrafts' noses were pointed northward, and their run was short relative to their weight. Ze'ev's "Chisel" formation took off first, followed by Nahumi's "Bunch" formation. The northern takeoff, improvised as a result of a sudden strong northwesterly wind, was a complete change in plan. It would obligate them to execute an arc turn backward and to pass dangerously and unexpectedly over the skies of Aqaba, which they had planned to avoid.

The last-minute change could wreak havoc on the entire operation. Aviem had intentionally lengthened the flight route so that they could stay out of range of the Jordanian radar as much as possible. Now, suddenly, they were revealing their presence and their intentions to thousands of vacationers in Aqaba. King Hussein himself saw them pass over his yacht, which was docked in the Jordanian port, but their southeastward flight to Saudi Arabia relieved him of any fear that his country might be threatened. Estimating that they were headed to Iraq, he acted on his obligation of solidarity and called his general command in Amman, telling them to warn Saddam Hussein. The "Butcher of Baghdad" was at the gulf front, decorating his soldiers. It is not known if the Jordanian warning was ever received. In any case, no enemy aircraft were seen on the horizon. The planes crossed the edge of the Eilat gulf, passing over the freighters, many of which were unloading weapons for Iraq's war against Iran. From the lead position it seemed that all the Jordanian, Saudi, and Iraqi detection systems were asleep.

Ninety minutes of loneliness awaited the pilots on their way to the target, and another hour and a half on the trip home. This was almost an eternity in terms of supersonic warfare, in which conflicts are generally measured in seconds. Before their departure, they were instructed to maintain electronic silence that would include not only the traditional radio silence but also complete shutdown of all radar systems and sensors. In this new age, even silent signals are translated to alarms in distant stations. Ze'ev led the force at three hundred feet, and was pleased that the desert vista was not a bland, monochromatic stretch, but rather an amazing spectrum of colors. At their speed of four hundred knots, the picture of the reddish landscape beneath them passed like a movie in slow motion. He lifted the formations up to five hundred feet to take the pressure off their eyes. For fifteen minutes they climbed over a strong sandstorm, descending again when it had cleared.

The fuel gauge indicated that the wing drop tanks were emptying. The difficult moment in which they would have to leave an actual Israeli souvenir on enemy ground, even in this remote desert region, was approaching. Aviem and Ze'ev had calculated the estimated spot ahead of time, and had ensured that it was not populated, even with a Bedouin tent encampment. Ze'ev wanted the release of all the aircrafts' tanks to be executed simultaneously, but this could not be coordinated on command. Even the rate of fuel use was not consistent among the aircraft. Those who had used less fuel would drop last, approximately five minutes after the first. Tension mounted. The tanks were dropped from low altitude. Ze'ev saw them smashing into the ground and breaking apart. Not a living soul was in sight. After dropping their tanks, the planes accelerated to 450 knots.

The expanse of brown-yellow desert bed was suddenly replaced by the greenery surrounding the Tigris and Euphrates rivers. This was the moment to break the electronic silence with one word on the radio. The pilots were ordered to push halon gas into the fuel tanks, which would prevent fire if they were struck by an antiaircraft shell. They flew over fields and orchards, where they saw people looking upward, following the path of the low-flying aircraft. They appeared unable to identify the aircraft or their target.

They crossed the Euphrates. Ze'ev was amazed that the Iraqi missile system was not responding. He had actually been more wary of a reception by Iraqi MiGs than of damage from the SA-6 batteries. No enemy aircraft appeared. The skies were clean. Their radar beams swept the area, breaking the electronic silence as they approached the target, but they did not detect a thing. "Watch out for antennas and poles," Ze'ev said openly on the radio. They were already deep within range of the Iraqi detection radar. Electric cables and high-tension wires presented the greatest danger. Ze'ev instructed them to climb and increase speed.

Using full engine power without afterburners, they accelerated to five hundred knots, closing in on the Baghdad suburbs and the bright strip of the Tigris River. The nuclear facility at Al-Taweeta was seventeen kilometers west of the city center. They would reach it without the residents of the capital noticing them. A large lake with an island in its center was the point where they would pull up. There they would push the throttle to the afterburner and climb to eight thousand feet to dive on the reactor.

Their attack gunsights were set on air-to-air, even though they saw no MiGs and no missiles.

The large lake with the island should have been right in front of them. The lake appeared, but without the island. "What is going on here?" Ze'ev asked aloud. The next day he learned that the waters of the Tigris had apparently flooded the island and covered it. But right now there was no time to check. They searched for the target and found it. The nuclear reactor complex was conspicuous in its poor suburban surroundings. A square wall surrounded it. The dome of the reactor protruded, almost at its center. It was clearer and brighter than the model target they had attacked in the exercises.

Ze'ev opened his afterburner, accelerating to six hundred knots. He flipped over and straightened out to place the white target in his gunsights. Steadying the aircraft, he descended in a steep dive at thirty-five degrees until he heard the computer's "pickle" beep, the signal to release the bombs. He pressed the button. Two tons dropped from 3,500 feet. He had been holding his breath, and now exhaled heavily. The tension and incredible forces were absorbed by the G suit; if they had not been, he would have blacked out. He executed another hard pull sideways and up in a quick maneuver to avoid any missile that might be on his tail, and released a smoke device to trick the infrared heat sensor of the missile, whether it had been fired or not. Pulling out of his dive, Ze'ev heard only the weak clicking of antiaircraft cannons. There were no missiles or MiGs, and even the ack-ack was not bad.

The eight aircraft descended on the reactor at five-second intervals, partially so that the "Chisel" pilots of Ze'ev's formation could estimate the precision and force of the hit. When it came time for Nahumi and the other "Bunch" pilots to place the reactor in their gunsights, a ball of flames was already glowing from inside the shattered dome. The last pair dropped its bombs into clouds of smoke. The bright flashes hypnotized the base commander as he pulled up, so that he lost his dive angle and was the only one who did not strike the "alpha" target, but instead destroyed nearby support buildings. The detonators of the bombs on each plane were timed so that one would explode at the top of the structure, while another was destroying the underground floors. Eight precisely dropped bombs would have been enough to cause complete destruction, but in all twelve 1,000-kilogram bombs were used. The concrete structure collapsed and crumbled, leaving not a trace of the reactor's core and other installations. Foreign journalists in Baghdad reported the next day that two bombs penetrated to the basement but did not explode. This death trap prevented the ruins from being cleared. The Osiris reactor had descended to a hellish end in forty-five seconds.

"Count off!" Ze'ev, flying over Baghdad, expected to hear that everyone had come out clean.

"Chisel Two, okay."

"Chisel Three, okay."

"Chisel Four, okay."

"Bunch One, okay."

"Bunch Two, okay."

"Bunch Three, okay."

Silence. Bunch Four was not answering.

"Bunch Four?"

No answer. Ze'ev and Nahumi were drenched in cold sweat.

"Bunch Four, are you okay?" Ze'ev's voice grew tense.

"Okay. I got out okay," he suddenly replied, to everyone's relief.

At home, he explained that he had been busy in his evasive maneuver and had not realized they were talking to him. He had forgotten his code name, which had not been used up to this point.

"Carbon, this is Chisel One. Chisel and Bunch are all charlie," Ze'ev reported to Aviem. "Charlie" was the code word for success. The command aircraft, flying in Israel, sounded incredulous.

"You're all charlie?"

"Affirmative. All charlie. Affirmative."

"All charlie!" Aviem transmitted to Central Control, and the two words sent a chill through Raful, Ivri, and the other top commanders around the loudspeaker on the command table. The chief of staff lifted the telephone and asked to speak with the Prime Minister at his home.

"Bunch One, this is Chisel One. What were your results?" Ze'ev asked Nahumi after the formations had regrouped. They had already climbed to thirty thousand feet over Baghdad.

"Perfectly good, except for a couple of undershots."

"Chisel One, this is Carbon. Good results?" Aviem asked.

"Affirmative. The target was apparently destroyed as planned."

"Injuries?"

"Maybe some ack-ack scratches on the body . . ."

"Home, and good luck . . ."

Over the Euphrates, they climbed to 42,000 feet. With their light wings, they flew home at six hundred knots, elated and hoping that the antiaircraft damage would not deteriorate. The minutes passed, and the flight remained smooth. There were no missiles and no MiGs. The only strange body that appeared on the radar screen was a "heavy," apparently a passenger airliner. Ze'ev smiled, for the surprise had been complete. All the debates with Aviem and the intelligence people over what was the more dangerous threat awaiting them in Baghdad remained unanswered. They did not have an additional drop of fuel that could be used for a defensive battle, even if they would shoot down their adversaries. The route home was shorter than the flight to Baghdad. Suspicious but unthreatening movement occurred over H-3, the Iraqi airfield on the Jordanian border, which was the only Iraqi base attacked during the Six-Day War. The Jordanian Air Force flight-control system was tensed toward the appearance of the Israeli aircraft coming from Iraq, but hesitated to get involved. Jordanian fighter aircraft in the air did not dare approach contact range.

Several seconds before the force crossed the Israeli border, Ivri did something very unusual. He took the flight controller's microphone, complimented Chisel and Bunch on their successful execution, and requested that they land at Etzion using the same degree of concentration they had exercised during the attack. The landing was smooth, like the takeoff. The ground crews stormed the aircraft, but did not find damages, and immediately refueled them for their flight to their home base.

Evening set in. They made their way home with full burners, flying at supersonic speed and creating a tremendous noise, which released all the tension and silence that had been forced upon them. The following afternoon, Ze'ev, on his way from his home to the base, picked up a hitchhiking soldier. "What do you think about the bombing of the Iraqi reactor?" the soldier asked, causing Ze'ev to almost lose control of the car.

"What are you talking about?" he asked the young man.

"What they just said on the radio," the soldier said.

The Israeli government released a statement about the bombing after Amman Radio mentioned it. The United States reacted as expected. Though they did not believe that the F-16s had executed the bombing, they temporarily delayed further shipments of the aircraft until the fury had blown over. Pentagon experts were surprised by the daring of the operation and by the conventional solution that had been used to destroy the nuclear threat. Beyond the diplomatic protests, experts wondered at the new level of strategic deterrence that Israel now possessed, and its effect on the nuclear arms race. They had difficulty accepting the fact that the F-16, in Israeli hands, had gone far beyond the calculations of the Americans who had designed it. In the midst of the storm, the U.S. military attaché in Israel invited himself to a meeting with Raful and Ivri and presented all that he knew of the results of the operation. The precision of the hits and the extent of the destruction had penetrated to the heart of the nuclear core. Ivri said that he had never seen such a devastating "opera." He summarized the operation with one word: "Overkill."

## The Lebanon War: Operation Peace for Galilee

In the meantime, the destruction of the missile system the Syrians had erected in Lebanon had been postponed. Weather problems led to repeated delays. Military and diplomatic opportunities were squandered. Aviem Sela believed that the solution had been found, and that the chance to prove this had been taken from him. He had yet to demonstrate his "greater theory" that aircraft had the advantage over the SAMs. At that time, the Syrian missile system had thirteen batteries, most of them in the Bekaa Valley and several along the Syrian border. The system comprised primarily mobile SA-6 missiles, with the backup of bunkered SA-3 batteries for moderate-altitude aircraft and a series of SA-2 batteries for high-flying aircraft.

An ongoing internal debate persisted between the IDF General Command and IAF headquarters about whether it was preferable to attempt the plan on a relatively thinner but less dangerous system. Ivri and Aviem preferred to deal with a denser system, for it was not worth expending years of labor, only to reveal the method and the special weapons by using them on a lesser adversary. Though many disagreed, Raful, like Ivri, wanted to strike at a large and diverse network and not at solitary batteries. He wanted to benefit from the lessons learned from the mistakes of the War of Attrition and the Yom Kippur War. As Brig. Gen. Avihu Ben-Nun, Ivri's deputy and the head of the IAF Attack Branch in the Yom Kippur War, had stated after the failure of Operation Dugman 5, which was to destroy the Syrian missiles, the IAF should not be frightened by losses, but should instead keep up the momentum and fight on to the end. The instruction that this time the IAF would not be deterred by losses, whatever they may be, was rooted in the belief that damage, if any, would be minimal. Therefore the attack would continue until all the batteries were destroyed, even if they were reinforced in the meantime.

The government approved the attack on the missiles on one of the transitional days between winter and spring, when the weather was extremely unstable. When the clouds covering the Lebanon mountains and the Bekaa Valley eventually cleared, Philip Habib, the U.S. envoy, closed in and promised to evict the missiles through diplomatic channels. The Syrians were stubborn, and though Begin repeated his threats of destruction, the missiles remained where they were. During this freeze, Israel executed Operation Opera over Baghdad.

On August 5, after the Israeli elections, Menachem Begin's second government took control in Israel, with Ariel Sharon as Minister of Defense. Two months later, on October 6, Anwar Sadat was assassinated in Cairo on the VIP platform of the parade celebrating the anniversary of the Yom Kippur War. In a first meeting with the new Egyptian president, Hosni Mubarak, Sharon promised that the IDF would not attack Lebanon, but would respond strongly to terrorist actions. The terrorist organizations were growing wily and avoiding direct conflict on Israel's northern border. They moved their strikes and began to attack Israeli and Jewish targets in Europe. In August they attacked Israeli embassies and El Al offices in Rome, Vienna, and Athens. In October they exploded a car bomb outside a synagogue in Antwerp. In April 1982, Yaakov Bar-Siman-Tov, an embassy worker in Paris, was murdered.

Sharon attempted to dictate, to the new government, a firm offensive line for dealing with terrorism that would send a clear message to terrorists around the world. The terrorist actions abroad, immediately after the inauguration of the new government and the beginning of the cease-fire, necessitated the destruction of the terrorist infrastructure in Lebanon. Raful, Sharon's subordinate from the paratrooper days, began to plan the Israeli action, to be called Operation Pines. Those who understood Lebanese history felt that the choice was either an expanded version of Operation Litani against the terrorist bases, or the establishment of a new diplomatic order in Lebanon, with a Christian government backed by Israel. The operation would need a convincing premise. Sharon felt that the terrorist strikes abroad were enough. The government and the public, however, were expressing differing opinions as to whether they could be seen as a violation of the cease-fire. Sharon needed the expulsion of the terrorists from Lebanon in order to balance the sense of responsibility that he felt after the painful final stage of the evacuation of the Sinai in April 1982.

Nearly a month had passed since the riots caused by the evacuation of the Jewish city of Yamit when the terrorists struck again, this time at the Israeli ambassador to London, Shlomo Argov. Terrorists belonging to the Abu-Nidal faction of the PLO set an ambush for him on June 3 opposite Hyde Park, and shot him as he walked out of the Dorchester Hotel. He fell to the ground unconscious, completely paralyzed. The following day, the government gave the IDF permission to execute Operation Pines. Yasser Arafat's claims that the attack on Argov had been executed without his permission and his declaration that Abu-Nidal was a "traitor" doing damage to the Palestinian cause were ignored.

On June 4, Ivri issued an all-encompassing alert order to all IAF bases. Herzle Bodinger, commander of the Ramat David air base, Israel's closest airfield to the front, briefed his squadron commanders before the first sortie. Late in the afternoon the Phantoms attacked the Beirut stadium and collapsed its concrete tiers, which protected the terrorists' enormous arms depots, constructed beneath them. The terrorists responded with heavy shelling of the Galilee, where residents once again returned to their bomb shelters under a shower of Katyusha missiles. On Saturday, June 5, the fifteenth anniversary of the Six-Day War, the first Israeli Merkava tanks toppled the fence along the Lebanese border, and the IDF entered Saad Haddad's security zone. The following day the government announced the beginning of Operation Peace for Galilee.

The operation was limited to terrorist bases located within forty kilometers, between the Israeli border and the Awali River, twice the amount of territory assaulted during Operation Litani. The Knesset approved the action with its military and geographic limitations. It seemed that the government had abandoned any hopes of a "greater plan" for a new order in Lebanon.

The first Israeli Skyhawk was shot down over Damour by ground fire. The international press displayed a picture of a body tied to a car being dragged through the streets of Beirut. Though they claimed it was the body of the pilot, he was returned to Israel after having been captured by the Fatah. The body was apparently that of an Israeli Cobra helicopter pilot who had crashed several kilometers north of the Israeli border. Realizing that the skies were filled with Israeli aircraft, the Syrians knew that any attempt to intervene would be suicidal. The missile batteries in the Bekaa Valley were also silent. Nonetheless, to instill confidence in their soldiers and to display solidarity with the Lebanese, they scrambled advanced MiG-21 aircraft and the new MiG-23 against Israeli armored columns on the third day. In a series of rapid dogfights, six MiGs were shot down, mostly by F-15 missiles. Two pilots parachuted and were taken prisoner. No Israeli planes were hit.

Ivri had instructed Aviem Sela to plan for his "greater theory" on the first day of the war. Aviem began to brief the force commanders who would participate in the joint operation. The preparations lasted three days, nearly nonstop. These long nights reminded him of the distant days after the Yom Kippur War, when he had been searching for a theoretical model to break the missiles. He recalled how things had moved from the War of Attrition until 1973, when thinking had regressed to conservative attack tactics instead of the search for a solution using sophisticated warfare. He was the first western pilot who managed to photograph the mobile and mysterious SA-6 from up close without being hit, thus reducing the threat. After 1973, when the IAF reached the conclusion that the missiles could be neutralized with a diverse and integrated force using well-calculated and organized trickery, it was Aviem who helped find the weak spots and human limitations of the existing control network. Later he pushed the project forward with a team that included Amir Nahumi, the F-16 squadron commander who had been the secondary leader in Operation Opera. The team developed a model until the electronic control system, rooted in a sophisticated and complex operation, was successfully tested in dry exercises. This special computerized center had enormous memory and the capability to process of millions of pieces of data in an instant, thus reducing the load on the central control system. It allowed the commanders of the IAF to make correct decisions more clearly, from a series of solidly based alternatives.

On June 9, the fourth day of the war, Israeli armored columns neared the Syrian lines. The support aircraft hovered within range of the missile batteries stationed in the Bekaa Valley. The searches of the villages, cities, and makeshift terrorist hideouts in the mountains had revealed weapons and munitions reserves that would have served a medium-sized standing army for several days of combat. This time the air support was generous, though there were still problems similar to those of the previous wars. Specific targets were not always defined for the pilots. On a front that included concentrations of civilian populations, with chases after terrorists who often stripped off their uniforms in order to survive, it was necessary to strike precisely to avoid uncontrolled, unnecessary, and immoral killing.

Until that morning the government had prohibited any provocation of the Syrian forces, which, early in the week, had still been a brigade force accompanied by armored and antiaircraft units. Within two days, however, the Syrians began to reinforce it with two armored battalions and attack helicopters who received cover from MiG-21 and MiG-23 aircraft. There was no indication that they intended to interfere in the war or to open a second front along the Golan Heights to remove the pressure from Lebanon. The intensified presence was threatening in itself, even if they limited their involvement just to Lebanon. The initiative was in their hands and gave them the advantage. Elimination of the threat, in case it materialized, would not be possible because of the reinforcement of the antiaircraft network in the Bekaa Valley. Nineteen missile batteries, more than half of them SA-6s, stretched from Mount Hermon in the south to Zahla in the north. The SA-6 network comprised two brigades, each containing six batteries in addition to a tight network of antiaircraft cannons and personal shoulder-held Strella missiles. The chief of staff instructed Ivri to plan an operation for the destruction of the missiles on short notice.

The operation was dependent on special approval by the government. Raful set the assault for 1200 hours. As the time approached, there was still no decision, for the ministers were hesitating. The attack time was delayed two hours.

. . . .

Two years later, in the summer of 1984, an extraordinary book was published in Damascus. *The Israeli Invasion of Lebanon* was a document written by a team of researchers under the sponsorship and supervision of the Syrian minister of defense, Mustafa Tlas. It was a detailed and critical documented summary of the Lebanon War and its lessons, from the Syrian point of view. The Syrian system, which is generally closed and censored, had never witnessed such a public self-flagellation. They admitted that the Israeli invasion of Lebanon had surprised them, and that they needed time to gather their wits. They realized that they did not have the strength to handle two fronts, the Bekaa Valley and the Golan Heights. Admitting their inferiority in the air and in their antiaircraft network, which was much larger than Israel had thought, they also noted the tremendous technological gap that appeared in their flight-control network. This effort to reveal their deficiencies and faults in the field of battle and to admit to Israel's military superiority indicated a healthy Syrian movement away from self-deception.

"Occasionally," the Syrians admitted in their research,

> enemy aircraft surprised ours by flying between the two mountain chains in Lebanon or from the sea. They were guided by excellent control systems from the ground and by detection and warning aircraft that were constantly in the air. The activation of the airborne control network of Hawkeyes along with Boeing 707s loaded with electronic surveillance equipment, which executed their missions over the Mediterranean, was well integrated with the activities of the quality F-15 aircraft armed with long-range high-execution air-to-air missiles. Thus the enemy was able to penetrate close to the Syrian border, even along Mount Hermon, without being detected by our forces. From there they were able to intercept our aircraft with complete surprise.
>
> In all of its sorties over Lebanon, the enemy used active blocking of our control systems and wireless blocking of the majority of our communications frequencies. Our aircraft were often immediately intercepted during their first stages of takeoff after electronic blocking was activated against them, disrupting the aircraft's communications and radar systems as well as the overall control systems. Thus the entire Syrian air response was essentially disrupted, and our General Command decided to limit air activities to the Lebanese skies alone

and not to attack in other areas. As long as the enemy did not attack our forces stationed in Lebanon, we maintained the status quo.

It was crowded in the Lebanese skies from the morning of June 9 until that afternoon. The first level, along the coast from Sidon to the outskirts of Beirut, was packed with Kfirs and Skyhawks assisting the ground forces and attacking terrorist targets in the refugee camps at low altitude. On the second level, at ten thousand feet and above, similar formations anticipated the flight controller's command to attack and were prepared to be sent to any area of the fighting. On the upper level, at high altitude, Hawkeye aircraft were providing continuous air control, precise coordination between planes in the air, and activation of electronic warfare measures against the Syrian systems. The routine activities of the day did not affect the operation that was about to begin.

The pioneers of the special mission force began to sneak in between the flanks, assisting the ground forces in the mountain areas. Among the targets they attacked at low altitude was the radar at the top of Jabel Baruch, which covered wide areas and might provide warning about the "concert" that was about to begin. West of the mountain, the F-15s and F-16s gathered, ready to intercept Syrian aircraft that might be scrambled against the attacking force.

The Prime Minister's office gave the green light at approximately 1330 hours. Returning to the Control Center, Ivri heard Raful's voice.

"Go. And good luck."

Aviem transmitted the code word to the squadrons. The forces were standing ready on the runways.

"Gabi" taxied his Kfir to takeoff position at Ramat David and sank into the concentration that precedes an operational sortie and liberates one from fears and sensitivities. For an entire year he had dreamed about his target. He wondered if he could make the dream real in the seconds that he had been allocated to charge at it from low altitude, then pull up, dive, and release his load of bombs on the missile battery, fleeing. He had been promised that, unlike other fliers in other wars, he would not be taking a "blockheaded" risk. Veterans of past wars were the leaders on this flight. They preferred not to recall previous conditions. Gabi found some confidence in the sense of being a component of an enormous machine, a part whose steps were calculated and guided by invisible wires.

"Scramble!"

The voice of the flight supervisor in the tower was, as always, direct, though somewhat parched.

The attack aircraft took off in pairs—Kfirs, Skyhawks, Phantoms, and F-16s loaded to capacity with various types of weapons, twice the quantity needed to ensure complete destruction of the missile batteries. Other aircraft were already in the air. They arranged themselves opposite the missile locations along the Bekaa Valley in levels, each level and its aircraft prepared to do its share in blocking communication, locating batteries, disrupting radar and guidance systems, and diverting missiles. Only after neutralizing all the threats and defensive belts did the first level of bombers attack their exposed and helpless targets. Gabi was finally able to release the light shiver of emotion that had built up in him when he saw "his" battery wiped off the map.

The Syrian research book described the events as an attack by many formations simultaneously, as all the Syrian detection, warning, and communications systems were blocked from Boeing 707 and Hawkeye aircraft and from ground stations. Pilotless aircraft transmitted data, and twenty-four Phantoms attacked, firing Shrike and Maverick missiles from long range. At exactly 1400 hours the Phantoms struck at the batteries' fire-control centers and silenced them. Immediately afterward, forty aircraft of different varieties attacked the batteries, destroying almost all of them within forty-five minutes. A third wave of Israeli aircraft located everything that was not hit and attacked it, eventually striking at all the other antiaircraft units. A fourth Israeli bombing wave attacked anything moving on the ground, including vehicles, armored units, and supply trucks.

Nineteen batteries and the equipment surrounding them were completely destroyed. It was a concentrated attack, using a variety of means, and executed with speed and a multitude of sophisticated weapons, at a quantity much beyond what was needed. The Syrians were not given a chance to check their damages and repair them, so that the mistakes of the Yom Kippur War were not repeated.

The Syrians were at a loss, for the attack on the missile batteries had developed into one of the largest air battles in history, the biggest since the Korean War. The Syrians claimed that 120 aircraft participated. Avihu Ben-Nun, the commander of the IAF Air Wing, stated that the Syrians alone scrambled approximately one hundred MiG-21 and MiG-

23 aircraft; therefore it can be assumed that a total of at least two hundred aircraft were flying in the Lebanese skies for those two hours. The scrambling of the Syrian planes was rapid and panicky, no less than the response of the missile battery commanders, who decided to protect themselves with smokescreens that merely attracted attention and made identification of the targets easier. The Syrian aircraft, which attempted to protect the batteries, were another example of the confusion and blindness that resulted from the disruption of the radar and communications equipment. The scrambling of the MiG aircraft bordered on unconscious suicide, for the missiles, now destroyed, had been placed in the Bekaa Valley as a protective umbrella for the Syrian ground forces and to ensure that the aircraft had clean skies.

The entry of the Syrian aircraft into the battle, unsure of whether the missiles were functional, placed them at a disadvantage. Essentially the missile system was neutralized. David Ivri could now allow himself to transfer command of the missile attack to Aviem Sela, so that he could manage the developing air battle. The F-15 aircraft from the backup position had an advantage, for they could see, but were themselves hidden. With the guidance of the warning systems and the airborne and ground-centered flight control, they could fire their missiles at long distances at a large percentage of the Syrian MiGs.

Herzle Bodinger had trouble believing the reports that were streaming into the war room of his base. The MiGs were rushing into the battle zone and falling like flies. The technological competition between East and West, in a clash of investments valued at billions of dollars, ended with a conclusive victory by the West. At least twenty-two MiGs, of both models, were shot down (in addition to seven others that had been downed since that morning), constituting between one-quarter and one-third of the Syrian force. Not a single Israeli aircraft was downed.

It was a special record. At this rate of zero losses, David Ivri decided to halt the attack and the air combat, and to return the Israeli force to its bases, even though three SA-6 batteries still remained in the area, having hidden themselves by shutting down their radar. In the IAF debriefing the following day, the remaining batteries were mentioned repeatedly. Ivri defended his considerations. He had been deterred by the dangers involved in searching for the batteries. The benefit of destroying them would be marginal at best, relative to the tremendous achievements of the attack. The batteries would not be worth the loss of even one aircraft.

The following day, Aviem revealed to an IAF journalist that they had used diversionary devices to confuse the missiles and their operators. Gabi had been amazed to see the missiles climbing from the valley toward him and his comrades, and then suddenly veering off and disappearing. The picture from the ground was similar. IDF soldiers watching the attack saw the SA-6 missiles fired toward the aircraft, dragging their orange trails behind them. The aircraft did not attempt to flee, and the pilots seemed indifferent to the threat chasing them. However, a moment before the fatal collision, the missiles broke from their paths and exploded in balls of fire and smoke after pulling out of range of the Israeli aircraft.

In an article titled "Lessons of the Air War in Lebanon," published in Moscow as the Syrian book was being released, Colonel Dubrov, a high-ranking officer in the Soviet Army, complimented the planners and formation leaders of the Israeli attack and referred to them as "initiators and inventors of the highest degree." He also said that even IDF soldiers learned of the hard hand of the IAF when an Israeli plane incorrectly identified the quickly shifting line of the front and mistakenly bombed an Israeli unit, killing fifty-three soldiers and wounding twice that number. His statements about the destruction of additional missile batteries were only half true. Though several launchers had managed to enter Lebanon and situate themselves in the Beirut suburbs, the colonel ignored the fact that three SA-8 missile batteries, of the most advanced type available, which had been brought to Syria after the attack on the Bekaa Valley system, had been destroyed two weeks later. *Aviation Week* magazine claimed that sophisticated protective systems for electronic countermeasures and even the expertise of the top Soviet officer in the missile network who had arrived in Damascus at the head of a research delegation and personally commanded the operation of the batteries could not help.

After the attack, aviation experts throughout the world competed at deciphering the secret technology that had shattered the SAMs' monstrous and invincible reputation. Like the Syrian book, *Aviation Week* mentioned the Hawkeye surveillance aircraft, which could simultaneously handle 150 combat targets and track Syrian aircraft that were still on the runway. The Boeing 707 was described as a flying fortress that fired electronic rays in every direction, disrupting radar systems. In this attack, it had caused the MiGs, which were scrambled to protect the missiles, to find themselves groping in the fog without directional flight control from the ground. Thus they were shot down one after the other. The journal stated that Israel's Zeev missile was a two-stage surface-to-surface artillery missile that could home in on radar waves emitted by the missile batteries. After the booster stage fell away, the second deadly stage, identical to the Shrike, would find its target.

Over the years, a number of sophisticated armaments produced by Israel have been revealed. Marketing materials represent only part of their operational possibilities.

The various pilotless aircraft produced by IAI and Tadiran were developed and improved beyond the transmission of television images of the front in real time. They were equipped with electro-optic systems for the precise tracking of targets, as well as with equipment for the disruption of radar systems. Elta developed a pod for electronic warfare that resembled a drop tank carried under an aircraft's wings. The first such pod was developed during the War of Attrition. Five generations of the device have since followed. It is three meters long and weighs 250 kilograms. As the aircraft enters the range of enemy missiles or radar-guided cannons, it receives the transmissions of the antiaircraft systems, analyzes them, and, according to need, transmits back incorrect signals that distance the missiles and cannot shells from the aircraft.

The missile diversionary devices known as Samson and Delilah were different in characteristics and prices. The Samson resembles a bomb that is suspended from the plane's wing and, when released, can maneuver in the air in a glide or in automatic, computer-directed flight. Its path is preprogrammed. From the moment it disconnects from the aircraft over a missile area, it homes in on enemy radar exactly like a plane. The batteries waste their missiles on it. If it is an evasive SA-6 battery, its location is revealed during the firing (as well as in the activating or extinguishing of the radar), and it becomes an easy target for manned aircraft. The Samson is efficient in all weather conditions and at night. Any aircraft can carry three Samsons in addition to its normal weapons, and can confuse an entire battery when dropping the diversionary devices from forty thousand feet. Before its use in Israel, it was offered to the United States for production purposes. The Americans refused. After the destruction of the Syrian missile system, they remembered the offer and regretted their lack of vision. Delilah is Samson's intelligent double, more flexible and expensive. It has an engine and excellent maneuverability, which create the impression that it is actually a plane. The most efficient diversionary method involves a Delilah along with several Samsons. A number of militaries have requested to purchase them.

Another weapon that was divulged was the Israeli version of the U.S. Shrike missile. Called the Purple Fist, it destroyed the radar of the missile batteries. The original American version resembled the Soviet Kelt missile, which was fired on Tel Aviv and the regional air-control station in the Sinai on the first day of the Yom Kippur War. It is an air-to-surface missile that detects and rides the radar waves of the center of the missile battery until it destroys the fire-control station and the operations center, silencing the battery's brain and killing its operators. The advanced Shrike is more intelligent than its predecessor, which could be confused or neutralized by the shutting down of the radar. The Israeli version was developed immediately after the Yom Kippur War for use against the SA-2 and SA-3 missiles. It "remembers" the target even if the electromagnetic ray it was following disappears, and continues to fly automatically toward the control center. It can also chase mobile radar such as the SA-6, and is protected against diversionary transmissions. The Purple Fist is a comfortable weapon for the pilot, for it is of the "fire and forget" type.

IAI publicized the Griffin, a laser-guided air-to-surface missile that excels in its strike, precise to within a radius of eight meters from the target at a firing range of five kilometers. The missile has a double guidance system in the nose and the tail. The nose laser sensor follows the laser indicator, which "illuminates" the target. The mechanism can also be placed on conventional bombs to guarantee maximum strike accuracy. Elbit developed the Ofer system, which homes in on heat sources and can also be added to other bombs, providing them with greater intelligence. Rafael, the national Israeli weapons development company, developed the Pyramid, a television-guided bomb, similar to the Maverick, which was given to Israel during the Yom Kippur War. In the nose of the American missile, which is carried by Phantom aircraft and is driven by solid fuel, is a guidance mechanism with a television camera eye. The system receives the picture of the target at the moment of firing, and the eye follows it and homes in, even if the missile has been fired from high altitude toward a massive target. This is also a "fire and forget" missile, for the Pyramid glides down to its target at an angle.

• • • •

The operation for the destruction of the Syrian missile batteries in Lebanon did not have advantageous opening conditions. The element of surprise was not used, for the attacks began on the fourth day of the war, when IDF battalions were already spread across Lebanon and were headed toward Beirut and were on the verge of a conflict with Syrians on the ground and within range of the missiles. Aviem Sela scrambled the aircraft under the assumption that the Syrians were waiting for them. He was amazed by the extent of their surprise. It is difficult to explain the Syrians' shock, unless they assumed that if they had not been attacked up to this point, they were not going to be attacked later. In the following days they abandoned the Lebanese skies, their forces, and their allies to the Israeli aircraft, which assaulted dozens of exposed targets. No efforts were made to stop them. One innovation in this period was the integration of air and ground forces, primarily artillery, in tactics based on the lessons of the successful attacks on the Egyptian missiles late in the Yom Kippur War. Even if the damage was eventually inflicted by conventional bombs, which, in three waves, pummeled the fire-control centers, the missiles, and the various support installations, the secret of Israel's success lay in the sophisticated control of the forces and in the precise coordination and timing of the various means used.

In the late-afternoon hours of June 9, dozens of ground crews in the northern and central bases were busy around the aircraft that had returned from the missile attack and the massive air battle. They were elated at the zero breakdown and damage rate and returned the aircraft to operational readiness at the lightning speed of the competitive cycle. Three armored and infantry brigades had begun to progress to the Bekaa Valley. The tanks were pressing forward to gain control of as much territory as possible between them and the Karoun Lake in the remaining hours of light. There were virtually no terrorists remaining in the region. It was almost completely in Syrian control. The penetration to the Syrian systems in the upcoming two days, through the roadblocks and tank ambushes that they had set, would change the character of the operation. It would no longer be a chase of irregular forces and destruction of their bases and supply depots, but a pressure attack on a professional army that was battered but still well armed and ready for battle.

At around noon, several small helicopters joined the mobile command center. They were not of the types used for assault transport or evacuation of wounded. Within several hours the combat helicopters were ready to introduce a new and surprising dimension into the armored battle, eliciting envy from anyone used to observing the battlefield through a turret or periscope. Ehud Barak, one of the deputy commanders of the ground force, had appreciated the helicopters since he first encountered them during his service as commander of one of the elite IDF commando units. The American Defender and Cobra were a different type of aircraft—small, flexible, and wily—that could preemptively strike armored forces in unfamiliar mountainous areas and in unplanned operations.

Barak gathered the pilots around the map. "You are to look for tanks or artillery and nail them," he said, pointing at a series of purple circles indicating Syrian armored positions in the Bekaa Valley. He then dispatched them as pioneers before the armored corps.

"Mish" noted to himself that the real war started for him at that moment. It would be a sharp firefight with a professional army. There were no longer the dilemmas and pangs of conscience surrounding the sorties earlier that week. For three days they had been ordered to block the terrorists' escape and to destroy pockets of resistance along the coast. Each day he had hesitated at least three times before pulling the trigger. How could he know if a civilian bus with a pile of mattresses on the roof or a black Chevrolet crossing the line of fire was an innocent vehicle or a camouflaged means of escape for the terrorists. Mish was a second-generation pilot in the IAF. His father, also a pilot, had sent him to the IAF Technical School in Haifa, from which he had emerged as an electronics technician. He had served in the IAF for one year on ground crew, gone to the officers' course, and, after another year in administration, volunteered for the Flight School. He had begun the course at twenty-one, five days after his wedding. During the Yom Kippur War he had still been a cadet, and his instructors had pressured him to go into the area of fighter aircraft. Mish, an outdoorsman by nature, had chosen the helicopters, vehicles that would keep him in the country's landscape, close to the trees and the flowers.

He had been sent to the Inverted Sword Squadron, and after a year he had participated in replacing the Bell 212 helicopters with the Cobra, entering the new age of helicopters in combat. The first six Bell Cobras arrived in Israel in the summer of 1975. This was a sophisticated version compared with the first ones, which had begun to fly in Vietnam. However, the IDF command, owing to the same emotional problems that had delayed the Sikorsky in the early 1960s, still had trouble accepting them. While the Bell 205 squadrons had been converted for combat missions with additions of the 30-millimeter Mirage cannons and 80-millimeter antitank rocket beehives, the replacements were not at the level of the originals. If so, the Bell Company would not have developed the Cobra. General Kinnard, the father of transport assault in the U.S. Army, tried to comfort those of us in the IAF who felt frustrated. "Ground forces commanders will always prefer the heavy, long-range fire power of the cannon or the attack aircraft. They will accept the flying mortars unwillingly, only as a second choice. So stop eating your hearts out. Even *our* military relates to the armed helicopter as a flying mortar."

Seven years and one war passed before it was decided to purchase the first Cobras. If they had come two years earlier, the Cobras could have replaced the aircraft that were downed during the Yom Kippur War, blocking the tanks in the Sinai and the Golan Heights under the umbrella of missiles. Mish participated in the interbranch team that developed theories of combat for the combat helicopters, which became the most efficient means of hunting tanks and blocking armored waves in surprise attacks until reserves could be mobilized.

The Cobras purchased in 1975 were modeled after those used by the U.S. Marine Corps. They still had the old triple-barreled 40-millimeter cannons in a forward turret, which fired 750 shells per minute, along with four weapons hangers under a pair of short wings that also carried antitank rockets. Its shape was reminiscent of a broad snake's head, twice the width of the body. The pilot sat behind the weapons-systems operator in a cockpit that constituted most of the helicopter's body. A year later, Shuki Livnat, the squadron commander, joined a group of fighter and helicopter pilots as part of an observer team in an integrated night exercise whose purpose was to evaluate low-altitude night attack. He boarded a CH-53 and did not return, for the helicopter, carrying fifty-four passengers, including paratroopers and aircrew, crashed in the dark of night near Jericho. Mish completed his flight instructor course and returned to the Cobras under the weight of the heaviest tragedy ever to befall the IAF.

The new breed of pilots manning the combat helicopters that appeared in the Lebanon War were strange to the generation of technologically focused fighter pilots who dealt with the enemy by pressing a button from a range of forty kilometers. Those who watched from the side could barely believe the calmness with which they entered these duels, reminiscent of the eighteenth century. They would aim their wrath toward the nearest tank or cannon, which would fire at them simultaneously. They would also hover at grass level among the snipers and machine gunners, who could hit them with even a stray bullet to the head or the fuel tank. Mish knew that these images concealed respect, envy, and perhaps a latent longing for the close-range air battles that had disappeared in the age of the F-15.

In late 1977, after debates and exercises with the commanders of the armored battalions, the Cobras were returned to the United States to be equipped with firing and guidance systems for Tow missiles, which could destroy tanks from a maximum distance of 3,750 meters, far from the tank's firing range. Until now, these missiles had only been fired from jeeps or armored vehicles. The Tow operator focuses the cross hairs in his gunsights on the target and fires the missiles. He is then able to control its flight through a fine wire that follows it through a small controlling stick in the optical navigation equipment. The new Cobra was programmed to carry eight missiles and six hundred cannon shells on every sortie. The shipment of the Cobras to the Hughes factories, which manufactured the Tow missiles, created a new era as IAF and armored corps engineers were preparing to introduce the Tow to the Cobra system in Israel.

The Defender, a light attack helicopter, was offered to the IAF at an excellent price. The United States had used the civilian model, the Hughes HO-6, during the Vietnam War for patrol missions alongside the Huey Cobra combat helicopters. The military version, the D-500, was developed three years before the withdrawal from Vietnam. The chances to prove its operational capabilities seemed greater in the Middle East than in any environments in which the American military was likely to use them at that time.

At first glance, it appeared to be a toy whose light weight (six hundred kilograms) and short body were the essential elements in its astounding executions. Mish would never forget his surprise when he first saw the Defender take off silently under its five rotor blades, barely raising a cloud of dust around it. The dizzying maneuvers and sharp turns (up to 110 degrees) of the small helicopter allowed it to fly quickly at ground level and to hide behind any plant, tree, or embankment without the noise of rotors to reveal its presence. Its flexibility made up for the limited weapons it could carry relative to the Cobra, only four Tow missiles on a pair of launchers, without a cannon.

The Hughes deal, which was concluded after a year and a half of contacts and tests, included thirty Defenders. The first ones arrived in December 1979. Their low price canceled the purchase plans for the Cobra beyond the first six, which had already been paid for and were about to arrive. As the pilots expanded their familiarity with the Defender, they became convinced that they now had the ideal attack helicopter. Two squadrons, called Northern and Southern, were formed on the same base in the center of the country. These squadrons would become the base for the absorption of the Apache assault helicopters in 1990. Like everyone else, Mish learned to fly the Defender and the Cobra in both roles, as pilot and systems operator.

The combat helicopters missed out on Operation Litani. In March 1978, the Cobra was still undergoing its transplant operation for the Tow missiles in the United States. Shortly after their return during the summer, the terrorists destroyed a house on the Israeli moshav of Margaliot, on the Lebanese border. Members of Saad Haddad's pro-Israeli militia tracked them to the refugee camp of Beit Al-Halil near Tyre. They had taken shelter in a two-story house not far from the coast. Mish was in the midst of a training sortie, one of the target range drills they were executing with the improved Cobras. Since live fire of the Tow cost $10,000 per missile, they practiced using missiles whose operational date had expired.

In the midst of the exercise, he was ordered to return to base and to prepare to attack an actual target. It was to be the squadron's maiden operational flight and Mish's first test of combat. Officers from IAF headquarters were waiting for the pilots in the operations room with aerial photographs on which they had marked the house. They had only an hour to learn the flight route and the details of the landscape, even if they would have the map and the photographs on their knees during the operation. The Cobra's reasonable speed (three hundred kilometers per hour) allowed them to manage comfortably in the terrain. The attack would take place at dusk, as the sun set against the eyes of the terrorists in the house.

Mish was allocated to the second helicopter, and would serve as the missile and cannon operator. His partner, Tzion Bar-Or, asked to fly. He was an amateur photographer, and did not want to miss the opportunity to photograph the events. They flew over the sea, far from the coast, at an altitude of twenty meters. Before Tyre, they readied themselves to identify the target, relying not only on the leader, but also on themselves. The navigation was easy. They approached to within three kilometers of the house and climbed to one hundred meters.

The refugee camp did not panic at their appearance, for the terrorists had yet to identify them as threatening. From the distance they looked like innocent and nonviolent patrol-and-rescue helicopters. They might even have belonged to the Lebanese Army. The Cobras hovered for a long moment. The leader aimed and fired first. Thin, hesitant fire began to come from the camp. The surprise was complete, and an aggressive helicopter with such strength was an amazing sight. Tzion continued photographing. It was Mish's turn to fire. He did not want to miss. He placed his eye against the gunsight, set the house in the cross hairs, and pressed the firing button as he moved the small steering stick that directed the missile along the wire that fed out of its belly. As long as the cross hairs remained on the house, the missile would race to its target. The shifting of the Cobra hovering in the air could be readjusted by small movements of the stick. A moment later, Mish saw the hit.

The Tow easily pierced the brick wall of the house. Its hollow closed mechanism, the missile head activated upon touch, emitted a burst of flames that destroyed everything around it. He saw no one running from the house after the four missiles struck both floors. The antiaircraft fire diminished and stopped, and Tzion's camera continued to snap its pictures. When he had used up his film, he said they could return home.

The Defender entered an operational routine at the end of July 1980, four months after the formation of the squadron. The Cobra was already hovering over a violent caldron of patrols, terrorist chases, and extermination of makeshift bases in the civilian surroundings. Eye contact between the helicopters and the small targets almost completely prevented injury to innocent parties, which would have been unavoidable from an altitude of thousands of feet. Because of this, IAF headquarters began to take missions from the fighter aircraft for allocation to the combat helicopters. The Defenders' first combat experience was in a night attack on terrorist positions and a radar bunker in the Rashidiyeh refugee camp in Tyre.

The IAF developed theories of combat from the imaginations of the ground forces' commanders and the aircrews, and from lessons of separate and joint exercises. Formations four and eight helicopters strong learned to synchronize their fire and to achieve accuracy in navigating the missiles to their targets. Though they prepared to face torrents of tanks that would roll across the Sinai or the Golan Heights in the next war, the script that developed in Lebanon in 1982 was very different from what they had expected. The war caught Mish in the midst of an intersquadron soccer game. The squadron was on alert starting in the morning hours, and the pilots related to it as part of the routine. After the assassination attempt against the Israeli ambassador in London the previous night, Israeli aircraft would spend the day bombing "terrorist targets in Lebanon," as the IDF military spokesman described them. Until the afternoon, the combat helicopters were kept out of the picture.

The operations loudspeaker called three teams to the briefing, of which two would head out to the sortie, while one stood as reserve. The terrorists had responded with heavy Katyusha fire on Israel's north, and the Cobras had been commanded to silence the towed missile launchers. An hour later it became clear that one silencing sortie would not be enough. The Katyushas continued to fall, and even grew stronger. Mish took off with the next pair, turned toward the sea, then cut northward parallel to the coast. After the border, he broke east and began to search the area. Evening was setting in. To their good fortune, there was a full moon. They easily detected the armored vehicles towing the Katyusha launchers, and blew them up with cannon fire. Then they exited, and a constant rotation of pairs continued throughout the night. Every cannon strafing reduced the shelling. By morning, the terrorists were hurrying to take cover the instant they heard the helicopters' rotors. The sorties continued, and the squadrons were ordered to head north and take position at emergency forward landing pads along the border.

During these hours, the Defenders' maiden war began. In their silent flight at vegetation level, they were able to detect and surprise any armored vehicle or artillery that the terrorists had hidden in the territory—even the Soviet T-34 tanks, which were entrenched and camouflaged against fighter aircraft attacks. After the first T-34 was destroyed, they celebrated, but soon lost count of the number of targets they had destroyed. At the conclusion of the war, it was decided that the helicopters would not be decorated with symbols of the ground targets they had destroyed. A tank simply was not a plane.

That Saturday evening the Cobras deepened their sorties and crossed north of the Litani River, chasing the artillery batteries as they retreated. For nearly an entire day they flew back and forth between Lebanon and Israel in a series of crazed runs of fuel-arm-attack. Mish thought the day would never end. Over the Zaharani ravine, which empties into the sea south of Sidon, they could hear, over and over, "Two calling One" from one of the other pairs. As the call went on, Two's voice grew more and more tense. Mish identified the speaker and knew that the helicopter flown by Amichai Spector and Yossi Keller must be missing. He still hoped that it was just the radio that had disappeared. No missiles defended the area in which they flew. The minimal antiaircraft fire, which caused no damage during the day, disappeared entirely at night. Their helicopter had apparently run into some object and crashed. "Two" requested that the area where "One" had last been heard be illuminated, but the request was denied. Searches of the area for Spector and Keller's distress signal would illuminate patrols and risk helicopters and the lives of the rescue crews.

During the first hours of Operation Peace for Galilee, the terrorists tried to elevate the spirits of the residents with victory chants, exulting that they had downed an Israeli plane. They dragged Keller's body through the streets of Sidon and made sure that the photograph was displayed by the international press. The dead pilot was not identified. The story of yet another young airman from Kibbutz Kfar Giladi in Israel's north, who had died defending his home, twenty kilometers from the farm, was not yet released in Israel. He was the fourth pilot from the kibbutz to die in combat.


Tuesday evening, after the capture of Sidon, the combat helicopters' real war began. Aviem Sela sent them to attack the radar station at Halda, on a hill south of Beirut. The mission had been planned for the Sky-hawks, but Aviem reconsidered and decided to use the Cobras. Two pairs approached the station and fired their Tow missiles from low altitude. The antennas and installations were destroyed, and the building began to burn. This maiden attack on a military target had been a success. Mish did not know that they were firing the first shot in the operation for the destruction of the Syrian missile system, which was to begin the following day. The Syrians also did not get the hint. The helicopters were barely active on the eastern front; until that evening they had simply silenced a number of terrorist positions in Fatah-land and shot at Syrian vehicles nearing the eastern battalion lines.

The level of danger in their real battlefield was greater than the danger awaiting them along the coast. However, the shift to an armored battle also increased the level of personal satisfaction. For the first time in IDF history, the crews of the combat helicopters received their intelligence picture and their operational briefing directly from the battalion commander. They took off on the missions after coordinating communications and observations with the armored corps commanders from a hilltop, surveying the area in which the Syrian tanks were to be found.

The shock of the helicopters' appearance affected the combat on the front, which had been stripped of its missile protection. A lone Sohoi that passed under Mish as he was about to land near a regiment of Israeli tanks did not receive any attention. The presence of the helicopters limited the initiatives of the Syrian tanks, a number of which took cover, allowing the Israeli armored corps to improve their positions. Along the front at Sultan Yaakub, the Syrians set a deadly ambush for the Israeli tanks. Even the helicopters were not able to assist them. Afterward, as the Israelis progressed into the Syrians' territory, toward the Beirut-Damascus road, the confusion of battle increased, and Mish's sense of confidence decreased.

On Friday, the sixth day of the war, Mish flew a Defender in a race to the Beirut-Damascus Road. The Israeli tank units had taken position five kilometers from the road, twelve kilometers from the town of Zahla. In the morning the Syrians had reinforced their position. The number of weapons they pushed into the Bekaa Valley indicated that the combat helicopter squadrons' dream of a massive battle might be realized. It was a race against the clock, for a cease-fire was to be declared that afternoon. Battalion intelligence reported a large force headed toward them. Some of the Defenders flew at high altitude over the mountainous region with its deep ravines, and found the Syrian force on a dirt road, closer than expected and before the Israeli force was prepared for the conflict. The Syrians had T-72 tanks, the best in Soviet armor, as well as armored personnel carriers and light vehicles towing Katyusha launchers. The helicopters pulled back toward the rear side of the mountain. In one of the ravines, they coordinated their activities while still hovering at vegetation level. They then set in on the column. From the mountain heights they identified their targets, and as they descended they began to feel turbulence, for there was a strong crosswind that they had not felt in the ravine. They lost the stability needed for accurate firing of the Tow, and while attempting to steady the helicopters, they also lost the element of surprise. They were exposed.

The Syrians fled quickly in every direction to take cover. Their confusion disrupted the hovering helicopters. The leader fired a missile toward an armored vehicle, which skirted around a hill. He decided to change his route to hit another. He was taking a risk, something quite different from the past days of easy strafings at stationary targets. Everyone was moving quickly, the frightened armored units, the pursuing helicopters, and of course the missiles. Though the Tow is connected to the helicopter by its guiding wire, it takes a well-trained team coordinated to the millisecond to score a hit under such conditions. The chances were infinitesimal. The navigator considered looking for a new target. Less than two seconds would elapse before the missile reached the end of the wire's range, so he decided to chase another armored vehicle. He dropped the cross hairs in the gunsight to an empty spot on the hill that connected to that imaginary line of the path the Syrian was following. The missile skipped over the hill, and a tremendous explosion followed. A column of black smoke indicated the location of the hit. The helicopter pulled to the side to clear the area for the next in line. A T-72 fired at him. He executed a climb in a 360-degree loop that placed him behind the tank. From short range, he fired a missile into its body, and an orange flame burst out of the steel armor, flipping the tank on its side.

As these events were occurring, Mish was in a Defender high and far from there, in the area of Jabel Baruch, providing support to an armored column breaking through to the Beirut-Damascus road. He had been scrambled to meet a force of Syrian tanks near the village of Ein-Diya. Mish identified fifteen T-62 tanks headed toward a deep canyon. He made contact with the Israeli armored commander and divided the targets with him, then headed to the canyon and destroyed his first tank. The Syrians showered him with cannon and machine-gun fire. Mish hid behind a rocky slope and planned to fire his second missile. As he hovered at fifty feet, a powerful explosion shook the cockpit and lit all the warning lights, including the one telling him to make an emergency landing. Only three seconds remained to organize the landing, and the rocks on the hillside threatened to crush his bones. He attempted to soften the landing, but in vain. The helicopter slammed into the ground, breaking its tail. Mish then understood what had happened. A Syrian shell had hit a rock, and its fragments had ripped into his engine, weapons systems, and gunsight. Several pieces of shrapnel were also lodged in the belly of his copilot, who pulled himself out of the helicopter and fell to the ground after taking several steps. Mish closed the throttles and disconnected the electrical systems. The three remaining live missiles could explode at any second, and the Syrian fire continued to chase him. The demolished helicopter lay exposed on a hillside overlooking the canyon. Tank and artillery shells flew above them, exploding only twenty meters away. Mish transmitted his distress signal to the Israeli armored forces and to the aircraft flying above, and told them about the wounded copilot. A Bell helicopter five kilometers away received the message and approached them in between the shells. Its pilot searched and found a landing spot on the hillside below them. Mish and the Bell's copilot lowered the wounded man to the helicopter as shells exploded every second. They made their way out safely, and the cease-fire took effect at 1200 hours.

Mish alone destroyed six of the dozens of tanks and armored vehicles that were hit by the combat helicopters during that first week. The fighter squadrons shot down eighty-seven Syrian aircraft during the first two weeks, and another five during the following weeks, including the first MiG-23 and MiG-25 to be shot down in world history. The only Israeli planes shot down were hit by ground fire and not in air combat. These included one Phantom, one Skyhawk, two Bell 212s, one Defender, and one Cobra. The Lebanon War, which took place in waves and with a sense of slow attrition, essentially ended three years later, in 1985, when the IDF withdrew.

David Ivri, who transferred command of the IAF to Amos Lapidot, concluded his service with a 124-to-0 victory in air combat, the IAF having achieved superiority against the enemy air defenses. Thus the tremendous change that had begun during Benny Peled's command, with its technological improvement in all aspects of the IAF's activities, had concluded.

It was Saturday night, September 28, 1985, and "Guy" was a member of the crack team that had gathered for a five-hour briefing before an unprecedented attack sortie that was to take off within three days. He was the highest-ranking officer in the group and also the oldest. IDF Chief of Staff Moshe Levi and IAF Commander-in-Chief Amos Lapidot had given their permission for Guy to participate if he wanted to.

On the morning of September 25, Yom Kippur, three terrorists had assaulted an Israeli yacht harbored in Larnaca, Cyprus. By noontime they had murdered the three Israelis on board in cold blood. The terrorists belonged to Force 17, a unit that had become the PLO's chief operational force after the Lebanon War. That evening the IDF General Command decided to strike at PLO headquarters. Minister of Defense Yitzhak Rabin stated that the PLO would not have immunity "anywhere in the world." His proclamation that "the long arm of the IDF would know how to reach them and punish them" left no doubt that the attack would be in the hands of the IAF.

Three years earlier, in early September 1982, 14,500 terrorists had withdrawn from Beirut in exchange for the removal of the IDF blockade of the western part of the city. While terrorist pockets still remained in areas of Lebanon not under IDF control, their command centers, including the headquarters of Yasser Arafat, the chairman of the PLO, were evicted from Lebanon. The president of Tunisia, Habib Bourgiva, was the only Arab leader who agreed to give them refuge. The command groups of the PLO and Force 17 chose a seaside vacation area on the northern end of Africa, opposite the shores of Sicily. The Hamas A-Shatt neighborhood lies approximately twenty kilometers southeast of the capital. Terrorist plotting continued under the innocent cover of the tourist villas and pensiones, which provide ideal sea and beach for those seeking sun in the early European autumn.

The terrorists delayed the renewal of their activities until after the Israeli withdrawal from Lebanon, which began in February 1985 and concluded in June of that year. It left a narrow security zone north of the Israeli border that was controlled by the Southern Lebanese Army, under Israeli auspices. On September 21 a terrorist squad infiltrated the security zone and fired several Katyushas into the Galilee. Airborne and armored Israeli forces began a hunt, capturing three terrorists. Above the village of Shihin, beyond the security zone, one of the helicopters was hit by an RPG. Its pilots and fighters escaped before it burned. Four days later the Israeli tourists were murdered in Larnaca.

An air attack on PLO headquarters in Tunis was one of the possibilities weighed the following day by the defense cabinet. The Minister of

Defense would make the decision. Prime Minister Shimon Peres also favored the plan, and persuaded the other ministers to agree. Elections to the Knesset, held in the summer of 1984, in the shadow of the Lebanon War, which had cost the lives of 625 Israelis, resulted in a tie between the Labor and Likud parties. They further decided to form a national unity government that would be controlled in turn by Shimon Peres of the Labor party and Yitzhak Shamir of the Likud, each for two years.

Of all the proposals presented to the cabinet, the attack on Tunis had the greatest chance of success with the lowest risk. Amos Lapidot described the flight route to the ministers, explaining that it would be beyond international routes and guarantee almost complete security and surprise. Lapidot assumed that enemy air forces in North Africa would not interfere and disrupt the mission, even if they noticed it. The Tunisian Air Force was small and not threatening, and there were no air defenses at the terrorists' headquarters. The only risk was in the long flight over the sea, 1,280 miles in each direction. The fighter squadrons had ten years' experience in long-range sorties that involved midair refueling. The Skyhawks and Phantoms had flown far beyond Israel's borders during Benny Peled's command. Since then, the means of refueling had been improved. F-15 and F-16 aircraft had been added, and had proven themselves by flying to Baghdad and back without refueling. The cabinet decided that the attack would take place four days hence, on the morning of Tuesday, October 1. They wanted to avoid injuries to tourists who fill the beaches on Sunday and desecration of the Jewish holiday of Sukkot, which was to begin on Monday.

Though the cabinet spent a long night deliberating the attack, IAF headquarters did not waste time. As the ministers were discussing the risks of the mission, Guy and his teammates were developing the operation plan as if approval were guaranteed. Technically, the F-15 was the most reliable aircraft. It could carry the required bombs a great distance and also defend itself in air combat. Designed with a maximum flight range of 2,800 miles and a maximum bomb load of five and a half tons, it was chosen for the mission. Since the destruction of the Iraqi nuclear reactor, the F-15 also had the advantage of a huge belly drop tank.

The ten aircraft chosen for the attack force were sorted according to their individual histories of reliability. In the four days that remained before takeoff, every bolt was checked, though the technicians did not know what the mission was. Only eight aircraft would participate in the attack, in two formations. An additional pair would serve as reserves and would accompany the formations to the point of no return, where the first refueling would take place. The planes were of the two-seat model in which the crew included a navigator to split the load with the pilot and relieve the loneliness. In a test run of the flight on September 27, immediately after receiving approval for the operation, they checked the planes' fitness for midair refueling and several attack runs.

The test run was the first step in the actual preparations, which began three days before the attack and did not conclude until takeoff. The aircrews studied the flight route, the refueling stations, and the timetables. They memorized the targets and bombing locations allocated to each specific aircraft. Israeli intelligence added more maps, sketches, and photographs daily. The ground crews rechecked all the planes' parts and replaced anything that might cause problems.

On Saturday night the planning groups and aircrews gathered for five hours of summary briefing. At 1300 hours, "Nir," the formation leader, presented the plans to the chief of staff, the IAF commander-in-chief, and top officers in IAF headquarters. Amos Lapidot emphasized the means that would prevent injury to civilians, from the attack methods to the types of weapons being used. The chief of staff instructed the aircrews to bomb only after definitive identification of their targets. Before entering the briefing auditorium of one of the squadrons, Guy urged the administrative officer of the base to run to a supermarket in the nearby town to buy "energy food" for the mission, dried fruit and soft drinks, enough to last twenty aircrew members half a day. Urine bags had already been prepared, a lesson from the long sortie to Baghdad.

At 0530 hours, everyone was in the squadron. Nir summarized the familiar briefing, emphasizing the important elements. The only detail about the target that remained unclear was the weather. Satellite photos revealed that clouds covered the gulf every morning, and this morning was no different. However, the forecast spoke of an improvement and, at worst, light cloud cover. At 0600 the team split up for forty-five minutes of aircraft checks and personal time. Each pilot and navigator received 250 grams of dried fruit and drinks. Nir recommended that they not overdo the drinking, so as not to burden their bladders.

Just before 0700 hours, Guy sat in his G suit, strapped into his seat. He started his engines without problems. The F-15 taxied slowly toward its heavy takeoff. Its wings were loaded to their maximum with bombs and Sidewinder air-to-air missiles on the hangers. The 20-millimeter cannons were loaded to capacity. Nir looked around and counted the aircraft by the identification numbers on their tails. He knew each of them by heart, for not a single aircraft had been replaced. Though an instant of hesitation struck Guy at the takeoff point, it dissipated as the wheels left the runway, off to six hours of flight. The number 1,280 on the navigational computer, the distance in miles to the target, meant three hours of flight to the objective. This was time enough to review and double-check the systems. They set out on their route and altitude, far from international flight routes, as their radar guaranteed early warning of any aircraft within a radius of one hundred kilometers. However, the skies were clear and clean, visibility was excellent, and the sun was at their backs.

At approximately 1000 hours, the refueling Boeing 707 was flying somewhere between Crete and Italy, at a point defined only on the maps and the navigational computer. Because of a political boycott on sales, the plane had been converted by IAI into a flying fuel tank. Here too, necessity was the mother of invention, for the Americans had refused to sell Israel the original Boeing KC-135 fuel tanks, which are equipped with a hydraulic telescoping refueling boom that can be used with advanced fighter aircraft. Instead they offered the Hercules tankers, which are similar in refueling method to the Stratocruiser tankers, which had often been displayed in IAF parades and were limited in their capabilities to serving the Skyhawks. The Americans considered the Hercules "tactical" equipment, while the Boeing was considered "strategic."

Design of the local version was completed in 1979, and an IAF transport Boeing was sent to IAI for installation of the system. About one year later it executed its first test flight. Fuel tanks filled its entire body except for a small passageway between the cockpit and the operator's station in its rear, from which the refueling boom was maneuvered to the aircraft receiving the fuel. The trial runs concluded in 1983. After two years the secret was revealed to the public, along with its technical advantages over the Western refueling aircraft. It had an electro-optical fuel-control system, the only one of its kind in the world.

The F-15s appeared on the horizon at the set time. The Boeing changed course to join their route. From the moment contact had been made with the flight leader, and the F-15 formations altered their speed to match that of the Boeing, "Rafel" crossed the narrow corridor and took control of the fueling mechanisms. The boom operator must be an excellent pilot and flight engineer. The television control system reduced the strain on the eyes that the operators of the American system had experienced. In this system, two cameras simultaneously transmit a vertical picture and a horizontal picture. A polaroid glass screen crosses between the displays. The operator watches them through glasses resembling those used to view 3-D movies. He sees the F-15 and directs the boom to the opening at its back using a small control stick, as if he were hovering outside of the aircraft. The boom's telescope stretches to fourteen and a half meters and can move twenty degrees in any direction. A third camera at the boom's wing root displays a close-up shot of the F-15's fueling aperture and allows for quick insertion. Contact is made, and hundreds of gallons are funneled in under pressure at double the quantity and speed of the Hercules.

Rafel refueled all of the F-15s, breaking the communications silence with short orders to the pilots coordinating their speed and direction so that he could shorten the connection process. The fueling location was also the point of no return and the last chance to pull out for technical or emotional reasons. Everything went as planned, and no one quit. The reserve aircraft refueled and returned home disappointed. The two quartets continued toward Tunis with the Boeing next to them for another refueling before the target, so that they could enter prepared to contend with any threat.

At 1110 hours, Guy saw the Hamas A-Shatt neighborhood of Tunis. The flat coastal strip stretched into the water straight in their path. Though clouds covered the gulf, they disappeared over the tourist town. The terrorist center lay not far from an island with yachts and luxury swimming pools, on the coast. To the F-15s, it was a series of innocent houses, similar to residential quarters. He had only seconds to identify his target, pull up, dive, and drop his bombs. Guy was to head toward a two-story residential building near the road, used by the terrorist organization A-Tzeeka. He reduced it to rubble. The Force 17 base was in a three-story building on the other side of the road, closer to the sea. Another aircraft demolished it. Two bombs destroyed Yasser Arafat's command center. The other aircraft struck at all the other targets. The head of the PLO was not present at the time and was saved. A house next door to the destroyed residence of deputy PLO chief Abu Al-Muatazam was not even scratched. The attack lasted mere seconds.

The accuracy of the hits would later be seen on the video films of the bombings, which were shown repeatedly at the squadron's home base. In the meantime, under the lasting impression of the pillars of smoke pouring out of the bombed building, they were making their way through the Tunisian skies unmolested. Not a single shell or missile was fired at them from the ground. No aircraft were scrambled to intercept them. The Tunisian Air Force radar was silent that day.

When they counted off, and everyone turned home unharmed, Guy was able to unwrap the dried fruit and eat it one piece at a time throughout the flight home. Over their base, the F-15s executed their "buzz" roll in salute to the ground crews. They were amazed upon stopping to see a large crowd storming the aircraft with embraces and kisses. At 1300 hours, while they were still on their way home, the BBC had reported the strike. The IDF military spokesman quickly revealed the secret. They had reason to be proud, for almost all the command posts had been destroyed. Seventy people had been killed and another eighty-six wounded, almost all of them terrorists. The following day, when Guy saw the post-strike photographs of Tunis, he stated that the damage and the statistics, impressive as they were, were unimportant relative to Israel's show of strategic strength.

Amos Lapidot took command of the IAF on the last day of 1982, and held that office for five years. He had been a member of the first Ouragan squadron under Moti Hod's command. In the Sinai Campaign he had flown a Mystère, covering for the Dakotas that had dropped Raful's paratroopers in the Mitla Pass. Amos's flight history was not full of daring tales, even though he had commanded a Mirage squadron during the Six-Day War. Aces have never become commanders of the IAF. Ezer Weizman and Moti Hod were men of inspiration and spirit. Don Tolkowsky, Benny Peled, and David Ivri were men of substance and intellect. Ultimately, particularly after 1973, the General Command and the government preferred men of organization and control. Lapidot, the man who had headed the Lavi Project, did not manage, as commander-in-chief, to win the war that buried it. He activated the new bases in the Negev and commanded the sortie to Tunis. After the small war in which Israel withdrew from Lebanon, the Syrians began to speak of "strategic balance" with Israel. They purchased additional MiG-23s and the advanced MiG-25. A month after Tunis, Nir took off on a reconnaissance flight over Lebanon, with no intention of engaging in conflict. The Syrians scrambled a pair of MiG-23s at him. Identifying their violent designs, he fired two missiles and downed both aircraft. Damascus stopped speaking of "strategic balance."

The IAF did not execute any extraordinary operations during Amos Lapidot's command. The attack on the terrorist headquarters in Tunis was considered part of ongoing security actions, though it again demonstrated the IAF's strategic capabilities in operations demanding daring, creativity, and precision, even at long range. These were years when operations were severely limited by budgetary constraints. Lapidot had to contend with his obligation to reduce the force under his command, trimming and even closing some units while not harming the levels of training. Throughout this time, however, he would have to continue to bear the burden of war against terrorism along the northern border and in Lebanon. He also had to continue to prepare the IAF for future conflicts using modern technology, new weapons, and high levels of sophistication as the tools in his hands were being decrementally reduced and cut from annual budgets.

He passed on this task to his successor, Maj. Gen. Avihu Ben-Nun, who took command of the IAF after serving as commander of the Planning Branch of the IDF General Command. In Planning Branch, Ben-Nun had encountered difficult budgetary limitations. The financial struggles that have plagued the IAF since its beginnings continue, and without "headline" operations, the preparation for war, which will be different from all others if it occurs, becomes all the more difficult, frustrating, and complicated. These efforts were made more difficult to a certain degree by the detection of corruption in the IAF's upper echelons. Brig. Gen. Rami Dotan, commander of the IAF's equipment division, was caught accepting bribes of millions of dollars from American suppliers. While he was sentenced to a lengthy prison term and stripped of his rank, his actions struck at the morale of the IAF, which had always been seen as an unblemished elite.

In mid-1990, a massive immigration of Soviet Jews to Israel began after decades of prohibitions by the Soviet government. Within two years, the already limited budgets would have to provide for the absorption of

400,000 immigrants who would need housing, employment, and time to grow accustomed to a Western market economy.

In the late 1980s the IAF shifted its focus to more innovative and sophisticated aircraft. It began to fly aircraft designed for the twenty-first century, the F-15, the F-16, the Phantom 2000, and the giant Sikorsky CH-53 Yasour 2000. It also received the Apache assault helicopters, which became heroes in the ongoing security missions along the northern border and in combat penetrations into Lebanon.

In May 1991 the IAF took part in a mission the likes of which it had never before executed. I participated in it, as a civilian pilot working for El Al. On the morning of May 23, I was awakened by a phone call after having just returned from a flight to the United States, and informed that I was to be on three-hour alert for a flight to Addis Ababa, Ethiopia, to transport new immigrants. An operation was about to take place that was enormous in the dimensions of its planning, control, and command. The IAF would be the central character in the mission.

In the past eighteen months I had flown dozens of flights to transport immigrants. The emotion of seeing them leaving countries whose borders were once closed had now diminished. Thus when it became the Ethiopians' turn, I saw this as just another flight. I was wrong. Even during the preflight briefing the following morning, I discovered translators, medical equipment, a special security team, and a plethora of special instructions. The rebel forces were about to capture the Ethiopian capital of Addis Ababa from the pro-communist leader Mengistu Haile Miryam. They agreed to delay their entry into the city for one day for a payment of $33 million. The agreement was reached with the assistance of U.S. President George Bush after covert negotiations. It gave the IAF and the IDF a window of several hours to extricate fourteen thousand Jews from Ethiopia. They congregated around the Israeli embassy and were transported in buses to the international airport, where they boarded IAF and El Al transport aircraft. I was in one of them. The IDF arranged the evacuation operation under the command of Deputy Chief of Staff Amnon Shahak. Amir Nahumi, the deputy commander-in-chief of the IAF for operations, oversaw the air activities.

Radio contact between the pilots in the long convoy that made its way for thirty-four hours from Addis Ababa to Lod revealed dozens of emotional moments. About half a dozen babies were born during the flights. The aircraft held double and sometimes triple the capacity for which they were designed. The passengers sat on the floors and squeezed against each other, unable to move. IDF soldiers who had immigrated to Israel several years earlier from Ethiopia served as translators and guides. For many of the passengers, this was not only their first flight, but also a flight from another world. It was rescue from a country ravaged by hunger and war. In addition to the complicated logistical organization of flying to a war-torn country, the IAF contributed eighteen Hercules C-130 aircraft and six Boeing 707s to transport the immigrants. It also provided the organizing and security forces, as well as F-15 fighter aircraft to protect the air train. Eight El Al aircraft also participated in the operation. The pride we all felt in this mission's success far exceeded that elicited by air combat operations in the near or distant past. The IAF saw itself carrying the weight of a national responsibility. It accepted this mission, as always, with dedication, professionalism, and efficiency.

The Iraqi invasion of Kuwait on August 2, 1990, elevated the level of alert of the entire IDF, and of the IAF in particular. Though Israel considers Kuwait one of its enemies and a financier of the terrorist organizations, it had never been involved in direct hostile actions against Israel. In that it was pro-Western and a country in which the West had a clear interest, the threat to it became a critical point for Israel as well.

Repeated declarations by Iraq's leader, Saddam Hussein, stating that Israel was destined to be one of his targets of attack, now received much greater immediate attention. As UN efforts to mediate a diplomatic solution to the crisis in Kuwait continued to fail, the level of alert in the IAF was raised. The organization of the military coalition that would fight for the liberation of Kuwait included forces from the Western countries. The United States feared, justifiably, that any inclusion of Israel in the armed force alongside enemy Arab nations such as Syria and Saudi Arabia and even Egypt, which had a peace agreement with Israel, would destroy any possibility of establishing the force. Israel was therefore excluded from the military forces that would fight Iraq.

The United States and its partners in the coalition guaranteed that they would take the task upon themselves without involving Israel. They also promised that if Saddam Hussein acted on his threats to attack Israel, they would disrupt and eliminate his plans.

On January 17, 1991, the Gulf War began. Israel was immediately attacked with Scud missiles carrying conventional warheads. These attacks continued throughout the war. A total of thirty-nine missiles were fired at Israel. While several of them landed in uninhabited areas, the majority hit population centers, primarily the cities of Ramat Gan, Tel Aviv, and Haifa. There were heavy damages to buildings and property. A large number of people were wounded. Luckily, there were only two fatalities. A number of civilians died from indirect results of the attacks; some suffered heart attacks, and others were suffocated by their gas masks.

The United States and Great Britain kept their promise to prevent the attacks against Israel. Part of the attack missions of the coalition's air forces and, according to reports, of the commando forces was to track and destroy the mobile and stationary Scud missile launchers situated in western Iraq. The elimination of the launchers was also vital for the prevention of missile attacks against coalition forces stationed in Saudi Arabia and the civilian population in Riyadh and other locations.

These actions had only limited success. Though the number of launchers decreased and the intervals between the attacks grew, Israel continued to be attacked until almost the final day of the war. With every missile fired against Israel, more and more voices were raised demanding that the IDF involve itself directly in destroying the sources of the missile attacks. Proponents of this idea had no doubt that the task should be given to the IAF and that it could find a comprehensive solution to the missile problem. Israel had adopted the slogan "Never again" into its national ethos after the Holocaust of the Second World War. Its passive response during the direct attacks was particularly difficult for the public morale. A number of people also decried what they characterized as Israel's lost ability to deter. "It cannot be," they claimed, "that Israel's cities will be bombed night after night and its civilians will close themselves off in sealed rooms as the IDF does nothing to defend them. Any enemy seeing that Israel is not responding will stop fearing the Israeli response, and the damage to Israel's security will be much greater than the actual damage inflicted by the missiles."

High-ranking officers in the IAF still claim that the IAF would have acted to silence the sources of the attacks in a much more efficient fashion than the coalition forces. It is possible that the first days would have been essentially the same, but from the third or fourth day, upon the completion of the building of the Israeli force and its organization in the field, all Iraqi movement would have been made impossible. Every source of fire would have been dealt with, using one sort of weapon or another.

Among the IAF's technological acquisitions during this period was the Patriot missile, considered the best antiaircraft missile in the world. These missiles, stationed in Israel during the Gulf War, were operated by American crews. Though the Patriot had already been proven effective against aircraft, its success against the Scuds was minimal; its primary importance was to boost public morale. After the conclusion of the Gulf War, however, the IAF's antiaircraft network absorbed the missiles.

# Epilogue

$J$anuary 1991 changed the face of the State of Israel and its defense consciousness. It now lives under the constant threat of biological, chemical, and—most frightening of all— nuclear weapons.

Israel was not assaulted with this type of weaponry during the Gulf War, either because Iraq had not yet reached the necessary technological level or because of the IAF's deterrent forces. The collapse of the Soviet Union and the ongoing disarmament has diminished the tensions between the superpowers. The nightmare of a missile striking New York or Los Angeles has also been eliminated. However, the Soviet Union's ability to restrain countries that were dependent on its supply of arms is now gone as well. Israel received belated expressions of appreciation for its bombing of the Iraqi nuclear reactor. It became clear that the attack had not eliminated the Iraqi nuclear threat, but rather postponed it. Israel had merely preceded the world in correctly reading the map.

In today's world, leaders like Libya's Muammar Khaddafi or Iraq's Saddam Hussein have proven that they will act on the most insane of their threats, as they hold a tremendous supply of chemical and biologic weapons. We are only a small step from witnessing nuclear weapons in the hands of a crazed leader.

This strategic threat places the IAF in a new role, for it is no longer dedicated solely to keeping the skies clean. Israel must develop defenses against missiles in order to apply itself to this generation of the missile threat. The advanced Chetz ("Arrow") missile, which will reach a speed of Mach 10 and will lock on its target from tremendous distances, is in advanced developmental stages. Its designers' goal is to produce a missile able to intercept surface-to-surface missiles while on their way to Israel, before they have completed half of their route and at the maximum altitude. Even if the target missile carried a nonconventional warhead, it would be demolished in the vicinity of the attacking country or its supporting neighbors.

Meanwhile, owing to its circumstances, Israel, more than most countries, has to utilize advanced antiaircraft defense. The Barak missile is a surface-to-surface missile for slow and low-flying targets, and is mainly suited for sea war. The Patriot has been modified and improved in accordance with its limitations discovered in the Gulf War. Neither missile, however, can replace or substitute for the Chetz. They do not fulfill even the most basic requirements.

Israel today faces a situation in which the West's obligations to it as a strategic asset are diminishing alongside the reduced East-West tensions. However, hostility toward Israel from fundamentalist Islamic elements is on the rise. Densely populated, Israel sits on a small territory that cannot withstand chemical pollution, let alone nuclear pollution, of its population centers. The threat of such a future war has only one meaning for Israel—a holocaust.

In an interview with the Israeli newspaper *Maariv* in April 1992, Deputy IDF Chief of Staff Amnon Shahak declared that "all methods are acceptable in withholding nuclear capabilities from an Arab nation." One year after millions of Israelis sat in sealed rooms and stared with commendable patience into their gas masks, the nation that asserts "Never again" has no choice but to clench its fists and gather its strengths, with the IDF and the IAF leading it. At the height of the Gulf War, as the front that they were to defend was penetrated, IAF helicopter and fighter pilots sat ready in their squadrons, waiting for an order that never came.

The Israeli airmen of the early 1990s are top professionals, with diverse knowledge. They operate sophisticated and expensive war machines, and believe their military service is a career choice that has provided them with the opportunity to prove their high levels of expertise. Few of them are idealists who signed up to defend the state. Flight is more a profession than a calling, and their lives are not focused on flight alone. Israeli pilots have many interests—computers, the arts, music, and girlfriends. As in any healthy country, they begin to think about their winter vacation as soon as the summer vacation ends. Only alerts and their heavy workload sometimes disrupt their personal needs, which they attempt to keep as separate as possible from their military lives. Nonetheless, one cannot disregard the level of excellence that continues to grow in the IAF.

IAF Commander-in-Chief Avihu Ben-Nun, who concluded his tour of duty in January 1992, complained bitterly that he could not conduct the IAF's work plan. The budget was cut or approved with great delays while being severely limited and constantly changed. It is difficult to maintain, train, and command an air force under such conditions, even in a quiet area in peacetime, let alone in such chaotic times as these. Israel and its neighbors have begun a long and arduous process of negotiating peace. Although the personnel of the IAF hope, like all Israeli citizens, that the negotiations will succeed, the possibilities of peace do not reduce the level of alert, preparation, and planning. Against the possibility of war, development, training, and absorption of personnel and equipment continues.

While they train to perform expertly on a moment's notice, the IAF's young pilots often express skepticism of the civilian network's ability to reach a decision or give a command in the necessary amount of time dictated by the war of the future. Such a decision will have to be made within minutes.

Maj. Gen. Herzle Bodinger took command of the IAF in January 1992. He is a new commander for a new period. Calm and calculating, he is known for his warm personality and wise approach. Israel's hope is that he will not only rebuild the Air Force, but also revitalize it.

Far from the heroics of dogfights, the newspapers, or the stories of glory, Bodinger must prepare his force for the possibility of entering an age of peace. Even more important, he must prepare Israel for a possible war that will be different from any that the Middle East has ever known. Pilots must be trained by building trust and deterrence, so that the IAF can serve as Israel's principal weapon in the nuclear age. The Middle East has its share of crazed leaders, any of whom could press the button.

# Index

A-4 Skyhawk bomber aircraft, 269–271, 272, 283, 426, 434
Abdullah (king of Jordan), 32
Adam, Yekutiel ("Kuti"), 405, 406
Adar (pilot), 377
Addis Ababa evacuation, 490–491
"Adi" (pilot), 356–357
Adir, Johnny, 36
Agassi, Yaakov, 115, 123, 124, 250
Agmon, Yoram, 182, 183, 184, 286, 304
Agranat Commission, 404
Airplane Company, 1, 6, 7–8
Air Service: aircraft procurement, 9–10, 12, 24–25; becomes Israeli Air Force, 26; formation of, 3, 4–6; pilots, 11; in War of Independence, 15, 16, 18–19, 20, 22
air-to-air missiles, 398–399
Air Transport Command, 42–44, 45, 59
Allouette jet helicopters, 163–164
*Almogit* (Israeli ship), 88
Alon, Joseph ("Joe"), 83, 93, 115, 158, 159
Alon, Mordechai ("Modi"), 40; in acquisition of Czech planes, 23, 24–25, 27, 46–47; as fighter pilot, 17, 18, 28, 30, 37, 226; killed in crash, 52; as squadron commander, 41, 52, 152
Alon, Yigal, 436
Alrom, Gidon, 404
Altman, Yekutiel, 116, 125
Amar, Abdal Hakhim, 107, 108
Amiel, Saadia, 266
Amin, Idi, 407, 409
Amir, Amos, 173–174, 176, 306–307
Amir (Zabeldovesky), Israel, 6, 26
Amiram (paratrooper), 381
Amnon (pilot), 157, 410, 411
Amos (pilot), 278, 279
Anilevitz, Mordechai, 93
Anklawitz, Morris, 117–118
Arab Legion, 27, 31–32
Arafat, Yasser, 261–262, 443–444, 462, 483, 487
Arens, Moshe, 421–422
Argov, Shlomo, 462
Arnan, Avraham, 166
Arnon (pilot), 357–359
Arolozor, Lev ("Zorik"), 209
Aryeh ("Lion") bomber aircraft, 420–421
Ashkenazi, Ephraim, 183
A Squadron: aircraft procurement, 6–7; becomes Panther Squadron, 26; formation of, 6; pilots, 7, 10–11; in War of Independence, 7–8, 15, 22, 25, 30–31, 43
El-Assad, Hafez, vii, 226, 311, 442–443
Aswan Dan, 97
Augarten-Carmi, Rudy, 56, 57, 66, 67, 68
Auster aircraft, 9–10

Avidan, Shimon, 28
"Avik" (pilot), 308
Avisar, Yaakov, 110, 111, 112, 113, 116
Avneri, Dror, 90, 115, 120, 121, 139
Avraham Field, 59
Avriel, Ehud, 24, 25

B-17 Flying Fortress bombers, 33, 35–36, 132, 145
Bacchus, Michel, 411
Bader, Douglas, 74, 395
Balak, Operation, 20–21, 25, 27, 44
Al-Baqr, Ahmed Hassan, 446
Bar, Menachem, 83, 85, 143
Barak, Ehud, 405, 473
Barak, Yair, 162, 321
Baraka, Mahmoud, 1, 2–3
Barak ("Lightning") aircraft, 413
Barak surface-to-surface missiles, 495
Bareket, Yeshayahu ("Shaike"), 93, 186, 187–188
Bar-Lev, Chaim: as brigade commander, 94, 137; as IDF chief of staff, 264, 273, 274; 290
Bar-Lev Line, 273, 337, 432
Bar-Or, Tzion, 476–477
Bar-Siman-Tov, Yaakov, 461
Beaufighter bomber aircraft, 51
Begin, Menachem, 432; and acquisition of bomber aircraft, 421; and bombing of Iraqi nuclear reactor, 449, 450, 451, 453, 454; and bombing of Syrian missiles, 461
Beirut Airport bombing, 265–269
Beit-Daras airfield, 20–21
Beit-On, Shlomo, 93
Bell Cobra helicopters, 473–474, 475, 476, 477
Bell 205 jet helicopters, 258, 259, 262, 263, 474
"Ben" (navigator), 308
Ben-Barak, Tzur, 180
Ben-Chaim, Yaakov ("Blackie"), 132, 133
Ben-Gurion, David: and acquisition of helicopters, 163; and acquisition of Meteor jets, 82; and acquisition of Mirage jets, 172; and border incidents, 162, 180–181; and Czech arms supplies, 21; and formation of Air Service, 4, 5, 6, 10; founding of Israel, 24; and IAF mission, 39, 69, 102, 151; and Negev airlift, 43, 44, 54; replaced as prime minister by Eshkol, 177; respect for World War II veterans, 4–5, 39, 70; and Sinai Campaign, 95, 102, 103, 145, 146, 147; and War of Independence campaigns, 9, 19, 55–56
Ben-Nun, Avihu, 172; and bombing of Syrian missiles, 461, 467–468; as IAF com-